THEORY OF INTERNATIONAL LAW

This book seeks to analyse various aspects of international law, the link being how they structure and marshal the different forces in the international legal order. It takes the following approaches to the matter. First, an attempt is made to determine the fundamental characteristics of international law, the forces that delineate and permeate its applications. Secondly, the multiple relations between law and politics are analysed. Politics are a highly relevant factor in the implementation of every legal order (and also a threat to it); this is all the more true in international law, where the two forces, law and politics, have significant links. Thirdly, the discussion focuses on a series of fundamental legal-political notions: the common good, justice, legal security, reciprocity (plus equality and proportionality), liberty, ethics and social morality, and reason.

Theory of International Law

Robert Kolb

• HART •
OXFORD • LONDON • NEW YORK • NEW DELHI • SYDNEY

HART PUBLISHING
Bloomsbury Publishing Plc
Kemp House, Chawley Park, Cumnor Hill, Oxford, OX2 9PH, UK

HART PUBLISHING, the Hart/Stag logo, BLOOMSBURY and the Diana logo are trademarks of Bloomsbury Publishing Plc
First published in Great Britain 2016

First published in hardback, 2016
Paperback edition, 2019

A catalogue record for this book is available from the British Library.

Library of Congress Cataloging-in-Publication Data

Names: Kolb, Robert, author.

Title: Theory of international law / Robert Kolb.

Description: Oxford ; Portland, Oregon : Hart Publishing, 2016. | Includes bibliographical references and index.

Identifiers: LCCN 2016020804 (print) | LCCN 2016020917 (ebook) | ISBN 9781782258803 (hardback : alk. paper) | ISBN 9781782258834 (Epub)

Subjects: LCSH: International law—Philosophy.

Classification: LCC KZ3410 .K657 2016 (print) | LCC KZ3410 (ebook) | DDC 341.01—dc23

LC record available at https://lccn.loc.gov/2016020804

ISBN: HB: 978-1-78225-880-3
PB: 978-1-50992-750-0
ePDF: 978-1-78225-881-0
ePub: 978-1-78225-883-4

Typeset by Compuscript Ltd, Shannon

ACKNOWLEDGEMENTS

Many thanks to the Schneiter Foundation (University of Geneva) for its generous financial support. I am also most grateful to Catherine Minahan for her highly competent, painstaking and precise copy-editing; she alone made the text readable.

CONTENTS

Part Two: International Law and Politics

Part Three: International Law and Certain Fundamental Legal-Political Notions

LIST OF ABBREVIATIONS

The usual abbreviations of the names of international organisations (such as, eg, UN) are not reproduced in the list below.

AADI	Annuaire africain de droit international
AFDI	Annuaire français de droit international
AJIL	American Journal of International Law
Ann	Annuaire
ASDI	Annuaire suisse de droit international
ASIL Proceedings	American Society of International Law Proceedings
ATF	Arrêts du Tribunal fédéral Suisse, Recueil officiel
AVR	Archiv des Völkerrechts
BYIL	British Yearbook of International Law
CYIL	Canadian Yearbook of International Law
EJIL	European Journal of International Law
EPIL	Encyclopedia of International Law
GYIL	German Yearbook of International Law
ICJ	International Court of Justice
ICLQ	International and Comparative Law Quarterly
IDI	Institut de droit international
ILC	International Law Commission
JDI	Journal du droit international
NILR	Netherlands International Law Review
NYIL	Netherlands Yearbook of International Law
ÖZöR(V)	Österreichische Zeitschrift für öffentliches Recht (und Völkerrecht)
RBDI	Revue belge de droit international
RCADI	Recueil des Cours de l'Académie de droit international de La Haye
RDI	Rivista di diritto internazionale
REDI	Revista española de derecho internacional
RGDIP	Revue générale de droit international public
RHDI	Revue hellénique de droit international
RIAA	Reports of International Arbitral Awards (United Nations)
RSDIE	Revue suisse de droit international et de droit européen
ZaöRV	Zeitschrift für ausländisches öffentliches Recht und Völkerrecht
ZöR	Zeitschrift für öffentliches Recht

TABLE OF CASES AND PRACTICE

1. International Jurisdictions

League of Nations Commission

United Nations Human Rights Committee

International Court of Justice

Permanent Court of International Justice

Permanent Court of Arbitration

World Bank Administrative Tribunal

International Criminal Tribunal for the former Yugoslavia

US Military Tribunal at Nuremberg

International Tribunal for the Law of the Sea

ILO Administrative Tribunal

Iran/USA Claims Tribunal

2. Regional Jurisdictions

European Court of Human Rights

EC Tribunal of First Instance

Court of Justice of the European Union

Inter-American Court of Human Rights

3. National Jurisdictions

Australia

Canada

Germany

Municipal Tribunals

Leipzig Trials following World War I

India

Israel

Italy

Philippines

South Africa

Switzerland

United Kingdom

United States of America

Municipal Tribunals

4. Arbitration

International Arbitral Awards, United Nations Reports

5. Diplomatic Practice

TABLE OF LEGISLATION

International Organisations

European Union

France

India

Philippines

Switzerland

United Kingdom

Military Tribunals

TABLE OF INTERNATIONAL INSTRUMENTS

Introduction

This is a shortened translation of my book *Théorie du droit international public*, published with Bruylant in 2013; but it is indeed also more than that. I decided to translate the text myself, which is certainly an idea falling to be discussed in view of my only relative mastery of Shakespeare's language. The advantage of this course is, however, that I have been able to adapt the text whenever new elements seemed to me to warrant some addition or modification. Therefore, a somewhat new text has emerged, which, on balance, is an exercise of greater interest than a mere facsimile translation. A translator proper could only have been aiming for faithfulness; I have been able to aspire to renewed creativity.

The present book is the product of my reflections and work on international law for more than 20 years. It has emerged from the crucible of interwoven and sometimes contrasting realities. Thus, international law is on the one hand a solidly built system of norms supported by a sound and aesthetic architecture: sources, subjects and responsibility, among other areas, fit together in a construction not far removed, in its well-balanced traits, from an immaterial cathedral. Yet there is also the claim that so many questions remain unsettled and uncertain in international law. This leads to the complaint: 'Its system is not established, its object is uncertain, its institutions remain sometimes in the shadow and no other science prompts to such a degree the sense of arbitrariness and relativity.'[1] Thus a gymnasium must be constructed to complement the cathedral.[2] Or to put it another way, on the one hand international law strives towards the rule of law, as much as towards international solidarity and cooperation for the common good: in the twentieth century this 'international community' limb within the law witnessed important developments. However, on the other hand, international law continues to be traversed by petitions of power politics, importing significant ambiguities and dissonances into its spectrum: the law thus presents itself as a maelstrom of different forces, centripetal and centrifugal, which account for its complexity and richness.

[1] R Quadri, 'Le fondement du caractère obligatoire du droit international public' (1952-I) 80 *RCADI* 583, our translation. See also on existence and effectiveness of the law, L Henkin, *How Nations Behave: Law and Foreign Policy* (London, 1968) 1: 'International Law ... must still constantly defend its existence. Even more earnestly must it defend its relevance to world events'. Others have noted a growing trend towards a self-destructive 'permissive pragmatism', ie a selective application of international law according to shifting interests: G Schwarzenberger, 'International Law and the Problem of Political World Order' in B Cheng (ed), *International Law: Teaching and Practice* (London, 1982) 62.

[2] JC Martin, *Les règles internationales relatives à la lutte contre le terrorisme* (Brussels, 2006) 561.

This volume seeks to construct these competing and countervailing forces into an edifice that is not perfectly coherent but the aim of which is to clarify the working of the system as a whole when perceived through the lens of all the differing legal and political realities that constitute it. In Part One, I analyse the main pillars of the legal system, allowing the reader to grasp its idiosyncracies: its history, its material domain, typologies, foundation and sources, the subjects of international law, the character of the international legal rule, residual rules, the effectiveness of the law, the role of public opinion, and the existence of an international society or of an international community. Part Two is devoted to the important problem of the relationship between law and policy, international law and power politics. It seeks to refine the analysis beyond the usually quite monolithic categories. The essence here is the relationship between law and realities. Part Three treats the relationship of international law with certain cardinal, legal-political notions, and the former's interpenetration by the latter, namely: the common good; justice; legal certainty; reciprocity, equality and proportionality; liberty; morals; will and reason; and sanctions. The gist of the matter is here the relationship of law with ideals (which, however, are themselves deeply coloured by realities).

The hope is that in-depth discussion of these notions will allow the reader to capture moments of international law outside the contexts in which they are most usually examined. The main goal is to provide a theory of 'living international law', on paths aside from those most usually taken.

One last word: in view of the relative length of the text, I have been somewhat sparing with footnotes, so as not to overburden it. The sources quoted are in different languages; they are most notably not confined to the English language. This seems to me the proper course for a book on *inter*-national law.

Part One

The Main Pillars of the Legal System

1

History and Characteristics of International Law

According to predominant modern opinion, law is a *set of rules* shaping decision-making processes. It is therefore an objective concept vested with a certain formalism, keeping some distance between the precept and the various social facts. The relative distance between the norm and the fact allows the impersonal and equal application of the latter to social actors. With that, a series of qualities we vitally attach to the law (or to the rule of law) is in most cases realised: the generality of the rule, the uniformity of its application, the clarity of the precept, the foreseeability and security of the law, reciprocity and regularity, the concept of obligation and the 'ought to be', as well as the sanctions under the rules. It should be noted that all these notions are in some way linked with the modern State.

In history, law was for a long time conceived of very differently. In primitive societies, the main legal notion was an authorisation given to elders, chiefs or other subjects vested with social prestige, to decide disputes arising in society. The decision-making process, not the rule, was at the heart of the matter. The act of deciding constituted the body of the law (enmeshed with religion, rites and social beliefs); whereas for us, today, the normative framework of the power to decide is the reason of the law. In ancient times, the decision created a sort of situational norm; today, the norm is seen as determining the situational decision. The ancient power of decision was thus a sort of *prius*; its domestication by the rule is a modern conception, linked with the idea of the rule of law: 'power or government of law, not of men'.

The final shift from a system based on decisions to a system based on rules came with the Natural Law School of the Enlightenment, which flowed from a new conception of the role of law with regard to power: the first must now limit the second. In the Roman law tradition, as had prevailed up to that time in Europe, power scarcely affected the law since it remained largely aloof from it. Roman law was essentially limited to regulating interpersonal relations between equals (citizens) and non-equals (eg citizens/slaves), that is, it principally contained rules of private law, *quod ad singulorum utilitatem* in the formula of Ulpian (Dig, 1,1,1,2). Political power had its own separate rules and reasons. Certain legal rules existed in this regard, for example on fiscal law (*fiscus Caesaris*), on sacral law (*jus sacrum vel pontificium*), on certain crimes against the State or Emperor, on alliances and on war. But these rules remained marginal within the legal system, and they were little studied in the many analyses of the jurisconsults. There is no doubt that this predominance of 'private law' stemmed from the conviction that the original political power could hardly be tamed by legal rules. This realistic vision, separating the law quite neatly from the *raison d'Etat*, and private law from public 'law', lasted for centuries. In the Middle Ages, still, lawyers were civil lawyers or canon lawyers, not public lawyers. In a certain sense, however, power relations penetrated into the private law system: some 'public law' relations were construed by analogy to private law concepts, such as, for example, the vast system of vassalage, based on contract law.

The emergence of the modern State consolidated territorial entities vested with sovereign power. Many factors contributed to the concentration of State power in the hands of its highest rulers, for example: mercantilism and a monetary economy; the creation of huge public administrations; the establishment of standing professional armies; the elimination of intermediary powers within the States, etc. This concentrated and expanding power, conscious of its might, purported to reject, as much as possible, the unwelcome pretense of the law to limit and control its expression. However, such exorbitant power, often in the hands of a monarch, was contrary to the interests of the new, rising middle class (bourgeoisie) enjoying economic autonomy and engaging in commerce. It is therefore understandable that the Natural Law School, dominated by exponents of this new class, sought to rein in this excessive power and to place it, at least partially, under the control of the law. Public law thus becomes the gist of the matter: only public law norms could limit the power of the State.[1] But if the main aim of the law is now to 'limit the power', it can no longer be conceived of as a simple decision-making process: bare decisions are the hallmark of power. In opposition to the fluctuations and flexibilities claimed by political power in order to keep its decisional leeway (now under the growing mask of sovereignty), law is called on to crystallise into rules if it wants to perform the new functions to be ascribed to it.

These new rules of public law are generally conceived of as having universal reach, in particular when they are linked with the rule of law: legality of action; separation of powers (in the words of Montesquieu, 'it is an eternal experience that man vested with power is tempted to abuse it'); equality of legal subjects and equality before the law; the notion of the legal person (connoting now the ability to enjoy subjective rights and to enforce them, contrary to the old notion of the subject being subjected to power); human liberties and human rights; non-retroactivity of law and the impersonal nature of legislation; publication of the laws; the prohibition of *ad hoc* constituted tribunals and the guarantee of the so-called natural judge; and so on. Private law itself penetrates into the halls of public law. It is now the State that legislates, codifies, ensures sanctions and grants procedural devices so as to realise private law and subjective rights of

[1] The power of the modern State cannot be compared even with that of the Roman Empire, which after all always remained a quite loose federation of peoples with notable local autonomy.

persons. Therefore, the law in its entirety becomes identified with the State, with its Constitution, with the guarantees of enforcement and sanction. Natural law, once codified, transits towards the positive law of the State. Ultimately, the whole legal phenomenon is subjected to the State model at the same time as the latter territorially consolidates and the constitutional movements reach their peak.

By these developments, legalistic and hierarchical State law is more and more markedly set in opposition to international law. The latter remains aloof from these powerful shifts towards centralisation, and continues to be the regulator of an anarchical society. The State organisation of the law, its construction as universal and general norms, the role of the various administrative bodies, as well as the centralised sanction mechanisms, all these evolutions make it difficult to extend the legal phenomenon, thus conceived, to international relations. In an international society dominated by equal powers without a common superior (coordinative character of international law), with its fragmentary and often bilateral norms, with its absence of organs entrusted with the enforcement of the law, how could one imagine a law sufficiently detached from power and its contingencies, ie a law limiting power and thus objectively applied? A significant number of lawyers have indeed denied a legal character to international law, obsessed, as it were, by strict municipal law analogies, in particular the notion of sanction. In this view, the modern law of the State reflects the entirety of the legal phenomenon: international law is not like internal law; thus, international law is not law at all. This is a radical attack.

From the preceding, we may emphasise two aspects. First, law has generally transited from a decision-making process (ie a model of movement) to a body of rules (ie a more static model). Primitive societies were dominated by decision-making. More advanced societies—like the Roman Empire—were in transition: they acknowledged rules, as in the Twelve Tables or in the Perpetual Edict, but the gist of the law remained rooted in judicial remedies (actions), and thus in the decisions of the jurisconsults and the praetor. Modern law is conceived, in the dominant view, as a body of very powerful rules. It flows from the general laws of the State, and its main aim is to limit power (as well as to allow private interaction). The law is thus itself considered to be a master, a sort of power on its own: only a power could limit another power. Seeking to limit political power, the law enters into a series of problematic relationships with the former. We could witness instances of this state of affairs in many contexts, for example the fate of the US anti-terrorist legislation after 9/11, and all its shifting fortunes in the US Supreme Court.[2] Secondly, public law consolidates at the time of the Enlightenment.[3] The phenomenon of law is thus now considerably enlarged. But the law is thereby irremediably centered on the State, being its 'unique true depositary. The conception

[2] See M Sassoli, A Bouvier and A Quintin, *How Does Law Protect in War?*, 3rd edn (Geneva, 2011) 128ff.

[3] Thus, the first professorships in public law in Germany were created in the 17th century: see M Mitteis and H Lieberich, *Deutsche Rechtsgeschichte*, 17th edn (Munich, 1985) 343.

spreads according to which there is no law outside the State with its legislator, its policeman and its judge.

International law is affected by both the developments mentioned in the preceding paragraph. The first issue raises the question of how a general law could be achieved in international society absent a legislator in the customary sense of the word. The only possible substitute for a law would seem to be a contract, which in international law is called a treaty. The positivistic current attached to that vision laid considerable stress on the principle *pacta sunt servanda*,[4] and devoted profound attention to the sources of the law. The second issue plunges international law into an ever-deeper crisis. How could a non-State-centered law exist? As different law? But would it then also be a primitive, defective or sick law, or a law in an embryonic state, *in statu nascendi* as it were, still in its infancy but called on to develop and strengthen itself in the wake of the progressive organic strengthening of international society itself? Such questions spark lively debate.

The time has come to reflect on the specificities of international law as a legal system. Can it display, at least to an acceptable degree, the objectivity and effectiveness we require from a legal system? What are the peculiarities engrafted upon it by the particular environment in which it has to function—that of international society? What are its weaknesses, and also its strengths? Before analysing the gravitational forces of international politics on international law, we should give some shape to the distinctive concept of law prevailing in international society.

I. Historical and Conceptual Aspects

A. The 'Two Histories' of Public International Law

1. *General Aspects*

The history of international law can be analysed in two different ways. First, we can try to reveal the roots of the public international law in force today, by rolling back events into the past. Secondly, we can try to bring together all the legal phenomena that have taken place among relatively independent peoples organised territorially and entering into relationships of minimum intensity, for all times and all places. The first perspective is limited: it is the history of one public international law, that is, of the public international law in force. The second perspective is universal: it examines the history of all public international laws in existence at any given time. Thus, the first perspective relates to European public

[4] In municipal law, there were some equivalent explanations centered on the social contract: see JF Spitz, 'Etat de nature et contrat social' in P Raynaud and S Rials (eds), *Dictionnaire de philosophie politique* (Paris, 1996) 255ff.

law, which has extended throughout the world via colonialism and has become the positive law of today.[5] The second perspective ushers in an analysis of the law among powers (*jus inter potestates*).[6] The interest in the latter is mainly to see if and how certain institutions and norms, being necessary to relationships between public collectivities, have crystallised in entirely different places at different times; and to see how these institutions correspond to or differ from those found in our positive international law. This also allows us to assess the role of contingency and necessity in the content of our international law, and thus to sharpen our understanding of the normative system. Such common norms are to be found, for example, in transactions (treaties), diplomacy, war, cooperation, etc. To the history of the victorious international law of today can thus be added the history of the defeated international laws, which ceased to exist at a certain moment in time. In sum, in historical perspective there is one single public international law valid today, with its own single history (*jus publicum Europeaum*); but there is also a plurality of international laws in most different regions of the world, and international laws that disappeared when the civilisations that developed them declined or were conquered. Under more favourable conditions, these other public international laws could have evolved to attain a level of sophistication similar to the public law of Europe. It is to be regretted that historical studies of international law have concentrated mainly, if not only, on the first limb and on the relations of Europe with certain bordering areas (Egypt, Assyria, Babylon, Mitanni, Hebraic Peoples, etc). Histories of the law in ancient India and China exist, but are rarely sufficiently developed and often lack critical focus. The time has come to correct this Eurocentric view. However, the enlarged scope of this enquiry poses its own practical problems (access to sources, existence of sources, capacity to understand the sources, existence of monographic studies, etc) and also theoretical problems. Among the latter, three are mentioned below.

i. Meaning of 'International Legal Order'

The main task for a holistic study of international law is to determine what constitutes an 'international legal order'. It would be erroneous to define such an order by exclusive reference to the criteria of modern Western legal thinking. This would be tantamount to implying that an international legal order could only exist if it had the characteristics of the public law of Europe. However, it is impossible to determine a legal phenomenon without referring to certain notions developed by legal science. The fact remains that law has been analysed scientifically mainly in Europe; this has been the only continent on which the legal phenomenon has, since the times of Roman law, crystallised into an autonomous science and art. However, the further the enquiry extends into ancient times, the less it will be

[5] W Grewe, 'Vom europäischen zum universellen Völkerrecht' (1982) 42 *ZaöRV* 449ff; W Grewe, *The Epochs of International Law* (Berlin/New York, 2000).

[6] W Preiser, *Frühe völkerrechtliche Ordnungen der aussereuropäischen Welt* (Wiesbaden, 1976); R Kolb, *Esquisse d'un droit international public des cultures extra-européennes* (Paris, 2010).

possible to find legal orders comparable to the European order. Law distinguished itself from other social notions only after a certain time; it was initially enmeshed in religion, rites, morals, social beliefs and so on. In its early stages, law also remained rudimentary, especially as regards its extension to relations between different peoples and collectivities. The concept of 'foreigner' was initially assimilated into that of 'enemy' (*hostis* denotes at one and the same time the foreigner and the enemy).[7]

In view of the above, it is necessary to distinguish between international legal orders in which the legal phenomenon crosses the threshold of a certain maturity ('order'), from sporadic international legal phenomena caused by the necessities inherent in haphazard contacts (armistices, exchange of prisoners) without any concomitant conception of a legal order nourishing and rooting them ('phenomena'). The order and the phenomena both suppose the existence of independent collectivities as legal subjects, granting some degree of recognition one to the other. The legal order additionally requires a series of regular interactions among the collectivities concerned, in peacetime and in war, coupled with a legal conscience, ie the conception that binding obligations are assumed towards the foreign entity under the threat of some sanction in the event of contravention. In sum, the phenomena require only the existence of sovereign entities having haphazard contact with each other and whose transactions can remain of an uncertain character;[8] the order supposes such regular and developed relationships as to crystallise an *opinio juris* for the existence of international legal bonds.

Now, when looking into the past, it appears that for most cultures and times we have no more than signposts for phenomena; it would be daring to affirm that they flowed from a legal order. However, in certain contexts, such as the Aztec America of the Triple Alliance (fifteenth century, see section I.A.3.i. below), or in the China of the era of 'Spring and Autumn' (771–481 BCE, see section I.A.3.v. below), real international legal orders had developed. The main distinctive characteristics of these orders with respect to simple phenomena were:

1. the existence of independent States (or of independent collectivities), recognising each other as subjects of law;
2. regular exchanges of a cultural, economic and political nature, supposing some legal regulation, or at least producing some legal consequences; and
3. the subjects participating in these exchanges were convinced that the conventional and customary rules for those interactions were legally binding and that their non-observance would trigger some sanctions.

[7] This 'strangeness' of the foreigner to some extent remains a feature of modern times. See the illuminating but strong words by M Bourquin, 'Stabilité et movement dans l'ordre juridique international' (1938-II) 64 *RCADI* 362.

[8] The argument that a legal phenomenon supposes a legal order (eg, to conclude a treaty there must exist a legal order regulating the law of treaties), so that the presence of the former induces the existence of the latter, cannot be so simply accepted. Behind the phenomena there was perhaps some legal order. But in most cases, we do not know whether this was actually the case.

These three distinctive elements can exist in a given situation to varying degrees. It is a matter of appreciation whether the degree of attainment is sufficiently developed to make the leap from a phenomenon to an order. It must also be noted that elements 1 and 3 are most often the consequence of the existence of element 2. When these three elements are present at a minimum, it is justified to speak of at least an embryonic legal order. If one or other of these elements is lacking (in particular the third, *opinio juris*, which is essential to the definition of proper legal rules and thus to a proper legal system), it will be appropriate to qualify the situation as consisting of more or less fragmented legal phenomena.

ii. Times of Transition

Another problem relates to times of transition and to the mixed spaces straddling federalism and internationalism. This difficulty is due to the continuous swing between phases of concentration of power (constitution of unitary States) and phases of dissolution of power (creation of international societies composed of independent entities). Mixed situations also exist in intermediary phases, for example with dependent States or relations involving complex vassalage. Such continuous oscillation impacts on the law: the latter shifts according to the political swing between common imperial or federal law (phases of concentration of power) and international law (phases of dissolution of power). Public international law is thus typically the product of the dissolution of empires, of federal or centralised States.[9] It is the fruit of loss, of distress, of dismantlement. The former experience of a common collectivity creates a series of bonds between the peoples concerned. These bonds also feed their relationships after the dissolution of the collectivity, and thus continue in the international space. Thus it is no surprise that historically, international legal orders have existed mainly in regions where there was a common empire (eg in China after 771 BCE), or at least a common culture (eg in Aztec Mexico in the fifteenth century). Conversely, between States that have not shared such common bonds, there have been only legal phenomena, not consolidated to the point of an international legal order. A common legal order supposes some sense of society or community. Such a sentiment does not develop with regard to wholly alien people and collectivities; or if it does, it supposes a significant amount of time over which such bonds can be constructed. The concept of society or community rests on that of race, culture, religion or other commonalities. But even once this is settled, fluctuating political fortunes and shifting social realities imply that the associated legal constructions will themselves constantly adapt. And it is difficult to pin down moving targets.

iii. Social Ideologies

A third problem concerns the social ideologies that sometimes favour the development of a legal system and sometimes are opposed to it. It is a matter

[9] See B Paradisi, *Storia del diritto internazionale nel medio evo*, vol I (Milan, 1940) 9–11.

of observation that historical phases alternate between those dominated by the paradigm of power policies and those dominated by the paradigm of respect for the law. It would certainly be wrong to view these two poles as neatly and purely opposed. In reality, both paradigms mix together to varying degrees at any moment of history. But it remains true that each time and space realises a new, complex balance between these two poles, and that the one will to a certain degree predominate over the other. Two important phases of Chinese history illustrate the point: the era of 'Spring and Autumn' (771–481 BCE) was geared towards chivalry and respect for the rules; that of 'States in War' (481–221 BCE) was dominated by a sort of Machiavellianism and power policies (see further section I.A.3.v. below). It is hardly necessary to emphasise that a true international legal order can flourish only in the 'moral' phases of international relations, based on a minimum of common convictions in the proper role of rules. 'Immoral' phases destroy the common bonds and the confidence between peoples, and tend to push the legal order towards its nadir, or sometimes to dismantle the order and usher back in the bare universe of phenomena.

2. *The Public International Law of Europe*[10]

The public law of Europe developed in the Middle Ages, but had been nourished by diverse sources since antiquity. Extra-European cultures situated around the Mediterranean contributed to its shaping.

i. The Near East

An early epicentre of international law phenomena was situated in the Near East starting in the fourth millennium BCE.[11] Egypt was at that time a unitary State. In Mesopotamia, there was a series of city-States, each relatively independent from the others. Important dynasties were those of Hammurabi (Babylon), the Hittites and Mitanni. All these collectivities entered into mutual political relationships. We therefore find treaties (eg treaties of amity and commerce, treaties of extradition, etc), commercial delegations vested with extraterritorial powers, or diplomatic missions benefitting from privileges and immunities. These rules were sustained by an *opinio juris*, as the great Codes of the region show (see, for example, the Ur-Nammu Code of the twenty-first century BCE).

[10] W Grewe, *The Epochs of International Law* (Berlin/New York, 2000); A Truyol y Serra, *Histoire du droit international public* (Paris, 1995); KH Ziegler, *Völkerrechtsgeschichte* (Munich, 1994) (2nd edn, Munich, 2007; S Laghmani, *Histoire du droit des gens* (Paris, 2003). See also G Stadtmüller, *Geschichte des Völkerrechts* (Hannover, 1951); A Nussbaum, *A Concise History of the Law of Nations* (New York, 1947); A Wegner, *Geschichte des Völkerrechts* (Stuttgart, 1936); TA Walker, *A History of the Law of Nations* (Cambridge, 1899). The following developments are a summary of the results of legal historic research as evidenced in the quoted monographs.

[11] See A Altman, *Tracing the Earliest Recorded Concepts of International Law, The Ancient Near East (2500–330 BCE)* (Leiden/Boston, 2012).

In the fifteenth century BCE, five powers dominated the region: Egypt, Babylonia, the Hittites, Mitanni and Assyria. The treaties of the Hittites are known: they contain some substantive regulation, accompanied by oaths and curses directed to the gods of each contracting power. The law of war was still under-developed in the region. Means and methods of warfare were rarely limited; the civilian populations of both sides were not protected; prisoners of war were seen as war booty and became slaves. Assyria remained notorious for its particularly brutal practices in war. Overall, the links between these cultures and the Judaic (since the ninth century BCE) and Western civilisations (particularly Greece) are manifest. The legal institution of the treaty has been influenced by the Near East tradition: thus, in the Greek Amphyctionic treaties we find the curses that were current in the Near East. Similarly, the doctrine of the just war was developed from the Bible, where God orders wars or where war is presented as a sanction following a wrong, for example when Israel is refused its right of passage.

ii. Ancient Greece

International law developed further in ancient Greece. With Greek colonisation occurring from the eighth century BCE, a network of cities spread all over the Mediterranean basin: Sinope, Trabzon, Tarrant, Sicilia, Alexandria (*magna graecia*). These city-States entered into mutual contacts and exchanges with neighbouring collectivities, for example with the Lydian Empire. In a short time, an international legal order became established between the Greek cities, tied together by a common culture and *opinio juris*. Treaty bonds were frequent and concerned a range of different objects: amphyctionies; symmachies (ie war alliances, such as the Peloponnesian alliance from the sixth century BCE); treaties of amity; peace treaties (which contained norms on territorial status, on the return of prisoners of war, on war reparations and arbitration clauses); arbitration treaties; treaties of commerce; legal assistance treaties (*symbolei*), etc.[12] Moreover, a quite detailed diplomatic law developed, with its privileges and immunities automatically accruing to certain persons, while others would enjoy such protections only through express assurances. Arbitration was frequently used by Greek city-States.[13] It should be noted that this mode of dispute settlement extended to highly important political questions, such as territorial settlements. Reference was not infrequently made to these arbitrations in the nineteenth and twentieth centuries to show that even disputes on so-called 'vital interests' could be arbitrated. It must also be noted, however, that such arbitration took place only between Greek

[12] DJ Bederman, *International Law in Antiquity* (Cambridge, 2001) 137ff.

[13] See G Tenekides, *Les relations internationales dans la Grèce antique* (Athens, 1993) 298ff; L Piccirilli (ed), Gli arbitrati interstatali Greci (Pisa, 1973); V Martin, *La vie internationale dans la Grèce des cités* (Paris, 1940) 487ff; A Raeder, *L'arbitrage international chez les Hellènes* (Kristiana, 1912); C Phillipson, *The International Law and Custom of Ancient Greece and Rome*, vol II (London, 1911) 127ff.

cities: it did not extend to powers alien to the Greek world. As a process of a legal-political nature embracing important questions, arbitration could take place only in the context of cultural proximity spawning the necessary mutual confidence.

On the other hand, the conduct of warfare remained virtually unregulated and was predominantly harsh.[14] The Near East tradition can be particularly felt in this field. The victorious power enjoyed mastery over the objects and the lives of the vanquished. Prisoners of war were generally sold as slaves. The civilian population was at the mercy of the victor. However, treaties and other agreements were regularly concluded, for example armistices, capitulations, safe-conducts, guarantees to spare the surrendering forces or the civilians, etc.

The law regarding aliens was comparatively highly developed. There were consuls (*proxenoi*), rules on asylum, isopolity (equal rights of citizenship; mutual political rights) and legal assistance treaties. It is manifestly in the ancient Greek world that the 'Western legal tradition' begins to take shape. It would be brought to full maturity by Rome in the centuries to come. This was the birthplace of the modern public law of Europe.

iii. Graeco-Roman Times

The Graeco-Roman times (from the fifth century BCE onwards) would develop further the legal institutions mentioned above.[15] Rome concluded treaties not only on technical matters, but also to regulate political questions of a certain importance: treaties of amity with other collectivities (*amicitia*); alliances and confederations, etc. Between equal partners such treaties were *foeda aequa*; when Rome predominated, a treaty was *foedum iniquum*. In diplomatic law, the inviolability of the envoy was now generally admitted. A violation of this principle constituted a just cause of war.

Arbitration continued to exist between Greek city-States, with Rome sometimes playing the role of the arbitrator (*Roma locuta, causa finita*). Conversely, Rome refused to subject itself to arbitration—the privilege of a Great Power.

The outbreak of war was now progressively enmeshed in a series of legal regulations flowing from the just war doctrine. The belligerents were defined as public collectivities: *liber populus qui nullius alterius potestati est subjectus—justus hostis*. Initially, a war was deemed to be just when it respected the procedure of fecial law (formally declared just war). Later, under the influence of Greek natural law and of orators such as Cicero, just war moved in the direction of the definition of material just causes of war—mainly defensive war, war punishing the commission of a wrong. Conversely, the laws of war (conduct of hostilities) remained rudimentary and harsh. The adverse party continued to be at the mercy of the victor: the fate of Carthage bears testament to that fact ('*delenda est Carthago*').

[14] On this issue, see the old but still fundamental study by JG Helm, *Die Rechtsstellung der Zivilbevölkerung im Kriege in ihrer geschichtlichen Entwicklung* (PhD, Frankfurt (Main), 1957).

[15] See still C Phillipson, *The International Law and Custom of Ancient Greece and Rome*, vols I and II (London, 1911).

The law of aliens continued to be refined and became part and parcel of a sophisticated *jus gentium*.

iv. The Transition from Antiquity to the Middle Ages

The time of transition from antiquity to the Middle Ages (400–800 CE) was replete with instability and regression.[16] The dominating political factors were the division of the Roman Empire in the reign of Theodosius (395ce) and the pressure of the so-called barbaric peoples on the Western Empire's northern boundaries. New States were created by these peoples (Visigoths, Ostrogoths, Franks, etc).

Starting in the the seventh century, Islam extended its reach. Byzantium (Constantinople), for its part, remained a vivid centre for international law. The Byzantine Empire entertained relations with other powers founded partly on international law, such as with Persia after the partition of Armenia in 389 CE. A peace treaty of 562 CE thus contained important clauses on commerce, the peaceful settlement of boundary disputes and on the protection of Christians in Persia. Mere international law phenomena existed between the Western Emperor and the Germanic *foederati*, as well as among the latter.

Overall, the legal institutions inherited from former times continued to exist but were reduced in scope and refinement. It was mainly Byzantium that kept alive rules on alliances, on diplomacy, on war and on aliens. It also developed the forms for concluding treaties. Thus, a procedure for maintaining respect for the instructions given to an envoy was introduced and formalised through ratification. In the law of war, the payment of ransom for liberating Christian prisoners of war in the hands of barbarians was gaining ground. In the law of aliens, certain remedies were granted to the foreigner against acts of the sovereign, notably in the context of commerce. Developments under the Frankish Empire (from the sixth century onwards) continued along the same lines.

v. The Middle Ages

The Middle Ages (800–1300 CE)[17] were dominated by the wars between the Pope and the Holy Roman Emperor for world domination (theory of the two *ministeria, sacerdotalis vel regalis*). This did not prevent the establishment of kingdoms and collectivities claiming their independence, treaty-making power, the right to go to war, and active as well as passive rights of legation. The maxim is '*rex imperator in regno suo*; *rex hodie videtur eandem potestatem habere in terra sua quam imperator*'. On these lines, a theory of fragmented sovereignty developed: sovereignty was not reserved to the person at the top of the hierarchy (Pope, Emperor, or even the king) but was enjoyed by whomever wielded a decision of last resort with regard

[16] On this epoch, see notably KH Ziegler, *Völkerrechtsgeschichte*, 2nd edn (Munich, 2007) 52ff, with ample bibliographic references.
[17] ibid, 71ff.

to any power, even if of only a local or partial nature. A town or person granted autonomy and empowered to dispense justice without any remedy to a higher authority was considered to be 'sovereign' with regard to that specific autonomy or power. By the same token, the vassalage of a collectivity or person did not deprive it of its autonomous power of action, or of its legal personality as regards its own external relations (eg the Kingdom of Sicily, vassal of the Vatican). This divided and multiplied sovereignty, the development of a great number of kingdoms, independent cities, federations and other entities enjoying some sovereign powers, the porosity of external relations in a world where the territorialisation of power was not yet established and where land boundaries were far from exercising their modern function—all these factors serve to explain why international relations were multiple and intense. Treaties between independent or partially independent entities significantly increased in number (alliances, peace treaties, treaties of amity, commerce and arbitration treaties, etc). The ratification procedure regarding the conclusion of treaties became a general practice.

Through the oaths inherited from olden times, the Church was now often involved in the conclusion of treaties: it would become the master of the oath and thus of the mutual *fides*. This would also trigger the applicability of canon law and of the jurisdiction of ecclesiastical tribunals over these treaties. By the same token, canon law influenced the conclusion of treaties: since faith was not a matter of mere external form, the tendency was to consider that treaty bonds did not suppose any specific form of treaty conclusion. Rather, the maxim was 'one man, one word': the commitment and resulting legitimate expectation created the binding force of the treaty.

Diplomatic law became increasingly involved. The various diplomatic functions were now distinguished (*legatus*, *nuntius*, *missus*, *procurator*, *orator*, etc) and the inviolability of the diplomat was generally recognised; however, diplomatic missions remained temporary ones, the first permanent mission being established only in 1450.[18] The reason for this lies in the profound suspicion a mission aroused: benefitting from privileges and immunities, working for a foreign power, it could easily engage in spying.

The Middle Ages also saw the emergence of an effort towards the maintenance of peace. Between the tenth and the twelfth centuries, the Catholic Church attempted to prohibit the use of force (private war) in certain places and on certain days by having recourse to Biblical analogies (for example, no violence on Fridays on account of Christ's Passion). These efforts were initiated under the terms of *Pax Dei* and *Treuga Dei*.[19] The sanction for breach essentially lay in excommunication. The German Emperors themselves issued decrees the aim of which was to secure the peace. However, all these efforts met with only relative successes. Conversely, a not wholly insignificant contribution to the peace was made by the use of

[18] See H Nicholson, *L'évolution des méthodes en diplomatie* (Neuchâtel, 1955) 41.

[19] See *Decretum Gratiani*, pars II, c 24, q 3, canones 23–24.

arbitration. Churchmen were frequently elected as arbitrators. Arbitration—for example between Italian city-States—was not limited to the application of the common or special law adopted by the parties but,[20] according to the customs of the times, extended to a conciliation and mediation function (*arbiter arbitrator et amicabilis compositor*).

In the domain of war, the main issue was to separate public from private wars (traces of this distinction can be found in Grotius). Since the thirteenth century, the doctrine of just war had played a primary role.[21] A just war essentially was a defensive war or a war to redress a wrong. Three conditions for a just war were laid down: the public authority of a prince or collectivity (*auctoritas principis*); the just cause, ie defence or reparation for a wrong (*iusta causa*); and the proper intention to pursue only permitted aims (*recta intentio*). The conduct of hostilities (*ius belli*) nevertheless remained quite brutal, notably as against the infidels (eg the conquest of Jerusalem, 1099) or against heretics (eg the Cathars, 1209, in Southern France).

As regards the law relating to aliens, the principal development was in consular law. The consul of the merchants played an eminent role. In the same period, Byzantium developed a sophisticated documentary system (*chrysobuls*) and perfected the practice of concluding treaties with the 'infidels'.

vi. The Late Middle Ages

In the late Middle Ages (1300–1500 CE) the modern European States progressively emerged, leading to the intensification of and increase in international relations. But there were few evolutions in the legal institutions mentioned above; the public law of Europe continued to develop according to the inherited lines.

The pretense of the Popes—however weakly effective—to distribute the newly discovered lands in the Americas (the most famous instance being the Bull *Inter Caetera* of 1456 leading to the Treaty of Tordesillas of 1494) and the emergence of the first rules for the protection of the civilians during warfare (covering the categories of the elderly, women, priests, those having religious functions, persons with infirmities, etc) should be noted.

The law of maritime warfare started to develop at this time, namely, the rules of neutrality and of neutral commerce.

vii. Spanish Dominance

This leads to the era of Spanish dominance (1500–1648). In this era, the public law of Europe was being made the object of doctrinal elaboration as a separate branch of law. This was the time of jurists and other philosophers, such as De Vitoria, De la Pena, Suarez, Belli, Ayala, Gentili or Grotius. The core of international law

[20] The sources of the law were: the particular law flowing from agreements, statutes or customs; the common law (*ius gentium*) and the common Roman-Canonical law; and subsidiarily the Natural and Divine Laws. See G Ermini, *Corso di diritto commune* (Milan, 1989).

[21] *Decretum Gratiani*, pars II, c 23; T Aquinas, *Summa Theologica*, II, II, 40, 1.

was geared towards the acquisition of territory and territorial titles. This evolution was the consequence of the great discoveries of the age. The issues discussed were the relations between the titles flowing from Papal Bulls, discovery, agreements, occupation of lands without masters (*terrae nullius*) and belligerent occupation. The question of the recognition of new States received some attention in the context of significant secessions, in particular the independence of The Netherlands from Spain in 1581. The doctrine of the freedom of the seas spread as an essential asset for commerce with the colonies (*mare liberum, non mare clausum*). The law of treaties was perfected, notably with regard to the procedure for conclusion, the absence of formalism and standard clauses. On the other hand, arbitration was in decline. The wide powers traditionally granted to arbitrators were no longer acceptable to the modern State, jealous of its sovereignty and aware of its power. The religious schism contributed to this state of affairs: its spawned tension and distrust.

The laws of war remained underdeveloped and displayed little humanity. The great treatise of Grotius, *On the Law of War and Peace* (1625), testifies to that effect. With significant intellectual honesty, Grotius does not pretend that the positive law of the public solemn war (the war between States) significantly limits the power of action of belligerents; and indeed actual practice is deleterious. Grotius even hesitates on the question of rape, before rejecting its lawfulness. He does not maintain that the reduction of the status of prisoners of war to slaves is prohibited. However, he proposes a series of restrictions (temperaments of war), which the sovereign should adopt and translate into war-related agreements. As he explains, *non omne quod licet honestum est*.

The doctrine of just war was led into crisis by the consolidation of the sovereign State. When every State is sovereign, and thus purports to be the sole judge of its proper causes of war, there remains little place for an objective and constraining doctrine of just war. Every State will consider its own causes to be just. At a time when the Pope and the Emperor are no longer recognised as oracles on the matter, when arbitration is not used for vital interests, when the assessment of the justness of a war is seen as an inalienable exercise of its sovereignty by each State, then the idea of just war can only be addressed by the conscience of the individual ruler. During the Spanish period of dominance here under discussion, the doctrine of just war had already been undermined by the acceptance that a war could be seen as subjectively just by both sides, since a party could fall into an inevitable error on the justness of its cause. This party would then subjectively be acting in good faith. While a war cannot be objectively just on both sides, subjectively it can be so. This admission was the first step towards the demise of the doctrine of just war. The doctrine cannot succeed when the objectivity of its criteria is abandoned through such relativistic devices.

Lastly, it should be noted that the law of maritime warfare developed considerably during this period. The sea gained in importance on account of colonial intercourse and the resultant commercial shipping of resources. The economic war at sea became part and parcel of warfare, as much as the more military war on land. In the Spanish period we notably see the development of the rules on maritime prizes.

In sum, it can be said that the fully-fledged international legal order of Europe stems from this period: we now see the emergence of 'classical' international law. The fundamental entity around which this classical law revolves, the sovereign State, consolidates precisely during this phase; so also, the law giving expression to this sovereignty could only develop alongside the modern State. The State eliminates the intermediary powers and establishes its exclusive internal sovereignty. The latter now becomes a single and supreme notion. The graduated and multi-layered sovereignty of the Middle Ages disappears. At the same time, the modern State secularises and rationalises itself. These are the times of the nascent bourgeoisie, of the rational natural law, of individualism. In municipal law, this state of affairs ushers in the great constitutions of modern times. International law is also affected by these evolutions: it constitutes itself into a discrete system, progressively distinguishing itself from municipal laws.

viii. French Predominance

The era of French predominance (1648–1815) witnessed the stabilisation of the public law of Europe through the great peace treaties of Münster and Osnabrück (Westphalia). The Treaty of Utrecht of 1713 established the principle of the balance of powers (*iustum potentiae equilibrium*) on the political level. Russia and Prussia become important Powers, and the US entered the international arena. The public law of Europe thus extended to entities situated apart from the old Continent. With the secession of the US, a certain tendency was established to recognise new States on the basis of criteria of effectiveness rather than legitimacy. The legal community of Europe lost its religious connotation; the *Res publica Christiana* of the Middle Ages was in decline. Its place was taken by a political-legal community acting as the administrator of the public law of Europe. International law was made the object of many monographic works. The consolidation of practice and precedents; the density of monographic treatment; relative social stability and other factors allowed a shift towards positivism (Zouche, Rachel, Textor, Van Bynkershoek or Moser).

The most accomplished account of the system of classical international law regulating the relations between sovereign States deprived of a common superior, is to be found in de Vattel's work, *Le Droit des gens; ou, Principes de la loi naturelle appliqués à la conduite et aux affaires des nations et des souverains* (1758). The modern territorial State is here at its apogee: public administration is established; mercantilism and economic policy emerge; modern armies are created; secularisation is accelerated, etc. The territorialisation of State and the development of power require certain and stable boundaries. International law applies itself keenly to that issue.

ix. The Evolution of International Law and English Dominance

The preceding paragraphs examined in brief the most important evolutions in the various branches of international law. The law of treaties had been modernised. Oaths had fallen into desuetude and the principle *pacta sunt servanda* had now firmly established itself. Agreements with the 'infidels' were routinely concluded. Diplomatic and consular law gained in importance and became tools of States' foreign policy. Permanent diplomatic missions were established. International arbitration made a reappearance through the Jay Treaties of 1794 between the US and the UK, although it would remain of marginal use till the nineteenth century. Mediation separated from arbitration and became a means of peaceful settlement of its own. The idea of maintenance of international peace was the object of various private reflections, such as in Kant's famous *Perpetual Peace* of 1795. The practice of war slowly started to humanise. A major contribution to this end was the reduction of the definition of war to a fight between professional State armies, with their discipline and rules of engagement. Conversely, the concept of 'just war' declined; it was incompatible with the dominant new idea of the competence of each State to go to war (*liberum ius ad bellum*).

The question of intervention to maintain the balance of power was now being discussed. With the reinforcement of international commerce, questions of neutrality, especially in sea warfare, posed new challenges and ushered in new rules. If a State was free to have recourse to war, another State, equally sovereign, should be free to remain aloof from that war, and in consequence to suffer minimum interference. Neutrality was also nourished by the concept of moral indifference to war: if any State appreciated for itself its causes of war, and if the recourse to war was therefore merely an expression of a general competence to use force, then the fact of remaining a stranger to that armed contest was not reprehensible for being a sort of non-assistance to a State under attack. Quite the contrary: by limiting the theatre of war rather than extending it, neutrality would contribute to the maintenance of peace.

Alien law also developed strongly over this time. Some rights were granted to aliens (minimum standard of treatment). The sources of such rights were internal legislation and treaties. The right of private reprisal remained active, however: when an alien suffered damage in violation of international law, his sovereign could allow him to take reprisals against persons of the nationality of the wrongdoer. The law of public reprisals (forcible measures short of war) also developed. Finally, the law of the sea would make great leaps forward. The concept of territorial waters stems from this period, in particular the famous cannon-shot rule for the extension of these waters: *potestatem terrae finiri ubi finitur armorum vis*. Towards the end of the eighteenth century, this maxim gave rise to the rule of an extension of three nautical miles. But not all States follow this rule.

This quick historical overview may be brought to a close by the era of *English domination* (1815–1914). This was the time of restoration, and later of nationalities. It was also the epoch of an unprecedented enlargement of international society, which extended to Central and Latin America, to Turkey, Japan, Siam, China and Persia. International law began its rise towards universality. The dominant conception was that some 'civilised' extra-European States would be admitted to the advantages of the public law of Europe. This was also the epoch of colonial imperialism, culminating in the Conference of Berlin of 1885. Colonialism led to a refined reflection of different forms of association between States: protectorates, colonies, extraterritoralities (capitulations), zones of influence, unequal treaties, etc. Effective occupation, as title for the acquisition of lands without masters, imposed itself.[22]

This was also the era of industrial revolution, of modern economy and the rise of international interdependence. The practice of States being at once more concentrated and also better documented, legal writings could focus on its systematisation. The tendency was towards moderate positivism. The main source of international law was the practice of States, more precisely their will as manifested either tacitly (customary law) or expressly (treaties) Natural law was pushed back into the consciences of political leaders. The number of treaties rose spectacularly. The European gatherings of Powers (a sort of international *de facto* government) were now important tools of multilateral diplomacy. There remained, however, an important difference between the Powers and the smaller States. It gave rise to a policy of intervention. A 'democratisation' of these international State gatherings was achieved at the Hague Conferences (called Conferences and not Congress, a lexical change of significance) of 1899 and 1907. Important political and legal rulings were adopted at such meetings, for example in Paris, in 1856, with its important Declaration relevant for warfare at sea.

The first technical international organisations were established during this era, giving rise to institutionalised international cooperation. These were administrative unions (such as the Universal Postal Union) or fluvial commissions (such as the Rhine Commission). These organisations were sometimes vested with non-negligible powers.

Modern arbitration took wing: there were numbers of important arbitrations in the nineteenth century (at least 177 have been counted).[23] The general competence of each State for deciding on war and reprisals was recognised; the doctrine of just war was finally dead. Consequently, neutrality developed considerably. The dominant idea of the era was the equality of belligerents in the *jus in bello* and the *jus ad bellum* (an idea still cherished by authors such as Carl Schmitt in the twentieth century). Concomitantly, the question of political intervention, notably also humanitarian intervention, continued to be discussed and gave rise to international practice. The conduct of hostilities was considerably humanised. This was a time celebrating civilisation and the ideal of progress, as exemplified

[22] Art 35 of the Final Act, Congress of Berlin, 1885.

[23] H La Fontaine, *Pasicrisie internationale, Histoire documentaire des arbitrages internationaux, 1794–1900* (Bern, 1902).

by Henry Dunant, the founding of the Red Cross, the Geneva Committee (later renamed the International Committee of the Red Cross), the first Geneva Convention on the wounded and sick military personnel in land warfare of 1864, etc. The ideal of humanity and civilisation also led to the fight against various scourges, such as diseases, piracy or human trafficking.

x. Conclusion

At the end of this brief review of the history of the public international law of Europe, three aspects can be emphasised. First, this international law has been marked by a constant thread of evolution from the times of the ancient Near East and Judaism, to Graeco-Roman civilisation, the Christian Middle Ages and modern Europe. The same legal institutions developed throughout, including, for example, the practice of oaths for treaties. Secondly, the growing cultural unity of Europe—to which Christianity made a great contribution—allowed the body of international law to develop with a significant degree of coherence. Relatively stable rules regarding the 'other', the 'alien', the 'enemy' suppose some degree of acceptance of the 'other' as being equal or quasi-equal. Only then can an *opinio juris* arise to sustain the legal order. This process is triggered by a common interest, common language (Latin), common cultural ground, common religion, common legal experience rooted in Roman law. Thirdly, this particular international law was able to consolidate to the point of being a perfected system, apt to be exported throughout the world, only on account of the fact that it maintained itself for centuries, enabling slow and controlled growth. In turn, this temporal basis was due to the fact that Europe remained for centuries the centre of world power. If Europe had been invaded at some time, the thread of its public law could have been broken—as occurred in connection with Mexican pre-Columbus international law (see section I.A.3.i. below), which unravelled following the arrival of the European conquerors.

3. *Extra-European Public International Law*

Our knowledge of international legal phenomena elsewhere in the world is closely linked with archeology and ethnology. It is quite difficult to obtain a clear idea of the relevant practices of ancient extra-European cultures. The difficulties stem mainly from three causes.

First, the ancient cultures were most often based on an oral tradition; written sources are lacking. In the event that written sources are available, it is not always possible to understand their content correctly, or even at all (as occurred, for example, with the symbols found on Easter Island). Most often, written sources, to the extent that they did exist, have been destroyed or are lost. The state of the sources is therefore in most cases dramatically insufficient for the reconstruction of phenomena as complex as the social and legal traditions of ancient peoples. It also has to be noted that it is often difficult to distinguish between myths, literature, political inventions, the personal views of the narrator and a reliable report on actual happenings. Ancient sources do not render that task easy—as is known, for example, from the ancient Indian sources.

Secondly, monographic studies on the institutions interesting for the lawyer are rare. It is most often necessary to refer to general historical works and to overall studies on this or that civilisation. But these sources make it hard to elicit the type of information needed for an understanding of international legal phenomena. A number of intermediary, and therefore somewhat detailed, studies of political and legal realities in those cultures must first be undertaken.

Thirdly, the general monographs mentioned are written by historians, who seldom display a sufficient sensibility for the legal side of the institutions they study. Their explanations remain in most cases too summary for the lawyer; the terminology is often loose and uncertain; the capacity to grasp normative phenomena in full is under-developed; overall, these studies rarely go beyond the point where the description would start to become rewarding for the international lawyer. Consequently, the lawyer will have to fill in the gaps left by having recourse to intuition more than to solid knowledge. It may well be that more detailed information simply does not exist. There is also the possibility that this information exists but that the historian did not give it pride of place on account of its irrelevance to his subject of enquiry or his view of its excessive sophistication. Legal institutions are complex intellectual realities. In order to achieve a proper knowledge of these matters, a number of good quality sources would be necessary. The more one goes back in time, the less such sources exist.

Notwithstanding such difficulties, it is possible to offer a brief overview of the legal phenomena and legal orders in the five regions of the world that remained for a long time without any direct ties to Europe: Pre-Columbian America; the Polynesian Islands; sub-Saharan Africa; India; and China.[24] Only a very superficial examination of their cultures and international legal rules will be offered here; for more detail, the reader is referred to the works quoted in the footnotes.

i. Pre-Columbian America[25]

International legal phenomena, and sometimes international legal orders, existed in Pre-Columbian America. Scattered legal phenomena had existed since ancient times in Central America, in the area of Mexico. The Olmecs (from 1000 BCE) had a culture allowing for the development of fairly sophisticated legal relationships. They enjoyed extensive commercial relationships with other peoples. Between 400–100 BCE a series of regional powers became established in the area. An international society must have existed, based on some degree of parity between the collectivities, which makes plausible an international legal order regulating their

[24] See Preiser, above n 6; and Kolb, above n 6. All the following pages are based on these two books, where the detailed quotations can be found.

[25] For a more detailed overview and a full quote of the sources, see Preiser, above n 6, 12ff; Kolb, above n 6, 31ff.

relationships. In this social and temporal context the Empire of Teotihuacan expanded (300–200 BCE). This expansion was economic and cultural rather than military. Conquest and control of territory was difficult in the vast and arid plains of Mexico; it would call for the maintenance of important and costly garrisons over extended areas. Thus the Empire consolidated itself on the basis of a detailed system of tribute: the public collectivities allied to the Empire benefitted from important commercial advantages on the markets of the capital as a counterpoint for the tributes paid. This system was initially based on a series of international agreements, which were in due course integrated into the imperial law.

In the southern, more humid areas, the Maya developed a network of city-States scattered throughout the jungle. The latter imposed a natural barrier; the cities were therefore subject to a significant degree of autarky. There was a series of independent kingdoms, conducting a low number of mutual relationships. However, wars of conquest were apparently frequent. They were fought at a level of low intensity. The aim of these wars was to impose on the vanquished the obligation to pay tributes and to open new commercial avenues. Progressively, a policy of dynastic marriages emerged. From the legal point of view, there existed rules on the treatment of prisoners of war (and their sacrifice to the Sun God), rules on the initiation of hostilities and rules governing commercial exchanges. Taking account of the common culture of the Maya peoples, it is probable that a fully-fledged legal order existed in the region. At the same time, this legal order could hardly have been strong and solid, in view of the endemic wars.

A similar model to that of Teotihuacan was developed by the Empire of the Toltecs around the tenth century. Its expansion was based on commerce and colonisation; but military power now played a greater role. There were rules on ritual warfare: an obligation to have recourse to war was defined in order to procure prisoners of war to be sacrificed to the Sun God. These wars were based on limitations in warfare so as to allow the capture of the prisoners alive. The aim of such limitations on the conduct of hostilities was not humanitarian but sacral: it was necessary to capture the prisoners alive because only then could they be sacrificed in due form to the Sun God. Other rules concerned non-ritual warfare (not limited in the same way) and diplomacy.

The Incas, in Latin America, consolidated their Empire starting in the thirteenth century. Between the thirteenth and the sixteenth centuries, the Incas perfected their State to an unprecedented degree. The organisation of public and private life reached a peak. Law was an important element of social organisation. The need for legal rules extended beyond the State to the international arena. There had been various international legal phenomena, but it seems that a fully-fledged international legal order could not develop because of the predominance of the Empire (and thus a concomitant lack of a sufficient degree of parity in international society). The phenomena in question were situated somewhere between international and federal law. With the consolidation and growth of the Empire, they were progressively attracted towards the federal pole. The following phenomena should be mentioned. First, a war could be initiated only through a certain procedure, which recalled Roman fetial law. The foreign collectivity had to be summoned and required to subjugate itself; the advantages of this would be laid out in detail, and conversely the terrible consequences of a refusal would be emphasised. To this effect, an embassy was sent to the relevant collectivity. Any attack on this mission was an independent and immediate cause of war. The procedure had as an aim the subjugation of foreign collectivities with the least expense and bloodshed. Diplomacy was given a chance before reverting to war. The opening of hostilities had to be preceded by various rites (fasting, sacrifices, prayers, consultation of priests, etc). The acquisition of territory was effected through annexation. A policy of dynastic marriages also developed as a tool of political expansion. Its aim was the progressive assimilation of collectivities and the conclusion of military alliances. These marriages were made in the public interest and had a legal component. The *jus in bello* of the Incas was a complex mixture of generosity and brutality. In international wars (which today would be called 'international armed conflicts') rules of war existed but were not always respected. On the other hand, the civil wars involving insurrectionists (which today would be called 'non-international armed conflicts') were conducted with the utmost harshness so as to discourage sedition. In international warfare, quarter was often denied. The fate of prisoners was left to the discretion of the captor. Sometimes such prisoners were treated with humanity and their wounds cared for, and they were also released; but more frequently, prisoners were killed, tortured or reduced to slavery. In sum, the prisoners were part of the war booty of the captor. This rule can be found everywhere in Pre-Columbian America. Other rules on international warfare included, for example, the obligation to conduct hostilities only in the daytime and not at night; the prohibitions on disturbing the peasants labouring in their fields, on destroying livelihood or on pillage; or the conclusion of agreements during warfare, such as armistices. This, if the law developed mainly in the context of federal norms, there were also some international legal phenomena, perhaps more as external projections of the municipal legal order rather than as objective international law norms.

American Pre-Columbian Law reached its zenith with the Aztecs (Mexica) in the fifteenth century. Between 1433 (Triple Alliance of the Aztecs, Tezcoco and Tlacopan) and 1521 (arrival of the Spaniards) an international legal order existed in Central America. The aforementioned alliance was based on a treaty. This instrument organised military campaigns of conquest or for the association of foreign collectivities with the detailed system of tribute inherited from the times of Teotihuacan. The confederation flowing from these associations remained limited in scope. The collectivities subjected to it retained an appreciable degree of independence and entered into separate treaty relations with the three confederated Powers. These Powers had moreover obliged themselves by a treaty to have recourse to war with the aim of capturing prisoners to be sacrificed to the gods (Flowers War). This type of war was governed by a series of tight treaty rules. Traditional warfare, on the other hand, was ruled by customary rather than conventional rules. It was based on a doctrine of 'just causes' of war, for example the refusal to pay tribute, punishment for refusing to entertain commercial relations, etc. There was a very detailed procedure for the opening of hostilities. An envoy would be sent to each collectivity, inviting it to subject itself to the Alliance. If the foreign collectivity ultimately did not accept the invitation, war could be waged on it. In the conduct of hostilities, the capture of enemy fighters would, if possible, be preferable to their killing, so as so secure victims for the ritual sacrifices. In this particular sense, combat was almost chivalric. This relative restraint in attacking enemy soldiers was one of the causes of the manifest inferiority of the indigenous forces when they faced the armies of the Spanish conquerors. However, attacks by night were allowed, as was pillage. There were also many peaceful relationships between collectivities, in particular between the three allied Powers. Each one of these collectivities having retained a significant degree of independence, their dealings remained largely dominated by international law rather than by the more tightly knit federal law. Thus, some treaties concluded among them organised cooperation for common interests, for example for the construction of an aqueduct that was completed in 1466. Overall, it can be said that the existence of a series of independent States in the Mesoamerican region, the close intercourse among them, the relatively developed municipal law systems and the sense of the binding nature of international agreements, support the existence of an international legal order in this region.

A few words may be added on the six 'Indian' nations of North America, which joined together in a Confederation from 1450 to 1777.[26] This 'union' was to some extent a precursor of the Geneva League of Nations of 1919. The main aim of the Confederation was to maintain the peace among its members, and to resolve disputes by diplomacy and collective negotiation. In order to achieve these aims, the Confederation established a system of collective security accompanied by a network of multilateral diplomacy. How can it be explained that nations in a still quite rudimentary condition could have raised themselves to such heights? The answer lies in the fact that before the Confederation was created, the region was riven by endemic war and conflict. Private vengeance constantly degenerated into widespread and destructive engagements. These constant wars destroyed men and resources in a region of vast plains able to nourish all their inhabitants. The North American Confederation succeeded in curbing the wars between its members, but not those between members and non-members. The Confederation was based on a 'Great Law', which preserved the sovereignty and independence of each member. Recourse to war was not generally prohibited: each member could declare war on a non-member, for example to force it into the Confederation as a 'peaceful' nation.[27] The principal organ of the Confederation was the Great Council, on which all members were represented. This was the deliberative organ, where the collective settlement of disputes took place. Decisions were adopted by unanimity.

[26] NC Crawford, 'The Long Peace Among Iroquois Nations' in K Raaflaub (ed), *War and Peace in the Ancient World* (Oxford, 2007) 348ff.
[27] ibid, 353.

Third nations, interested in some decision of the Confederation, were consulted. The confederated entities concluded a series of treaties between themselves. It is remarkable that war did not break out between the members of the Confederation for the 200 years of its existence; and that, on the contrary, war remained frequent with regard to non-members, be it for defensive or for offensive purposes. The municipal 'rule of law' thus contrasted with the international 'rule of nature'. Consequently, international law was quite sharply divided: pacific and progressive within the Confederation, in advance of its times by centuries and the precursor of Geneva; regressive and primitive outside the Confederation, where a precarious state of transactions and the rule of force dominated. The North American Confederation collapsed with the arrival of the European conquerors and their wars of extermination against the 'Indian' communities.

ii. The Polynesian Islands[28]

In the seventh and eighth centuries, the Polynesian Islands were the object of massive immigration from the north. The newcomers were ruled by a cast of aristocrats called the Ariki (or Ari'i). The collectivities created on various islands consolidated themselves into States. The common bonds between these States progressively eliminated the legal and political divergence of previous times. A powerful and stable order was imposed. It was strengthened through a system of vassalage based on a policy of marriages, adoptions and proxeny. The common religion and culture created a bond among the various collectivities. They were relatively independent one from the other, but united by cultural bonds and reciprocal allegiances. Thus, an international legal order had some chance to establish itself in the Polynesian space. However, restricted intercourse between distant islands did not allow for the development of this legal order beyond some rudimentary state. Moreover, there were different rules in different regions. The following main rules may be mentioned:

1. there was a common place of sanctuary and a series of ritual international rules in connection with it;
2. there were days on which warfare was prohibited;
3. there existed rules on meetings of the States for the discussion of common concerns;
4. there was a series of recognised causes for recourse to war, such as reprisals, the capture of persons for cannibalism, the resolution of power policy disputes, wars commanded by the gods, etc.;
5. there were rules for the avoidance of conflict, such as the sacrifice of a young, innocent girl;

[28] For a more detailed overview and full quotation of the sources, see Preiser, above n 6, 55ff; Kolb, above n 6, 89ff.

6. there were also rules on *jus in bello*, but warfare remained on balance very brutal (women and children were appreciated for their tender flesh, quarter was generally refused, prisoners of war were most often killed). However, parliamentarians were normally respected; there were sometimes places for the care of the wounded; and in some situations warfare was moderate (as was also the case against the Western conquerors).

Taking account of the relative paucity of intercourse between these distant collectivities, it may be more prudent to speak of international legal phenomena rather than of a fully-fledged international legal order. However, the cultural and religious ties that existed also allow us to project these phenomena into a legal order based on some *opinio juris*. The information that has come down to us does not permit a definitive answer to this question.

iii. Sub-Saharan Africa[29]

Peoples living to the south of the Sahara Desert have conducted international relations only in certain areas and during certain periods of history. It is difficult to identify the content of these relations, due to the widespread absence of a written tradition before the arrival of Islam and of the Europeans. Were the collectivities of sub-Saharan Africa drawn together in a net of close peaceful and bellicose relations sufficient to develop some common order? Did these relations give rise to rules of public international law? Such questions cannot be answered in any simple and straightforward manner. In most of the areas examined here no international legal order could emerge, mainly due to the paucity of mutual intercourse (limited in many cases to incursions for booty). Autarky and segregation prevailed in the huge African spaces. The individuality of each people or tribe was too pronounced, the tendency to remain aloof from others too great, aversion to neighbouring tribes or peoples too significant to be able to produce a sense of common interests, or at least, of necessity, a consistent body of rules to govern mutual relationships. However, in certain areas international legal phenomena did exist in significant numbers. This triggers the consequence that fully-fledged international legal orders could indeed have consolidated themselves at certain times. The most detailed information we possess for sub-Saharan Africa stems from the Guinean region, that is, the region where Guinea and Benin are now situated. International legal phenomena were particularly frequent in this area. Conversely, the availability of information is much less solid for areas towards the south of Africa. Collectivities and tribes lived there in small, quite primitive unities, entertaining few external relationships. The conditions for supporting the emergence of an international legal order were thus unfavourable in that part of the continent.

[29] For a more detailed overview and full quotation of the sources, see Preiser, above n 6, 71ff; Kolb, above n 6, 107ff.

The region of Upper Guinea provides an example of the development of phenomena (or perhaps an order) of international law. This region encompassed the Empire of the Yoruba, and the Kingdoms of Benin, Ashanti and Dahomey. The organisation of these collectivities was based on Sacral Kingdoms. For a long time they kept apart from Christianity or Islam. The Yoruba (emigrating from the region of Ethiopia) created a series of towns in the region of western Nigeria and eastern Benin. The various cities were interlinked by bonds of religion and culture, as well as by common ancestors. These cities grew into independent States linked together by a weak federal pact, which progressively consolidated after the sixteenth century. The administration of the city-States was thus based on an appreciable degree of autonomy. The oldest kingdom enjoyed a privileged status in foreign affairs: it offered its services to settle disputes between city-States; and it counselled the city-States on the opportunity or not to declare war. The Yoruba cities were small, comprising the main town and surrounding villages. Toward the south, expansion was limited by dense tropical forests. The vassals paying tribute to the cities were thus to be found in the immediate vicinity of the centre. Only one of these cities, Oyo, expended to become an Empire (in the seventeenth century). This expansion was facilitated by the surrounding savannah, which allowed easier movement. The city-States did not have neatly delimited territories. Boundaries in the modern sense were not drawn. There was indeed no need for sharply delineated frontiers; the limits were situated somewhere within the vast surrounding spaces, not marked by a line.

These States in the region of Upper Guinea had a series of peaceful and bellicose relationships among themselves and with third powers. Our information on the later relationships between these entities (ie after the arrival of Islam and the Europeans) is that they were good. This allows us to track the social and legal institutions back to the times before contact with Arabia and Europe. As far as the peaceful relationships were concerned, diplomacy and treaties enjoyed pride of place. But it is probably only following the introduction of Islam that diplomatic tools were refined and a written language imposed, so that treaties could be concluded otherwise than orally. Diplomatic exchanges were intense. Missions were exchanged between Ghana and Morocco; Oyo and Dahomey had diplomatic missions at least from the eighteenth century; the diplomacy of the Fante and Ashanti was famous and celebrated locally. The main aims of these diplomatic missions were political and commercial. It seems that there also existed permanent missions, whose main task was to control the proper payment of tribute (Songhai, Ashanti). In certain regions the consular function was developed, notably for the Haussa State. Throughout the region, the mistreatment of a diplomatic envoy was an autonomous cause of war. Diplomats carried certain symbolic emblems attesting to their accreditation, notably sticks, whistles or swords (Ashanti, Dahomey). The envoys were magnificently dressed so as to impress their hosts and obtain free passage. A detailed protocol regulated their reception. The envoys enjoyed immunities. In some collectivities, the law of immunities reached a certain degree of sophistication. Thus, the Yoruba distinguished immunities according to function: diplomatic functions were covered by immunities; but immunities were denied for espionage or hostile acts. The Ashanti were known for their scrupulous respect for diplomatic law. However, some isolated cases of arbitrary imprisonment of diplomatic envoys remain in the annals.

The majority of treaties concluded in the region concerned the termination of hostilities or commercial matters. A boundary treaty of the Central Sudan region (sixteenth century), written in Arabic, has come down to us. There is also series of peace and alliance treaties between Oyo and Dahomey, covering the years 1730 to 1748. The procedure for the conclusion of treaties was solemn and aimed at producing a sense of sacred duties. An oath was proclaimed during a ceremony in which an elephant and a slave were sacrificed, and the blood of the contracting parties was mixed together. As is so often the case with 'primitive' peoples (similar procedures can also be found in ancient China or Rome), the naked pact was not legally binding: only the oath created the binding force. Sometimes hostages were delivered to guarantee respect for the treaty obligations. These hostages were frequently members of the other party's royal family. The unilateral relinquishment of the treaty obligations through a particular ceremony was permitted in certain cases, which we would now view as akin to a doctrine of *rebus sic stantibus*.

In the context of the *jus ad bellum*, there were several recognised causes of war: acquisition of territories (territorial expansion and tribute); acquisition of resources (pillage, war booty, access to commercial routes, capture of slaves or women, capture of persons for sacrifices); power policy wars and wars to settle boundary disputes; wars to respond to wrongs committed against passing travellers, raped women, incidents connected to hunts, witchcraft, and general reprisals. It was not unusual for wars to be declared under the pretence of reprisal, whereas in reality they were based on power policy concerns. Expansion was often pursued by imposing a duty to pay tribute, rather than by incorporation of the 'conquered' lands. However, not all territorial expansions were the result of a policy of military aggression. Some were the fruit of subtle diplomacy. Thus, Wegbadja (1650–80), King of Dahomey, obtained the subjugation of a number of tribes of the Abomey heights. A series of relationships also existed with European powers, notably France and Spain. The city of Alada, situated on the coast, since the seventeenth century had attracted the attention of European traders. The slave trade quickly became a pillar of external relations in the region. Summing up, the regional *jus ad bellum* was based on the traditional conception of the ancient world: freedom of recourse to war and consequential power policies. The causes of war oscillated between redress for a wrong and territorial expansion. But the 'political' wars (expansion) prevailed over the 'legal' wars (redress).

In the context of *jus in bello*, the sources show the existence of both moderate and unbridled warfare. The Igbo conducted very moderate warfare for certain causes, for example the failure to pay dowry. In many cases, however, non-combatants were not spared. With the advent of artillery in the nineteenth century, warfare was pitched at a higher level of intensity. There were nevertheless several customary rules on the conduct of war in the region. First, a declaration of war was a common occurrence; sometimes an envoy was sent; in certain cases, a time-span of three days was offered for the adverse party to accept the claims presented (this can be seen as foreshadowing a cooling-off period). There were few rules for the protection of the wounded or sick: this might have been due to the lack of proper medical knowledge, but some exceptions existed, which show that care was provided. Frequently, the flesh of the wounded was eaten in cannibalistic feasts. Prisoners of war were the property of the captor. Most often, they were reduced to slavery for the benefit of the captor; alternatively they were sold or ritually executed (in the Borno Empire or in Dahomey). In later times, some important prisoners were kept alive for ransom or as hostages. War booty was recognised; it encompassed horses and weapons. In most cases, half of the booty became the property of the soldiers. Following the arrival of Islam, its very precise rules on the distribution of booty were frequently applied. Weapons of different types were used, including poisoned or incendiary arrows. Attacks by night were rare, but troop movements were often made under cover of darkness. Ruses were frequent and expected. In the forests or in fluvial regions, war was carried out by ambushes, ie by a quasi-guerilla tactic. Certain examples of maritime warfare are also known: in the war between Dahomey and Badagry (1783–84), the King of Lagos blockaded the coast against the war canoes of Badagry, to the benefit of Dahomey. It must also be noted that the Ashanti respected rules of chivalry in their fight against English forces; it is difficult to suppose that they would have fought any differently in their local wars.

The African continent was the theatre of endemic warfare between tribes, chiefdoms, villages, collectivities, kingdoms and empires. War was the most frequently occurring international phenomenon. It served as much for conquest as for the vindication of rights previously breached. Its spectrum ranged from great collective wars to small, semi-private exchanges. The significant presence of warfare explains the development of a number of rules of *jus in bello*. However, political fragmentation among the various collectivities and the enormous spaces of the African continent do not allow us to identify a single customary African law on warfare. There are many examples of particular rules on the conduct of warfare or the treatment of persons applicable in different places. The declaration of war, however, is a custom generally observed in the various regions of Africa. There is no such declaration for raids of reprisal. The declaration, when it occurred, was frequently uttered by diplomatic envoys. Negotiation for a peaceful settlement was sometimes attempted in order to avoid the escalation into war. The Nupe of Nigeria had the custom of sending an envoy to declare an ultimatum. Such envoys were considered to enjoy the privilege of inviolability. For the conduct of warfare, the rule about not fighting at night-time can be found in various African regions; the rule was applied, for example, by the Nupe, mentioned above. In certain regions different types of weapons were to be found, according to the type of war at issue. Thus, for wars between closely connected villages, the only admissible arms were machetes and sticks. The Zulus of Southern Africa distinguished between the weapons to be used, depending on whether the war was a war of conquest, of subjugation (without conquest of territory) or long-distance. Very occasionally, one can also come across efforts to renounce weapons that cause superfluous or excessive suffering.

The treatment of those captured was normally harsh and cruel. African war witnessed many executions, massacres, tortures and instances of enslavement. However, certain collectivities respected women and children (thus, in certain Kenyan collectivities it was prohibited to kill women except when inevitable and militarily necessary). Other collectivities refused any quarter to any persons captured (eg the Gallas of Ethiopia). The Nuer rarely attacked women and children; however, the latter could be captured and integrated into the family of the captor, and sometimes women who had been captured were taken as spouses by their captors. Certain collectivities respected private property; others practised pillage on a grand scale. Occasionally, private pillage was prohibited and any seizures depended on authorisation granted by the military commanders. The burning of villages and food supplies of the enemy was a frequent event. Male prisoners of war were generally executed; alternatively they might be adopted into the family of their captor (notably in Central or Eastern Africa), or ransomed or else sold as slaves (for example in the regions of Nigeria or Dahomey); or they might be inducted into the army of the captor (notably in the communities of northern Nigeria); or enslaved within the captor's community. Prisoners of war would also sometimes be put to death under the law of reprisal. In certain regions close to Egypt, notably in Ethiopia, phallotomy (mutilating the male organ) was practised as a sign of the courage of the warrior and as a trophy of war. The Ibos killed prisoners of war to collect their skulls. Generally there was no care for the wounded or for sick soldiers; but aftercare for the wounded and sick in an army's own ranks was sometimes available following a battle. The termination of armed conflicts of a certain magnitude took place through emissaries and negotiation. Primitive forms of mediation and political arbitration existed. The payment of war reparations was not infrequent, for example with the Ibos of Nigeria.

This brief overview has revealed a host of international legal phenomena. However, in most cases they remained too diffuse and insufficiently influenced by the sense of a common legal obligation to be considered a fully-fledged legal order. There nevertheless existed a number of precise customary rules, which enable us to situate this African international law somewhere between mere dispersed phenomena and a fully consolidated legal order. As we have already seen, a legal order was ultimately shaped after the seventeenth century in certain African regions, such as the coastal Guinean area.

iv. Ancient India[30]

An international legal order developed on the Indian subcontinent only at certain stages of a history stretching over more than 5,000 years and producing cultures of

[30] For a more detailed overview and a full quotation of the sources, see Preiser, above n 6, 118ff; Kolb, above n 6, 151ff.

high standing. There are limited traces of such orders in the Indus culture, between 1350 and 1000 BCE, and at the time of the Aryan culture, towards 600 BCE. After the sixth century BCE, kingdoms slowly began to emerge: tribes settled on a part of the territory and the population became stable. The creation of important towns accelerated the division of labour and cultural progress. Relations between these collectivities were governed by an international legal order with both bellicose (law of war) and pacific (diplomacy, treaties, tribute, cooperation) limbs. A sense of legal obligation was not lacking within these great aristocratic republics, but it was less well developed in the case of absolutist and monarchic States, which were largely prone to conquest and power politics. However, even as regards such States, the reality of international relations imposed certain legal and political limitations. Thus, however much the sense of legal obligation was precarious, it was not completely absent. When analysing the European Middle Ages or the Renaissance, the existence or absence of a legal order has never been measured solely on the basis of a factual propensity to violate certain norms, or from statistics showing the prevalence of breaches: an analysis of Indian international legal orders should not be made the subject of more exacting demands. Some particular difficulties in the analysis of ancient Indian international law nevertheless fall to be mentioned. First, Indian historiography has displayed a marked tendency to rely essentially on ancient written sources (literature, chronicles, etc). These sources contain more than one pitfall. They are hardly sufficiently critical and, further, they do not distinguish between different historical periods. They inevitably mix up reality, myths, moralism, speculation and the subjective view of the writer. Secondly, in India there has been a significant rift between the law in books and the law in practice. Thus, frequently, the particularly generous, progressive and humanistic Indian law of war is praised: in the texts (eg the Code of Manu) and in the sacred tradition, the applicable rules are indeed of a remarkably pacific character. But in reality, Indian history is replete with endemic wars, and their conduct was hardly less brutal than those in Europe or in the Near East. Thus, there are inscriptions in the temples that exalt and glorify war. A god or goddess of peace, such as the Greek Eirene, was entirely unknown in ancient India. It is therefore proper to take account of the rules and reports in the texts, but this should be made without too much reliance on their content. It would be similarly inadequate to attempt to write the history of European warfare on the sole basis of papal prohibitions, or the history of municipal societies merely in the light of legal codes.

Notwithstanding the difficulties outlined above, it is appropriate to give a general overview of the international legal institutions and rules of ancient India. These institutions and rules changed considerably according to the time and place in which they appeared. Here, they will be presented synthetically, without distinctions due to time or space. The global view of these core rules shows a fairly well developed international legal order. It frequently contained institutions and rules later found in the European international legal order:

1. *Diplomacy*. Diplomatic missions had been known since the time of the late Vedic States (sixth century BCE). In conformity with the practice of all ancient

peoples, these were only *ad hoc*, and not permanent, missions. Diplomatic privileges were granted, notably, the inviolability of the ambassador and of his closest staff. These persons could not be imprisoned or impaired as to their physical integrity. The powers of the envoy were clearly distinguished: sometimes he could negotiate and conclude agreements on his own authority; at other times he could only transmit messages. In the event that an envoy exceeded his powers, he could be punished in his home State. It is not clear whether the legal acts performed in excess of his authority were internationally valid or void.

2. *Treaties*. Treaties were considered to be sacred. The bond was not rooted in the operation of the principle *pacta sunt servanda*, nor in the conviction of the binding nature of the pledged word, but rather in the ceremony of conclusion culminating in an oath. There were means of guaranteeing performance of treaties, for example the delivery of hostages. This bears witness to the fact that the 'holiness of treaties' was in many cases more theoretical than real, and that the will of the parties to perform their duties had to be buttressed by sanctions or guarantees. A doctrine *rebus sic stantibus* was known: in the event of a considerable change of circumstances, the treaty could cease to bind the parties. Kautilya mentions the situation where a weak State was coerced to conclude a treaty, but where in due course the power situation changed. In such a case, says Kautilya, it would be legitimate for the formerly weak State to repudiate that treaty. The point is not to question the validity of the treaty on account of the initial coercion; it is rather to allow for a political 'change of circumstances' doctrine on account of the mobility of power. Many treaties in ancient India concerned territorial questions. Those treaties were bilateral. Multilateral or normative (law-making) treaties were unknown.
3. *The rights and duties of States*. Various fundamental rights of States were recognised: the right to self-preservation; the right to territorial integrity and sovereignty; the equality of States in the conclusion of treaties (*jus tractatus*); but also a right of intervention by force for 'humanitarian' causes, in particular against the oppression of the local population—a distinctly political matter.
4. *The right to use force (jus ad bellum)*. The just and recognised causes of war were manifold and overlapped, as in practically all ancient cultures. There were restrictive and centripetal 'legal' causes of war, as there were expansive and centrifugal 'political' causes of war. The former were centered on reparation for a wrong, and to some extent also on the self-preservation of a State. The latter were extremely varied: the extension of power and conquest (sacral duty of the king); the maintenance of the balance of power; intervention in the event of oppression of a population. As a practical—rather than legal—matter, the king was advised to have recourse to war only if he was sufficiently certain of the superiority of his own force. The advice was also given to use armed force only as *ultima ratio*, after having attempted to solve the matter by peaceful means. If it appeared possible to obtain the advantages

pursued without having recourse to war, the peaceful means should be preferred. In sum, there was no legal regulation significantly restraining the use of force; the matter was influenced by political considerations, all the more so since 'political' causes of war were always at hand. It is true that the textbooks elaborated on some restrictive doctrines on recourse to war; they were, however, rarely followed in practice. The most remarkable text is doubtlessly the Mahabharata, an epic cosmology of the Vedic era, in which a doctrine of just war was developed.[31] A war was reputed to be just if three conditions were met: (i) the war was of last resort, ie all pacific means to try to settle the dispute had failed; (ii) the subject matter of the war was lawful; (iii) the rules of the law of armed conflict were respected. We may identify here the conditions of necessity/proportionality of a just cause and of *debitus modus*. The authority of the king, prominent in the European doctrine of just war, was not explicitly mentioned but was implicit; and the *recta intentio* was inherent in condition (ii). Condition (iii) is a criterion of just war extended in time. Thus, a war can become unjust during the fighting, even if it was initially just, if the belligerent exceeds the means of conducting that war. As can be seen, our Occidental doctrine of a just war was already foreshadowed in ancient India.

5. *The laws of war (jus in bello)*. This subject matter attracted the significant attention of international legal doctrine. In the textbooks, Indian warfare is remarkably humanised and generous. In reality, it was severe and harsh, breaches of the rules of war being frequent. In the era of the Vedic States, war was declared on a regular basis. In later times, it was accepted that in the event of 'wars by ruse', a declaration of war was not required. In the wake of these developments, the absence of a declaration of war did not entail a breach of international law. The ancient rule had thus fallen into obsolescence: more precisely, the old rule had been overcome by a new, more permissive one, initially rooted only in certain categories of war. The conduct of hostilities was regulated in detail, notably in the Mahabharata and in the Code of Manu. The belligerents were required to distinguish between combatants and non-combatants; only the former could be attacked and the latter had to be spared (except in 'wars by ruse'). The list of non-combatants was quite generous: it included, for example, sleeping persons, naked persons, disarmed persons, the Brahmin (priests), mendicants joining their hands in supplication, persons who were surrendering, persons engaged in combat with another combatant, peasants and civilians, persons eating or drinking (in certain texts also persons engaging in sexual intercourse), etc. Such lists reflect a moral and chivalric view of war. It should be added that in the textbooks, a series of places and localities were protected from attack: religious buildings, civilian houses, agricultural land, foodstuffs and crops, etc.

[31] See LR Penna, 'Humanitarian Law in Ancient India' (1983) 22 *Revue de droit pénal militaire et de droit de la guerre* 1236.

Attacks at night-time were condemned. There also existed a rule on the matching of forces: cavalry should fight only against adverse cavalry; foot soldiers only against foot soldiers, etc. Weapons had to be carried openly. Certain weapons were prohibited—for example, fire weapons, poisoned weapons, arms having an excessive or indiscriminate effect—and certain textbooks also prohibited weapons containing barbs. In these prohibitions one sees the first signs of a view according to which weapons causing excessive suffering should be banned. It was laid down that wounded or sick combatants should be taken to a safe place. A medical body existed to provide some care. Normally, the wounded or sick had to be released after their treatment. However, only loyal combatants benefitted from these generous rules.

The treatment of prisoners of war had to be humane. In the post-Vedic era, enslavement was prohibited, as was any attack against the physical integrity of prisoners. Some medical care existed for the prisoners, who had to be liberated at the end of the war. In the ancient Vedic times they were released against a ransom, while they were obliged to work as quasi-salves during their captivity.

Brahmin India also knew a law of belligerent occupation. It was advised not to annex conquered territories and to maintain local customs and traditions. However, to the extent that the local population resisted against the occupier, it could be tamed by all available means, including destruction and pillage.

In sum, the modern eye will recognise a series of rules of modern international humanitarian law. It is unfortunate that these rules were not sufficiently respected in Indian warfare in practice. What were the sanctions laid down in the textbooks for violation of *jus in bello*? There were two types of sanction. The first was of a religious nature: the transgression was viewed as sacrilege, as showing contempt for the gods; the law-breaker was ostracised and banished to await divine punishment. The second was of penal nature: for certain offenses, the death penalty was prescribed.

There were some other consequences of war. For example, it automatically interrupted ordinary diplomatic intercourse between the belligerents; it restricted relationships between persons of the enemy nationality; it suspended most treaties; it triggered the application of elaborate rules on contraband of war, etc. A law of neutrality (*asana*) also saw the light of day. It mainly concerned maritime warfare in the context of neutral commerce, and devised criteria for the determination of the hostile destination of goods.

v. Ancient China[32]

In order to properly analyse the international law in ancient China, it is necessary to distinguish between three phases in its history. They have given rise to distinctive international legal systems. First, there was the era of 'Spring and Autumn'

[32] For a more detailed overview and full quotation of the sources, see Preiser, above n 6, 153ff; Kolb, above n 6, 183ff.

(771–481 BCE), based on the formation of an international society among States enjoying relative independence one from the other. The culture of this era was geared towards chivalry and respect for the rules (this constituted a notable basis for *opinio juris*). Secondly, the era of 'States at War' (481–221 BCE), during which States consolidated their power basis and now practised shameless power policies. Territorial expansion constituted the core of foreign policy. Chivalry and the propensity to observe the law significantly decreased, while power plays and political calculation dominated. Thirdly, the era of the Chinese Empire (after 221 BCE), which was based on a 'world order' dominated by the Empire. The latter was at the centre of a system of tributaries. The existence of a common culture (language, religion and tradition, for example Buddhism, allegiance to the Empire, etc) strongly supported the emergence of an international legal order. Each of these international legal systems is examined in further detail below.

The Era of 'Spring and Autumn'

The era of 'Spring and Autumn' was characterised by the emergence of three of the most important institutions of public international law: diplomacy, conferences and treaties. There were also rules on the opening and the conduct of hostilities.

Diplomatic exchanges were at the same time frequent and intense. However, no permanent embassies were exchanged; rather, special missions were sent out. The inviolability of the person of the ambassador and his suit was recognised. Insults or assaults against the diplomatic mission were a just cause of war. The diplomatic exchanges covered a wide range of subjects: official visits; the solicitation of military aid or the search for alliances; funerary gifts following the death of a king; requests for arrest or extradition of criminals; the notification of the conclusion of a peace agreement and complimentary gifts; requests for mediation in a dispute; during warfare, the proposing of armistices or peace agreements, etc. In particular, there were many alliances; they culminated in a system involving the balance of power.

Conferences among the Chinese States were frequent, notwithstanding the numerous political divergences and clash of interests between them. This accounts for a certain degree of solidarity among the Chinese States, furthered by a common cultural tradition. The conferences added a layer of multilateral diplomacy to the traditional bilateral diplomatic relationship. The object of the conferences was to discuss matters of common concern, to try to settle disputes or to forge confederations of States. The most celebrated conference took place in 546 BCE, when the Chinese States tried to conclude an agreement on disarmament and to establish a federation so as to maintain the peace. The insurmountable differences in interests and significant mistrust throughout the conference led to its failure. However, the similarity to the Hague Conferences of 1899 and 1907, as well as to the League of Nations, should be noted.

Hundreds of treaties (*meng*) were concluded between the Chinese States. They were generally bilateral, but multilateral treaties were also known. The object of the treaties was often of a political nature: mutual military assistance; defensive and offensive alliances; extradition; establishment of amicable and commercial relations; the exchange of territories, etc. The treaties were normally quite concise. The preamble laid down the aim and spirit of the instrument; the text would set out the mandatory provisions; and an oath, as well as a curse clause, would conclude the commitments. The principle *pacta sunt servanda* was not unknown in its substance. However, as in all ancient cultures, the obligation was not inherent in the agreement or in the pledged word, but rather flowed from the oaths sworn to the divinities. In older times these treaties were concluded in accordance with a very strict ceremony: a blood oath was accompanied by the sacrifice of an animal, whose ear was cut; the blood flowing from the ear was smeared on the mouths of the contracting parties; and finally the animal was buried with a copy of the treaty written in red on a jade tablet. However, treaties were also concluded without this strict ceremony. The oath would in any case remain at the core of the binding force of the agreement. Normally, treaties were concluded *intuitu personae*, ie attaching to the person of a king rather than to the abstract entity of the State. When the king died, it was customary for the new ruler to swear on the treaty in his own name. Frequently treaties were reinforced by specific guarantees: hostages were one of the most common means in this regard.

In the context of the prevention of war, ancient China has a particular place among the old cultures. True, war was conducted in China, as elsewhere (during the 'Spring and Autumn' phase with considerable chivalry), but it was not exalted as a glorious enterprise. All the most important texts written in the region, from Confucianism to Lao-Tse, Se-Ma, Mencius, Sun-Tse, Yang-Kiu and others, insisted on the fact that having recourse to war was a sign of weakness and a cause of irreparable destruction. Hence, war was to be avoided; in any event, it should only be accepted as a means of extreme last resort. Sovereigns should seek to achieve their goals by negotiation. Good offices and mediation by third parties were indeed frequently resorted to in order to obtain a peaceful settlement. Lastly, the use of deceit was recommended to the extent that it could help avoid recourse to arms. As can be seen, this was not simply a moralist attitude but a political calculation: the point was to obtain the required result with the least effort, expenditure and destruction. In certain texts, a 'just war' doctrine seems to take shape: war is used simply as a means of last resort to curb an insurrection, in cases of self-defence or if the other party refused to grant redress for a considerable wrong. Moreover, the advice was to accept compromises so as end any war as soon as possible. It stands to reason that with this background, the actual conduct of hostilities was in this era limited and rule-orientated (before degenerating into 'total warfare' in the 'States at War' era, below). In the actual international policy of the region, the following causes of war were put forward: to obtain a territorial gain or some other object; to counter a threat or to act pre-emptively; to curb an insurrection, or to intervene in a dispute regarding dynastic succession; and to react to a wrong, notably the breach of a treaty or a promise, an attack on one's own territory, or the lack of customary courtesy towards a sovereign or its envoys. These causes of war gained momentum and expanded in the transition from the 'Spring and Autumn' era to the 'States at War' era. And the discretionary political motives to wage war progressively predominated over the legally limited causes of war.

In the context of the law of war, the era of 'Spring and Autumn' is noted for its spirit of chivalry. However, it would be wrong to think that cruelty or unscrupulousness were absent in practice. The norms are but an approximation of real social conduct; sometimes, they can be ineffective. Unexpected attacks were prohibited: the adverse parties would agree a time and place for the battle. Only aristocratic warriors would fight each other, so the armies were quite small. Hostilities were limited to the combatants, unnecessary destruction was prohibited, and the treatment of the injured or sick persons, as well as of prisoners of war, was generally humane. The annals of Lu attest to the chivalric character of the hostilities. In 707 BCE, the King of Zhou excluded the Prince Zheng from any participation in the administration of the Empire. The latter, having been offended, refused to attend an audience. The King unleashed military operations against the Prince, but suffered a military reverse: he was injured by a spear. That evening, the Prince sent a diplomatic mission to the King to present his condolences. Another episode is no less revealing. The Duke of Song, named Xiang, warred against the powerful State Chu (638 BCE). The Song troops were ready to start fighting, but the forces of Chu were still crossing the river. One of the Song counsellors, knowing the strength of numbers of the adverse forces, proposed to take the strategic advantage of attacking while they were still crossing the river. However, the Duke of Song refused to do so, arguing that such a course would be violating the principle that an attack is not allowed while the adversary is in a difficult position. He continued to refuse to countenance any hostile act for as long as it took the adverse forces to form themselves after the river crossing.

The equality of States was formally guaranteed. However, the *jus ad bellum* of those States holding the most power allowed them to practise conquest and territorial expansion. There were also protectorates, situated midway between full independence and complete subjugation (annexation). The protected State lost its competence on matters of foreign policy but preserved its municipal autonomy. Protected States notably lost the right to participate in the meetings of fully independent collectivities. The numerous alliances between two or more equal States did not result in their joining a federation. These cooperation agreements created at most limited confederations in which the independence of the States was preserved and their freedom of action was limited only to the extent necessary for the common enterprise. International diplomacy and summit meetings were remarkably well developed. Good offices and mediation were frequent occurrences.

It should also be noted that violations of conventional or customary international obligations did occur. It would nevertheless be wrong to conclude from this that the local actors were deprived of a sense of legal obligation. The sources reporting the violations or the controversial decisions not to respect the law bear witness to the careful balancing of interests that led to such decisions. The absence of any moralising commentary in the relevant passages allows us to conclude that the passages were not interpolated by a later Confucian author. The binding nature of the legal obligation was thus present in the minds of the decision-makers. In the majority of cases, violation of the law was studiously avoided.

The above facts shows that an international legal order existed in the region during this period. It is rare to find the same rules being applied in a localised space among subjects of the law who themselves are largely unaltered, over such a long time (three centuries).

The Era of the 'States in War'

The era of the 'States in War' operated on the basis of a wholly different paradigm. The independence of the various States now tended to become absolute. Allegiance towards the Emperor dissolved. Hence, power policy rapidly gained ground; legal and religious bonds faded away. Aggressive wars spread quickly. They were fought for intensely political reasons and therefore lacked moderation and restraint. The legal phenomena and institutions identified in the previous phase continued to exist, but the sense of faithfulness to the law became eroded. The Chinese international legal order was torn apart by a weakening of the sense of legal obligation. Thus, international law was reduced to sparse phenomena, more or less precarious according to context. The existence of an international legal order and the exercise of power policies would seem to be antinomic, but they were not mutually exclusive: the stronger the one, the weaker the other. Reality constituted some mixture of these two extremes. Even if an ideology premised on power policies were able to dissolve an international legal order, it would not be able to do away with international legal phenomena, which are inevitable in any society with international contacts. This also means that fidelity to the law cannot be comprehensively denied: it has to be ascertained for each phenomenon in its unique context. The only general appraisal that can be offered is that a fully-fledged international legal order could not prosper in the shadow of a significantly growing power policy culture.

The Empire

The period of the Empire was characterised by the emergence of a federal type of law with some elements of international law. It stands to reason that these international elements were not emphasised in Chinese historiography, since they ran counter to the belief in the primacy of the Chinese Emperor as the son of Heaven. The international elements stemmed from the fact that the States grouped together in the Chinese tributary system never ceased to enjoy formal independence. The Sinocentric system had an important commercial side. Commercial advantages were the main incentive for States to subject themselves to China and accept its claim of superiority. The tributary system within which they were merged was an extremely elaborate and complex system of vassalage. It was built on the pillars of economy, security and protocol. In fact, it was based on a series of special commercial agreements accompanied by aspects of policy and protocol. It was meant to benefit both treaty partners. This allowed the system to last for centuries. It developed substantially during the Tang Dynasty, between 618 and 907 ce; the last tributary mission was sent by Nepal in 1908. According to certain sources, the system comprised at its zenith 72 tributary entities. Between 1662 and 1911, more than 500 tributary missions were sent into China on behalf of 62 countries. The tributary States were obliged to periodically send missions of allegiance to the Emperor; they had to present gifts (but also received presents, in many cases even more valuable) but they could take advantage of the visits to organise commercial exchanges. For China, the main asset was the recognition of its superiority, the allegiances sworn and the construction of a system of military fortification. The 'subjected' States would gain economic (lucrative commerce and receive precious gifts), political (legitimation and the prestige of the rulers) and military (protection by China) advantages. The internal autonomy of the States parties remained unaltered; intervention in their internal affairs was excluded in principle.

With the formation of a unitary Empire, the basis for an intra-Chinese international law crumbled. The associated States now lost the right to entertain direct relations with external powers, China being the sole remaining subject of international law. Federalisation had gone full circle. The Empire itself refused to treat with external powers on an equal footing: China would enter into relations with external powers only as a superior dealing with an inferior. The Chinese world was thus now hierarchically structured; it was not built on the relations between equally sovereign States. The soil was thus not favourable for the nurturing of an international legal order, supposing, as it does, the existence of States recognising one another as being equal, independent and sovereign. However, the Chinese principle of inequality was workable only in theory; in practice, the Emperor had to accept inroads, according to the strength of the external power and the circumstances. In a series of situations entailing relations with foreign powers, the Chinese Emperor had to put the principle to one side and proceed on the basis of equality. In such circumstances, international law relations were established. This was the case, for example, as regards relations between the Emperor and the Oriental Huns or with the Empire of Tibet. The same was true for the relations with Russia, starting in 1618.

4. *Encounters between the Public Law of Europe and the International Law of Other Regions*

In certain cases, the public law of Europe and the international law of other regions encountered one another. Thus, for example, a number of European powers concluded treaties with Morocco and Tunis during the Middle Ages. Some of these agreements were of a political nature: alliances, agreements to fight piracy, agreements for subsidies. We might recall the Treaty concluded by Frederic II with the Sultan of Egypt in 1229, or the Treaty concluded by Alphonse of Aragon with the King of Morocco in 1282.[33] It is interesting to study these encounters from the

[33] FA von der Heydte, *Die Geburtsstunde des souveränen Staates* (Regensburg, 1952) 251ff.

perspective of how the legal obligation was construed. It is impossible to claim that the bond lay in some universal international law, superior to the State legal orders, which had as yet not developed. The agreements were thus held to be binding either on account of the oath expressed by each party to its own gods (the treaty was thus in reality the sum of two unilateral engagements), or alternatively on account of the pledged word, which each party regarded as sacred. The international legal phenomenon flows from the coming together of two 'constitutional laws', ie from the external projection of two internal legal orders. The construction is at once ingenious and dogmatically interesting. Overall, it can be said that such a construction will be considered satisfactory only in periods when international contact is still sporadic and underdeveloped. With its strengthening, the necessity for a truly common and superior legal order emerges. But it remains the case that, in its beginnings, international law was inextricably linked to agreement and to municipal laws. The experience of legal regulation on the internal plane then spills over into the international arena. Initially, there will be many municipal law analogies, notably with contract law. Later, the new unique body of international law renders it easier to conclude international transactions, and stabilises them once made. It is no longer necessary to have recourse to the doubling of legal orders, with the concomitant difficulty that the obligation for each State rests, in the last resort, on a legal order which 'belongs' to only one party. The whole delicate problem of legal self-limitation is thus theoretically and practically solved—apart from the fact that Jellinek would again attempt it in the nineteenth century.

5. *Conclusion*

This long section has had the aim of clarifying the historical basis of international law, to aid understanding of when such a law developed and to make clear the fact that there have been public international legal orders and phenomena at all times and throughout the world. International law is thus in this sense a universal and unavoidable reality. It takes shape each time minimally constituted and independent public collectivities entertain reciprocal relations founded on the absence of a common superior. A common cultural bond facilitates this emergence, allowing States to pass more quickly from isolated phenomena (expressing the unavoidability of contacts) to the firmer ground of legal orders (expressing the solidity and quality of the legal bond). As a part of reality, each legal order is a historical phenomenon: it emerges and fades away according to social and political parameters. Philosophy, when it wants to speculate on constant and variable elements of the law, on justice or the security of the law, or on any other cardinal question, will be able to do so with a certain profoundness only if it takes these historical realities keenly into account. It will certainly not be limited to reproducing these realities, and may go beyond them by proposing new blueprints. But philosophy cannot ignore these realities if it wants to avoid merely abstract systems whose usefulness is greatly diminished by the lack of experience. This was the reason for devoting a substantial amount of space to the historical aspects of the subject at the beginning of our journey in this book.

This brings us now to another question: what is the object of public international law? Which subject matters does it regulate? Can we say that these subject matters are completely contingent, changing radically according to time and place? If that were true, what would be the common reference point allowing us to identify something as part of public international law? Would it be only the actors, ie the States? Have the historical developments examined above not shown that there are certain common rules and institutions throughout the times and cultures analysed, notwithstanding all the differences in the detail of positive law? In short: what is the material scope or domain of public international law?

II. The Substantive Subject Matter of Public International Law

A. Introductory Remarks

Public international law is traditionally defined through its subjects rather than through its objects. It is considered to regulate 'horizontal' relationships among independent public collectivities in areas where these subjects want to create some sort of legal bond.[34] A fully-fledged legal order develops only after the most primitive stages of social organisation. The development of such a legal order—as we have seen—will be quicker if the collectivities at stake share a common cultural, religious or political background; and it will be slower in the opposite situation. It is only in modern times, after the secularisation of public institutions and the significant growth of interdependence, that a universal international legal order has seen the light of day.

This definition of international law through the structural element of its subjects suggests that the content of the law is not relevant in this context. The collectivities can agree to any question they perceive as being of international concern as part of the international legal order. If that is true, any object whatsoever can be regulated by international law; and the objects it does regulate may change radically over time. A treaty may, for example, be the vehicle for States to agree on matters of private international law, or to unify their internal private legal regulations. The treaty will then require the States parties to adopt the necessary municipal legislation to fulfil their obligations under the convention. The subject matter remains one of private international law or of municipal private law. However, through the treaty these matters are also inserted into the international legal order. Their content remains of a private international law or private law nature, but the instrument in which they are contained is part of public international law. There is here

[34] WG Grewe, *The Epochs of International Law* (Berlin/New York, 2000) 7; A Truyol y Serra, *Histoire du droit international public* (Paris, 1995) 2.

a certain blend between the two legal orders through the subject matters that are regulated. In most cases both the content and the 'container' are rooted in public international law. This occurs when States regulate matters of public law that are part and parcel of international relations, such as the creation of an international institution. If the sole fact that States incorporate a certain subject matter into the international legal order suffices to make it the subject of international law, it may appear difficult to define international law through its object. When international law can accommodate any object whatsoever, the possibility to proceed to a definition of its province through these objects is epistemologically impossible. This is all the more so if one considers that the content of international law will change according to the social and political conceptions dominant at any particular time.

There are certain schools of thought that have taken the position outlined. They have claimed that international law is entirely indifferent as to content; and that it is impossible to define *a priori* a certain material domain of international law, apart from the fact that certain matters could sensibly be regulated only by the international legal order.

B. The Impossibility of Defining International Law Through its Subject Matter: Kelsen

The thesis that international law cannot be defined by its subject matter has been defended with his usual conceptual clarity by Hans Kelsen and his followers. Here is the argument made by this eminent author:

> There does not exist any subject matter that is reserved to national law by its nature and could not be regulated by international law. There is no subject matter that remains exclusively the competence of the State and unable to be regulated by a general or particular norm of international law. There is no subject matter that could not be the object of an obligation flowing from such a norm of international law. International law can indeed regulate any subject matter, even those which are normally regulated by municipal law, eg the form of government, acquisition and loss of nationality, social policy, religion, immigration, custom dues, criminal law matters as well as civil law matters, and matters of criminal or civil procedure.... If no subject matter is, by its own nature, solely or essentially in the domain of the domestic jurisdiction of States, that means that every subject matter can be regulated by international law. The material domain of validity of the international legal order is thus unlimited. Hence, it is impossible to define international law by its object, ie by the subject matters regulated by its norms. ... If there is no subject matter which cannot be regulated by international law, there are some subject matters which can be regulated only by it, ie to the exclusion of the municipal legal order whose validity is limited to a territory and its population. The initial aim of international law is to delimit the territorial, personal, temporal and material scopes of the national legal orders and thus to establish among them a form of coordination. This function can be performed only by the international legal order and not by a national legal order limited to a territory and a population. By the same token, the creation and application of norms of international law, in particular the conclusion of treaties and the establishment

> of international tribunals, can be regulated only by international law and not by national law. The latter is conceived as the law of only one State, ie a legal order whose validity is limited to a specific territory and to the population residing there.[35]

Kelsen therefore admits that certain subject matters can rationally be regulated only by the international legal order, ie that they are in a sense 'necessary' to that legal order. Substantive relativism is limited and not absolute. Moreover, notice that substantive relativism was in any event operating only in one way: international law can regulate any subject matter whatsoever, and there is thus no domain reserved for municipal law; conversely, since municipal law cannot regulate certain subject matters that are in essence international, there is consequently a domain reserved for international law. Thus, it is possible to reflect on the various necessary and contingent contents of international law. A degree of definition of international law by its content is not excluded. A rich dialectical web shifting over time opens up for our enquiry.

C. 'Necessary' and 'Contingent' Subject Matters of Public International Law

It stands to reason that most subject matters subjected to international regulation will vary over time according to the type of subjects of the law, the distribution of power, the predominant ideology and interests, conceptions as to what is 'internal' and what is 'international', and a series of other variables. However, we can be more precise in our reflection on this question.

Historical analysis shows that, since antiquity international interdependence has grown considerably, and that therefore the material scope of international law has significantly increased. In the remote past, international law regulated only some limited subject matters. Today, it governs a wide array of questions and domains. No branch of human activities has remained untouched by significant international dimensions. These international concerns create the need for international regulation. In certain cases, it will be sufficient to try to unify municipal law through a treaty regime; in other cases, all regulation has to take placed at the international level.

This notable increase in the material scope of international law has been noted by many authors. They add to their analysis the significant extension of the spatial scope of international law (universalisation) and of its personal scope (new subjects of the law, notably the individual).[36] The extension of the personal scope of

[35] H Kelsen, 'Théorie du droit international public' (1953) 84 *RCADI* 111, 112–13, 116–17, our translation. See also H Kelsen, 'Théorie générale du droit international public' (1932-IV) 42 *RCADI* 178. Among the followers of Kelsen, see, eg, P Guggenheim, *Traité de droit international public*, vol I (Geneva, 1967) 65. Kelsen's conception has been accepted even by non-followers, see eg A Truyol y Serra, 'Théorie du droit international public' (1981-IV) 173 *RCADI* 38.

[36] See, eg, M Sørensen, 'Principes de droit international public' (1960-III) 101 *RCADI* 5ff; P Weil, 'Cours général de droit international public: le droit international en quête de son identité' (1991-VI)

international law also contributes to the growth of its material diversity. When a series of different legal subjects is recognised, the particular dealings of those subjects will enter at least partially into the domain of public international law. Before such subjects were recognised as possessing some degree of international personality, their dealings were regulated only by municipal law, or by some transnational law. As a result of the recognition of the individual as a subject of international law, the question of how a State treats its own nationals has become a matter of international law, whereas formerly it was exclusively a question of internal law, with the exception of peculiar treaty obligations (eg minorities treaties). From that extension we can trace the development of human rights law and international criminal law. Indeed, the treatment of criminal law matters is another good example of the foregoing. Traditional international law limited itself to defining a crime, and to enjoining States to suppress it it in their criminal legislation and to prosecute it via their tribunals.[37] Ancient customary law thus defined piracy *jure gentium* and conceded universal jurisdiction with regard to it. The Hague Convention IV of 1907 on the laws and customs of land warfare left to the States parties the competence to prosecute war crimes, without laying down any duty in this regard. After World War II, international criminal tribunals were created, whose mission was to prosecute some offences directly as defined by international law. The most sensitive part of State sovereignty was thus affected—this can still be seen today, with the International Criminal Court and its changing fortunes.

This evolution, making the individual a subject rather than just an object of international law, would also lead to the increased blending of international and municipal law, as well as of transnational and international law.[38] When international law ceases to be purely inter-State, a series of questions arises touching on private interests. The answers to these can today be legally grasped only when one combines the sources of municipal and international law (or transnational law) in order to take account of all the relevant regulations. Thus, labour law is a combination of internal legislation and practices, and a series of international conventions and practices centered on the International Labour Organisation. The same can be said for intellectual property (with the World Intellectual Property Organisation), commercial law (with the World Trade Organisation), environmental law (with the United Nations Environment Programme), investment law (with the International Centre for Settlement of Investment Disputes), etc. It should be added that international law has also extended towards the realm of non-law. Soft law phenomena have gained such momentum since the 1960s that ignorance of them can hardly be justified in the context of most questions of international law. Any modern manual of international law will show the degree to which this has become

237 *RCADI* 83ff; C Tomuschat, 'International Law: Ensuring the Survival of Mankind on the Eve of a New Century' (1999) 281 *RCADI* 56ff.

[37] N Politis, *Les nouvelles tendances du droit international* (Paris, 1927) 95ff; M Travers, *Le droit pénal international*, vol V (Paris, 1922).

[38] W Friedmann, *The Changing Structure of International Law* (London, 1964) 5ff.

true. In sum, modern international law is the result of a multiple 'Big Bang': extension of its material scope; extension of its personal scope; a blending of the legal orders and—at least for a certain time—the progress of monism; and a blending with non-legal sources, though the soft law engagements can in practice even be 'harder' and more compelling than some hard law obligations.

If we now compare the primitive legal orders, analysed in section I. above, with the modern international legal order, it should become possible to identify those subject matters that may be found at every stage of international law. The question is: which are the truly necessary rules of international law, those without which an international legal order is not possible? A perusal of ancient and modern sources allows us to say that there are four subject matters:

1. war and the regulation of hostile relationships (*jus ad bellum* and *jus in bello*);
2. diplomacy and special missions for negotiations;
3. transactions, notably treaties;
4. cooperation (extradition, common installations, etc).

The quality and the extension of these four branches vary considerably according to region and time. However, nowhere are traces of these four subject matters completely absent. Transactions are not only a matter of settlement of disputes; they also encapsulate the domain of the 'sources' of the law—treaties have traditionally been fundamental sources of international law. In most primitive societies, the treaty probably precedes customary international law: between isolated peoples common rules will not yet have developed in practice; only the treaty can end their isolation, and it is based on the sum of interacting municipal laws, as described above. On the other hand, in the context of States descending from a common empire or having a common culture, a customary law may precede treaties: this was the case, for example, for the rites (*li*) and the law (*fa*) in ancient China during the 'Spring and Autumn' era (771–481 BCE—see section I.A.3.v. above).[39] Each one of these four branches supposes some treatment of the question of who is a subject of the law. Only those subjects are entitled to declare and conduct war, can send embassies to another subject, can conclude treaties, etc. The rather phenomenological nature of ancient legal systems, where there is not yet a mature legal science, hides these questions regarding the sources and subjects behind more concrete aspects. It would, however, be a mistake not to acknowledge their implicit presence.

Modern international law is founded on the following structures, buttressed by a series of contingent subjects matters of greater or lesser importance:

1. the sources of the law, ie the law-creating processes and the places where the law can be found;

[39] L Zhaoije, 'Traditional Chinese World Order' (2002) I *Chinese Journal of International Law* 40ff; see also generally W Tieya, 'International Law in China: Historical and Contemporary Perspectives' (1990-II) 221 *RCADI* 195ff.

2. the subjects of the law, their determination and their competences or rights and obligations;
3. the relationships between international and municipal legal systems;
4. international responsibility, ie the rules on the legal consequences of breach of rules of international law;
5. settlement of disputes, either by the use of force (ancient law) or by peaceful means (modern law);
6. the law of common spaces, notably the high seas and the extra-atmospheric space;
7. war and diplomacy.

This skeleton of international law is fleshed out by other subject matters, some more eminent (eg the rules on the use of force or fundamental human rights law), some more marginal (eg intellectual property or meteorology). International law has existed for centuries, however, without any general prohibition on the use of force and without any rules for the protection of human rights. This is not to say that such subject matters would not be regarded as fundamental today, nor that their influence on the substance of modern international law is not profound. The point is only that these subject matters remain contingent, in the sense that a public international law order can exist without them.

The seven structures listed above do not share the same importance when considered from a diachronic perspective. The sources and subjects of the law are absolutely necessary to any international legal order, even if in primitive times they were not made the object of explicit treatment. Diplomacy is equally fundamental: sources could not exist without it, ie treaties could not be concluded. We are thus here at the hard core of subject matters necessary for an international legal order. The following subject matters do not occupy the same level of eminence:

1. War

From a strictly analytical point of view, it is possible to say that war has always existed alongside humanity.[40] Because of this, all international legal orders have developed rules governing war. But it would be wrong to conclude from this that war will inevitably always remain a part of international life. It is not impossible that it could be laid to rest universally, as it has been within the European Union. There is no compelling reason why peaceful settlement procedures could not be used in place of war some day. Therefore, the regulation of war is not absolutely necessary to any international legal system. In other words, it is not placed at the same level of necessity as diplomacy or transactions. The only truth is that as long as public war remains a reality, international law will have to regulate it. If the fact of war were to fade away, international law would cease to regulate it—and that

[40] And it has usually been a byword for barbarity. See the still interesting 19th-century monograph by C Letourneau, *La guerre dans les diverses races humaines* (Paris, 1895).

would hardly be to its detriment. Rather, the international legal order would probably gain in force and strength.

2. Relationships Between International and Municipal Law

In the primitive or less advanced legal systems of the Americas, in sub-Saharan Africa, in Asia or in Australia, as well as in early Europe, the problem of the relationship between municipal and international law did not exist. Obligations assumed in external relations were not founded on the conception of an objective international legal order with its own set of norms. The rough jurisprudence of primitive peoples could not elevate itself to analytical levels of such refinement. It should be added that, in these ancient times, the concept of an internal legal order distinct from social morals, rites and religion did not exist. As we have already seen, engagements of an international nature were fundamentally based on oaths sworn to local deities. Clauses invoking curses were often added. Thus, article 15 of the Compact between Hattusil (of the Hittites) and Ramses II (of Egypt) of 1292 BCE stipulated that the thousand gods of Hatti and the thousand gods of Egypt would destroy the houses, the lands and the servants of the he who failed to respect the clauses of the agreement.[41] The treaties were inscribed in two copies, one for each Power. The international norms thus created were initially part and parcel of internal law, or, better, of the legal-religious tribal order. In other words, they were part of the section of municipal law touching on external relations (from which, even up to the nineteenth century, we find the construction of treaty obligations as 'external public law').

It is only when internal legal orders progressively consolidated themselves as being distinct from morals and religion, and when an international legal order developed as a set of objective norms, that the question of the relationship between these two orders could take shape. Today, the question is inescapable. The delimitation of the scope of application or of the respective reach of the several municipal legal orders can indeed rationally be performed only through international law. If such delimitation were the result of municipal legal orders, there would be overlapping and conflicting unilateral claims and ultimately chaos. We also have to take into account the fact that the international legal order does not develop all the rules necessary for its proper functioning; it will refer in part to the internal legal orders, which will furnish some necessary complements, such as organs for the enforcement of international duties. International law will often concentrate on the creation of rules (sources) but leave their implementation and enforcement to the organs of the State. International society does not yet have all the organs necessary for the implementation of all the norms produced at the international level. The jealous protection of State sovereignty, but also considerations of subsidiarity,

[41] See G Contenau, *La civilisation des hittites et des mitanniens* (Paris, 1934) 146ff (the text of art 15 can be found at 151); V Korosec, *Hethitische Staatsverträge, Ein Beitrag zu ihrer juristischen Wertung* (Leipzig, 1931) 58ff.

contribute to this state of affairs. Hence, international law will need to cooperate with internal law in a sort of sharing of work. From the fact that the two legal orders are thus in necessary relation one to the other, the question of their legal relationship is posed. But this question has not always arisen throughout history, and it has not always had the same weight—say at the time of Vattel—that it has today.

3. *The Law of Common Spaces*

This branch of international law is quite old, but it is not strictly necessary to the existence of an international legal order. The law of common spaces supposes the consolidation of States, a certain degree of social evolution and in particular a certain threshold of international intercourse. Only at these stages of development is the need to define one or several commonalities—*res communis omnium* (better: *res extra commercium*)—felt. The space most clearly destined to be the subject of such a law is the high seas. They cannot be dominated to the same extent as a piece of land; an element essential for the acquisition of property, or sovereignty over it, namely, that it can be occupied for the exercise of uncontested power, is manifestly lacking. It is hardly an accident that domination over the territorial sea (which was to be assimilated to State territory at the beginning of the twentieth century) was initially defined as a function of the reach of cannon placed on the shore (the 'cannon-shot' rule).[42] That rule was later translated into the fixed distance of three nautical miles. It is within this restricted area that the actual display of State power was considered to take place.

Furthermore, the high seas provide routes for commercial exchanges. They could therefore not be appropriated under the sovereignty of one State to the exclusion of all others. The excluded powers would not accept such a pretence, which would hamper their commercial and war-related capacities. Thus, from quite early times the high seas were considered to constitute a common space subject to rules of international law.[43] The first traces can be found in antiquity, notably at the time of the Roman Empire.

Modern international law now recognises other common spaces too: Antarctica (with some limitations) and extra-atmospheric space. The degree of necessity of this branch of international law is linked to the development of territorial States and of international commerce.

[42] A Raestad, 'La portée du canon comme limite de la mer territoriale' (1912) 19 *RGDIP* 598ff; HSK Kent, 'The Historical Origins of the Three Miles Limit' (1954) 48 *AJIL* 537ff. See also P Jessup, *The Law of Territorial Waters and Maritime Jurisdiction* (New York, 1927).

[43] And see the famous Selden/Grotius dispute on *mare clausum* and *mare liberum*: WG Grewe, *The Epochs of International Law* (Berlin/New York, 2000) 257ff.

4. *Pacific Settlement of International Disputes and International Responsibility*

These interlinked subject matters, the pacific settlement of international disputes and international responsibility, fully penetrate into the body of international law only at a late stage, that is at the end of the nineteenth century and at the beginning of the twentieth century. True, the issue of sanctioning violations of the law is much older; so also is the question of how to settle disputes. However, these questions were apprehended differently in older systems of international law. The two subject matters were for a long time enmeshed in the legal institutions of diplomacy, transactions and war. If a dispute arose between certain collectivities, they could resolve it through negotiation (diplomacy). Such a dispute could rest on the claim of a violation of some legal rule; this would be tantamount to putting into motion a claim of responsibility. If the negotiations were successful, the dispute was resolved. There is here the creation of a set of new rules of international law, contained in the treaty which the collectivities concluded to resolve their dispute. Consequently, the law of settlement of disputes and of responsibility initially constituted a mechanism involving diplomacy and the sources of the law. If negotiation was not successful, the purportedly aggrieved State could have recourse to reprisals or war in order to 'settle' the dispute. In the latter case, one would pass from the law of peace to the law of war.[44] From this vantage point, ie from a legal perspective, the war would have the function of resolving the dispute and ensuring punishment for the wrong inflicted. If a State was not powerful enough to have recourse to this ultimate means, it would either have to accept this diminution of its standing, or alternatively seek powerful alliances. In short, war was the ultimate measure for sanctioning a breach of international legal obligations.

On the political plane, clearly, war was not always declared or conducted to punish previous unlawful conduct. Frequently, the allegation of a wrong was only a pretext: often, a State would not invoke a right that had been violated but some vital interest;[45] and it was often difficult to disentangle the spheres of rights and of mere interests (eg in the context of arguments such as the balance of power or the Monroe Doctrine). However, from the legal point of view, war could thus be analysed as a hybrid instrument, for lawful sanctions and for the settlement of disputes.

[44] With reprisals, on the contrary, the law remained the 'law of peace'. Thus, some legal contraints were to be respected when, say, the territory of another State was made the object of forcible measures: this is the gist of self-defence or self-preservation precedents like *The Caroline* of 1837. See JB Moore, *Digest of International Law*, vol II (Washington, 1906) 409ff. See also RY Jennings, 'The Caroline and McLeod Cases' (1938) 32 *AJIL* 82ff.

[45] This is still sometimes the case today: see, eg, the declaration of Turkey in 1995 that the extension of Greek territorial waters from 6 to 12 nautical miles (the latter being the ordinary extension of the territorial sea under the rules of the Montego Bay Convention on the law of the sea, 1982, art 3) would be considered by Turkey as a *casus belli* in view of the fact that it would drastically affect vital Turkish interests. See BBC, World Broadcasts, EE/2326 B/7, 10 June 1995. It is needless to insist on the incompatibility of such statements with art 2, § 4 of the UN Charter.

Thus, the law on the settlement of disputes and the law on State responsibility were not developed as fully-fledged and autonomous branches of international law; rather, they were ancillary to other legal institutions, ie to treaties and war. The situation began to change when modern international law attempted to prohibit the use of war (and later the use of force). If war was no longer to be recognised as a legal means to settle disputes, other avenues had to be explored to that end. Hence, rules on State responsibility and on the pacific settlement of disputes now had to be developed. While in the nineteenth century eminent authors could still write that an international law of State responsibility was inconceivable because it would be incompatible with State sovereignty,[46] an astonishingly modern theory of State responsibility was developed by the great Italian international law teacher Dionisio Anzilotti at the very beginning of the twentieth century.[47] It became progressively clear that the effort to keep the peace could only lay claim to some degree of success if alternative and effective means to settle the real disputes of the world were devised. If aggrieved States were not offered any effective avenue to channel their legitimate claims, the threat of military action would continue to materialise. No State would be able to accept that its rights could not be enforced while at the same time it was deprived of any means of effective self-help. Thus, concomitantly with the development of a law against war, there was developed a law on the pacific settlement of disputes: the Hague Conferences (1899/1907), the League of Nations Covenant (1919, which was based on the fundamental rule under articles 12–15 of the Covenant: no recourse to war without a prior attempt to achieve pacific settlement);[48] and later the UN Charter (1945, article 2, § 4, chapters VI and VII).[49] In sum, only in the modern system of international law could the branches of peaceful settlement of disputes and the responsibility of States find their place as autonomous subject matters. They became fully realised during the transit from classical to modern international law, ie from the nineteenth to the twentieth centuries.

5. *The Degrees of Necessity*

The preceding sections show that there are different degrees of 'necessity' with regard to the content of the international legal order. Certain subject matters are truly necessary in the strictest sense: the sources, the subjects and the transactions (cooperation and diplomacy). Other subject matters are only relatively necessary: they become so only at a certain stage of development of the international legal order (common spaces, the relationships of international/internal law), or are so only because they happen to have always been with us (war). Still other subject

[46] T Funck-Brentano and A Sorel, *Précis de droit des gens* (Paris, 1877) 224: 'L'idée d'une responsabilité réciproque des Etats est contradictoire avec l'idée de souveraineté.'

[47] D Anzilotti, *Teoria generale della responsabilità dello Stato nel diritto internazionale* (Florence, 1902).

[48] See R Kolb (ed), *Commentaire sur le Pacte de la Société des Nations* (Brussels, 2015) 555ff.

[49] See B Simma, DE Khan, G Nolte and A Paulus (eds), *The Charter of the United Nations, A Commentary*, 3rd edn, vols I and II (Oxford, 2012) 200ff, 1069ff, 1237ff.

matters are necessary only to a particular international legal order, for example an international legal order trying to suppress violence among its members (the law of State responsibility and the law of pacific settlement of disputes; the law on the maintenance of international peace). Lastly, some branches are contingent, in the sense that they can be made the object of international law but can also remain aloof from it. These can be important branches of the law as it stands today (eg human rights law), or be rather more marginal branches (eg the law of intellectual property).

D. Branches that were Part of International Law and Have Ceased to be Part of It

It may be rewarding to shed some light on certain subject matters that were historically parts of certain international legal orders and which have been abandoned over time. This is a sort of contribution to the relativity of many of the contents of international law, in the sense of the words of Hans Kelsen quoted in section II.B. above. All these are contingent parts of international law.

1. Sacral Causes of War

In a series of more or less primitive international societies, there were several recognised causes of war. The two most ancient causes were the appropriation of resources (wars of pillage) and vengeance (wars in response to a perceived wrong).[50] It is true that the first type was a predatory war of a typically anti-juridical nature, whereas the second was a war of reprisal of a typically legal nature. However, both types of wars were permitted by the legal order; in this larger sense, both were legal wars. A third category of causes has to be added to these. There existed in some societies wars that were commanded by the law and by religion, ie divine or sacred wars. Thus, in Pre-Columbian America, and more particularly in the area of the Triple Alliance among the Aztecs (Mexica), Tezcoco and Tlacopan (in 1433 ce; see section I.A.3.i. above), the gods of war demanded human sacrifices in great numbers. The religion of the Aztecs was built on the belief that the survival of the world depended on these sacrifices. The Sun God was to be constantly nourished with human blood so as to sustain his course while crossing 'hell', symbolised by the night, rising again in the skies the following morning. In accordance with this belief, wars launched in order to capture persons to be sacrificed were not only allowed but mandatory. This sacral cause of war was part of the positive law of the region.[51]

[50] See Letourneau, above n 40.

[51] J Soustelle, *Les Aztèques à la veille de la conquête espagnole* (Paris, 1955) 239; WL Bernecker, H Pietschmann and HW Tobler, *Eine kleine Geschichte Mexicos* (Frankfurt, 2007) 14; A Knight, *Mexico, From the Beginnings to the Spanish Conquest* (Cambridge, 2002) 152ff; MC Meyer and WL Sherman, *The Course of Mexican History*, 4th edn (New York/Oxford 1991) 67ff.

In the *Jus Publicum Europeaum*, the just causes of war were part of natural law; but they also had some effect in the realm of international law.[52] Thus, in memory of the wars God (Jahweh) had commanded the Jewish people to wage, there existed the category of wars that were just simply because they were ordered by God (*quod Deus imperat*).[53] Therefore, a 'divine' just cause of war was to be found in some interpretations of international law of the time.

Compare this with the entirely different international law of the nineteenth century: the question of objectively just causes of war disappears and gives way to the sovereign competence of each State to declare war for any cause that will seem just to it. The result is that international law is not concerned with the causes of war but only with the formal declaration of war.[54] This is the time of emergence of the doctrine of indifference of international law with regard to the causes of

[52] On the law of antiquity: H Hausmanninger, 'Bellum iustum und iusta causa belli im älteren römischen Recht' (1961) 11 *Oesterreichische Zeitschrift für öffentliches Recht* 335ff; S Albert, *Bellum iustum: Die Theorie des gerechten Krieges und ihre praktische Bedeutung für die auswärtigen Auseinandersetzungen Roms in republikanischer Zeit* (Lassleben, 1980); S Clavadetscher-Thürlemann, *Polemos dikaios und bellum iustum: Versuch einer Ideengeschichte* (Zurich, 1985); M Mantovani, *Bellum Iustum—Die Idee des gerechten Krieges in der römischen Kaiserzeit* (Berne/Frankfurt, 1990); A Calore, *Forme giuridiche del 'bellum iustum'* (Milan, 2003). On the Middle Ages: J Salvioli, *Le concept de guerre juste d'après les écrivains antérieurs à Grotius*, 2nd edn (Paris, 1918); A Vanderpol, *La doctrine scolastique du droit de la guerre* (Paris, 1925) 28ff; G Hubrecht, 'La guerre juste dans la doctrine chrétienne, des origines au milieu du XVIe siècle' (1961) 15 *Recueil de la Société Jean Bodin* 107ff; FH Russell, *The Just War in the Middle Ages* (Cambridge/London, 1975); WG Grewe, *The Epochs of International Law* (Berlin/New York, 2000) 105ff; A Vanderpol, *Le droit de la guerre d'après les théologiens et les canonistes du Moyen Age* (Paris/Brussels, 1911); H Gmür, *Thomas von Aquino und der Krieg* (Leipzig, 1933); G Beesterm-Iler, *Thomas von Aquin und der gerechte Krieg: Friedensethik im theologischen Kontext der Summa Theologicae* (Cologne, 1990). On the concept in general: H Wehberg, 'Le problème de la mise de la guerre hors la loi' (1928-IV) 24 *RCADI* 151ff; D Beaufort, *La guerre comme instrument de secours ou de punition* (The Hague, 1933); R Regout, *La doctrine de la guerre juste de Saint Augustin à nos jours* (Paris, 1935); Y De La Brière, *Le droit de juste guerre* (Paris, 1938); E Reibstein, *Völkerrecht—Eine Geschichte seiner Ideen in Lehre und Praxis*, vol I (Freiburg Br/Munich, 1958) 121ff; GIAD Draper, 'The Just War Doctrine' (1978) 86 *Yale Law Journal* 370ff; P Haggenmacher, *Grotius et la doctrine de la guerre juste* (Paris, 1983) 250ff, 597ff; P Haggenmacher, 'Mutations du concept de guerre juste de Grotius à Kant' (1986) 10 *Cahiers de philosophie politique et juridique* 117ff; JB Elshtain, *The Just War Theory*, (Oxford/Cambridge (Mass), 1992); M Walzer, *Just and Unjust Wars: A Moral Argument with Historical Illustrations*, 2nd edn (New York, 1992); K Szetelnicki, *Bellum iustum in der katholischen Tradition* (Fribourg, 1992). On the relations with the Islamic doctrine of just war: R Steinweg, *Der gerechte Krieg: Christentum, Islam, Marxismus* (Frankfurt, 1980); J Kelsay and JT Johnson, *Just War and Jihad: Historical and Theoretical Perspectives on War and Peace in Western and Islamic Tradition* (New York/London, 1991). In the newer literature, see notably: JW Lango, *The Ethics of Armed Conflict: A Cosmopolitan Just War Theory* (Edinburgh, 2014); CE Gentry and AE Eckert (eds), *The Future of Just War: New Critical Essays* (Athens/London, 2014; J Neusner, BD Chilton and RE Tully (eds), *Just War in Religion and Politics* (Lanham/Boulder/New York, 2013); AF Lang Jr, C O'Driscoll and J Williams (eds), *Just War: Authority, Tradition and Practice* (Washington, DC, 2013); NJ Rengger, *Just War and International Order: The Uncivil Condition in World Politics* (Cambridge, 2013); T Brooks (ed), *Just War Theory* (Leiden, 2013); RJ Regan, *Just War: Principles and Cases* (Washington, DC, 2013); F Allhoff, NG Evans and A Henschke, *Routledge Handbook of Ethics and War: Just War Theory in the Twenty-First Century* (London, 2013); C Nadeau and J Saada, *Guerre juste, guerre injuste: histoire, theories et critiques* (Paris, 2009); and see also F Rigaux, *De la doctrine de la guerre juste à la prohibition du recours à la force* (Brussels, 2003).

[53] J Van Kan, 'Règles générales du droit de la paix' (1938-IV) 66 *RCADI* 438.

[54] See I Brownlie, *International Law and the Use of Force by States* (Oxford, 1963) 19ff.

war: each sovereign State possesses a *liberum jus ad bellum*; it is free to engage in a duel with another State; the law then limits itself to attaching some *jus in bello* consequences to this public contest, which is considered by definition to be just on both sides and is fought under the polar star of equality of arms.[55]

The twentieth century would again distinguish between 'legitimate and illegitimate' wars. But the criterion was now not that of justice, but rather one of legality, ie of conformity with the rules of positive law as enshrined, for example, in the Covenant of the League of Nations for the States parties to that treaty.[56] Under the Covenant, the following wars were unlawful: wars of territorial conquest (annexation, article 10 of the Covenant) and unmediated wars (ie any war declared or commenced before having fully gone through the procedures of peaceful settlement of disputes under articles 12–15 of the Covenant). The 'unjust', or more precisely illegal, cause was thus determined in the first case by a substantive criterion (annexation) and in the second by a formal criterion (non-use of procedures).[57] In the system of the Charter of the UN, unlawful wars are all those which are undertaken in the absence of a circumstance precluding wrongfulness, such as self-defence (article 51 of the Charter), the authorisation of the Security Council (an evolutionary interpretation of Chapter VII of the Charter) or the consent of the local government to military action on its territory (customary international law). It is easy to grasp the variations of international law on this question in different eras.

2. Dynastic Succession

At the end of the fifteenth century, the maxim of the balance of powers started to take shape in the European arena. It would reach its zenith in the eighteenth and nineteenth centuries. With the rise of that maxim, dynastic succession became a question of common concern and entered into the body of international law.[58] We have already seen that dynastic marriages were issues of international law in other parts of the world too, as, for instance, in the Mesoamerican Pre-Columbian international law (see section I.A.3.i.). According to the way dynastic succession was to be managed, the balance of powers could be more or less easily maintained or, conversely, upset. When republican forms of government started to gain ground

[55] See, eg, P Haggenmacher, 'Mutations du concept de guerre juste de Grotius à Kant' (1986) 10 *Cahiers de philosophie politique et juridique* 107ff.

[56] This evolution from equality to discrimination was sharply criticised by some conservative authors such as C Schmitt, *Die Wendung zum diskriminierenden Kriegsbegriff* (Munich, 1938).

[57] JB Whitton, 'La neutralité et la société des Nations' (1927-II) 17 *RCADI* 477; N Politis, *Les nouvelles tendances du droit international* (Paris, 1927) 101–02. For a fuller account, see R Kolb (ed), *Commentaires sur le Pacte de la Société des Nations* (Brussels, 2015).

[58] There are still traces of this question in international law textbooks of the 19th century. See, eg, GF de Martens, *Précis du droit des gens modern de l'Europe* 2nd edn, vol I (Paris, 1864) 208ff, notably at 214–15, with many references. The title of the chapter is emblematic: 'Des Droits qui peuvent appartenir à une nation sur la Constitution de l'autre'; the principle of the balance of powers is mentioned.

and the 'balance of powers' concept was put into retreat, the issue of dynastic succession disappeared from the province of international law.

3. *The Duties of a Nation Towards Itself (Self-preservation)*

In the wake of European modernity with its anthropocentric revolution, the objective system of natural law dissolved into a system comprising a series of subjective natural rights of any subject thought of as being originally free.[59] From this perspective, it is understandable that the authors would be concerned with natural rights as regards others, as much as with natural rights as regards oneself. The rights as regards oneself were not simply a matter of morals. Rather, it would be possible to claim these rights before a third party, in order to escape from certain legal obligations assumed towards it, invoking the primacy of the right to self-preservation. This was a sort of old-fashioned *jus cogens*. We can find traces of this approach in the public international law of the time.

The most eminent authors in this regard were Wolff[60] and de Vattel. The latter, in his famous volume on the *Law of Nations* of 1758 (Book I, Chapter II and following), enumerates the 'interior' rights of a nation, notably the right of self-preservation, but also the rights to culture, to agriculture[61] and to maintain public roads.[62] He says clearly that in the event of conflict between a fundamental right as regards oneself and an obligation towards another, the former prevails, 'les devoirs envers soi-même prévalent, en cas de collision, sur les devoirs envers autrui'.[63] Thus, this subjective system of natural rights has an immediate effect on the construction of international law.

[59] E Opocher, *Lezioni di filosofia di diritto* (Padua, 1983) 101ff. On the history of these subjective right, see P Pavan, *Diritto dell'uomo e diritto naturale* (Rome, 1966) 355ff; F Castberg, 'Natural Law and Human Rights' (1968) 1 *Revue des droits de l'homme* 14ff; R Marcic, *Geschichte der Rechtsphilosophie* (Freiburg, 1971) 67ff; EBF Midgley, 'Natural Law and Fundamental Rights', (1976) 21 *American Journal on Jurisprudence* 144ff; G Oestreich, *Geschichte der Menschenrechte und Grundfreiheiten im Umriss*, 2nd edn (Berlin, 1978); MC Peces Barba, *Teoria dei diritti fondamentali* (Milan, 1993); D Merten and HJ Papier (eds), *Handbuch der Grundrechte*, vol I: *Entwicklung und Grundlagen* (Heidelberg, 2004) 3ff; A Facchi, *Breve storia dei diritti umani*, (Bologna, 2007); F Rigaux, 'Les fondements philosophiques des droits de l'homme', (2007) 18 *Revue trimestrielle des droits de l'homme* 307ff.

[60] C Woolf, *Jus Gentium Methodo Scientifica Pertractatum* (1749), ch I.

[61] E de Vattel, *Le droit des gens ou principes de la loi naturelle* (1758), ch VII.

[62] ibid, ch IX.

[63] ibid, book II, ch II, § 25; Préliminaires, § 14: '[L]es devoirs envers soi-même l'emportant incontestablement sur les devoirs envers autrui'. Vattel applied this rule in several contexts: book II, ch I, § 2 (duties of assistance and solidarity among nations); book II, ch II, § 25 (commerce with other nations); Book II, ch VII, § 94 (prohibition on foreigners entering into the territory); book II, ch IX, § 123 (in certain cases, necessity prevails over humanity: 'Mais si ce vaisseau [demandant l'entrée dans un port à cause d'une tempête] est infecté de la peste, le maître du port l'éloignera à coups de canon, et ne péchera ni contre la justice, ni même contre la charité, laquelle, en pareil cas, doit sans doute commencer par soi-même'); book II, ch XII, § 170 (necessity and treaty obligations); book II, ch XVIII, § 332 (primacy of vital State interests); book III, ch VI, § 92 (military assistance is not due, even if provided by treaty, if the public salute of the State is at risk). Necessity can thus also affect perfect conventional rights and obligations: book III, ch VII, § 107; book III, ch VII, § 122, 125. This part of Vattel's doctrine has been harshly criticised in some writings of the 20th century: C Van Vollenhoven, *Du droit de paix, De iure pacis* (The Hague, 1932) 133.

The obligations towards oneself would usher in, at the end of the nineteenth century, a more detailed system of 'fundamental rights' of the State.[64] These rights were abandoned in the twentieth century, in the wake of the strengthening of an objective international law, more robust against subjectivist challenges and 'vital interest' exceptions.[65]

III. Types of International Law

A. Universalism, Supranationalism and Internationalism

Certain types of international relations recur throughout time and influence the international legal order regulating international society.[66] There are three basic types of relations that can apply to collectivities:

1. *universalism*, ie the existence of an empire;
2. *supranationalism*, ie forms of federalism or mixed political regimes among powers in hierarchical settings;
3. *internationalism*, ie a system based on the existence of a series of equal and independent powers.[67]

In Europe, universalism corresponds to Roman antiquity, with the Empire and the *pax romana*; supranationalism corresponds to the complex system of the medieval Christian Republic, with its plurality of powers, collectivities and kingdoms placed under the umbrella of the Pope and the Emperor; and internationalism reflects the atomised and egalitarian system of independent powers of post-Westphalian times. The typology can also be found in other areas of the world. In Latin America,

[64] On these fundamental rights, see, eg, L Duguit, *Traité de droit constitutionnel*, 3rd edn, vol I (Paris, 1927) 715ff; G Gidel, 'Droits et devoirs des nations. Théorie classique des droits fondamentaux des Etats' (1925-V) 10 *RCADI* 537ff; L Le Fur, *Précis de droit international public*, 3rd edn (Paris, 1937) at §§ 638ff. See also A Pillet, *Recherches sur les droits fondamentaux des Etats dans l'ordre des rapports internationaux et sur la solution des conflits qu'ils font naître* (Paris, 1899); A Pillet, 'Recherches sur les droits fondamentaux des Etats' (1898) 5 *RGDIP* 66ff and (1899) 6 *RGDIP* 503ff; P Fauchille, *Traité de droit international public*, vol I, pt I (Paris, 1922) 395ff; WG Phillimore, 'Droits et devoirs fondamentaux des Etats' (1923-I) 1 *RCADI* 29ff; S Séferiadès, 'Principes généraux du droit international de la paix' (1930-IV) 34 *RCADI* 343ff; E Kaufmann, 'Règles générales du droit de la paix' (1935-IV) 54 *RCADI* 574ff. Due to US interventionism, the doctrine of fundamental rights and duties of States maintained itself for a longer time in Latin America: H Rolin, 'Les principes de droit international public' (1950-II) 77 *RCADI* 353, 354. For a Latin American viewpoint, see, eg, RJ Alfaro, 'The Rights and Duties of States' (1959-II) 97 *RCADI* 95ff, the word 'fundamental' being dropped.

[65] See, eg, the clear position taken by H Lauterpacht, *The Function of Law in the International Community*, (Oxford, 1933).

[66] See also P Vinogradoff, 'Historical Types of International Law', *Bibliotheca Visseriana*, vol I (Leiden, 1923) 1ff.

[67] On this classification, see J Van Kan, 'Règles générales du droit de la paix' (1938-IV) 66 *RCADI* 318ff.

the Inca Empire occupied a similar position to the Roman Empire, governing a phase of universalism. Various collectivities and peoples were incorporated into the imperial orbit through alliances and other treaties, on the basis of greater equality (*foedus aequum*) or lesser equality (*foedus iniquum*). The result was the ushering in of a vast system of imperial law with various autonomies. The Inca Empire used the tools of federation, federal administrative staff and autonomies organised through agreements. Conversely, in the Chinese world of the second millennium BCE, the universal powers witnessed the consolidation of local power of a series of vassals, leading to a complex and dual constitutional system. Progressively, with the consolidation of local power, the system shifted, as in Europe with the Westphalian treaties,[68] to a regime favouring internationalism (841 BCE).

Each of these types of social organisation leads to a distinctive form of international law:

1. *Universalism*. This is based on the predominance or hegemony of one power in a certain region. In that area, any law between 'independent powers' tends to contract into an imperial or sometimes federal law (according to the degrees of autonomy granted). This imperial or federal law does not, however, lose any international or horizontal element, which is typical of international law. When autonomies are granted to the peoples knitted together in the imperial or federal bond, there are at least some relations between these collectivities in which they confront each other as independent equals. Moreover, the central power will sometimes have had relations with its constituent collectivities based on equality rather than on command. In other words, these relations will have been based on international law, perhaps through the instrument of treaties. This treaty-based approach would occur more frequently when the empire was weak and the constituent collectivities could claim a greater amount of local power. Furthermore, the abolition of international boundaries between the collectivities so knitted together leads to the development of various types of *jus gentium*, ie systems of transnational law, where disparate actors entertain relations crossing the internal boundaries separating the collectivities. The empire thus tends to fuse together public and private international law phenomena. Finally, if the empire dissolves, the peoples formerly linked by it will easily accept a system of common rules of international law, since they are used to living together in a setting comprising a common culture and law.[69]
2. *Supranationalism*. The constitutional functions are here distributed on two levels: one universal, the other particular (a sort of *divisio regnorum*). It is a frequent occurrence that in a region dominated by an empire, particular

[68] The shift from supranationalism to internationalism is ordinarily a slow process. The Westphalian Treaties were not a distinct turning-point but the beginning of an accelerated process of change. See B Fassbender, 'Die verfassungs- und völkerrechtsgeschichtliche Bedeutung des Westfälischen Friedens von 1648' in I Eberich et al (eds), *Frieden und Recht* (Stuttgart, 1998) 9ff.

[69] See B Paradisi, *Storia del diritto internazionale nel medio evo*, vol I (Milan, 1940) 9–11.

collectivities will progressively consolidate their power and claim *de facto*, and later *de jure*, independence (*civitates superiorem non recognoscentes*). The new entities are territorially based. Through centralisation and rationalisation of public functions, which are easier to organise in smaller entities, they gain economic and military strength. The result is the coexistence of superior and inferior powers, brought together in federations, each having its own peculiarities. The political and legal regime of supranationalism is mixed in every respect. It is situated somewhere between federal and international law, between concentration on one entity and the juxtaposition of a series of independent entities. The State is not dissolved in the common space, yet it is not wholly independent from it either. Thus the constant mix between vertical elements, centered on allegiances, and horizontal elements, centered on independence. This type of social regime was typical in the European Middle Ages.

With the formation of modern States within the empire, the decentralisation of the system increases. The international elements of the system grow, to the detriment of its universal and supranational elements. The old federal law slowly shades into the new international law. If there is a consolidation of the central power, local autonomies are progressively reduced and the system returns to universalism. In supranational systems there is not yet a clear-cut distinction between domestic and international affairs. Internal and international law still form a cluster of norms within a common space. International law deals with public and private law aspects. It contains transnational and public international rules, for example the *jus armorum* binding the individual warrior, as well as rules on the conclusion of treaties. The main legal characteristic of the supranational system is therefore the blend between internal and external law. It main political feature is its instability: no detailed power-sharing between a series of competing centres is likely to last for long. The system tends to oscillate between the consolidation of central power, and thus the return to the empire, and the dissolution of the common bonds, ushering in a society of independent sovereigns. This is a power struggle exacerbated by the competing layers of power. The regime of supranationalism therefore is typically to be found in times of transition. However it can also be entrenched in a common, purposive structure, such as the European Union. The intention is here to create a lasting edifice, leading to some form of federation.

3. *Internationalism*. This regime is based on a society composed of a plurality of independent and atomised powers. It is often accompanied by the search for a balance of power. International law is here at its peak: it is essentially based on the concept of the coordination and cooperation of independent States. Coordination is founded on the necessities of coexistence and the exercise of the will of States. Commands from a superior power do not exist; all international regulations tend to be set out in agreements. Only agreements, as 'horizontal' engagements based on free will, are likely to be accepted by the sovereign entities as being their law. There is no sole legislator, executive or judge; these constitutional functions are rather split between as many States

as exist, so that two or three States, by concluding an agreement, may exercise a legislative function; by stipulating for some common control organ, may exercise an executive function; and by electing an arbitrator or a judge, may bring into play some judicial function. As can be seen, a sharp contrast between the common (international community) and the particular (State) is created. Hence also a sharp antagonism, in European legal history, between the authors attached to the medieval tradition of international law, emphasising the pre-eminence of the law (natural law) and the importance of the community, and modern writers, emphasising rather the *raison d'Etat*, the sovereignty and the free will of States. With the territorial consolidation of the State, internal and international society progressively oppose each other. International boundaries and domestic jurisdiction reinforce this state of affairs. Consequently, international and municipal law are now shaped as two distinct poles of legal regulation; in due course, dualistic theories pop up. By the same token, international law is separated from its transnational elements. These are now domestic matters, to be regulated by internal law. Thus, for example, the treatment of aliens is now fundamentally an internal matter and not a matter of international law (customary international law would, however, develop the 'minimum standard of treatment' doctrine, notably in the nineteenth century).[70] Individuals are in this phase under the sole sway of municipal law. International law retracts into inter-State law, exclusively public in nature and purely international in reach. It is placed in the space *between* States. The evolution of Europe since 1648 is an example of a system of internationalism.

These three types of organisation are thus based on unity (universalism), duality (supranationalism) and plurality (internationalism). International power is in principle at its peak in the universal system (the power maintains law and order, see Dante's *De Monarchia*), challenged in the supranational system (tensions between the various centres of power) and weak to non-existent in the internationalist system (where there is relative anarchy and a relative weakness of the law, deprived of mechanisms of regular and organised sanction by a common superior).

Synthetically it can be said that international law is the law for the regulation of relations of parity between relatively[71] independent public collectivities, ie a law of horizontal public relations at whichever level these are situated (internationalism). However, modern inter-State international law is but one model of international law, even if perhaps the most perfected model we have ever had. But there is international law elsewhere too. Each federal law contains some elements of international law, for example through the autonomies granted to the federated entities, or else by direct referral to international law norms, as in the case of

[70] On this minimum standard doctrine, see, eg, A Roth, *The Minimum Standard of International Law Applicable to Aliens* (Leiden, 1949); E Borchard, 'The Mimimum Standard of the Treatment of Aliens' (1939) 33 *Proceedings of the ASIL* 51ff.

[71] Absolute independence being a chimera.

boundary delimitations between federated entities.[72] For the sake of argument, we might also say that if extraterrestrial civilisations were to enter into contact with humanity, the legal relations between humanity and those aliens could only be regulated by a new[73] system of international law. And perhaps there would be a rule of inter-celestial international law stipulating its primacy over any terrestrial international law.

From the point of view of its content, international law is thus part of public law, inasmuch as it deals with public power. From the point of view of its structure, however, international law belongs to the family of private law, ie a law between equals, applied here to the dealings between public collectivities. In this way, international law bridges the two great branches of the law and assimilates heteronomous bodies into one single system. In its form as 'horizontal' and yet 'public' law, international law is a perennial phenomenon. There will never be a situation where relationships of subordination will completely replace or oust relationships of parity. Public law will never completely erase private law, even between public collectivities. In this sense, international law is immortal. Some of its aspects would survive even a federalisation of the world.

There are other classifications of international society, which are, however, more useful from the standpoint of political science than from the perspective of an international law typology. Thus, it has been proposed[74] to distinguish between an 'anarchical' international society, where power policies completely predominate and where there is an absence of legal commitment (a sort of Hobbesian state of nature or of generalised war); a 'universal' international society, where there is a *civitas maxima* imposing a set of federal law (Kant's world State, which the people regrettably do not want to realise); and an 'international' society based on a plurality of subjects practising power politics but yet not alien to legal commitments stabilising their dealings in certain subject matters (a Grotian international society enmeshed in the law). This classification is useful only in its last branch. For the rest, there never existed in reality purely predatory international societies (Hobbes)[75] or a world State predicated on the rule of law (Kant). As models of thought, the categories proposed by Bull may obviously be of interest.

[72] For Switzerland, see, eg, the *Nufenen* case (1980) or the *Plaine Morte* case (1994), decided by the Federal Tribunal: Arrêts du Tribunal federal, Recueil officiel, vol 106, Ib, 154ff and vol 120, Ib, 512ff. For US American law, see, eg, the *Georgia v South Carolina* case (1990) 91 *ILR* 439. US Supreme Court. When there is a succession of states within a Federal State, eg because of a separation of one part of a federated State so as to form a new federated State, the rules of international law on State succession are often applied by analogy, as was the case in Switzerland when the new Canton of Jura was formed after a separation from the Canton of Bern (1977): see Y Lejeune, 'La pratique jurasianne en matière de succession aux traités et concordats internationaux' (1984) 40 *ASDI* 30ff; U Kohli, *Die vermögensrechtliche Auseinandersetzung zwischen den Kantonen Bern und Jura* (Bern, 1986).

[73] Not our system of international law, which would be a purely municipal law for the aliens, by which they could not be bound. Substantively, the new international law would probably resemble in many aspects our current international law.

[74] H Bull, *The Anarchical Society—A Study of Order in World Politics* (London, 1977).

[75] Even if, as we have seen, there were spaces and times where power politics predominated, as in China of the 'States at War' era—see section I.A.3.v. above.

B. Law of Subordination and Law of Coordination

There is a natural tendency—fraught with some danger—to compare international and municipal society as well as their respective legal orders. From such a perspective, international law will often be criticised for not being like the municipal legal order, ie as being less perfect than the latter. This tendency to excessive assimilation is wrong on a series of accounts. Most importantly, international law and internal law regulate wholly different societies. Their utility must be measured not on the degree of resemblance they manage to achieve, but rather on the appropriateness with which they fulfil their functions in the social context into which they are cast. Moreover, there will often be an exaggeration of the perfection of internal law, with its executive and judicial organs. The observer will tend to see the matter dogmatically: the lack of centralised sanction signifies ineffectiveness; on the other hand, the presence of centralised sanction signifies the effectiveness of the legal order. There is no doubt that the presence of sanctions influences effectiveness, but the whole matter of effectiveness remains one of degree and of taking stock by empirical analysis

The foregoing does not mean that all analogies between the municipal and the international legal orders have to be rejected. Such analogies of private or public law have for a long time enriched the body of international law; gaps within international law have thus been filled. Analogies are also unavoidable in the sense that the lawyer will naturally tend to apply to international legal phenomena the tools learned when studying jurisprudence. However, these analogies have always to be mindful of the differences of context, structure and function.

Now, if international law is sufficiently different to resist a direct comparison with internal law, but at the same time not so different as to defeat any municipal law analogy, how should one view the degree of similarity and difference? Manifestly, the differences are greater on the structural than on the substantive level. International law can indeed regulate every subject matter, and does so: its content ranges from classical international matters to criminal and administrative law. The difference is here not marked with respect to municipal law. On the structural level, there exist three fundamental types of law: (i) the State model (law of subordination); (ii) the international model (law of coordination); (iii) mixed models (law of federation, eg the EU). The two first types must be analysed carefully, because they constitute the two basic types. The point will not turn around an evaluation of these models, but only on the presentation of their characteristic features.

1. The Law of Subordination (State)

This is the type of law developing within an organised public collectivity, such as the State, with its 'internal' law. The public collectivity has here consolidated itself and centralised the main public functions, legislature, executive and judicial power. These powers now unfold autonomously. The members of the society are subjected to them. Consequently, the subordination of the members of society, the presence of a superior authority and the vertical system are the touchstones of this type of law. It does not matter that the State is free to renounce acting through its public power, in some areas, by concluding contracts with its subjects. The gist of the matter is that the State can, alone and with full discretion, determine the extent to which it will have recourse to the one or to the other: agreement or authority.

In this type of the law, there is a certain predominance of public law. Private law, concerning the horizontal relations between members of the society, needs the State machinery to realise itself. The contract is part and parcel of private law; but its enforcement (distinct from spontaneous compliance) is based on the execution mechanisms offered by the State, ie on public law. The enactment of private law itself, for example in a civil code, is based on legislation of the State which is 'public' law. This verticality of the law tends to usher in a strong type of law: its adoption and its enforcement are guaranteed by public power and by the concept of the 'rule of law'. The sanctioning of breaches of the law is organised and centralised. There are clearly some blind spots, as is the case with the sanctioning of constitutional law norms at the apex of the system. There will probably be no remedies for the violation of the constitution by the supreme legislator or judge. But this is all at most a marginal limitation on the perfection of the system as it appears on the paper. The subordination model of the law is considered by the modern observer as giving rise to 'perfect' legal systems, possibly to the only systems of law deserving of this name. Thus, the law of subordination tends to be equated with law *tout court*. The conception is that to be a legal norm, a certain provision must be constructed according to this type of legal structure. Conversely, if it is not, it cannot be truly law. The fact remains that this type of law is historically a recent phenomenon: in Europe, this model is only some centuries old, having developed with the consolidation of the modern State in Westphalian times.

2. *The Law of Coordination (International Law)*

This is the type of law developing among powers or persons independent one from the other. These entities are not subject to a common superior. Thus they are not under the control of a single and centralised legal order emanating from such a common superior. Each collectivity encounters the others—which are more or less equal to it—in a context of independence, sovereignty and mutual recognition. The sovereignty of each collectivity is the touchstone of this type of law. The main public functions have not been centralised: the legislature, executive and judicial power consequently remain at the level of each collectivity. The latter will itself exercise the functions of legislation, executive action or judicial determination of the law through its own organs. This remains true even if common norms of international law fall to be applied. The main public functions therefore remain decentralised. Each collectivity will exercise these powers internationally too, for example by concluding an agreement, which is an exercise of 'legislative' power. Legislation will not be unitary and centralised but fragmented and partial. This is the structural basis for the fragmentation of power in international society. This is also the basis for the general competence of self-judgement of each State. Sovereignty being at the heart of the system, the 'me' projects selfishly into the outward space; it there encounters other selfish 'me's' and thereby provokes friction.

As can be seen, this type of law is 'horizontal': equality and independence are at its root. Consequently, private law predominates over public law. This is certainly not true from the point of view of the content of rules, which express relations of public authority. But it is true from the structural point of view, since the subjects deal with one another on a footing of equality. This type of the law is generally considered to produce a weak legal order. The law is constantly in danger of being subverted by the gravitational force of particular interests and power policies. In this type, legal policies and policies in general are much more inextricably linked to the legal norms than in any other type.[76] No impartial organ acting on the basis of the law (rule of law) has been able to tame the relationships of power. A law of this type concentrates on the production of norms (sources). In the domain of the execution of norms, decisive progress is rendered impossible by the shield of sovereignty and the equality-based nature of the society. This type of the law may often be brushed aside with some impatience by the modern man in the street. But we may at least notice that it is much older than the subordination law model examine above.

The features of international law as coordinative law imply a series of legal consequences. The most important among them are as follows:

1. In the first place, there are consequences on the *creation and the modification of the law*. Absent a centralised legislator, law is essentially created through agreements among States. Law can be created only by injunction or by agreement; if there is no injunction, there must be agreement. But agreement is particularly difficult to obtain on the universal plane among almost 200 jealously sovereign entities, each one acting according to its real and perceived interests of the moment. Once created, this law is lacking in unity and in coherence. It is fragmented, as much as the sovereignty it reflects is itself fragmented. The agreed law will not bind all States, but only those ratifying or expressing it; and it will not apply to all the parties for the same temporal span. On the other hand, customary international law will often be difficult to determine in a society as split and heteroclite as the international one; political context and the accelerating needs of the 'international community' will not render the matter easier. It also stands to reason that any change in the law is complicated. Every State party to an agreement is vested with the right not to accept an alteration of the legal regime to which it has not consented. When a multilateral treaty needs to be adapted to new circumstances, and if not all States agree to the proposed new version, which is the most frequent case, the legal

[76] See the very strong account in G de Lacharrière, *La politique juridique extérieure* (Paris, 1983).

position is cumbersome: the new treaty will apply among those States that have ratified the new version; the old treaty will apply among those States that have not ratified the new version but who are parties to the old version; the old treaty will equally apply between States that have ratified the new version and those that have ratified only the old one; and, lastly, the treaty will not apply at all, in whichever version, to States that have ratified neither one, or between States that have ratified one of the two versions and States that have ratified neither. When a treaty is modified more than once, the splitting up of legal regimes becomes still more complex, since even more variants have to be contemplated. The formulation of treaty reservations will add to these complications. Thus, not infrequently, power relations may here resolve the difficulties and refashion the treaties. This is all the more true since an organised procedure of 'peaceful change' does not exist in international law. For customary international law, a modification is not necessarily any easier. A small number of States, if sufficiently determined and representative, can impeach the formation of any new rule. Practice and *opinio juris* will hardly become 'general' if those States dissent. The veto tactic is here collectivised: a single State cannot use it as a sword, as it can with treaty law; but a small group of States can do so.

2. Then there are consequences on the *execution of the law*. In the absence of a centralised executive, each State judges for itself the legal rights and obligations it has assumed. It is true that this is also the usual staring point in municipal law: the parties to a contract will first of all interpret and apply, each one for itself, the clauses of the contract. The main difference lies in the fact that in the event of a dispute, there will be a judge to hear the case and to decide it independently and impartially. The self-judging momentum is a starting point, but it is not necessarily the point of arrival. In international law, the pervasive rule of sovereignty renders such a two-tier solution impossible. Any general subjection to the power of decision by a judge or a third party would be tantamount to relinquishing sovereignty. It may be useful to recall that the very concept of sovereignty is based on a supreme power of decision. If a judge were authorised to decide simply on the referral of a case by one party, without the consent of the other party, the latter could no longer be considered sovereign. In order to have a settlement of disputes compatible with the exacting notion of sovereignty, it is necessary to base the competence of the judge or third party on the consent of the State. In such a situation, the exercise of judicial power is an exercise of sovereignty and not a relinquishment of it; the same is true for the conclusion of any treaty, not only that agreeing to the competence of the judge or any other third party for the settlement of a dispute.[77] Alternatively, there remains only the realm of 'private

[77] See PCIJ, *Wimbledon* case, ser A, no 1, 25; PCIJ, *Exchange of Greek and Turkish Populations* opinion, ser B, no 10, 21.

justice', flowing directly from the power of self-judgment already discussed. In other words, when there is no agreement to engage in a third-party review of a dispute, each State can enforce the law as it perceives it. On the whole, it is thus inexact to claim that international law is deprived of sanctioning mechanisms. A sanction for breach of the law exists, even if primitive or not deserving of that name in the strict sense: in the past it was war, today there are still reprisals and counter-measures. It stands to reason that this self-judging mechanism is hardly satisfactory: it constantly endangers international peace through the risk of degenerating reprisals and concomitant uses of force; and it does not serve international justice, through its dense net of self-centred and self-righteous projections where the powerful have a greater say than the weaker. In effect, a powerful State can have recourse to very trenchant reprisals, and even the threat of them will in most cases determine the outcome. For a weaker State, the the opposite is the case.

3. Further, the consequences bear on the *quality of the law* produced. Any legal order contains some norms of a dispositive nature, where the members of society can substitute for the general rule special rules of their choice in the exercise of their private autonomy (eg contractual rules), and norms of an imperative nature, where the superior common interest dictates a unitary and non-derogable regulation binding all members of society to the same degree. In the latter case, the attempt to produce a contrary legal regime leads to nullity; and there are public organs vested with control functions. Modern international law has also sought to develop such notions as collective interest and peremptoriness: *jus cogens* (peremptory norms), obligations *erga omnes*, international crimes, 'absolute' human rights, etc. However, such notions, to be really effective, suppose a series of conditions: a society where a set of quite generally accepted values has emerged; and where collective organs are vested with the power to determine and to apply the collective interest norms through binding competencies. On the other hand, such collective interest norms, when applied by each State individually, often risk being detached from their high-reaching aims, deteriorating into a policy of self-interest and selectivity, which ends up discrediting the whole process. Thus, it might be possible to select 'humanitarian interventions', by force or otherwise, by marshalling some collective interest norms, while in reality pursuing highly particular policy interests. Could one really condemn a State acting in this way: would it be ready to risk its men and women, and its funds, in an intervention for which there are no other interests than pure and lofty humanity? The foregoing shows that international law often remains limited to the creation of contingent and particular norms, shaped by the timely interests of the States and caught up in their power plays. On the other side, there is a genuine need for a true international governance with respect to urgent and global common concerns. The precarious conjunction of 194 foreign policies is hardly sufficient to meet these needs and concerns. The protection

of the natural environment is a topical example. The insufficiency of proper mechanisms of regulation in international law is palpable here. There are, nevertheless, some international institutions whose work remains invaluable in these fields. But they are not vested with powers of decision. The political responsibilities remain exclusively with the national constituencies. A way out of this quagmire is not yet visible. Elective democracy, and therefore the need to leave important decisions to the local peoples, impeach any significant effort towards greater international institutional power. Pressing needs at the international level, however, increasingly drive inroads into this old-style division of work, where decisions were taken inside and sometimes coordination sought outside.

3. *Conclusion*

In opposition to the vertical 'State law' model international law thus proposes its horizontal model. Clearly, there is a series of limits to this all too simple opposition. The most visible are the mixed models of organisation within often quite complex systems of federation. This is the case notably for the European Union, which allies elements of subordination (supranationality) and elements of coordination (sovereignty of its Member States).

It may be argued that the coordinative model does not produce a legal order deserving of the name 'law'. This type of judgment will be analysed in more detail in the next two chapters concerning the so-called 'primitive nature' of international law, as well as its lack of effectiveness. We may note here that international law is fundamentally based on sovereignty: this is at once its *raison d'être* (without a plurality of sovereign entities there would not be an international legal order but only one internal legal order) and its greatest threat (sovereignty signifies a power not tamed by superior organs, with the consequence of a certain degree of anarchy). Therefore, essentially linked with sovereignty, international law will never be able to be wholly different from what it is and has been throughout history. Peoples cannot without contradiction cherish, to a sometimes absurd degree, their sovereignty and independence, and at the same time acerbically criticise the anarchical state of the world and the concomitant relative weakness of the legal phenomenon. There is a clear choice: either one maintains sovereignty to a high degree, and accepts an international legal order whose bite will remain limited; or one is ready to organise an institutional international society progressively through a transfer of powers, and thereby benefit from an increase of the rule of international law. The choice of the peoples is fairly clear at the beginning of the twenty-first century: even on the regional European plane, there is no propensity to limit to any degree local freedom and sovereignty; all the more is it fanciful to hope for such a paradigm change on the universal plane. We shall therefore continue to live with an international legal order based on coordination and rooted in the sovereignty of a plurality of States.

C. Inter-State Law and Transnational Law

Municipal law can be defined as the legal order regulating a national society, whereas international law can be defined as the legal order regulating international society. Any legal order regulates a society; both notions are inextricably linked. But what is 'international society'? There is no *a priori* substantive definition that would be equally valid for all times. What international society is depends on a series of factors of an historical nature. It thus shifts in time. This is true for the type of subjects of international law, the 'public collectivities'; for the distribution of power in a certain area (imperial imprint, federations, independent States); for the dominant conceptions of what belongs to the domestic sphere; for the degree of interdependence and the sense of international solidarity reached, etc. That international law regulates international society is a definition of synthetic nature, thus valid for all times. But the determination of a concrete international society can be made only by taking into account the historic facts of a given time. Thereby one can join, one to the other, the necessary and the contingent poles, the fixed and the mobile assets.

In our times, there are fundamentally two ways to define 'international society'. On one side, it is defined as the society of States. On the other side, international society is defined as a transnational society of different actors plunging, in their various dealings, into international space (ie crossing the boundaries of a State). The first conception remains predominant, except, perhaps, for within US scholarship.

1. *International Law as Inter-State Law*

According to this conception, international law mainly regulates relations between States.[78] Not all relations between States are legally regulated, but some are, and this is the realm of international law. The same is true for municipal law: love and friendship are not regulated legally in all their aspects but only in some areas (eg marriage, when love develops into that bond). So it is also for States: only a part of their foreign relations is bound by legal rules, under convention or customary law; the rest is left to their discretionary policy. It is observable that States are keen to keep a number of their dealings aloof from the legal realm They are at pains to keep a significant (even if progressively reduced) domain of freedom of action in which policy considerations of expediency and interest will prevail, and where the ability to adapt to quickly changing circumstances will be paramount.[79]

[78] See, eg, A Truyol y Serra, 'Théorie du droit international public' (1981-IV) 173 *RCADI* 36.

[79] This is also the root of the rule of international law—no longer strictly applied—whereby there is a presumption of freedom of action: if no rule of international law binds a State to do or to abstain from doing something, that State may act as it sees fit. The domain of this freedom has, however, in any case significantly diminished, since there are hardly areas of foreign policy where no general principle with some legal colour will be wholly absent (eg proportionality, good faith, etc). See the interesting reflections of A Bleckmann, *Grundprobleme und Methoden des Völkerrechts* (Freiburg/Munich, 1982) 72ff, 180ff.

Thus, if international law is essentially inter-State law, it presents itself as a '*jus inter potestates*', a law between powers.[80] This is also to say that international law is a 'political' or 'public' law, a law of 'public power'. Since the nineteenth century, it has been accepted, however, that the 'powers' comprise certain other quasi-State subjects. This is the case for belligerents or insurgents, later movements of national liberation; to a certain degree *de facto* regimes, deprived of recognition as a State. Other entities exercising public functions also became accepted as the subjects of rights and duties under international law: international organisations; the International Committee of the Red Cross; the Holy See; the Sovereign Order of Malta, etc.

Finally, in the twentieth century, the link of the subjects with public authority was severed: the individual was now recognised as a partial and limited subject of international law. This subject would be vested only with those rights and duties accorded to him by the States, and he could not acquire other rights and duties, say, by concluding treaties (having no treaty-making power). This change of paradigm, whereby private subjects penetrated into the arena of international law, brought with it the demise of the formerly neat separation of international and municipal law. The new situation allowed for the progressive interpenetration or blending of the legal orders, at least from the perspective of the content of the respective rules. However, the gravitational orbit of international law has remained unaltered: international law remains mainly the legal order of and for sovereign States. This fact is graphically manifested in the domain of the creation of the law: State practice is paramount in the formation of customary international law, and treaties are essentially inter-State.

2. *International Law as Transnational Law*

In this larger conception, international law regulates all relations that transcend a national boundary and cannot therefore be governed by one, municipal, legal order.[81] International law formally becomes the legal order of all relations trespassing across national legal orders. International law encompasses public relations (between States) and private relations (between individuals when crossing a national boundary). Public and private international law tend thus to merge into one another, the *jus gentium* and the *jus inter gentes*, to become one single phenomenon. The material fact to which international law is attached is the 'international relation' instead of the 'relation between States'. Thus, transnational

[80] The expression has been used by M de Taube, 'La situation actuelle du Pape et l'idée d'un droit entre pouvoirs (jus inter potestates)' (1907) I *Archiv für Rechts- und Wirtschaftsphilosophie* 360, 510ff.

[81] See Truyol y Serra, above n 78, 43ff. On transnational law, see amongst others G Handl, J Zekoll and P Zumbansen (eds), *Beyond Territoriality: Transnational Legal Authority in the Age of Globalization* (Leiden, 2012); G Shaffer (ed), *Transnational Legal Ordering and State Change* (New York, 2013); R Nickel and A Greppi (eds), *The Changing Role of Law in the Age of Supra- and Transnational Governance* (Baden-Baden, 2014).

law is not orientated towards public power. It includes, importantly, private and corporate dealings.

There are different schools of transnational law. One has a sociological stamp (Politis, Scelle, also the New Haven School with McDougal), combating State power in favour of individual empowerment, or binding the State to pursue certain values centered upon a free world order.[82] Other schools tend to construct an international law of the world community, branded by some idealistic elements (Jessup, Jenks, Tanaka, Cançado Trindade).[83] Still others are at pains to define a constitutional law of the international community, often around the UN Charter, and taking account of universal values (Fassbender, Peters, etc).[84] These schools of thought often take as a point of reference the law still to come (*lex ferenda*). If they do not always correctly describe the law as it is, they nourish debates on how it ought to be, and are therefore prone to influence practice and opinion in the sense of their proposals.

Transnational law phenomena will increase, and possibly predominate, in phases when State power tends to regress or to dissolve. Thus, in the last few years, many public functions have been privatised, even in the core State functions like the making of war.[85] Conversely, international law phenomena will impose themselves in phases when State power consolidates and strengthens.[86] Neither of these realities is fixed and firm; both shift over time, and so will the gravitational orbits of international law. We might just notice that State power has not yet weakened to the point where the 'inter-State' aspect of international law has lost its predominance.

3. *Conclusion*

It may be important to stress that no one of the two poles is inherently superior to the other from an axiological point of view.[87] Each phase in history establishes its legal structures as a function of its material needs and of its ideological representations. That the opening of international law to private actors is not inherently superior to the closing of international law to States appears, for example, in the context of certain problems accompanying the privatisation of war.[88] By the

[82] For further details, see A Truyol y Serra and R Kolb, *Doctrines sur le fondement du droit des gens* (Paris, 2007) 91ff.

[83] Truyol y Serra, above n 78, 43ff.

[84] See, eg, J Klabbers, A Peters and G Ulfstein (eds), *The Constitutionalization of International Law* (Oxford, 2009).

[85] See, eg, F Francioni and N Ronzitti (eds), *War by Contract* (Oxford, 2011).

[86] This was the case, eg, in the 19th century, and thus the classical reverberation of this State-centered international law in the famous monograph by D Anzilotti, *Cours de droit international* (Paris, 1929).

[87] But such a claim is not infrequently made, notably in the US: see, eg, AM Slaughter, 'A Liberal Theory of International Law' (2000) 94 *Proceedings of the American Society of International Law* 240ff; AM Slaughter, *A New World Order* (Princeton, NJ, 2004).

[88] H Tonkin, *State Control over Private Military and Security Companies in Armed Conflict* (Cambridge, 2011); L Cameron and V Chetail (eds), *Privatizing War: Private Military and Security Companies under Public International Law* (Cambridge, 2013); J Pattison, *The Morality of Private*

same token, it is not to be assumed that classical international law, with its expulsion of the individual as a subject of law and with its hermetic water-tightness to human rights, was on any account better than modern international law. It is thus adequate to renounce dogmatic and *a priori* views and to analyse carefully each question on its own merits.

IV. Phases of Development of International Law

A. Classical and Modern International Law

With a certain degree of schematisation and thus of lack of nuance, we can distinguish two main phases of development of European public international law, which were then exported to the whole world: classical international law and modern international law. Both are explored in further detail below.

1. *Classical International Law: Mainly Coexistence and Predation*

Classical international law, in its heyday from the eighteenth century to the nineteenth century, was quite idiosyncratic, if not paradoxical.[89] It united two apparently contradictory realities, namely, the protection of coexistence and the allowance of predatory conduct. Poorly equipped with rules orientated towards the interests of humanity or of the international community, it was mainly at pains to delimit and to protect the spheres of action of each State taken individually: territorial integrity, domestic jurisdiction, fundamental rights and freedoms of States, the will and contractual power of States. Territory, diplomacy and war were its cornerstones. Obligations were often of a negative nature, ie to abstain from doing something. Subjective rights of States were at their peak; they took the almost constitutional shape of 'fundamental rights' of States. The system was geared towards the realisation of a minimum order between antagonistic States,

War: The Challenge of Private Military and Security Companies (New York, 2014); C Seiberth, *Private Military and Security Companies in International Law: A Challenge for Non-Binding Norms* (Cambridge, 2014); G Andreopoulos and J Kleinig (eds), *Private Militarly and Security Companies and the Quest for Accountability* (London, 2015); E Moyakine, *The Privatized Art of War: Private Military and Security Companies and State Responsibility for their Unlawful Conduct in Conflict Areas* (Cambridge, 2015).

[89] On classical international law characteristics, see mainly W Friedmann, *The Changing Structure of International Law* (London, 1964) 60ff; G Schwarzenberger, *The Dynamics of International Law* (Abingdon, 1976) 107ff; G Abi-Saab, 'Cours general de droit international public' (1987-VI) 207(I) *RCADI* 319ff; S Villalpando, *L'émergence d'une communauté internationale dans la responsabilité des Etats* (Geneva, 2005) 61ff. But see also the reservations of E Jouannet, *Le droit international liberal-providence: une histoire du droit international* (Brussels, 2011) 83, regarding a too-sharp opposition of the two phases. It is certainly true that elements of cooperation and common concerns were not absent in the 17th to 19th centuries.

the gain of the one being considered the loss of the other in a sort of zero-sum game. Cooperation between States existed but was essentially voluntary, embryonic and mostly limited to technical concerns (mail, telegraph, rivers, etc). The execution of the law was based on self-regulation and reprisals. Formal equality of States was cherished, but great powers enjoyed pre-eminence.

Nonetheless, classical international law had also its other, darker side, which relativised considerably the protection of coexistence. It was also a law of predation. The legal order authorised each State to pass from peace to war by a simple discretionary declaration of war. This *liberum jus ad bellum* was considered an inalienable part of its sovereignty.[90] Once this declaration of war was made, the state of war was unilaterally established and all the main guarantees of coexistence lapsed: the stronger party could impose its will on the weaker, the latter's territory could be annexed—*vae victis*, and then also *vae neutris*, through the extension of economic warfare at sea. Moreover, a great part of the globe was left to colonial acquisition and to the partitioning of humanity into three circles comprising civilised, barbaric and savage peoples.[91] In peacetime, the intervention of the great powers in the affairs of smaller States was a common occurrence, notably through the congresses of powers of the nineteenth century.[92] In sum, this international law promoted the inequality of States, unequal treaties, the discretionary use of force, the freedom of annexation of foreign territory, colonialism, etc. It was also marked by the absence of certain important branches of the law, notably State responsibility and peaceful settlement of disputes.

On the whole, it can be said that classical international law is predicated upon realism. Unable to domesticate force by law, incapable of taming sovereignty by rules, it accommodates these facts and carves out a dark spot in its legal body. Classical international law was initially a 'servant' of States. It was instrumental in the sense that it offered States the tools they needed for their foreign policy, in matters of treaties, diplomacy and war. This also explains why the question of its violation was not paramount: an essentially subservient law is easily observed; must one worry about sanctions for its breach? The law flows from the sole will of the States and tends to condone all their deeds: *quod fieri not debet, factum valet*;

[90] See I Brownlie, *International Law and the Use of Force by States* (Oxford, 1963) 20; N Politis, *Les nouvelles tendances du droit international* (Paris, 1927) 100–01. For a discussion of the various projects to limit this right to wage war, see S Amos, *Political and Legal Remedies for War* (New York, 1880).

[91] It would be wrong to think that only the somewhat eccentric J Lorimer, *The Institutes of the Law of Nations*, vol I (Edinburgh, 1883) 101, upheld this notion. It can also be found in the textbooks of moderate and progressive authors, such as H Bonfils, *Manuel de droit international public*, 3rd edn (Paris, 1901) 82.

[92] K Wolfke, *Great and Small Powers in International Law From 1814 to 1920, From the Pre-History of the United Nations* (Wroclaw, 1961). See also M Schulz, *Normen und Praxis, Das Europäische Konzert der Grossmächte als Sicherheitsrat 1815–1860* (Munich, 2009); S Hoffmann, *Organisations internationales et pouvoirs politiques des Etats* (Paris, 1954) 23ff. Even a liberal author could claim that the powers united in congress could create binding norms for third States: JC Bluntschli, *Le droit international codifié* (Paris, 1870) 101, art 110, 'Lorsque les états rassemblés en congrès général européen sont d'accord sur certaines dispositions, celles-ci deviennent obligatoires pour tous les états européens'.

quod fieris, ipsum valet. This has as a further consequence the relative normative poverty of classical international law. There is little inclination to fight against the 'is'. International law is there mainly to empower States to act, rather than to compel them not to act. Positivism and voluntarism predominate. In the ultimate analysis, classical international law is replete with syncretism and of norms that must be considered as being contradictory from the axiological point of view—for example the norms on the protection of the territorial integrity of States on the one hand (in peacetime) and the rule on the freedom to resort to war and annexation on the other hand (wartime).

2. *Modern International Law: Coexistence, Cooperation and Community Values*

Modern international law seeks to overcome the manifest weaknesses of its classical counterpart. It does not abandon the layer of simple coexistence among reserved, prudent or sometimes hostile States. But it adds to this minimum layer some new layers of law that considerably enrich its structure and functions. These new layers are cooperation and community values. The modern law seeks to improve the relations between States by guaranteeing some degree of equality, justice, order and peace, ie by imposing some community values. It thereby transcends the mere interests of States taken individually. From this vantage point it is a militant law, fighting inequality, intervention in internal affairs, use of force, violation of human rights. It promotes the peaceful settlement of disputes, international cooperation and confidence building, human rights and humanitarian law, decolonisation. It is a law addressing the common concerns of humanity: nuclear weapons, the depletion of the environment, the humanitarian cause, development and wealth issues, etc. By all these aspects, modern international law becomes at least in part messianic. There is no question of slavishly following effective State practice and abdicating when confronted with illegal facts. Thus doctrines of non-recognition of illegal situations now flourish. By the same token the absolute predominance of the will of States, central to the older positivistic doctrines, is broken. Positivism and simple will orientation are insufficient to tackle the urgent common concerns mentioned above. Hence, international law now considerably increases its normative density. Through general principles and analogies, and a customary law liberated from the old doctrine of the tacit agreement, it extends its reach beyond the expressed will of States. The 'ought' takes an increasingly important place in its body at the expense of the mere 'is', especially the illegal 'is'. International law does not limit itself to providing instruments to the States so that they can fulfil their foreign policy wishes; it also seeks to delimit and to organise the powers of each State, taking into account the common good. There lies the emergence of the idea of the international community. By all these developments, modern international law links up with the best legal tradition: the role of law is not purely instrumental; it must also be normative. Law is not there simply to condone; it is also there to direct. Without losing contact with realities and with what States want, the legal order must try to transcend and direct the facts of life. In short, if modern international law has not ceased to provide instruments for States to use in their dealings, it has now also become a 'master' and not just a servant. It is understandable that the question of the violation of the law and its punishment now appears in a wholly new light. The new partially 'messianic' law is not so easily and spontaneously complied with as was the old instrumental law.

This modern international law is enshrined mainly in the long list of fundamental norms contained in article 2 of the UN Charter. This provision contains an extremely condensed overview of the main rules of modern international law. It was later completed by Resolution 2625 (1970) of the UN General Assembly, on 'Friendly Relations' between States. These Charter provisions have decisively influenced customary international law. In this narrow sense, the Charter has been more than just one treaty amongst others. It did not simply add a new particular international law to the layer of general international law; it rather modified the old general international law, casting it in a new direction. The effect of the Charter was felt on two planes: (i) it served as a basis for interpretation and understanding of the traditional rules of international law; and (ii) it operated to modify some rules of traditional customary law, expressing a new general legal opinion. In legal terms, the Charter is a source of interpretation and of abrogation. It is the great staple of modern international law.

B. First Phase of Development of Modern International Law: The 'Juridisation' of International Society

1. *The Sunset of the Middle Ages*

The passing away of the structures proper to the Middle Ages, with its universal community (*Respublica Christiana*) and its system of vassalage, ushered in a crisis of political, legal and philosophical thought. The shifting political parameters influenced new human thoughts about society and law. The Middle Ages had been dominated by Aristotelian and Thomistic thought, whereby finality was more important than causality, and moral theology prevailed over science.[93] In this conception, the phenomena of reality are essentially an externalisation of the evolution of things towards the aim that is inherent in them. Thus, the seed planted already contains the program for the ripening and later the ripe fruit. Its evolution in time is but an unfolding realisation of this inherent finality (entelechy). The whole world of realities is dominated by this finalistic thought. Consequently, reality is not simply identical to the observable facts, determined by causal laws, as we would consider it today. The dimension of the inherent finalities inoculates

[93] On this issue, see the interesting developments by H Welzel, *Naturrecht und material Gerechtigkeit*, 4th edn (Göttingen, 1990) 28ff, 108ff.

into these objects a distinct meta-empirical bent. Reality itself becomes a value—and hence the great scholastic maxim, *bonum et ens convertuntur*, which cannot be understood with a purely empirical conception of reality, where the 'is' is not in all cases the 'good'. By the many finalities, which are interlinked, the things of this world are ordered into a cosmos, a coherent whole. The finalities point towards a unity to be found in the aim of aims, in the immobile motor of the movement of things. Teleology thus opens to theology. This edifice is most visible in the impressive construction of Thomas Aquinas, on the basis of the philosophy of Aristotle. The obsession with unity straddles the medieval political universe and dominates it. The supreme rule of the Middle Ages is that all things are reduced to the ultimate unity (*omnia naturalia unum reducentur*). From there flows the claim of the necessary political unity of Christian mankind, rooted in the single body of God (*humana universitas quoddam totum ad regna particularia vel ad gentes*). Hence also the claim for a universal monarchy (*unus princeps totius universi*)—Dante would still sing its praises.

At the end of the Middle Ages, methods based on causality and empirical science would progressively take the place of the finalistic credo. Reality is thus severed from the layer of values imported into it; it now becomes an external and naked fact, observable by empirical and physical methods. Each object must be reduced to its constituent elements, and the relations of cause to effect traversing it must be studied.[94] This causal method is now applied also to political phenomena, namely to the State.[95] The time of the study of atoms, of infinitesimal mathematics has come. The interest of Man now concentrates on the particular rather than on the universal, on the empirically observable unit rather than on the metaphysical unity. This new empirical orientation of thought has effects on the conception of the law: the act by which the positive legislation is passed by power and authority is the cause of all law and thus its ultimate basis. It is an observable fact, whereas the value of the law, its justice, is but a universalistic fiction rooted in subjective judgement. Justice is an unreal essence, not a real existence. Power also ensures the enforcement of the law. Power reinforces its anchoring in the hard facts of reality. Hence the famous maxim: *auctoritas, non veritas facit legem*.[96] This rise of positivism would reach its heyday in the nineteenth century.

[94] Which was done, say, by Galileo Galilei when he verified the downward attraction of objects falling to earth. He did so on the Tower of Pisa. On the other hand, in the Middle Ages, the belief had been that the movement of things was inherent in their finalistic nature.

[95] See particularly the Preface of Hobbe's *De Cive*.

[96] For an interesting analysis of this famous utterance of Hobbes (*Leviathan*, book II, ch 26), see O Höffe, *Politische Gerechtigkeit* (Frankfurt, 1987) 130ff. According to this author, the 'non veritas' sentence implied only a rejection of the absolute legal moralism, ie an unjust law is not by this simple fact invalid. The 'auctoritas' does not necessarily imply all types of power but can be read as referring to an authorised power.

2. *The Dawn of the Modern World*

There is an almost ideal correspondence between this orientation of thought towards the particular elements rather than towards the general essence and the atomised international society of sovereign States taking the place of the traditional concept of an ecumenical international community. Legal doctrine would thus attach to the description of an international society composed of individual States considered in themselves, with their individual rights and duties. This new paradigm marks profoundly the most influential monograph on international law of the time, namely de Vattel's *Le droit des gens* of 1758. The sovereign State is its hallmark; the international community is completely absent; de Vattel even casts away the fictitious *civitas maxima* upheld by his master, Wolff. The international community is thus brushed aside: it is not an empirically observable reality. Consequently, there remains only the law of each single entity, each one taken for itself. The law is completely State-centred. It was only a matter of time before authors could be found indulging in outright negation of international law: since there was no institutional organisation at the international level, able to legislate and to impose the execution of its norms on the single States, international law remained a pure postulate (Austin would later say a 'positive morality')[97] ; hence it was not true law. In short, international law was too much 'essence' and too little 'existence' to satisfy the standards of modern causal methods.

One of the first authors to depart from the old finalistic methods was Niccolo Machiavelli. The 'ought' (morality) and the 'is' (causality) were completely separated. Effective power had its own causal laws. They were stronger than all moral concepts. Spinoza would then apply these precepts to international law, which he identified with power. This tradition then wound its way through Hobbes and later came down to Austin, and in the twentieth century to Morgenthau, Kennan, Aron or, more recently, Goldsmith and Posner.[98] Hobbes, influenced by Occam and Bacon, was certainly the father of this school of thought. The sole aim of the law he recognises is to secure safe living together in society. Thus, an ideal but ineffective legal order has no value in itself, since it cannot realise that supreme aim. It only postulates, whereas it should effectively guarantee. In fact, security can be granted only through the sword. This leads Hobbes to emphasise dramatically the realistic elements in the law, ie the effectiveness of legal norms. To guarantee

[97] In his Lectures on Jurisprudence or the Philosophy of Positive Law (1st edn, 1869).

[98] See generally R Kolb and A Truyol y Serra, *Doctrines sur le fondement du droit des gens* (Paris, 2007) 21ff. On Morenthau, see the interesting analysis in M Koskenniemi, *The Gentle Civilizer of Nations, The Rise and Fall of International Law 1870–1960* (Cambridge, 2001) 413ff. The most celebrated passage of R Aron, *Paix et guerre entre les nations*, 8th edn (Paris, 1984) 691 is as follows: '[La politique internationale] a été toujours, par tous, reconnue pour ce qu'elle est: politique de puissance, sauf à notre époque par quelques juristes ivres de concepts ou quelques idéalistes qui confondent leurs rêves avec la réalité' ('International politics have always been recognised for what they are: power policies, except by certain lawyers drunk on concepts or by certain idealists taking their wishes for reality'). And JL Goldsmith and EA Posner, *The Limits of International Law* (Oxford, 2005); on this book, see the critique of H.J Cremer, 'Völkerrecht—alles nur Rhetorik? ' (2007) 67 *ZaöRV* 267ff.

security, the law must be able to be sanctioned. The contents of the law can be whatever is desired; only the sanction is the necessary proof of its reality. Consequently, if the law depends entirely on security and sanction, ie on the power of the lawgiver to impose it, it follows that true law can exist only within the modern State. Only there does one find the social organisation geared towards mechanisms of regular enforcement of the law. Hobbes therefore draws the logical conclusion that among States there is only a natural society, at best regulated by moral norms. In the absence of security, there is an endemic state of war of all against all in such a natural society. And there is no law proper.[99]

3. *Resistance of Tradition*

In the face of these new conceptions there is a doctrinal thread eager to uphold the older legal tradition. It attempts to adapt to the new political and social realities the heritage of the medieval Christian Republic. Its main aim is to avert the excessive concentration of sovereign power, in the municipal sphere (modern constitutionalist movements) and in the international sphere (construction of a new international legal order among States). The legal tradition of the Middle Ages was nourished by three sources. First, on the universal plane, there was the old *jus gentium*. It applied to all the individuals and peoples, since it was considered to be based on natural justice, reason and equity. Secondly, still on a general plane, there was Roman civil law. It had been inherited by the European States as a matter of succession from the Roman Empire. This branch of the law had been considerably developed through its multiple contacts with canon law. Thirdly, on the local plane, there was the *jus proprium* flowing from the autonomous legislation of towns, guilds, leagues, etc. It stands to reason that only the first two sources could be used for the construction of a new international law. The principles of civil law were interesting because of their horizontal reach, ie their application to dealings between equals, who were granted a progressively significant portion of private autonomy. The secular work on this old civil law had purified it from its contingent aspects and brought is closer to natural law precepts (*ratio scripta*). The *jus gentium* was still more useful. It purported to be based on the most universal idea accessible (the common reason of all peoples), and could therefore be put most easily into service to construct a common legal order for all States. Whenever the civil law remained too entangled in formalism (as in certain parts of

[99] There are interesting variants of this realistic theory up to the 20th century. Thus, the eminent Swiss lawyer W Burckhardt wrote—contrary to Hobbes and Austin—that international law is true law but is at the same time devoid of positivity. In short, international law is non-positive law. The existence of a legal order among States is for Burckhardt a postulate of reason. However, this law will remain purely natural, ie an aspiration to justice, as long as international society is not organised. Organisation here means the creation of organs for the sanctioning of breach of rules. The conception is substantively the same as that of Hobbes and Austin: fully-fledged law supposes social and institutional organisation, acts of will and the sanction of the sovereign. See W Burckhardt, *Die Organisation der Rechtsgemeinschaft* (Basle, 1927) 374ff.

contractual law, where *nuda pacta* had no legal protection and thus the principle *pacta sunt servanda* was not of general application),[100] the *jus gentium* tradition would prevail.

The doctrine attached to this legal tradition was split into two schools, and there was also a mixed or synthetic conception. The first was rooted in scholastics, remaining as faithful as possible to the classical Aristotle–Aquinas view. The second was rooted in rationalism, and thus more heavily influenced by modern theories on empirical methods:

1. The first line of thought is to be found in the works of Grotius. His system is based on an attempt at synthesis between the old Aquinas tradition and the new needs of an atomistic society (by comparison, de Vattel would lay stress only on the second aspect). The synthesis at stake is characterised by an equilibrium between natural law and positive international law, ie the law based on rational deduction and the law based on induction from actual practice. Hence the two stages of the Grotian edifice: the necessary law (natural) and the voluntary law (created). The many authors close to the Grotian system tried to uphold this effort at synthesis, for example Rachel. But there was a progressive tendency to lean more heavily towards the positive law element by, for example, van Bynkerhoek. The two mentioned poles of the law would later lead into a new synthesis through the idea of an international law based on some vague 'common consent of nations', beyond the individual voluntary acceptance of each of its rules by each individual State.

[100] In Roman law—which exerted a known influence on European legal thinking and practice—there was initially a rigid contractual formalism in the civil law (*jus civile*). The contracts clothed with legal protection were enumerated: contracts re *verbis (stipulatio)*, *litteris* and *consensu*. By contrast, contracts that did not fulfil the formal requirements of any of these categories were called *nuda pacta*, or simply *pacta*. They were not legally protected: *ex nudo pacto actio non oritur*. It was, however, accepted that they could give rise to some procedural exceptions against the action of the other party. An analogous application of the Roman civil law principles to international covenants could not be suitable. The kings and other rulers of the States were sovereign. They could not be forced to observe the forms of the old civil law; and the categories of contracts were hardly suitable for public treaties. Thus, the classical authors of international law, Grotius, Gentili or de Vattel, and also Vitoria and Suarez, had been influenced by the *jus gentium* tradition and, as far as the Catholic authors were concerned, also by the law of the Church. From this tradition they could draw the rule *pacta (nuda) sunt servanda*. On these issues, see R Kolb, *La bonne foi en droit international public* (Paris, 2000) 87ff; L Seuffert, *Zur Geschichte der obligatorischen Verträge* (Nördlingen, 1881); W Scherrer, *Die geschichtliche Entwicklung des Prinzips der Vertragsfreiheit* (Basle, 1948). See further H Dilcher, 'Der Typenzwang im mittelalterlichen Vertragsrecht' (1960) 77 *Zeitschrift der Savigny-Stiftung für Rechtsgeschichte, Romanistische Abteilung* 272ff; E Bussi, *La formazione dei dogmi di diritto privato nel diritto comune*, vol I (Padua, 1937) 217ff; J Roussier, *Le fondement de l'obligation contractuelle dans le droit classique de l'Eglise*, PhD (Paris, 1933); J Bärmann, 'Pacta sunt servanda—Considérations sur l'histoire du droit consensuel' (1961) 13 *Revue internationale de droit comparé* 18ff; B Schmidlin, 'Zum Gegensatz zwischen römischer und moderner Vertragsauffassung: Typengebundenheit und Gestaltungsfreiheit' in *Essays in Commemoration of the Sixth Lustrum of the Institute for Legal History of the University of Utrecht* (Assen, 1979) 111ff; KP Nanz, *Die Entstehung des allgemeinen Vertragsbegriffs im 16. bis 18. Jahrhundert* (Munich, 1985). For Grotius, see *De jure belli ac pacis*, Prolegomena, § 15; book I, ch 3, § 16; and most importantly book II, ch 11. See also M Diesselhorst, *Die Lehre des Hugo Grotius vom Versprechen* (Cologne, 1959).

2. The second line of thinking is that of Pufendorf. Pufendorf was influenced by Hobbes, from whom he takes over the cardinal concept of the sanction as the distinctive element of the law. Law is based on the command of some superior, divine (natural law as the command of God) or civil (civil law as the command of the sovereign). These commands are underlined with a sanction; the sanction is the hallmark and the indicator of the existence of law.[101] Law thus rests on an act of will, since the command is an act of will. In international society there is no superior authority. Consequently, there is no superior command and no sanctioned law. Hence, international law cannot be part of positive law. At this juncture, however, Pufendorf departs from Hobbes. He distinguishes the physical world, dominated by causal laws, from the world of obligations, based on moral considerations—*entia moralia*.[102] Moreover, for Pufendorf the state of nature is a state of peace and not a state of endemic violence; but it is a state of precarious peace in the absence of a sanctioned law. Based on these two assumptions, a legal order among States remains possible. This law will relate to the duties flowing from reason, ie to the *entia moralia*. International law is consequently purely natural and non-positive; it is based on rational postulates, constructed on indications of reason; practice comes into the play only marginally. The teaching of Pufendorf on the *lex imperfecta gentium* would be taken up by his disciples—Thomasius, Cocceius, Barbeyrac, Heinecke, Burlamaqui and later Burckhardt[103]—with slight variations.
3. A distinct school of thought, which can nevertheless be linked to that of Pufendorf/Hobbes for the purposes of international law, is the one espoused by Leibniz, followed to some extent by Wolff, de Vattel, Nettelbladt, Darjes and Püttner. The law is still anchored in the moral world—as with the *entia moralia* of Pufendorf. Its mission is not to describe facts; it is to impose rights and obligations. Consequently, the law cannot be deduced from facts, ie from empirical reality; it must flow from a value, ie the idea of justice. International law is therefore a universal precept of justice and manifests itself as a rule of reason. It is not dissociable from morals.[104] Since the law is based on a series of injunctions flowing from right reason, it cannot depend from its sanction, which is a mere fact. Moreover, the law calls for coherence. Thus, the various rights and obligations can only be deduced through reason from the most general precepts. Strictly empirical data have to be ignored: a fact can be just or unjust, legal or illegal; its existence does not turn it into law. As can be seen, the separation of the 'ought' and 'is' leads to a purely deductive method. This would still influence authors like Kelsen in the twentieth century, albeit in

[101] *De jure naturae et gentium* (1672), book I, ch II, a VI and book II, ch VI.
[102] ibid, book I, ch I.
[103] *Die Organisation der Rechtsgemeinschaft* (Basle, 192[illegible]) 374ff.
[104] Neminem laedere (jus strictum); suum cuique tribuere (jus aequum); honeste vivere (jus pietatis).

the context of a normative-positivistic construction of law. Still more precisely: the method followed is rationalistic, *more geometrico*. From these theoretical assumptions flows a strange identification of natural with positive international law. In natural society there is a law binding only in conscience (morals); in international society there is a positive international law deduced from the supreme precepts of reason and binding as law. The whole international law is therefore purely rational. It is based on self-sufficient juridical norms independent from social and institutional organisation. The evolution of this school of thought would progressively lean towards a greater place made for State practice, as is evidenced in the work of de Vattel.

4. *Continuity and Reform*

It is not easy to grasp the precise interplay between the two great schools of thought of the times described, the one leaving international society in the hands of the mechanical play of causal laws, limiting itself to observing the changing constellations of power, and the other trying to enrich the received legal tradition with the necessary new elements for constructing an international juridical order.[105] Several factors contributed to the predominance of the doctrine of legal continuity. Among those were principally the irreducible necessity of living together (with its interdependencies), and the need for a minimum order to consolidate the gains obtained through political action and to impose the desired charges. This confirms the maxim that where there is a society there is also law—even if there has hardly been any society less prone to be subjected to the rule of law than the international one, dominated, as it is, by sovereignty and power. It has to be noted that the transformation of the person-based medieval system into the modern territorial-based system has been progressive. In particular, the Westphalian Treaties of 1648 did not mark a brutal point of rupture; they were inscribed as part of a flow of events. This state of affairs, ie the gradual nature of the shift, facilitated some degree of continuity in legal tradition.

The above-mentioned continuity was essentially based on frequent reference to doctrinal works. At the start of modern international society, legal writings by the most qualified publicists were the main source of international law. Grotius was a particularly important point of reference. He offered a fully-fledged rationalisation of international relations and avoided too sharp a divorce from international practice (as was the case, for example, with Pufendorf or Leibniz). It is known that kings were reading Grotius' *De jure belli ac pacis* (1625). The attraction of

[105] As has been said (our translation), 'The first line of thinking is based on a tendency towards synthesis and universality, and also, in line with the best theological tradition, is based on a Christian and limited conception of State power in view of the necessities of social life. The second line of thinking reveals a fragmented vision, quasi-anarchical, of international society, with the conception of a State power jealous of its prerogatives, oriented towards expansion and subordinating the social relations to its will'. L Cavaré, *Le droit international public positif*, 2nd edn, vol I (Paris, 1961) 11–12.

the Dutch internationalist's works also hinged upon his intellectual honesty. In analysing positive international law, Grotius neither invented nor postulated; he avoided a purely ideological stance. At the same time, he would not refrain from indicating what reason indicated the best solution to be, and recommended it to the conscience of rulers. Such a system was manifestly quite attractive: there was at once a realistic exposition of actual practice, but also a blueprint of the best solutions to adopt.

It has to be emphasised that diplomacy—especially at the times of Grotius—tends to refer to principles of law, of justice and of equity. These concepts formed a bridge to the legal order, to *jus gentium* and to Roman law.[106] As has rightly been said,[107] the States never gave any hint that they considered themselves absolved from any legal obligations in their mutual dealings. A purely natural international society had never existed; it was a simple doctrinal fiction. On the other hand, it must be emphasised that the law drafted to govern international society maintained itself at some minimum level, contrary to the constitutionalist movements on the municipal plane. It was limited to being essentially a law of coexistence (with some predatory elements), a law to push back a natural society exempted from any legal rights and obligations. What a difference between this essentially limited legal body and the broad constitutional guarantees within the modern State! International law is mainly there to delimit the respective spheres of competence and to impose to some degree the maxim *alterius non laedere* (do not harm the other), while allowing for the important exception of the competence to wage war. When law is thus received in modern international society, it must suffer from a diminution and share its victory with the threatening shadows of power. Hence the ironic words *Ordnung im Kleinen, Unordnung im Grossen*[108]—the law provides for order in small things and leaves disorder to the great matters. From there flows the ambiguity of this first phase of 'juridisation' of international society. This legal penetration remained precarious and unstable; it was caught up in the fight between the countervailing forces of law and power. This line of development would lead to the great wars of the twentieth century.

The aim of this section has been to show that at the time of formation of modern international society, an apparently significant choice had to be made by writers and practitioners. On one side, it was claimed that a legal order is impossible for the relations among independent States. Such a law could not have the qualities the modern spirit assimilates to any law, namely a centralised sanctions mechanism. On the other hand, it was claimed that international law existed in and was based on the *jus gentium* tradition, as well as on analogies with civil law and on a series of new constructions under the banner of natural justice and equity.

[106] H Wheaton, *Histoire des progrès du droit des gens*, 4th edn, vol I (Leipzig, 1865) 109–10.

[107] See, eg, A Verdross, 'Die allgemeinen Rechtsgrundsätze als Völkerrechtsquelle', *Essays in Honor of H Kelsen* (Vienna, 1931) 360; G Balladore Pallieri, *Diritto internazionale pubblico*, 8th edn (Milan, 1962) 5–7.

[108] A Hold-Ferneck, *Lehrbuch des Völkerrechts*, vol I (Leipzig, 1930) 88.

However, in practice, this choice was not a true one. When dogmatism and reality clash, only the latter prevails. International relations needed some minimum regulation; they needed the legal dimension, for example the legal tools for concluding and managing treaties. The States themselves wanted such an order. Moreover, when the constitutional movements legalised the municipal sphere, it was impossible to imagine that law could halt sharply at the boundaries of the State, not covering any of its external relations. The concepts of law at the municipal level always have repercussions in the international sphere.[109] The juridisation of international society has thus been nourished by the necessities of life, the existence of a common legal culture and the sway of internal constitutional movements.

C. Second Phase of Development of Modern International Law: The 'Constitutionalisation' of International Society

1. *The Positivistic Twist*

The progressive absorption of the legal phenomenon by the State ushered in a progressive restriction of its sources. This reached its apogee in the nineteenth century. A substantial monism—extending from the sources to the foundation of the law—shaped understanding of the formal expressions of the law. According to predominant will-orientated positivism, law was limited to the commands or expression of the will of the sovereign, set out in the procedures tailored to that end. Outside these commands or will (legislation, contract) there was no law. A series of factors had contributed to this significant restriction.

First, during the Enlightenment the school of natural law had sided with the cause of the construction of modern liberal-constitutional States. To that effect, natural law was put into writing in the constitutions (public law) and in the codes (private law). Once achieved, these important codifications caused the critical spirit to ebb. The exigencies of reason having been codified, attention now turned towards the exegetic methods allowing comprehension and mastery of the constitutions and codes. Codification was thus necessarily accompanied by some positivistic bent towards legal science. There was a shift in the epicentre of interest from the existence and foundation of rules towards the systematic exposition of the codified norms (which has been called 'legal dogmatic'). The *lex lata* and the *lex ferenda* were thus neatly distinguished. Any non-exegetic question was expelled into the non-legal lands. Policy and law dissociated to a degree never known before. The modern legal science to which we are accustomed was birthed in the nineteenth century.

[109] This link has been rightly stressed in legal doctrine: see, eg, D Schindler, 'Gedanken zum Wiederaufbau des Völkerrechts' in D Schindler, *Recht, Staat, Völkerrecht* (Zurich, 1948) 238. It has already been discussed very clearly by C Schmitt, see R Kolb, *Deux textes de Carl Schmitt* (Paris, 2009) 61ff.

Secondly, positivistic thinking was furthered by industrialisation and the progress of natural sciences. Scientific evolution had presented natural sciences as a model for all sciences, and as an indispensable vehicle for human progress. From there flowed the scientific dogmas and the faith in progress so typical of the nineteenth century. The dominating theories believed in the holistic apprehension of all types of realities though facts and their observation. This era saw the birth of sociology, biology and even of materialistic determinism. The maxim was *verum ipsum factum*—something is true to the extent that it is a fact; and if something is true, it must be a fact. Fact became the sole object of scientific truth. Legal positivism fitted perfectly into that scheme, since it was based on an empirically verifiable fact: the expression of legislative will.

Thirdly, a change of dominant paradigm operated to buttress positivistic tendencies. The time-honoured rationalism, abstract and deductive, had progressively ushered in rigid and repetitive schemes of analysis. There came a reaction against this rule of abstract reason and technical rationality. Burke went so far as to coin the phrase 'terrorism of reason'. This was also the era of the discovery of historical contingencies (through the historical school of law and the *Volksgeist*), of a certain radical individualism (Fichte), of attention to the irrational (Bergson), of a certain exaltation of the will (Schopenhauer, Nietzsche). After the French Revolution, moreover, the issue of nationalities took root. It emphasised the particularity of peoples. A gulf opened up between the particularistic perspective and the old, universally common reason of all peoples. Further, national sovereignty, so fiercely and often lately won by some peoples—notably in Germany and Italy—became exalted and revered. The sovereignty of the people sublimated popular will; the latter then constituted the highest material source of the law. International law, created through the executives of States, was progressively subjected to parliamentary control and procedures of municipal assent. No foreign law might imposed without agreement. All these evolutions strengthened the will element of the law to the detriment of natural law aspects. Positivism progressed, with its concentration on will and with its dogmas regarding the completeness of legislative law, of subsuming facts to normative contents and of legal conceptualism.[110]

This reductive approach would be progressively abandoned when the stability and quietude of social reality of the nineteenth century gave way to the traumas and crises of the early twentieth century. Positivism within the State would remain engrafted onto a network of constitutional and legal norms, as well as onto a vivid legal tradition and evolving judicial jurisprudence. But its reach was entirely different in international affairs, ie in the law between States. As a coordinative system, international law is not the expression of an integrated society being regulated by a constitution and by codes. Nowhere other than in the context of international law were the principles of the completeness of the law, of formal syllogism, of a

110 See N Bobbio, *Il positivismo giuridico* (Turin, 1996). For international law, see, eg, J Kammerhofer and J d'Aspremont (eds), *International Legal Positivism in a Post-Modern World* (Cambridge, 2014).

conceptual jurisprudence and the like more aloof from reality and from the true capacities of the legal system. A positivistic conception founded on such municipal law experiences here had the effect of completely fragmenting the international legal phenomenon. Pushed to its ultimate logic, this positivism meant that general international law could not exist: only particular norms of international law could see the light of day; they would flow from agreements among a certain number of States. Since the agreement—the sole basis of international law—was always a matter of 'privity of the parties', a truly general or common law was impossible; even if all States happened to agree on a rule, there would remain the fact that it would not bind a new State. This consequence was indeed drawn by many positivistic authors, such as Triepel[111] and to some extent Cavaglieri.[112] As a consequence, international law developed only thinly; it was formed of a series of unattached islands and rocks scattered throughout the international seas, each one accommodating the expressions of will and power of the transient moment. Such a phenomenon could hardly aspire to the noble title of a 'legal system' ruling a society; indeed, such law was geared only towards the individual States and their will. It fringed upon the conception of an 'external constitutional law'. The large spaces left unoccupied by international law were left to competing powers. While material interdependencies progressed, the state of the law was premised on disorder, and thereby manifested its increasing separateness from the evolving social facts.

2. The Anti-positivistic Reaction at the Beginning of the Twentieth Century

The political instability of the end of the nineteenth century, the emergence of the social and working-class tensions, and the weaknesses of the positivistic method opened the gates to the decline of that method. In legal science, the reaction came initially from the neo-Kantian school of Marburg and Heidelberg, with Stammler at its head. If positivism was not discarded altogether, there was rejection of its purely empirical variant. There was a search for an *a priori* form of the law, a form that must pre-exist so that the observer can classify as 'legal' most differing social phenomena spread over time.[113] The critique against positivism became more fundamental after the cataclysm of the Great War. The common point of all these critical writings was that the foundation of the law must be rooted in some objective reality, ie in a fact or a supreme norm situated beyond the realm of empiricism. It was considered to be impossible to construct a fully-fledged legal system on the sole basis of empirical data, or on a meeting of wills, which itself is an empirical fact. The reason for this criticism was a logical one. It flowed from the

[111] H Triepel, *Völkerrecht und Landesrecht* (Leipzig, 1899) 84.

[112] A Cavaglieri, 'Règles générales du droit de la paix' (1929-I) 26 *RCADI* 323.

[113] See mainly his most mature publication, R Stammler, *Lehrbuch der Rechtsphilosophie* (Berlin/Leipzig, 1922) 46ff. This school of thought influenced the Vienna Circle, including Merkl and Kelsen.

difference between the 'is' and the 'ought': for a will to produce a legal norm, it is necessary to suppose a legal power attributing to the will the capacity to produce such law-creating effects.[114] Moreover, a legal order rooted only on empirical facts will not be able to represent a 'legal system', ie a law deserving of that name. It will remain a uncoordinated heap of various accidental facts, haphazardly occupying an ill-defined normative space. The lawyer, accustomed to the theoretically perfect ordering of municipal law, could hardly be expected to deal with such extensive and messy international legal phenomena. His training and ideology would push him to construct the international space so as to obtain a fully-fledged legal order. That the latter might display some idiosyncrasies with respect to the municipal legal order could be conceded; but if it could not form itself into a 'system', this would seem to condemn the very idea of law in the international sphere: however, since there had to be a legal order in international affairs, international law had to be systematised.

Lastly, it must be emphasised that the positivistic construction of law had a strong political imprint, even if it did much to conceal the policy elements behind the veil of pure legal technique. Will-orientated positivism is manifestly the theory *par excellence* of omnipotence of power. Whoever is the sovereign—by establishing the ultimate power of decision over a territory—controls the creation of the law, and it will bind itself internationally only when this involves an expression of will: *sic volo, sic jubeo*. A law based only on command (internally) and on the meeting of wills (internationally) was considered insufficient at the beginning of the twentieth century. It no longer corresponded to the needs of the time. After the Great War, the core issue had become the 'organisation' of international society in order to extract it from the anarchy and decentralised power that had led to the War.[115] How could anarchy continue to prevail in an increasingly interdependent world? How could future wars be avoided on such a basis? As was said lucidly some years later by Rousseau, '[The international law system] rests mainly on the primacy of the sovereign wills. However, nothing solid or sustainable can be constructed on such a foundation. We are unfortunately in a domain where politics keep the law stalemated.'[116]

Against the positivistic heritage, four significant critical schools of thought emerged: (i) the theory of pure law of the Vienna School (Merkel, Kelsen); (ii) the theory of social objectivism (Duguit, Scelle, Politis); (iii) the reborn theory of natural law (Pillet, Verdross); and (iv) the theory of the institution

[114] As to this frequent argument, see, eg, A Verdross, 'Règles générales du droit international de la paix' (1929-V) 30 *RCADI* 285ff; M Bourquin, 'Règles générales du droit de la paix' (1931-I) 35 *RCADI* 50.

[115] The organisation of international society was the life's work of some important international lawyers of the first part of the 20th century, eg, Hans Wehberg. See C Denfeld, *Hans Wehberg (1885–1962)* (Baden-Baden, 2008) 158ff.

[116] C Rousseau, 'Un siècle d'évolution du droit international (1873–1973)' in University of Neuchâtel (ed), *Le droit international demain* (Neuchâtel, 1974) 22.

(Hauriou, Romano).[117] It is understandable that the anti-positivistic reaction was to make itself felt in particular in the realm of international law. It was clearly that branch of law that was in greatest need of reconstruction on a more solid basis. This is manifest if we consider the needs of modern international law when compared with classical international law. Municipal law was ordered under a constitution; international law was disordered and deprived of a constitutional order.[118] The critical authors thus leaned quite naturally towards the idea of some 'constitution' equipped with flexible supreme principles and tying together society. Postulating the existence of a constitution was tantamount to founding international law on an objective basis, and to reconciling law and power. A constitution is indeed mainly nothing more than the general organisation of powers and competencies. The point was no longer to 'juridify' international society, so as to avoid a legal vacuum, but rather to objectivise the social functions with a view to avoiding the fragmentation of the legal phenomenon provoked by positivistic approaches. It is hardly a surprise that the critical schools flourished mainly in Italy and Germany, the two States where positivism had had its brightest heyday. A part of the German school, normative in its outlook, linked the constitution of the constitution to a series of substantive values going beyond the mere ordering of competencies. The constitution was thus to translate into legal reality some exigencies of justice and of the common good of international society.[119] The Italian school remained rather sociological. It sought to root the constitution in the existing social institutions, the law being merely the expression of a social reality in its ordered aspects. Thus, international law took shape in the structures of the social reality called 'international society'.[120] In both situations, international law was a true system of law founded on an objective fact, ideal (justice, the common good) or real (social institution).

3. *Consequences for International Law*

Several important consequences from the foregoing flow for the concept of international law. *First*, this law is now construed as a system in itself and not as an ill-defined middle path between universal natural law (obligatory in conscience) and a practice-orientated voluntary law (accidental and haphazard). The first

[117] On these schools of thought, see R Kolb and A Truyol y Serra, *Doctrines sur le fondement du droit des gens* (Paris, 2007).

[118] As has been said in uncompromising terms, 'International law in fact is a law without constitution ... Unconnected with a society, it cannot adjust itself to its needs ... There is in fact, whatever the names used in the books, no *system* of international law ... What is to be found in the treatises is simply a collection of rules which, when looked at closely, appear to have been thrown together or to have been accumulated, almost at haphazard. Many of them would seem to be more appropriately described as materials for an etiquette book for the conduct of sovereigns and their representatives than as elements of a true legal system': A Zimmern, *The League of Nations and the Rule of Law (1918–1935)* (London, 1936) 98.

[119] See mainly A Verdross, *Die Verfassung der Völkerrechtsgemeinschaft* (Vienna/Berlin, 1926).

[120] See mainly S Romano, *L'ordinamento giuridico* (Pisa, 1917).

modern manuals of international law were indeed written at the beginning of the twentieth century: they are based on a systematic exposition of the law condensed into general categories, such as the 'State', the 'subject of the law', the 'jurisdiction', etc. Compared to the manuals of the nineteenth century, the effort at synthesis is remarkable. The older textbooks were a collection of particular rules addressed in lengthy and usually convoluted passages.[121] Thus, the State was not treated according to its general elements, such as territory, population and government; rather, the different forms of existing States were presented one after the other, and single State regimes were discussed. Particular elements neatly prevailed over general ones. The tide now turned. The aim was to determine the general foundations, principles and concepts of the system. Moreover, legal science does not limit itself to registering the 'is'; it frequently projects into the future, criticises the realities of power and calls for reforms; it therefore sometimes becomes messianic and hence politically coloured.

Secondly, the international community and its exigencies slowly occupied the limelight; the State by itself did not remain the ultimate reality and aim of international law. From there flowed the concept of a universal international society and of a general international law, binding all States. Thus, general international law became the silent expression of a general international society; particular international law was no longer the final touchstone of international law. The general lecture courses at the Hague Academy were now given a title that itself reflected significant progress: 'Règles *générales* du droit de la paix'.[122] The first lecturers (such as Cavaglieri)[123] asked themselves whether such general rules could indeed exist and what their content could be. This focus on general international law was at that time a true breakthrough. Moreover, international society would progressively expand to encompass all peoples and different types of subjects. It would relinquish the old concept of the three circles comprising civilised, barbaric and savage humanity.[124] International society was no longer the Concert of European Powers, into membership of which one was co-opted. The new League of Nations was based on the strict equality of States, as manifested mainly in the voting rules under article 5 of the Covenant. The time-honoured positivistic concept according to which there could exist States living apart from international society and

[121] The textbooks of the 19th century were thus often quite long. See, eg, P Pradier-Fodéré, *Traité de droit international public européen et américain* (Paris, 1885–1906) 8 vols. Compare the monograph by Anzilotti, above n 86.

[122] Emphasis added. On these courses, see R Kolb, *Les cours généraux de droit international public de l'Académie de droit international de La Haye* (Brussels, 2003).

[123] Cavaglieri, above n 112, 323–24; he tempers this statement, however, by admitting certain general rules (ibid, 326).

[124] The famous, already quoted dictum (see text connected to n 91 above) has been uttered with particular clarity by J Lorimer, *The Institutes of the Law of Nations*, vol I (Edinburgh, 1983) 101: '[H]umanity, in its present condition, divides itself into three concentric zones or spheres—that of civilised humanity, that of barbarous humanity, and that of savage humanity.'

from international law was abandoned.[125] International society and participation in it were now considered to be based on social necessity.

The external emblem of this progressively organised new community of States was the League of Nations with its Covenant. It constituted an embryonic world government, attempting to centralise certain law-creating agencies and certain aspects regarding the execution of the law. In its wake the first World Court was established, the Permanent Court of International Justice. The Secretariat was formed as a permanent executive branch. The Assembly was constituted in the hope that all the States of the world would become members. The League itself was far from being a State, but it exhibited certain features pointing in that direction. Through institutions such as the League, the new international law of cooperation would take shape. It would have an influence on the conception of the international society, and in particular on its universality.

The densification of international law posed new problems in its relationships with municipal law. The cooperation, but also the conflict, between the two legal orders became more intense.[126] The proper reach of each of these legal orders manifested itself in the lingering question of the reserved domain of municipal law, so-called 'domestic matters'. The question of the delimitation of jurisdiction of the various States became urgent in an increasingly interdependent world, where States no longer limited their policies to simple Manchester Liberalism.[127] New subjects of law entered onto the scene: this was the time of the creation of a series of international institutions. The individual emerged as a subject of international concern (minorities, refugees). The new needs led to an attack on the notion of 'egoistic' sovereignty, taken to mean an omnipotent and arrogant power.[128] Some authors now rejected sovereignty altogether as a notion of law; others limited it to a relative concept, granted and governed by legal rules, and meaning essentially

[125] Such a concept was still upheld by the most purely positivistic authors, eg, Cavaglieri, above n 112, 344ff.

[126] Great theories are shaped on the precise relationship between the two legal orders, ranging from the dualistic (H Triepel, 'Les rapports entre le droit interne et le droit international' (1923) 1 *RCADI* 73ff) to the monistic (H Kelsen, 'Les rapports de système entre le droit interne et le droit international public' (1926-IV) 14 *RCADI* 227ff).

[127] The Manchester School of Liberalism argued, inter alia, that free trade would result in a more equitable society, making essential products available to all.

[128] N Politis, 'Le problème des limitations de la souveraineté et la théorie de l'abus des droits dans les rapports internationaux' (1925-I) 6 *RCADI* 1ff; S Séferiadès, 'Principes généraux du droit international de la paix' (1930-IV) 34 *RCADI* 353ff; G Scelle, 'Règles générales du droit de la paix' (1933-IV) 46 *RCADI* 371ff. In the words of RJ Dupuy, *Le droit international*, 7th edn (Paris, 1986) 4, '[T]ous les partisans de la paix par le droit se sont attaqués à la notion de souveraineté, obstacle majeur à la primauté du droit international sur ses sujets, les Etats. La démarche est d'une logique indiscutable, mais elle oublie que la souveraineté est une notion historique et que l'histoire ne se défait pas à coups d'arguments logiques.' ('All defenders of the idea of peace through law have attacked the notion of sovereignty, a major obstacle for the primacy of international law over its subjects, the States. The claim is of an undisputable logic. But it forgets that sovereignty is a historical notion and that history cannot be dismantled through logic.')

certain competencies or jurisdiction. For the same reason, the 'fundamental rights of States' were progressively abandoned: self-judging and sweeping notions such as 'self-preservation' were considered untenable. Such examples could be multiplied. They all show the effort to impose higher degrees of an organised society by relinquishing all-too individualistic positivism.

D. Third Phase of Development of Modern International Law: The 'Community Orientation'

1. *Progress of the Idea of an International Community*

The idea of the constitution pursued at the beginning of the twentieth century was essentially directed against positivistic reductionism, and culminated in the affirmation of an international society being universal in scope. The 'community orientation' phase in the second half of the twentieth century was centered on an anti-individualistic reaction. It affirmed the existence of an international community vested with its own interests. In part, these two orientations have the same aims, and certainly the later efforts took the same path as the earlier ones, but those later efforts also clearly go beyond the reach of their predecessors. The difference is between a society (legal organisation of coexistence with a degree of cooperation) and a community (preponderance of certain common interests and a degree of presence of a communitarian spirit).[129] The basis of the first orientation remains the socialised individual, the basis of the second is the collectivity.

2. *Progress of the Communitarian Spirit in International Law*

Since the mid-twentieth century, a series of threats and challenges common to all humanity has forged a sense of common destiny. This concept of a planetary solidarity first developed in a negative context, in the face of common existential dangers.[130] Thus Friedmann concluded his general course of 1969, held at the Hague Academy, with the dramatic claim that the survival of Man on Earth

[129] Sometimes, in legal language, 'the community' (or 'legal community') is simply a term used to designate the existence of a legal order in a society. See, eg, AP Sereni, *Diritto internazionale*, vol I (Milan, 1966) 83ff.

[130] See eg M Bourquin, *L'Etat souverain et l'organisation internationale* (New York, 1959) 144: 'Il serait nécessaire, en tout cas, d'accorder plus d'importance que nous ne le faisons aux dangers et aux intérêts qui nous sont communs. Ce qui divise les hommes est grave assurément; mais s'ils continuent à se laisser dominer exclusivement par leurs dissensions, quelque justifiées qu'elles puissent être, il est à craindre que la marche des événements ne les éclaire trop tard sur leur erreur.' ('It seems necessary to grant more importance than we are used to do, to the dangers and interests that we have in common. Humanity is divided on important questions, assuredly; but if man continues to be dominated only by his dissensions, however justified they may be, the unfolding of events could reveal too late the error committed.') This sentence occurs in the chapter on atomic energy.

would probably depend on a significant increase in the capacity to cooperate.[131] The threats in question were of different types. First, there was the danger of new destructive wars, possibly of a thermo-nuclear nature. The tension surrounding Cuba in 1962 influenced such apprehensions. Secondly, after the experiences with totalitarian and lawless regimes, there was the issue of human rights, that is, the cause of human dignity and rights. The respect for such rights and freedoms was linked to the maintenance of peace. It was claimed that there could be no peace in the long run if human security was not guaranteed. Thirdly, there was, at least from the 1960s, a more vivid perception of economic and social interdependence, notably in the relations between north and south. A particular social and economic situation somewhere in the world could lead, for instance, to massive migration in the international space, which would affect third States.[132] Fourthly, there was increased awareness of ecological crises, pollution, deterioration of the atmosphere, depletion of resources, extinction of species, overpopulation, etc. Through all these evolutions, there was created a place in the collective psychology—at least in the West—for the understanding that what happens at the South Pole can affect a man living in Alaska.

The anti-positivistic reaction found at the beginning of the twentieth century had essentially been a matter for the doctrinal elite. The new concepts concerning community orientation had a much wider audience. Public opinion had been galvanised by symbolic acts with a certain force, such as when Garry Davis, an American, tore up his passport in front of the cameras and proclaimed himself a citizen of the world. The maxim 'Unite or die' (*s'unir ou périr*) was gaining ground. The politicisation of part of the popular masses flowed from such evolutions, in which a part of civil society wanted to play an active role. Moreover, interdependence continued to grow in all fields; it called for further international regulation[133] and later ushered in globalisation. In the wake of this, the political organisation of international society and its law seemed, at least partly, to belong to earlier times. As with every social transformation, legal doctrine seeks the right answers and continuously adapts its constructions of the law. To answer the needs of the beginning of the twentieth century, it was necessary to provide international law with an objective basis; in order to respond to the new challenges, it was necessary to accentuate the community layer of international law.

[131] W Friedmann, 'General Course in Public International Law' (1969-II) 127 *RCADI* 39ff, 246.

[132] An example is the expulsion of Uganda's Asian minority population by General Idi Amin in 1972, which led to the forced migration of more than 50,000 individuals.

[133] For example, in Switzerland, between 1947 and 1982, federal legislation increased 131%, cantonal legislation increased 124% and federal legislation concerning international law norms increased 293%. See W Linder, *Schweizerische Demokratie* (Bern/Stuttgart/Vienna, 1999) 148.

3. *International Law and Progressively Defined Community Interest:* Utilitas Publica[134]

Through its constitutionalising cure, international law had been objectivised in its foundation more than in its sources, which remained essentially bilateral and relativist. Fragmentation of power in international society led to a number of particular legislators each concluding separate agreements and treaties, or following various customary practices. The consequence was a great number of legal entitlements of relative reach (*inter partes*); they were superimposed over and juxtaposed to each other. There were a number of agreements between some parties, as opposed to one piece of legislation created for all members of society. International law thus tended to remain a huge collection of unilateral, bilateral and multilateral acts applicable to different subjects. The rule was dominated by the subject of the law, and not vice versa. Each subject was the guardian of its own interests; it concluded agreements as a function of those interests. In this aspect of its configuration, international law presents itself as a type of private law: the State is not considered the bearer of a public function linked to an external common good, but rather as a person possessing private autonomy and deciding, as master, how to adequately defend its own interests. Private interest (*utilitas singulorum*) prevails over collective interest (*utilitas publica*). It stands to reason that such a vision of law is based on a contractual and patrimonial conception, on the ethics of 'contract, responsibility and property'. The law organises the respective spheres of action of each autonomous subject. The 'public' aspect of the law is limited to defining these spheres of each subject, ie in granting and delimiting its jurisdictions. Moreover, rights predominate over obligations; the duty is mainly the logical corollary of the subjective rights granted. Thus, international law tended for a long time to occupy a reduced layer of 'public' law, regulating the conflicts between jurisdictions, and a deep layer of 'private' law, based on powers of legal action attributed to the subjects of international law taken individually. Such a law is poor in common values. At the end of the nineteenth century, Jellinek wrote, with good reason, that any unlawful act could be elevated into the rank of positive international law if only it were made the object of an agreement.[135]

The second half of the twentieth century saw a reaction against this state of affairs. Its main aim was to pursue the quest for the objective construction of international law. The goal was to extend this effort beyond the theory of the foundation of international law so as to import it into the sources, and therefore into the heart of positive law. The argument went as follows: the new challenges in international society disclosed the necessity for the extension of international

[134] See, eg, B Simma, 'From Bilateralism to Community Interest in International Law' (1994-VI) 250 *RCADI* 217ff.

[135] G Jellinek, *Die rechtliche Natur der Staatsverträge* (Berlin, 1880) 59.

law's public law layer at the expense of its private law layer—in the same way that municipal law evolved between the nineteenth and the twentieth centuries, for example through social legislation. Consequently, in areas of collective interest, State individualism would have to cede its place to the requirements of the common good. International law would have to present itself in these domains as the 'law of humanity', geared towards this higher aim.[136] Thus, after an international law of coexistence and later of cooperation had seen the light of day, an international law of humankind was called on to develop itself, ie a law of the international community geared to the challenges and threats of the modern world. As has been emblematically written, 'This new dimension of international law, which is the law of the international community, has been added to the traditional dimensions of the legal order regulating the inter-State relations of coexistence and cooperation.'[137]

Legal doctrine developed various concepts in order to reinforce the 'public layer' of international law. Their common purpose was to organise legally the precedence of certain common interests over the individual powers of States. Thus, the Charter of the United Nations was considered a sort of constitution of the international community.[138] Concepts such as *jus cogens*, *erga omnes* obligations, and world order treaties or international crimes (of States and individuals) were forged. These sought to ensure control of common values in the areas of validity of legal acts, of *locus standi* to bring claims, of construction of treaty rules and of the sanctions in the context of certain breaches of the law. In particular the concept of *jus cogens* was vested with the role of a supra-constitutional international law, limiting in law and fact the powers of action of States in international and in municipal law.[139] Today, *jus cogens* is often presented as an all-round limitation on the autonomy of States.[140] Parallel efforts were made to ensure the legal

[136] As Thomas Aquinas wrote, 'lex est quaedam rationis ordinatio ad bonum commune'. See *Summa theologica*, II, I, q 40, a 4.

[137] JA Carrillo-Salcedo, 'Droit international et souveraineté des Etats' (1996) 257 *RCADI* 146.

[138] See, eg, B Fassbender, *The United Nations Charter as the Constitution of the International Community* (Leyde/Boston, 2009); R Chemain and A Pellet, *La Charte des Nations Unies, Constitution mondiale?* (Paris, 2006). See also J Crawford, 'The Charter of the UN as a Constitution' in G Abi-Saab and H Fox (eds), The Changing Constitution of the United Nation (London, 1997) 3ff; TM Franck, 'Is the United Nations Charter a Constitution?', *Essays in Honor of T Eitel* (Berlin, 2003) 95ff; J Klabbers, A Peters and G Ulfstein (eds), *The Constitutionalization of International Law* (Oxford, 2009); MW Doyle, 'The UN Charter: A Global Constitution? ' in JL Dunoff and JP Trachtman (eds), *Ruling the World? Constitutionalism, International Law and Global Governance* (Cambridge, 2009) 113ff; B Fassbender, 'Rediscovering a Forgotten Constitution: Notes on the Place of the UN Charter in the International Legal Order' in JL Dunoff and JP Trachtman (eds), *Ruling the World? Constitutionalism, International Law and Global Governance* (Cambridge, 2009) 133ff.

[139] See, eg, A Orakhelashvili, *Peremtory Norms in International Law* (Oxford, 2006).

[140] See, eg, the Trial Chamber of the International Criminal Tribunal for the former Yugoslavia, *Furundzija* case, decision of 10 December 1998, §§ 153ff: the prohibition of torture being of a *jus cogens* nature, various consequences are envisaged, eg, the international law nullity of contrary municipal norms granting amnesty, the applicability of universal jurisdiction, etc. Art 139, § 3, of the Swiss Constitution provides for popular initiatives that are contrary to peremptory norms of international law to be rendered void. This has to be decided by the Federal Assembly.

preponderance of international human rights, the maintenance of peace and the protection of the environment. Hence the multiplication of special regimes, such as in reservations to treaties (limitation of the power to reserve), the limitation of devices for opting out and of the power to denounce a treaty;[141] in the context of material breach of treaties (savings clause in article 60, § 5, of the Vienna Convention on the Law of Treaties of 1969 for 'humanitarian treaties' and limitation of the power to adopt countermeasures according to article 50 of the ILC Articles of State Responsibility 2001); in the context of subsequent treaties (no derogation from world order treaties through *inter se* agreements lowering the applicable standards); in the context of succession of States to treaties (pressure in the practice of international organs towards automatic succession to world order treaties, in particular treaties of a humanitarian nature); or in the context of various norms and powers under international law, eg the circumstances excluding wrongfulness, counter-measures or the law of immunities. There was here an attempt at the vertical reconstruction of international law in the sense of so-called common values and interests. In each branch of international law, the old private layer with its bilateralism was to some extent attacked and fought back. Integral legal regimes, which cannot be fragmented through special agreements or derogation, began to spread and grow. A new international law of humankind or of common causes sought to emerge from the traditional landscape of the international law of States.

4. *Appraisal of these Evolutions*

The benefits and the dangers of these evolutions have to be correctly appraised. On the one hand, it is appropriate to pay due tribute to the attempt to give legal expression to certain common State interests, or to interests of the international community. Who could doubt the sense of increased environmental protection, or of action against excessive climate change? The same is true as regards nuclear weapons and their proliferation; the fight against diseases and pandemics; the protection of people against massacres, etc. Generally speaking, it is difficult to imagine that a society, having reached the density and quality of the international society of the twenty-first century, could live without a increasing layer of 'public law' that seeks to promote functions linked to the common good—and not only to regulate bilateral relationships. It remains true, however, that these evolutions are in but the first stage. Therefore, it would be preposterous to expect the immediate, coherent and perfect organisation of such functions, just as it would have been foolish to expect a fully-fledged inter-State international law in the times of Grotius.

[141] See, eg, the reactions to the withdrawal of North Korea from the Nuclear Non-Proliferation Treaty. See the *Annual Report of the UN Human Rights Committee*, General Assembly Official Records, Supplement No 40, UN/Doc. A/53/40), 1998, § 413.

On the other hand, it would be unrealistic to ignore the multiple ambiguities and problems raised by these evolutions. The effort towards a community-orientated legal layer stops all too often at the level of norms and is not translated onto the plane of institutions. The way is cleared for some normative federalism; but the latter remains based on organic relativism. In simpler terms, the 'common good'-orientated public law needs common institutions to define it and apply it properly. If every single entity can aspire to define and promote for itself the 'common good', the danger is that the community will be a handy facade behind which private interests will remain the true motor of action. Hence, the community layer remains limp and ineffectual. It affirms, postulates and sometimes triumphantly proclaims; but it does not possess the means to realise its own ambitions. Thus the 'common good' is ultimately reduced to the unilateral and subjective appreciation of States *uti singuli*,[142] with its inevitable consequences of selectivity, subjectivity, politicisation, threats to social peace and possible amplification of conflicts. It may be nice to speak of humanitarian intervention or humanitarian protection, or of 'responsibility to protect', but the afore-mentioned consequences can have deleterious effects on the realisation of such aims.[143] In the event of action through the Security Council of the United Nations, politicisation is not avoided, but at least there is a brake on idiosyncratic action by individual States, or by self-proclaimed coalitions of the willing. Conversely, when each State acts on its own account (eg because the Security Council is considered to be 'blocked' or 'stalemated' by an inopportune veto)[144], the observer frequently has the impression that States proclaim noble causes as a pretext for, at bottom, a

[142] On this aspect of international law in general, see P Klein, 'Les prétentions des Etats à la mise en œuvre "unilatérale" du droit international' (2010) 43 *RBDI* 141ff, especially at 163ff.

[143] On the concept, see, eg, C Focarelli, 'La dottrina della "responsabilità di proteggere" e intervento manitario' (2008) 91 *RDI* 317ff. For a very critical third-world survey of the question, see VS Mani, 'Humanitarian Intervention Today' (2005) 313 *RCADI* 9ff. Among the recent literature on the responsibility to protect, see A Orford, *International Authority and the Responsibility to Protect* (Cambridge, 2011); AJ Bellamy, SE Davies and L Glanville (eds), *The Responsibility to Protect and International Law* (Leiden, 2011); A Rausch, *Responsibility to Protect: Eine juristische Betrachtung* (Frankfurt, 2011); J Hoffmann and A Nollkaemper (eds), *Responsibility to Protect: From Principle to Practice* (Amsterdam, 2012); J Genser and I Cotler (eds), *The Responsibility to Protect: The Promise of Stopping Mass Atrocities in Our Time* (New York, 2012); G Zyberi (ed), *An Institutional Approach to the Responsibility to Protect* (Cambridge, 2013); P Hilpold (ed), *Responsibility to Protect: A New Paradigm of International Law?* (Leiden/Boston, 2015).

[144] The concept of a blocked or stalemated Security Council is open to manipulation. The Council will be considered blocked only when the opposition has used his veto, never when the veto is used by oneself. Thus, in Western media, one rarely reads that the Council is 'blocked' when the US has used its veto (or threatens to use it) to protect Israel. The Council is 'blocked' only when Russia or China use the veto. However, in recent times the statistically most frequent veto or threat of veto has been that of the US. An abuse of the right of veto clearly remains possible. But each use of the veto is not a 'blockage' of the Council or an abuse. The veto is part and parcel of the political decision-making process. The law of the UN has also developed some avenues to fight against excessive veto practices, eg through Resolution 377(V) of the UNGA, called the Dean Acheson Resolution. On this latter Resolution, see I Brownlie, *International Law and the Use of Force by States* (Oxford, 1963) 333–36.

highly self-interested and selective foreign policy.[145] Hence the current objections in the context of humanitarian interventions: Why here and not there? Why in Kosovo[146] and not in Angola? Why in Iraq and not in Sudan? Why in Libya and not in Syria? That some objective motives may exist to distinguish the situations is not the point; it is the perception of matters in society at large that is important here. And that perception is manifestly often negative.

This state of affairs gives way to certain paradoxes. First, international law regulates a society riddled by power struggles, with a marked propensity to adopt power policies. Therefore, more than other branches of the law, international law can attain a certain degree of effectiveness only if it is sustained by an appreciable degree of assent of States. To obtain such assent, it must accommodate the interests of States. Furthermore, this assent depends on maintaining a certain distance of the law from the more or less vivid political or ideological struggles permeating international society.[147] Bold public order normative layers not sustained by solid State will and practice, may contribute to weakening the credibility of the law, and thus ultimately to reducing its role and relevance.[148]

Secondly, the main evolution of the law, from its primitive to more mature stages, is to limit and tame the powers of each individual subject of a society. Thus, the fight against 'unilateralism', in particular the unilateral use of force, has been prominent for a long time in the life of international law. Unilateral action is neither a means to ensure peace, nor a means to ensure justice. Now, in the absence of common organs vested with powers of execution in the context of the public law layer, legal doctrine often reverts to the States and postulates some enlargement of their powers of action. Thus, the system of 'private justice' or of unilateral

[145] That good causes are often taken as pretexts for bad policies is a known historical fact. With regard to the law, see, eg, E von Hippel, *Die Perversion von Rechtsordnungen* (Tübingen, 1955) 10ff.

[146] This intervention marked a return and victory of 'legitimacy' over 'legality', with a sort of Directory of Powers intervening in a part of Europe, as was the case in the 19th century. The intervention opened the gates for future interventions, and ultimately inspired even the annexation of Crimea by Russia in 2014. For a measured view of the Kosovo precedent, see B Simma, 'NATO, the UN and the Use of Force: Legal Aspects', (1999) 10 *EJIL* 1ff. For a more systemic view, see M Kohen, 'The Use of Force by the United States after the end of the Coild War and its Impact on International Law' in M Byers and G Nolte (eds), *United States Hegemony and the Foundations of International Law* (Cambridge, 2003) 197ff.

[147] This is the reason why a certain degree of formalism is inherent in the legal rule: legality, equality, reciprocity, generality and abstraction. If the rule is excessively individualised, ie opened to particular circumstances, it disappears. It then leads to a discretion, which is essentially political. In international law, there has in the past been an attempt to keep a certain distance with regard to ideological struggles, eg in the context of the doctrine of 'peaceful coexistence' and its textual expression, the Friendly Relations Resolution, no 2625 (1970) of the UNGA.

[148] Thus, eg, if *jus cogens* is used as a tool of general legal hierarchy in order to render entire branches of international law void (such as the law of State immunities), the legal order will become a plaything of ideological battles. In this logic, if 'human dignity' (as a human right) is at the apex of the system, and is *jus cogens*, it will prevail over all other norms of international law, which can then selectively be called null and void, or at least rendered inapplicable in the particular situation. No legal system can survive such a course. On the dangers of such a use of *jus cogens*, see R Kolb, *Peremptory International Law—Jus Cogens* (Oxford, 2015).

action is reinstalled, to a disquieting degree, in international relations. Its anarchical side tends to give a free ride to power. Without the expropriation of the unilateral powers in order to vest them in common organs, the development of public law layers may mean, at the end of the day, the incidental reinforcement of the private law layer of the law. It may be observed, moreover, that the attempt to create common organs vested with the necessary competences to take care of collective values is constantly resisted by the very same States that regularly proclaim themselves the guardians of the 'fundamental values of the international community'. There is often fierce resistance with regard to the even partial ceding of sovereignty. The result is then as follows: the domain of action that the common interest had dictated needed to be taken out of the hands of individual States is progressively restored to those States in the name of the protection of community values. Instead of progressing, international law could regress. In technical terms: the density and configuration of the primary rules of a legal order cannot outweigh by too much the maximum limit allowed by the infrastructure of the secondary rules of the system, ie its institutional setting. The two must grow together, with a certain harmony. An excessive proliferation of primary rules, which the secondary level is not equipped to digest, will lead to the regression, the weakening and sometimes the destruction of the legal order.

Apart from the paradoxes, there is also a series of other problems linked with the modern 'public law' layer of international law. The first of these is connected to the determination of common values and the norms to which they give rise. It is doubtful that the Western conception of such values could automatically be considered to be the universally applicable standard. For example, the Western Group thinks that human rights are its proper heritage, and that it has to defend such rights—as a fundamental common value—everywhere in the world. It stands to reason, however, that the West defends *its* conception of human rights, centered on individual and political rights. An even summary perusal of UN practice, especially of the Organisation's organs vested with competences in the field of human rights, reveals that the Western conceptions in this area clearly present a minority view.[149] Considering the strength of the various State groupings in the UN, and the dominant social and political conceptions within each of these groups, this hardly comes as a surprise. In particular, third world States have a conception of human rights that continues to be coloured heavily by the right to development, collective rights, the right to self-determination of peoples, social, economic and cultural rights, the right to peace, etc. But this simple reality will rarely be reflected in the Western press and debates. True, oppressive political regimes sometimes misuse these differences of emphasis as a pretext to justify their violations of civil and political rights of the individual—be it by the old argument that they lack the means to respect them ('development first, human rights thereafter'), or by

[149] See H von Senger, 'Die Schweiz, europäische Staaten und die Volksrepublik China im UNO-Menschenrechtsrat' (2011) 130 *Revue de droit suisse* 323ff.

the cynical argument of cultural relativism (an argument used by governments and not by victims).[150] But there remains the fact that it is not enough to proclaim a purportedly collective interest in Washington, London, Paris or Berlin, thinking that it is thereby necessarily universal. On this account, there is no way round taking seriously the *opinio juris* of all States, ridding oneself of excessive self-assertiveness and Euro-centrism (or any other 'centrism'). The many great UN Conferences at world level have engaged in crystallising collective interests: Environment, Population and Development; Human Rights, Social Development; Women; Human Settlements; Racism and Racial Discrimination; Organised Crime, etc.[151] But even these Conferences remain enmeshed in divergent State interests, as the Kyoto Protocol on Climate Change of 1997 and its follow-up instruments aptly illustrate.

To sum up, in the absence of international organs composed of persons with a strictly international allegiance, the definition of the common interest passes through the distorting lens of some 194 particular foreign policies. How is it possible, then, to expect something sufficiently common and reasonably strong to woven out of the multiple threads of such processes? Even in the best case, characterised by a *bona fide* effort to define the common interest in precise norms, there will remain the problem that the execution of these norms is left to the individual States, and that each one will interpret for itself the meaning of the various provisions and their mutual relationships. This subjectivism may be chased out of the front door, but it will come back in through the window.

The concepts promoted under the banner of 'fundamental values' have not yet been able to resolve these problems satisfactorily. If any progress is to be made in this context, only institutional advances will offer adequate solutions. However, it is hardly imaginable that States and peoples, both fiercely protective of their sovereignty, will consent to the necessary limitations on their freedoms to achieve such institutional progress. Quite to the contrary: in the last few years, specific movements emphasising national independence, freedom from international constraints and protectionism have gained ground. Even in organisations geared towards integration, such as the EU, where solidarity should be at its strongest, there has been a reaction against the centralisation of powers in Brussels. Within the State, the more the common good is endangered, the more the people are ready to sacrifice themselves for the survival of the nation. In international society, the higher the stakes, as is the case as regards the maintenance of peace, the more solidarity fractures as the people revert to their national allegiances. This individualistic state of mind plainly and contradictorily coexists with the perception of common dangers and challenges.

[150] This was rightly noted by many authors: see, eg, R. Higgins, 'General Course on Public International Law: International Law and the Avoidance, Containment and Resolution of Disputes' (1991-V) 230 *RCADI* 137.

[151] On these Conferences, see AA Cançado Trindade, 'International Law for Humankind: Towards a New Jus Gentium' (2005) 317 *RCADI* 247ff.

The state of affairs described above provides a good indication of the obstacles to be overcome on the way to a true realisation of common values in the international legal order. Ultimately, the necessary institutional leap calls for the federalisation of the world. Thus the realisation of the doctrine of fundamental values supposes the promotion of a universal federal law instead of a traditional, sovereignty-based public international law. Such federalisation of the world is for the time being a political Utopia. And figuratively speaking, it paradoxically is based to some extent on the 'killing' of the international legal order in favour of a new federal legal order.

The result is that international law will, for now, continue to trek along a mountain ridge exposed, on the one side, to the forces of unclearly defined international generosity and, on the other side, to the forces of ever-changing State unilateralism. The community leap within international law is today irreversible, as far as we can see; its concrete expression, however, will remain chaotic and unsatisfactory because of the structure of international society, based on the parity of its members. A horizontal setting cannot at the same time be a vertical one; it cannot be the one and have at the same time the qualities of the other. It can in this context only try to craft shaky 'diagonals', built on sandy foundations. It stands to reason that nothing solid can emerge. However, there is no reason to abandon every effort just because the forces of resistance might or will be fierce.

2

Foundation, Sources and Structural Principles of International Law

I. General Aspects

The subject of the foundation of international law is part of the theory of law; it is common to all of its branches. Therefore it is impossible to discuss the foundation of public international law without taking into account the question of general jurisprudence. Due to the decentralised structure of international society, the subject of the foundation of international law shares a long history with the issue of sources. In a society characterised by parity, agreements will constitute a fundamental legal source. For a number of authors, it is tempting to view the agreement or the expression of will as at one and the same time the positive source of international law and its ultimate foundation.[1] This temptation will be the greater the more a society is impregnated with the values of individualism and liberalism. Therefore, such a construction will find pride of place in an international society dominated by the even stronger concept of sovereignty, rather than the milder private autonomy of municipal society.

The law-creating agencies and the justification of the norms thus produced are the pillars on which each legal order rests.[2] The very roots of the legal order within a society are here at stake. The sources and the law are essentially linked: one signifies the other. Therefore, a crisis in the sources indicates a crisis in the law; and a crisis in the law reveals a crisis in the sharing of social power. Conversely, crises in the law and in society find their initial expression in the system of sources and then in the realm of the execution of the norms produced.[3] This very close link between society, law and sources flows from the fact that the sources are but a legal

[1] See A Truyol y Serra and R Kolb, *Doctrines sur le fondement du droit des gens* (Paris, 2007) 59ff.

[2] N Bobbio, *La consuetudine come fatto normativo* (Padua, 1942) 12.

[3] This was the case, for example, as regards the crisis occurring in connection with Roman law at the end of the Middle Ages. Developed by casuistry, this body of the law had grown opaque over the centuries. It was full of controversies and developed a plethora of excessively contextual rules. Thus, this body of law allowed the judge to apply the rules with a great degree of discretion, ie in an arbitrary way. In a society that progressively centralised, and in which commerce expanded with the new middle classes, such a legal setting could no longer be countenanced. From this there flowed a crisis as regards the traditional sources and the promotion of the ideas of legalism and codification. See A Cavanna, *Storia del diritto modern in Europa, Le fonti ed il pensiero guiridico*, vol I (Milan, 1982) 194ff.

rationalisation of power within society. The power to create legal norms, or the power to confer a legal status on social norms, is an eminent expression of power in the strict sense. The apparent formalism of the legal doctrine of sources hides but imperfectly this close link with the distribution of social power.[4]

The place of power policy in international relations—which has even led to instilling doubts as to the existence of an 'international law'—confers an even greater urgency on the identification of the sources and the foundation of the law than it could possibly have in the municipal context. Within the question of the foundation of international law arises its existential dimension. The partial transformation and domestication of power through legal rules remains the cardinal problem besetting international law. It dominates logically and chronologically the issue of the weakness of the existing means of forced execution of the law.

II. The Relationship Between the Foundation and the Sources of International Law

What is the precise relationship between the foundation of and the sources of international law? The theory of sources responds to the following questions: *How* is the law created and in which categories does it appear? *How* is a rule recognised as being part of the law? There are two distinct aspects in this questions. The first deals with the voluntary creation of the law on the basis of the legislative model. The second takes account of the fact that there is also the spontaneous creation of legal rules in the social body, in jurisprudence or by legal science (eg general principles of law). Moreover, it is possible to approach the issue of the sources from two distinct angles: the one active, the other passive. The active aspect focuses on the production of rules (law-creating agencies, *Erzeugungsarten*); the

[4] Thus, in England, the judicial corps, emerging from the Inns of Court, was vested with important powers and was able to successfully defend them. This legal tradition has its roots in the centralisation of the Norman State from the 11th century. This centralisation was due in significant part to the judiciary, which opposed the more widespread feudal forces. The judges were the guardians of the rule of law. Having thus gained an important position within the State, and being the oracles of the common law, they were able to resist any excessive interference by the king or parliament. This distribution of social power led to a system that could not adhere to a closed set of sources centered on legislation: case law and all the material sources inspiring the judge (reason, public policy, the consequences of a decision, experience, legal maxims, etc) continued to be fundamental in the sources of English law. On the other hand, in some States of Continental Europe, the judges represented the ancien régime, opposed to the emerging bourgeoisie. The latter, when coming to power, sought and managed to curtail the powers of the former. This was one of the main reasons for the strict legalism adopted, ie the subjection of the judge to the legislation, the doctrines regarding the clarity and completeness of the law, the prohibition on 'interpreting' the law, etc: in such jurisdictions the legislation was all the law and its sole source. As can be seen, the different evolution of social power leads to different doctrines of sources. On this issue, see ibid, 479ff, with many references.

passive aspect focuses on the normative categories in which the law will appear once created, or on the places where it can be found (law-containing agencies, *Erscheinungsformen*). Often these two aspects will be just the two sides of the same coin: the process of production and the finished product. Thus, the legislative process is a source of the law because it constitutes a fact of law creation. On the other hand, the piece of legislation is a vehicle for the norms that can be found or consulted there. There are, however, also situations where the active and the passive aspects are not so joined. Not all the sources are based on acts of voluntary creation. There are sources and norms that are latent in the legal body and are revealed by legal learning. This is the case, for example, as regards the general principles of law. They are not 'created' but are 'discovered' in a given legal environment. In this sense, they are not characterised by deliberate production (active aspect) but rather by the ability to handle a given legal experience (passive aspect). This absence of a true law-creating process explains why general principles of law are viewed with suspicion by purely positivistic authors,[5] who consider the whole process to be indicative of meddling by the judge in the domain of the legislator (ie a violation of the principle of separation of powers). However that may be, the construction of sources always makes reference to a set of facts, that is, to a sociological process. The point is a rationalisation of normative facts: the sources describe the way through which the law is generated by the bearers of normative power within a society, or in which the law is revealed by an expert lawyer able to handle the whole system of norms thus created.

The question as to the foundation of the law is different: *Why* must one obey the legal rules? *What* is the ultimate justification of the law? The fact of the creation of a rule does not carry with it the justification of that rule; the 'is' is not the 'ought'. The issue goes beyond the sociological perspective and ushers in metaphysics. The point is no longer centered on normative facts but on normative reasons; it does not bear on causality but on finality. The question of the foundation of the law in the large sense encompasses the whole domain of legal metaphysics, ie the question of justice, in general or in a particular legal order (just law, *richtiges Recht*). It stands to reason that this is an important question, which legal positivism has entirely cast beyond the confines of legal enquiry, and sometimes even beyond those of philosophy of law. From this perspective the question as to the foundation of the law is always a critical one: the ideal model passes judgment on the real legislation of a given legislator; it identifies the measure of the efforts still to be made, and the imperfections still present. The spirit constantly challenges and questions itself, judging the concrete products situated in space and time. This critical function is of the utmost value: it does not permit repose on a bed of false certainties, infused with the hypnotic aroma of self-satisfaction. In short, the issue of sources will concentrate on notions such as the law (legislation), rules of the executive, judicial decisions, contracts, treaties, customary law and general

[5] See eg K Strupp, 'Les règles générales du droit de la paix' (1934-I) 47 *RCADI* 335.

principles of law, whereas the issue of foundation will deal with notions such as justice, will and the necessities of coexistence (*ubi societas, ibi jus*).[6]

Legal doctrine has often perceived the difference between the foundation of law and its sources as involving the polarity of interrelated notions: between the origin and the manifestation of law; between the reason of the law and its modes of positive validity; between legal justification (*Sollen*) and social genesis (*Sein*); between reason and will; between the formal and the finalistic causes, etc. This beneficial tension between two opposing and yet connected poles has been diminished by certain overly ambitious theories, which have attempted to reduce the process to only one controlling factor. Such theories have either lowered the foundation to the level of the sources, or elevated the sources to the level of the foundation. An example of the first course can be found in the theories of divine law, or in the context of excessively rationalistic natural law theories. Foundation and sources coagulate in the divine will or in the omnipotent rationality. The foremost example of the second category can be found in will-orientated positivism. The will of the legislator is here at one and the same time the foundation and reason of the law *and* the only source of the positive rules. All these theories are dangerous in their reductive tendencies. On the one hand, they atrophy and asphyxiate the living experience of the law by an abuse of deductive methods; on the other hand, they anaesthetise any critical spirit against the imperfection of human endeavours. However, the law is a complex and multi-faceted reality; it cannot be reduced to a

[6] In terms of legal philosophy, it is possible to view the difference between sources and foundation in the light of the ontological difference between 'essence' and 'existence'. An object exists in two ways: ideally it has a general presence (essence); but in the order of real things it has a particular presence (existence). It is possible to think of justice as a series of qualities (virtue, subjective propensity to give to each what is due to him or her, equality, equity, etc); but we can also qualify a particular behaviour as just. In the latter case, the mental image and the reality partially coincide in the domain of the essence (value of justice, *modo transcendentalis*); but they differ in the domain of their reality (idea or concrete action, *modo accidentalis*). Reality covers in part the idea; but the two remain distinct in the form of their existence. Translated to our problem, it appears that the question of the foundation of the law reflects the general idea of the law, whereas the source reflects its concrete realisation. The one is placed on the level of the essence (legal values), the other one the plane of existence (sociological facts). Both form a complex and interrelated duality. The bridge between both levels is the general principles of law: they flow from the experience of the conditions of justice, ie realise a complex synthesis between the 'ought' (essence) and the 'is' (existence). In other words, the general principles are concretisations of the requirements of justice, eg: good faith, protection of legitimate expectations, equity, equality and reciprocity, proportionality, *pacta sunt servanda*, legal security, *neminem laedere* (hence also non-intervention), the principles of the rule of law such as legality, separation of powers, generality and abstraction of the law, *nullum crimen sine lege*, the publicity of the law, the requirement of the natural judge, etc. By taking into the account the principles of the law, it becomes possible to perceive the legal system as a body constructed around a set of fundamental gravitational points—as the tree is constructed around its trunk. But the principles do not constitute a close or rigid system (H Coing, *Grundzüge der Rechtsphilosophie*, 4th edn (Berlin/New York, 1985) 208: 'Die Grundsätze der Gerechtigkeit, die sich entwickeln lassen, geben uns daher immer nur Elemente der Ordnung, Teilstrukturen, und schliessen sich nicht zu einem selbständigen, anwendbaren System zusammen.' They remain flexible and fragmentary, inspirational points for the creation and interpretation of the law, as well as for the pursuit of legal policies. On the whole, the Protestant precursor of Grotius, Winkler, was right when he proclaimed that 'In tota iurisprudentia, nihil est quod minus legaliter tractari possit quam ipsa principia' (B Winkler, *Principiorum juris* (Leipzig, 1615) lib I, cap II, first phrase).

mono-causal entity. Elements of ideals, of finality and of positivity must all find their place in the different functions concerning the legal order: production of the law, critique of the existing law, application of the existing law, etc. All these aspects are linked to the law. The interpretation and application of the norms is not the sole internal function of the legal phenomenon. Thus, for example, a solid knowledge of jurisprudence and principles is necessary for the legislator when he enacts legal norms. Consequently, these one-sided theories are excellent for what they include, but defective for what they exclude from their perspective.

III. The Basis of Obligation in International Law

A. General Aspects

What is the theoretical foundation of international law, ie where lies the basis of international obligation?[7] And, more concretely, why must one obey the legal rule? Why is it just to obey legal rules at all? This question goes to the root of the legal phenomenon; it is hugely important and grave, not a matter for gratuitous speculation. It has to be admitted that the positive lawyer often has little reason to address this question. He or she shelves it in the realm of philosophy of law, where it is then placed beyond the reach of his or her competence. Is it useful at all to discuss whether a rule is just or valid with reference to criteria situated outside the box of the positive law system? Might not the question be left wholly to the moralist, the historian or others? Clearly, this is the simplest path. It is certainly true that any person may choose the subject matter to be treated and to delimit it in a certain way. Therefore it is all but illegitimate to confine the analysis to the positive law as it stands. This is what the lawyer is asked to do in most cases. Such a limitation on perspective and outlook is often called 'positivistic'. But this is only partially true. Such a positivism is at best what has been called a 'thematic' positivism.[8] To take the system of positive law as a starting point and as an end point is not a positivistic choice. The lawyer will then simply not take any position *at all* on the basis of obligation of the positive law rules. There is no negation of the role of values, justice or other related concepts, since these aspects are simply thematically excluded from the enquiry. This type of 'positivism' is thematic in the sense that the author claims to be limiting himself to the analysis of positive law, without offering any critique, without reflecting on its basis, without measuring it against the exigencies of justice. It stands to reason that this is a legitimate perspective for a lawyer; in certain cases, it will even amount to a professional duty.

However, this narrowing of perspective has led to the paradox that those who know the law, and who could thus speak out on these matters with well-founded

[7] See the general treatment of the issue in Truyol y Serra and Kolb, above n 1.

[8] O Höffe, *Politische Gerechtigkeit* (Frankfurt, 1987) 115.

knowledge, often refrain from doing so; and those who have but an insufficient knowledge of the legal system, namely philosophers, political scientists or sociologists, express themselves on the matter. That the latter speak out is not to be regretted; that the former abstain from doing so is a cause for greater concern. Historically this has led to the fact that lawyers have sometimes been blind with regard to questions of the justice of the law (as in some instances in Germany during the 1920s and 1930s)[9], but also that they have completely neglected to address the issues of creation of the law or legislation.[10] The lawyer expressed himself on the law as an end product; he did not mean to deal with the rational modalities of its creation, with its link to certain fundamental principles or the like, holding that these were questions of legal policy placed beyond his remit. Thus 'thematic positivism', however legitimate it may be, has led to a regrettable limitation of perspective. It has excessively isolated itself from legal policy and philosophy, which, although remaining distinct from the law in the strict sense, enjoy such close relationships with it that they do not deserve the ostracism and silence to which they have been subjected.

In international law, this positivistic separation, strongly developed in municipal systems, could not gain the same strength. Material and rational factors in the creation of international law, as well as questions relating to its justification and existence, have long been treated by international lawyers. International legislation is too precarious a process to allow concealment behind the veil of formal sources. Moreover, the important differences in ideology and interest among States have kept alive the issues of justice and of justification of the rules—amongst others, the challenge of the third world to the received rules. The existence of international law being constantly contested, the question of its foundation could even less be ignored.[11] This inclination to reflect on the existence and foundation of the legal order can be seen as a sign of its persistent primitiveness. Is the necessity to return to such questions not the hallmark of poorly assured foundations and of excessive precariousness? It is nevertheless also possible to see in this fact the manifestations of a greater richness and depth in international law than are to be found in internal law. Instead of taking too much for granted, the international lawyer is constantly forced to refer back to fundamental questions. He thus pays close attention to realities and underlying forces, and also maintains a refreshing modesty. Consequently, his or her reflections will offer a more comprehensive and

[9] BC Frenzel, *Das Selbstverständnis der Justiz nach 1945* (Frankfurt, 2003).

[10] The issue has returned to the agenda only relatively recently: P Noll, *Gesetzgebungslehre* (Reinbek (Hamburg), 1973) 9ff. At the time of Enlightenment, the great lawyers were mainly specialists in the art of legislation: H Coing, *Die obersten Grundsätze des Rechts* (Heidelberg, 1947) 153–54. This attention to the subject even went beyond the circle of lawyers: K Haakonssen, *L'art du législateur—La jurisprudence naturelle de David Hume et d'Adam Smith* (Paris, 1998).

[11] It has been stressed that, contrary to the municipal lawyer, the international lawyer must first rebut various challenges and attacks against the very existence of his discipline. In this sense, the international lawyer has always to start his reflections by asking what are the bases of international law, like a 'masochist among masochists': P Weil, 'Cours general de droit international public: Le droit international en quête de son identité' (1992-VI) 237 *RCADI* 41.

mature set of results. Both ways of thinking have some degree of justification, but the second deserves to be emphasised.

Taking a bird's-eye view of the matter, there are three ways in which to conceive of the law and its foundation. The law can be considered from the perspectives of values, validity or effectiveness.[12] Thus, the foundation of the law can be a value (natural law), or may be created and sanctioned by a power (positivism), or may be taken as the fact of the observation of the rule in practice (sociologism). This is also the order in which the doctrines developed throughout history. Natural law has been shaped since ancient times. One of the first literary fragments from Ancient Greece—by Anaximander—postulated the existence of a cosmos, ie the existence of a superior order in the universe. The Stoics would later develop the rationalistic doctrine of international law. Positivism appears at the juncture with modern times: it presupposes the existence of the State and modern methods of legislation and law enforcement. In its voluntaristic version it is, however, much older. The will of the ruler as a source of law had already been affirmed by the Roman Emperors in our era,[13] and later in Byzantium and by the theological doctrines that saw God as an almighty legislator. This was, for instance, a belief held by the Franciscans. The struggle between reason (natural law) and will (positivism) is the great theme of occidental legal history.[14] Sociological theories were starting to develop in the nineteenth and twentieth centuries. The new ideals of the natural sciences were transferred to legal theories. The main criterion of sociology is the study of facts and of the laws of causality, rather than speculation about values. Therefore, these theories renounce seeking a foundation of the law beyond the determination of facts. The law carries its justification within itself: if it exists, it is justified. From the maxim that 'where there is a society there is a law', we may also deduce the duty to obey the rules thus created by the social body. But there remains the difficulty of explaining how facts become legal rules, if the distinction between the 'is' and the 'ought' is not to be completely jettisoned.

B. Legal Positivism

Legal positivism is a relatively recent doctrine, but its roots reach back to the relativism of the ancient sophists and to the nominalism[15] of the Middle Ages. For the nominalists, ideas and concepts do not really exist; they are but extrapolations

[12] See, eg, L Lombardi Vallauri, *Corso di filosofia del diritto* (Padua, 1981) 144ff.

[13] F Calasso, *Medio evo del diritto, Le fonti*, vol I (Milan, 1954) 42ff.

[14] H Welzel, *Naturrecht und materiale Gerechtigkeit*, 4th edn (Göttingen, 1990); G Fassò, *La legge della ragione* (Bologna, 1962).

[15] In nominalism, existence precedes essence: there are no general ideals, concepts or values; every idea is realised in the concrete objects of this world. Thus, nominalism prepared the path for positivism: if there is no general essence, there is no universal natural law; there are only particular laws, flowing from the will of whomever has the power to legislate. Duns Scot, Occam, d'Ailly, Gerson, Biel and Vasquez were famous nominalists.

of the mind. Reality only knows particular objects. Hence, it is not in the reason, which is a general concept, but in the will of God, which is a particular reality, that the source of obligation has to be found. Applied to the law, this leads to fragmentation: there are as many laws as there are wills to impose them. The law is atomised, multiplied, particularised. Universal law disappears from view.

Modern positivism emerged from the triple impulsion of religious reform (with its fragmentation of values), fascination with modern natural science (with its exact methods), and the consolidation of an absolute and centralised power within States. The anthropocentric revolution also had its part to play in the matter. Man put himself at the centre of the cosmos. Being its supreme subject, it stands to reason that all law must be referred to him: he creates the law; he disposes of the law; the law derives only from his mind and will. The objective cosmos of superior values imposed on Man dissolves into a subjective cosmos where Man projects his will into time and space. This subjective bent would lead to German and Italian Idealism, for which all reality lies in the spirit of individuals or in the spirit of the world, with its supreme reality: the State (Hegelianism). The will of individual subjects thus becomes the supreme source and also the foundation of the law. Man and State make all reality subject to their free deliberation and disposal. Formerly transcendent, the law now becomes immanent. It is the mere product of the intelligent will of Man.

The common ground between these positivistic doctrines is the rejection of metaphysics. Each scientific reality must be reduced to observable facts. As already discussed, this leads to concentration on specific enactments and legislation, and to the rejection of 'non-positive' natural law. The latter, indeed, is postulated rather than enacted, thus its existence cannot be proven. From there flows a series of features of positivism: individualism and empiricism; relativism; State- and will-centredness; and formalism. Conversely, values are rooted in personal opinions and cannot be made the object of scientific truth. Being irrational, they are expelled from the legal phenomenon. The split between the moral and the legal 'sciences' is thus radical. This is the reason why the content of positive law norms is indifferent; it can be anything, provided the norm has been adopted through the correct procedure. Hence, only the form of the law is scientifically determined; its content is a purely political matter. The law is form; policy is content. From this perspective, the law is reduced to a school of legal exegesis, an '*allgemeine Rechtslehre*', ie the explication of the powers and techniques for the creation, interpretation and application of legal norms. The lawyer explains the functioning of the clock, but does not venture into the question of the energy that sustains that functioning.

From these general assumptions flows a series of concrete consequences for the construction of the legal order.[16] First, positivism holds that each piece of legislation and each norm produced according to the recognised law-creating agencies

[16] See, eg, N Bobbio, *Il positivismo giuridico* (Turin, 1996) 127ff. On the limits of positivism, see the interesting study by EJ Lampe, *Grenzen des Rechtspositivismus* (Berlin, 1988). On the background of positivism, see also W Ott, *Der Rechtspositivismus* (Berlin, 1976).

is necessarily valid. Law is a fact, not a value. Secondly, the law lies exclusively in the legislation; and each piece of legislation is law. The whole legal phenomenon is thus attracted by and concentrated within the State. The reason why one must obey the law is not a legal one; it is tantamount to regarding the existence of the State as a common superior. Thirdly, the separation of powers is strictly upheld: the lawyer is a simple applier of the law; he or she must never usurp the functions of the legislator. Hence, too, we see the great suspicion with which judicial developments of the law are viewed. Restrictions on the power of the judiciary are found in both dictatorial and democratic regimes. In the former, judges must not encroach upon the will of the great dictator; in the latter, judges must not limit the exclusive competence of the democratically elected legislator. The legislator has a monopoly over any change to or development of the law. This also means that the judge owes absolute submission to the law (law is law; '*Gesetz ist Gesetz*'). Fourthly, the law is always clear and contains answers to the questions posed (there are no gaps, *lex semper loquitur*). Where no norm is posed, no law exists. There is then possibly a space without law, in which each party remains free to act as it sees fit. Moreover, there are no true contradictions within the law; contradictions are only apparent and can be resolved by interpretation. Fifthly, the law supposes a sanction, or at least a procedure of 'enforceability'. It is basically a command by the superior to the inferior, reinforced by mechanisms of sanction. As can be seen, some of these postulates rendered it difficult for positivistic lawyers to conceive of the existence of an international legal order: there is no legislation in the proper sense, there is no command by a superior, there is no general mechanism of centralised sanction; in short, there is no State. The translation of positivism into the international legal order took some time. Authors like Anzilotti succeeded in that enterprise, at least in part, by substituting agreement for the command of a superior.[17]

Overall, the premises on which positivism is constructed entail certain important consequences for the features of a legal system. First, as already said, the law is completely State-centred; there is in principle no law outside the State. Secondly, positivism is a doctrine of power: the legislator is omnipotent; its will is not limited by any constraint.[18] Having expelled from the law any element that oversteps the systematisation of a given legislative will, there is not even the possibility of some doctrine of legislation to guide those persons having the function of enacting the laws. The will is the only source of the law: thus law is power. In other words: *justum quod jussum*. Thirdly, between the concurrent values of justice and legal security, positivism will countenance the second and ignore the first. Considering all these assumptions and consequences, it is no surprise that the principles of the 'rule of law' have not been developed by positivistic schools of thought but rather

[17] See mainly D Anzilotti, *Droit international* (Paris, 1929).

[18] As Ortolan has rightly observed, the essence of positive law resides in power. Quoted in E Creasy, *First Platform of International Law* (London, 1876) 14.

by the ideological natural law schools from the times of the Enlightenment.[19] These principles are not so much based on power as on the effort to limit it. The above-mentioned orientation towards power also shows that the claim for the ideological neutrality of positivism is at least partially unfounded. The ideology of positivism may be implicit but it is nonetheless clear: it sides with power as constituted and gives free rein to its commands. Contrary to what is often done, it is inexact to mix the doctrine of 'positive law' with the doctrine of legal positivism, ie to conflate a term that designates the law in force at a given moment with the doctrine of absolute power of a formally valid will. The term 'positive law' goes back to the Middle Ages and was used, for example, by Abelard.[20] It declines to respond on the basis of obligation. Making a positive law analysis is therefore not tantamount to being a positivist—but more probably to being a lawyer.

Given the experience of totalitarian regimes and war in the twentieth century, and the utter perversion of legal institutions up to the climax that was the concentration camps,[21] the rising star of positivism lost some of its attraction.[22] A doctrine that gives free rein to the will of the powerful was no longer considered to be wholly satisfactory. To the extent that the omnipotence of the legislator is abandoned, the positivistic intensity of any given doctrine will diminish, since facts and values situated beyond the command and the will of the legislator are then necessarily taken into account; and this is no longer positivism in the strict sense. The ultimate foundation of the law then shifts towards these further facts or values. This is not to say that it is impossible to follow a moderate or enlightened positivism. The only point is to show that without recourse to a moral or otherwise extra-legal criterion, it is impossible to distinguish between legal norms that have all been enacted through the applicable procedure.

Having emphasised the intellectual roots of positivism and its problems, it is only right to focus on some of its strengths and benefits. Three aspects may be mentioned. First, positivism has stressed the virtue of obedience to the law, and thus equality and legality. It is true that in perverted legal orders such obedience may become an evil in itself; but in the great number of non-perverted legal orders

[19] H Coing, *Die obersten Grundsätze des Rechts* (Heidelberg, 1947) 150ff.

[20] See S Kuttner, 'Sur les origines du terme droit positif' (1936) 15 *Revue historique de droit français et étranger* 728.

[21] F von Hippel, *Die Perversion von Rechtsordnungen* (Tübingen, 1955). See also O Kirchheimer, *Politische Justiz* (Neuwied/Berlin, 1965); I Müller, *Furchtbare Juristen* (Munich, 1987); and on a more theoretical plane, H Durth, *Der Kampf gegen das Unrecht* (Baden-Baden, 2001). For the Nazi regime, see H Pauer-Studer and J Fink (eds), *Rechtfertigungen des Unrechts, Das Rechtsdenken im Nationalsozialismus in Originaltexten* (Berlin, 2014).

[22] It must be added that strict positivistic obedience existed only on the European Continent and not in common law countries. The balance between the great constitutional bodies in England, the power of the judiciary and a more pragmatic tradition tempered the reach of positivistic doctrines. Thus, for example, the principle of 'reasonableness' remained here a constant auxiliary source of law. The sources of law and their foundation were never completely divorced. The same can be said with regard to the strength of the rule of law in a moderate and liberty-imbued society.

or non-perverted legal branches, this is a hallmark of the proper functioning of society. In our complex modern societies, it would be impractical, and even impossible, to live with constant and radical subjective challenges to the enactments of the legislator. A certain degree of contestation is certainly salutary, if only as a first bulwark against perversion, but it stands to reason that the social stabilisation flowing from generalised obedience to the law triggers significant social benefits and constitutes a political virtue. Even if I find some rule unjust, I will sacrifice myself and obey it for the common good.

Secondly, positivism has sometimes favoured intellectual honesty and the search for facts, instead of the travesty of personal speculation, *post festum*, as an expression of the law in force. There must be a certain ability to distinguish between things as they are and things as we would wish them to be. Clearly, no one of us can fully see all things 'as they are'; but there remains the truth that there are facts, and that it is possible to remain close to or to move further away from them. To search for the reality of facts is not to act like Alice in Wonderland. Positivism has in certain cases favoured the propensity to signal the perspective chosen: here I speak about positive law, and I take seriously State practice and legal opinion, whether I like it or not; there I speak out in my personal capacity on the law I would prefer to see (*lex ferenda*), in order to change the law where it is unsatisfactory. It is possible to bend the norms slightly to better the process of their interpretation. The legislator does not ask the judge to be subordinate to the point that he or she will apply unreasonable norms. Quite the contrary: the social expectation is that the judge (or any other legal operator) will reasonably apply the law. But the matter remains one of degree. The average positivist, however, will not infrequently be better armed against manipulation than the self-confident, illuminated actor, completely imbued with his good cause, not caring for the complexities of the problems or for the world outside his box, and practising a do-it-yourself 'human-rightism' or a 'jus cogensism' within a bluntly ideological setting.

Thirdly, positivism has contributed to the strengthening of certain important constitutional values, notably the separation of powers and the pre-eminence of the political body elected by the people. It has insisted on the fact that judges and legal operators are bound by the law created through legislation, and are thus limited in their search for extensive interpretations It stands to reason that these constitutional principles cannot be viewed as absolute. Thus, democracy cannot be divorced from the rule of law; minorities have to be protected against the excesses of the majority; certain fundamental rights and freedoms of Man must remain as firewalls against majority decisions, etc. But there remains the fact that a certain modesty of the legal operator with regard to political decisions is a value in itself. I may have my own opinion, but within certain limits I have to respect that of the majority. By insisting on this virtue of self-limitation, positivism upholds a fundamental principle for the proper functioning of a democratic society.

C. Sociological Doctrines

The sociological doctrines of the law push to its ultimate consequences the causal method that was at the root of positivism. From this vantage point, they appear to be the most perfected positivistic doctrines. From a series of other aspects, however, they distinguish themselves from the positivistic assumptions. Most importantly, they refuse to consider the law as an artificial phenomenon, framed by arbitrary and changing wills identified with the State. From the sociological perspective, the law precedes the State and the will of its organs. The law is a social product. It emerges from the interaction of social forces. The legislator only has the task of giving expression to it, without specifically being called on to create it. The core aspect of the validity of the law is not its adoption through a formally unimpeachable procedure but the effectiveness of the norm in social reality.

There are objectively and subjectively framed sociological doctrines. Objective theories lay emphasis on the regularity and effectiveness of expected social behaviour. This is the case, for example, as regards the legal realism defended by Oliver Wendell Holmes[23] or by the Uppsala Legal School.[24] The law here presents itself as a cluster of social facts, culminating in the predicable decisions of tribunals or in the effective threat of sanctions. There are also the doctrines of social solidarity promoted by Duguit, Scelle or Politis in France.[25] The law is here the result of material interdependencies within the social body. Subjective sociological theories, on the other hand, lay emphasis on the legal conscience or conviction of the subjects of law. The law is what is socially considered as being such. The subjective element of social conscience takes the place of the reality or expectation of external behaviour. The subjective branch has been defended, mainly in Germany, by authors such as Bierling or Jellinek,[26] and later in more developed forms by Ehrlich[27] or Weber. The German form of sociology is favourable to the State (contrary to the French school noted above, which is liberal and anti-State); it therefore leads back to positivistic lands.

Sociological doctrines have a relatively recent pedigree. Their roots lie in the reaction to the abuse of deductive methods by the later natural law school of the Enlightenment. In place of the unity and fixity of abstract reason, the nineteenth

[23] See the studies on US Legal Realism: G Tarello, *Il realismo giuridico americano* (Milan, 1962); GJ Aichele, *Legal Realism and Twentieth-Century American Jurisprudence* (New York, 1990); WW Fisher (ed), *American Legal Realism* (New York, 1993); JH Schlegel, *American Legal Realism and Empirical Social Science* (Chapel Hill, 1995); M Martin, *Legal Realism* (New York, 1997); MA Rea-Frauchiger, *Der amerikanische Rechtsrealismus* (Berlin, 2006); J Zarembie, *Legal Realism and American Law* (London, 2015).

[24] See the references in A Truyol y Serra and R Kolb, *Doctrines sur le fondement du droit des gens* (Paris, 2007) 27ff. And see also Martin, above n 23.

[25] Truyol y Serra and Kolb, above n 24, 91ff.

[26] On the latter, see M Stolleis, *Geschichte des öffentlichen Rechts in Deutschland*, vol 2 (Munich, 1992) 450ff.

[27] See M Rehbinder, *Die Begründung der Rechtssoziologie durch Eugen Ehrlich*, 2nd edn (Berlin, 1986).

century would progressively substitute the plurality of historical experiences of a plurality of different peoples (nations). The law thus became linked to the history and culture of different peoples; by this token, it became automatically relative, changing and multiple. If positivism filled from the top the gap left by the demise of natural law (by the command of the superior), sociological theories sought to fill that gap from the bottom (law as an emanation of social forces). The earliest construction of this type is to be found in the Historical School of Law of Friedrich von Savigny.[28] Politically conservative, opposed to the codifications of the modern State (which were considered to artificially petrify the law and to attempt to cut it off from its living source, the people), this conception considers the law to be indissolubly linked to the national culture of a given people at a given moment of history (*Volksgeist*). The question is no longer geared towards the discovery of a universal law valid for all peoples and all times. On the contrary, the law becomes a never-ending process of growth and change, emerging from the historical life of a people. It is a customary law resulting from the action of social forces. Consequently, there are only particular laws for each society, that is, as many legal orders as there are peoples.

What is the foundation of this sociological law? Where lies the basis of obligation? For its followers, there is no reason to seek any other justification than the very existence of the people, with its culture and society: *ubi societas, ibi jus*. A common approach of the sociological theories is therefore to reduce the question of the foundation of law to that of its sources. The existence of society automatically justifies the rules generated in the social body and imposed therein as being the law. A separate question as to the foundation of these rules has no specific sense according to this conception—no more than it could have had in the context of positivism. However, there remains the lingering question as to why what emerges in fact must also be obeyed. How can one explain this great leap from what 'is' to what 'ought to be'? Must the 'is' really carry its justification within itself? To this question no sociological doctrine has been able to give a satisfactory answer, apart from that of expelling the question from the legal universe altogether. Contrary to their anti-metaphysical starting point, sociological theories rely here on a highly disputable postulate: the radical unity of what is and what ought to be. This conception sweeps away certain problems that may seem speculative; but it also eliminates any critical approach and criterion of distinction for appraising the law. Every legal piece becomes equivalent and relative. By this token, the above-mentioned conception revolts against one of the most cherished convictions of the human spirit, namely, that the mere fact (*le fait accompli* as the French say) does not carry within itself its justification. What 'is' is not automatically what ought to be. As a phenomenon of reality the 'is' cannot be ignored, in particular at the level of the sources of law. But it cannot pretend to dispose of that further

[28] On this school, see, eg, D Strauch, *Recht, Gesetz und Staat bei F. C. von Savigny*, 4th edn (Tübingen, 1963); G Marini, *Savigny e il metodo della scienza giuridica* (Milan, 1966). See also the useful general study of G Wilhelm, *Zur juristischen Methodenlehre im 19. Jahrhundert* (Frankfurt, 1958).

question relating to the foundation of the duty to obey the rule. Antigone cannot be so easily gagged, Creon cannot so easily triumph. Indeed, a legal rule imposes a duty, an obligation. The category of the 'you shall' (in the sense of a *Sollen*) is a prescriptive and not a descriptive reality. Only the compulsion to do, the *Müssen*, belongs to the world of facts and of mere causality. Therefore, the sanction or the force, for example, can explain only the compulsion to act as a *Müssen*, but not the reason of the action under a *Sollen*. The latter supposes manifestly some form of a value. If one wants to escape from the monstrous determination of the causal world, ie from the harsh dictates of the *fait accompli*, the suppression of any value is impossible. Only the latter allows us to find a criterion in order to distinguish among the 'is' and to offer the basis of a criticism. It is on that basis, for example, that we do not consider completely equivalent the laws of some primitive societies regulating human sacrifice and the modern legal system of British Constitutionalism. If the foregoing is true, there is ever a resurgence of some form of natural law, the function of which is essentially to test the quality of any given legal reality.

The strength of sociological doctrines has been to emphasise the realities in the context of the creation of the law, to show and explain the differences among the various national legal systems, to link the law to the life of societies, to introduce the time factor in the comprehension of the law and to inject some concreteness into the construction of the law. The number of factors contributing to the creation and application of the law is considerably larger and more diverse here, when compared with the sole omnipotence of the legislator in the context of positivism. The concomitant weakness of these doctrines is that they fail to indicate precisely how the law is made. They often remain very vague on this issue, indicating that the law emerges 'spontaneously' from the social forces. Their elaboration of the sources often remains summary, customary law predominating over all other law-creating agencies. It stands to reason that such a construction can at best fit primitive or underdeveloped societies, mainly of a rural kind, and not the highly complex post-modern industrial societies, with their huge need for constant regulation of technical matters.

D. Natural Law Doctrines

The plural 'doctrines' is necessary here: the doctrines of natural law are multiple and sometimes opposed in content and outlook.[29] In a larger sense, all Western

[29] There is an extremely rich literature on the subject. See, eg, AP d'Entrèves, *Natural Law* (London, 1951); L Strauss, *Droit naturel et histoire* (Paris, 1954); F Flückiger, *Geschichte des Naturrechts*, vol I (Zollikon/Zurich, 1954); E Wolf, *Das Problem der Naturrechtslehre* (Karlsruhe, 1955); Annales de philosophie politique, *Le droit naturel* (Paris, 1959); J Messner, *Das Naturrecht*, 4th edn (Innsbruck/Vienna/Munich, 1960); H Welzel, *Naturrecht und materiale Gerechtigkeit*, 4th edn (Göttingen, 1962); G. Fasso, *Il diritto naturale* (Turin, 1964); J Sauter, *Die philosophischen Grundlagen des Naturrechts* (Frankfurt, 1966); J Finnis, *Natural Law and Natural Rights* (Oxford/New York, 1980) (2nd edn, Oxford, 2011); G Garancini, *Diritto naturale e storicità del diritto* (Milan, 1981); J Hervada, *Introduction critique au droit naturel* (Bordeaux, 1990); A Sériaux, *Le droit naturel*, 2nd edn (Paris, 1999).

reflections about the law from antiquity up to the nineteenth century have revolved around the concept of natural law. Natural law was the crucible of legal philosophy as a whole. This fact alone serves to explain the multiplicity of doctrines sailing under its coloured banner. The common core of natural law doctrines is that they seek for elements that are imposed on the human being when creating and administering the law. This is the heart of the term 'natural'. But this latter term is confusing because it is ambiguous: sometimes it indicates an ethical cosmos (nature in the transcendental sense), sometimes it is reduced to the observation of causal forces dominating reality (nature in the empirical sense, eg 'the larger fishes eat the smaller ones'). The history of natural law doctrines is complicated by the interaction between these two wings. On the one hand, there were spiritualistic, ideal or ethical natural law theories (which are today often regarded as 'the' natural law theories); they were founded on values such as justice, reason or the natural sociability of the human being. These doctrines gave rise to a perfect body of law that was sometimes opposed to, sometimes called on to complement and always provided a measuring rod for positive law. On the other hand, there have been existentialist or empirical natural law theories. They founded the law on nature understood as a reality. Thus instincts, cries for self-conservation and self-aggrandisement, the law that the stronger prevails over the weaker, the struggle for survival and the like were placed at the core of the doctrines. A long thread links the sophists to Hobbes, Spinoza to Schopenhauer or Nietzsche. However, after Hobbes, this latter line of thinking affiliated itself to positivism and the modern conceptions of State power. Natural law was now progressively identified with the first line of thought.

What are the common aspects of the spiritualistic natural law theories (and to some extent also of the empirical ones)? *First*, natural law concerns elements that are prior to and exterior to any voluntary act of Man. These elements are imposed upon him as a series of givens (*Vorgegebenheiten*). The spiritualistic doctrines seek the foundation of the law in the given of a transcendental idea representing a supreme value: God, justice, the common good or some conception of Man in his moral and physical needs. Therefore, these doctrines reject the idea that law could ultimately be founded on the arbitrary will of some persons invested with power, be it formally (positivism) or informally (sociologism). The dogma '*voluntas quia voluntas facit jus*' is rejected. Thus, the foundation of the law is not seen in a mere fact but is rooted in a value. It is often recognised that even an unjust legal order must be obeyed because it provides for some legal certainty, which is

For a markedly catholic conception: G Ambrosetti, *Diritto naturale cristiano*, 2nd edn (Milan, 1985); C Maio, *Principi generali e fondamentali di diritto positivo e naturale* (Reggio Calabria, 1963). For a negative perspective: A Leinweber, *Gibt es ein Naturrecht?*, 3rd edn (Berlin/New York, 1972). Among the newer literature, see RH Helmholz, *Natural Law in Court* (Cambridge, Mass, 2015); AM Emon, M Levering and D Novak, *Natural Law* (Oxford, 2014); FJ Contreras Palaez (ed), *The Threads of Natural Law* (Paderborn/Heidelberg, 2013); PF da nha, *Rethinking Natural Law* (Heidelberg, 2013); JD Charles, *Retrieving the Natural Law* (Grand Rapids, Mich, 2008); AM Gonzalez (ed), *Contemporary Perspectives on Natural Law* (Aldershot, 2008); P Simon, *Le droit naturel, ses amis et ses ennemis* (Paris, 2005).

itself a value.[30] But to be well-founded as a *legal* order and not just as an order of compulsion, these doctrines would require something more than a simple fact or effectiveness. From there comes the objectivism of natural law schools. At the top of the system is placed a value. *Secondly*, in the negative, the idea of a common law for all peoples and all times is not a common core of spiritualistic natural law doctrines. That feature is common only to a series of rationalistic natural law doctrines ranging from the Stoics to the Enlightenment. Thus, in both the Middle Ages and in modern times, the mutability of natural law has been emphasised.[31] At best, it can be said that certain principles or categories of legal thought are valid throughout time and space. They do not form a fully-equipped legal order but only a fragmentary set of precepts and principles guiding the legal order towards the requirements of justice—and whose absence tends to pull the law towards injustice.[32]

In this sense, the concept of natural law offers something eternal: it corresponds to a fundamental need of the human spirit and soul. Confronted with the experience of events, Man must be able to revert to an idea of justice without having to irremediably accept the fact as it stands and the constraints of whatever power. There is little place for absolutes in this world, and yet, paradoxically, that is what renders natural law indispensable. Legality and legal certainty, important as they are, cannot completely eradicate the quest for justice. As was written by Politis, some months before his death and during the terrible events of World War II, '[w]hen in a human society rules of positive law become idle or arbitrary because of a lack or hypertrophy of power, the feeling of justice, which never deserts the heart of men, pushes the latter to look upward so as to attach their hopes of salvation to permanent and superior precepts, which the ancient Greeks called the non-written laws'.[33] It is therefore possible to proclaim the death of natural law, to emphasise that it is not a scientific concept, to stress its deficiencies and drawbacks; and yet, it remains at least dormant, ready to return once more, especially in times of oppression and revolution. Taking account of what has been said, natural law is a pole star for difficult times. In a well-operating society, rich, ordered and self-satisfied, it will be easy to push aside any natural law and to stick to a solidly constructed edifice of positive law. This will be all the more so if all sections of the population are called on to benefit from social advantages—not to enjoy the same shares, but at least to be included in the process of participation.[34] Conversely, in times of oppression and crisis, the legal and social order will be put into question

[30] See T Aquinas, *Summa Theologica*, II, I, 96, 4. On Aquinas's conception of natural law, see R Bagnulo, *Il concetto di diritto naturale in San Tommaso d'Aquino* (Milan, 1983).

[31] Aquinas, above n 30, II, II, 57, 2. For modern times, see the formal (neo-Kantian) natural law theory of R Stammler, *Wirtschaft und Recht nach der materialistischen Geschichtsauffassung*, 4th edn (Berlin, 1921) 174; R Stammler, *Lehrbuch der Rechtsphilosophie* (Berlin/Leipzig, 1922) 167ff.

[32] See the highly interesting study by K Larenz, *Richtiges Recht* (Munich, 1979).

[33] N Politis, *La morale internationale* (Neuchâtel, 1943) 7, our translation.

[34] This criterion on inclusiveness and participation is emphasised by some authors as a fundamental tenet of political justice: see, eg, O Höffe, *Politische Gerechtigkeit* (Frankfurt, 1987) 379ff.

to their very roots. Recourse will then be had to principles and precepts transcending the positive given. These are the moments of history when natural law conceptions will manifest themselves. They will accompany or presage important changes in the legal or social order. Natural law is thus a concept that will be active in times of transition. This was the case, for example, when European societies passed from absolutism to modern individualism (the Enlightenment) or when Germany passed from the Third Reich to the Bonner Democracy.

What have been the most important historical phases of development of natural law in the Western world?

1. In *Greek antiquity*, the concepts of law and justice were linked to that of a cosmos ordered by deities. Progressively, through cognitive optimism and the belief in the primacy of reason over will, the Greek thinkers would rationalise the cosmos and cut off the religious ties. This was the time of the emergence of natural law. Law, in this conception, was part of the natural order of things. This order could be known by reason. Being inherent in things, the law was a given and not just a human creation. This thought was at its height with the Stoics after which it was exported to the Romans (Cicero, Epictetus, Seneca, Marcus Aurelius) and their *jus naturale vel gentium.*
2. In the *Christian Middle Ages*, natural law oscillated between reason and will. Hebraic and Christian cultures marked a departure from Greek intellectualism. The latter was based on the equation: cosmos = rational order = cognisable by man. Christendom was initially dominated by voluntarism anchored in the impenetrable commands of God. There was a division between the world and the heavens (*civitas terrena, civitas Dei*). A veil covers reason, corrupted by the original sin. Man cannot know anymore, and he cannot claim to be able to know; he must therefore merely obey the commands of God. Natural law tends to become the positive law flowing from the will of God. The freedom of God is unlimited: one might mention the tribulations of Job, the sacrifice of Isaac, the union of Hosea and the prostitute, and other biblical episodes buttressing this state of affairs. This tradition was upheld by Paul, the Franciscans, Victorinus, Augustin, Duns Scot or Occam—and later by Luther and Calvin. Universalism and reason gave way to individualism and will. The schematic generalisations of reason were rejected in favour of the individual act of faith. From there a subjectively skewed natural law emerged, which was the transcription of the commands of God into the heart of Man.

   At the other end of the spectrum, the intellectualistic tradition of ancient Greece was revived by Thomas Aquinas. He affirmed the primacy of divine wisdom over divine will. This construction was then taken up by da Rimini and by the Spanish Scholastics (de Vitoria, Molina, Gabriel Vazquez). According to this school of thought, natural law is the rational participation of man in the finalistic order of the universe. The order of things can be at least partially known by human reason; God himself has provided Man with reason so as to enable him to participate in the cosmos. The order of the cosmos is not only physical, but also moral. The law is the expression of this latter aspect. Natural law thus becomes again an objective reality, the expression of the ordered cosmos. The tensions between here and there, world and heaven, human justice and divine justice, are relaxed through an edifice of remarkable harmonisation.

3. *The Enlightenment* was based on a system of rationalistic natural law. This was the time of modern constitutionalism. The natural law doctrines advanced by various thinkers were now politically tainted: absolutism (Hobbes), liberalism (Locke), democracy (Rousseau). The growing arm of natural sciences would propose a method to be used for the law too: the construction of a complete system of norms by way of safe deductions from some supreme principles representing the 'nature of man' or the 'nature of things'. Since reason is common to all human beings, the law deduced therefrom must perforce be common and universal. The result was a vast system of speculative law, deduced from a combination of principles such as *suum cuique*, *honeste vivere*, *neminem leadere*, *pacta sunt servanda*, *sufficientia vitae*, *homo animale sociale*, *tranquillitate civitatis*, *securitate*, *quod vis ut alii tibi faciant tu et ipsis facias*, etc. This process was also based on a secularisation of the law. Any ties with religion were severed. One of the famous phrases of the time was that this law would exist even if God did not exist. The apex of this deductive method can be found in the works of Leibniz (especially in *Nova methodus discendae docendaeque jurisprudentiae*, 1667) or Wolff. Modern critics of natural law often refer to the excessively deductive natural law of the Enlightenment. But it has to be accepted that this expression of natural law thinking is an episode in a multi-secular history. Even during this time, the systems were complex, in the sense that natural law would not simply prevail over positive law—quite the contrary, often the law emerging from settled practice would not be displaced by the law indicated by reason (but would be used to criticise the existing deficiencies).[35]
4. The *modern tendencies* in the context of natural law have completely abandoned the idea of deducing a fully-fledged and immutable system of rules from some supreme precepts. A system of law cannot be based merely on deduction from certain principles; it cannot ignore local and temporal experience; it cannot ignore changes in emphasis and ideological baggage; it cannot ignore the fact that a balancing of countervailing principles and solutions must still be made by the legislator. Justice and its supreme principles do not encompass all the concrete choices on which a legal order needs to be based. If it were otherwise, this would signify the end of history; any legislator would be superfluous; cultural and ideological differences would be only

[35] For the articulated system of Grotius, see P Haggenmacher, *Grotius et la doctrine de la guerre juste* (Paris, 1983); P Haggenmacher, 'Grotius et le droit international—Le texte et la légende' in A Dufour, P Haggenmacher and J Toman (eds), *Grotius et l'ordre juridique international* (Lausanne, 1985) 115ff. See also generally M Giuliano, *La comunità internazionale* (Padua, 1950)11ff.

apparent; only one moral and legal opinion would be correct, and all the others would be wrong. Such holdings are manifestly contrary to experimental truth. Therefore modern natural law theories accept the historical contingence and mutability of law. Their effort assists in a better understanding of the great principles of justice that form a framework for positive law. The aim is to find the changing ingredients for a 'just legal order' here and now. Religious natural law doctrines continue to operate on the basis of a strong 'given' (Ellul, Brunner, Fuchs, Ambrosetti), while secular authors are more modest and more measured in this regard (Marcic, Ryffel, del Vecchio). The common core of these modern doctrines lies in the search for a synthesis between the necessary and the contingent. If the necessary cannot be defined too boldly because that would be tantamount to negating life, the contingent cannot be absolute either, since that would obliterate civilisation and justice.[36] The starting point must be the domain of liberty, and thus of the contingent. Liberty allows Man to shape his destiny. It frees Man from the oppressing yoke of those who pretend to know better than him. Moreover, since human knowledge is relative, partial, uncertain, and linked to time and place, a complete normative system of natural law is impossible. No natural law will ever be able to be a system of positive law.[37] It follows that the effectively applicable law in a given society must be left to a very large degree to the unfolding and changing opinions crystallised in the political process. This is the eminent part left to positive law. However, according to the doctrines discussed here, the liberty of Man is not absolute. There are some 'givens' that are beyond the reach of Man's arbitrary will. This domain is first of all constituted by the idea of Man himself, ie by his individual finality and value (fundamental human rights, the idea of 'human dignity') as well as by his social needs (common good, equality, justice). Natural law is thus not an autonomous system of law. It contains only some supreme principles of justice, so as to avoid, as it were, a *reductio ad Hitlerum* of law. It is an open and fragmentary body of principles, to be complemented by the positive legal orders with their institutions and sanctions. This body of principles has a critical function: it will serve as measuring rod for the realisations of positive law and as a benchmark to push the latter in the direction of the former. Therefore, natural law expresses certain exigencies of a just law, and sometimes unconsciously or consciously directs the endeavours of the legislator and the judge. In a certain sense, the objective

[36] As has been said, 'Eine vollkommene Gleichgültigkeit gegenüber der Wahrheit, die bloss "subjektiv" ist und der man nur noch die Bedeutung eines gelegentlichen "Mittels" zum eigenen Zweck zuerkennt, aber keinerlei verpflichtenden Eigenwert' leads to the perversion of legal orders: F von Hippel, *Die Perversion von Rechtsordnungen* (Tübingen, 1955) 54.

[37] Hence also the futility of comparing the two orders and thus to emphasise the contradictions of natural law, as Kelsen did. See H Kelsen, 'Naturrecht und positives Recht' (1927/1928) 2 *Revue internationale de la théorie du droit* 71ff; H Kelsen, 'Die Idee des Naturrechtes' (1927) 7 *Zeitschrift für öffentliches Recht* 221ff. On some aspects of Kelsen's conception of natural law, see, eg, S de Benalcazar, 'Kelsen et l'approche historiciste du droit naturel classique' (2008) 48 *Droits* 219ff.

> of this natural law is not to form a bridge to heaven, but rather to avoid the descent into hell.[38] The natural law will then signify a struggle for the 'just law' in the face of a corrupted positive legal order with its sanctioning arm.

Since the beginning of the twentieth century, with the return of objectivistic legal theories, moderate natural law doctrines have found their way back into international law.[39] But this return was much more limited after the 1950s.[40] A series of factors led to this result: the division of values in the modern pluralistic world, to which the emancipation of the third world added a significant chapter; the overwhelming increase in pluralism of interests and conceptions in modern international society; and the preponderance of the political factor during the Cold War. All these evolutions lowered belief in the capacity to define an 'objective' law that would be superior to the positive legal system. The effort to devise natural law standards has quickly moved back to philosophers and has been mostly abandoned by lawyers.

What are the drawbacks and deficiencies of natural law doctrines? Their positive contributions have already been noted, so that it now becomes necessary to look to the dark side. It stands to reason that the criticisms levied against natural law will differ according to the type of natural law doctrine at stake. It also stands to reason that certain natural law doctrines can unfold only in some regions of the world. Thus, a Christian or Catholic natural law could hardly offer a suitable basis for an international law discussion, given the double fact that international society is secular and also that Christianity is but one among many other religious beliefs. By the same token, it is easy to attack all too ambitious theories of natural law: they manifestly exaggerate the given with respect to the domain of human freedom in shaping his fate in the varying contexts of history. Going beyond such partial or sectorial criticism,[41] what is the common ground in the critique of natural law? There seem to be three fundamental criticisms directed against the conception of a law higher than the man-made positive one: first, that natural law is anti-historic; secondly, that it is anti-scientific; thirdly, that it is anti-pluralistic. Thereby it is supposed that historicism, science and pluralism are essential assets and axioms

[38] As D Hammarskjold, former Secretary General of the UN, once said of the United Nations. On this eminent personality and his life, see M Fröhlich, *Dag Hammarskjöld und die Vereinten Nationen* (Paderborn/Munich/Vienna/Zurich, 2002).

[39] For details, see A Truyol y Serra and R Kolb, *Doctrines sur le fondement du droit des gens* (Paris, 2007) 103ff.

[40] It also happened that the renaissance of natural law after World War II, as occurred in Germany, quickly led to dogmatic overstretching and thus to discredit. Thus at least one tribunal founded on natural law the prohibition of sexual intercourse between engaged but not married persons. See A Kaufmann, *Rechtsphilosophie*, 2nd edn (Munich, 1997) 31–32.

[41] There are also other criticisms that do not go to the heart of the matter. Thus, natural law is not based only on the idea of immutable laws; it is not necessarily meant to constitute a complete legal order, etc. Moreover, natural law may be based on 'hidden' ideologies—but this is true of all doctrines, including positivism, which is the legal theory par excellence of (unbridled) power. Lastly, natural law does not necessarily confuse the 'is' and the 'ought', since 'nature' must not be taken in an empirical sense but can also be taken in a figurative and moral sense. On these points, see O Höffe, *Politische Gerechtigkeit* (Frankfurt, 1987) 92ff.

that cannot be curtailed or given up. Let us consider each one of these criticisms in a little more detail:

1. The argument regarding the *incompatibility of natural law with historical mutability* is as follows. Experience shows that there is no objective law that is invariably valid. Ethnology and history show a great variety of social and legal conceptions. Moreover, the needs of Man have changed so considerably over time as a result of manifold social changes, that the effort to freeze history in the form of some natural law is doomed to fail. Man and his institutions are necessarily linked to time; *panta rei*, everything moves. This line of argument is decisive against the speculative natural law of a deductive nature, which purported to flesh out a fully-fledged legal order from a handful of supreme precepts of a social and moral nature. The criticism is also convincing against all too ambitious doctrines of natural law, namely those developed by the Catholic Church or by other religious movements. The rules presented as being valid *ex jure naturali* in one century had later to be given up or modified. Who would today countenance the argument that any effort to protect animals against mistreatment is a perversion of the divine natural order, with the rider that by showing compassion to animals the latter are almost placed on the same footing as human beings instead of remaining fundamentally inferior?[42] Conversely, the criticism loses some weight when it is directed against the more modest theories of natural law, which confine the latter to a fragmentary system of principles of justice. It is also clear that humanity progressed in its transit, from the most primitive societies to modern ones, not necessarily through its acts but at least through its conscience. It is not astonishing that certain principles of justice can thus be found in all minimally developed societies, eg the principle that agreements have to be respected. It is not astonishing either that the great private crimes of the criminal codes indicate behaviour that is considered reprehensible in all such minimally developed societies: murder, arson, theft, fraud, etc. These same acts and deeds are condemned in all the great sacred books. Thus, the hardest core of the various criminal codes presents itself as a sort of inner circle of natural law. This is a matter of negative philosophy: it is about ruling out a core of socially harmful actions; it is about saying what is radically unjust. But there are other principles of natural justice of a more positive nature. For example, the rule *audiatur et altera pars*, ie the duty to hear all the parties in a judicial or equivalent procedure (due process of law, fair trial).
2. It has been claimed, further, that natural law is *not scientifically defensible.* Positive law can be known, since it is produced through a law-creating agency. Natural law is not so created; it therefore remains a matter of subjective

[42] This argument was indeed made by L Taparelli, *Saggio teorico di diritto naturale*, 6th edn (Palermo, 1857) 59–60. The sensitivity of Jeremy Bentham on this point is so much more profound. He claimed that animals must be protected because they are able to suffer and thus possess a soul: J Bentham, *An Introduction on the Principles of Morals and Legislation* (London, 1789), ch VIII, § 1.

opinion or speculation. It pretends to be 'objective law', but in reality it is based on subjective opinions and differs from one thinker to another. Ultimately, each one of us can believe in it or not, construct it that way or another—and indeed there have been innumerable doctrines of natural law. Such a 'discourse law' cannot fulfil the urgent tasks of regulation in a complex modern society. Additionally, it is argued that natural law is caught in a vicious circle. In the words of the German legal philosopher Zippelius:

> This is the reason why natural law doctrines lay emphasis on just some of the many elements constituting reality, saying that there the 'true nature' of things is being manifested. However, by this process there is an evaluative selection. Certain ethical criteria have here already been projected into the natural order of things. At this stage, the natural lawyer pretends to deduce precisely these elements from the 'true nature' of man, of the institution or of the object at stake. This operation is simply a vicious circle. When one examines the basic values which have served to inform the selection mentioned, one is often referred back to traditional conceptions of justice or simply to the personal preferences of the author.[43]

Thus, it is possible to deduce from the nature of Man the common ownership of goods (based on the natural equality of man) or a social Darwinism without limits (based on the right of the strongest). By the same token, it can be observed that natural law has served to justify monarchy as much as it has served to justify democracy.[44]

On the whole, it is not possible to satisfactorily rebut these arguments. It is true that natural law is not founded on a scientific conception of law; it is rather based on an act of faith with regard to the existence of some cosmos and some objective principles of justice. This cannot be proven; it can only be thought or believed. However, since positivism presents its own weaknesses, in particular to be all too open to arbitrary power, there remains the fact that a choice has to be made by balancing the stakes. That is to say that the question is not yet resolved.[45] Moreover, while the construction of the sources must rest on positive law conceptions, the issue of the basis of legal obligation is another matter, where a richer array of considerations must prevail.

3. Lastly, natural law is accused of being *anti-pluralistic*. The claim is that holders of natural law conceptions seek to impose their position as being founded on an objective truth. Thereby, they seek to enforce a cut-off effect on critical

[43] R Zippelius, *Rechtsphilosophie* (Munich, 1982) 101, our translation.

[44] In the Middle Ages and during the Renaissance, natural law often served to justify some forms of absolutism, since it was allied to the doctrine of God's arbitrary will (voluntarism), expressed through his representative on Earth. See G Fassò, *La legge della ragione* (Bologna, 1964) 93ff, 114ff.

[45] It thus remains possible to postulate, as did Immanuel Kant, some primacy of the practical over theoretical reason: the freedom of Man cannot be proved (theoretical reason), but we all gain from supposing that it is true (practical reason). From there we also see the 'as-if' philosophy. In still other words, it is often profitable not to discuss the truth of assumptions but to measure the validity and practicality of a doctrine in considering its practical social consequences. As to such criteria, see CS Peirce, *Collected Papers*, vol V: *Pragmatism and Pragmaticism* (Cambridge, Mass, 1965) 1ff.

discourse. However, nobody can pretend to speak out for objective truth. Such a position would simply amount to imposing a subjective point of view under the supposed mantle of objectivity. Is that not tantamount to denying that the other is an equal partner in the search for truth? Is it not tantamount to placing oneself above the other? Does it not rely on dogmatism and *a priori* thinking?

Again, this criticism is to a certain extent well-founded and non-rebuttable. However, the cardinal point is the degree to which the speaker resorts to such authoritarian cut-off arguments. There is no reason to wholly abandon the search for truth or the idea of a 'given', since we have in any case to suppose, to some degree, that what we utter in this search is founded on reality. If that were not true, rational and serious discourse would not be possible. It would become a simple game, and thus ultimately a sham. Thus the following question may be asked: why would it be outrageous to affirm, under the guise of natural law principles, that the *Bonner Grundrechtsdemokratie*[46] is a better legal regime than that of the German Third Reich?

E. Conclusion

What, then, is the ultimate foundation of legal obligation? Each one of us will give the answer he or she prefers, be it positivistic, sociological or natural law-orientated. The following elements may, however, be added for reflection. Notwithstanding all its important weaknesses, a moderate and limited doctrine of natural law[47] is useful for understanding the ultimate foundation of law (as opposed to the construction of the sources of positive law). On this plane, it constitutes perhaps the lesser evil. Its aim is to keep visible the necessity for some equilibrium between law and justice, or between positivity and justice. Natural law admits some form of dialectic relationship between both notions. It therefore presents itself as a doctrine of harmonisation between the ideal and the real elements within the legal process.[48] It is the only doctrine seeking such a sweeping synthesis. Positive law

[46] This expression is used by W Fikentscher, *Methoden des Rechts*, vol IV (Tübingen, 1977) 651ff.

[47] In the rather too restrictive but still important words of M Bourquin, 'Règles générales du droit de la paix' (1931-I) 35 *RCADI* 77: '[I]l y a dans le droit naturel quelque chose d'irréductible. C'est la norme fondamentale, dont l'unique objet est de conférer un caractère obligatoire aux règles en vigueur. Au delà de cette borne, il s'égare dans les sables mouvants. En deçà, il est inexpugnable.' ('There is something irreducible in natural law. This is the fundamental norm, whose function is to confer a binding character on the positive rules. Beyond this milestone natural law loses itself in the shifting sands; within this boundary, it is invincible.') The words 'unique objet' appear to be too restrictive.

[48] That the law is a cluster of ideal and real elements has been shown by E Fechner, *Rechtsphilosophie*, 2nd edn (Tübingen, 1956) 21ff. This is a series of elements that the legislator has to take into account when legislating, ie a series of relatively moveable 'givens'. There are three main real elements: (i) biology (eg the need for the protection of children, who are not yet self-sufficient, hence a certain family law); (ii) economy (eg the existence of feudal or industrial structures, hence a certain economic law); (iii) politics (eg the prevailing distribution of power, hence a certain constitutional law). There are also three main ideal factors: (i) reason (eg the idea of equality and reciprocity, paramount in contract

should not be immune from any limitation and from any guidance so as to plunge it into a boundless arbitrariness. These eminently pragmatic arguments remains valid even in the face of all the theoretical shortcomings of natural law doctrines.

The above-mentioned aspects concerning the general legal phenomenon are also relevant to international law. Some features of international law have even predisposed it to remain close to particular natural law conceptions: its universality and 'ecumenism'; its absence of formalism; its rational construction since the times of the Roman *jus gentium*; the place it makes for equitable considerations in many of its subject matters, etc. To ensure proper functioning, however, a positivistic setting needs a much denser and richer legal experience than that prevailing in international society. In particular, it needs a regular legislator, creating the law to be applied. On the other hand, it must be admitted that the extreme pluralism of values and conceptions in international society makes it more difficult to base the law on values, justice or natural law. Whose justice? That of the Western world, or that of the Third World? That of the investors, or that of the 'exploited'? This is not to say that certain principles are not common; it is merely to emphasise that the task, once concrete, is arduous. It is even more so in international society, where a common cultural, political and axiological basis is lacking, or is at least significantly reduced in scope. But this is no reason to abandon the effort. For example, there remains the fact that the State is not self-sufficient and that a people can attain the necessary degree of self-fulfilment only through participation in international life and in the common effort to solve the threats to and problems of humanity as a whole.[49] In the long run, international society can only prosper if its keeps alive a link with an order geared towards peace and justice. What that means in concrete terms has to be determined in the political process. Universal sociability and striving for the common good supposes some universal law (international law) and some universal values (natural law). The legislator has to consider these values and the interests at stake. The bridge here connects with the realm of the sources of positive law.

History shows that notwithstanding its crises and critics, natural law has regularly re-emerged from the mists of time, for example to affirm the application of principles of justice for the American Indians (non-believers); to construct the principles of the rule of law at the time of the Enlightenment (and we still live under the regime constructed from these principles); to oppose perverted and tyrannical legal systems (eg Nazi Germany); to emphasise the inalienability of fundamental human rights (eg after World War II); and so on. Vocabulary may change, natural law may be designated differently, but the core remains. Natural

law); (ii) values (eg war-related, patrimonial or liberal social ideals, hence a totalitarian, corporatist or liberal legal order); (iii) religion (hence a certain law on God's judgments, on family, etc). In a certain sense, the ideal factors have a greater density than the real ones. They serve at one and the same time as signposts for the legislator (and are thus to this extent real factors of which to take account) and as guidelines for the finality of the law. They are thus both the cause and the aim of the law.

[49] See already the famous words of F Suarez, *De legibus*, book ii, ch XIX, § 9.

law is thus seemingly ageless.[50] This is a law that has suffered from various vicissitudes and from which the hubris of triumphalism has not always been removed. But this is also a law that has now transformed into a moderate and tamed[51] set of principles for the ultimate foundation of the legal phenomenon.

IV. The Sources of International Law

A. General Aspects

Some important uncertainties still persist in the construction and understanding of the sources of international law. By reason of their decentralisation and mobility,[52] these sources are more difficult to systematise then their municipal counterparts. The latter have been clarified through the vertical and authoritative structure prevailing within the State, and through a pluri-secular jurisprudence. Moreover, important divergences remain alive across the various legal traditions, in particular between those States dominated by a common law conception and those influenced by the Roman law heritage.[53] Both come together and confront each other in the realm of international law. These differences in perception and sensitivity add to the theoretical uncertainties.

The sources of international law are influenced by both the Roman and the common law traditions. Their formalisation, as expressed in Article 38 of the Statute of the International Court of Justice, is only partial. The system remains mainly open-ended. Moreover, each source has distinct characteristics and plays its own role. Together, the sources provide the international legal system with a balanced set of law-creating agencies, responding to the concurrent needs of stability and flexibility, of detailed regulation and leeway in the law. The duality of the main sources, with their particular roles (treaties/customary law), recalls the dual common law system with its interplay of common law and statute law.

[50] H Rommen, *Die ewige Wiederkehr des Naturrechts* (Leipzig, 1936).

[51] F Gény, *Science et technique en droit privé positif*, vol II (Paris, 1927) ch IX.

[52] They remain much more significantly linked to the events and situations occurring in the social body than most internal law, which is more distanced from such social and political facts.

[53] Continental Europe has been marked by a significant degree of formalisation in the law-creating processes. This has been manifested in the strict category of 'formal sources' of a positivist stamp. Such a system is based on the primacy of the legislator. The law tends to be reduced to the statute. Extra-statutory sources, for example customary law, are brought back to the statutes, which refer to them and thus make them legally relevant. Conversely, in the common law legal orders there has never been a formalised set of formal sources, but rather a series of real sources. Here, besides the statute and precedent, were counted as sources of the law all those facts that could influence the decision of the judge: reason, public policy, values, legal maxims, etc (ie what the Continental lawyer would call 'material sources'). See, eg, the very open-ended doctrine of sources of R Phillimore, *Commentaries upon International Law*, vol I, 3rd edn (London, 1879) 14ff. On the whole question, see also the remarkable study by J Esser, *Grundsatz und Norm in der richterlichen Fortbildung des Privatrechts*, 4th edn (Tübingen, 1990).

The plurality of the sources means that an appraisal of their working must always take into account the whole set of agencies and not only one or another in isolation. It may be useful to briefly recall the main functions each one of the main sources of international law has within the legal-political system.

1. Treaties

Treaties are increasingly important vehicles of regulation in modern international law. In the estimation of the UN Treaty Service, there are today approximatively 100,000 treaties in force. Their number is increasing.

The treaty fulfils two main functions in the body of international sources. *First*, treaties are orientated towards the pole of stability and ensure a sometimes appreciable degree of legal certainty. The function of the treaty is to stabilise certain relations between a number of States when they wish to extract a particular subject matter, for a certain time or *sine die*, from the instability of ordinary international intercourse. The agreement bears on certain matters, and legitimate legal expectations concerning reciprocal behaviour are built up. This is the reason why the violation of treaties is regarded with opprobrium, and why *pacta sunt servanda* is sometimes super-elevated to the lofty world of the 'sanctity' of treaties. The above-mentioned stabilising function is particularly important in international relations, when one considers their fluctuating character, the role of power policy, the insecurity wrought by constant governmental changes and revolutions, the rapid shift in positions and interests, the significant tendency towards unilateralism, egoism and anarchy, as well as the weight of many other contingent factors. The treaty allows States—without forcing them to do so—to extract or shield certain subjects from the worst aspects of these fluctuations. They do so when their interests seem to indicate the advisability of such a course in the short, medium or long run. The treaty is then a welcome instrument: it binds and provides stability; but at the same it is an optional vehicle, in the sense that each State can make up its mind as to whether it wants to ratify it or accede to it. Thus, the treaty allies discipline and freedom; constraint and sovereignty. It seems to be ideally tailored for a society of sovereign *primadonne*. Moreover, in the process of conclusion, the treaty offers the greatest leeway for accommodating the most variegated desires, which can be individualised down to the shadowy realm of reservations. However, once it is concluded, the pole star of the treaty is faithfulness to the agreed content and the restriction of unilateralism. The thread running through the Vienna Convention on the Law of Treaties (VCLT) of 1969 is the fact that treaties are bi- or multilateral undertakings creating legitimate expectations among the treaty partners, and that harmful unilateral action is therefore not allowed in connection with them. Anti-unilateralism is the cornerstone of the law of treaties. This is nothing less than a legal formalisation of the binding character of treaties and of the stability of treaty relationships.

Secondly, treaties allow States to plunge into and to adopt complex and detailed legal regimes, package deals, articulated institutional settings, well-balanced procedural regulation and the like. Such precise legal regimes could not have been created through the instrumentality of customary international law. The latter is too generic and floating to be able to regulate detailed subject matters: an international organisation such as the International Monetary Fund could hardly function on the basis of customary rules alone. In short, a treaty allows States to exercise a true 'legislative activity' by analogy to the international plane, ie international social engineering, which is indispensable to the governance of the modern world.

2. *Customary Law*

The main functions of customary law are distinct and autonomous in comparison with those of treaties. *First*, customary law corrects the orientation of treaties towards stability by ensuring some flexibility in and adaptability of the law. It allows international law to remain close to the practice of States, so that it does not suffer from an excessive gap between its normative injunctions and the facts and opinions found in reality. This function, releasing potential tensions, is all the more essential in international relations, where the formal modification of treaties—the other main source of the law—is rendered extremely arduous by the requirement for consent. A treaty is a consensual bond; therefore its modification requires in principle the agreement of all the States parties. If such unanimous agreement is not forthcoming, the treaty may be derogated from by special agreements *inter se* or partially revised (within the limits of Article 41 of the VCLT of 1969). The treaty will then fragment into a plurality of legal relationships, ushering in a significant complexity: the non-revised treaty will be applicable between States that have not ratified the new version and remain parties only to the old one; the non-revised treaty will also apply between States bound on the one hand by the old treaty and on the other hand by the new one; conversely, the new treaty will apply between States that have ratified or acceded to the new treaty One might easily imagine the complexity of the situation after more than one revision or derogation. There are different rules in the context of certain institutional treaties, where such a procedure would be impossible to manage. Thus, through Articles 108–109 of the UN Charter, a qualified majority of UN member States can bind the minority to the revised version of the Charter, the latter being, however, allowed to withdraw from the Organisation. Nevertheless, the requirements for such a Charter revision are so exacting that formal Charter revisions are extremely rare. The Charter evolves and adapts through subsequent constitutional custom, as happened, for example, as regards the veto according to Article 27, § 3, of the Charter and the role of abstention of one of the permanent members, or as occurred in connection with peace-keeping operations. Customary law thus allows the blunting of the sharpest edges of treaty rigidity: certain norms will reflect general customary law and bind all the States notwithstanding the complexities of the legal situation under conventional law (state of ratifications, reservations, suspensions, etc). Customary law will allow the law contained in treaties to develop by the device of 'subsequent practice' of the parties, which is of paramount importance for ensuring that the law keeps pace with political events.

Secondly, on the general plane (ie not in regional or particular settings) customary international law produces norms of 'general international law'. These are norms that apply to all States and bind all the States of the world, and sometimes even other subjects of international law. Together with the general principles of law, customary law is the only source producing norms of 'common law'. These may be largely derogable by treaties and special legal situations (acquiescence, estoppel, recognition, etc); they nevertheless create a common ground of norms applicable to all the main subjects of the law. They provide, in other words, at least a network of subsidiary legal norms. Conversely, treaties always remain, technically speaking, sources of particular international law. This is so even in the case of universally ratified conventions. For example, the four Geneva Conventions on international humanitarian law (1949) have been ratified and acceded to by 'all' the States of the world—up until the moment a new State emerges, often in the context of instability and warfare. This State is not yet bound by the Conventions. Hence, in the context of the international armed conflict between Ethiopia and Eritrea (1998–2000), Eritrea had not acceded to the Conventions almost right up to the end of the conflict. The legal consequence was that the Geneva Conventions were not applicable in the dealings between the parties. The arbitral commission hearing a series of complaints in the context of this armed conflict could thus not formally apply the Geneva Conventions and had to fall back on norms of customary international law.[54] Without this backing of customary rules or general principles, international law would reveal a significant number of gaps. No legal order can produce only norms of particular law. It must contain at least some general rules on the production of the law, and needs some 'bridges' between the islands of the particular norms produced. By the same token, the treaties themselves must be based on a series of customary rules relating to their conclusion, their validity, their termination, etc. In short, without the unifying glue or staples of customary international law, an objective legal order would not exist. At best there would be shifting and scattered phenomena of law that are not linked together, as in primitive societies.

3. *Interplay Between and Common Features of Treaties and Customary Law*

Summing up, it can be said that the treaty represents the pole of stability and certainty, and customary law the pole of flexibility and adaptation. Moreover, the treaty allows the shaping of complex legal regimes and the blossoming of particular international law tailored to special needs and wishes. This particular international law will usually (apart from *jus cogens* norms) enjoy priority over the general

[54] See XXVI *RIAA*, eg, at 37–40. In the case of the Geneva Conventions of 1949, the Commission could find that the applicable customary and conventional norms were largely the same.

law by virtue of the *lex specialis* principle. Conversely, customary international law creates a common law of principles and rules, stapling together the innumerable rules of the particular law. Thus if each source, taken in isolation, displays some functional weaknesses and presents itself as a non-saturated molecule, the interplay between them will offer a significant equilibrium and the answer to the most urgent normative needs of international society.

The two main sources of international law also have features in common. One of the most significant is the fact that both sources are of an 'historical' nature, ie moving sources closely allied to the underlying social and political facts. In municipal law, legislation, especially in the context of private law, tends to abstract itself to a greater degree from the facts of social and political life, and sometimes even seems to 'petrify' in codes and laws. The aim of such legislation is mainly to influence social behaviour rather than to be influenced by it. There is no equivalent to this in international law, not even in the context of so-called 'codification'. The hiatus between the sources and political life is here significantly smaller. True, the treaty seeks a certain stabilisation of normative regimes, but this remains relative: subsequent practice as special customary law can change the treaty at any time; the latter will therefore remain constantly linked to the events and attitudes shaped by the contracting parties. Customary law is in itself modelled by the practice and legal opinions of States or other subjects of the law; thus, the distance between the law and society remains small. This proximity of the legal norms to the social facts is one of the reasons for the difficulties found in the legal constructions of the sources of international law. Legal science is able to elaborate a well-structured doctrine of sources when the latter are significantly formalised. Once it is confronted with geometrical lines, the scientific spirit is equipped to draw general categories and systems from them. On the other hand, when the realm of sources remains open-ended and highly permeable to social life, the lines are broken and become uncertain. Policy constantly makes inroads into the realm of the law; it permeates everywhere, lifting some veils and breaking down the regularities. The lawyer approaching a question will often find confused situations, shadowy areas and half-ways difficult to translate into neat legal categories. It must be understood, however, that this is not a technical 'weakness' of the system of international sources; the latter are no more defective than their municipal counterparts. The point is simply that international sources are cast in a different society, whose reality and distribution of power they aptly reflect. The sources are linked in this order of things, whose wheels their mission it is to oil. They are not there to revolutionise the system so as to present a well-ordered, federalised world law. Such a law would be a political postulate and not an issue of sources.

B. Customary International Law

International customary law does not simply and solely consist of (and indeed has never simply consisted of) a normative consolidation of social behaviour, ie what was once called an *inveterata consuetudo*. In a decentralised society, customary law moreover plays too significant a role to be limited to accompanying rules of written law of whatever origin. International customary law covers a range of very different phenomena: the consolidation of an ancient bilateral practice or of prescriptive titles; the emergence of rules by practice and legal opinion; the normative generalisation of multilateral treaties; subsequent practice within a treaty regime or some other regime of particular law; quasi-legislative processes within international institutions, where the will of the participants and their *opinio juris* often fill the gap left by an insufficient or absent practice (as also in some branches of international law, such as human rights law and international humanitarian law, where customary rules are tilted more towards the legal opinion of the relevant actors than to their effective practice: 'do what I say, don't do what I do'); the formation of general principles of the law, which more often direct practice than flow from it; the providing of some constitutional foundations of the international legal order, eg *pacta sunt servanda* or considerations of humanity, and many others, etc.

Considering these variegated functions, it stands to reason that customary international law cannot be cast in a simple and unique frame; it cannot be reduced to the sole predominant mould of (effective) practice plus (legal) opinion. Clearly, this classical form of customary law is the most frequent result of unwritten norms. Intellectual honesty commands us to stick to its requirements in all areas of contingent rules, ie in all contexts where the practice of States (and possibly of some other subjects of the law) is and must remain the touchstone of normativity. But there are other forms of customary rules. For example, there are customary rules formed by necessity or by projection, as for axiological first principles, or in some human rights matters, where, for example, the prohibition of torture is maintained by relying on legal opinion (more precisely by the absence of contrary legal opinion) rather than by scrutinising all too closely a State practice formatted by the fact that a majority of States in the world indulge in physical and mental assaults on human dignity. This shows that international customary law is not only a 'process', dominated by the creative elements of practice and opinion, but also a 'result', that is a place where rules can be found and can be normatively clothed. Customary law is a sort of auxiliary receptacle for all unwritten, and sometimes also written, law, whose characteristic is to be considered as 'general international law', ie law applicable to all States, or even to all subjects of international law. The weakness of the formal expression of customary law—a vague conception of 'practice' and an uncertain requirement of 'opinion'—allows such a significant extension of its legal spectrum. This legal playground, and the fact that the most important rules of the international legal order are situated within the customary realm, however, also account for the existence of ambiguities and conflicts within the legal order.[55] Again, this is not so much an expression of some

[55] For an overview of the main legal traditional constructions of customary international law, see G Gianni, *La coutume internationale* (Paris, 1931). For a general discussion of customary international law, see M Mendelson, 'The Formation of Customary International Law' (1998) 272 *RCADI* 155ff. For

weakness of international law but concerns the search for an optimum adaptation to the needs of the society which that law is to regulate.

Even when one remains confined to the traditional field of customary norms, where practice precedes the norm, the problems are significant.[56] The link that the human spirit establishes between the relative regularity of a behaviour and a rule of law cannot be expressed in any equation delivering certain results. This link cannot be translated into general and immutable terms. The inductive process leading from the regularity to the rule supposes the taking into account of all the *relevant* elements of practice that must have been reduced to their *comparable* features. The italicised words show that a selection, an evaluation, a comparison and an analogy remain necessary[57] (examples will be given below). Conformity in the manifestation of facts is based ultimately on a particular classification, and thus on some form of *a priori* framework. The process of 'preparing' the precedents to make them comparable is all but an exact one: contingent elements will have to be discarded (but what is contingent?) in favour of the true *ratio*; the elements to be compared must be placed on a roughly similar level of abstraction or concretion, etc. Thus, if one compares concretely the practice on State immunities, it may seem haphazard and messy: here immunity is granted, there it is not. At a slightly higher level of abstraction, though, the practice seems much more ordered: when the acts at stake are *jure gestionis*, immunity is not granted; when the acts are *jure imperii*, immunity is granted. Everything that rises converges; the higher the chosen level of abstraction, the more likely it is to find a common practice and thus a rule, but also vice versa. However, the interpreter is not confined to a particular level of concretion or abstraction; he or she may choose that level himself. Moreover, and on a more practical level, the practice of most States of the world is simply not known, since it is not published or otherwise rendered accessible. There would also remain the necessity to weigh up the different elements of practice; not all of them reflect the same degree of importance—some are at the core, while others are on the periphery. The issue would also remain whether certain States are particularly representative or interested in a subject matter, as the International Court of Justice (ICJ) suggested in the *North Sea Continental Shelf* cases,[58]

a discussion of the doctrine of the two elements, practice and opinion, see P Haggenmacher, 'La doctrine des deux éléments du droit coutumier international dans la pratique de la Cour internationale' (1986) 82 *RGDIP* 5ff; GJH van Hoof, *Rethinking the Sources of International Law* (Deventer, 1983) 85ff. See also SFDI, *La pratique et le droit international* (Paris, 2004); J Kammerhofer, 'Uncertainty in the Formal Sources of International Law: Customary International Law and Some of its Problems' (2004) 15 *EJIL* 523ff; BD Lepard, *Customary International Law* (Cambridge, 2010). For a classical treatment, see H Thirlway, *The Sources of International Law* (Oxford, 2014) 53ff. And for an overarching perspective, see J d'Aspremont, *Formalism and the Sources of International Law* (Oxford, 2011). For paradoxes in customary international law, see R Kolb, 'Selected Problems in the Theory of Customary International Law' (2003) 50 *NILR* 119ff.

[56] See the very instructive passages in C de Visscher, *Théories et réalités en droit international public*, 4th edn (Paris, 1970) 170ff.

[57] Analogy does not yield certain legal results, since it is always in part based on an evaluation: see A Kaufmann, *Rechtsphilosophie*, 2nd edn (Munich, 1997) 75ff.

[58] *North Sea Continental Shelf* [1969] ICJ Rep 43, §74.

and what the influence of this fact would be on the weighing of practice and opinion. Can it be that the law of the sea is formatted more by States with coastlines than by land-locked States? Would it be correct to say that States possessing the ability to shuttle in outer space should have a greater say over the status of that space? Or that States possessing the atomic bomb should have a greater input on this issue than those States having no such bombs? Why should the 'sending' States carry more weight in such matters than the 'receiving' ones? There also remains the issue of legal opinion. It is there to ensure a proper passage from the 'is' to the 'ought', ie to convert into the legal realm what are initially simple facts devoid of legal significance. The attentive observer cannot fail to feel that in many cases the issue is not really geared towards the real psychological facts prevailing in the ministries, which are difficult to grasp and to qualify. Rather, general notions, such as legal security, reasonableness, justice, the common good or particular interests, have a significant share in the reasoning. The aim is to distinguish between what seems to be dictated by the need for a certain conformity to the general (or in self-interpretation: particular) interest at a given moment, and what rather seems due to accidental circumstances or idiosyncratic motives. The former can more easily be generalised, while the latter cannot.

On balance, a growing formalisation of customary law does not seem either possible or desirable. It would prevent customary law from displaying the functions of flexibility and adaptation that are of paramount importance in international society. In other words, the deficiencies in the formal expression of customary law—often expressed by the lofty but simplistic term 'ambiguities'—are deliberately maintained: they allow a more flexible evolution of the legal body than the requirements of practice and opinion, taken all too seriously, would grant. This is of the greatest importance in a society where the peaceful amendment of the law, so as to allow it to keep pace with quickly changing social or political events, is so poorly developed. In municipal law, this task is usually performed by a centralised legislator. It possesses the decisive weapon that is the majority to impose any desired new law on all members of society. In international society this course is impossible; sovereignty does not allow it to take root. Hence, customary law and its flexibilities is a sort of minor substitute. The result is less certainty of the law; but conversely it also allows for a greater degree of adaptation so as to avoid the trap of 'irrelevance'. Uncertainty versus adaptation and non-irrelevance; the exchange rate is not necessarily unfavourable.

The time has come to give some examples of the difficulties encountered in isolating the elements to be compared in the context of customary precedents. These difficulties can be used instrumentally by legal operators: when they want to affirm the existence of a legal rule, the course chosen will be to place themselves at a considerable level of generality or abstraction so as to be able to insist on the similarities with other cases and to construct a chain of precedents; conversely, when operators wants to deny the existence of a legal rule, the course chosen will be to place themselves on a much lower level of generality, where all the contingent and particular facts come within the equation, so as to be able to deny the similarities of the elements and to find that there is no common practice. An example of the first course can be found in the *North Sea Continental Shelf* cases (1969). There, the ICJ construed customary rules on the delimitation of continental shelves around a vague and very general proclamation by President Truman based on 'equity'.[59] An example of the second course can be found in the *Asylum* case (1950) of the ICJ.[60] The practice of granting asylum in embassies of Latin American States revealed a series of fluctuations and political motives, when considered closely and meticulously.[61] It is remarkable that the Latin American Judges of the Court conversely admitted the existence of a regional customary rule by looking at the matter from a higher and more principled perspective.[62] Indeed, in its principle the practice could seem sufficiently common; in its concrete modalities, it differed significantly. By the same token, acquisitive or liberatory prescription (laches) can be said to exist when one looks merely to the general principles of acquisition or time-bar; but it can also be denied when one looks to the particular modalities in different legal orders, notably with regard to the time that has to lapse before the legal effect accrues. This selective legal technique is also used to brush away some rules considered to be too strict, too formal or too outdated. This was the case, for example, when the ICJ held that the law of the sea rule according to which straight baselines should not exceed 10 nautical miles, could not be applied to all coastal situations, in particular in the context of coastlines as irregular as that of Norway.[63]

Another technique consists in deducing a rule from a common ground between legal systems (like general principles), even though the effective practice of States is not necessarily aligned on it. Thus, Judges Vorah and McDonald have argued that between the criminal law rule found in common law jurisdictions, according to which compulsion or duress are merely reasons to mitigate the sentence handed down, and the Continental law rule, according to which compulsion or duress in certain circumstances will exonerate a defendant from criminal responsibility, the rule of international law should be situated in the middle common ground, so that compulsion reduces the degree of criminal culpability.[64] But such extrapolations can easily lead to difficult conundrums. Let us imagine that there are in a given society a republican party, a monarchist party and an aristocratic party. Each one enjoys one-third of the popular vote. By logical deduction, it is possible to say that there is a clear anti-republican majority in this society; and a rule could be construed from this. It stands to reason, however, that this same deduction could be made as regards any one of the three parties: there is also a clear anti-monarchist majority; and a clear anti-aristocratic majority. The issue is then simply the starting-point the legal operator decided to adopt. Conversely, the most precise extrapolation would

59 *ibid*, 46ff.
60 *Asylum* [1950] ICJ Rep 266.
61 *ibid*, 276–77.
62 See notably the dissenting opinions of Judges Alvarez and Azevedo, *ibid*, 290ff, 332ff.
63 *Norwegian Fisheries* [1951] ICJ Rep 131.
64 *Prosecutor v Erdemovic*, 7 October 1997, ICTY.

basically be that there is no majority in this society, and thus no rule supported by a majority—at least if no further information is provided. In any case, the reduction *ex pluribus* and the induction of a rule from such a starting-point leaves us with intricate problems of construction. Such awkward problems do actually occur in the context of the construction of customary rules.

Still other difficult issues pop up. Thus, for example, the question arises how to ascertain failures to act, which are a form of negative practice. Such failures to act will most often not be visible, or at least not be contained in the available records. Moreover, to be able to assess their relevance, it would be necessary to know how many material acts actually took place in relation to which the failure to act manifested itself, eg the lack of protest occurred. For example, the question may be whether a State has the right or duty to arrest ships sailing in its territorial waters or other zones of jurisdiction, when the engines of such ships present a significant danger to the environment. Let us assume that there has been no such arrest over the last 20 years. This failure to act can be given a legal sense only when the legal operator knows how many ships presenting the required elements of danger to the environment passed through the relevant waters of States, and also how many times the coastal State was put on notice of the existence of the danger. If no such ship passed through the relevant waters of States, the failure to act has no legal significance; it did not flow from legal considerations but simply reflects the circumstantial absence of the situation able to trigger the action. If such ships passed through the relevant zones but no action was taken, and if the danger to the environment was not known, the failure to act has again no legal relevance in the context of the formation of customary international law (but may have relevance in the context of international responsibility, if it signals negligence with respect to the duty to enquire as to the existence of such dangers). The relevant information will not always be easily available. From the point of view of its role in the formation and termination of the law, passivity therefore remains shrouded in mystery.

Practice itself is a far less clear element than it might seem at first sight. Apart from the old debate about whether only actual practice can be taken into account, or whether verbal practice is also relevant,[65] there is the fact that international life generates practice in clusters of very different intensity. There are subject matters where practice is produced every day. Thus, there hardly one day passes without some decision of national authorities, particularly municipal tribunals, on issues of State or diplomatic immunity being issued. On the other hand, there are subject matters where the circumstances allow action to be taken only very rarely. This is the case, for example, regarding the right of angary, and even more the right of angary with regard to aircraft.[66] This state of affairs considerably relativises the number of precedents necessary to buttress the existence of a rule. In the first situation, hundreds of concordant precedents may well not reflect a customary

[65] See M Akehurst, 'Custom as a Source of International Law' (1974/1975) 47 *BYIL* 1ff.

[66] On the concept of angary, see ER Van Bogaert, 'L'angarie' (1974) 21 *NILR* 251ff. For an older account, CL Bullock, 'Angary' (1922/1923) 3 *BYIL* 99ff.

rule, because there may be the same or a greater number of divergant precedents. Conversely, in the second situation, two or three precedents spanning one century may be considered to fix a customary rule, if only two or three situations calling for the relevant action ever arose and if in all these cases substantially the same course of conduct was chosen. Other questions are linked to the weight to be accorded to particularly important States, or to States particularly interested in certain subject matters. Should their practice carry greater weight? Can that be squared with sovereign equality? Would that not pose problems in drawing the right lines? Is any effective practice equivalent in the context of the formation of customary norms, or must practice contrary to international law be discarded? Must a distinction be made in this regard for 'international crimes' or 'serious violations of *jus cogens* norms', where unlawful practice would be devoid of any legal impact in the formation of customary law? Or would even the violation of a marginal bilateral treaty diminish the value of the precedent by claiming that the law cannot accord law-creating value to a breach of the law?[67] The issue has been discussed, for example, in the context of torture, especially after the events of 9/11.[68] It has also been discussed in the context of practice attempting to modify any established customary rule.[69] In certain cases, it is claimed, States must violate the older rule in order to establish the newer one, that is, the new practice needs to depart from the old one. Or must verbal declarations proclaiming the demise of the old law precede this new practice, so that shifting legal opinion has perhaps already abrogated the old rule?

To these difficulties, one must add the pronounced relativity of the constitutive notions of customary law: uniformity, continuity and generality of practice. The nature of this relativity is twofold: first, impossibility to quantify; secondly, mutual relatedness. As to the first point, the notions are all gradual and therefore sometimes suppose a strong evaluative element. The legal operator must have a good deal of experience of international relations and international law, so as to limit his creativity to what States are ready to accept. As to the second point, like the universe, which is a unity of time and space, the various elements of customary law are related one to the other and mutually reinforce themselves. Thus, a certain weakness in continuity can be compensated for by a greater uniformity in the relevant acts or by their greater generality, and vice versa. Additionally, weaknesses in the material expression of practice can be countered by some greater vigour of the subjective element (legal opinion). Thus, in human rights matters, practice may sometimes be shaky, but legal opinion may be expressed in firm terms. This may amount to no more than the expression of hypocritical stances. However,

[67] For some general reflections on the maxim '*ex injuria non oritur jus*', see GG Fitzmaurice, 'The General Principles of International Law Considered from the Standpoint of the Rule of Law' (1957-II) 92 *RCADI* 117ff.

[68] See, eg, the discussion (and the plea that new practice has reduced the scope of the prohibition) in TH Cheng, *When International Law Works—Realistic Idealism after 9/11 and the Global Recession* (Oxford, 2012) 227ff.

[69] See A Bleckmann, 'Völkergewohnheitsrecht trotz widersprüchlicher Praxis?' (1976) 36 *ZaöRV* 374ff. And M Akehurst, 'Custom as a Source of International Law' (1974/1975) 47 *BYIL* 21ff.

it occurs more often than not in the law that persons are to be judged by what they say rather than by what they actually do. The requirement for 'generality' of the practice is itself triply relative. First, it is relative in the senses mentioned above. Further, it is relative in the sense that its absence does not preclude the formation of a customary rule but may simply limit its reach *ratione personarum* (regional, local, particular custom).

If the law is not an exercise in exact sciences, customary law is even the less caught in such geometric schemes. Here we have one of the domains of the law where geometrical approaches based on firm and clear lines are inadequate. Thus, Continental municipal lawyers often have the greatest difficulties with customary international law. It is based on legal phenomena to which these persons are not accustomed and in which they have not been trained. Caught up in their daily practice of seeking the law in handy State legislation, such persons are often highly concerned about the 'uncertainties' in and the 'arbitrariness' of the formation of customary international norms. However, this must be kept in proportion. There are entire subject matters of international law where the customary rules have been well settled and highly certain for centuries, as is the case, for example, on many issues relating to diplomatic and consular law. Conversely, there are subject matters in transition, where the legal rules are far from firm and certain; but here the shifting customary rules, with their own flexibility, ensure that legal rules are also changed, which would not otherwise occur due to the absence of a centralised legislator.

In sum, the two main and complementary functions of customary international law within international society emerge fairly clearly. First, in those stable domains where States have matured well-balanced practices that have arrived at their point of optimum equilibrium, the traditional equation 'practice plus *opinio juris*' aptly reflects the current needs and the actual law-creating agency. Secondly, in those shifting or oppressive domains where States are engaged in power struggles, flexible and indefinite approaches to the customary processes allow the law to evolve step by step as a function of events, and to ensure equitable adjustments or differences between several groups of States at regional or local levels. Certainty in stable matters, embellishment in shifting matters—that is the profound functional duality of customary international law. By these devices, the customary part of the legal order is particularly well adapted to the peculiar needs of international society.

C. General Principles of Law

The uncertainties as to the definition and construction of the notion of 'general principles of law' are even greater than those we have witnessed in the discussion of customary international law.[70] Overall, it is correct to say that 'few legal questions

[70] For a detailed discussion by the present author, see R Kolb, *La bonne foi en droit international public* (Paris, 2000) 24ff, with many bibliographic references.

have aroused in the contemporary literature of international law so many discussions and controversies'.[71] A significant doctrinal current has denied that general principles of law form a distinct source of international law, or alternatively has confined them in notions such as 'material sources' or 'equity'. In particular, positivistic authors have never appreciated the general principles,[72] whereas the naturalistic authors were fond of them.[73] The reason lies in the fact that such principles are not made but are found by the lawyer as secular expressions of legal wisdom and practice. This seems to contradict the fundamental positivistic *topos* that law is to be found only in 'legislation'.

For many authors, there are two types of general principles of law: principles of international law; and municipal law analogies. The principles of international law are part and parcel of customary law. The qualification as principles serves to denote the supreme systematic importance of these norms and the fact that they give rise to several normative concretisations: for example, from the non-use of force principle one derives rules such as the duty of non-recognition of situations created by unlawful force, the prohibition of annexation, the voidness of coerced treaties, etc. On the other hand, there are common principles of the municipal legal orders suitable for a transposition into the international legal order when the latter presents a gap. For example, arbitral tribunals of the nineteenth century and beginning of the twentieth century were often confronted with claims for which there was no clear customary rule and no conventional rule at all. They did not simply reject the claim as not being founded on any sound legal basis but considered whether some principle known in the common legal experience of internal law could be transposed by analogy into international law. Thus, when a claim was presented a long time after the triggering events, arbitral tribunals asked themselves whether some rule on the application of a time-bar for negligent failure to present the claim earlier was to be applied. They sometimes applied such a rule by analogy to the municipal law principles.[74]

Taken largely, the general principles of law are part of unwritten law. They range from supreme norms (*pacta sunt servanda*, good faith) to simple maxims of the law (*qui habet commoda ferre debet onera*, he who has the benefits must also bear the burdens)[75], or even to the technique of municipal law analogies in private or public law (eg the search for a definition of what is encompassed in the term 'rape', which had never been defined in international law but on which the municipal law experiences cast light).[76] General principles may thus span most different legal

[71] C Rousseau, *Droit international public*, vol I (Paris, 1970) 372.

[72] See, eg, K Strupp, 'Les règles générales du droit de la paix' (1934-I) 47 *RCADI* 330ff.

[73] See, eg, A Verdross, *Die Quellen des universellen Völkerrechts* (Freiburg, 1973) 120ff.

[74] See, eg, *Gentini Case* (1903), X *RIAA* 551ff.

[75] On this maxim, see R Kolb, 'La maxime "qui habet commoda, ferre debet onera et contra" (celui qui a les avantages doit supporter aussi les charges et vice versa) en droit international public' (2004) 37 *RBDI* 12ff.

[76] Such an enquiry occurred in the ICTY's *Furundzija* case, Trial Chamber judgment of 10 December 1998, §§165ff.

tools and rules: constitutional principles (including the primacy of fundamental norms over particular law norms or *jus cogens* techniques); logically necessary rules (*pacta sunt servanda*); principles inherent in every legal order in some way or the other (good faith, reasonableness); principles of international law (non-use of force, peaceful settlement of international disputes, self-determination of peoples, etc); rules of legal technique (eg *lex posterior derogat legi priori*); legal maxims (eg 'nobody can profit from his own wrongdoing'); some low-profile common legal rules (eg the admissibility of indirect evidence in legal process)[77]; techniques of analogy and of transposition of the reason inherent in legal rules (the issue here tends to merge into that of interpretation).

What are the main functions of the general principles of law within the international legal order? There are several functions to be discussed. Some of them are not unimportant.

1. *Logical Function*

From the logical point of view, there are some general principles that must be supposed to conceive a legal order. Without these principles, the construction of the sources would fall into a vicious circle. Thus, for example, the principle *pacta sunt servanda* is a necessary normative proposition in any developed legal order. Practically speaking, it stands to reason that if the pledged word were not binding, an international legal order would be impossible. Moreover, a derogation from this principle is logically impossible. It is thus a type of *jus cogens*. If some actors agreed not to honour their agreements, they would at least have to honour their agreement not to honour, which again supposes the rule *pacta sunt servanda*. Finally, from a violation of the principle there could never flow its legal inexistence or desuetude. The principle remains a logical and axiological premise. This aspect brings out the particular legal complexion of such primary principles within the legal order. They are on this account different from ordinary customary rules based on practice and opinion.[78] The result is that such principles are intensely normative and are not based on induction to be valid. Their number is extremely limited; to the rule *pacta sunt servanda*, good faith may be added.

2. *Axiological Function*

Some general principles serve to maintain the fundamental unity of the system of international law beyond its almost infinite variety (*unitas in varietate*). They guarantee some minimum common ground of values, functions and concepts without which the legal order would dissolve into concurrent and unrelated legal blocks. Verdross has aptly insisted on this aspect: 'The positive international law

[77] See, eg, the *Corfu Channel* (Merits) [1949] ICJ Rep 18.

[78] D Anzilotti, *Cours de droit international* (Paris, 1929) 44–45. We might also recall the already quoted Winkler, who was correct when he proclaimed that '[i]n tota iurisprudentia, nihil est quod minus legaliter tractari possit quam ipsa principia' (Winkler, above n 6, lib I, cap II, first phrase).

contained in customary and conventional rules is composed of a number of isolated rules and precedents. In order to become a system, these rules and precedents need some directing principles'.[79] He adds, '[w]ithout these principles … international law would not only be silent on many matters, but also scattered into a mass of detailed rules and precedents which no common link would unite'.[80] This particular form of normativity leads to principles that can serve as starting-points for deductive or concretising reasoning. The legal operator will avoid pure legal conceptualism or usurpation of the legislative function by carefully considering the social necessities, the acceptability of certain deductions for the States and the existing international practice. It may thus occur that a principle can be abstracted from the scenes of practice through a meticulous analysis by analogy, deduction and induction.[81] The principle will then not be simply subjectively postulated; it will have its roots in some complexion of international practice. Once shaped, the principle will develop some autonomy and be able to format further legal arguments. It may serve to develop the law, to fill gaps within the law, to elaborate new rules or to sustain a deductive conclusion. Thus, for example, the principle *pacta sunt servanda* can be extracted (apart from its logical necessity) from the practice with respect to agreements, contracts and treaties and then serve as normative pillar to deduce or to accompany—together with the principle of good faith—the binding character of unilateral acts such as promises (*promissio vel pollicitatio est servanda*).[82] Through such a course, the value of faithfulness and legitimate expectation is also being transported throughout the legal system.

3. *Normative Function*

The principles reinforce the reach and the density of international law. As has been aptly said:

> By introducing general principles of law recognized by civilized nations into the sources of applicable law, the drafters of the Court's Statute purported to develop to its utmost degree the domain of judicially applicable law, and, as has been claimed, to push to apogee the productivity of the sources.[83]

[79] A Verdross, 'Les principes généraux du droit applicables aux rapports internationaux' (1938) 45 *RGDIP* 50.

[80] *ibid*, 52.

[81] See the interesting developments in K Engisch, *Einführung in das juristische Denken*, 3rd edn (Stuttgart, 1956) 134ff. According to a famous definition, the principle is as follows: 'Principes de droit: Propositions premières dégagées de l'ensemble du système juridique par voie de synthèse, considérées comme exactes et susceptibles, en conséquence, de justifier des déductions dans l'ordre juridique' (J Basdevant (ed), *Dictionnaire de la terminologie du droit international* (Paris, 1960) 472). See also M Virally, 'Le rôle des "principes" dans le développement du droit international' in M Virally, *Le droit international en devenir* (Paris, 1990) 201–02, 204, 212.

[82] See the reasoning of the ICJ in the *Nuclear Test* cases, [1974] ICJ Rep 253, 267–68, §§43ff and 472–73, §§45ff.

[83] C de Visscher, *Théories et réalités en droit international public*, 4th edn (Paris, 1970) 419, our translation.

There are several functions here. *First*, the general principles complement the customary and conventional rules by filling potential gaps. It is debatable whether true gaps exist in the legal order, this being a question that will be considered later. For present purposes, it suffices to notice that through the principles, the normative content of international law is increased to the detriment of the residual domain of State freedom.[84] Thus, if any rule in one of the other recognised sources of international law is lacking, the general principles can serve as the last possible pillar on which to erect a legal reasoning so as to 'discover' some auxiliary rule. When State conduct impinges on a legitimate interest of another State, or creates some damage to that other State, but no norm of international law expressly prohibits this course, there is the possibility of looking at the matter through the lens of some principle, eg good faith, abuse of rights, proportionality, or the principle that a State may not allow the use of its territory in a way that breaches the rights of other States ('principle not to allow use of territory injurious to other States').[85]

Secondly, principles provide a tool for the interpretation of customary or conventional norms.[86] Thus, municipal norms contested from the point of view of international human rights law are often evaluated in the light of general principles relating to necessity and proportionality.[87] Good faith and reasonableness[88] are used as a standard for the interpretation of discretionary powers of States, notably when the latter have extraterritorial effect or affect rights or interests of third States.

Thirdly, general principles of law influence the formation of conventional and customary rules of international law, and sometimes also of rules of internal law (legislation).[89] Thus, in international humanitarian law, the whole normative process is profoundly influenced by the fact that each rule is a compromise between the countervailing principles of humanity on the one side and military necessity on the other. These are two fundamental general principles of international humanitarian law.[90] By the same token, in the context of the law relating to the expulsion of foreigners, the rules have been elaborated so as to take account of the gravity of the motives for expulsion and therefore of proportionality.[91]

[84] P Guggenheim, *Traité de droit international public*, vol I, 2nd edn (Geneva, 1967) 296–97.

[85] As to the latter, see the classical reasoning of the *Trail Smelter* arbitral tribunal (1941), III *RIAA* 1963ff. The principle was repeated by the ICJ some years later in the *Corfu Channel* case, above n 77, 22, and later became a pillar of international environmental law.

[86] H Lauterpacht, *The Development of International Law by the International Court* (London, 1958) 158ff; W Friedmann, 'The Uses of General Principles in the Development of International Law' (1963) 57 *AJIL* 286.

[87] See, eg, W Kälin and J Künzli, *The Law of International Human Rights Protection* (Oxford, 2009) 99ff; F G. Jacobs and RC White, *The European Convention on Human Rights*, 2nd edn (Oxford, 1996) 304ff.

[88] O Corten, *L'utilisation du 'raisonnable' par le juge international* (Brussels, 1997). See, on this issue, eg, the *Iron Rhine Railway* case (2005), XXVII *RIAA* 100ff, in particular §204.

[89] See P Reuter, *Droit international public*, 6th edn (Paris, 1983) 119.

[90] C Rousseau, *Le droit des conflits armés* (Paris, 1983) 21.

[91] This subject has become considerably more controversial politically over the last few years, and is now under consideration at the International Law Commission: see <www.legal.un.org/ilc/>.

Fourthly, general principles allow the judge to introduce some flexibility into the law to be applied, and sometimes to develop international law.[92] This need is characteristic of new areas into which international law progressively extends.[93] The development of the modern law of maritime delimitation around the concept of 'equitable principles' (in its phase between 1969 and the 1990s) is an interesting example.[94] For a long time, the international law of environmental protection remained anchored in the main principle of the law of neighborhood, namely, '*sic utere tuo ut alienum non laedas*'. In other words, a State could not use or allow the use of its territory in a way that trespassed on the territory of neighbouring States, if the damage so caused crossed the threshold of a certain gravity. Only progressively has that body of the law been enriched by a much larger perspective, where, however, the *sic utere* principle has continued to play a dynamic role.[95]

4. *Unifying Function*

The application of the same or of similar general principles across the different branches of the law—and even across the legal orders—accentuates the unity of the legal phenomenon. In addition to the axiological and systematical unity mentioned above, there comes a certain practical unity of common legal experiences and of common legal language. The general principles allow a certain fluidity of the master ideas of the law throughout its provinces. By way of analogies, there key ideas can be transported from one legal branch to another.[96] The principles are in this regard like a currency that allows exchanges. Thus, it has been demonstrated how general principles have contributed to a progressive interrelation of private and public law, which were once separated with significantly greater rigidity.[97] Necessity and proportionality, or good faith/reasonableness, are some principles common to all legal science. An impressive example of this unifying and centripetal function of principles can be seen in the law of international spaces. This law has been formatted by UN General Assembly resolutions, where the mention of

[92] See, eg, the classical works by H Lauterpacht, *Private Law Analogies and Sources of International Law* (London, 1927) and B Cheng, *General Principles of Law—As Applied by International Courts and Tribunals* (London, 1953).

[93] For a long time this has been the case in the context of international contracts: see, eg, P Weil, 'Principes généraux du droit et contrats d'Etat', *Essays in Honor of B. Goldman* (Paris, 1982) 387ff.

[94] P Weil, *Perspectives du droit de la délimitation maritime* (Paris, 1988).

[95] On the international law of the environment and its development, see, eg, U Beyerlin, *Umweltvölkerrecht* (Munich, 2000); P Sands, *Principles of International Environmental Law*, 2nd edn (Cambridge, 2003); AC Kiss and D Shelton, *International Environmental Law*, 3rd edn (New York, 2004); PW Birnie, AE Boyle and C Redgwell, *International Law and the Environment*, 3rd edn (Oxford, 2009); see now also D Bodansky, J Brunée and E Hey (eds), *The Oxford Handbook of International Environmental Law* (Oxford, 2007).

[96] Analogy is a fundamental tool of human reasoning in general and of legal reasoning in particular. It was used extensively by the glossators of the Middle Ages, when trying to harmonise the various passages of the *Corpus Juris* by 'concordantia discordantium' and by 'procedere ad similia': see A Steinwenter, 'Prolegomena zu einer Geschichte der Analogie', *Essays in Honor of F. Schulz*, vol II (Weimar, 1951) 345ff.

[97] W Friedmann, *The Changing Structure of International Law* (London, 1964) 281ff.

principles outweighed by far the precise technical elaboration in detailed norms. Thus, the law of outer space is governed by principles such as non-appropriation, freedom of use, peaceful use, due regard to the activities of other States, exploration and exploitation as a common heritage of mankind, cooperation, etc. One finds these principles in Resolutions 1721 (XVI) of 1961, 1962 (XVIII) of 1963 and 2222 (XXII) of 1967, and later in the Outer Space Treaty of 1967.[98] The legal regime of the deep seabed is to some extent similar. The 'common heritage of mankind' aspect has been emphasised in Resolution 2749 (XXV) of 1970 and in Articles 133 et seq of the Montego Bay Convention on the Law of the Sea.[99]

5. *Correcting Function*

General principles may add precision to the scope of application of a conventional or customary rule of international law, and sometimes have even derogatory force.[100] This occurs in the context of supreme principles, not of auxiliary or subsidiary ones.[101] When the legal operator has to reconcile a plurality of norms applicable at the same time to the same facts, principles will often guide his way.[102] Equity has performed this function in some cases. It may temper some unjust rigour in the application of one norm by allowing other norms to be taken into account. Thus, the legal operator could develop an 'equitable exception' by careful distinguishing. In a highly interesting decision of the Swiss Federal Tribunal,[103] the question arose in the context of a limitation imposed by federal legislation (the so-called *lex Friedrich*) on the free disposal of their properties by the owners of land. This legislation applied to the purchase of Swiss land by foreigners. The federal legislator (the legislation had been adopted by popular vote against the advice of the Government) had omitted to harmonise this new law with a series of existing treaties. Among these treaties was the Agreement of 1862 between France and Switzerland relative to the Dappes Valley. This valley had in 1862 been definitively ceded to France, which in turn had retroceded certain lands to Switzerland. The lands retroceded had been acquired by the Canton of Vaud. Must the new federal legislation be applied to these lands, or could one argue that French purchasers would have a right to acquire such lands in which they had a long-standing equitable interest? The Federal Tribunal started by emphasising that the Treaty of 1862

[98] R Wolfrum, *Die Internationalisierung staatsfreier Räume* (Berlin, 1984) 269ff.

[99] AC Kiss, 'La notion de patrimoine commun de l'humanité' (1982-II) 175 *RCADI* 99ff. Part XI of the 1982 Convention has in the meantime been modified by a more market-orientated legal regime: see, eg, DH Anderson, 'Resolution and Agreement Relating to the Implementation of Part XI of the UN Convention on the Law of the Sea: A General Assessment' (1995) 55 *ZaöRV* 275ff. For the effect of this revision on the Law of the Sea Tribunal, see T Treves, 'The Law of the Sea Tribunal: Its Status and Scope of Jurisdiction after November 16, 1994' (1995) 55 *ZaöRV* 421ff.

[100] A Favre, *Principes du droit des gens* (Freiburg, 1974) 295.

[101] M Akehurst, 'The Hierarchy of the Sources of International Law' (1974/1975) 47 *BYIL* 278.

[102] A Verdross and B Simma, *Universelles Völkerrecht*, 3rd edn (Berlin, 1984) 389.

[103] *Office fédéral de la Justice v Morel et Commission vaudoise de recours en matière foncière*, judgment of 15 July 1982 (1983) 34 ASDI 199–200.

did not contain an express provision on such a right of purchase, since at the time it was supposed to exist under generally applicable legislation; the restrictions issued one century later could not be foreseen.[104] But the whole spirit of the Treaty was manifestly based on the existence of such a right. It had been a fundamental basis for retroceding the lands to Switzerland.[105] The federal legislation ought thus to be interpreted restrictively, so as to reconcile it with the Treaty. The Tribunal thus accepted an 'equitable exception' for a special case manifestly not considered by the legislator. Behind the technical arguments of the Tribunal, there loom large the principles of equity, good faith and reasonableness. They allowed the bending of an overly rigorous norm.

6. *Adapting Function*

The more a norm is formulated in general and abstract terms, the longer it will be able to last; conversely, the more individualised and concrete the formulation of the norm, the less it will be equipped to survive the erosion of time. The general norm does not contain precise and situated normative elements. Such elements would need to be constantly adapted in the light of changing social conditions. The general norm rather encapsulates constant aspects of human life and elementary conditions of justice, such as the duty to hear the other party (*audiatur et altera pars*), the respect for the pledged word, the protection of legitimate expectations, etc. Each epoch can then elaborate the meaning and reach of such general injunctions, for example by determining what it considers to be a 'legitimate' expectation. On the other hand, the more the norm contains concrete elements, the more it is rooted in a particular socio-political context. This is why the general principle of good faith can traverse many centuries with little alteration, while a concrete administrative provision on technical matters will require constant adaptation. This explains why general principles, which are among the most general and abstract norms of the legal system, provide a certain degree of permanence and unity of the law across time. The particular norms that must be changed, adapted or made more flexible can sometimes be remoulded in the light of the general principles and their concretisations.

This adapting function is all the more important in a legal order that is defective from the standpoint of mechanisms of change. It is true that most international norms are *derogable*, ie the general rule can be substituted *inter partes* by

[104] *ibid.*

[105] *ibid*, 200: 'On peut donc supposer que, si la législation suisse sur l'acquisition des immeubles par des personnes à l'étranger avait existé en 1862, les négociateurs du traité concernant la vallée des Dappes n'auraient pas manqué de soumettre à un régime particulier les transferts de terrains situés dans la partie de territoire cédée à la Suisse. [...] Dès lors, on se trouve aujourd'hui en présence d'une lacune proprement dite, qu'il y a lieu de combler selon le principe général énoncé à l'article premier [du Code civil, c'est-à-dire: *modo legislatoris*]'. Summing up: the Federal Tribunal considers that if the federal legislation restricting the purchase of land had existed in 1862, the treaty would have made an exception for the French purchasers; thus, there is now a gap in the law, which has to be filled by the judge acting as a legislator. The gap is filled by the principles mentioned.

a special provision. But the *modification* of the general norm often remains difficult. Multilateral treaties provide for unanimous consent to modifications with effect *erga omnes partes*; bilateral treaties can be changed by the consent or the subsequent practice of the two States; customary norms of general scope suppose a sufficiently general practice and legal opinion (it is, however, not necessary that the new practice and opinion are actually displayed by the vast majority of States, it being sufficient that some States practice and consider legal a certain course, and that the majority of the other States do not oppose or protest against that course, especially when they are particularly affected by it). In the end result, international law, centered on individualistic sovereignty, has always suffered from a distinctive lack of means of peaceful change. In this environment, the general principles offer themselves as vectors of a minor—but not necessarily less effective—process of legal change. They may induce new interpretations of old-style norms; insert into the body of the law new equitable exceptions; create new norms by judicial development of the law; and so on. The principles thus have a palliative effect on the illness characteristic of international law, consisting in the tendency to constantly privilege the past over the future. In short, the principles may contribute to allowing the law, at least to some degree, to keep pace with the exigencies of time. Certainly, one must not exaggerate this function. The judge is not the legislator, and he or she cannot simply re-invent the law as he or she sees fit. But the issue lies elsewhere: between the all and the nothing lies the something; and sometimes it is possible to adapt and slightly reshuffle, even if it is not possible to rebuild.

Some examples follow. It may occur that a certain domain of the law has become too rigid in view of new developments within social life. It may also be difficult to expect a formal modification of the law. The jurisprudence has then sometimes—as we have seen in the previous section—attempted to adapt the law. It could try to do so by instilling into it some equitable exception justified by new circumstances. The latter could be linked back to some hypothetic will of the law-giver: if the new facts had been known, the legislator would have.... The rule on the exhaustion of local remedies in the context of diplomatic protection offers an example. In *Panevezys-Saldutiskis Railway* (Preliminary Objections),[106] the Permanent Court of International Justice admitted that there were exceptions to that rule, for example when municipal tribunals were not in a position to decide, or when the remedy could not lead to a change in the decision. This means that the rule of exhaustion of local remedies has been tempered when confronted with situations in which it would be unreasonable or inequitable to require its application. International practice shows that many other equitable exceptions to this rule have been accepted in the growing case law, albeit in a piecemeal and sometimes haphazard way. The rule has been said to be inapplicable in the case of direct damage between States, including damage to diplomatic personnel or other persons

[106] *Panevezys-Saldutiskis Railway* (Preliminary Objections) (1939) PCIJ Series A/B no 76, 18.

covered by international immunities;[107] if the damage is caused outside the territory of the wrongdoing State (since it would be inequitable to require a foreigner to exhaust remedies in a territory with which he or she has had no voluntary connection);[108] if it is excluded by treaty;[109] if the defendant renounces the benefit of the rule after the judicial organ has been seized[110] (renunciation may be implicit if there are clauses providing for the arbitration of a class of disputes); if there are no appropriate remedies for the dispute at stake,[111] in particular if the remedies are illusory or ineffective[112] by reason of objective circumstances (municipal judicial organisation,[113] the state of municipal law,[114] the nature of the competent organ,[115] excessive delays,[116] a substantial risk of increasing the damage,[117] etc) or by reason of subjective circumstances (the dependence of the tribunals on the executive, the bad faith or notorious xenophobia of the judges,[118] etc); if the remedy is only one for revision of the judgment and not an ordinary appeal or cassation;[119] possibly also if the question is limited to points of law to the exclusion of any point of fact;[120] if an estoppel calls into question the claim that the remedies have not been exhausted;[121] and so on. Moreover, the rule of exhaustion is satisfied even when the municipal procedures do not have exactly the same subject matter as the international procedures, provided that the substance of the claim has been presented at the internal level and that there has been the maximum possible

[107] *Phosphates in Morocco* (1938) PCIJ Series A/B no 74, 28. The interpretation and application of a treaty, even in the context of individual rights and obligations, is never subject to the rule: *Switzerland v Germany* (1958) 25 *ILR* 42ff; *Aerial Services (France v US)* (1978) 54 *ILR* 322ff; *Ireland v UK* (1978) 58 *ILR* 263 (ECtHR).

[108] This is a controversial matter: see CF Amerasinghe, *Local Remedies in International Law* (Cambridge, 1990) 138ff.

[109] *Amoco* (1982) 1 *Iran/US Claims Tribunal Reports* 493. This is also the case under the ICSID system under the Washington Convention of 1965, Art 26 (1965) 4 *ILM* 536. See also *Uzielli* (1963) 40 *ILR* 149ff; *Gallardo* (1981) 67 *ILR* 578.

[110] *Müller v Austria* App no 5849/72 (Commission Decision, 16 December 1974).

[111] *Altesor v Uruguay* (1982) 70 *ILR* 253; *Nielsen v Denmark* (1961), Communication no 343/57, European Commission of Human Rights Report; *Englert v FRG* (1987) Series A no 123, 51–53; *Velasquez Rodriguez* (1988) 95 *ILR* 233, 270ff (Inter-AmCtHR). See also the concluding observations of the Belgian Government in the *Barcelona Traction* case, ICJ, *Memorials, Pleadings and Documents*, vol I, pt III, 218–19, and vol III, 602.

[112] See CF Amerasinghe, *Local Remedies in International Law* (Cambridge, 1990) 166ff, 193ff.

[113] This may occur, for example, if the supreme tribunal depends on the executive on a particular question the international legality of which is disputed: see *Salvador Commercial Company* (1902), XV *RIAA* 476–77; *Valentine Petroleum* (1967) 44 *ILR* 91–92.

[114] Eg, when the decision flows from a formal law over which the judge has no power of review: see *Rhodope Forests* (1933), III *RIAA* 1405.

[115] Eg acts of Government: *Finnish Shipowners* (1934), III *RIAA* 1490ff.

[116] *El Oro* case (1931), V *RIAA* 191 (9 years). See CF Amerasinghe, *Local Remedies in International Law* (Cambridge, 1990) 203ff.

[117] *De Sabla* (1933) 28 *AJIL* 607, implicitly.

[118] *Brown* (1923) VI *RIAA* 120, 129. See CF Amerasinghe, *Local Remedies in International Law* (Cambridge, 1990) 193ff.

[119] *Salem* case (1932), II *RIAA* 1190.

[120] *Aerial Services (France v US)* (1978), XVIII *RIAA* 469.

[121] See R Kolb, *La bonne foi en droit international public* (Paris, 2000) 565ff.

action in the light of internal procedures and laws.[122] The conjunction of all these exceptions, developed in the case law, has blunted the sharp edge of the rule and brought it into line with equitable considerations. A German author had proposed as early as the 1930s that the rule should be cast aside each time there are 'valid motives' to spare the aggrieved party its observation.[123] Overall, the developments mentioned placed the rule directly under the control of equity and ultimately *inter fauces justitiae*. Equity has penetrated the normative injunction to the point of dominating it altogether. This means that a general principle of law has served as a vehicle for a transformation of the law, in substitution for the formal legislator.

Another example can be found in the *Norwegian Fisheries* case (1951).[124] The rule of international law is to measure maritime zones from baselines situated on the coastline. These lines follow the low-water mark. However, there exist some extremely irregular coastlines, replete with fjords, islets, rocks, fringes, banks and other complications. It would be difficult to draw practicable maritime lines by following the haphazard course of such coasts. This is the reason why many States have in such circumstances had recourse to straight baselines. Is this practice compatible with the rule of international law? This is far from being obvious. The practice of straight lines is at variance with the rule discussed. Moreover, it allows the coastal State to claim areas of the high seas by extending the reach of its maritime zones. When seized of the question, the ICJ admitted nevertheless that such straight baselines are compatible with international law in some conditions. An equitable and reasonable exception is thereby carved out of the rule. The conditions for the acceptability of straight baselines are defined by the Court in a passage resembling an act of judicial legislation.[125] These conditions are as follows:

1. the straight baselines must not significantly depart from the general direction of the coastline;
2. they may encompass certain waters so intimately linked with the coast that it is justified to treat them as internal waters;
3. economic interests of the coastal State attested by a long usage can be taken into account.[126]

The conditions outlined by the Court were finally inserted by the formal legislator into Article 4 of the 1958 Geneva Convention on Territorial Waters and later in Article 7 of the 1982 Montego Bay Convention on the Law of the Sea. The principles of reasonableness, of equity, of practicability, of good faith and of legal security have influenced the judicial reasoning.

[122] *Elettronica Sicula (ELSI)* [1989] ICJ Rep 46, §59.

[123] E Kaufmann, 'Règles générales du droit de la paix' (1935-IV) 54 *RCADI* 457.

[124] *Norwegian Fisheries*, above n 63.

[125] As the Court had already done for the conditions of validity of reservations to multilateral treaties: *Genocide Convention* [1951] ICJ Rep 20ff.

[126] *Norwegian Fisheries*, above n 63, 132–33.

D. Treaties

The international treaty is considered to be the source of international law most akin to the sources of municipal law: on the one hand on account of the voluntary creation of its rules; and on the other hand on account of the certainty and objectivity of the rules it sets out.[127] However, this conception corresponds to reality only to a certain degree. The treaty is a significantly polyvalent source; it does not fit entirely the traditional model of State law. Its functions and typology are varied: there are transactional treaties limited to the exchange of goods; there are normative treaties posing general rules in areas of common interest; there are institutional treaties containing the founding act of international organisations or organs, etc. Institutional treaties fuse together a series of wills geared at least in part towards a common goal. There is a difference here with respect to treaties balancing opposing interests in a *do ut des* network. There are also treaties regulating matters essential for humanity as a whole (so-called 'world-order treaties'), and there are other treaties regulating only secondary matters (eg the Rio Arrangement of 26 October 1979 concerning certain postal matters). There are treaties securing a precise and reasonably complete regulation of a subject matter, and

[127] On the law of treaties: A Aust, *Modern Treaty Law and Practice*, 2nd edn (Cambridge, 2007) (now 3rd edn, 2013); S Bastid, *Les traités dans la vie internationale* (Paris, 1985); L Bittner, *Die Lehre von den völkerrechtlichen Vertragsurkunden* (Stuttgart, 1924); H Blix and JH Emerson, *The Treaty Maker's Handbook* (New York, 1973); E Cannizzaro (ed), *The Law of Treaties Beyond the Vienna Convention* (Oxford, 2010); J Combacau, *Le droit des traités* (Paris, 1991); M Craven and M Fitzmaurice (eds), *Interrogating the Treaty: Essays in the Contemporary Law of Treaties* (Nijmegen, 2005); S Davidson (ed), *The Law of Treaties* (Aldershot, 2004); I Detter, *Essays on the Law of Treaties* (Stockholm, 1967); TO Elias, *The Modern Law of Treaties* (New York, 1974); M Fitzmaurice and O Elias, *Contemporary Issues in the Law of Treaties* (Utrecht, 2005); P Fois, *Il diritto dei trattati* (Naples, 2009); AF Frangulis, *Théorie et pratique des traités internationaux* (Paris, 1934); E de la Guardia, *Derecho de los tratados internacionales* (Buenos Aires, 1997); J de Dios Gutiérrez Baylon, *Derecho de los tratados* (Mexico City, 2010); G Haraszti, *Some Fundamental Problems of the Law of Treaties* (Budapest, 1973); O Hoijer, *Les traités internationaux* (Paris, 1928); DB Hollis, *The Oxford Guide to Treaties* (Oxford, 2012); K Holloway, *Modern Trends in Treaty Law* (London/New York, 1967); J Klabbers, *The Concept of Treaty in International Law* (The Hague, 1996); J Klabbers and R Lefeber (eds), *Essays on the Law of Treaties* (The Hague, 1998); C Laboissière Muzzi, J Soares Amaral and L Melillo Cardozo, *A Convenção de Viena sobre o Direito dos tratados (1969)* (Curitiba, 2013); A Maresca, *Il diritto dei trattati* (Milan, 1971); AD McNair, *The Law of Treaties* (Oxford, 1961); MG Monroy Cabra, *Derecho de los tratados*, 2nd edn (Bogotá, 1995); V de Oliveira, Mazzuoli, *Tratados internacionais*, 2nd edn (Sao Paulo, 2004); A Orakhelashvili and S Williams (eds), *40 Years of the Vienna Convention on the Law of Treaties* (London, 2010); P Reuter, *Introduction to the Law of Treaties* (London/New York, 1989); JF Rezek, *Direito dos Tratados* (Rio de Janeiro, 1984); S Rosenne, *Developments in the Law of Treaties, 1945–1986* (Cambridge, 1991); I Sinclair, *The Vienna Convention on the Law of Treaties*, 2nd edn (Manchester, 1984); AN Talalajev, *Das Recht der internationalen Verträge* (Berlin, 1977); C Tams, A Tzanakopoulos and A Zimmermann (eds), *Research Handbook on the Law of Treaties* (Cheltenham/Northampton, 2014); M Villiger, 'The 1969 Vienna Convention on the Law of Treaties: 40 Years After' (2009) 344 *RCADI* 9; E Vitta, *Studi sui trattati* (Turin, 1958). See also the Commentaries to the VCLT of 1969: O Corten and P Klein (eds), *The Vienna Convention on the Law of Treaties, A Commentary*, vols I–II (Oxford, 2011) (2,071 pp); O Dörr and K Schmalenbach (eds), *Vienna Convention on the Law of Treaties, A Commentary* (Heidelberg/Dordrecht/London/New York, 2012) (1,423 pp); ME Villiger, *Commentary on the 1969 Vienna Convention on the Law of Treaties* (Leiden/Boston, 2009) (1,057 pp). And lastly see also R Kolb, *Introduction to the Law of Treaties* (Oxford, 2016).

there are others of imprecise and vague content. The latter offer only some general criteria for political action, notably in the domains of economics, development or environment.

This varied typology and taxonomy of treaties explains that the choice to devise unitary rules on treaties through the Vienna Convention on the Law of Treaties of 1969, justified as it is in principle, poses some problems in certain specific contexts. Thus the rules on successive treaties on the same subject matter[128] are not in all points entirely suitable for world order or human rights treaties: the later treaty should not always prevail *inter partes* by virtue of the *lex posterior* rule if the standard of protection is thereby lowered.[129] Conversely, the rules on interpretation of treaties as enshrined in Articles 31–33 VCLT (1969) can be applied to all treaties because they leave considerable room for manoeuvring and adaptation. The legal operator will thus be able to apply them at one end of the spectrum to a bilateral treaty of a transactional nature (where the intention of the parties may in some cases play a greater role than the VCLT seems to admit) and at the other end of the spectrum to a multilateral treaty setting objective norms, eg an institutional treaty, where dynamic and teleological factors, subsequent practice, mobile inter-temporal references and the reduction of importance of preparatory work will prevail.[130] If the rules on interpretation had been drafted in a more rigid way, the uniform approach would have been manifestly problematic.

The application of treaties is coloured by the usual difficulties relating to the decentralisation of the international legal fact. All the interactions between the law and the life of treaties can be captured in a double lens: on the one hand the ideal aspiration to reduce the plurality of interests to the unity of the agreed legal regime; and on the other hand the relentless task of splitting up the unity apparently reached into the plurality of the real interests at stake. This permanent tension between the normative universalism and the real particularism creates and nourishes the main difficulties in the application of the agreement. Thus,

[128] See in particular Art 30, §3 VCLT.

[129] See K Zemanek, 'The Legal Foundations of the International System' (1997) 266 *RCADI* 225ff. The application of the *lex posterior* rule, as enshrined in Art 30, §3, VCLT, may thus not be adequate for human rights treaties. Indeed, the later treaty may lower the standards of the earlier, especially if it is universal and follows in time a tougher regional treaty. But this odd result will not ensue as regards the ECHR by reason of the express clause contained in Art 53 ECHR. It provides for the priority of the human rights instrument offering the wider protection. The ECHR would thus prevail for the parties when it offers greater protection. Even in other situations, the lowering of standards is not always acceptable. It is possible to argue that the parties to the later universal treaty did not intend to derogate from an earlier, more protective regional agreement; that the norms in the regional convention are more precise, ie are *lex specialis* and not automatically superseded by a later, more general norm; that the treaties are not on the 'same subject matter' in the sense of Art 30 VCLT by reason of the regional speciality; that the conditions for a derogation from the more general treaty under Art 41, § 1, letter b, of the VCLT are not fulfilled, etc.

[130] These rules have been applied even to State contracts under investment law: see, eg, *Eurotunnel* Award, Permanent Court of Arbitration, Partial Award of 30 January 2007, §92 (consulted on <www.pca-cpa.org>). On this award, see M Audit, 'The Channel Tunnel Group Ltd and France-Manche SA v UK and France, Partial Award on Jurisdiction' (2008) 57 *ICLQ* 724ff.

the apparent unity of the treaty can often be broken down into a large number of special regimes through reservations. This perilous tendency has spawned the emergence of some ultimately insufficient limitations, such as the 'object and purpose' test of Article 19 VCLT. The insufficiency of the limitations stems from the fact that there is no objective control of the validity of reservations in general international law, and that the matter thus rests on unilateral claims. A multilateral treaty concluded between 'n' parties can be split down into 'n (n-1): 2' bilateral relationships. This means that a treaty concluded between virtually all States of the world, say 194 States, could technically, through reservations, be multiplied to comprise 18,721 special regimes. Fortunately, in practice the problems with reservations have not been so much quantitative as they have been qualitative. These problems occurred mainly in certain areas of international law, such as human rights treaties.[131] The pressure of an invisible 'world community', and in particular of Western States taking a moralising stance not always devoid of hypocrisy, pushes each and every State to feel obliged to ratify human rights treaties, so as not to be branded the notorious bad guy of international relations. But there are some States—such as Djibouti or Saudi Arabia—where, for cultural and religious reasons, the Convention on the Elimination of Discrimination Against Women (1979) or the Convention on the Rights of the Child (1989) unfortunately cannot be applied according to their letter and spirit. The content of these conventions contradicts too openly and too sharply certain social norms and conceptions on family, infused with Islamic, and sometimes even sharia, beliefs. Pushed towards ratification, these States seek to take away with the left hand what they have to concede with the right hand. They formulate reservations of such a sweeping nature that the object and purpose not only of those conventions but of any convention are thereby reduced to naught. Thus, Djibouti has formulated a reservation to the 1989 Convention noted above, according to which it does not consider itself bound by provisions incompatible with 'its religion and traditional values'.[132] These being entirely subjective notions, which Djibouti is the only State to know, the reservation is tantamount to saying that the Convention does not bind Djibouti, or, more

[131] On reservations in human rights treaties, see, eg, JA Carrillo Salcedo, 'Droit international et souveraineté des Etats' (19960 257 *RCADI* 181ff; B Simma, 'From Bilateralism to Community Interest in International Law' (1994) 250 *RCADI* 364ff; L Lijnzaad, *Reservations to UN Human Rights Treaties* (Dordrecht, 1994); I Ziemele (ed), *Reservations to Human Rights Treaties and the Vienna Convention Regime* (Leiden, 2004); A Pellet and D Müller, 'Reservations to Human Rights Treaties' in *Essays in Honour of B. Simma (From Bilateralism to Community Interest)* (Oxford, 2011) 521ff; I Ziemele and L Liede, 'Reservations to Human Rights Treaties' (2013) 24 *EJIL* 1135ff. See also the short overview in W Kälin and J Künzli, *The Law of International Human Rights Protection* (Oxford, 2009) 125ff. And see Human Rights Committee, General Comment 24 (52), General comment on issues relating to reservations made upon ratification or accession to the Covenant or the Optional Protocols thereto, or in relation to declarations under article 41 of the Covenant, UN Doc CCPR/C/21/Rev.1/Add.6 (1994). Compare also C Redgwell, 'Reservations to Treaties and Human Rights Committee General Comment No 24' (1997) 46 *ICLQ* 390ff, and the *Eurotunnel* Award and Audit, above n 130.

[132] See *Multilateral Treaties Deposited with the Secretary General*, vol I, UN Doc ST/LEG/SER.E/19. This is periodically updated.

precisely, that it is subjected to a purely potestative condition, so that Djibouti is free to make up its mind, in every single case, whether it will apply the instrument or not. How this can be squared with the binding nature of treaties and the rule that municipal law cannot be invoked as an excuse for not honouring the conventional obligation (*pacta sunt servanda*, Articles 26–27 VCLT) is not clear. The point is not to pass judgment on the social orders of those States, which we may well regret; the point is rather to insist on the fact that it is not through human rights treaties that such firmly entrenched social conceptions can be wiped out. The law of treaties here becomes the hostage of political gambling, and of pressures and counter-pressures situated in the twilight.

Another question has been whether world order treaties, and in particular human rights treaties, should be treated differently from other treaties, say in matters of interpretation, of validity of reservations, on account of termination, etc. There is no reason for this, apart from the obvious fact that the particular object and purpose of such treaties will have some effect within the four corners of treaty law. Sometimes, the law provides for a specificity for some treaties, and then this *lex specialis* has to be followed. This is the case, for example, under Article 60, §5 VCLT and related customary law, with regard to termination of 'humanitarian treaties' (ie human rights and law of armed conflict treaties of a humanitarian nature).[133] Conversely, there are also treaties concluded to consolidate power positions or influences of one group of States over other States. Even these treaties have to be appreciated in the light of the general rules on the law of treaties, without being oblivious to the special context in which they are cast. The political background of these instruments and their tendency to be affected by political fluctuations nevertheless make them frequently more vulnerable than other instruments to fundamental changes of circumstances and revision. There is here potentially some encroachment on the conventional armature overlaid with *pacta sunt servanda*.[134] This may be the case, for example, for treaties concerning zones of influence, alliances or (anciently) protectorates.

The modification of treaties does not occur only according to the formal modalities as expressed in its clauses. These provisions, if they exist at all, remain subject to the subsequent practice of the States parties. The latter can manifest

[133] On this provision, sponsored at the Vienna Conference by Switzerland, see B Simma and C Tams, 'Article 60' in O Corten and P Klein (eds), *The Vienna Convention on the Law of Treaties, A Commentary*, vol II (Oxford, 2011) 1366–68; T Giegerich, 'Article 60' in O Dörr and K Schmalenbach (eds), *Vienna Convention on the Law of Treaties, A Commentary* (Heidelberg, 2012) 1045–47. See also M Gomaa, *Suspension or Termination of Treaties on Grounds of Breach* (The Hague/Boston/London, 1996) 106ff; C Laly-Chevalier, *La violation du traité* (Brussels, 2005) 448ff.

[134] The opinion held by some German writers in the 1920s and 1930s, according to which there are 'legal treaties' and 'political treaties', the former with an ordinary application of international law and the latter with a primacy of the 'vital interests'-exception as subjectively interpreted by each State, has rightly been rejected since the end of World War II. It would amount to negating any legal value to treaties of a 'political' nature, without the category being definable in any objective sense. For such an old-fashioned opinion, see eg C. Bilfinger, 'Les bases fondamentales de la communauté des Etats' (1938-I) 63 *RCADI* 140ff.

a new agreement (applicable as *lex posterior*); and it creates legitimate expectations as to the continuity of the behaviour previously experienced (good faith). The ink of the treaty once adopted is hardly dry before possible modifying forces are at work.[135] The *Franco-American Air Services* case (1963)[136] and the *Houston Contracting Company* case (1988),[137] or still, in diplomatic practice, the German-Swiss Convention of 1952 on the assistance of indigents,[138] are emblematic in this regard. For subsequent practice of a 'constitutional nature', one might recall the interpretation given to Article 27, §3 of the UN Charter through a persistent practice of the members of the Security Council, whereby the abstention of one of the five permanent members was not computed as a veto, contrary to the clear wording of the provision. From the first meetings of the Council, during the Greek and Iranian crises after World War II, there was acceptance of this new practice.[139] It enriched Soviet foreign policy with a new instrument of action: abstention to show dissatisfaction, a negative vote to veto the decision.

Customary international law may generally derogate from a treaty by virtue of the *lex posterior* rule. But this will be a rare occurrence, since the later customary rule will infrequently relate directly to the treaty norms (*lex posterior generalis non derogat legi priori specialis*). Moreover, the legal regime of successive treaties (Articles 30, 41 VCLT) remains quite uncertain, apart from the reach of some general principles. Legal operators will often be guided by case-to-case considerations. This state of affairs is tantamount to admitting a locally insufficient penetration of the legal discipline into the body of the law of treaties. The recent tendency to accord some primacy to 'world order treaties' in a hierarchical setting does nothing to simplify matters. Priorities and derogations are then claimed according to the closeness of a treaty's content to the international public order.[140] But this public order and the priorities to which it gives rise should be organised carefully if one wants to avoid a relentless subjectivism, which would ultimately deal a fatal blow to *pacta sunt servanda*.[141]

There remain uncertainties with regard to certain questions relating to time or the number of States parties. Here are two examples. *First*, what shall be done with respect to objections formulated in relation to late reservations? What shall be done if a reservation is lodged after ratification or accession, ie too late from the point of view of the applicable law (Articles 2, §1, letter d, and 19 VCLT)? Practice has relaxed the time requirement applicable according to the VCLT. The depositary, or the reserving State directly if there is no depositary, will consult

[135] See the very solid monograph by W Karl, *Vertrag und spätere Praxis im Völkerrecht* (Berlin, 1983).

[136] *Franco-American Air Services* (1963), XVI *RIAA* 60ff.

[137] *Houston Contracting Company* (1988) 20 *Iran/US Claims Tribunal Reports* 56.

[138] (1998) 8 *RSDIE* 630.

[139] G Day, *Le droit de veto dans l'Organisation des Nations Unies* (Paris, 1952) 115ff. On the crisis of collective security in the first years of the UN, see F van Langenhove, *La crise du système de sécurité collective des Nations Unies, 1946–1957* (Brussels/The Hague, 1958).

[140] See A Orakhelashvili, *Peremptory Norms in International Law* (Oxford, 2006).

[141] See R Kolb, *Peremptory International Law (Jus Cogens)* (Oxford, 2015).

the other parties, laying down a certain time for objections (normally 90 days, according to the seminal practice of the UN Depositary). If there are no objections within this time, the reservation is considered to be accepted; if there are objections, the reservation is rejected. The question would then arise whether the reservation can be applied at least between the late reserving State and those not having objected. Certain unexpected problems can then surface. Here is one example from Swiss practice.[142] How does the time limit of 90 days relate to the ordinary limit of 12 months to react to a reservation (Article 20, §5 VCLT)? Treaty parties might, during the 90 days, react to the admissibility of the reservation in view of its *lateness*. But they might also seize that occasion to express themselves on the *substantive admissibility* of the reservation, eg its compatibility with the object and purpose of the treaty. Normally a time limit of 12 months is applicable to this latter aspect, by virtue of the previously mentioned provision. Can the 90-days practice of the depositary derogate from this longer time limit? In other words, can the rights of the States parties be thus curtailed? The question arises all the more since States react most often to both aspects, lateness and substance, by the same legal act. The Swiss Legal Directorate did not take a final position on this issue. It made a vague reference to the circumstances and to consultation of the parties.[143] The legally correct position would probably be to apply the 90-day timespan to both issues, in view of the fact that, according to the applicable law, a reservation cannot in principle be lodged at all after ratification/accession. Thus, the 12-month delay does not formally apply at all in such cases. If objections are to be made, whichever aspect they bear, they would have to be made in the extraordinary shorter time-span apparently accepted in this regard. Considerations of legal certainty buttress this position. The reservation being late, and the exigency of legal certainty being important in the context of treaties, the point must be settled quickly. This is all the more so since the treaty is already in force and the parties must know how to apply it. In another instance of a late reservation to a convention of which Switzerland was the depositary, there had been three objections within the stated time of 90 days. Thus, the reservation could not be registered as such by the depositary. However, the aspects of the reserving declaration not implying a modification of the rights and obligations under the treaty could continue to stand as a free-riding interpretative understanding. Moreover, the question was again raised whether the objection made within the 90 days must refer solely to the lateness, or whether it could also cover substantive aspects of the reservations; and whether after the 90-day limit the depositary must impose a new time limit of 12 months, or perhaps of nine months (12 months minus 90 days), for substantive objections.[144] The better view is, as already said, that the 90 days must be considered the applicable time limit for both types of objections.

142 (2010) 20 *RSDIE* 516.
143 *ibid*, 517; see also 519.
144 *ibid*, 519.

Secondly, there exist questions relative to the entry into force of an amendment to a multilateral convention. Article 40 VCLT left open some crucial questions, which have had to be resolved by relevant subsequent practice. One of these questions relates to the moment of entry into force of the amended version of a multilateral treaty. Assume that a treaty clause provides that the amendment shall enter into force for all States parties when two-thirds of the States parties have ratified it. The amendment is adopted, say, on 1 January 2000; the Convention has at that time 60 States parties. On the 1 January 2015, 40 States have ratified the amendment. Does the amended treaty enter into force if there are now 90 States parties to the original convention? In other words, is the relevant date for the two-thirds of the States parties the date of the adoption of the amendment (2000), or the date of its entry into force (2015)? If it is the former, 40 ratifications bring the amendment into force; if it is the latter, the amendment will enter into force only when 60 States have ratified or acceded to it, and possibly the figure will change again if further States become parties to the original treaty. From this theoretical perspective, the date of the adoption of the amendment would be the better point of reference. It provides for legal certainty: the number of ratifications needed is known from the outset and remains fixed. Moreover, as a majority of the States voted for the amendment, it seems straightforward to facilitate its entry into force rather than to delay it. As far as the newcomer States are concerned, Article 40, §5 VCLT presumes that they want to be bound by the amended version (once it entered into force), provided no different intention is indicated. However, this simple solution would possibly impose an amendment ratified by only a minority of the States parties on a majority of them; for example, in our example, 40 States out of 90. This is the reason why the Secretary General of the UN, as depositary of treaties, has adopted the practice of using the 'moving target': the relevant date is that of the purported entry into force of the amendment. At that date two-thirds of the States parties must have ratified or acceded to the amendment. Thus, in our example, 60 ratifications and/or accessions will be required—or possibly 61, 62, etc, as further parties participate in the treaty. If the newcomer States expressly accede to the original treaty and the revised version, they will be counted as having accepted the amendment.

Such examples could be multiplied. Their aim has been to show that the treaty, a source of certainty and stability, cannot be any more certain and stable than the environment in which it is called to operate. This environment is characterised by rapid changes and by the decentralisation of power. These facts impose their own exigencies on the treaty. However, it should not be overlooked that in the very great majority of cases, treaties offer an appreciable degree of protection. Out of the roughly 100,000 treaties currently in force in the world, only an infinitesimal number, ie some hundreds, cause any problems of note. This remains an excellent record for treaty law. This is so true that States, mindful of the strength of the legal obligations incurred by treaties, increasingly hesitate to engage in multilateral regimes and prefer more mobile and flexible soft-law instruments.

E. Soft Law

What is the role of soft law within the sources of international law? What is the meaning of this concept? Here is a current definition:

> Rules whose normative value is considered to be limited because the instruments containing them are not legally binding or because the provisions at stake, contained in a binding instrument, do not create obligations under positive law or create only obligations of a low binding character.[145]

The phrase 'soft law' can thus relate to two distinct phenomena: on the one hand, it may indicate the softness of the *instrument*, ie the fact that the support itself is not binding in law (recommendations, gentlemen's agreements, programs, etc); on the other hand, it may refer to the softness of the *content*, ie the fact that the norms at stake are vaguely formulated so that there is no clear legal obligation flowing from them ('use best efforts to', etc). An example of a treaty containing a series of soft norms is the Framework Climate Change Convention of 1992.[146]

It has been claimed that the existence of soft law reveals the fragmented and complex political configuration of international society. In light of the speed of historical change, international society would need pick up the pace in the production of flexible new norms. Traditional sources could not ensure the necessary swiftness of response; nor could they guarantee the necessary flexibility; nor were they necessarily adapted to certain new areas of international law. In their first phase, soft-law instruments were complementary to the law and remained politely outside its realm. In their second phase, these norms were progressively instilled into the international legal body. The ancient positivistic equation 'law = bindingness' was thus watered down.[147] Legal doctrine has emphasised certain corollary legal effects that soft-law texts may display:[148] a duty to take account of the recommendations; the non-availability of 'domestic jurisdiction' arguments; permissive effects; triggers for estoppel; the duty to give reasons for contrary conduct; the reversal of burdens of proof; the influence on the formation of customary or conventional law; the influence on interpretation of hard law, etc.

There are also some more disquieting effects. Soft law has not remained confined to areas that hard law cannot encompass immediately or at all; it has stretched progressively to touch all areas of international law. The result has been a certain degree of dilution of the normative content and certainty of the international legal order. Thus, for example, soft law has increasingly made its way into treaties. It has

[145] J Salmon (ed), *Dictionnaire de droit international public* (Brussels, 2001) 1039, our translation.

[146] (1992) 31 *ILM* 849ff.

[147] For a positive appraisal of soft law, see G Abi-Saab, 'Eloge du "droit assourdi": Quelques réflexions sur le rôle de la soft law en droit international contemporain' in *Essays in Honor of F. Rigaux* (Brussels, 1993) 59ff.

[148] See, eg, M Virally, 'La distinction entre textes internationaux ayant une portée juridique entre leurs auteurs et textes qui en sont dépourvus', *Annuaire IDI*, 1983, 166, 328ff. See also W Heusel, *'Weiches' Völkerrecht* (Baden-Baden, 1991).

coloured legal opinion in the context of the formation of customary international law and concomitantly weakened the need to show an effective practice (hence the emergence of a 'soft custom'). It has also formatted general principles of its own, such as the 'obligations to cooperate' in environmental matters, the 'duties of due regard', the obligation of 'equitable use and share' in natural resources, etc. It is true that certain of these developments express a need to make the law more flexible. But it also occurs that the aim of the indeterminate formulae is to give States room to manoeuvre in a way that is utterly incompatible with the most elementary certainty of the legal injunction. In such cases, international law is weakened more than served.

Conversely, it also occurs that agreement on some soft guidelines may be better than no agreement at all. The soft norms can give a certain direction to the development of the law and canalise the discretionary powers of States. In other cases, these soft engagements serve rather to mask the absence of real agreement behind the use of dilatory formulations. Here, it might be sometimes better to openly admit the lack of consensus rather than to cloak it in vague and incantatory words, creating expectations that will fall to be disappointed. In this case, the perception of many non-initiated observers is that international law has—once more—failed in its mission and glaringly demonstrated its ineffectiveness. The integrity of the law might be better served by an open admission of the lack of any agreement to create an obligation, accompanied by a severe critique of the timidity of States having led to this result, rather than by cobbling together a fanciful obligation that will not be respected. It is current experience that an all too frequent hiatus between proclamations and realities (even through intelligently crafted formulations that leave constant leeway for argument) tends to weaken the image of, and ultimately respect for, the legal order. The reality of international life shows, however, that soft law has continued its steady climb, and that many important normative instruments of the day—eg in the context of private military companies[149]—are cast in this mode.

It is possible to summarise the main reasons for the development of the soft law phenomenon and its main advantages and dangers. First, the main reasons for the development of soft law are as follows:

1. the considerable increase in the number of States after 1945 and the considerable division in ideological beliefs, which has rendered it more difficult to find compromises and agreement on hard obligations;
2. the considerable diversification of the actors, spanning civil society, eg through a myriad of non-governmental organisations (NGOs), which cannot become party to hard-law instruments (treaties);
3. the constantly increasing mobility and complexity of the questions to be regulated, which need frequent and quick revisions of the technical norms, where the conventional process is much too burdensome;

[149] See M Sassoli, A Bouvier and A Quintin, *How Does Law Protect in War?*, vol I, 3rd edn (Geneva, 2011) 172ff, with many references.

4. an increasing fear of engaging oneself through hard-law instruments and of being caught in a net of limitations upon freedom and sovereignty;
5. the existence of an agreement on some rules and principles, but also on the choice not to render them binding in law, especially when States are not prepared to assume international legal responsibility for breaches or non-conforming behaviour. This may occur, for example, when States want to test a certain regime and only later, enriched with experience, possibly cross the line into accepting hard obligations.

Secondly, the main advantages of the soft-law process are as follows:

1. There is sometimes a real hunger for norms, so that it seems impractical to wait for the possible future formation of hard norms. Many actors demand standards to govern their action, and fear the emptiness of pure discretion (the present writer has witnessed this tendency in the army, where the commanders are not always happy with the answer 'there is nothing specific or clear-cut').
2. There is a possibility to experiment with the working of soft provisions, with all their flexibility, before agreeing on a binding legal regime at a later date. Thus, States first signposted the law of outer space by the adoption of some principles contained in Resolution 1962 of the UN General Assembly; only with the experience of some years' space-faring did it became possible to adopt the Outer Space Treaty of 1967.
3. The soft norms can be adopted quickly to address urgent needs, and can be adapted with celerity to react to changes in the relevant environment.
4. Soft law allows the association of non-State actors in the normative process. Thus, the normative expressions are extended and to some extent 'democratised', ie founded on a larger and more inclusive participation. Within inter-State relations, the soft law may be the expression of the many as against the few. The resolutions of the UN General Assembly are an example in point. True, these resolutions are no longer granted high esteem in the West, since the third world States dominate the Assembly and have their conceptions expressed there. It was different when the UN was still dominated by the Western States, as was the case between 1945 and 1960.
5. Soft law allows, when necessary, the ensured confidentiality of the adopted norms. This may be an important asset in military matters or commercial secrets.

Thirdly, there are also drawbacks of soft law, essentially as follows:

1. There is a constant tendency to blur the normativity and to merge the law and the non-law into each other, ie law and policy. The hard law may be affected by a loss of credibility and solidity.[150]

[150] This aspect has been emphasised by P Weil, 'Vers une normativité relative en droit international?' (1982) 86 *RGDIP* 5ff (English translation in P Weil, 'Towards Relative Normativity in International

2. The use of soft norms may mask the absence of any true agreement, and therefore create illusory expectations on compliance. This state of affairs has been witnessed more than once in the context of the natural environment, even if the relevant norms were not all deprived of effect.
3. It may occur that that consciousness of the non-binding nature of the norms created leads the negotiators into a feckless over-reaching and superficiality, where illusory norms are adopted in the knowledge that ultimately they engage with little or nothing. Public opinion and the media can then be waved off with apparent success. Overall it would, however, be wrong to consider that hard-law norms are generally well-respected and that soft-law norms have a poor record. Examples, such as the famous Helsinki Final Act of 1975,[151] show that soft law may have a considerable vitality and accomplish far from negligible political-legal results.

Soft-law instruments nourish the development of a series of 'vines' attached to the body of international law. They sometime enhance its resistance and diversify its reach, while at other times they smother it. Initially, soft law was a separate source of normativity; it then quickly became an inherent normative modality within each source of international law. As an instrument blurring or reinforcing normativity, soft law adds to the complexity of the international legal order. It is possible to subscribe to the following considered description:

> These instruments [of soft law] are situated in the context of the binding norms, and it is as difficult to sever them completely from the legal universe as it is to precisely define their effects. It is possible to deplore the risks of intellectual confusion ensuing. However, if States engage on this path, this shows that they have an interest in doing so. Notwithstanding, or perhaps because of the imprecision of their status, soft law norms perform in the eyes of the States useful functions.[152]

It remains to be observed that very often today, soft law functionally operates as law. We have here entered into the realm of the 'as-if'.

F. Final Considerations

From the standpoint of its sources, international law is characterised by the following features:

1. There is the extreme breadth of the normative spectrum, ranging from the universal principle to the particular norm geared towards a unique situation.

Law ?' (1983) 77 *AJIL* 413ff); P Weil, 'Le droit international en quête de son identité' (1992-VI) 237 *RCADI* 213, 230ff. See also the discussion in U Fastenrath, 'Relative Normativity in International Law' (1993) 4 *EJIL* 305ff.

[151] JF Prévost, 'Observations sur la nature juridique de l'Acte final de la CSCE' (1975) 21 *AFDI* 129ff. For an appraisal of the results of this Act, see W Heusel, *'Weiches' Völkerrecht* (Baden-Baden, 1991) 166ff.

[152] J Combacau and S Sur, *Droit international public*, 8th edn (Paris, 2008) 53.

2. There is a poly-normativity and an overlap of the sources, eg the contemporaneous applicability of conventional and customary norms, the coexistence of nascent and dying norms, etc.
3. There is the existence of a series of bilateral and relative legal situations, ranging from prescriptive titles to *inter se* modification of rules, to special regimes, to regional and local customs, to reservations or persistent objections, etc.
4. There is an absence of any hierarchy of sources. The applicable norms are in most cases an expression of States' practice, and therefore there is no reason to grant them any hierarchically different status. However, there is an increasing tendency to instill some primacy at the level of the substance of norms, notably through the *jus cogens* technique.
5. There is a normativity of significantly different quality, spanning from soft to hard law, and sometimes blurring the line between *lex lata* and *lex ferenda*.
6. We have to note the tendency often to individualise legal situations beneath some set of quite generic principles or rules.
7. There exists a number of material gaps in the law, for example cases where it has proved impossible to adopt a norm on account of too great a divergence between States and their interests. This sometimes renders necessary contrived legal arguments, through extensive interpretation, postulation of customary rules not yet well matured, the praying into help of some general principles or analogies, etc.
8. There is a pronounced tendency to preserve the acquired and current law by reason of the difficulties involved in changing it (*quieta non movere*).

These particularities of the international legal order explain the complex and sometimes adventurous law-creating processes, and the difficulties involved in their doctrinal rationalisation. However, these difficulties have also their advantages. They force the mind to remain critical, confronting it constantly with unexpected problems and requiring from it a considerable degree of flexibility and willingness to adapt.

The sources of international law express the idea of some objective law in a society traversed by subjective forces. These forces seek to individualise the rule as much as possible, so as to mould it to their particular needs and interests. The aim is to subject the rule to the fluctuations and contingencies that are inseparable from political action. The more a rule is contextualised and complex, the more responsive it will be to attempts to bend it to particular political agendas. At the same time, the objective side of international legal rules tends to resist such attempts at instrumentalisation. The norms impose their injunctions on States. The result is a highly interesting struggle by the law in defence of its integrity and of policy for the realisation of its aims. Law and politics are in this regard fused together in a never-ending *pas de deux*.

V. The Structural Principles of International Law

International law is based on a series of structural features, which now fall to be discussed. In the light of these structural aspects, the material principles and norms of international law appear in a new framework. The structural aspects to be discussed below do not form part of international law but explain and underlie it; they abstract from its nature and functioning a series of explanatory criteria.

A. International Law as Horizontal 'Coordinative Law'

This is certainly the most intimate aspect of international law, to which all the other aspects refer. International law is a law without a common superior; a law without a central legislator, policemen or judge; an anarchical law evolving in the shadows of sovereignty. International law can thus be called a 'law of coordination', because it is marked by the absence of a common superior authority in relation to the individual subjects composing international society.[153] In other words, the fundamental constitutional functions (legislative, executive, judicial) have not been centralised through common organs entrusted with the pursuit of the common good and representing the public collectivity. These functions remain scattered within the various States comprising international society. Each one retains a fraction of these powers that it can use unilaterally. The vertical relationship found in the presence of a superior order is thus largely absent from international law. Basically, it remains a horizontal law coordinating the relationships between sovereign subjects, each one '*superiorem non recognoscens*'.[154] This also means that

[153] See on this issue, among many others, P Reuter, 'Principes de droit international public' (1961-II) 103 *RCADI* 438ff; R Monaco, *Manuale di diritto internazionale pubblico*, 2nd edn (Turin, 1971) 13ff; H Mosler, 'General Course on Public International Law' (1974-IV) 140 *RCADI* 31; F Berber, *Lehrbuch des Völkerrechts*, vol I, 2nd edn (Munich, 1975) 16ff; A Truyol y Serra, 'Cours général de droit international public' (1981-IV) 173 *RCADI* 46ff; P Weil, 'Le droit international en quête de son identité, Cours général de droit international public' (1992-VI) 237 *RCADI* 203ff. This feature has been forcefully defended in Germany, see eg J Hatschek, *Völkerrecht* (Leipzig/Erlangen, 1923) 1ff.

[154] The absence of a superior authority must not be taken in absolute terms. Even if there exist some superior institutions, a legal order may remain coloured by the basic structure of horizontality. The main point is that there is no regular superior authority, and that any that exist are based only on special agreements, ie on particular international law. Thus, the powers of the Security Council, though not supranational, under ch VII of the UN Charter, can be described as a gentle form of world federalism. But this 'international government' is strictly limited as to its scope, since it can take action only in the context of threats or breaches to international peace; and even then, it is devoid of its own mechanisms of enforcement, so that the cooperation of States to implement its decisions again becomes crucial. This has been shown graphically in the context of the listing procedures and sanctions against terrorists.

the cornerstone of international law is the equal sovereignty of the States.[155] What in municipal society is the prerogative of public organs, in international society remains the prerogative of each subject taken individually.[156] Thus, private law predominates over public law. The legal order is mainly the result of the exercise of these individual powers. By concluding agreements, the States legislate: they exercise their power to create the law, and thereby also bind themselves to a certain type of conduct. But the implementation of the obligations largely falls back on the unilateral level of self-control and self-implementation. Here again, common mechanisms of control can be introduced only by agreement, ie by particular international law.

The coordinative character of international law is a structural given; but it may evolve. It is therefore impossible to deduce norms of positive law from this structural given. The structural principles are but a snapshot of the legal body at a certain moment. They cannot be used as criteria for judging if a norm exists (which is solely a matter of sources). They also cannot be used to deny the ability of the legal order to change, and possibly not to be fully coordinative anymore (as in the EU). The following argument would thus be wrong: because of the coordinative character of international law, any decision can only be taken with the unanimous agreement of all the States represented.[157] This argument was often raised at the time of the Hague Conferences (1899 and 1907) and later in the League of Nations, where it was reflected in Article 5, §1 of the Covenant.[158] But it has been abandoned in many contexts since then, as the voting rules in the UN[159] and in most international conferences show. International law has not become any less coordinative for this reason: the concrete positive law modalities of voting, and thus the concrete meaning of coordination in this particular context, have just evolved.

The coordinative character of international law still accounts for many of its most intimate features. Here are some examples: the autonomy of the legal bond (contract, not statute); the tendency to favour unanimity in the absence of contrary agreement; the difficulties of peaceful change; the absence of hierarchy among the sources; the relativity of legal situations, which generally apply *inter partes* and not *erga omnes*; the predominance of private law tools over public law

[155] Sovereignty is on the one hand the condition for the existence of an international legal order and also its greatest existential threat. If there was no sovereignty, there would be not international law but federative world law; but since sovereignty means power in a decentralised society, the law and its enforcement remain constantly on the edge of ineffectiveness and weakness. As has been aptly said, 'The fundamental difficulty of subjecting States to the rule of law is that States possess power': JL Brierly, *The Law of Nations*, 6th edn (Oxford, 1963) 48.

[156] See, for German legal history, O von Gierke, *Das deutsche Genossenschaftsrecht*, vol I (Berlin, 1868) 89, where similar structures existed.

[157] See F Berber, *Lehrbuch des Völkerrechts*, vol I, 2nd edn (Munich, 1975) 17.

[158] See the critique in N Politis, *Les nouvelles tendances du droit international* (Paris, 1927) 27ff. For a modern commentary on Art 5 of the Covenant, see G Bartolini, 'Article 5' in R Kolb (ed), *Commentaire sur le Pacte de la Société des Nations* (Brussels, 2015) 205ff.

[159] See mainly Arts 18 and 27 of the UN Charter, voting rules for the General Assembly and the Security Council.

tools; the emphasis placed on the States (basic unit) rather than on the collectivity (community), including the fundamental rights of States, rights of necessity, reservations and other exceptions; the domestic jurisdiction; the territorial organisation granting exclusive and plenary control over delimited spaces; resistance against the recognition of new subjects of the law, eg the long discussions about the status of individuals in international law; the free choice of means principle in the context of the peaceful settlement of disputes; the requirement of consent to be subjected to a mechanism of pacific settlement of disputes; the existence of many rules requiring abstention from action (non-use of force, non-intervention, etc); the importance of reciprocity as a means to enhance respect for the law; the difficulty of promoting a universal public order; the increased importance of unilateral acts in changing legal situations; the absence of a crystallised system for sanctioning violations of the law, etc.

The absence of common superior organs also renders arduous the uniform handling of international facts. International law is most often composed of strands of unilateral, bilateral and multilateral acts, which interact in a certain creative disorder. It is only exceptionally that these multiple acts can be appraised by some common organ, vested with binding powers of decision. Only then are these acts reduced to their objective meaning. In most cases, the power of qualification, interpretation, appreciation and application of the various acts remains subject to the wishes of the subjects of the law themselves.[160] From there flows the particular importance of recognition and of other unilateral acts in the international legal order.[161] Principles like that of good faith, requiring that parties behave mutually according to standards of legitimate expectations, are particularly important in such a naturally chaotic environment.[162] This also explains the mainly bilateral nature of international legal interactions, and the frequent bar on the 'third party' (*pacta tertiis nec nocent nec prosunt*).[163] The inorganic nature of international society has as the effect of creating a multiplicity of special legal positions above and below the main sources of the law, be it through reservations, or special derogatory agreements and the like. A uniform approach to international normativity is thus in most cases impossible.

Moreover, the absence of centralised organs explains the absence of a proper international policy, ie a policy geared towards the common interests of States and humanity. Since each State concentrates within itself the main constitutional functions, and since it jealously guards its particular interests and destiny, the policies proposed on the international plane are but the sum of policies of individual

160 G Abi-Saab, 'Interprétation et auto-interprétation. Quelques réflexions sur leur rôle dans la formation et la résolution du différend international' in *Essays in Honor of R. Bernhardt* (Berlin, 1995) 14ff.

161 See J Verhoeven, *La reconnaissance internationale dans la pratique contemporaine* (Paris, 1975) 817ff; RL Bindschedler, 'Die Anerkennung im Völkerrecht', *Berichte der Deutschen Gesellschaft für Völkerrecht*, vol IV (Karlsruhe, 1961) 2–3.

162 R Kolb, *La bonne foi en droit international public* (Paris, 2000).

163 P Weil, 'Le droit international en quête de son identité, Cours général de droit international public' (1992-VI) 237 *RCADI* 282ff.

States, with all the influences the particular interests impose. The world is governed by the interaction of some 194 national policies. It stands to reason that collective interests find it difficult to secure a foothold in such an environment. They are mainly represented by NGOs and civil society. However, NGOs are deprived of any political powers and of a clear democratic legitimation—not to speak of their frequent lack of sufficient transparency. The result of antagonistic interests and of opposing policies can be illustrated by the issue of the natural environment and climate change since the Rio Conference in 1992. The lack of 'international policies' in this area is the result of the education of the masses: individuals within particular States have, since their youth, been steeped in the culture and interests of their own nation; it is in this context that domestic politics are organised and anchored. The international sphere remains a universe far aloof from the save havens of habit, culture and concrete life.

The absence of common superior organs has a particularly important impact on the issue of interpretation of norms of the law. In international society, interpretation is not naturally considered to be a constitutional function, ie a legal process. It is rather quite often situated in the context of unilateral policies and interests.[164] Self-interpretation prevails over other forms of legal construction. In internal law, self-interpretation is also the ordinary modality of interpretation, and the starting-point for the implementation of contracts. But in the event of a dispute, there is the possibility to take the matter before a judge. The judge will resolve the particular dispute and formulate interpretive guidance for the future. Possibly, the law may then be adapted to changing circumstances. In international society, this constitutional function of interpretation is but weakly developed. Common organs will formulate binding interpretations in only a few cases; moreover, these will be limited to the parties and often entangled with issues of particular law. Frequently, the interpretation proposed will not be binding at all; the States may thus maintain their own views on the matter (as did, for example, many dissenting States after the Advisory Opinion of the ICJ in *Certain Expenses*, 1962).[165]

The precision and consistency of the jurisprudence is also quite different in municipal and in international society. In internal law, there is a continual flow of cases, which allows tribunals to regularly express opinions on various subjects. If there is crisis and change, the more problematic cases will most probably end up being sent for adjudication. In international society, many years may elapse before a certain subject is considered by the judges. Thus, for example, at the ICJ, issues of State immunity were squarely treated only in 2012—in the *Jurisdictional Immunities* case[166]—even though the Court had been in existence for almost 70 years. Moreover, international case law is more often linked to the particular

[164] See the highly interesting monograph by G de Lacharrière, *La politique juridique extérieure* (Paris, 1983) and a tentative answer in R Kolb, *Réflexions sur les politiques juridiques extérieures* (Paris, 2015).

[165] See E Luard, *A History of the United Nations*, vol II: *The Age of Decolonization, 1955–1965* (London, 1989) 443ff. As to the opinion of the Court, see [1962] ICJ Rep 151.

[166] *Jurisdictional Immunities* [2012-I] ICJ Rep 100.

circumstances of highly individualised cases and thus is less generalisable. If crisis and violence erupt, there will be no adjudication.

Lastly, it must be borne in mind that in municipal society, disputes are often resolved by the application or enforcement of the existing law. In international society, on the other hand, disputes are more often resolved by the creation of new law, ie by the conclusion of an agreement between the States in dispute. The free choice of means in the settlement of disputes and the rulings of the PCIJ/ICJ, which really are merely an 'alternative to a friendly and direct settlement between the parties',[167] are emblematic hallmarks of this state of affairs. The result is that interpretation is less able to legally regulate the body of applicable rules in international law than it is in municipal law. The law remains in a more fluid, or semi-fluid, state. It resists the penetration of legal technique, which would imply regularity and impersonality. The law is subject to fluctuations and to important inroads necessitated by political contingencies. In municipal law, the function of interpretation has the double value of policy orientation (when adapting the law to evolving needs) and constitutional legal action (when keeping the law within the four corners of legal discipline). In international law, the policy function remains active but, absent the institutional setting, the constitutional function vanishes. The latter is at best a fluctuating and feeble *ad hoc* function, the threads of which cannot be brought together to form a coherent whole. It would be wrong to say that there is no 'law' in the international legal order (ie that international law is not law at all); the truth is rather that there is little pre-eminence or rule of law in international relations.[168] The steps from regularity to rule, and from rule to ruled behaviour, are and will remain arduous. All the preceding considerations lead to the point that power aspects frequently prevail over legal ones.[169]

As we have seen, the coordinative element in international law is at the heart of all its constructions. It has served to deny the legal nature of international law, to perceive it as a merely nascent legal order, or to conceive of international law as a different type of law. It has also served to suggest that international law is the most evolved form of a legal order, based not on the naked fact of constraint but on the free meeting of minds and spontaneous implementation by the subjects.[170] The debate goes on in the context of the content of the legal order. For some authors, general principles of law have an enhanced role in a legal order based on coordination, since they will have to fill its numerous gaps. Good faith, for example, becomes fundamental in a legal order based on consent. For other authors, the coordinative structure of international law implies that the vague and open-ended

[167] *Free Zones of Upper Savoy and the District of Gex* (1929) PCIJ Series A no 22, 13; *Boundary dispute (Burkina Faso v Mali)* [1986] ICJ Rep 577, §46; *Passage through the Great Belt (Finland v Denmark, interim measures)* [1991] ICJ Rep 20, §35.

[168] JA Pastor Ridruejo, 'Le droit international à la veille du XXe siècle: normes, faits et valeurs, Cours général de droit international public' (1998) 274 *RCADI* 32, 37.

[169] K Zemanek, 'The Legal Foundations of the International System—General Course on Public International Law' (1997) 266 *RCADI* 36.

[170] R Marcic, *Rechtsphilosophie* (Freiburg, 1969) 191, 209 ff, 218.

principles are a non-negligible danger to the stability of the law. Absent a regular judge, they allow the single States too much room for self-serving interpretations and manipulations of a highly subjective complexion. The institutional gap here triggers normative impoverishment. All these debates will remain with us.

B. International Law as 'Primitive' Law?

The so-called primitive character of international law is as often affirmed in legal doctrine[171] as it is challenged.[172] The issue is thus much debated, unlike the coordinative character of the international legal order. The gist of the matter is that the term 'primitive' (which easily carries with it a value judgement) may mean several different things.[173] In most cases, the authors affirming primitiveness have in mind the consequences of the coordinative character of international law,

[171] See among the many: H Kelsen, 'Théorie générale du droit international public' (1932-IV) 42 *RCADI* 131; H Kelsen, 'Théorie du droit international public' (1953-III) 84 *RCADI* 32, 44, 96; H Kelsen, *Reine Rechtslehre* (Leipzig/Vienna, 1934) 131ff; P Guggenheim, *Traité de droit international public*, vol I (Geneva, 1953) 22ff; P Guggenheim, 'Les principes du droit international public' (1952-I) 80 *RCADI* 27; R Piédelièvre, *Précis de droit international public*, vol I (Paris, 1894) 7; JB Whitton, 'La règle pacta sunt servanda' (1934-III) 49 *RCADI* 219; H Lauterpacht, *The Function of Law in the International Community* (Oxford, 1933) 406; H Lauterpacht, 'Règles générales du droit de la paix' (1937-IV) 62 *RCADI* 118; R Ago, *Scienza giuridica e diritto internazionale* (Milan, 1950) 106, fn 2; JP Cot, *La bonne foi en droit international public*, Cours de l'Institut de Hautes Etudes Internationales (Paris, 1968/1969) 12, 33; JP Cot, 'La bonne foi et la conclusion des traités' (1968) 4 *RBDI* 141; J Kunz, 'The Meaning and Range of the norm pacta sunt servanda' (1945) 39 *AJIL* 196; P Vellas, *Droit international public*, 2nd edn (Paris, 1970) 16ff; J Barberis, 'La liberté de traiter des Etats et le *jus cogens*' (1970) 30 *ZaöRV* 24; L Cavaré, *Le droit international public positif*, vol II, 3rd edn (Paris, 1969) 322; JM Mössner, *Einführung in das Völkerrecht* (Munich, 1977) 4–5; B Conforti, 'Cours général de droit international public' (1988-V) 212 *RCADI* 183–84; JPA François, 'Règles générales du droit de la paix' (1938-IV) 66 *RCADI* 256ff; WL Gould, *An Introduction to International Law* (New York, 1957) 580ff; Q Wright, 'The Strengthening of International Law' (1959-III) 98 *RCADI* 112; B Simma, *Das Reziprozitätselement im Zustandekommen völkerrechtlicher Verträge* (Berlin, 1972) 17ff; H Hart, *The Concept of Law* (Oxford, 1961) 226.

[172] G Vedel, 'L'idée d'évolution, la société internationale et le droit des gens' (1939) 46 *RGDIP* 15ff; A Hold-Ferneck, *Lehrbuch des Völkerrechts*, vol I (Vienna,1930) 79–80; A Verdross and B Simma, *Universelles Völkerrecht*, 3rd edn (Berlin, 1984) 33; F Berber, *Lehrbuch des Völkerrechts*, vol I, 2nd edn (Munich, 1975) 19; AP Sereni, *Diritto internazionale*, vol I (Milan, 1956) 106; A Truyol y Serra, 'Cours général de droit international public' (1981-IV) 173 *RCADI* 119; P Weil, 'Le droit international en quête de son identité, Cours général de droit international public' (1992-IV) 237 *RCADI* 203ff; G Abi-Saab, 'Cours général de droit international public' (1987-VII) 207 *RCADI* 123–25. For a general discussion, see M Virally, 'De la prétendue "primitivité" du droit international' in M Virally, *Le droit international en devenir* (Paris, 1990) 91ff. See also M Barkun, *Law without Sanctions: Order in primitive Societies and the World Community* (New Haven, 1968); and R Prieto Bances, 'Derecho internacional y derecho primitivo', *Essays in Honor of L. Sela Sampil*, vol 1, (Oviedo, 1970) 165–79.

[173] In relation to what legal orders or criteria is international law primitive? Is this primitiveness necessary or curable? If primitiveness is meant to signify the relative underdevelopment of international law in certain aspects, how are these aspects selected? Why are only these aspects selected? How are the several aspects weighted? Is the primitiveness nothing other than the sum of the weaknesses, defects and gaps in a legal order at a given moment? If it is that, is the word 'primitiveness' really appropriate? Does the primitiveness judgment refer only to structural aspects of the legal order, or must one also take into account its normative content, which may be significantly more modern? In other words, does primitiveness refer only to the secondary norms relating to the organisation of the legal society, or must the primary norms relating to substantive rights and obligations also be taken into account?

ie the effects of its relativism and pluralism (decentralisation or decentration). The ensuing weakness of the legal phenomenon and the constant threat of excessive political influence may be seen as a sort of 'underdevelopment' of the law. In this regard, international law seems to resemble the law of those societies existing before the emergence of the State with its municipal legal order, involving fragmentation of the sources and private justice in the enforcement of the rules. Thus, Kelsen would write in 1932:

> General international law thus presents in all aspects the features of a primitive legal order: 1) Essentially customary creation of its general rules; ... 2) Absence of specialized organs for legislating and adopting sanctions; .. 3) Collective responsibility and responsibility for result.[174]

There are different schools of thought regarding the primitiveness of international law. Those affirming it and those denying it are examined more closely below.

1. *The Affirmers of Primitiveness*

The bulk of legal doctrine affirming primitiveness does so in regard to the structural aspects of international law, ie the consequences of its coordinative rather than subordinative character.[175] These consequences have already been discussed in section V.A. above. For a number of the authors, the consequences are inescapable. International law cannot ward them off; if it did, it would cease to be an international legal order and transform itself into some federal legal order.[176] This

[174] Kelsen, 'Théorie générale du droit international public', above n 171, 131. In Kelsen, *Reine Rechtslehre*, above n 171, 131, there are the following developments, which we may here leave untranslated: '[D]as Völkerrecht ist noch eine primitive Rechtsordnung. Es steht erst am Anfang einer Entwicklung, die die einzelstaatliche Rechtsordnung bereits zurückgelegt hat. Es zeigt zumindest im Bereich des allgemeinen Völkerrechts und sohin für die ganze Völkerrechtsgemeinschaft noch weitgehende Dezentralisation. Es gibt hier noch keine arbeitsteilig funktionierenden Organe zur Erzeugung und Vollziehung der Rechtsnormen. Die Bildung der generellen Normen erfolgt im Wege der Gewohnheit oder durch Vertrag, das bedeutet: durch die Glieder der Rechtsgemeinschaft selbst und nicht durch ein besonderes Gesetzgebungsorgan. Und ebenso auch die Anwendung der generellen Normen auf den konkreten Fall. Es ist der sich in seinen Interessen verletzt glaubende Staat, der sich selbst zu entscheiden hat, ob der Tatbestand eines Unrechts vorliegt, für den ein anderer Staat verantwortlich ist. Und wenn dieser das behauptete Unrecht leugnet, fehlt es an einer objektiven Instanz, die den Streit in einem rechtlich geregelten Verfahren zu entscheiden hat. Und so ist es auch der in seinem Recht verletzte Staat selbst, der gegen den Rechtsverletzer mit dem vom allgemeinen Völkerrecht eingesetzten Zwangsakt, mit Repressalie oder Krieg, zu reagieren befugt ist. Es ist die Technik der Selbsthilfe, von der auch die Entwicklung der einzelstaatlichen Rechtsordnung ausgegangen ist. Demgemäss herrscht das Prinzip der Kollektiv- und Erfolgs-, nicht das der Individual- oder Schuldhaftung. Die Unrechtsfolge richtet sich nicht gegen den—als Organ des Einzelstaates fungierenden—Menschen, der den Unrechtstatbestand absichtlich oder fahrlässig gesetzt hat, sondern gegen andere, die an ihm in keiner Weise beteiligt und nicht imstande waren, ihn zu verhindern. Repressalie und Krieg treffen nicht die Staatsorgane, die mit ihrer dem Staat zurechenbaren Handlung oder Unterlassung das Völkerrecht verletzt haben, sondern die Masse der das Volk bildenden Menschen ...' See also the consequence noted in A Bleckmann, *Grundprobleme und Methoden des Völkerrechts* (Freibourg/Munich, 1982) 153–54.

[175] This is the case, for example, with Kelsen and Guggenheim, in the works cited above n 171.

[176] TE Holland, *Elements of Jurisprudence*, 6th edn (Oxford, 1893) 339; J de Louter, *Le droit international public positif*, vol I (Oxford, 1920) 59. See also the whole monograph by E Zitelmann, *Die Unvollkommenheit des Völkerrechts* (Munich/Leipzig, 1919); W Burckhardt, *Die Organisation der*

means that international law must perforce remain 'primitive' if it is to remain international law at all. Its evolution can take place only within its own frame of reference. Hence, it can be more or less primitive, realise some improvement on this or that aspect, but it cannot cease to be 'primitive'. The latter trait is a necessary given on which international law stands or falls. In other words, a non-primitive international law is a contradiction in terms. From the political perspective, this way of thinking may easily lead to keeping international law in a subordinate position: this legal order will then always remain a lower law, a law at the outer border or on the fringes of the legal phenomena, a law at the vanishing point of jurisprudence. The anarchy of legal qualifications and the absence of an organised centralised sanction condemns the international legal order to eternal juridical damnation. Born under a maleficent star, it has to perform Sisyphean forced labour throughout its existence without reaping adequate results.

According to another point of view, international law's primitiveness designates only the insufficiencies and imperfections of that legal order in its present form of organisation.[177] Primitiveness is not here a necessary given. It is a sum of historically contingent defects. The destiny of international law is to develop itself towards the strands of a more perfected legal order. The ultimate model must be the vertical, subordinative and organic legal system of the modern State. Thus, '[i]nternational law can be considered as part of the law only if its actual imperfections are considered to be transient. … If they are considered to be permanent, international law completely disappears from the province of law'.[178] This leaves the following alternative: either international law is considered to be necessarily primitive, and then it is not part and parcel of law; or international law is considered to be temporarily imperfect, and then it is a legal order whose weakness will disappear progressively, in the wake of its constant development. Primitiveness is here but a catchword for all the imperfections of the legal order at a given time. Politically, the perspective has completely changed. An optimistic outlook can be proposed to the reader. International law may be as imperfect as it is today. However, there is the implicit promise that it will evolve and progressively perfect itself. Perhaps even that the reader can contribute to its happy destiny and rising star. Such a perception is entirely in line with the important functions assigned to international law, notably to ensure international order and keep the peace within international society. The robust qualification of 'primitiveness' serves here merely as an expression of the disappointment that international law is not yet already more perfected. In a sense, the primitiveness in this context has positive connotations: international law will live, and its imperfections will fall.

Rechtsgemeinschaft (Basle, 1927). On these last two authors: A Truyol y Serra and R Kolb, *Doctrines sur le fondement du droit des gens* (Paris, 2007) 54ff; GA Walz, *Wesen des Völkerrechts und Kritik der Völkerrechtsleugner* (Stuttgart, 1930) 88ff, 97ff.

[177] Lauterpacht, 'Règles générales du droit de la paix', above n 171, 118–21.

[178] *ibid*, 119, our translation. The English original could be found in the *Collected Papers* of Sir Hersch Lauterpacht.

2. The Deniers of Primitiveness

Many of the deniers of international law's primitiveness criticise the point of reference of that judgement. This point of reference is manifestly the 'perfected' legal order within the State, ie municipal law. Thus international law is accused of not being like internal law. However, by definition international law could not be like internal law. International law is regulating a significantly different society. It must be judged in its capacity to adequately accomplish the functions required from it within its own society. In this regard, it seems inadequate to take as the exclusive basis of induction for all legal phenomena and for the perfection of all law the legal order of the modern State. Law existed before the State emerged; and it was different from the modern law because it regulated a society organised in a different way. Thus, 'the point is not so much, indeed, to insist on a difference of "development" between international law and municipal law; it is to understand that there is a difference of structure'.[179] And '[i]nternational law is a different law much more than a primitive law'.[180] In simple terms, international society has its own structure and needs; thus, international law has also its own structure so as to suit the parameters of the society it is meant to regulate. In political terms, this leads to the result that international law should not evolve and perfect itself by emulating the standards of municipal law. That would be tantamount to postulating a senseless race. If that emulation occurred, international law would no longer be adapted to the features and needs of international society. It could then perhaps be qualified as 'perfect', but it would cease to have any usefulness for the relations occurring in real international society. In this sense, it would be 'perfect' in the theoretical sense and wholly 'imperfect' in the practical sense; it would float through the air and cease to be applicable in practice. In sum, from this perspective, international law is a fully-fledged legal order.[181] And it is not working its way towards a greater perfection according to standards borrowed from the municipal law experience.[182]

[179] Truyol y Serra, above n 172, 119. See also G Barile, 'La structure de l'ordre juridique international, Règles générales et règles conventionnelles' (1978-III) 161 *RCADI* 21; Weil, above n 320, 203ff; Verdross and Simma, above n 172, 33; Berber, above n 172, 19; Virally, above n 172, 98: 'International law is not at a stage of evolution less advanced than the majority of municipal laws: in relation to the latter, it presents itself … as a different type of law' (our translation).

[180] Virally, above n 172, 92.

[181] Hence the criticism levied against authors denying the legal nature of international law, such as J Austin, *Lectures on Jurisprudence or the Philosophy of Positive Law*, vol I, 5th edn (London, 1885) 79ff. On this author, see, eg, A Truyol y Serra and R Kolb, *Doctrines sur le fondement du droit des gens* (Paris, 2007) 34–36; GA Walz, *Wesen des Völkerrechts und Kritik der Völkerrechtsleugner* (Stuttgart, 1930) 4ff, 56ff.

[182] An opinion often held by legal philosophers, eg, I Vanni *Filosofia del diritto* (Bologna, 1920) 81; G del Vecchio, *Lezioni di filosofia del diritto*, 3rd edn (Rome, 1936) 230–31; W Schönfeld, *Die logische Struktur der Rechtsordnung* (Leipzig, 1927) 56; H Ryffel, *Rechts- und Staatsphilosophie* (Neuwied, 1969) 188; N Bobbio, *Il positivismo giuridico* (Turin, 1996) 156. On this aspect, see GA Walz, *Wesen des Völkerrechts und Kritik der Völkerrechtsleugner* (Stuttgart, 1930) 88ff. *Contra*, H Henkel, *Einführung in die Rechtsphilosophie*, 2nd edn (Munich, 1977) 124.

Other authors challenge the qualification of primitiveness on the basis of an analysis of the material content of the international legal order.[183] International law is primitive neither in its primary rules, which are as developed as those of the most modern internal legal orders and are often destined to be incorporated into them, nor in its secondary rules on the creation and application of the material norms, which are even more sophisticated than those of the municipal orders because they regulate a more complex society.[184] Primitive societies are based on sacral and formalistic rules; international society has rules that have entirely different parameters from this point of view. Non-formalism predominates here even more markedly than in internal societies. The term 'primitiveness' is dangerous, since it connotes a series of unwarranted value judgements.

Lastly, there is an opinion that international law is not a primitive legal order but rather the most perfected law existing and imaginable.[185] International law is based on an exacting notion of inclusiveness and 'democracy': the subjects of the law participate directly in the law-making and none can be bound against its will. Municipal law norms must often be imposed on the recalcitrant by force; in international law there is free and informed adhesion to the norms. From this perspective, municipal law is primitive. It rules the conduct of the self-interested and irresponsible, who constantly attempt to escape from the empire of the law and who have to be compelled through the threat of sanctions. Conversely, international law regulates relations among much more thoughtful and mature subjects, who have carefully calculated the relative advantages and disadvantages of each action, and who are generally sympathetic to the rules to which they were free to bind themselves.

3. *Conclusion*

Seen from the structural point of view (the only one where the judgement of primitiveness may have some justification)[186], international law is based on a social-legal organisation that resembles the legal orders of the European Middle Ages. This is the case notably with regard to the decentralisation of power. In this equation, there are two basic types of law: either the State-type model based on subordination and which is 'non-primitive'; or the decentralised model based on coordination and which is 'primitive'. The word 'primitive' must here obviously be taken as a simple reference to the characteristics of the centralised or decentralised legal models, and not as a value judgement (but for that very reason the term is

[183] Abi-Saab, above n 172, 123–24.

[184] *ibid*, 124.

[185] R Marcic, *Rechtsphilosophie* (Freiburg, 1969) 191, 209ff, 218.

[186] There is generally agreement that from the point of view of its substance, international law is not primitive. Quite to the contrary, its rules and procedures are highly developed: see G Ziccardi Capaldo, *Diritto globale, Il nuovo diritto internazionale* (Milan, 2010).

also inadequate). Some common traits between international law and the legal orders of the European Middle Ages may be briefly recalled:

1. the horizontal distribution of power, from the clans to the Roman paterfamilias, and in the Middle Ages to the jurisdiction of the various holders of power;[187]
2. the recourse to private justice, ie to reprisals and unilateral action;[188]
3. the splitting-up of the sources (graphically called in the German language '*Rechtszersplitterung*') into a multiplicity of rules with different scopes of application;[189]
4. the role of general principles trying to unify the scattered body of particular rules;[190]
5. the difficulties of changing the law because of requirements of unanimity and the protection of vested rights,[191] etc.

Having said all that, is international law really a 'primitive' law? At the end of the day, the issue is merely one of the definition of terms. However, the danger of the term 'primitive' is to imperceptibly shift from a purely descriptive dimension, concerning the coordinative structure of international law, to a normative judgement connoting the necessity of progress and change, the maximum approximation of municipal legal experiences, and so on. It is not true that the imperfections of international law cannot be smoothed out; it is not correct to say that progress is impossible if international law has to maintain its fundamental characteristics. A world State appears utopian for the time being.[192] But less than a world State remains open to determined efforts at political reform. In any case there remains the fact that international law must respond to the needs of international society and international political realities, not to some pre-conceived ideal of a legal

[187] See, eg, F Calasso, *Medio Evo del diritto*, vol I (Milan, 1954) 499ff.

[188] See, eg, for the Germanic law circle, E Kaufmann, 'Fehde' in A Erler and E Kaufmann (eds), *Handwörterbuch zur deutschen Rechtsgeschichte*, vol I (Berlin, 1971) 1083ff.

[189] A Cavanna, *Storia del diritto moderno in Europa—Le fonti e il pensiero giuridico*, vol I (Milan, 1982) 200ff. On the relations between the *jus proprium* and the *jus commune* according to the *lex specialis* (*jus commune viget ubi cessat statutum*), see G Ermini, *Corso di diritto comune*, vol I (Milan, 1989) 17ff. On the progressive terriorialisation of the law, see SL Guterman, *From Personal to Territorial Law* (Metuchen, 1972); O Stobbe, 'Personalität und Territorialität des Rechts und die Grundsätze des Mittelalters über die Collisio statutorum' (1963) 6 *Jahrbuch des gesamten deutschen Rechts* 21ff.

[190] Eg in canon Law, PG Caron, *Aequitas romana, misericordia patristica ed epieichia aritotelica nella dottrina dell'aequitas canonica* (Milan, 1971); C Lefebvre, 'Equity in Canon Law' in RA Newman (ed), *Equity in the World's Legal Systems* (Brussels, 1973) 93ff. See also in general A Cavanna, *Storia del diritto moderno in Europa—Le fonti e il pensiero giuridico*, vol I (Milan, 1982) 120ff and JL Barton, 'Equity in the Medieval Common Law' in RA Newman, (ed), *Equity in the World's Legal Systems* (Brussels, 1973) 139ff. For the Germanic legal orders, see E Kaufmann, *Aequitatis iudicium, Königsgericht und Billigkeit in der Rechtsordnung des frühen Mittelalters* (Frankfurt, 1959) notably 93ff.

[191] Compare F Kern, *Recht und Verfassung im Mittelalter* (Basle, 1953) 84–85; N Politis, *Les nouvelles tendances du droit international* (Paris, 1927) 28ff; and N Politis, *La justice internationale* (Paris, 1924) 198ff.

[192] Immanuel Kant had spotted this point when he affirmed that peoples do not want such a State, in his *Perpetual Peace*, section ii, second final article.

order.[193] Viewed from this perspective, international law is overall well-equipped. It could play a greater role if States wished it to do so; but as long as this is not the case, it is there to respond to the concrete setting in which it is called on to operate. Overall, it is dangerous to consider that a coordinative legal order is deficient, defective or imperfect *per se*. True, the modern mind perceives the absence of organised and centralised sanctions as a fundamental weakness. But the price to be paid for a system of fully-fledged sanctions would be the severe curtailing of sovereignty and independence to the benefit of some supranational organ. It has therefore to be clearly understood that the fight against the 'primitiveness' of international law implies a significant abandonment of sovereign independence to the benefit of collective discipline. Whether that is desirable or not, and to what extent it may be so, is not a legal question but an eminently political one. Some degree of 'primitiveness' will thus be seen by many as concomitant with independence; and it may then have positive connotations. In between, there remains the possibility to partially organise sanctions in a growing network of particular legal regimes.

Summing up, it would be better to abandon the term 'primitiveness', which is too much of a loaded gun. Rather, the 'imperfections' of the coordinative legal order, or perhaps just neutrally its 'features', should be placed at the heart of a discourse that ultimately concerns the 'organisation' of international society between the world State and the anarchical parity-orientated society.

C. International Law as Individualised Law

Each legal order oscillates between two legal values that it seeks to realise: on the one hand the generality and typicality of the legal provision, guaranteeing legal certainty and equality; and on the other hand the individualisation and flexibility of the legal provision, ensuring its equitable application, the taking into account of varied particular circumstances, the capacity to adapt to new problems and, in short, the quest for nuanced justice. The less a legal order is developed, the stronger the hold of political actors; and the more the relations it regulates are irregular, the more this legal order will lean towards the spectrum of individualisation. But what is the exact meaning of 'individualisation'?

The rules of legal orders are situated somewhere on the sliding scale between generality and abstraction, speciality and individualisation.[194] The degree of these qualities varies from legal order to legal order, and from legal branch to legal branch. Thus, for example, in private law the rules tend to be of a significant generality and abstraction. They open up a certain distance between the normative realm and the

[193] Virally, above n 172, 98; Truyol y Serra, above n 172, 119.

[194] The term 'generality' refers to the number of subjects bound by the rule, 'abstraction' to the number of situations covered by the rule. The more general a rule is, the more subjects it applies to; the more abstract it is, the more situations it covers.

spontaneous social facts. In the context of constitutional law, on the other hand, some rules are much more particularised. The constitutional space is often characterised by a relative closeness between the law and facts, by the greater weight of political aspects, and by a concomitant diminution of the impact of regularity and equality. International law often prefers concrete and individualised regulation to the general and abstract.[195] More precisely, there are more rules in the individualised spectrum in international law than in other legal orders. In internal societies, the individual subject rarely has the political weight to impose his particular requirements on the legal order. He or she is part of a society composed of millions of interchangeable and anonymous subjects, confronting one another in typical contractual or delictual situations. Legal dogma can here elaborate further on the typical aspects of legal transactions. The politically branded relationships among States cannot be reduced to typical categories such as those of seller and purchaser, or testator and heir. The cession of a territory will never acquire the same typification as the sale of a car in private law, nor will the disappearance of a State be handled in the same unhurried way as the funeral of a natural person. For example, the disappearance of a State will take place in an historically unique setting and involve social and political convulsions of great magnitude. As has been aptly emphasised:

> These profound differences flowing from the ethnic and historic individuality of nations, from the inequality of their physical and economic constitution, from the reduced number of States when compared with that of individuals, from the eminently political character of their aims and from the irregularity and lesser frequency of their mutual relations, have as a consequence a predominance of the particular over the general situations.[196]

The consequences of the individualisation of the rules of international law are manifold: a diminution of the weight of legal certainty and of equality; more frequent recourse to general principles and standards; the difficulty of codifying the law; the importance of political means to settle disputes; the greater impact of political considerations and fluctuations, etc. Certain areas of international law tend towards individualisation more than others. This is the case, for example, as regards the law of State succession or the law of the sea. In both branches, historical, economic, local and special circumstances have a heavy impact on

[195] F Berber, *Lehrbuch des Völkerrechts*, vol I (Munich, 1975) 22ff; JL Brierly, 'Les règles générales du droit de la paix' (1936-IV) 58 *RCADI* 16; JL Brierly, *The Outlook for International Law* (Oxford, 1944) 40; AP Sereni, *Diritto internazionale*, vol I (Milan, 1956) 97; A Hold-Ferneck, *Lehrbuch des Völkerrechts*, vol I (Vienna, 1930) 82ff; H Mosler, 'Völkerrecht als Rechtsordnung' (1976) 36 *ZaöRV* 27; M Virally, 'Panorama du droit international contemporain' (1983-V) 183 *RCADI* 39, 169–70; D Schindler, 'Contribution à l'étude des facteurs sociologiques et psychologiques du droit international' (1933-IV) 46 *RCADI* 265; A Ross, *A Textbook of International Law* (London/New York/Toronto, 1947) 58–59; J Stone, *Legal Controls of International Conflict* (New York, 1954) 330. And see generally A Verdross, 'Abstrakte und konkrete Regelungen im Völkerrecht' (1937/1938) 4 *Völkerrecht und Völkerbund* 212ff; G de Lacharrière, *La politique juridique extérieure* (Paris, 1983) 63ff.

[196] C de Visscher, *Théories et réalités en droit international public*, 4th edn (Paris, 1970) 165–66.

international normativity.[197] The law on the delimitation of maritime spaces has long been dominated by a set of shifting criteria to be applied to individual circumstances,[198] even if the tide has now turned to the benefit of geometrical criteria (equidistance).[199] Other issues are based on some more generalised rules, as are the rules on reparation in the Articles of State Responsibility of States of 2001.[200]

D. International Law and Fragmentary, Empirical and Uncertain Normativity

International law is empirical and fragmentary in nature[201] because of the erratic structure of international society. The decentralised political structure means that the norms are themselves scattered and do not fit into a coherent whole. Moreover, legislation is drafted to have varied effects: some norms bind some States, other norms bind other States. There are only some norms binding on all existing States (and possibly all existing international law subjects). The normative density of international law depends on the international power constellations, in particular the degree of consonance or dissonance between interests and ideologies at a given time.[202] Thus, certain subject matters will be densely bound with rules, while others will remain in normative underdevelopment. As has been said with some exaggeration, but not without a degree of justification:

> International law in fact is a law without constitution ... Unconnected with a society, it cannot adjust itself to its needs ... There is in fact, whatever the names used in the books no *system* of international law ... What is to be found in the treatises is simply a collection of rules which, when looked at closely, appear to have been thrown together or to have been accumulated, almost at haphazard. Many of them would seem to be more appropriately described as materials for an etiquette book for the conduct of sovereigns and their representatives than as elements of a true legal system.[203]

[197] For State succession there is the following dramatic—and somewhat exaggerated—appraisal, '[there is a] persistent doubt whether there really exists such a thing as an accepted international law of State succession, or whether it is not rather still a receptacle of contradictory and incoherent practices and views' (JHW Verzijl, *International Law in Historical Perspective, State Succession*, vol VII (Leiden, 1974) 2). It is understandable that in such a setting, individualised rules will prevail over general ones: A Verdross and B Simma, *Universelles Völkerrecht*, 3rd edn (Berlin, 1984) 608.

[198] See, eg, R Kolb, *Case Law on Equitable Maritime Delimitation, Digest and Commentaries* (The Hague/London/New York, 2003).

[199] See, eg, the latest decision on this matter by the ICJ, *Maritime Dispute (Peru v Chili)*, judgment of 27 January 2014, §§ 177ff.

[200] Arts 34 et seq.

[201] L Delbez, *Les principes généraux du contentieux international* (Paris, 1962) 18.

[202] C Schmitt, *Die Kernfrage des Völkerbundes* (Berlin, 1926) 63ff. On the heterogeneity of the legislative process, see also G Abi-Saab, 'La coutume dans tous ses états ou le dilemme du développement du droit international général dans un monde éclaté', *Essays in Honor of R. Ago*, vol I (Milan, 1987) 53ff.

[203] A Zimmern, *The League of Nations and the Rule of Law (1918–1935)* (London, 1936) 98.

Periods of international tension trigger a weakening of the international legal order.[204] They put a brake on the development of customary international law and give some priority to precarious equilibria obtained by transient agreements. In extreme cases, this can lead to what has been called 'pactmania' (*pactomanie*). Such tensions can be generalised, as was the case during the 1930s or in the first phase of the Cold War. In the wake of general distrust and lack of sufficient will to cooperate, the legal phenomenon atrophies. Important subject matters remain deprived of any chance of progress, eg disarmament, atomic energy questions, etc. The irregularity and ideological deformation of practice hardly allows for its consolidation into customary rules (eg in human rights matters, in the domain of economic exchanges, etc). Conversely, the tensions can also be limited to certain subject matters. Thus, at the beginning of the twentieth century, the investment of capital abroad and migratory movements gave an impulse to economic nationalism and protectionism. The increasing disequilibrium between the importing countries (Latin America) and the exporting countries (Europe) of capital and manpower augmented the tensions between the States of these two continents. The political instability of the Latin American countries exposed them to military intervention by European powers (*politique de la cannonière*, gunboat diplomacy).[205] The reaction of the aggrieved States was to take a bitterly hostile position against any form of interventionism. This state of affairs rendered impossible the emergence of universally accepted rules on State responsibility, on the standard of protection of foreigners ('minimum standard' or 'national standard') and on diplomatic protection. In the second half of the twentieth century, these tensions completely disappeared. This paved the way to a solution on the matters mentioned above.[206] The same analysis could be made in the context of expropriation from and compensation of foreign investors. The issue was highly controversial in the 1960s and 1970s, when decolonised States purported to cast off the ties of the coloniser in economic matters by expropriating assets for which they could not possibly provide prompt, full and effective compensation.[207] When these tensions disappeared after 1990, a network of bilateral investment treaties, often quite favourable to the investor, saw the light of day. It may also happen that apparently technical aspects are unsuitable for legal regulation at a particular time because of latent political tensions. Thus, the question of the right to participate in multilateral treaties was dominated by political tensions between the different blocs of States. Since then, the problem has lost its political underpinning and has tilted back towards the idea that multilateral treaties should be open as much as possible to the participation of all States willing to become parties.

[204] C de Visscher, *Théories et réalités en droit international public*, 4th edn (Paris, 1970) 95ff, 166ff.

[205] AM Dorman and TG Otte (eds), *Military Intervention: From Gunboat Diplomacy to Humanitarian Intervention* (Dartmouth, 1995).

[206] C de Visscher, *Théories et réalités en droit international public*, 4th edn (Paris, 1970) 299ff.

[207] MH Muller, 'Compensation for Nationalization: A North-South Dialogue' (1981) 19 *Columbia Journal of Transnational Law* 35ff; R Dolzer, 'New Foundations of the Law of Expropriation of Alien Property' (1981) 75 *AJIL* 553ff.

The evolution of international law is thus marked, as regards many subject matters, by a haphazard evolution according to changing opportunities and windows in time. An important number of its rules are based on induction from particular acts and the will of legal subjects, notably the States. This approach leaves certain glaring gaps in the interstices between the scattered acts and wills. These are consequently international relations not governed by legal rules, or not governed by clear legal rules. True, no legal order regulates all existing social relations. But there is hardly any legal order more cautious and restrictive than international law in regulating politically relevant international relations and subjecting them to some form of rule of law. There is obviously the possibility to seek refuge in some general principle, or to call into play some analogy. However, such a course is tantamount to admitting that a subject matter is not regulated by precise primary legal rules. This is also the reason why so many international disputes are difficult to classify in clear categories. They leap-frog between politics and law. Governments do not want to regulate the underlying subject matters by precise legal rules because they consider these questions too intimately linked with the conservation or the development of important State interests or of State power.[208] The mission of international law as regards order and peace is consequently reduced when compared to that of municipal law. Unable to resolve such important conflicts under its sway, international law prohibits at least the use of force in addressing them. The fragmentary character of the regulation increases some States' distrust of the international judge.[209] In the absence of clear rules and of legal certainty, submission to the judge's decision may seem all too risky. These States submit to the judge disputes of minor importance, or at best those of medium importance, while continuing to impede any progress in important international relations and/or obstruct the path to resolving more important questions.[210] Important issues will in most cases be reserved for direct negotiation, or bluntly consigned to the realm of self-controlled unilateral action.

It would, however, be wrong not to mention the fact that international law has made great strides in its normative development since the first part of the twentieth century. Some decades ago, it was common to lay stress on the defects of this non-codified legal order, showing itself to be in a state of uncertainty as regards almost all its subject areas.[211] Since then, many subject areas have been codified, for

[208] It occurs that such matters are regulated, but in such cases—at least for some States—the regulation is more often than not merely lip service rather than real commitment. One might think of human rights norms.

[209] This was the reason for the failure of the international prize court, proposed in 1907–08: see N Politis, *La justice internationale* (Paris, 1924) 129ff.

[210] M Virally, 'Le champ opératoire du règlement judiciaire international' (1983) 87 *RGDIP* 281ff, 309; and H Tourard, 'Le champ opératoire: nouvelles perspectives?' in C Apostolidis (ed), *Les arrêts de la Cour internationale de justice* (Dijon, 2005) 11ff.

[211] See, eg, the brisk analysis by AH Feller, *United Nations and World Community* (Boston, 1952) 133: 'The trouble with international law is not that it is not law, but that there is not enough of it. The rules cover only a small part of the relations between states; many of the rules are vaguely defined or their meaning is disputed; there are too many loopholes, too many opportunities for evasion and quibbling.'

example the law of treaties, diplomatic and consular intercourse, the succession of States, refugee law, the law of the sea, etc. In certain subject matters, this codification has produced a mass of extremely detailed rules, as in the area of international humanitarian law (law of armed conflict).[212] But even in such areas there remain some uncertainties and gaps, for example in the law of non-international armed conflict, where the codified rules largely lag behind the current state of customary international law.[213] Thus, the number of norms multiplies and sometimes even proliferates. This creates in turn a feeling of the absence of proper articulation and of disorder. This scattering and superposition of norms has launched a post-modern discourse on the 'fragmentation' of international law due to the overlap of numerous norms and sources.[214] In the past the fragmentation was due to a relative paucity of norms; now it is discussed in the context of the great number of poorly articulated norms.

The main consequences of the fragmentary character of international law in the sense discussed above (to the extent it still prevails) are as follows:[215] (i) an important number of rules of international law have a limited scope and tend towards the spectrum of particularisation and circumstance-relatedness; (ii) the rules tend to be self-contained unities, which means that it is more difficult to expand them by interpretation or by analogy (the speciality of international rules); (iii) in other situations legal argument will often bring into play some general principles able to construct bridges between the scattered norms (eg good faith and its concretisations, equity, sovereignty, non-intervention, sustainable development, *sic utere tuo…*, *uti possidetis*, etc); (iv) legal security is reduced in scope and impact, the many particularised rules limiting it considerably. As has been emphasised by an eminent international lawyer, '[i]nternational law formulates a significant number

212 D Schindler and J Toman, *The Laws of Armed Conflict*, 4th edn (Leiden/Boston, 2004).

213 For a (non-generally accepted) study of the rules of the two Additional Protocols of 1977 to the Geneva Conventions of 1949 representing customary law, see the ICRC study: JM Henckaerts and L Doswald-Beck (eds), *Customary International Humanitarian Law*, vol 1: *Rules*, vols II and III: *Practice* (Cambridge, 2005). Updates on the website of the ICRC at <www.icrc.org>.

214 See M Prost, *The Concept of Unity in Public International Law* (Oxford/Portland, 2012).

215 P Weil, 'Le droit international en quête de son identité, Cours général de droit international public' (1992-VI) 237 *RCADI* 203ff, has laid stress on many consequences of the fragmentary character of international law. They are presented as a weakness of this legal order. First, international law is incomplete in its normativity: the decentralisation of the law-creating process produces many gaps; the principle of effectiveness thus also looms large and threatens the legal rule. Secondly, international law suffers from uncertain normativity: there are too many standards and soft norms, which merge the law and the non-law into each other. Thirdly, international normativity is scattered: there is poly-normativity, ie many layers of legal rules exist on the same subject matter. For example, there can be an overlap between declining customary rules and customary rules *in statu nascendi*, where neither the old rule is completely dead nor the new rule firmly established. Further, there can be the coexistence of customary and conventional rules on the same question, as, for example, in the context of the use of force. There is also normative plurality through special legal situations, eg local custom, reservations to treaties, recognition and objection, prescription, etc. Self-interpretation of the rules will further complicate the matter, with a tendency to have international law fragmented into a series of divergent subjective representations (*ibid*, 222). Lastly, there are questions raised by the absence of a hierarchy of international norms.

of its rules in a very abstract form, ie in the form of general principles'.[216] The very fragmentation and individualisation of many international rules call for the presence of general principles as a corrective force.

E. International Law as Permeable and Non-Formalistic

Unlike internal law, international law has never been cast as a rigid system of sources and institutions, erecting a barrier between it and other social norms or facts. Such a rigid conception could be envisaged only in the context of codifications in the municipal sphere, when the law was identified with the code and was meant to contain rules for all possible cases (*lex semper loquitur*). Rather, international law has always been open to social, moral and political factors. Its universal character and its independence from the State legal orders has immunised it to some extent against the legalistic dogmas of positivism. Since ancient times, it has tended to remain close to the conception of a rational and necessary law. The importance of its customary element has kept it in touch with the social realities. Centralised organs have been unable to insert a barrier between its growth and the social or political facts of life.

International law is highly permeable to policy.[217] The influence of politics can be felt mainly on two planes. First, the normative body of international law is considerably permeable to policy considerations. As we have seen, the individualisation of many rules of international law allows States to take contingent and self-orientated considerations into account in the process of implementation of the law. Secondly, policy is not simply an external factor that has made its way

[216] P Reuter, 'Quelques réflexions sur l'équité en droit international' (1980) 15 *RBDI* 168. See also M Virally, 'Le rôle des principes dans le développement du droit international' in M Virally, *Le droit international en devenir* (Paris, 1990) 195ff.

[217] On the relations between law and policy, see Part Two of this volume. In legal doctrine: F Berber, *Lehrbuch des Völkerrechts*, vol I, 2nd edn (Munich, 1975) 24ff; W Friedmann, *The Changing Structure of International Law* (London, 1964) 45ff. See also E Giraud, 'De la valeur et des rapports des notions de droit et de politique dans l'ordre international' (1922) 29 *RGDIP* 473ff; C de Visscher, 'Quelques réflexions sur la notion du politique en droit international public et privé', *Essays in Honor of T. Perassi*, vol I (Milan, 1957) 401ff; Q Wright, 'Law and Politics in the World Community', *Essays in Honor of H. Kelsen (Law and Politics in the World Community)* (Berkeley/Los Angeles, 1953) 3ff; I Brownlie, 'The Relation of Law and Power', *Essays in Honor of G. Schwarzenberger* (London, 1988) 19ff; WG Grewe, 'Aussenpolitik und Völkerrecht in der Praxis' (1998) 36 *Archiv des Völkerrechts* 1ff; JC Hsiung, *Anarchy and Order: The Interplay of Politics and Law in International Relations* (Boulder, 1997); D Kennedy, 'The Disciplines of International Law and Policy' (1999) 12 *Leiden Journal of International Law* 9ff; L Ferrari-Bravo, 'Quelques notes à propos du fondement de la politique étrangère en droit international public', *Essays in Honor of M. Bedjaoui* (The Hague, 1999) 173ff; O Schachter, 'The Rule of Power in International Law' (1999) 93 *ASIL Proceedings* 200ff; M Byers (ed), *The Role of Law in International Politics* (Oxford, 2000); AL Paulus, 'Law and Politics in the Age of Globalization' (2000) 11 *EJIL* 465ff; N Paech, *Völkerrecht und Machtpolitik in den internationalen Beziehungen* (Hamburg, 2001). For some authors international law is only the result of power struggles: AV Lundsted, *Superstition or Rationality in Action for Peace* (London, 1925); GF Kennan, *American Diplomacy, 1900–1950* (Chicago, 1951); H Morgenthau, *Politics Among Nations*, 5th edn (New York, 1967). See also G Schwarzenberger, *Power Politics: A Study of World Society*, 3rd edn (London, 1964).

into the alien body of international law. International law is also political in itself, by its proper object. It concerns the public or political relations between States. Therefore, as Montesquieu wrote, it is the 'political law of nations in their mutual relationships'.[218] The object of international law is external policy (or international policy) as much as the object of civil law is private relationships or the object of criminal law is crimes. There is therefore constantly a double weight of policy on international law, especially in some areas such as peaceful change, the distinction between political and legal disputes, necessity or conservation arguments, the doctrine *rebus sic stantibus*, the use of vague or dilatory formulae in legal texts, etc.

International law also entertains close relationships with ethics.[219] The universal character and the precariousness of international law have constantly kept it in contact with moral values and considerations of justice. Any developed legal formalism supposes a much more advanced institutional system, social data moulded in greater uniformity and a higher degree of convergence of interests than exist in international society. The autonomy of the law with respect to its profounder justifications can occur only in periods of social tranquillity and as long as social life is not upset by instability and crisis.[220] Such periods of pervading stability did not exist in the international relations of the twentieth century. This is the reason why international law has been shaped by content and value more than merely form and technique. It is paradoxical only to a superficial eye that the instability of international relations has brushed away any easy assurances and forced the observer to reflect deeply on the foundations and justification of law in international society. As has been aptly said, 'given that between States the obligations are not ensured by power [a superior authority], it is necessary that they be strengthened by ethics'.[221] This is one of the reasons why we have long found so many references to justice and equity in international practice.[222] It would be all too easy to see in these only hypocrisy and self-interest, even if these traits are never completely absent.

From the preceding, it can easily be gathered that international law is not formalistic. Sovereign States can commit themselves through many types of legal

[218] Montesquieu, *De l'esprit des lois*, book x, ch I: 'la loi politique des nations considérées dans le rapport qu'elles ont les unes avec les autres'.

[219] F Berber, *Lehrbuch des Völkerrechts*, vol I, 2nd edn (Munich, 1975) 31ff; WF Römer, *The Ethical Basis of International Law* (Chicago, 1928); B Landheer (ed), *Ethical Values in International Decision-Making* (The Hague, 1960); KG Giesen, *L'éthique des relations internationales—Les théories anglo-américaines contemporaines* (Brussels, 1992); A Boldizar and OI Korhonen, 'Ethics, Morals and International Law' (1999) 10 *EJIL* 279ff; MW Janis (ed), *Religion and International Law* (The Hague, 1999); R Weiler (ed), *Völkerrechtsordnung und Völkerrechtsethik* (Berlin, 2000). For a theological approach, see, eg, W Huber, *Gerechtigkeit und Recht, Grundlinien christlicher Rechtsethik* (Gütersloh, 1996) 21–22, 362ff.

[220] C de Visscher, *Théories et réalités en droit international public*, 4th edn (Paris, 1970) 164ff.

[221] M Huber, *Grundlagen nationaler Erneuerung* (Zurich, 1934) 56.

[222] See eg the Memorandum of the Portuguese Government to the British Government of 2 January 1873 calling for the application of principles of the law of nations informed by justice, equity and the nature of things. See V Bruns, *Fontes Juris Gentium (1871–1878)*, Series B, sect I, vol II, §1, 60. Another example can be found in. Phillimore, *Commentaries Upon International Law*, vol I, 3rd edn (London, 1879) 15.

acts, without being bound to forms that in municipal society have the aim of protecting the individual against precipitancy, ignorance or other failures. Thus, in the conclusion of treaties, international law considers the true intention and the legitimate expectations created, not the realisation of any particular form. Some examples of informal treaties may be mentioned here.[223] In the *Aegean Sea Continental Shelf* case of 1978,[224] the ICJ was confronted with the plea that a 'joint press communiqué' signed by the Ministers of Foreign Affairs of the States concerned could constitute a treaty binding upon them and conferring jurisdiction to the Court to hear the case. The ICJ had this to say on the issue, '[o]n the question of form, the Court need only to observe that it knows of no rule of international law which might preclude a joint communiqué from constituting an international agreement'.[225] In the *Maritime Delimitation and Territorial Questions (Qatar v Bahrein)* case of 1994,[226] the ICJ had to deal with minutes of negotiations having been signed by the Foreign Ministers of the States concerned. The Court held that the minutes were not simple records of a meeting, giving an account of discussions and summarising points of agreements and disagreement; rather, the minutes enumerated commitments to which the parties consented. And the Court concluded, '[t]hey [the minutes] thus create rights and obligations under international law for the Parties. They constitute an international agreement'.[227] In the *Pulp Mills* case of 2010,[228] the ICJ affirmed that a common press release constituted an agreement between the two States parties to the proceedings, obliging them to create a negotiating framework.[229] There is also ample authority on this point from other tribunals. Thus, in the *International Military Operations (German Participation)* (1994) decision of the German Federal Constitutional Court, emphasis was laid on the fact that international agreements can be concluded in any form, such as an exchange of notes or a verbal understanding.[230] In the *Newfoundland/Nova Scotia* arbitration (First Phase, 2001),[231] it was emphasised by the tribunal that there are no specific requirements of form in international law for a treaty to which the parties have agreed. Or, in the words of a celebrated Latin-American Judge:

> It is well known that international law does not impose any given form for the conclusion of an agreement, provided that there is sufficient evidence of the intention of the parties to create rights and obligations, ie, to produce legal effects. There is no legal

[223] Further examples may be found in *The Hoshinmaru (Japan v Russian Federation)* (2007) 143 *ILR* 24, §§86–87 (ITLOS). The Tribunal recognised that agreed minutes could constitute a treaty, but held that in the particular case there had been no agreement on certain matters.

[224] *Aegean Sea Continental Shelf* [1978] ICJ Rep 39.

[225] *ibid*, §96.

[226] *Maritime Delimitation and Territorial Questions (Qatar v Bahrein)* [1994] ICJ Rep 121.

[227] *ibid*, §25.

[228] *Pulp Mills (Argentina v Uruguay)* [2010-I] ICJ Rep 65.

[229] *ibid*, §138.

[230] *International Military Operations (German Participation)* (1994) 106 ILR 336: 'Their actual form … [is] immaterial'.

[231] *Newfoundland/Nova Scotia* (Arbitration) (2001) 128 *ILR* 449, §3.15.

> distinction between formal and informal agreements, because the validity of a treaty does not depend on the adoption of any form; it therefore is up to the parties to choose such form as they think fit for assuming international obligations.[232]

The finding on non-formalism is generally accompanied by a twin assertion, namely that the only aspect that is decisive is the existence of an intention to undertake legal commitments. Thus, the Eritrea/Ethiopia Claims Commission award in *Pensions, Eritrea's Claims 15, 19 & 23* (2005) stated that what really counts in the conclusion of an agreement is the intention to create legal obligations.[233] Similarly, in the above-mentioned *Newfoundland/Nova Scotia* arbitration (First Phase, 2001), it was stated that:'[w]hat matters, ultimately, is the intention of the Parties to be bound by the agreement under international law'.[234] The intention of the parties must be determined by a case-to-case analysis of the context, ie by way of interpretation.

Overall, international law thus presents as a phenomenological legal order devoting a large share to the pursuit of material finalities such as peace, the settlement of disputes, the protection of human beings or the environment, etc.

F. International Law Between Coexistence and Cooperation

According to a famous distinction adopted in particular by Wolfgang Friedmann, international law is composed of a classical layer of 'coexistence' and a modern additional layer of 'cooperation'.[235] The law of cooperation thus does not take the place of the older law; it adds to it, and on some issues dispenses with the old rules. It would also clearly be wrong to consider that cooperation or common interests were unknown to international law before the twentieth century.[236] There remains the fact, however, that there has been a partial shift since the nineteenth century, towards giving a greater emphasis to collective interests.

In a nutshell, the distinction between the law of coexistence and cooperation is as follows. Traditional international law was essentially a body of rules centered on the *coexistence* of sovereign States. Its main aim was to fit and serve the interests of single States, while ensuring to each one, in principle, its territorial integrity

232 Individual Opinion of JM Ruda, *WHO Regional Office*, Advisory Opinion [1980] ICJ Rep 123.

233 *Pensions, Eritrea's Claims 15, 19 & 23* (2005) 135 *ILR* 512.

234 *Newfoundland/Nova Scotia*, above n 231, §3.15.

235 W Friedmann, *The Changing Structure of International Law* (London, 1964) 60ff; W Friedmann, 'General Course in Public International Law' (1969-II) 127 *RCADI* 91ff. See also G Schwarzenberger, *The Dynamics of International Law* (Abdington, 1976) 107ff; G Abi-Saab, 'Wither the International Community?' (1998) 9 *EJIL* 250ff; S Villalpando, *L'émergence de la communauté internationale dans la responsabilité des Etats* (Geneva, 2005) 61ff. See also more generally B Simma, 'From Bilateralism to Community Interest in International Law' (1994-VI) 250 *RCADI* 217ff.

236 See the interesting study by E Jouannet, *Le droit international liberal-providence, Une histoire du droit international* (Brussels, 2011). English version: E Tourme-Jouannet, *The Liberal-Welfarist Law of Nations: A History of International Law* (Cambridge, 2012).

and political independence.[237] The law was individualistic and State-centered. As has been said, '[t]he international law of coexistence is a set of rules of abstention, of adjustment and delimitation between different national sovereignties'.[238] The law of coexistence is mainly horizontal in structure (delimitation of powers) and negative in content (duties not to do). It tends towards ideological neutrality by seeking the minimum international order necessary to guarantee the life in common of the existing sovereign States. The rights of the ones are reflected in the obligations of the others (bilateralism). Sovereign equality is a cornerstone of this layer of the law. The game is zero sum: the advantage of the one is considered to be the loss of the other. The obligations themselves are of result rather than of means; this leaves a discretionary power for States in their implementation. Conservative in its assets, the law of coexistence favors positivistic approaches. Its pole star is stability. International law therefore presents itself as a type of 'private law'. The State is not considered to be the subject of a public function linked to the common good, but rather as a person gifted with private autonomy deciding autonomously how to best protect and further its interests. Private interest prevails over at least partly absent public interest. From the point of view of content, the law concentrates on diplomacy, war and transactions (agreements), on contract, property and wrongful acts; and on issues of reciprocity. The 'public' aspect of international law is concentrated on the delimitation of the respective spheres of action and competences; it is not integrated through a concept of the common good. Hence, international law presents itself as a restricted body of public law rules regulating the conflicts between the subjects, and a large body of private law rules granting legal powers of action to the subjects.

Modern international law has developed an additional layer of *cooperation*.[239] Since the end of World War I, there has been an increasing number of areas where interdependence has created the urgent necessity for collaboration of States in the attainment of common goals. These areas have involved questions on sanitation (eg the typhus epidemics in Eastern Europe at the beginning of the 1920s), the maintenance of peace, the control of armaments, the protection of human rights, the protection of the environment, etc. This need for cooperation has led to the blossoming of international organisations, where cooperation can take place

[237] But this protection of territorial integrity is applicable only to peacetime relations. The discretionary right of States to declare war (*liberum jus ad bellum*) allows a State to invade foreign territory and even to annex it. By the same token, the law of the 19th century did not develop strict rules on non-intervention. The Concert of Europe intervened in internal affairs and the European States regularly intervened in the affairs of third States, eg in China, Japan or Latin America. On some of these aspects, see TG Otte, 'Of Congress and Gunboats: Military Intervention in the Nineteenth Century' in AM Dorman and TG Otte (eds), *Military Intervention: From Gunboat Diplomacy to Humanitarian Intervention* (Dartmouth, 1995) 19ff.

[238] W Friedmann, *The Changing Structure of International Law* (London, 1964) 92.

[239] In practical terms, the League of Nations has in many areas greatly contributed to this state of affairs. See FP Walters, *A History of the League of Nations* (London/New York/Toronto, 1960).

in practice.[240] The public law aspect of international law has been strengthened: for example, powers of decision by simple majority have been granted to international organs. The vertical structure of international law has been reinforced (by the many powers of international organs, sometimes of supranational organs) and positive duties are now more numerous. The cornerstone of the law of cooperation is interdependence or solidarity. From this perspective, the issue is not simply zero sum: the gains of the other are not simply the losses of the other; there are common gains and common losses. Obligations of means are now more numerous, so that the leeway given to States' discretionary powers diminishes.[241] Having a progressive outlook and putting into question received realities, the law of cooperation is less favourable to positivistic approaches. State individualism is sometimes seen to give way to the grand design of the law of an international community, with its own collective interests and needs.

It is not useful at this point to take a final stand on the merits of each of these forces, centrifugal on the one side, centripetal on the other. It is, however, important to grasp that international society is now dominated by the conflict between an individualistic law, which becomes increasingly insufficient, and a communitarian law, which is too weakly organised to inspire legitimate confidence. The interaction between these two forces will continue to mark the international law of the twenty-first century.

G. International Law as Non-self-sufficient Law

International law is the sole legal order largely deprived of self-sufficiency. Thus, it is rich in mechanisms of law creation but contains hardly any organic structure for the implementation and enforcement of the rules created. From there flows the necessity for a workshare with municipal legal orders. Roughly speaking, international law provides the sources, internal law the organs for implementation. International law produces norms that are common to States; municipal law could not produce such norms, since they would not be common. But international law does not possess substantial means for implementation and enforcement. The organic growth that would be necessary for such a function is strenuously resisted by States out of fear of creating too much supranational power and too penetrating an inroad into their sovereignty. Thus, international law refers to internal law and to the organs of the States a great share of the duties of implementation and enforcement. States are thus under an obligation to put their organs at the disposal of international law so as to implement its norms. In monistic systems,

[240] For the UN system, see R Wolfrum (ed), *United Nations: Law, Policies and Practice*, 2 vols (Munich/Dordrecht/Boston/London, 1995).

[241] A good example can now be found in the *Whaling* decision of the ICJ, judgment of 31 March 2014, §§51ff.

the international law norms are automatically part of the municipal legal order ('international law is part of the law of the land'). In dualistic systems, the international norm must first be transformed into municipal law by an act of legislation. This occurs only for written norms. For customary rules, all the world's systems are monistic. But it is rare that a customary norm of international law has to be implemented in internal society, apart for certain subject matters such as, say, the law of non-international armed conflict. In a sense, international law is therefore genetically incomplete; it calls into aid another legal order to ensure its full and proper functioning.

This state of affairs has led to certain sophisticated and progressive theories, such as the '*dédoublement fonctionnel*' of Scelle.[242] The gist of this theory is that there is a mandate to the internal organs to implement international law rules as organs of the international community. When implementing and enforcing rules of international law, the municipal organs are no longer merely municipal organs but international law organs too. Their function is double, whence the term 'functional doubling'. In an extreme version, the internal organ is even primarily an organ of the international community when it applies international law. There is here a vision of embryonic world federalism and the primacy of international interests over municipal ones. This theory is, to say the least, in advance of the facts of international life. In reality, municipal organs apply municipal law first and foremost, and are more sensitive to the interests of their State than to remote or sometimes lofty international interests.[243] It remains true that these municipal organs will in most cases apply international law. But they will also colour it with varying political and legal conceptions. It is hard indeed to perceive in this process the function of an impersonal and neutral execution of the law.

The dependency of international law on municipal law can be traced in three ways. First, international law operates a significant number of referrals (*renvois*) to the municipal legal orders. The normal occurrence is that a legal order makes a formal or material referral to another legal order in the context of the implementation of a precise legal norm. This happens regularly in private international law. It will, for example, refer to a foreign legal order for the application of the law of the *lex fori* to a transaction linked with the foreign legal order. This also occurs when the State legal order refers to canon Law for a religious marriage, to which the State legal order attaches some effects. The magnitude of such referrals is wholly different in the international legal order. The referral to municipal law concerns whole subject areas. Thus, the organs competent to conclude treaties, or otherwise to engage the State, and the procedures to this effect, are largely determined by municipal law. International law limits itself to defining some specific legal consequences for its own needs, for example the effects of the violation of

[242] G Scelle, *Précis de droit des gens*, vol I (Paris, 1932) 56; G Scelle, 'Règles générales du droit de la paix' (1933-IV) 46 *RCADI* 358; G Scelle, 'Théorie et pratique de la fonction exécutive en droit international' (1936-I) 55 *RCADI* 87ff.

[243] C de Visscher, *Théories et réalités en droit international public*, 4th edn (Paris, 1970) 169.

internal procedures on the validity of the treaty concluded (Article 46 VCLT).[244] Similarly, the organisation of the State remains a matter for internal legislation, to which international law refers. It then attaches certain legal consequences to this internal organisation, for example in matters of international responsibility.[245]

Secondly, there are numerous subject matters in which international law is nourished by municipal law. Thus, international customary law evolves through municipal law acts, eg for State immunity or the extension of maritime zones. Internal legislation and jurisprudence are of the essence in such subject matters. The same is true when States adopt unilateral acts (eg recognition, promises).

Thirdly, according to what has already been said, international law depends largely on municipal law in the context of implementation and enforcement. In analytical terms, this means that the municipal legal orders are to some extent integrated in the constitutional scheme of international law. The implementing function is particularly visible in the context of treaties concerning individuals, eg human rights or criminal law. In most cases, such treaties are limited to the harmonisation or unification of applicable norms. The States parties assume the duty to modify their municipal legal orders so as to be able to implement their international obligations domestically. This close relationship exists for any norm addressed to a State. Some municipal organ must then be able to act so as to realise its normative injunction. The functional merger of international and internal law is thus very pronounced.

[244] See, eg, ME Villiger, *Commentary on the 1969 Vienna Convention on the Law of Treaties* (Leiden/Boston, 2009) 583ff.

[245] J Crawford, *The International Law Commission's Articles on State Responsibility* (Cambridge, 2002) 91ff; J Crawford, *State Responsibility* (Cambridge, 2014) 113ff.

3

The Subjects of International Law

I. General Aspects

It is redundant to insist on the fact that the number and plurality of the subjects of international law have increased considerably since the nineteenth century, and in particular since 1945;[1] that international organisations and even individuals have emerged as subjects of the law;[2] that this evolution has ushered in a fragmentation, functionalisation and gradualism of the concept of 'subject' according to a changing array of rights and obligations;[3] or that the emergence of the individual as the bearer of international rights and obligations has modified the structure of international law by a progressive interpenetration of the international and the municipal spheres, ie of the international and the municipal domains.[4] It is not much more useful to explain the several doctrines on international legal personality in the current discussion.[5] Neither is it fruitful to try to put the several legal doctrines of personality into their larger socio-cultural context.[6] All these have already been aptly covered. The object of this chapter is something else: the aim is to scrutinise the concept of 'international legal personality' from certain fundamental definitional aspects, including its paradoxes and circularities.

The concept of legal personality is generally defined in the following terms:

> Subject of international law: entity capable of having rights and obligations having their source in public international law.[7]

[1] See, eg, M Sørensen, 'Principes de droit international public' (1960-III) 101 *RCADI* 7–8.

[2] H Mosler, 'The International Society as Legal Community' (1974-IV) 140 *RCADI* 48ff.

[3] *Reparations for Injuries* (Opinion) [1949] ICJ *Rep* 178 '[t]he subjects of law in any legal system are not necessarily identical in their nature or in the extent of their rights'. It has been claimed that the concept of legal personality is not severable by degrees, but that the capacities (ie the rights and obligations flowing from the personality) can vary: C Dominicé, 'La société internationale à la recherché de son équilibre' (2013) 370 *RCADI* 178.

[4] E Menzel, 'Das Völkerrecht und die politisch-sozialen Grundstrukturen der modernen Welt' in G Picht and C Eisenbart (eds), *Frieden und Völkerrecht* (Stuttgart, 1973) 401ff.

[5] See in this regard JE Nijman, *The Concept of International Legal Personality* (The Hague, 2004).

[6] See to that effect R Portmann, *Legal Personality in International Law* (Cambridge, 2010).

[7] J Salmon (ed), *Dictionnaire de droit international public* (Brussels, 2001) 1062, our translation. See also amongst others, Dominicé, above n 3, 139.

And:

> Legal personality: capability to have rights or be subject to obligations.[8]

The constitutive element of legal personality is thus seen in the *ability* to have rights and obligations under a legal order. There may in reality be no subject actually possessing such rights or duties; but what is essential for legal personality is rather the entity's ability to acquire such rights and duties. It is more a potentiality than an actuality. Moreover, an entity may be a subject in one legal order but not in another; it depends on whether the particular legal order recognises that entity as the bearer of rights and obligations. The subject of the law as such will possess a general set of rights and obligations, for example States with their sets, international organisations with another set, individuals with still another set, and so on. The States have the largest spectrum of rights and duties. This is why they are referred to as the principal subjects of international law. The international legal order is indeed made by States and principally exists for them.

The number of rights and duties also varies from subject to subject within the same category. The ability to possess these rights and duties will be identical in principle, but the actual rights and duties will not be. Thus, State X may be party to a treaty to which State Y is not a party. State X will then have rights and duties under the treaty that State Y will not have. The total number of rights and duties in a given category of subjects increases the more a subject is party to special legal relationships, eg agreements, unilateral undertakings, prescriptive situations, acquiescence, etc. Even general international law does not necessarily apply equally to all subjects of international law. It will certainly apply to all States, but it is not proven that it also automatically binds all international organisations or other subjects. Certain customary rules are manifestly not applicable to international organisations, since they suppose the existence of a territory. Other customary rules may be altered when they apply to an international organisation: for example, if the Security Council of the UN is bound by a series of customary *jus cogens* norms, it is not excluded that these norms will not have exactly the same scope and complexion for the Council as they have for States.[9] After all, for example, while the prohibition on the unilateral use of force is a peremptory prohibition applicable to States (subject to the self-defence exception, the invitation onto the territory exception and the authorisation of the Security Council exception), there is no such general prohibition applicable to the Council. The UN Charter gives it the right to use force (Article 42). However, these modulations in the actual number and nature of the rights and obligations are a question of the scope of capacity of a subject. The question of legal personality is situated on a preliminary plane, that is it concerns the capacity to have such rights and obligations in the first place.

Considering now this notion of legal personality, certain perplexing questions arise. First, if legal personality flows from the capacity to possess rights and duties,

[8] Salmon (ed), above n 7, 819, our translation.

[9] See the reflections in R Kolb, *Peremptory International Law (Jus Cogens)* (Oxford, 2015) 85–86.

how, then, can these rights and duties be explained, since apparently they must have been created by the subjects themselves? Is there not a vicious circle here? One may obviously define the subject as a first notion severed from all experience. Thus the vicious circle would be avoided, but the notion of the subject would be purely dogmatic and ignore the real historical entities that have been vested with such legal positions. Alternatively, one could define legal personality as a secondary notion, flowing from the experience of real entities having possessed relevant rights and obligations. But then one falls into the trap of circularity mentioned above. This seems something of a conundrum: are we necessarily caught between dogmatism or circularity? Secondly, if one considers that legal personality is linked to a certain density of the rights and duties (ie subjective legal positions) possessed, and that one or some rights and obligations that an entity may enjoy do not automatically make it a subject of the legal order, other problems appear. What would here be the required density of the subjective legal positions?[10] Thus, individuals may not seem to be a subjects of international law, since they possess only the rights and duties granted in treaties but not the power to create rights and duties themselves, for example through treaty-making power. And if one adopts this way of looking at international legal personality, what is the legal position of those entities that do not qualify as a subject? Can there be legal capacity without legal personality? Or does legal capacity perforce suppose legal personality?

II. The Question of Circularity Between the Sources and the Subject

The problem we face can be graphically illustrated by the contrary positions of two eminent international lawyers. Quadri,[11] on the one hand, considers that the notion of legal personality is *a priori* and cannot flow from experience or induction. The norms do not make the subject; on the contrary, the subjects create the norms. The definition of the subject is thus unique and cannot be fragmented into different numbers of rights and obligations.[12] The approach is *ante rem*; legal dogma predominates in order to avoid the above-mentioned vicious circle.

[10] C Tomuschat, 'International Law: Ensuring the Survival of Mankind on the Eve of a New Century', (1999) 281 *RCADI* 160: '[T]he position may be taken that identifying a special category of subjects of international law makes sense only with regard to entities which have a certain freedom of action at the international level and which engage in international transactions beyond a framework rigidly fixed once and for all in their constitutive instruments. Then, the capacity to conclude treaties would stand out as the main element permitting identification as a subject of international law.' See also *ibid*, 142.

[11] R Quadri, 'Cours général de droit international public' (1964-III) 113 *RCADI* 373, 376; R Quardi, *Diritto internazionale pubblico*, 5th edn (Naples, 1968) 389, 391.

[12] The result is that the State is the only subject of international law: Quadri, 'Cours général de droit international public', above n 11, 433.

Conversely, for Barberis[13] the attribution of legal personality supposes an exhaustive review of all norms of the international legal order so as to determine to what entities rights and obligations sanctioned by the international legal order are granted. Legal personality is thus a notion linked to experience: the norms create the subject, not the reverse. The legal personality is part and parcel of effectiveness. The definition of the subject can therefore be variable, the rights and obligations of various subjects being different and multiple. The accent is placed on diversity and flexibility. The approach is *post rem* and empirical.

One way to escape from this sharp opposition rests on postulating two types of legal subjects.[14] The first subjects are necessarily linked to the fundamental structure of a society, ie its constitutional setting.[15] Thus, for example, the Westphalian territorial order of 1648 (or at least what it progressively became) was centered upon the notion of the sovereign State. It stands to reason, therefore, that the sovereign State was the natural and *a priori* subject of that system, as much as the individual is the natural subject of the municipal legal order. The State is not granted legal subjectivity by some legal norms; it is an original historical fact, which carries with it some legal effects, such as, in particular, legal subjectivity. Effectiveness is the source of that grant. But it is an effectiveness recognised by the relevant actors in society. In other words, the legal personality of States is inherent in the modern international legal order. These natural subjects, ie the States, can then create or recognise[16] further subjects according to their political agendas, and also according to the pressure of social facts. These other entities will be derived subjects of the law. Their subjectivity flows from the grant originating in norms of the system created by the primary subjects, ie the States. Their rights and duties will differ according to the extent of the grant.[17] Thus, in short, if one wants to escape from the vicious circle, it is necessary to postulate some original subjects of the law, consubstantial to the structure of a given legal order; and if one wants to avoid excessive dogmatism, it is necessary to add subjects flowing from a creative

[13] J Barberis, 'Nouvelles questions concernant la personnalité juridique internationale' (1983-I) 179 *RCADI* 168. See also H Kelsen, 'Théorie générale du droit international public' (1932-IV) 42 *RCADI* 142ff; H Accioly, *Traité de droit international public*, vol I (Paris, 1940) 81: 'Les personnes internationales sont les êtres ou organismes dont la situation juridique est régie par le droit international public, et dont les droits et devoirs sont déterminés par lui.'

[14] See FA von der Heydte, 'Rechtssubjekt und Rechtsperson im Völkerrecht', *Essays in Honor of J. Spiropoulos* (Bonn, 1957) 250; G Balladore Pallieri, *Diritto internazionale pubblico*, 7th edn (Milan, 1956) 98. See also G Gidel, 'Quelques idées sur la condition internationale de la Papauté' (1911) 18 *RGDIP* 604.

[15] See on this point A Verdross, *Die Quellen des universellen Völkerrechts* (Freiburg, 1973) 20.

[16] There are authors distinguishing three layers of subjects: the original subjects; the subjects created; and the subjects recognised. The second layer comprises the subjects created by the States, such as an international organisation; the third comprises subjects already existing but recognised in their personality, eg the individual. See C Dominicé, 'La société internationale à la recherché de son équilibre' (2013) 370 *RCADI* 145. In a large sense, categories two and three merge into one another, since in both cases the subjects are clothed with legal personality by the States.

[17] H Mosler, 'Réflexions sur la personnalité juridique en droit international public', *Essays in Honor of H. Rolin* (Paris, 1964) 238–39, 242–43, 250.

will or from a social fact. In concrete terms, the States are the primary or natural subjects; all the other entities are derived subjects of international law, created, or at least recognised, by the community of States.

III. The Quantity or Quality of the Subjective Legal Positions

The State appears as holding all the legal positions recognised in the international legal order. States can obviously modulate the extent of these rights and duties by undertaking various legal engagements via different sources (agreements, unilateral acts, estoppels, etc). The derived subjects do not have a single starting-point as regards the rights and obligations held. The subjective legal positions vary according to the function that international law accords to these subjects.[18] There must be at least one norm granting an entity one right or imposing one obligation[19]—without that, the legal personality could in no case be recognised. There is thus a sort of continuum, from the possession of all possible rights and obligations under international law to the possession of but one single right or obligation. Where is the boundary line for the recognition of international legal personality? Or is there none, legal personality extending the full length of this spectrum?

The question is of increasing relevance in view of the growing number of entities with different limited functions, such as NGOs, fluvial commissions, international committees, international courts, etc. Tomuschat has analysed this question in his general course at The Hague Academy.[20] He mentions a series of entities vested with some limited international powers:

1. Expert committees, eg in the area of human rights, such as the Human Rights Committee under Article 28 of the International Covenant on Civil and

[18] The legal personality is here closely linked to the powers of these subjects. See RY Jennings, 'General Course on Public International Law' (1967-II) 121 *RCADI* 346.

[19] The most famous example is the *Blockadebrecher* mentioned by Kelsen, ie the person violating an international blockade and incurring responsibility for that act under international law. Since one norm of international law is directly addressed to that person, he is a subject of international law. See H Kelsen, 'Théorie générale du droit international public' (1932-IV) 42 *RCADI* 153, which reads as follows in the original version and which we may leave untranslated: 'Supposons valable une norme de droit international en vertu de laquelle le navire neutre qui (en tentant de sortir d'un port bloqué ou d'y pénétrer) viole un blocus régulier peut être saisi et confisqué avec toute sa cargaison par l'Etat qui maintient effectivement le blocus: cette norme implique que, dans la mesure où le blocus a un effet juridique vis-à-vis des navires de commerce neutres, tous les propriétaires de ces navires sont directement obligés par le droit international de s'abstenir de rompre le blocus, sous peine de saisie et, le cas échéant, de confiscation du navire et de sa cargaison. Ces actes de contrainte, en tant que conséquences de la rupture du blocus, sont des sanctions prévues (et même prévues directement) par le droit international, dirigées contre un individu directement déterminé par le droit international: le propriétaire du navire qui a commis la violation du blocus.'

[20] C Tomuschat, 'International Law: Ensuring the Survival of Mankind on the Eve of a New century' (1999) 281 *RCADI* 141ff.

Political Rights (ICCPR) of 1966. The Committee has some international powers vis-à-vis States, notably the power to require periodic reports under Article 40 ICCPR; it may express opinions on these reports. The powers of the Committee are, however, strictly defined in the ICCPR; it has no autonomy to conduct an 'international policy' like, for instance, States.

2. International Courts and Tribunals, including arbitral tribunals. In the context of arbitration, the organs can be *ad hoc*, existing for one single dispute, or hear a number of cases and therefore be of some relative permanence (eg the Iran/US Claims Tribunal). The International Criminal Court is an international organisation constituted by the Assembly of States Parties under Article 4 of the Rome Statute of 1998. The Court also maintains diplomatic contacts with States in view of the cooperation necessary in the arrest of fugitives, the submission of evidence and the enforcement of judgments. The Law of the Sea Tribunal at Hamburg has been granted an internal legal personality (Article 2 of the Agreement on Privileges and Immunities of the Tribunal). This provision does not also automatically grant an international legal personality. It may be noted, however, that some tribunals conclude headquarters agreements. These can be subjected to international law and then trigger implied legal personality.[21]
3. There are further hybrid entities, situated somewhere between international and municipal law. This is the case, for example, as regards the Chamber of Human Rights under the Dayton Agreement of 1995.[22] This is an organ that can be seized by any person claiming that his or her human rights have been violated in the territory of Bosnia-Herzegovina. The applicable law comprises a series of international conventions on human rights. Similar considerations could be presented to the Claims Commission in Bosnia-Herzegovina; its statute is largely anchored in international law.[23] There are moreover National Truth Commissions, such as that established by the UN in Guatemala in 1994; it enjoys international privileges and immunities.[24]
4. There is a significant number of NGOs exercising the most varied international functions. Some of these NGOs have a consultative status within international organs such as ECOSOC or the Human Rights Council of the UN. They sometimes submit an *amicus curiae* (expert opinion) to international

[21] There had been voices since the beginning of the 20th century calling for recognition of the international legal personality of international courts and tribunals. See, eg, K Strupp, *Eléments du droit international public universel, européen et américain*, 2nd edn (Paris, 1930) 38–39. This author writes that any entity exercising international power is a subject of international law, eg a Bank for international settlements.

[22] General Framework Agreement for Peace in Bosnia and Herzegovina (1996) 35 *ILM* 89, 130. See K Oellers-Frahm, 'Die Rolle internationaler Gerichte im Friedensprozess in Bosnien und Herzegowina nach dem Abkommen von Dayton' in *Essays in Honor of G. Jaenicke* (Berlin, 1998) 263ff; P Szasz, 'The Protection of Human Rights through the Dayton/Paris Peace Agreement on Bosnia' (1996) 90 *AJIL* 309ff.

[23] P van Houtte, 'Mass Property Claim Resolution in a Post-War Society: The Commission for Real Property Claims in Bosnia and Herzegovina' (1999) 48 *ICLQ* 625ff.

[24] C Tomuschat, 'Between National and International Law: Guatemala's Historical Clarification Commission' in *Essays in Honor of G. Jaenicke* (Berlin, 1998) 991ff.

tribunals. These rights of NGOs are granted by international instruments, in particular treaties. Some NGOs possess a right of petition, eg with regard to the Inter-American Commission on Human Rights; or even a right to bring a claim, as, for example, according to the 1995 Protocol to the European Social Charter. There are NGOs with a considerable amount of power and influence, eg the International Olympic Committee.

5. Further, there are transnational corporations that have been granted certain international rights through contracts concluded with States. They may seize an international arbitral tribunal. Some authors view this process as constituting some degree of international legal personality.[25]

The aspect common to all these entities is the exercise of some scattered international functions and concomitant powers. For most authors this is not tantamount to possessing international legal personality. For the latter, it is necessary for an entity to participate in exercising some important powers and competencies under international law. The most frequently mentioned functions are: the capacity to conclude treaties (*jus tractatus*); the capacity to present international claims; the incurring of international responsibility for breach of the law; the capacity to stand before an international tribunal; and the possession of international privileges and immunities.[26] Certain authors add that an entity must possess rights *and* obligations, not just certain powers, to be a subject of the law.[27] Among the factors mentioned above, some are manifestly more important than others: if an entity possesses the right to conclude treaties, it must *eo ipso* be considered a subject of international law. In the most restrictive view, only 'Powers' are clothed with international legal personality, ie entities capable of pursuing their own autonomous international policy.[28] This is the case, for instance, as regards certain movements of national liberation or of insurgents. If one goes further and requires that the Power in question possesses sovereignty, ie the maximum amount of international autonomy, then this amounts to limiting international legal personality to States.[29]

[25] W Friedmann, *The Changing Structure of International Law* (London, 1964) 223.

[26] See, eg, M Sibert, *Traité de droit international public*, vol I (Paris, 1951) 87.

[27] N Mugerwa, 'Subjects of International Law' in M Sørensen (ed), *Manual of Public International Law* (London/Melbourne/Toronto/New York, 1968) 249. However, the possession of a subjective right always imposes a corresponding obligation.

[28] S Romano, *Corso di diritto internazionale*, 3rd edn (Padua, 1933) 61: '[L]e persone internazionali sono sempre, per usare una espressione del linguaggio diplomatico, delle *Potenze*. Però è da tener presente, che non ogni subordinazione, … è incompatibile con quel minimo di indipendenza richiesta dal diritto internazionale, e quindi tutto si riduce ad una questione di misura e di grado che non si può determinare *a priori* e con un principio generale. Inoltre, poichè la comunità internazionale ha carattere politico, i suoi membri sono o essi stessi degli enti politici o almeno dei soggetti che rivestono delle qualità che hanno direttamente o indirettamente rilevanza politica' (original emphasis). We may again leave that sentence untranslated. Some authors have contended that any political body that is a part of the international community possesses international legal personality: see F Capotorti, *Corso di diritto internazionale* (Milan, 1995) 17.

[29] This is the conclusion of P Weil, 'Le droit international en quête de son identité, Cours général de droit international public' (1992-VI) 237 *RCADI* 100ff. Any extension of legal personality to other subjects is ultimately based, according to Weil, on a fiction disguising the true power relations.

What position may we take with regard to the question posed? There are two main possibilities here. The first identifies legal personality with the possession of any international competence, power, right or obligation, ie any subjective legal position held directly by virtue of international law. Legal personality will then be extended to a great number of entities whose capacities (ie scope of powers) will vary greatly. The second restricts legal personality to the possession of some key powers showing a certain political autonomy (*jus inter potestates*). What combination of criteria is relevant here is not entirely clear, but the capacity to conclude treaties, to bring claims on one's own behalf and the onus of international responsibility should be determinative in any case. Legal personality will then be restricted to only some entities, while the great number of other persons possessing some international functions will have legal capacity without legal personality.[30] In practice, this means that they can exercise the functions international law assigns to them, but nothing more. The reason for denying international legal personality to such entities lies in the fact that no supplementary right other than those granted can be exercised. The recognised subjects of international law will here be mainly States and quasi-State entities (non-State belligerents, insurgents, movements of national liberation), and also some entities historically recognised as subjects (the Holy See, Maltese Order, ICRC). This limits the subjects of international law to certain named and known entities.

The distinction operated between capacity and personality is also reflected in certain other theories. First, we may find it in the above-mentioned conception according to which there are natural or original subjects and derived ones. The former have a general legal personality, the latter a functional one, ie the latter are essentially determined by their capacities. Secondly, the distinction subject/capacities is close to that between active and passive subjects of international law.[31] The former is a fully-fledged member of the international community and participates in the making of international law; the latter is only an addressee of international legal norms, without capacity to participate in the law-creating process. Thirdly, the question can also be approached through the lens of legal orders of different generality.[32] There would exist on the one hand the subjects of the universal international legal order, vested with a general legal capacity; and there would be on the other hand the subjects of particular international legal orders, clothed with a limited and functional capacity, which is limited precisely to the scope of the particular law from which they draw their subjective legal positions. We might mention in passing that some authors have ventured to claim that all subjects of international law are functional, in the sense that their spectrum of powers is in any case variable. Each subject has certain functions, for example to

30 See, eg, G Morelli, 'Cours général de droit international public' (1956-I) 89 *RCADI* 537ff.

31 A Favre, *Principes du droit des gens* (Freiburg, 1974) 309–10. On the capacity of a non-State entity to contribute to the formation of customary international law, see M Mendelson, 'The Formation of Customary International Law' (1998) 272 *RCADI* 198ff; R Kolb, *La bonne foi en droit international public* (Paris, 2000) 37–39.

32 G Ottolenghi, *Corso di diritto internazionale pubblico* (Turin, 1956) 71–72.

cooperate, settle disputes, claim rights, etc; legal capacities and legal personality are thus necessarily limited and functional.[33]

At the end of the day, the issue of legal personality turns on some assumptions. It rests on a definition of terms, as much for what it certainly includes (States in international law, individuals in municipal law) as for what it probably excludes (minor entities). The most that can be asked is to be clear on the use of the term in personal parlance and scientific work. When it is understood that the concept of legal personality remains distinct from the concrete array of powers, rights and obligations of a given subject, there may be little reason for not adopting the broad view of international personality. There remain, however, some awkward questions even here: should some terrorist groups then be called subjects of international law because a UN Security Council resolution imposes certain sanctions, ie international obligations, on them? From the point of view of legal technique, there may be little to fear from this statement; but politically, it is difficult to accept it.

[33] RY Jennings, 'General Course on Principles of Public International Law' (1967-II) 121 *RCADI* 346–48.

4

Questions of Method and the Structure of Rules in International Law

I. Method in International Law

In many sciences, questions of method have elicited keen reflection and efforts to pin down one method or another; not so in international law.[1] The method is not linked to the material object of a science but to the ways of knowing it.[2] A certain degree of consonance on the accepted ways of demonstrating and coming to a conclusion about the object at stake ensures some rational unity in the realm of science and allows the result reached to be controlled. For the law, the most relevant questions are, for example: What questions shall I ask? From what assumptions must or may I start? What are the means for reaching a conclusion? As we have seen, the political permeability and the individualisation of the international legal rule have hampered or forestalled fruitful efforts in the context of methodology. International law has developed empirically by the accretion of successive haphazard acts and facts. Pragmatism has had greater weight than systematic or methodological considerations. Uniformity and codification find it more difficult to gain a foothold in international law than in any other branch of the law, as is the case with the elaboration of a universally accepted method. Too many schools of thought exist, and there is no firm basis for an integrated legal culture, such as exists in the municipal legal orders. There are also important problems of terminology: the legal concepts used often have a different meaning according to context and user; this makes an international legal discourse more prone to pitfalls and misunderstandings.[3]

[1] See mainly H Kruse, 'Völkerrecht als Forschungsgegenstand' in G Erler (ed), *Völkerrechtliche Forschung* (Göttingen, 1955) 9ff; M Bos, *A Methodology of International Law* (The Hague, 1984); C Dominicé, 'Methodology of International Law' (1984) 7 *EPIL* 334ff; O Corten, *Méthodologie du droit international public* (Brussels, 2009).

[2] *Habitus intellectualis instrumentalis, nobis inserviens ad rerum cognitionem adipiscendam.*

[3] In the elegant words of N Politis, 'Le problème des limitations de la souveraineté et la théorie de l'abus des droits dans les rapports internationaux' (1925-I) 6 *RCADI* 19, which for this very reason may remain untranslated, 'On ne saurait assez attirer l'attention sur les graves inconvénients que comporte

The reasons for this methodological disaffection have been manifold. *First*, for a long time, entrenched and very general theoretical discussions on the construction of international law predominated. The focus on these fundamental questions obstructed the view as regards the more detailed issues of method located at a lower point in the edifice. And what common ground could be found between the sociological approach of social solidarity (Duguit) and the transcendental logic of normativism (Kelsen)? Thus, questions of existence, foundation and the basics of international law dominated the field following World War II. The elaboration of methodological avenues would suggest that such questions had been resolved; they had not.

Secondly, too many aspects of international law remain uncertain; this is inhibitive to the progress of method. Thus, in the *Nuclear Weapons* Opinion (UNGA, 1996),[4] the ICJ would take up the much debated fundamental question of whether international law is attributing competences to its subjects, or whether it merely limits original competences retained by the States. The scope of what is allowed under international law may differ according to which conception is adopted. The issue was put squarely before us in the famous *Lotus* decision of the PCIJ in 1927.[5] Have we made significant progress since then? Perhaps, but only in the last decades.

Thirdly, international law is an extremely heterogeneous legal order. Its material object is almost unlimited, as we have already seen. It is harder to establish methodological rules in such a scattered universe. It is no accident that in municipal law, questions of method have predominated largely in the context of private law, whereas their development has been weaker in the context of public law, notably in the context of constitutional law (but with the exception of criminal law). Constitutional law suffers from a lack of unity of its material object. In international law, the range of objects is broader again. We have also seen that the implementation of international law often occurs through the internal legal systems. The effect of this sharing of work implies a further fragmentation in the approaches towards international law.

Fourthly, the actors in international law vary. Not only lawyers work within with this legal order. And even the lawyers come from prodigiously different cultures, with different outlooks, training, ideological backgrounds, language and the like.[6] Many of them are today attracted either simply by practice, or else by ideological

une terminologie vicieuse. Il est impossible, dans la lutte des idées, d'arriver à un accord, d'approcher d'une solution, de réaliser un progrès, si l'on ne réussit pas à s'entendre sur le sens et la valeur des termes employés dans la discussion. Il est dangereux de se servir d'expressions inexactes, de locutions équivoques, de mots évocateurs d'idées fausses ou périmées. La pensée en est entravée et parfois elle s'arrête faute de pouvoir faire l'effort nécessaire pour percer le nuage qui la sépare de la réalité.'

[4] *Legality of the Threat or Use of Nuclear Weapons* (Advisory Opinion) [1996-I] ICJ Rep 238, §21.

[5] *SS Lotus (France v Turkey)* (1927) PCIJ Series A no 9, 4ff.

[6] Even between common law and civil lawyers, the finding of a common ground may pose problems. The conflict between the two traditions was, eg, most visible at the ICTY in the *Erdemovic* case of 1997 ((1997) 111 *ILR* 298ff). The issue of duress was difficult to handle, since in common law it is a defence only giving rise to a lower sentence, whereas in civil law it may be a circumstance precluding punishment altogether. The common law judges postulated a sort of absolute duty not to kill, even if

approaches. The method is secondary in their conception. The relevant acts of international law are themselves not regularly performed by lawyers but rather by administrative personnel, diplomats, politicians, etc. It is rare that a legal adviser will first formulate the act and format it according to legal exigencies. But the participation of many non-lawyers in international legal processes has meant that the legal content of the materials is considerably diluted. International law is staffed with persons having made some interdisciplinary study, having heard some lectures on constitutional or international law, having studied international relations and the like. These individuals will then participate in the formulation of legal content in various committees or elsewhere. They are often devoid of sufficient knowledge of legal technique and legal argument. However interesting their contributions to international law may be, they will invariably instill into the legal body a series of fluctuations, imprecisions, confusions. For a methodological study of the law, their contributions will not infrequently sail under an unidentified flag.

Fifthly, as already mentioned, the political and individualising tendencies of international legal norms add to the difficulties of the method. When rules are heavily contextualised, it renders systematisation more difficult. There are too many circumstances to take into account; thus the classification becomes either too simplistic, or overly complex. In both cases it loses its justification. Method is geared towards regularity and formalism; large fluctuations and contingencies, as well as political motives, reduce its impact. Moreover, the typification of legal situations under international law is significantly less developed than in municipal law. This can be seen in many of its disputes: the length of the relevant time-span to be taken into account (in territorial disputes, frequently many centuries); the plurality of historical and psychological factors; cultural, economic, political and other issues inextricably linked to the object of the dispute; the role of the practicability of any solution devised, etc. Here the method tends most often to disappear behind the result. As we have already seen, the issue in the settlement of disputes is generally that the dispute is settled and that the States can live with the result, much more than that the dispute is settled by the application of rules of international law (rule of law).

Ultimately, it appears that systematic and methodological 'purity' are not required assets in the international legal order; there are other, much more urgent problems and issues to tackle. The reverse side of the coin is that international law,

your own life is thereby jeopardised (and policy reasons were adduced to that effect). Judge Cassese voiced staunch opposition from the civil law perspective, criticising the reasoning of his common law colleagues as being founded on extra-legal arguments contrary to the principle *nullum crimen sine lege*. The divergence also existed on the starting-point for the reasoning: the common lawyers considered that the common ground of the two main legal systems had to be taken into account, ie lesser blame on a person who killed under duress—hence a reduction of the sentence. On the other hand, the starting-point was the application of the general rule on duress as a fully-fledged circumstance precluding punishment, given that the common law exception to this rule for cases of murder had not been received in international law. There is here a manifest mutual incomprehension and a clash of views. It had a heavy impact on the reasoning. It must be added, however, that even within the same supreme court of a State, there can be diametrically opposed reasoning.

more easily than other legal orders, may give the impression that any operator can arrive at any legal result on whatever path. This may weaken the authority of the legal order and of the legal conclusions reached in a particular case. Therefore, even if it is true that methodology is not the main preoccupation in international law, it would be going too far to say that this must remain the last word on the matter. The lack of agreed unity is particularly problematic in certain areas, for example in the context of conceptual and terminological confusions. Such fluctuations are particularly awkward for the lawyer.

II. Conceptual and Terminological Problems

There are three frequent sources of confusion in international law:

1. *Conceptual confusions.* The sense of a legal concept is here viewed differently, which leads to uncertainties and misunderstandings. Thus, an agreement becomes impossible either because of some claim that a concept cannot be used in a way different from the one utilised by those making this claim (this is the case, for example, in the context of sovereignty, see section II.A.1. below); or the confusion flows from the fact that many authors are not sufficiently aware that the concept is being used with different shades and meanings, thus projecting into it a unity that it does not possess (this is the case, for example, in the context of good faith, see section II.A.2. below).
2. *Systematic confusions.* The confusion here stems from the fact that a term or concept is used with different meanings in two or more legal traditions, or that the context of an identical rule is not the same in two or more legal traditions (eg common law and civil law). The problems are here linked to the conversion of legal terms from one system to the other. This necessitates an understanding of the conceptual and environmental aspects embedded in each system (see section II.B. below).
3. *Terminological confusions.* The confusion has its origin in the insufficient definition of certain terms of international law. Each author can thus use these terms with differing meanings, multiplying the sources of misunderstanding. A good example can be found in the law of war through the terms 'seizure' and 'requisition' (see section II.C. below).

Let us consider some examples in each of these categories.

A. Conceptual Confusions

1. Sovereignty

The first example of conceptual confusion occurs in the context of *sovereignty*. This notion gave rise to lively debates at the beginning of the twentieth century, when the creation of the League of Nations and the nascent conscience of international interdependence triggered the need for revision of traditional thinking.

During the Middle Ages and up to the eighteenth century, sovereignty was configured as a limited and relative notion.[7] It referred in the first place to a notion of independence, ie the faculty to make final decisions, without any appeal to a higher authority. This meant that the concept could apply to any type of jurisdiction: in respect of that particular jurisdiction, the sovereign power was that which made the final decisions. The territorial State had not yet appeared, thus the concept did not describe the abundance of centralised powers, as it did in later centuries. The result was that there was no one sovereignty (of the State) but many sovereignties (of many bearers). The claim of independence, which was inherent in royal sovereignty, was manifested in the struggle against the universal powers—the Pope and the Holy Roman Emperor. The king pretended to be 'emperor in its own kingdom', ie to be independent in his decision-making from the overbearing authority of those universal powers.

With the territorialisation of the State starting in the sixteenth century, a further aspect was added: interior sovereignty, manifested in the centralisation of supreme powers within the State and the elimination of the particular 'sovereignties' of various entities and persons. Politically, this corresponded to an effort to erase the powers of the intermediate bodies, whose consent was necessary to legislate. This was the main preoccupation at the time of Bodin.[8] But the sovereignty of the king remained circumscribed: it was subject to the common law and to a series of constitutional laws of the Holy Roman Empire. It was also subject to divine and natural law, to international law and to some customs or private acquired rights.[9] In other words, it was not an absolute power.

From the eighteenth century a concept of absolute sovereignty started to develop in political theory. It was rooted in the pretence of States to be the highest authority on earth, not subject to any superior whatsoever. Thus, sovereignty began to be considered 'the absolute and non-controllable power of States to behave, in their external and internal relations, as they saw fit, without any other restrictions than the ones freely accepted'.[10] Hence, sovereignty now became a weapon against any non-voluntary limitation, for example against the binding nature of external laws. It was designed as the ultimately supreme power to do whatever one wanted, which was international anarchy. This conception had its roots in Machiavelli, Hobbes and Spinoza, and later in Hegel and Austin.[11] It is not difficult to grasp that such a conception of sovereignty is at odds with the existence of a binding international

[7] See the study by A Truyol y Serra, 'Souveraineté' (1990) 35 *Archives de philisophie du droit* 313ff; H Quaritsch, *Souveränität—Entstehung und Entwicklung des Begriffs in Frankreich und Deutschland vom 13. Jahrhundert bis 1806* (Berlin, 1986). For the Middle Ages, see, eg, F Calasso, *I glossatori e la teoria della sovranità* (Florence, 1945).

[8] Truyol y Serra, above n 7, 316–17; Quaritsch, above n 7, 39ff.

[9] J Bodin, *Les six livres de la République* (1576), book i, chs 2, 4 and 8.

[10] N Politis, *Les nouvelles tendances du droit international* (Paris, 1927) 18–19.

[11] Truyol y Serra, Souveraineté, above n 7, p319–321.

legal order. This is the reason why certain authors of the twentieth century denied that 'sovereignty' could be an international legal concept at all.[12] Having in mind only absolute sovereignty, they affirmed that the very idea of 'limited sovereignty' was a contradiction in terms and therefore a logical impossibility:[13]

> To admit that sovereignty could be reduced would indeed be tantamount to recognizing that it does not exist at all, since by very definition it is a notion deprived of any restriction. One is independent or one is not independent. It has been said with good reason that a limited independence is already dependence.[14]

Many other arguments have been added: for example, that the original distribution of jurisdiction among States must have been performed by some superior international law, lest there be only an international space subject to total anarchy;[15] that not the State but only the international community, as the highest entity, could be called sovereign;[16] that States possess only powers linked with duties at the service of some common weal, and not unlimited subjective rights;[17] that a society based on (absolute) sovereignty did not square with the needs of the new interdependent world at the time of the League of Nations,[18] etc. This rejection of the notion can also be found in recent writings on international law.[19]

This leads to a paradoxical situation. While the majority of international lawyers consider sovereignty to be the cornerstone of international law, that is that this legal order exists only because there are sovereign States that must be

[12] H Krabbe, *The Modern Idea of the State* (New York/London, 1927) 233ff; H Kelsen, *Das Problem der Souveränität und die Theorie des Völkerrechts*, 2nd edn (Tübingen, 1928) 22ff; G Scelle, *Précis de droit des gens*, vol I (Paris, 1932) 7–8, 81ff; N Politis, *Les nouvelles tendances du droit international* (Paris, 1927) 18ff; J. W Garner, 'Des limitations à la souveraineté nationale dans les relations extérieures' (1925) 6 *RDILC* 36ff; L Duguit, *Traité de droit constitutionnel*, vol I (Paris, 1921) 551ff; G Salvioli, 'Les règles générales de la paix' (1933-IV) 46 *RCADI* 56ff and G Salvioli, 'Studi sui caratteri dell'ordinamento giuridico internazionale' (1921/1922) *Rivista di diritto internazionale* Series III, vol 1, 20ff; A Verdross, *Die Einheit des rechtlichen Weltbildes auf Grundlage der Völkerrechtsverfassung* (Tübingen, 1923) 31ff, 34; DJ Hill, *L'Etat moderne et l'organisation internationale* (Paris, 1912); S Séferiadès, 'Principes généraux du droit international de la paix' (1930-IV) 34 *RCADI* 360–63; JL Brierly, 'Règles générales du droit de la paix' (1936-IV) 58 *RCADI* 23ff; L Le Fur, 'La souveraineté de l'Etat et le droit international', *Les Lettres* (Paris, 1925) 87ff; C Rousseau, 'L'aménagement des compétences en droit international' (1930) 37 *RGDIP* 423; G Jèze, *Principes généraux du droit administratif*, vol I, 3rd edn (Paris, 1925) 339. See generally E Giraud, 'Le rejet de l'idée de souveraineté' *Essays in Honor of G. Scelle*, vol I (Paris, 1950) 253ff; J Mortelet, 'Le principe de la souveraineté de l'Etat et le droit international public' (1926) 33 *RGDIP* 104ff; C Rousseau, 'L'indépendance de l'Etat dans l'ordre international' (1948-II) 73 *RCADI* 181ff.

[13] S Séferiadès, 'Principes généraux du droit international de la paix' (1930-IV) 34 *RCADI* 360; C Rousseau, *Droit international public*, vol II (Paris, 1974) 63.

[14] N Politis, *Les nouvelles tendances du droit international* (Paris, 1927) 22–23.

[15] *ibid*, 24. See also L Le Fur, 'Le droit naturel ou objectif s'étend-il aux rapports internationaux?' (1925) 6 *RDILC* 78; J Ralston, *Le droit international de la démocratie* (Paris, 1923) 173.

[16] S Séferiadès, 'Principes généraux du droit international de la paix' (1930-IV) 34 *RCADI* 360, 363.

[17] C Rousseau, *Droit international public*, vol III (Paris, 1977) 9.

[18] N Politis, 'Le problème des limitations de la souveraineté et la théorie de l'abus des droits dans les rapports internationaux' (1925-I) 6 *RCADI* 9ff.

[19] Apart from the writings on globalisation and the erosion of sovereignty, there is a conceptual critique along the lines of our concern at this juncture in L Henkin, 'General Course of Public International Law—International Law: Politics, Values and Functions' (1989-IV) 216 *RCADI* 26.

coordinated,[20] others argue that international law cannot exist at all if the notion of sovereignty is upheld. It is manifest that there is principally a conceptual disagreement here. If sovereignty is necessarily an absolute and boundless power (absolute sovereignty), it must be condemned from the point of view of the legal order; if sovereignty is a power to decide and act in the last resort subject to the constraints of international law (relative sovereignty), the concept is entirely compatible with international law. History shows that for a long time sovereignty was a relative and limited concept. Relative sovereignty is therefore not a contradiction in terms; but there remains the fact that the concept has often been abused in international politics, so that the flavour of absolutism sometimes permeates through it. Thus the concept has been somewhat discredited. In any case, the social and legal realities expressed by the concept are undeniably with us: the fact was and remains that States are independent from the point of view of law and have the power of decision in the last resort. Whether this is called 'sovereignty' or some other term[21] does not much matter; what is important is that the concept must be designated by some word. In this light, protracted disputes on the logical impossibility of the concept of sovereignty are not helpful. We must proceed to substance.

2. *Good Faith*

A confusion of a slightly different type occurs in the context of the concept of *good faith*.[22] Good faith refers to two distinct concepts, one subjective the other objective in nature. In the Latin languages, both aspects are covered by the same concept: *bona fides*, bonne foi, buona fede, buena fe, boa fé, from which the English 'good faith' is derived. Germanic languages distinguish both aspects by referring to them by different terms: *Treu und Glauben* for the objective aspect, and *guter Glaube* for the subjective one.[23] In the objective sense, good faith designates the well-known principle of law, which is the basis for, amongst others, *pacta sunt servanda*, the protection of legitimate expectations, acquiescence and estoppel, etc. In the subjective sense, good faith designates a mental state of affairs, ie the fact of knowing or not knowing a certain fact. As a legal doctrine, it here means an excusable error due to absence of knowledge. Thus, it is said that the purchaser was acting in good faith since he did not know that the object he purchased had previously been stolen. Both concepts have their legal standing and their legal effects; but they are quite different one from each other, the first being a legal principle and the second referring to a fact. The two aspects have not been sufficiently separated—which is

[20] EN van Kleffens, 'Sovereignty in International Law' (1953-I) 82 *RCADI* 5, 127–30. See also *SS Lotus* (1927) PCIJ Series A no 9, 18–19; and *SS Wimbledon* (1923) PCIJ ser A no 1, 25.

[21] As, eg, the word 'reprisals' has been replaced with the word 'counter-measures', so as to avoid the connotations of force the former word has progressively obtained through the practice of 'armed reprisals' and by being often related to armed reprisals in time of armed conflict.

[22] On this concept, see among others R Kolb, *La bonne foi en droit international public* (Paris, 2000).

[23] See Arts 2 and 3 of the Swiss Civil Code.

where the confusion arises.[24] Thus, Zoller claimed in her monograph that good faith does not play any significant role in international law.[25] This statement could manifestly only be made because the subjective aspect was meant: it would be quite wrong to extend this statement to the objective aspect. In order to be clearer, the distinction between the two needs to be examined, otherwise there will remain a constant source of confusion.

B. Systematic Confusions

The cohabitation of civil and common law concepts within the body of international law is a source of possible quibbling and misunderstanding. It renders more arduous the transfer by analogy of municipal law concepts into the international legal order.[26] The differing conceptualisations of the two systems sometimes obscure the determination of the common roots of the regulations, ie the underlying principle to be transferred by analogy to international law. An example is the concept of the abuse of rights. Known to civil law systems, it is absent from common law systems. But there is a series of particular norms in the common law that are based on the same basic idea and which, taken together, can serve as a basis for induction[27]—for example trespass in private law and the misuse of authority in public law.[28] The same is true for the concept of 'public order', meaning a set of fundamental values of a legal system embodied in a series of sometimes hierarchically superior norms. The term 'international public order'[29] is not wholly satisfactory, neither is the term 'public policy'. An example of concepts of the common law that have no civil law equivalents can be found in the procedural laws: affidavits, subpoenas (eg *subpoena duces tecum*), etc.[30] There are

[24] Or the distinction is not made properly at all: see, eg, E Zoller, *La bonne foi en droit international public* (Paris, 1977).

[25] *ibid*, 335ff, 351.

[26] Analogies with municipal law have in the past been an extremely important device for the development of international law. See on this point KH Ziegler, 'Die römischen Grundlagen des europäischen Völkerrechts' in *Ius commune*, vol IV (Frankfurt, 1972) 1ff; H Lauterpacht, *Private Law Sources and Analogies of International Law* (London, 1927); ES Creasey, *First Platform of International Law* (London, 1876) 83ff; B Paradisi, *I fondamenti storici della comunità giuridica internazionale* (Siena, 1944); J Kosters, 'Les fondements du droit international' in *Bibliotheca Visseriana*, vol IV (Leyde, 1925) 156ff; A Miaja de la Muela, 'Aportaciónes históricas y actuales del derecho romano al orden internacional' in *Essays in Honor of Santa Cruz Teijeiro*, (Valencia, 1974) 531ff; G Barile, 'La rilevazione e l'integrazione del diritto internazionale non scritto e la libertà di apprezzamento del giudice' in *Comunicazioni e studi*, vol 5 (Milan, 1953) 177ff; AD McNair, 'The Debt of International Law in Britain to the Civil Law and the Civilians' (1953) 39 *Transactions of the Grotius Society* 183ff.

[27] On the process in general, see J Esser, *Grundsatz und Norm in der richterlichen Fortbildung des Privatrechts*, 4th edn (Tübingen, 1990) 28ff, 87ff, 141ff, 242ff.

[28] B Cottier and M Sychold, 'Qu'en est-il de l'abus de droit dans les pays qui ignorent cette institution?' in B Widmer and B Cottier (eds), *Abus de droit et bonne foi* (Freiburg, 1994) 325ff.

[29] G Jeanicke, 'International Public Order' (1984) 7 *EPIL* 314ff.

[30] C Bassiouni and P Manikas, *The Law of the International Criminal Tribunal for the Former Yugoslavia* (New York, 1996). For subpoenas, see JA Carrillo Salcedo, 'The Inherent Powers of the International Criminal Tribunal for the Former Yugoslavia to issue "subpoena duces tecum" to a

also concepts on which there is only partial correspondence: this is the case as regards estoppel in municipal law when compared to the civil law *venire contra factum proprium*.

International criminal law illustrates these difficulties. A perusal of the judgments rendered after World War II on the most differing legal bases reveals the divergences between common and civil lawyers.[31] The preponderance of common lawyers on the bench of the tribunals to some extent overshadowed the extent of the difficulties. For example, important fluctuations occurred in the assessment of the subjective elements (*mens rea*) of crimes: *intention*, *dolus directus* (of different types) and *dolus eventualis* on the one side; intention and recklessness on the other side. Another example can be found in the distinction or confusion between crimes by omission and negligence.[32] Tensions flowing from different criminal law conceptualisations still exist in the criminal tribunals of today, eg in the ICTY. The above-mentioned *Erdemovic* case of 1997 is a good example.[33] We may here just recall that the issue turned on the legal effect of duress in the context of homicide: could the accused excuse the murder committed by him because he was compelled to commit it under threat of danger to his life, or could this coercion only be taken into account in mitigation when sentencing him for the crime?[34] This controversy gave rise to acrimonious exchanges between the judges of the two traditions.[35]

C. Terminological Confusions

There are numerous uncertainties regarding the precise legal meaning of a series of terms of international law. It sometimes happens that the great majority of operators agree on a certain use of the term; divergent uses remain confined to the

Sovereign State', *Essays in Honor of N. Valticos* (Paris, 1999) 269ff; P Malanczuk, 'The International Criminal Tribunal's Power to issue subpoena duces tecum', *Essays in Honor of P. de Waart* (The Hague, 1998). 260ff; JM Favre, 'Le mécanisme du subpoena dans la jurisprudence du Tribunal international pour l'ex-Yougoslavie' (1997) 43 *AFDI* 403ff. For rules on evidence, see WA Schabas, 'Le Règlement de preuve et de procédure du Tribunal international chargé de poursuivre les personnes présumées responsables de violations graves du droit international humanitaire commises sur le territoire de l'ex-Yougoslavie depuis 1991' (1993/1994) 8 *Revue québécoise de droit international* 112ff; Y Nouvel, 'La preuve devant le Tribunal pénal international pour l'ex-Yougoslavie' (1997) 101 *RGDIP* 905ff; H Ascensio, 'The Rules of Procedure and Evidence of the ICTY' (1996) 9 *Leiden Journal of International Law* 467ff.

[31] United Nations War Crimes Commission, *Law Reports of the Trials of War Criminals*, vols I–XIV (London, 1946–49).

[32] See the *Informal Paper* of the ICRC of 17 February 1999.

[33] *Erdemovic* (1997) 111 *ILR* 298ff. On this case, see LC Green, 'Drazen Erdemovic: The International Criminal Tribunal for the Former Yougoslavia in Action' (1997) 10 *Leiden Journal of International Law* 363ff; K Oellers-Frahm, 'Die Erdemovic-Rechtsprechung des Jugoslawientribunals: Probleme bei der Entwicklung eines internationalen Strafrechts, dargestellt am Beispiel des Notstandes' (1998) 58 *ZaöRV* 389ff; D Turns, 'The International Criminal Tribunal for the Former Yougoslavia: The Erdemovic Case' (1998) 47 *ICLQ* 461ff.

[34] See above n 6.

[35] See, eg, the harsh words of Judge Cassese in his dissent in (1997) 111 *ILR* 298, 395, §11.

margins. But it also happens that a series of concurrent definitions are juxtaposed and possibly remain unrelated. A vivid illustration of the latter situation is offered by the two terms, 'seizure' and 'requisition', in the context of the law of armed conflict.[36] The meaning to be accorded to the words already varies in the context of the law of belligerent occupation, the law of conduct of military operations and the law of maritime prizes. The dominating opinion distinguishes the meaning of the terms as a function of the nature of goods appropriated: assets that can be used for military operations are seized, other objects are requisitioned (but they must in any case be destined for the use of the army or the occupying authorities).[37] For other authors seizing is limited to maritime warfare, whereas requisitioning is limited to land warfare.[38] For still others, seizure concerns public property, requisition private property.[39] There are authors who consider that 'requisition' covers all appropriations for the needs of the army, whereas 'seizure' is limited to moveable goods taken as war booty.[40] There are also those who consider that both terms largely overlap and can be distinguished only on account of two elements: requisition applies to immoveable and moveable property, while seizure is limited to moveable property; and requisition is limited to private property or to assets of the local public authorities in occupied territory, while seizure covers private and public property.[41] Lastly, some authors affirm that requisition refers to a legal regime, whereas seizure is simply the fact of appropriation of a certain asset.[42]

The existence of such terminological fluctuations is not in itself an evil. To some extent, it is unavoidable in a society deprived of a central legislator capable of imposing a unitary definition of the law and its vocabulary. The problems lies in the fact that such a multiplicity of approaches is a constant source of confusion and quibbling. Each author tends to convey the idea that his definition is generally accepted; that it is *the* meaning of the term at stake. This impression is then reinforced for the reader. Therefrom flows a series of apparent certainties, which will later fall to be disappointed. This in turn creates a sense of frustration and a loss of orientation. Such frustration is much deeper than the sense of complexity

[36] See Arts 23, letter g, and 52 of the Hague Regulations of 1907 (Hague Convention IV on the laws and customs of land warfare).

[37] M Greenspan, *The Modern Law of Land Warfare* (Berkeley/Los Angeles, 1959) 293ff, 296, 300; FA von der Heydte, *Völkerrecht*, vol II (Cologne/Berlin, 1960) 324–25; P Jessup, 'A Belligerent Occupant's Power Over Property' (1944) 38 *AJIL* 458–59; AD McNair and A Watts, *The Legal Effects of War* (Cambridge, 1966) 394–95.

[38] L Oppenheim and H Lauterpacht, *International Law*, vol II: *Disputes, War and Neutrality*, 7th edn (London/New York/Toronto, 1952) 474–76.

[39] P Fauchille, *Traité de droit international public*, vol II: *Guerre et neutralité* (Paris, 1921) 254ff, 281ff. The conditions for requisition are stricter.

[40] LH Woolsey, 'The Forced Transfer of Property in Enemy Occupied Territories' (1943) 37 *AJIL* 285.

[41] G Schwarzenberger, *International Law—As Applied by International Courts and Tribunals*, vol II: *The Law of Armed Conflict* (London, 1968) 269, 291ff.

[42] C Rousseau, *Le droit des conflits armés* (Paris, 1983) 166–70, 167. There are also some arbitral awards based on this understanding, notably *Tesdorpf v Germany* (1923), I *RIAA* 107, where the arbitrators emphasise that seizure does not transfer property.

arising from the various definitions that were correctly understood from the very beginning.

D. Conclusion

The lesson to be learned from the foregoing three sources of confusion is that efforts at clarification are necessary on many levels of international law. The main point is to eliminate sources of misunderstanding and the waste of energy provoked by the imprecision of the tools to be used. Greater clarity can help to improve the scientific construction of international law, which supposes communication and inter-subjectivity. Greater clarity also allows the better practical functioning of the law, which depends on legal certainty. There are manifestly cases where the States—as legislators—do not wish certain provisions to be clear and unambiguous. But it would be foolish to add to these cases of voluntary ambiguity the complication of avoidable confusion.[43]

However, it is illusory to believe in rapid and decisive progress. International legal doctrine and international legal operators are multifarious, and come from the most varied cultural and educational backgrounds. Lawyers and non-lawyers intermingle, more than in municipal law contexts, in the making and shaping of international law. The diplomatic and political nature of international law—with the frequent search for compromise and dilatory formulae—does not improve the situation. All these elements account for a certain degree of formal or conceptual weakness of international law. In other words, international society is not so much in search of a scientifically solid and conceptually coherent body of the law as requiring a flexible and multi-faceted body adapting to extremely varied circumstances in the largest society existing, namely in world society. The foregoing should not mean, however, that international lawyers could or should not try to improve the situation by a succession of modest steps, as and when feasible.

III. What Place can be Made for Method in International Law?

Method is a path for arriving at knowledge. In the context of the law, there are different methodical aspects. Some relate to interpretation: textual, teleological, systematic interpretation; *argumentum ab aucoritate, a simili, a contrario, a fortiori, ad absurdum*, etc. Others relate to logic, such as the avoidance of gaps in reasoning,

[43] This is true all the more if the claim that international law is still in its infancy is true: T.M. Franck, 'Fairness in the International Legal System, General Course on Public International Law' (1993-III) 240 *RCADI* 23ff.

contradictions and insufficient premises: eg *fallacia consequentis*,[44] *quatertio terminorum*,[45] *fallacia ambiguitatis*[46] *and petitio principii*.[47] Lastly, there are general techniques: induction, deduction and analogy. These last shall concern us here.

Induction starts with the particular facts and attempts to extract a general rule from them. Its truth is thus empirical and linked to experience; it is *a posteriori*. For example, one can observe that any object thrown into the air comes down on the ground; thus, there is a law of gravity. Facts that are contrary to the rule inducted either disprove it or lead to its correction. An induction can be fully successful only if it is founded on the totality of the relevant real data. However, this is hardly ever possible,[48] and thus in most cases induction is incomplete. It leads to a hypothesis, holding that the objects observed have had quality '*x*' up to now, but not that they will continue to have it in the future. For example, all ravens observed so far have been black: thus the hypothesis stands that ravens are black; but this does not exclude the possible discovery in future of a raven of another, so far unseen colour.

Deduction, on the other hand, starts from the principle and works back from it to the particular facts. Its truth is rational and of an *a priori* nature. It is therefore a truth that the human spirit holds firm at a given time: things must or ought to be '*x*'. This judgement cannot be refuted by a contrary fact: the 'is' and the 'ought' are not placed on the same plane. Deductions can be of general reach (eg from the premise 'you shall not kill', the necessity for a criminal law provision prohibiting intentional and negligent homicide, or even abortion, is deduced) or of particular reach (taking then the form of a syllogism: it is prohibited to kill under the threat of criminal sanction; A has killed B; A will be punished).

Induction is the main method of the natural sciences (geared towards the 'is'), while deduction is an important method for the normative sciences (geared towards the 'ought'). There is, however, no firm and entrenched opposition between these two methods. There is no reasoning of a purely inductive or purely deductive nature. Thus, even the natural sciences work with assumptions,

[44] The argument is: 'Since A is necessary for B, B is also necessary for A', which is an error. Example: A will be acquitted if he acted in self-defence; A is acquitted; thus he acted in self-defence. The error lies in the fact that A may have been acquitted for other reasons.

[45] A term is used more than once in a chain of argument but with different senses. Example: Judge Abi-Saab is intelligent like a fox; foxes have four legs; Judge Abi-Saab thus has four legs.

[46] A conclusion is enunciated, but there is no precision as to one of its necessary elements. Example: if *x* is done, the trial will be lost. But there is no precision as to which of the two parties will lose. This situation is frequent in international law, especially with presumptions 'in favour of sovereignty'. No precision is expressed as to the sovereignty of which State—since in a relationship there is more than one party!

[47] The deduction flows directly from the assumption subjectively made, and is thus defective (one supposes what has to be proved). Example: God is the perfect being; thus God exists (otherwise he could not be perfect). In international law, there are frequent defective examples of this type, eg it is claimed that *jus cogens* is international public order, and that thus it must be universal and cannot be regional.

[48] Such an observation can occur only for a limited category of facts situated in the past, or at least terminated in the present. If future facts have to be envisaged, the matter turns into a hypothesis.

and even legal science knows about the influence of facts on the rules (even if 'effectiveness' is itself transformed into a legal concept).[49] Moreover, the method used also depends on the aim pursued: the application of the law to a single case is based on deduction, while the formulation of a principle by the analysis of the case law is based much more on induction; or deduction will be used if the aim is to establish a definition or an assumption, whereas induction may be used to establish a mere provisional hypothesis.[50] The main point remains that both methods have to be combined.

Certain legal theories have placed too much emphasis on one of the methods to the detriment of the other. Their results have therefore been insufficient and defective. Thus, some rational natural law theories of the Enlightenment (eg Wolff)[51] exceeded the bounds of what could be obtained by deduction. On the other hand, some positivistic theories sought guidance only from sparse facts of international practice, significantly impoverishing international law. The law then became a simple 'ratification chamber' of the accomplished fact, or a simple receptacle of power policies.[52] In short, the method of international law as a whole would be limited to classifying facts; it would largely resemble an inquiry into the formation of a rule of customary law through the analysis of State practice. But a legal order cannot simply consist of a compendium of facts: this would be at best a guide to usages. Legal prescriptions cannot be grasped without a normative element going beyond the simple fact. Thus the formation of customary international law is not based on practice alone, but also on legal opinion.[53] Moreover, a legal order can contain many rules flowing from practice, but it must also contain some rules flowing from axioms (general principles, first normative propositions). Without

[49] On the principle of effectiveness in international law, see notably F Couveinhes-Matsumoto, *L'effectivité en droit international* (Brussels, 2014).

[50] A sentence of the type 'ravens are black' can be a definition or a hypothesis. If it is the former, it will express an unalterable truth. Thus, the discovery of a non-black raven will have the effect of classifying that bird into a new category, called, for example, 'baven' (eg if it is blue). Concomitantly it will be said, 'This bird is blue, thus it is not a raven.' If the sentence is a hypothesis, it will express a rationalisation of facts observed. Therefore, the discovery of a blue bird will lead to the abandonment of the assumption that ravens are black. From here flows the well-known 'trial and error' method of Popper. There is, however, a fundamental difference between ravens and legal phenomena. The former belong to observable nature, and thus to natural science. The latter are not based on physically observable facts but on spiritual realities: these have no tangible reality and are thus much more complex to grasp. In the normative sciences, it is thus necessary to start from the assumption of the character of the object to analyse (axioms); otherwise it would be impossible to understand which manifestations are part of the legal phenomenon and which are not. These axioms here replace the absent physical body of the object to be scrutinised. Moreover, the 'ought' orientation of the law explains the more limited reach of induction: the sociological reality is not the normative injunction. From the fact that homicides become constantly more frequent, I cannot deduce—without further enquiry—that the rule prohibiting homicide has been abolished or is no longer applicable.

[51] On his system, see, eg, B Winiger, *Das rationale Pflichtenrecht Christian Wolffs* (Berlin, 1992).

[52] See, eg, G Schwarzenberger, *The Inductive Approach to International Law* (London, 1965).

[53] Even those authors who have denied any role to legal opinion have finally abandoned their views. On this question, see, eg, M Akehurst, 'Custom as a Source of International Law' (1974/1975) 47 *BYIL* 31ff.

the support of the latter, it could not function properly:[54] it would dissolve into a series of haphazard positions without proper links or unity. In practice, this would mean that the legal order would not contain answers for many lingering or at least open questions.[55] Consequently, the legal order is composed of many types of different norms with many different functions. Principles fill the gaps and govern the dynamics of the law (*lex lata* pushed towards *lex ferenda*). Their dynamism is limited by their small number and by a series of contingent facts (ideological consonance in a given society at a given moment, distribution of power, pressure of more or less urgent social and political transformations, political stability or instability, the importance law is accorded in the political system as a whole, etc). In short, there are some legal rules based more on axioms (deduction) and others based more on practice (induction). Ideal and real factors are related in the body as a whole, the 'is' and the 'ought' refer one to the other, facts are related to the norm and the norm is related to the facts.[56] The method of the law is eclectic: it is situated constantly between deduction, induction and analogy.

In the next section, we shall see how these methodological tools can find their way into a legal order characterised by the significant individualisation of its legal rules. As we have already seen, international law often enunciates fact-intense or circumstantial legal rules. How does this state of affairs impact on its methodology?

IV. The Individualisation of International Law Rules and its Consequences

A. Generalising and Individualising Perspectives

Any object appears in our eyes as a sum of qualities that can be considered on two different planes. First, the object can be considered as a manifestation or as an element of a broader category of which it is part. This perspective allows the formulation of types, for example the different types of fruits. It is a generalising perspective. Conversely, we may also consider an object in its unicity, ie in

[54] 'It stands to reason that good faith … cannot be observed by empirical methods. As an ever-present element of any legal system, it constitutes a rationalization of a certain way of correct conduct required of everyone.' (C Tomuschat, "International Law: Ensuring the Survival of Mankind on the Eve of a New Century' (1999) 281 *RCADI* 322) See R Kolb, *La bonne foi en droit international public* (Paris, 2000) 1ff.

[55] Thus, some arbitrators could affirm the subsidiary responsibility of the member States of an international organisation based, inter alia, on the principle of good faith: see *Westland Helicopters* (1984) 80 *ILR* 613.

[56] Legal facts cannot be understood as such without being mentally referred to the elements of some norm, and conversely the norm cannot be understood in the abstract without some mental reference to the facts it seeks to cover and cases that may arise under its command. See the reflections in A Kaufmann, *Rechtsphilosophie*, 2nd edn (Munich, 1997) 86–88.

the particular elements that distinguish it from all other objects, even ones of the same type. This may be the case for the shape of a particular fruit. The perspective is here individualising. Now, each object is at one and the same time a type and an individuality. Thus, Katrine is on the generalising plane a collie—dog—vertebrate—animal—being. At the same time, Katrine is an individual being presenting a set of qualities that no other dog has ever had, nor ever will have. This example shows, moreover, that the two perspectives are gradual. 'Collie' is already a much more individualising judgement than 'animal'.

The law is caught between these two poles. In the modern conception, legal rules are orientated mainly towards the pole of generality or typicality.[57] It stands to reason that a rule cannot descend to the circumstantial level of unicity lest it be completely dissolved. The search for a regulation of social life through normative precepts according to standards of equality and foreseeability limits the degree to which legal norms can embrace circumstantial and individual features. Thus, legal regulation is mainly addressed to typical situations, for example buyer/seller, tenant/landlord, judge/parties, testator/beneficiary, or proprietor, shareholder, etc. It is not to a particular shareholder that the norms are addressed, but to the recurring and rational problems involved in the context of shares or stocks. But this orientation towards generality is not uniform. It first depends on the subject matter: there are parts of the legal order where a general approach prevails (eg in the law of insurances), and others where an individualised perspective reigns (eg the meting out of criminal sentences, where the individual culpability and personality of the accused must be taken into account). Secondly, legal orders also evolve over time: the older a legal order, the more it will contain individualised provisions; the younger a legal order, the more it will tend to produce general norms. Thirdly and lastly, the equation varies between legal orders: municipal private law tends towards generality and typicality; international law and canon law tend much more towards individualised rules.

From a general perspective, each legal order constantly wavers between the values to which is it equally committed: generality, legal certainty, equality, practicability, normativity on the one side; particularity, individuality, equity, taking into account of differences and concrete facts on the other side. The less a legal order is developed, the more the direct impact of social facts and political realities; the more the relationships it regulates are haphazard and irregular, the more this legal order will tend towards the spectrum of individualisation. The distribution of power in international society and the weight of political factors clearly impress upon international law a considerable tendency towards an individualisation of its rules. We have already discussed this issue: a situation of State succession will never possess the same degree of typicality as the passing over of private property.

[57] The legislator will thus seek a general regulation balancing the relevant ideal factors (dominating social and political values) and real factors (past legal experience, usages of the subject matter to be regulated, expected results of a given regulation, etc).

There are different legal techniques through which an individualisation of the legal rule can be achieved. We may discuss them first in the context of general jurisprudence, before turning to the specific area of international law. When the legislator wants to open a certain regulation to circumstantial factors, individualising vectors will be inserted into the body of the rule. A mandate is thus given to the legal operator to take account of all the contextual aspects to which the norm makes indirect reference. This opening or aeration of the legal norms can be analysed as a recourse to gaps *intra legem*, or as a delegation of partial legislative powers to the legal operator. Such vectors of individualisation are of three types:

1. *explicit individualization clauses*, such as the referral to 'particular circumstances' or 'special circumstances', eg in Article 6 of the 1958 Geneva Convention on the Continental Shelf;
2. *equity clauses*, which refer to a balancing of relevant circumstances so as to reach an equitable result in the particular case;
3. *legal standards*, which refer to social average behaviour as a measuring rod, as well as to the socially accepted and dominating values (eg reasonableness, *bonos mores*, due diligence, proportionality, etc). Some standards have a normative scheme, such as the protection of legitimate expectations under the principle of good faith; others refer the operator to the rationalities of the specific case without further indication (eg what is reasonable).

The more a norm is precise and circumstantial, the more it will exclude the flexible taking into account of further aspects of individualisation; conversely, the more a norm is generally formulated, as are the standards, the more it will allow the flexible taking into account of a wide array of specificities linked to the particular case. Thus, if the legislator wants to sharpen the sanction for theft committed with a 'dangerous weapon', he can insert that very term into the norm, or alternatively he can enumerate the weapons he considers dangerous. In the former case, the legal operator has much greater leeway for considering all the relevant circumstances of a particular case in the judgement as to whether an object was or was not such a dangerous weapon. The clause can cover new weapons, not known to the legislator at the time of the adoption of the norm; or it can lead to the inclusion of an object that was dangerous only in the particular circumstances, for example a pen that was used to attack the eyes of the victim (a pen can hardly be said generally to be a weapon, and even less to be dangerous). The standard is, however, not merely an instrument of individualisation. It differs, in this perspective, from equity clauses. By referring to social normality, the standard requires the operator to seek and secure a *quod prelumque fit* test. The equity clause, on the contrary, is based on a delegation of legislative power for highly atypical cases where the rule, based on average and normality, would create an undesirably inequitable result.[58] It must

[58] See Aristotle, *Nicomachean Ethics*, book v, ch, X. Compare Art 1 of the Swiss Civil Code.

be added that standards do not indicate the precise level of individualisation or abstraction the operator may reach. Thus, for example, the 'dangerousness' of a weapon, when qualified as such in a criminal provision, can refer to the abstract danger created (eg firearms) or to the concrete danger created in the circumstances (eg a knitting needle used in an attack on the victim's face). Dangerousness is here a standard. Reference to the abstract danger guarantees a better legal foreseeability. Conversely, reference to the concrete danger ensures equitable conclusions, for example taking account of the fact that an attack with a rifle used as a stick may in the circumstances not be dangerous.

From a temporal perspective, there are important reversals leading from individualisation towards generalisation. In legal practice, there progressively emerge regularities, similarities and typical features. These will lead to systematisations. The lawyer thus retreats from case law to embrace categories (*Fallgruppen*). Therefore, the individualising trend of a standard progressively creates a generalising stream in which normative contours take shape. It is through practice that the various facets of the principle of good faith emerged, for example the protection of legitimate expectations, the prohibition of abuse of rights, estoppel, the faith due to the finality of agreements, the responsibility for appearances deliberately created, the duty to announce jurisprudential reversals in the domain of public law (where applicable), etc. Ultimately, individualisation is thus not separable from generalisation. In each legal order the two streams flow side by side and nourish one another. They are as inseparable as Castor and Pollux.

B. The Individualising Perspective in International Law

1. *Historical Aspects*

International law has passed through different phases in which its degree of individualisation has varied. In the nineteenth century, it was mainly considered as the public law governing the external relations of European Powers.[59] Being the law of the chancelleries dealing with concrete problems, the body of rules tended to be at once diffuse and concrete. Even in legal doctrine, international law was not discussed at that time in the general categories we are accustomed to see today, for example the 'State'. The issue was broken down into the concrete statuses of States, for example independent States, unions of States, federal States, half-sovereign States, vassal States, neutral or neutralised States, etc. Within each of these types, specific situations were addressed, for example Belgium, Greece, Romania, the

[59] Bluntschli could thus write that when the European Powers assembled in a Congress decided on a certain matter, their decision became binding for all European States (JC Bluntschli, *Le droit international codifié* (Paris, 1870) 101). This rule may not have expressed the positive law as it stood, but it is highly characteristic.

Swedish-Norwegian Union, the British Empire, Austria-Hungary, the US, the German Confederation and later Empire, the Belgian Congo, etc. Similarly, treaties were not explicated through their general features, such as conclusion, validity, interpretation, modification, conflict, third States, termination, etc. After a summary account of the concept of treaties and a reminder of the pervading principle *pacta sunt servanda*, authors directly passed on to concrete categories of treaties, such as political and alliance treaties, law of war agreements, peace treaties, economic and commercial compacts, treaties of guarantee, etc. In the terminology of modern codification, one could say that the special part of the code was still far more developed than the general part. This also had the consequence that the treatises of the nineteenth century were hugely detailed and—from our perspective—overly long, often indulging in a level of moralising.[60]

At the beginning of the twentieth century, in the phase we have called the 'constitutionalisation' of international law, there was a reaction against this concrete typology. An effort was now made to formulate general categories and to leave behind the specific. This era saw the birth of many of the general concepts we are used to seeing today, for example the 'subjects of the law', the 'State' with its three or four constitutive elements (territory, population, government, sovereignty), the 'treaty', 'international responsibility', 'peaceful settlement of disputes', etc. The code of international law was progressively filled in with a general part. In the second half of the twentieth century, there was a partial return to a greater degree of individualisation. Some had warned of the danger of excessively abstract and formal structures, hardly suitable for an international society embroiled in complex conflicts of interests (West/East, North/South, etc). Flexibility, policy and equity were to have a greater share in international law and in the revision of a series of old-fashioned rules.[61] The new international economic order and the new law of the sea were hallmarks of these tendencies; the same can be said of the modern fluvial international law.[62] In addition to these political evolutions, it may be said that international law continues to be at bottom a system of law regulating bilateral State relationships. Thus, the majority of treaties in the world are bilateral. In a field like investment law, there are some multilateral treaties and a huge number of bilateral treaties (so-called BITs, bilateral investment treaties). This bilateralism and the related particular law (subsequent practice, acquiescence, estoppel, etc) tend to maintain a high degree of individualisation in the body of the law. We are thus far from seeing a unitary code.

[60] For such an old-fashioned treatment of international law, see, eg, P Pradier-Fodéré, *Traité de droit international public européen et américain*, vols I–VIII (Paris, 1885–1906).

[61] See, eg, M Bedjaoui, *Pour un nouvel ordre économique international* (Paris, 1978). And see generally A Cassese, *International Law in a Divided World* (Oxford, 1986).

[62] L Caflisch, 'Règles générales du droit des cours d'eau internationaux' (1989-VII) 219 *RCADI* 9ff.

2. Techniques of Individualisation within International Law

Such techniques can first of all be observed in the context of conventional norms. Some techniques are situated on the level of secondary rules, ie rules on the formation, modification and termination of the conventional bond. This is the case, for example, with reservations,[63] allowing States to modulate the content of their conventional engagement to their particular needs or wishes. And indeed, certain States have not hesitated to lodge reservations with regard to entire value systems, such as 'internal traditions' or 'sharia law'.[64] Frequently, the State also reserves to itself the right to determine whether the conditions of the reservation are met (self-judging reservations). The individualisation of the norm is here so radical that there remains no obligation at all—which is incompatible with the treaty bond. Another technique of secondary law is rooted in 'opting in' or 'opting out' clauses. The most celebrated 'opting in' systems are those of the optional clause on the jurisdiction of the ICJ under Article 36, §2 of the ICJ Statute and of Article 20, §1 of the European Social Charter. Systems of 'opting out' can be found, for example, in Articles 21–22 of the Constitution of the World Health Organisation, or in Articles 37, 54 and 90 of the Constitution of the International Civil Aviation Organisation. Still another technique consists of umbrella agreements to be completed by a series of more concrete protocols. This technique allows States to accede to a set of protocols according to their individualised needs and abilities. The international law of the environment knows many examples of this type, for example under the 1987 Convention on the Ozone Layer. Other techniques are placed at the level of primary rules, ie the substantive rules of international law setting out rights and obligations for States. The legislator inserts into the conventional norms vectors permitting flexibility, allowing the circumstances of the particular case to be taken into account. Here too, we find the explicit individualisation and equity clauses, as well as standards. Some examples of each of these categories follow:

1. *Individualisation clauses*. Some individualisation clauses refer the legal operator to the 'circumstances' in general, without further precision. Thus, Article 59 of the Montego Bay Convention on the Law of the Sea (1982) stipulates that conflicts of jurisdiction between coastal States and third States in the exclusive economic zone should be resolved on the basis of equity and 'in the light of all the relevant circumstances'.[65] This provision allows any debate

[63] See the basic rules on reservations in Arts 19–23 VCLT. On reservations, apart from the works of the ILC (A Pellet, Special Rapporteur on the Law and Practice Relating to Reservations, available at <http://www.un.org/law/ilc/>, under 'reservations to treaties', 'analytical guide'), see F Horn, *Reservations and Interpretative Declarations to Multilateral Treaties* (Amsterdam, 1988); RM Riquelme Cortado, *Las reservas a los tratados: Lagunas y ambigüedades del régimen de Viena* (Murcia, 2004).

[64] E Lijnzaad, *Reservations to UN Human Rights Treaties* (Dordrecht, 1995); I Ziemele (ed), *Reservations to Human Rights Treaties and the Vienna Convention Regime* (Leiden, 2004).

[65] On this provision, see S Karagiannis, 'L'article 59 de la Convention des Nations Unies sur le droit de la mer (ou les mystères de la nature juridique de la zone économique exclusive)' (2004) 37 *RBDI* 325ff; SN Nandan and S Rosenne, *United Nations Convention on the Law of the Sea 1982, Commentary*,

on the general status of the zone to be tempered: does it come within the regime applicable to the high seas, or does it fall under some sovereignty of the coastal State? In Articles 69, §3 and 70, §4 of the same Convention it is stipulated that when the harvesting capacity of a coastal State approaches a point which would enable it to harvest the entire allowable catch of the living resources in its exclusive economic zone, this State shall cooperate with the land-locked and geographically disadvantaged States of the region in order to conclude equitable agreements for the participation of the latter States. The matter is referred to special equitable agreements, ie to individualisation by further agreements. In Article 6 of the Convention on Non-Navigable Use of International Waterways (1997) there is clause enjoining the States parties to use the watercourse equitably and reasonably by taking account of 'all relevant circumstances'. These are geographic, hydrographic, hydrologic, climatic, ecological or otherwise natural circumstances; the economic and social needs of the States concerned; the needs of the populations dependent on the resources of the waterway in each State; the effects of the use; the conservation and protection of the resources, etc (§1, letters a to g). However, not all individualisation clauses refer to 'circumstances'. Thus, Articles 197 and 207, §4 of the Montego Bay Convention on the Law of the Sea (1982) refer, in the context of the protection of the marine environment, to regional particularities, ie 'characteristic regional features'. In Article 22 of the Statute of the ICJ it is written that the Court may, 'when it considers it desirable', sit and exercise its functions somewhere other than at its seat in The Hague. The effect of such individualisation clauses is the same.

2. *Equity clauses.* Such clauses are often inserted into instruments where issues of distributive justice have a significant role to play, for example in the context of the sharing of resources or goods. Thus, the Vienna Convention on State Succession in matters of Goods, Debts and Archives (1983) stipulates, in Articles 37, §2, 40, §1 and 41, that the debts of the predecessor State shall pass on to the successor State in an equitable proportion, considering also the goods, rights and interests that pass over to that State. The Montego Bay Convention on the Law of the Sea of 1982 makes often reference to equity. As we have seen, this is the case, for example, in Articles 69 and 70 of the Convention relating to the participation of landlocked and geographically disadvantaged States in the harvest within the exclusive economic zone of coastal States of the region. Article 160, §1, letter g of the same Convention stipulates that the Assembly of the Seabed Authority shall decide on the equitable apportionment of the economic and financial advantages flowing from activities in the area. Articles 5 and 6 of the above-mentioned Waterways

vol II (Dordrecht/Boston/London, 2002) 569. More generally, F Orrego Vicuna, 'La zone économique exclusive: régime et nature juridique dans le droit international' (1986-IV) 199 *RCADI* 19ff; G Andreone, 'The Exclusive Economic Zone' in DR Rothwell, A Oude Elferink, KN Scott and T Stephens (eds), *The Oxford Handbook of the Law of the Sea* (Oxford, 2015) 159ff.

Convention of 1997 calls for an 'equitable and reasonable' use of the shared resource. Often equity refers to the reparation of damage: thus, Article 12 of the Convention on the Responsibility for Damages caused by Space Engines (1972) provides for an equitable determination of the indemnity. Elsewhere, Article 44, §3 VCLT excludes the severability of vitiated treaty clauses from the rest of the treaty, inter alia when it would be 'unjust' to apply the rest of the treaty without the severed clauses. Such equity clauses operate a quite radical individualisation of the norm at stake. Explicit individualisation clauses call on the interpreter to take into account the special facts of the various situations. Equity clauses are not limited to such a 'factualisation' of the norm; they also lower its normative content by requiring the seeking of a solution that is just in the individual case. The individualization is in a sense twofold: factual and normative.

3. *Standards.* Standards may be half-abstract and half-concrete. The individualisation induced is here less radical, since the standard refers back to social normality or the average. There are a great number of standards in international law. Thus, Articles 56, § 2 and 87, § 2 of the Montego Bay Convention on the Law of the Sea of 1982, or Article 9 of the Outer Space Treaty of 1967, enjoin every State exercising its rights in certain spaces to also exercise 'due regard' with respect to the rights and obligations of other States in these areas. A very frequent standard is 'reasonableness': see, for example, Articles 147, §§1 and 3 of Montego Bay Convention, 'reasonable regard'; Article 144, §2, letter a, of the Montego Bay Convention, 'fair and reasonable terms and conditions'; Article 206 of the Montego Bay Convention, 'reasonable grounds'; §63 of the Jurisdiction and Admissibility Judgment of the ICJ in the *Nicaragua* case (1984), 'reasonable time',[66] etc. There are other standards too: 'every possible assistance' (Article 5 of the Outer Space Treaty, 1967); 'appropriate measures' (Article 2 of the Convention on the Prevention and Suppression of Offences Committed against Persons enjoying International Protection, 1973); 'extent strictly required by the exigencies' (Article 4 ICCPR);[67] 'as far as practicable' (Article 206 of the Montego Bay Convention) 'where the evidence so warrants' (Article 218, §1 of the Montego Bay Convention); 'legitimate interests' (Article 125, §3 of the Montego Bay Convention), etc. We might also recall the historically important clauses excluding certain matters from arbitration ('vital interest' clauses, eg Article 1, §2 of the Arbitration Treaty between Switzerland and Japan, 1924).[68] In the absence of well-settled social normality in international relations, the application of such clauses in international

[66] *Military and Paramilitary Activities in and against Nicaragua (Nicaragua v United States of America)*(Jurisdiction and Admissibility) [1984] ICJ *Rep* 420, §63.

[67] See M Nowak, *UN Covenant on Civil and Political Rights, Commentary*, 2nd edn (Kehl/Strasburg, 2005) 83ff.

[68] On these vital interest clauses, see the criticism of H Lauterpacht, *The Function of Law in the International Community* (Oxford, 1933) 3ff, 26ff.

law leads more easily to a value judgement by the legal operator. This state of affairs reduces the typological impact of standards, and thus also their relative objectivity.

3. Consequences of Individualisation

What is the concrete consequence of this range of individualisation on the international legal order? There are several aspects here. Individualisation diminishes legal security; it increases recourse to general principles and legal standards; makes codification of the law more difficult; explains the preference shown to flexible political means for solving disputes over recourse to the international judiciary, etc. There are moreover areas of international law particularly marked by individualisation. Thus, in the law of the sea, a dominant role is played by various historical, economic and local considerations.[69] The law of maritime delimitation has for a time been influenced by the doctrine of the unicity of each coastal situation.[70] The law of State succession is also considerably marked by the individualising approach.[71]

The main consequences of individualisation are, first, that international law often accompanies conflicts rather than truly regulating them; it is an instrument to be used flexibly for their resolution, rather than a rule to be applied for their settlement. In other words, international law is sometimes ambulatory rather than ordering. Secondly, the principle of effectiveness looms relatively large in such a legal order. The distance of the law from the facts of life is less than that of private law in the municipal legal order. Thirdly, international law remains highly permeable to political influence. Its lack of distance from political factors could be criticised if its norms were less circumstantial. Conversely, the opening of international law to special circumstances does allow power issues to find their way into its body. In this regard, the individualisation clauses have quite different effects in international law and in municipal law. In the latter, such clauses essentially constitute a delegation of competence to the judiciary, ie to an organ independent from the political branches of government. The aim of the judge will be to objectivise the conditions of application of the clauses through jurisprudence.

[69] The individualising approach can be found, eg, in the definition of historical waters (eg historical bays; or see, eg, the treatment of the Gulf of Fonseca in *El Salvador v Honduras* [1992] ICJ Rep 591 and the criticism of Judge Oda, at 735ff); on the impact of economic factors (eg preferential fishing rights), see the *Fisheries Jurisdiction* cases [1974] ICJ Rep 24ff); or on the relevance of local situations (eg in the drawing of baselines), see *Norwegian Fisheries* [1951] ICJ Rep 133).

[70] R Kolb, *Case Law on Equitable Maritime Delimitation* (The Hague/London/New York, 2003); P Weil, *Perspectives du droit de la délimitation maritime* (Paris, 1988). See in particular the *Gulf of Maine* case [1984] ICJ Rep 313, §158. See also *ibid*, 290, §81.

[71] As early as 1929, Cavaglieri could write that the only general rule in this context was the principle of unjust enrichment for patrimonial debts: 'Règles générales du droit de la paix' (1929-I) 26 *RCADI* 371. Another author could hold that the only general rule was '*res transit cum onere suo*': K Strupp, 'Les règles générales du droit de la paix' (1934-I) 47 *RCADI* 471, 479. In particular, there are many individualised rules in the Vienna Convention on State Succession in Goods, Debts and Archives of 1983.

In international law, such clauses are not a delegation but rather the maintenance of discretionary power in favour of the political branches of each State. They will not principally be used in the context of precepts such as justice, reciprocity, equality or proportionality, but rather will be kept in the environment of fluctuating political interests. The absence of a regular judge in international law renders more difficult and lengthier, as well as plainly subordinate, the process by which such clauses could be objectivised. Particular interests thus maintain considerable influence on the international legal order. It should not be forgotten, however, that the foregoing is a matter of degree, and that the individualisation of norms is not equally strong in all areas of international law. The law of treaties, for example, contains significantly fewer individualised rules than the law of the sea or the law of State succession.

5

The 'Lotus Rule' on Residual State Freedom

I. General Aspects

The issue of the relationship between freedom and regulation depends on the construction of the relationship between the State and the international community. This, in turn, depends on the relationship between power and law, between sovereignty and the common good. Here one is confronted with the many balancing exercises necessary between the centrifugal and centripetal forces that exist in every living body, and in international law too. The reasoning here can take as its points of departure two separate bases: either the individual State, or common interests. In a positivistic conception, the State and its own needs have primacy. The State is originally vested with unlimited powers; the law is only an *ex post* projection of its free and unconditional will; the law is fully subsidiary and limits the original freedoms only to the extent of the State's will; thus, international law is an external reflection of the State's 'me'. The consequence of this view is a Hegelian conception of the State, with the State enjoying the preponderance of power and a relative atrophying of the law. Conversely, in the community-orientated conception, international law, with its ordering purpose, is the starting-point; the original delimitation and attribution of State jurisdiction can be performed only through an international legal order superior to the State, otherwise pure anarchy would be unavoidable; the law sets up its own requirements in opposition to the State's will; it regulates the jurisdiction of each unit so as to render the freedom of the one compatible with the freedom of the other; the needs of life within society and the protection of the 'other' constrain the freedom of the State, which is therefore not originally unlimited. Thus, according to one theory, the law is constructed around the State and is a function of it; according to the other theory, the law is consolidated around the international community. On the one side, it is the law of individual collectivities; on the other, it is the law of the collectivity of collectivities.

The struggle between these two basic conceptions can be found in every branch of international law, and in particular with regard to the competences. It is also present in the conception of a classical law of coexistence (centered on sovereignty) and a modern law of cooperation (centered on community). But its main expression is certainly the apparent presumption in favour of general freedom: 'what is not prohibited is permitted' (the so-called *Lotus* rule).[1] The era of State-centered positivism was clearly favourable to this apparent rule of residual freedom. If international law is only the product of the will of States, it follows that where there is no will there is also no rule, and hence no legal obligation; the original freedom prevails, and is unhampered. There is a gap of sorts, but this gap is filled by an automatically applicable rule, holding that by virtue of its sovereignty the State remains free to behave as it sees fit.[2] Such a construction is tantamount to saying that the international legal order is necessarily complete and that a gap in the proper sense cannot arise at all: a gap signifies only freedom; and thus the gap disappears.

This aggressive conception of the residual rule was adopted by the majority in the Permanent Court of International Justice (PCIJ) in the *Lotus* case of 1927 (in the context of criminal jurisdiction flowing from the collision of two ships on the

[1] On this residual freedom rule, see, among many others, H Lauterpacht, *The Development of International Law by the International Court* (London, 1958) 359ff; H Lauterpacht, 'Some Observations on the Prohibition of "non liquet" and the Completeness of the Law' in *Essays in Honor of J.H.W. Verzijl* (The Hague, 1958) 196ff; J Stone, 'Non Liquet and the Function of Law in the International Community' (1959) 35 *BYIL* 124ff; J Stone, 'Non Liquet and the Judicial Function' in C Perelman (ed), *Le problème des lacunes en droit* (Brussels, 1968) 305ff; J Salmon, 'Quelques observations sur les lacunes en droit international public' in C. Perelman (ed), *Le problème des lacunes en droit* (Brussels, 1968) esp 316–17; A Bleckmann, 'Die Handlungsfreiheit der Staaten' (1978) 29 *Österreichische Zeitschrift für öffentliches Recht und Völkerrecht* 173ff; A Bleckmann, 'Die Völkerrechtsordnung als System von Rechtsvermutungen' in *Essays in Honor of H.U. Scupin* (Berlin, 1983) 407ff; A Bleckmann, *Grundprobleme und Methoden des Völkerrechts* (Freiburg/Munich, 1982) 25, 232ff; U Fastenrath, *Lücken im Völkerrecht* (Berlin, 1991) 239ff; I Stribis, *La manifestation des lacunes en droit international* (Athens, 2009) 97ff; C Focarelli, *International Law as Social Construct* (Oxford, 2012) 278ff. Interesting remarks on the rule can be found in M Bourquin, 'Règles générales du droit de la paix' (1931-I) 35 *RCADI* 101ff; F Castberg, 'La méthodologie du droit international public', (1933-I) 43 *RCADI* 342ff; G Salvioli, 'Les règles générales de la paix' (1933-IV) 46 *RCADI* 21ff, 62; L Le Fur, 'Règles générales du droit de la paix' (1935-IV) 54 *RCADI* 302; J Basdevant, 'Règles générales du droit de la paix' (1936-IV) 58 *RCADI* 593ff; JL Brierly, 'The Lotus Case' in JL Brierly, *The Basis of Obligation in International Law* (Oxford, 1968) 143–44; GG Fitzmaurice, 'The General Principles of International Law Considered from the Standpoint of the Rule of Law' (1957-II) 92 *RCADI* 50ff; GG Fitzmaurice, 'The Law and Procedure of the ICJ, 1951–54: General Principles and Sources of Law' (1953) 30 *BYIL* 8ff; H Mosler, 'Völkerrecht als Rechtsordnung' (1976) 36 *ZaöRV* 37ff; A Verdross and B Simma, *Universelles Völkerrecht*, 3rd edn (Berlin, 1984) 388. See also generally L Siorat, *Le problème des lacunes en droit international* (Paris, 1958). The following critiques are favourable to the rule, eg: H Kelsen, 'Théorie du droit international public' (1953-III) 84 *RCADI* 113, 121–22; H Kelsen, *Reine Rechtslehre* (Leipzig/Vienna, 1934) 100–02; H Kelsen, *General Theory of Law and State* (Cambridge, Mass, 1949) 146–49; H Kelsen and R Tucker, *Principles of International Law*, 2nd edn (New York, 1966) 438–40; E Kaufmann, *Das Wesen des Völkerrechts und die clausula rebus sic stantibus* (Tübingen, 1911) 49; W Rebbe, *Der Lotusfall vor dem Weltgerichtshof* (Leipzig, 1932) 26–27; P Guggenheim, 'Principes de droit international public' (1952-I) 80 *RCADI* 64; P Guggenheim, *Traité de droit international public*, vol I (Geneva, 1967) 264; G Schwarzenberger, *A Manual of International Law*, 5th edn (London, 1967) 245; I Seidl-Hohenveldern, *Völkerrecht*, 7th edn (Cologne/Berlin, 1992) 136, fn 537; W Wengler, *Völkerrecht*, vol I (Berlin, 1964) 870; G Hoffmann, 'Die Grenzen rechtlicher Streiterledigung im Völkerrecht' in *Berichte der deutschen Gesellschaft für Völkerrecht*, vol 9 (Karlsruhe, 1969) 29; R Quadri, *Diritto internazionale pubblico*, 5th edn (Naples, 1968) 212–13; G Balladore-Pallieri, *Diritto internazionale pubblico*, 3rd edn (Milan, 1941) 336; AP Sereni, *Diritto internazionale*, vol I (Milan, 1966) 99.

[2] This is as true for legal situations on the territory of a State as it is for extraterritorial action.

high seas).[3,4] Certainly the negative formulation of the question posed to the Court in the special agreement conferring jurisdiction played a decisive role in the answer of the PCIJ.[5] As is known, the legal issue revolved around the criminal jurisdiction of Turkey with regard to French seamen who had caused the death of Turkish citizens on board another ship on the high seas. Was the criminal jurisdiction limited to the flag State of the ship that caused the accident (France)? Or could Turkey claim concurrent criminal jurisdiction based on the passive personality principle? For the Court, the residual freedom, which here allowed concurrent criminal jurisdiction, was founded in the principle of sovereignty: 'all that can be required of a State is that it should not overstep the limits which international law places upon its jurisdiction; within these limits, its title to exercise jurisdiction rests in its sovereignty'.[6] Thus, a State does not need title or authorisation under international law; it simply must not be hampered or estopped by a rule of international law. The issue has resurfaced in a series of later cases, in the International Court of Justice (ICJ),[7] and also in supranational entities like the European Community[8] (as it then was).

[3] This criminal law context is emphasised by some authors, with the claim that the Court did not formulate the residual freedom as a general principle applicable to all areas of international law: see, eg, Focarelli, above n 1, 280.

[4] *SS Lotus* (1927) PCIJ Series A no 9, 18–19, 19: 'It does not, however, follow that international law prohibits a State from exercising jurisdiction in its own territory, in respect of any case which relates to acts which have taken place abroad, and in which it cannot rely on some permissive rule of international law. Such a view would only be tenable if international law contained a general prohibition to States to extend the application of their laws and the jurisdiction of their courts to persons, property and acts outside their territory, and if, as an exception to this general prohibition, it allowed States to do so in certain specific cases. But this is certainly not the case under international law as it stands at present. Far from laying down a general prohibition to the effect that States may not extend the application of their laws and the jurisdiction of their courts to persons, property and acts outside their territory, it leaves them in this respect a wide measure of discretion which is only limited in certain cases by prohibitive rules; … In these circumstances, all that can be required of a State is that it should not overstep the limits which international law places upon its jurisdiction; within these limits, its title to exercise jurisdiction rests in its sovereignty.' See also Dissenting Opinion Loder, *ibid*, 34–35; Dissenting Opinion Weiss, *ibid*, 44–45; Dissenting Opinion Finlay, *ibid*, 57; Dissenting Opinion Nyholm, *ibid*, 60–61; Dissenting Opinion Moore, *ibid*, 92–94; Dissenting Opinion Altamira, *ibid*, 95, 101–02.

[5] *ibid*, 5: 'Has Turkey … acted in conflict with the principles of international law by instituting …?' The issue was not formulated positively, ie 'Has Turkey acted in conformity with international law by instituting …?' The formulation in the special agreements can determine judicial outcomes, as the classic *Alabama* arbitration of 1873 had already graphically shown. On the *Alabama* arbitration, see N Politis, *La justice international* (Paris, 1924) 36ff.

[6] *ibid*, 19. But the PCIJ two years later introduced an exception to this residual freedom: see *River Oder* (1929) PCIJ Series A no 23, 26: the Court cannot accept that any doubt in the grammatical interpretation of a text should lead to the freedom of the State; all other methods of interpretation in order to ascertain the intention of the parties must first be exhausted.

[7] See the *Nuclear Weapons* opinion (UNGA), *Legality of the Threat or Use of Nuclear Weapons* [1996-I] ICJ Rep 238, 247. On this case see J Salmon, 'Le problème des lacunes à la lumière de l'avis "licéité de la menace ou de l'emploi d'armes nucléaires" rendu le 8 juillet 1996 par la CIJ' in *Essays in Honor of N. Valticos* (Paris, 1999) 197ff; D Bodansky, 'Non Liquet and the Incompleteness of International Law' in L Boisson de Chazournes and P Sands (eds), *International Law, The International Court of Justice and Nuclear Weapons* (Cambridge, 1999) 153ff. The issue came to the fore again in the *Kosovo* opinion, *Accordance with International Law of the Unilateral Declaration of Independence in Respect of Kosovo* [2010-II] ICJ Rep 425, §56. On this case see A Peters, 'Does Kosovo Lie in the Lotus-Land of Freedom?' (2011) 24 *Leiden Journal of International Law* 95ff.

[8] See eg the Opinion of Advocate General Darmon in the European Court of Justice in *Ahlstöm* (1988) 96 *ILR* 179. The rule is also often invoked in international criminal law, notably when the issue

Manifestly, the reach of the residual rule of freedom is different in the international and in the municipal contexts. First, private individuals enjoy their freedom (*Privatautonomie*) only within the four corners of State legislation and the mandatory jurisdiction of tribunals. The municipal legislator can act at any time to remedy a legal situation that it considers to be unsatisfactory. None of these conditions prevails on the international plane. Hence, a 'liberal' principle (in the European sense of the word) in the internal context is transformed into a principle of 'anarchy' in international society.[9] Secondly, the application of the residual rule leads to the equal treatment of two unequal situations: one where the legislator has not adopted a rule because he did not consider the situation that might arise at all; and the other where the legislator has considered and weighed up the consequences, and has willingly refrained from adopting a rule in order to allow each subject a free choice (qualified silence). In the first case, unlike the second, the legislator has expressed no will. The legal equivalence of the two situations must be justified by specific argument, since at first sight it may appear dubious to treat them alike. Thirdly, the residual rule seems to better accommodate the domain of public law where the State intervenes in the freedom of its subjects, notably in the fields of criminal law (eg *nullum crimen sine lege*) or of fiscal law (eg the principle of legality). Conversely, it is more difficult for the rule to find a foothold in the branches of private law, where the issue is rather to adjust the spheres of action and of subjective rights. Here, in many cases, the residual rule does not indicate a satisfactory legal solution at all, since the dispute is ultimately not resolved by it. The point in dispute is about the friction between and concurrence of subjective legal positions; to say that there is a rule of residual freedom would here mean that both subjects remain free and that therefore the friction and dispute continue. Thus, in international law, what could it mean to apply the rule of residual freedom to the issue of delimitation of territories? At most, it would be tantamount to abstaining from delimiting, ie leaving it to the States in dispute, entangled in the conflicting web of their unilateral actions. International law is structurally of a 'private law' configuration; it regulates the relationships between equals. This explains why the residual rule of freedom—notwithstanding the pole star of sovereignty—is not as easy to settle in its realm as it might seem at first sight.

It must be emphasised that, currently, the relevant gaps within international law are the gaps in practice, ie the situations where the law should give a response and does not (gaps *de lege lata*). We have to distinguish this situation from that where the legal operator is not satisfied with the existing rule because it leads to inequitable results (gaps *de lege ferenda*). In this latter context, modifications or

turns round the universal jurisdiction of municipal courts: *Jorgic* case (26.8.1997), Oberlandesgericht Düsseldorf, 2 StE 8/96, 152.

[9] As has been said by C Rousseau, *Droit international public*, vol I (Paris, 1970) 378, 'The principle may be admissible in municipal law, where there are organs competent at any moment to adopt a legal regulation imposed on the subjects and where there is a sanctioning machinery. This principle cannot, however, be normally applied in international law.' (our translation)

developments of the law are at stake. Legal science does not easily admit that the judge is authorised to fill in such deontological gaps, since that would be tantamount to legislating. The issue in this latter context is the ability to refuse to decide or the ability, in extreme cases, to decide *contra legem* (or rather, *contra tenorem legis* but not *contra tenorem juris*).

II. Origin of the Residual Rule

The residual rule is rooted in an individualistic and atomistic perception of society. It is therefore easily understandable that it is the product of the times of the Enlightenment. Indeed, its tenor flows from the great principles of the modern European constitutional State: rule of law, safeguard of the individual freedoms, separation of powers, creation of the law by the elected legislature and not by the judge, etc. Moreover, the anthropocentric revolution and the needs of growing international commerce pushed towards the recognition of individual freedom as the basic tenet. Consequently, the law was perceived as a body of limitations to original human freedom.[10] The law was seen as a necessarily complete body: each one of its injunctions is but an exception with respect to the underlying freedom rule. Legal obligation and freedom are mutually exhaustive categories: everything that is not prohibited or mandatory by virtue of a legal rule remains within the scope of freedom.

Roman law had not known such a sweeping and mechanical rule. There are only some interpretative presumptions protecting the freedom in particular equitable contexts.[11] Neither was a general residual rule known in the Middle Ages. The universalistic and finalistic vision of the world inhibited the creation of a rule bluntly based on the interests of individual human subjects. But some hints can be found in the late Scholastics, eg with Francisco de Vitoria in the context of the right to travel unhampered.[12] The rule would then flourish in the context of the modern codifications. We can find passages in Pufendorf[13] and Leibniz,[14] and later in the positivists.[15] However, the eventual turn of the tide towards modern legal methods, and in particular the development of sociological conceptions of the law, reduced

[10] See I Kant, *Metaphysik der Sitten* (1797), 'Doctrine of Law'.

[11] See eg Dig, 50, 17, 20; Dig 12, 4, 16. There are such presumptions in procedural law too, eg *in dubio pro reo*, implicit in Dig, 48, 19, 5; *neganti nulla probatio*, Codex, 4, 19, 23; *in obscuriis minimum est sequendum*, Dig, 50, 17, 9 and 34.

[12] Omnia licent, quae non sunt prohibita aut alias sunt in injuriam aut detrimentum aliorum: *De Indis*, sect III, tit I, prob 3.

[13] *De officio hominis et civis*, book I, ch II, §11.

[14] Specimen difficultatis in jure seu dissertatio de casibus perplexis, ch XII–XVII.

[15] K Bergbohm, *Jurisprudenz und Rechtsphilosophie* (Leipzig, 1892) 375ff; E Zitelmann, *Lücken im Recht* (Leipzig, 1903) 19; D Donati, *Il problema delle lacune dell'ordinamento giuridico* (Milan, 1910) 28ff. On the whole issue, see S Romano, *Osservazioni sulla completezza dell'ordinamento statale* (Rome, 1925) 3ff; E Jung, *Von der logischen Geschlossenheit des Rechts* (Berlin, 1900).

the scope of this residual rule in the municipal context.[16] The complex social engineering of the twentieth century could no longer accept the simple presumption of residual freedom. The strong individualistic bent of the rule would nevertheless suit the positivistic construction of international law around the omnipotence of the will of States or the normativistic theories of Kelsen. In international law, the rule seems ideally to reflect the domain of State sovereignty. And as we have seen, the *Lotus* Court was able to adopt it as the basis of its reasoning.

III. Relativity of the Residual Rule

It is important to note the double relativity of the residual rule. It is limited with regard to the meaning of 'prohibited' and with regard to the branches of law at stake.

First, there is the question as to the scope of what is 'prohibited' (all that is not *prohibited* is permitted). It stands to reason that this term must be taken in the large sense, ie to cover every type of legal regulation, prohibiting, obliging or permitting—and perhaps even encouraging (soft law). Further, it is important to be clear about the exact juncture at which the rule operates the shift towards freedom. This juncture can be placed at quite different points, namely the absence of:

1. explicit regulation;
2. implicit injunctions (to be ascertained by interpretation);
3. injunctions obtained by analogy;
4. injunctions obtained by general principles of law;
5. injunctions obtained by considering the overall rationalities of the legal system; and
6. injunctions obtained by taking into account the general values of the legal system or the social necessities of the time.

The scope of application of the rule is reduced while passing from 1 to 6. The maximum reach of the rule is at level 1: freedom will prevail as soon as there is no explicit regulation, by way of an argument *a contrario*. This is the case in some formalistic branches of the law, such as criminal or tax law. The minimum reach of the rule is at levels 5 and 6: freedom could be admitted only if the basic legal and social values did not indicate that the solution thus reached was inequitable. This is the case in some non-formalistic branches of the law, such as canon law. What has been said for the prohibitive rule is equally true for the reverse rule of authorisation by the law, that is, the conception according to which there must be a rule granting a competence or a right to do something. The authorisation can rest in an

[16] See the critiques in L Brütt, *Die Kunst der Rechtsanwendung* (Berlin, 1907) 77ff; G Del Vecchio, 'Les principes généraux du droit' in *Essays in Honor of F. Gény*, vol II (Paris, 1934) 69ff. For the modern law, CW Canaris, *Die Feststellung von Lücken im Gesetz*, 2nd edn (Berlin, 1983) 50.

express, implicit, analogous, general principles-related or value-based legal rule. In this regard, the two theories of residual freedom and of necessary authorisation can converge quite largely in the circles 4–6, while they would diverge strongly in the circles 1–2. In particular, general principles can be construed either as limitations to discretionary powers (prohibitive rule) or as authorisations to act in a domain not expressly regulated (permissive rule). It should be noted that much confusion on the role of our rule stems from the fact that the authors do not explore the point between 1 and 6 at which the *a contrario* argument concluding the residual freedom shall take place. Some authors seem to imply that the rule—if admitted—renders impossible any gap in the law, and would thus operate before an analogy could be considered[17] (which is tantamount to saying that it should apply after circles 1 and 2, and before circle 3). Other authors seem even stricter in their virulent critique of the rule: they assume that it would apply every time there is a minimum of obscurity within the law, ie between circles 1 and 2.[18] Most authors in international law would apply the rule at best only after having considered the avenues of analogy and the general principles of law[19] (which means after circle 4). This conception is certainly due to the recognition of the general principles of law as a formal legal source in Article 38, § 1, letter c of the ICJ Statute.[20]

Secondly, as already suggested, the scope of the rule is not the same in the different branches of the law, and still less in the different legal orders. The rule has stronger standing when the question is about State interventionism in the branches of public law. This is the domain called *Eingriffsverwaltung* in German administrative law: criminal law, tax law, public charges, etc—but not, for example, social contributions by the State. The rule has less standing in coordinative branches of the law as private law, and still less in canon law, which is geared towards the realisation of moral aims. Thus, for example, in canon law there is no strict principle of legality in the context of crimes (*nullum crimen sine lege*), but this stern course is tempered by the general principle of misericord (ie compassion). In international law, a relevant distinction is that between the exercise of territorial or domestic jurisdiction (where the presumption of freedom is stronger) and the exercise of extraterritorial jurisdiction or of jurisdiction affecting legally protected interests of third entities (where often a permissive norm would have to be shown, at least

[17] A Bleckmann, 'Die Völkerrechtsordnung als System von Rechtsvermutungen' in *Essays in Honor of H.U. Scupin* (Berlin, 1983) 410–11.

[18] L Lombardi Vallauri, *Corso di filosofia del diritto* (Padua, 1981) 49–51.

[19] See, eg, JL Brierly, 'Règles générales du droit de la paix' (1936-IV) 58 *RCADI* 145ff, 147; E Kaufmann, 'Règles générales du droit de la paix' (1935-IV) 54 *RCADI* 485–87; GG Fitzmaurice, 'The General Principles of International Law Considered from the Standpoint of the Rule of Law' (1957-II) 92 *RCADI* 50, 51–52, 54, 55ff; H Lauterpacht, *The Development of International Law by the International Court* (London, 1958) 360–61; A Verdross and B Simma, *Universelles Völkerrecht* 3rd edn (Berlin, 1984) 388; M Miele, *Diritto internazionale*, 3rd edn (Padua, 1972) 40; R Kolb, 'Universal Criminal Jurisdiction in Matters of International Terrorism' (1997) 50 *Revue hellénique de droit international* 85.

[20] On this provision, see A Pellet, 'Article 38' in A Zimmermann, C Tomuschat, K Oellers-Frahm and C Tams (eds), *The Statute of the International Court of Justice, A Commentary*, 2nd edn (Oxford, 2012) 731ff.

for extraterritorial action). Moreover, the place of the rule is different in the context of the law of coexistence and in the context of the law of cooperation. In the latter, in view of the common interests and finalities (eg protection of the environment, sharing of resources, work within international organisations, etc) the rule is of less assistance.

IV. Objections Against the Residual Rule

There are many objections against the residual rule. Some are rooted in the general theory of law, others are placed specifically within the pale of international law.

A. Objections Under the General Theory of Law

There are so many and such ingenious objections here that a certain selection and simplification must be welcome. Some arguments concern more than one category and are thus presented more than once, each time from a slightly different perspective.

1. Logical Objections

A first argument is that there is a logical hiatus between the premises and the conclusions drawn. It is impossible to directly and without further justification conclude that something that is not prohibited is thereby automatically permitted. The law contains categories other than the prohibited or the permitted, eg indifference or voluntary lack of regulation. Thus, there also exists the category of the 'neither prohibited nor permitted', which is equivalent to a real lacuna.[21] However, it has to be said that the defect is not truly placed on a logical level. According to

[21] See the argument presented by J Salmon, 'Quelques observations sur les lacunes en droit international public' in C Perelman (ed), *Le problème des lacunes en droit* (Brussels, 1968) 316–17. *Contra*, A Conte, 'Décision, complétude, clôture—A propos des lacunes en droit' in C Perelman (ed), *Le problème des lacunes en droit* (Brussels, 1968) 76, holding that the formula 'neither prohibited nor permitted' can be replaced by the argument *a contrario*, which is always legally admissible. Prof Salmon, for his part, argues that it is certainly not illogical to admit the residual rule, but remains reserved on its propriety. D Bodansky, 'Non Liquet and the Incompleteness of International Law' in L Boisson de Chazournes and P Sands (eds), *International Law, The International Court of Justice and Nuclear Weapons* (Cambridge, 1999) 162–64, gives an example: if two tennis players ignoring the rules of the game meet and agree that each ball falling within the lines gives one point and each ball falling beyond the lines gives zero points, and later a ball falls on the line, there is a gap in the regulation that cannot be solved by the residual rule. Logically, we are in the 'neither/neither' configuration. But we might add that this is not true for all unregulated matters between the two players. If we now imagine that a point is gained but the ball touched the net, the player having thus scored could argue that the point must be accorded, since the aforementioned regulation does not rule out the possibility of scoring after having touched the net ('not prohibited').

the followers of the residual rule, the sphere of 'neither prohibited nor permitted' is assimilated to the domain of freedom. Each time something is neither prohibited nor permitted, the subject must remain free. This equation can be attacked from many angles, but not under the logical one.

A second, related argument sees in the operation of the rule a consequential fallacy. A legal norm may positively dispose, but it cannot be assumed that it thereby also intends to negatively liberate: the norm pronounces on the consequences of its application, but does not take any position on the consequences of its non-application.[22] But again this is not a logical issue: it is precisely because the norms may not dispose anything on their negative side that the residual rule is postulated to usher in the realm of freedom. The true scope of the rule is that the argument *a contrario* shall in such cases prevail over any analogy.

Thirdly, it has been said that a legal norm cannot exist only by reason of logic, ie by way of a residual conclusion. The validity of the freedom accorded must necessarily rest on a legal norm produced by the sources of the law; logic alone cannot create a legal provision.[23] Indeed, it is added, the residual rule does not impede development of the law by the judge; it only requires that a certain behaviour be not prohibited and permitted at the same time (non-contradiction). In other words, it is not placed on the level of substantive law but rather on the level of logic requiring the avoidance of a contradiction.[24] But again there is nothing illogical in having a substantive residual rule. After all, criminal law has such a rule, whereby something that is not prohibited is therefore not punishable. There is nothing illegal or illogical in such a course.

Contrariwise, and fourthly, it has been argued that the residual rule is not logically necessary: it is possible to admit the existence of gaps in the law, which the legal operator can fill either by normative extension (analogy) or by normative restriction (freedom) on a case-by-case basis and without the operation of a rigid rule.[25] While this argument is manifestly true, it does not preclude the existence of a residual rule in certain branches of the law. This rule could even be created by the legislator.

Lastly, the argument has been presented that the residual rule is based on a circularity (*petitio principii*): it supposes what has to be proved.[26] The gist of the argument is that the residual rule is based on the assimilation of the whole law to a

[22] CW Canaris, *Die Feststellung von Lücken im Gesetz*, 2nd edn (Berlin, 1983) 49–50. Canaris write: 'Wenn das Gesetz an den Tatbestand T_1 die Rechtsfolge R knüpft, so ist damit keineswegs auch umgekehrt gesagt, dass aus dem Nichtvorliegen von T_1 ohne weiteres der Nichteintritt von R gefolgert werden könne, dass also nicht auch der Tatbestand T_2 dieselbe Rechtsfolge haben kann.' This sentence corresponds to the argument made in the text in section III. above. *Contra*, AWH Langhein, *Das Prinzip der Analogie als juristische Methode* (Berlin, 1992) 121.

[23] A Soeteman, *Logic in Law* (Dordrecht/Boston/London, 1989) 141.

[24] ibid, 141–42. See also K Meessen, *Völkerrechtliche Grundsätze des internationalen Kartellrechts* (Baden-Baden, 1975) 79.

[25] F Somló, *Juristische Grundlehre*, 2nd edn (Leipzig, 1927) 401.

[26] E Betti, *Allgemeine Auslegungslehre als Methodik der Geisteswissenschaften* (Tübingen, 1967) 644. For international law, see C de Visscher, 'Contribution à l'étude des sources du droit international' (1933) 14 *RDILC* 418, fn 42.

particular set of sources: eg *quod non est in lege, nec in jure*. Therefore, the conclusion would be that there are no legal norms outside the formal State legislation. This is nothing more than a petition of principle. And it is also too narrow a view in regard of legal experience. The truth in this argument is manifestly that the residual rule, if admitted, must be placed in the context of the above-mentioned circles 1–6; if this is not done, there remains a fundamental ambiguity.

2. *Theoretical Objections*

A first argument is that the residual rule may fit certain legal domains regulating State interventionism, but that it cannot provide any legal solution in the situation of concurrent subjective rights or in the context of apportionment of assets. For example, if the law provides for an 'equitable' sharing of water resources between neighbours, what could the impact of the residual rule possibly be? What could be its role when the issue turns around the delimitation of land? An application of the residual rule in this context could only mean that the judge leaves the dispute unresolved.[27]

A second argument is that the residual rule inhibits the proper development of the law by imposing rather static views: it postulates completeness of the law, and suggests thus that there is no need to develop it.[28] This danger is particularly pronounced in an underdeveloped and fragmentary legal order such as international law: the operator will then be trapped by the existing imperfections, without the possibility of furthering improvements.[29] This objection is certainly well founded; but it is true essentially if the residual rule is applied too early, ie towards circles 1 to 3, and much less so if the residual rule is applied late in the process, in the higher circles 4–6. The objection goes therefore more to the proper extension of the residual rule than to its existence.

Thirdly, it has been claimed that the residual rule could fit the model of the Manchester liberal State in the nineteenth century, but hardly the model of the modern State with its multiple missions.[30] The remark is welcome, but it does not rule out that the residual rule could be assigned a certain well-considered place.

Fourthly, the argument is that the residual rule is not part and parcel of the positive law, since no such rule could be found in the domain of the applicable sources. Therefore the residual rule is based on a pure doctrinal construction or

[27] A Soeteman, *Logic in Law* (Dordrecht/Boston/London, 1989) 140.

[28] E Betti, *Allgemeine Auslegungslehre als Methodik der Geisteswissenschaften* (Tübingen, 1967) 644–46; M Virally, *La pensée juridique* (Paris, 1960) 170. This argument has also been made in international law, where the residual rule has been criticised for simplifying excessively the legal reality: see, eg, P de Visscher, 'Cours general de droit international public' (1972-II) 136 *RCADI* 22.

[29] C de Visscher, 'Contribution à l'étude des sources du droit international' (1933) 14 *RDILC* 418, fn 42; C de Visscher, *Théories et réalités en droit international public*, 2nd edn (Paris, 1955) 411, fn 2; P Reuter, *Droit international public*, 6th edn (Paris, 1983) 61. Lastly, as has been said, 'L'ordonnancement juridique ne se résume pas en un ensemble d'interdits: il exprime des valeurs et consacre des droits' (M Virally, *La pensée juridique* (Paris, 1960) 170). In English, 'The legal order cannot be reduced to a sum of prohibitions: it expresses values and grants rights.'

[30] L Siorat, Le problème des lacunes en droit international public (Paris, 1958) 34.

postulate.[31] However, this objection is not decisive. In a legal system, not all applicable rules are based on express rules created by the legislator. Thus, the secondary rules relating to the application of the substantive rules are often developed by legal science: rules on interpretation, technical legal rules (such as *lex specialis derogate generali*). Moreover, when the law provides no regulation for a certain situation, a solution must be found. It is not impossible to assign some role to the residual rule in such contexts.

Fifthly, it has been claimed that the residual rule could not simply provide a particular liberty for one subject; because of the bilateral structure of rights and obligations, the liberty of one subject must correspond to the obligation of another subject not to interfere with that liberty; therefore, the application of the residual rule does not lead simply to the freedom of one subject, but also to the creation of a new prohibition inhibiting any behaviour contrary to the conceded freedom.[32] This ingenious objection calls for two answers. On the one hand, it may be acceptable to apply the residual rule in some cases, even if that implies the concomitant creation of some obligation in another subject. The freedom and the obligation could both be accepted. On the other hand, it must not be true that every freedom conceded rests on the bilateral obligation not to interfere with it. The legal order knows of some freedoms that are not matched by corresponding obligations. Thus, when the law concedes the ability (rather than right) of self-defence, this does not imply an obligation by the other party to suffer the defensive action without reacting to it. There is no corresponding obligation to remain passive (*pati*). It might thus occur that the residual rule leads to a freedom on both sides: on the one hand to behave as is seen fit, and on the other hand to react in a discretionary manner to that first behaviour.

Sixthly, it has been said that the residual rule subjects the application of the substantive rules of the law to a precarious fact: the procedural position of the claimant and defendant.[33]

3. Practical Objections

A whole series of authors have emphasised that the (strict) application of the residual rule has negative consequences: it inhibits the development of the law and its adaptation to current needs;[34] it leaves unresolved the collision of concurrent jurisdictions;[35] it extracts from the domain of the questions to be tackled by the judge a class of cases left to political discretion if not vagaries;[36] it can produce

[31] K Engisch, 'Der Begriff der Rechtslücke' in *Essays in Honor of W. Sauer* (Berlin, 1949) 95; E Ehrlich, *Die juristische Logik*, 2nd edn (Tübingen, 1925) 223.

[32] L Lombardi Vallauri, *Corso di filosofia del diritto* (Padua, 1981) 47–48.

[33] *ibid*, 48.

[34] L Cavaré, *Le droit international public positif*, vol I, 3rd edn (Paris, 1973) 243; GG Fitzmaurice, 'The Law and Procedure of the ICJ, 1951–1954: General Principles and Sources of Law' (1953) 30 *BYIL* 10.

[35] F Castberg, 'La méthodologie du droit international public' (1933-I) 43 *RCADI* 344–45.

[36] E Betti, Allgemeine Auslegungslehre als Methodik der Geisteswissenschaften (Tübingen, 1967) 645–46.

results that are shocking to the moral sense,[37] for example by treating differently materially similar situations,[38] etc. These criticisms are all well founded, but their strength manifestly depends on the exact scope of the residual rule in our scale ranging from 1 to 6 (see section III. above).

A second argument is that the residual rule has hardly ever been applied in practice. The tribunals have for centuries developed the law and filled gaps within it (by analogies and general principles) without availing themselves of the doubtful advantage of the residual rule.[39] Again, this argument is well founded, but it manifestly concerns circles 1 and 2 more than circles 4–6 of our classification.

4. *Conclusion*

Overall it can be said that there are many and decisive arguments for precluding an application of an extensive residual rule (circles 1 and 2), but that no decisive argument has been advanced against a subsidiary application of the rule in circles 4–6, possibly after the last circle.

B. Objections Under International Law

A series of objections already mentioned under the flag of the general theory of law (see section IV.A. above) have also been advanced in the context of international law. The decentralised structure of international society sometimes gives them a dramatic overtone. In this regard, it must be noted that the whole historical development of jurisdictional rules under international law has given rise to sharp doctrinal divides. For one school of thought,[40] the construction of international law as a legal order that is not based merely on a prohibition of certain conduct would be tantamount to claiming that originally everything was prohibited. If an authorisation is needed in order to act, initially there could have been no authorisation at all, and hence no behaviour would have been legally well-founded. Only progressively, by a series of authorisations, would international behaviours of States have been founded in law. But according to this argument this conclusion is at once absurd and contrary to historical reality. Appealing as it may be, this theory is hardly very solid. If we applied the contrary rule, as the author suggests, this would lead to the no less absurd result that initially everything was permissible among States, before the emergence of some prohibitive rules. But this does not correspond to historical

[37] A Favre, *Principes du droit des gens* (Freiburg, 1974) 31.

[38] F Bydlinski, *Juristische Methodenlehre und Rechtsbegriff* (Vienna/New York, 1982) 236: 'Die praktische Anwendung des "allgemeinen negativen Satzes" müsste ständig zu Ergebnissen führen, die jeder Vernunft und Gerechtigkeit spotten, vor allem weil ständig offensichtlich Gleiches ungleich behandelt würde.'

[39] *ibid*, 236; and P Foriers, 'Les lacunes du droit' in C Perelman (ed), *Le problème des lacunes en droit* (Brussels, 1968) 20–22.

[40] W Rebbe, *Der Lotusfall vor dem Weltgerichtshof* (Leipzig, 1932) 26.

reality either, and certainly not to the modern legal order emerging after the Westphalian Peace Treaties.[41] Quite to the contrary: the jurisdiction of States from its birth was territorially and personally limited. An international legal order would have been a contradiction in terms if that had not been true. We may now review the various arguments advanced against the rule in the international legal order.

First, it has been claimed that international law could not carry a general presumption of freedom.[42] The rule could at best apply in context, eg for activities on the territory of the State and not for activities with extraterritorial reach.[43] For action on a State's own territory, covered by the traditional domestic jurisdiction rule, there is a general presumption of freedom limited by prohibitive rules. This solution is rooted in the principle of territorial sovereignty. In the extraterritorial domain, the sphere of legal interests of third States is directly affected. Hence, a State must produce a legal title (authorisation) for being allowed to act.[44] Sometimes, the affectedness of third States is considered from a closer perspective: an authorisation to act would be required if legal interests of third States were affected, but not if simple interests of third States were touched.[45] By the same token, it has been said that the residual rule could find some place in the law of coexistence, but that it could have no place in the modern law of cooperation where a effort towards common aims is demanded.[46] Thus, it has been said that Article 56 of the UN Charter, imposing a general duty of cooperation, has abrogated the old rule on residual freedom.[47]

Secondly, it has been claimed that the residual rule is based on an erroneous conception of sovereignty.[48] The latter concept flows from international law. It is not possible to deduce legal obligations from it, or conversely to use it for affirming the lack of existence of legal obligations. Indeed, sovereignty is concerned only with the *exercise* of jurisdiction and not with the initial distribution of competences.[49] The residual rule would create unlimited original powers, contradicting the rules

[41] See JL Brierly, 'The Lotus-Case' in JL Brierly, *The Basis of Obligation in International Law* (Oxford, 1958) 142ff, 144.

[42] JL Brierly, 'Règles générales du droit de la paix' (1936-IV 58 *RCADI* 147; M Bourquin, 'Règles générales du droit de la paix' (1931-I) 35 *RCADI* 103ff; A Bleckmann, 'Die Handlungsfreiheit der Staaten' (1978) 29 *OzöRV* 183ff.

[43] V Bruns, 'Das Völkerrecht als Rechtsordnung' (1933) 3 *ZaöRV* 460; A Bleckmann, 'Die Handlungsfreiheit der Staaten' (1978) 29 *OzöRV* 185; M Bourquin, 'Règles générales du droit de la paix' (1931-I) 35 *RCADI* 103. See also in the *Lotus* case, above n 4, 60–61, the Dissenting Opinion Nyholm.

[44] A Bleckmann, 'Die Völkerrechtsordnung als System von Rechtsvermutungen' in *Essays in Honor of HU Scupin* (Berlin, 1983) 416; H Waldock, 'General Course on Public International Law' (1962-II) 106 *RCADI* 166.

[45] Bleckmann, above n 44, 416.

[46] U Fastenrath, *Lücken im Völkerrecht* (Berlin, 1991) 239, 246; M Lachs, 'The Development and General Trends of International Law in Our Time' (1980-IV) 169 *RCADI* 37.

[47] K Zemanek, 'The Legal Foundations of the International System' (1997) 266 *RCADI* 70, fn 165.

[48] C Rousseau, 'L'aménagement des compétences en droit international' (1930) 37 *RGDIP* 423; H Lauterpacht, *The Function of Law in the International Community* (Oxford, 1933) 96; O Schachter, 'International Law in Theory and Practice' (1982-V) 178 *RCADI* 242.

[49] JL Brierly, 'Règles générales du droit de la paix' (1936-IV) 58 *RCADI* 144.

of international law on the distribution of original jurisdiction. This in turn would lead back to the concept of absolute sovereignty.

Thirdly, it has been claimed that the residual rule would lead to important international conflict, since it leaves unresolved a series of disputes arising from concurrent jurisdictions or from the exercise of concurrent subjective rights.[50] What is not prohibited is indeed permitted to anyone. Thus, two series of actions could be equally justified, even if absolutely contradictory.[51] The anarchical bent would remain even if one applies the rule that the earlier exercise of the freedom would prevail over the later one (*prior tempore, potior jure*).[52] The problem is rendered even graver in the international legal order, which does not always clearly fix the domain of jurisdiction and which knows of many concurrent sets of powers.[53] It is also recalled that many rules of international law deal with the apportionment of resources, damages, etc. The residual rule could have no concrete role in their regard. To apply it would be tantamount to refusing any solution for the dispute.

Fourthly, some authors keenly distinguish gaps from areas of residual freedom. Thus it has been said that a State can perform any action with regard to which international law positively establishes that it is not prohibited; but it cannot act freely in the area where rules of international law are simply lacking (gaps).[54] In the case of a gap, there is no agreement of the States on the applicable rule: it therefore cannot be said that the action is permitted or that it is prohibited; it is neither.[55] The gap is filled by having recourse to different criteria, and not only by the postulate of a residual freedom. The judge will seek to draw inferences from general principles of law. If none is available, only the legislator can decide the issue.

Fifthly, many authors have insisted on the particularly negative consequences of the residual rule when applied to international law, that is, in the context of a fragmentary legal order, having a series of gaps, devoid of a centralised legislator able to respond quickly to deficiencies, etc.[56] There are relatively few 'prohibitive' rules in international law; the residual rule would thus leave too much room for anarchy.[57] It has been added that the rule may have its justification in municipal law, where it limits the interventions of the executive and preserves individual

[50] C Rousseau, 'L'aménagement des compétences en droit international' (1930) 37 *RGDIP* 423; L Le Fur, 'Règles générales du droit de la paix' (1935-IV) 54 *RCADI* 302.

[51] F Castberg, 'La méthodologie du droit international public' (1933-I) 43 *RCADI* 344.

[52] This criterion has been suggested by R Quadri, *Diritto internazionale pubblico*, 5th edn (Naples, 1968) 212–13, who accepts in this case the legitimacy of the 'struggle'.

[53] P Reuter, *Droit international public*, 6th edn (Paris, 1983) 61.

[54] G Salvioli, 'Les règles générales de la paix' (1933-IV) 46 *RCADI* 21–23, 62; G Salvioli, 'Il caso del Lotus' (1927) 19 *Rivista di diritto internazionale* 543.

[55] The category 'neither prohibited nor permitted' is emphasised by C Focarelli, *International Law as Social Construct* (Oxford, 2012) 283.

[56] GG Fitzmaurice, 'The General Principles of International Law Considered from the Standpoint of Law' (1957-II) 92 *RCADI* 50, 52; C Rousseau, *Droit international public*, vol I (Paris, 1970) 378.

[57] C Rousseau, 'L'aménagement des compétences en droit international' (1930) 37 *RGDIP* 424.

freedoms; but international law is not concerned with the interventionism of a superior power.[58]

Sixthly, the argument is that the residual rule would subject the application of the substantive rules of international law to the hazards of the procedural position of States, either as claimants or as defendants.[59] In view of the uncertainty of a number of rules of international law, States taking part in a judicial procedure would have an interest in manoeuvering themselves into the position of defendant so as to benefit from the presumption of freedom

> [T]he outcome of a great many of disputes would depend largely on the accident of which side was plaintiff and which defendant; and a party to a dispute would only have to maneuver itself into the position of defendant … in order to benefit at once from a presumption in favor of the legality of its action, deriving from sovereignty…[60]

But it must be added that a party is claimant or defendant essentially with regard to individual claims. Thus, the general position of defendant does not liberate a State from the burden of proof with regard to all the allegations it produces. It is clear, however, that the position of defendant may carry some advantages, as does a formulation of the special agreement, conferring jurisdiction, in negative terms, as occurred in the *Lotus* case ('Is it contrary to international law…?' rather than 'Is it in conformity with international law…?').

Lastly, it has been said that international judicial and arbitral practice does not reveal that the rule has been applied at all.[61] Where the law has been silent, the judges have rather attempted to develop the law by analogies and through recourse to general principles of law. There is thus a sort of absence of any practical need for the rule. The role of general principles of law has been particularly emphasised in this context: '[w]ithout putting States to the necessity of invariably proving that their actions are in positive conformity with international law, it requires of them something more than action which is merely not contrary to it'; there is duty 'to act in good faith and with due regard to the position of other States, and, in particular, to avoid abuses of rights'.[62] There are even authors who have claimed that each time an action is likely to destroy the legal community as such (eg the use of nuclear weapons), there must be a norm in the legal order prohibiting that behaviour.[63] Other authors have held that soft-law sources equally pre-empt the residual freedom, as they also roll back the reserved domain.[64]

[58] F Castberg, 'La méthodologie du droit international public' (1933-I) 43 *RCADI* 342.

[59] GG Fitzmaurice, 'The Law and Procedure of the ICJ, 1951–1954: General Principles and Sources of Law' (1953) 30 *BYIL* 12; H Lauterpacht, *The Development of International Law by the International Court* (London, 1958) 362–63.

[60] Fitzmaurice, above n 59, 12.

[61] J Basdevant, 'Règles générales du droit de la paix' (1936-IV) 58 *RCADI* 596, 600ff.

[62] GG Fitzmaurice, 'The General Principles of International Law Considered from the Standpoint of the Rule of Law' (1957-II) 92 *RCADI* 50, 58.

[63] H Mosler, 'Völkerrecht als Rechtsordnung' (1976) 36 *ZaöRV* 44.

[64] G Abi-Saab, 'Cours général de droit international public' (1987-VII) 207 *RCADI* 210.

C. Objections to the Authorisation Theory

According to the theory of authorisation, a State must produce a legal title allowing it to perform an action; otherwise the action is not lawful. This conception predominates in municipal public law. Conversely, it has been scarcely defended in the realm of public international law. We have to note that this construction is subject to the same relativity as the opposing residual freedom doctrine. Its role and place may fluctuate as a function of the legal order or legal branch considered. Moreover, the authorisation can flow from an express or an implicit provision, from an analogy, from a general principle of law or from the values underpinning a legal system. Especially in the circles 4–6 described above, the two theories of prohibition or authorisation may converge: for example, a general principle can be seen as a limitation on a power to act (prohibition), but it can also be construed as an authorisation for some action (legal title). What objections have been voiced against this theory in international law?

The main criticism seems to be that the rule is hardly practicable.[65] The creation of international law norms is often delayed, difficult and partial. The legal titles flowing from the norms are often bilateral or otherwise limited. Thus, there would exist an excessive brake on State action if a legal title fitting the situation had to be sought in all cases. In sum, the theory of authorisation supposes a significantly denser legal order, accompanied by a legislator able to act at all times to fill possible gaps. In a sense, the necessity to produce an authorising title would lead to an excessive block on the capacity to act and to live[66]—for individuals and for States. As has been said tongue in cheek: for a private law transaction, the law would have to prescribe the exact time where it should take place, the form of payment, the fact whether it is necessary to wear a tie or not, whether it is necessary to smile or not, etc.

As we have seen, in both cases we have good arguments against an application of the theories in circles 1–2, but not for the application of the residual rule in the remoter circles 4–6.

D. Scope of the Residual Freedom Rule in International Law

What is the scope and role of the rule on residual freedom in international law? There is no overall and unequivocal answer to this question. It rather seems that the residual rule may be a valid legal argument in certain contexts, in most cases being placed amongst other available arguments. It also stands to reason that the

[65] A Bleckmann, 'Die Völkerrechtsordnung als System von Rechtsvermutungen' in *Essays in Honor of HU Scupin* (Berlin, 1983) 413.

[66] C Cossio, 'Panorama der egologischen Rechtslehre' in A Kaufmann (ed), *Die ontologische Begründung des Rechts* (Darmstadt, 1965)279–80. See also A Soeteman, *Logic in Law* (Dordrecht/Boston/London, 1989) 148.

application of the rule must be of last resort: only when no analogy or general principle can be found to provide a solution within the four corners of the law, and when the fundamental legal values inherent in the legal order are not thereby sacrificed, could it possibly be considered that each subject remains free to act as it sees fit. If the liberty conceded unreasonably injures the interests of a third person or preponderant collective interests, the legal operator should not have recourse to the residual freedom argument (ie to an *a contrario* argument). Moreover, the residual rule remains limited to areas where legal obligations are relevant; it cannot extend to areas where concurrent subjective rights or jurisdictions are at stake. Such a reduced and tamed residual freedom to some extent corresponds to the needs of life. The function of the law is not to regulate any and every aspect of social life. Its mission is to provide regulations when other persons need to be protected, or when the general interest so requires In this light, it is not unreasonable to conceive of the province of law as an inherently limited area, bordered by spaces of liberty, when there is no reason for the law to be extended there. This modest construction also better corresponds to the *opinio juris* of States. Indeed, States do not consider that they have to produce a legal title for every one of their actions; in many areas, they consider their actions to be unfettered so long as there is no legal rule requiring particular conduct. Consequently, by limiting the operation of the residual rule to our circles 4–6, we can at once protect the autonomy of the subject and the integrity of the law. A fair balance thus seems to have been achieved between the concurrent forces of freedom and order. In particular within a legal order characterised by so many normative and institutional uncertainties as international law, the residual rule cannot be a *prius* presumed on the basis of sovereignty. It must remain a confined *posterius*, subordinated to the application of all the possible sources of the law, including the principles and the fundamental values of the legal system. In this sense, the residual rule flows from the law and remains governed by the exigencies of the legal order.

The place of the rule also varies according to the different branches of international law. It has an important role in the context of criminal international law, with the legality principle (*nullum crimen sine lege*), which is but a special expression of the residual rule: there is no punishable crime if no positive law offence is defined in an applicable provision. As has already been said, the role of the residual freedom is more important in the exercise of territorial jurisdiction than in the exercise of extraterritorial jurisdiction, and in the 'law of coexistence' than in the 'law of cooperation' (eg the protection of the environment).

We must note that the rule has its own *leges speciales* in particular branches of international law. Thus, in the law of armed conflict, and specifically in the law relating to the means and methods of warfare (conduct of hostilities), the approach has constantly been, since the times of the Hague Conventions II of 1899 and IV of 1907, to prohibit certain conduct (eg the use of certain weapons) and not to authorise a belligerent to use only enumerated means and methods to overpower the enemy. There would be no point in the law of armed conflict telling belligerents everything that they can do; the list of permissive action would be endless. Moreover, the legal result of any omission in the list of accepted conduct could have the result of prohibiting that action. This would produce a too far-reaching domain of prohibition. The general rule must remain that what is necessary to overpower the enemy must in general terms be regarded as lawful.[67] On the other hand, this 'prohibitive rules' approach is tempered by some sweeping norms contained within the law of armed conflict. This is the case, first of all,[68] with the so-called Martens Clause, which is considered to be part and parcel of modern positive international humanitarian law.[69] A modern version of this Clause reads as follows:

> In cases not covered by this Protocol or by other international agreements, civilians and combatants remain under the protection and authority of the principles of international law derived from established custom, from the principles of humanity and from the dictates of public conscience.[70]

There is some debate as to the precise scope of this clause. There is no doubt, however, that it limits the residual freedom of action of States even when there is no explicit prohibition in the body of the law of armed conflict. At a minimum, the Clause it taken to mean that if conduct is not expressly prohibited, it is not thereby meant to be automatically lawful. A belligerent must first check whether this action would be compatible with the requirements of humanity and public

[67] The attribution of rights approach would also produce some other legal difficulties. Indeed, if the law of armed conflict conferred a 'right' of belligerent action, this would mean that belligerent A would have a legal entitlement to realise a conduct *x*, with the concomitant duty of the other belligerent B to suffer this very action. But no belligerent feels itself bound to passively accept the regular belligerent action of the adverse party. Quite on the contrary, everything possible and lawful is done, and may be done, in order to oppose this conduct, to minimise its effects or even to neutralise it. See G Balladore-Pallieri, *La guerra* (Padova, 1935) 163.

[68] A second provision having such a general reach is the one relating to 'humane treatment' of the protected persons, a provision to be found in all four Geneva Conventions (GCs) of 1949: Article 12/12/13/27 GCs I–IV. This legal situation justifies the conclusion that the prohibitive approach still has a certain reach in the so-called 'Hague Law' (relating to the means and methods of warfare) but that it has been largely restricted, if not abandoned, in the 'Geneva Law' (relating to the protection and humane treatment of persons *hors de combat*).

[69] US Military Tribunal at Nuremberg, *Krupp* case (1948) 15 *Annual Digest of Public International Law Cases* (now *ILR*) 622. On the Martens Clause, see, eg, F Münch 'Die Martens'sche Klausel und die Grundlagen des Völkerrechts' (1976) 36 *ZaöRV* 347ff; S Miyazaki, 'The Martens Clause and International Humanitarian Law' in *Essays in Honour of J Pictet* (Geneva, 1984) 433ff; T Meron, 'On Custom and the Antecedents of the Martens Clause in Medieval and Renaissance Ordinances of War' in *Essays in Honour of R. Bernhardt* (Berlin, 1995) 173ff; VV Pustogarov, 'The Martens Clause in International Law' (1999) 1 *Journal of the History of International Law* 125ff; A Cassese, 'The Martens Clause: Half a Loaf or Simply Pie in the Sky?' (2000) 11 *EJIL* 187ff; R Ticehurst, 'The Martens Clause and the Laws of Armed Conflict' in N Sanajaoba (ed), *A Manual of International Humanitarian Laws* (New Dehli, 2004) 312ff (see already in (1997) 37 *IRRC* 125ff); MN Hayashi, 'The Martens Clause and Military Necessity' in HM Hensel (ed), *The Legitimate Use of Military Force, The Just War Tradition and the Customary Law of Armed Conflict* (Aldershot, 2008) 135f; G Distefano and E Henry, 'Final Provisions, Including the Martens Clause' in A Clapham. P Gaeta and M. Sassòli (eds), *The 1949 Geneva Conventions, A Commentary* (Oxford, 2015) 155. On the reduced efficacy of this Clause before 1949, see G Best, *War and Law Since 1945* (Oxford, 1994) 250.

[70] Art 1, §2 of the 1977 Protocol Additional to the Geneva Conventions of 12 August 1949, and relating to the Protection of Victims of International Armed Conflict (AP I).

conscience, and an appeal is made to him to reject the conduct if it does not comply with these notions. Thereby, the Clause rebuts any mechanical application of the principle, inherent in prohibitive bodies of law, namely that 'what is not prohibited is allowed'. In short, if something is inhuman and incompatible with public conscience, it is not allowed simply because there is no specific prohibitory rule. As can be seen, the Martens Clause is a direct counterbalance to the residual rule. Both rules pull in opposite directions; one moderates the other.

Within special areas of the law of armed conflict relating to the conduct of hostilities, such as weapons law, other rules operate a similar check on the residual freedom. Thus, if a particular weapon is not prohibited by a specific norm (say in a treaty), it is not thereby automatically lawful to use that weapon. It must first be tested whether that weapon causes what is called 'unnecessary suffering' as compared with the military advantage of its use.[71] If the suffering appears unnecessary, the weapon is prohibited. In short, the body of the law of armed conflict recognises some general principles the role of which is to reverse (or even to bring to fullest power, if the principles are themselves seen as prohibitions) the 'prohibitive' approach, in order to secure the better protection of persons against the sufferings and evils of war.

Lastly, we might also emphasise that certain specific rules of the law of armed conflict reinforce the residual freedom principle. Thus, it has been claimed that the exception relating to 'military necessity' contained in various rules of the law of armed conflict[72] is nothing more than a particular application of the *Lotus* freedom: while the law imposes a certain number of obligations on a belligerent, thereby limiting its action, it also accords through specific exemptions a freedom in certain contexts, so as to take account of inescapable military necessities.[73] Thereby, 'black holes' are punched into the body of the law; these black holes are positive law expressions of the residual freedom. We might note, however, that, contrary to the *Lotus* situation, the freedoms are here granted by an express rule of international law. And it is more than doubtful whether they give rise to an unfettered discretion.

On the whole, the reader may detect the complex balance between freedom and constraint in various branches of international law—and the pervasive presence of some aspects of the residual freedom rule as visible or invisible invitees.

[71] Art 35, §2 AP I. See, eg, WH Boothby, *Weapons and the Law of Armed Conflict* (Oxford, 2009) 55ff. The ICJ has recognised that this principle is part of positive international law: see *Legality of the Threat or Use of Nuclear Weapons* (Advisory Opinion) [1996-I] ICJ Rep 257, §78.

[72] Eg for the destruction of private property, Art 23, letter g, of the Hague Regulations of 1907.

[73] See G Schwarzenberger, 'Military Necessity: A Misnomer' in *Essays in Honor of S. Séfériadès* (Athens, 1961) 13ff; G Schwarzenberger, *International Law, As Applied by International Courts and Tribunals*, vol 2: *The Law of Armed Conflict* (London, 1968) 128

6

The Effectiveness of International Law

I. General Aspects

Is international law effective?[1] Does it have any real weight in international affairs? Or are the sceptics on the right track when they claim that relations between States are power relations where the stronger holds sway over the weaker? If this were true, international law would be but a palliative and chimerical cloak, destined at best to impress naive believers. A significant number of persons consider that the resolution of the problem thus posed depends on the establishment of a regular sanction for the breaches of the law. When sanctioning mechanisms are regular and strong, the law perforce is effective; when they are not, the law is necessarily feeble. The issue is from this perspective not one of experience but of preconception. Moreover, the spontaneous execution of the norms hardly enters into the equation, all the more since it is regularly not even on the radar. The reasoning is thereby inverted, the pathological cases of deviance and defiance being placed at the centre of attention. The questions are simply: How can we compel the recalcitrant? How can we tame the wrongdoer? *Hic sunt leones.*

In truth, the question of the effectiveness of a legal order is considerably more multifaceted and must be addressed on several different levels. First, there is the issue of spontaneous compliance. The more there is such compliance, the more the legal order will be effective. Manifestly, such a spontaneously accepted order will be more effective than another where the commission of many unlawful acts has to be regularly sanctioned through some well-oiled mechanisms. Secondly, there are the compliance and implementation mechanisms, the function of which is to inform States and other subjects of the existing rules and of the best ways of implementation. Even a summary perusal of international realities shows that violations of the law are not always based on deliberate ill will. Frequently the States or local actors have important gaps in their knowledge of the relevant rules, or simply lack the appropriate means for implementing them. The quest for the better effectiveness of international law will not be satisfied by the improvement of sanctions; it rather hinges on the provision of means for the better application

[1] On this issue, see the still important monograph by L Henkin, *How Nations Behave*, 2nd edn (New York/Washington/London, 1968). See also R Kolb, *Réflexions sur les politiques juridiques extérieures* (Pedone, Paris, 2015); TH Cheng, *When International Law Works* (Oxford, 2012).

of the obligations. Thirdly, and very much in last place, come the sanction mechanisms. The law has been violated; there must be remedies.

Throughout legal history, the imposition of sanctions in the event of violation of the law was a question of policy rather than of law. Legal doctrine limited itself to exposing the rules and their sources, and to addressing the issue of normative conflict. With the advent of the modern State, the question of sanctions was encompassed by the concept of the rule of law. Thus, it was to some extent legalised. But the execution of the law has to some extent remained a 'political' question, in the sense that the social body must be ready to marshal its own will and energy to sustain the meting out of the sanction. In municipal law, this fact becomes evident when the violation of the law is attributable to a potent social actor, or when there are mass breaches. In international law, where there is no centralised executive, this fact is even more visible. If the social body lends its strength to the execution of the law, the latter will emerge reinforced from the challenge; if this does not occur, the law is weakened and possibly fails. However much a society is developed and refined, and thus entrusts legal sanctions to specialised and central organs, there remains this social responsibility to take care of the legal order. Institutional procedures would lose all their weight without a proper backing of social forces.

In international law, where there are no regular centralised sanctioning mechanisms, the States remain the masters of the law's fate. Their legal policy will reinforce it, or will weaken it. Thus, for example, if the States do not oppose aggressive wars (Ethiopia, 1935; Goa, 1962; Pakistan/India, 1965; Iraq, 2003, Ukraine, 2014, etc); if they do not react adequately in the event of massive violations of international humanitarian law (Rwanda, 1994; Chechnya, 1999; territories occupied by Israel; Syria, 2011–..., etc); if their opposition in the face of international disputes is merely ideological, pursuing a partisan policy instead of making a real effort to respond to the situation on the ground (Congo, 1960–63; Indochina after 1962, etc); if all that happens, the law is weakened or fades away, and vice versa. It would be short-sighted to deny that this is first and foremost a function of legal policy and not simply one of law. In short, the execution of the law is only partly a legal question. Here is the rule, and there are the consequences attached to it. Here is the norm, and there the vagaries in its application. Here is the 'ought', and there are the realities of the world. Even when the issue of execution is partly legalised, as in Article 94, §2 of the UN Charter with regard to the execution of judgments of the ICJ, the heart of the matter remains the will to cooperate in that execution. To be sure, Article 94, §2 offers a power to the Security Council to decide on measures of implementation, which could technically include the use of force. But nothing is said about the will to exercise that power; this is not a legal question. The law must thus rely in this context on certain political conditions, which it cannot create itself.[2]

[2] As has been said by an eminent constitutional lawyer, the rule of law rests on conditions that the legal order alone cannot create but must presuppose. See EW Böckenförde, 'Die Entstehung des Staates als Vorgang der Säkularisierung' in EW Böckenförde, *Recht, Staat, Freiheit, Studien zur Rechtsphilosophie, Staatstheorie und Verfassungsgeschichte* (Frankfurt, 1991) 112.

It is a fact of observation—mentioned above—that many persons base their reasoning on our subject matter on a simple and linear assimilation, seemingly replete with good sense. In an 'anarchical' society with no superior power, the law must perforce be weak. It is bound to remain a chimera, and will be used by the powerful to cloak their interested action. It will thus be used to justify whatever position. Without a controlling influence, legal injunctions remain in such limbo that it is perhaps even improper to speak of law at all.[3] The gist of the matter is thus an assimilation of decentralisation and ineffectiveness. Control and effectiveness are merged one into the other: if there is control, there will be effectiveness; and if there is no control, there will be no effectiveness. If the recalcitrant subject cannot ultimately be forced to obey the legal prescription, the latter remains an aspiration and does not rise to become a legal injunction. But the law does not deal mainly with aspirations; it is based on rules. Examples are not lacking: How were Japan and Italy treated after their aggression in Manchuria in 1932 and in 1935? Where were the sanctions against the coalition of States that attacked Iraq in 2003 without any valid legal entitlement? What will happen as regards Russia and the annexation of Crimea in 2014? We might note in passing that all these examples relate to the supreme question of war and peace, ie the use of force. The preceding developments imply, at the end of the day, that there is true law only within the State with its vertical scheme of organisation. This would also imply that there was no (true) law before the emergence of the modern State—or should an exception perhaps be made for the Roman Empire with its Roman law?

It is certainly correct to consider that the organisation of international society and the lack of really effective solidarities at the universal level have as a consequence that the law may be weak in certain contexts. This is essentially the case in matters relating to vital interests such as the use of force (but even here powerful sanctions may be meted out, as the example of Iraq after the annexation of Kuwait in 1991 shows; but selectivity remains, this case not being treated like others). However, vital interests as perceived by States at a given moment do not cover the whole spectrum of international law. They may relate to the most important and visible part of the legal order, namely the use of force. Statistically, we are speaking here of the visible 1–2 per cent of the iceberg. It would be odd indeed if the performance of international law as a whole were measured only with regard to this sole, if important, province. Technically, the mistake would be the same as if we were to find international law to be effective overall just because postal mail is distributed satisfactorily all over the planet (since this is based on an implementation of international law through the universal postal conventions). Moreover, it is to some extent peculiar to compare the effectiveness of international law with that of municipal law through the sole lens of internal law tools, notably the centralised executive. International law cannot have such an executive, since that would be

[3] JL Goldsmith and EA Posner, *The Limits of International Law* (Oxford, 2005). On that monograph, see the justified critique in HJ Cremer, 'Völkerrecht—alles nur Rhetorik?' (2007) 67 *ZaöRV* 267ff. Among the deniers of the role of international law, see also the well-known words by R Aron, *Guerre et paix entre les nations*, 8th edn (Paris, 1984) 691.

tantamount to living in a world federation and not in an international law setting. This fact suggests that in analysing its effectiveness, we have to go beyond the hammer of the sanction and put together a much more varied toolbox of factors contributing to the adequate response by the law to the real needs of international society. In other words, international society has its own exigencies; international law must be measured first of all as to its aptitude to respond to these needs, and not as regards its capacity to approximate as much as possible to the municipal law model.[4] The proper functioning of the system must be measured in accordance with its own functions and surroundings, and not by the projection of imaginary missions and parameters which are, and will remain, alien. In passing, we might note that municipal laws are by far not as effective as the short equation presented above suggests. How many breaches of the law are effectively sanctioned in internal law? How many thefts, how many road traffic offences? How effective is the Somali legal order? Or that of Iraq? Or that of Central Africa? All the foregoing may be summarised as follows: We should mistrust *a priori* conclusions drawn from such premises as 'decentralisation', and should rather look for the results of painstaking empirical data. The reality will be portrayed much more accurately by induction from reality than by deduction from some dogma.

A last general question must be posed. What is a violation of international law? The observer often seems to know that there has been one. But international law often works with open and discretionary norms,[5] where more than one interpretation is reasonably possible. The question of what constitutes a violation has not yet been settled. A good example can be found in the law of armed conflict. Article 51, §5, letter b of Additional Protocol I to the Geneva Convention (1977), considers that collateral civilian damage (to persons or objects) is lawful as long as it does not become 'excessive' with regard to the military advantage pursued.[6] The provision does not require strict proportionality; rather, the collateral civilian damage of an attack is acceptable if there is no clear excess with regard to the military advantage sought. In warfare, a belligerent may attack only military objectives; but these he must remain free to attack, even if there is collateral damage. The latter is unfortunately a frequent occurrence in our densely populated world. However, when civilians die in a bombardment, there are hardly any journalists

[4] By the same token, it would be wrong to consider that the UN administration is not as effective as the Swiss federal administration and to draw negative inferences from this finding. The point is that the UN administration does not have the same financing and powers as the Swiss administration; in particular it is deprived of executive (supranational) powers. The UN administration's effectiveness must be measured in the context of its own social and legal environment. When seen in this light, the informed observer will see that it is astonishingly effective. It has been noted by an international lawyer who cannot be considered to suffer from lofty idealism that very hard work is performed within the UN, often under exceedingly difficult conditions: S Sur, 'La créativité du droit international, Cours général de droit international public' (2012) 363 *RCADI* 273.

[5] *ibid*, 22.

[6] For a discussion of this provision and of the whole issue, see, eg, I Henderson, *The Contemporary Law of Targeting* (Leiden/Boston, 2009) 198ff; J Holland, 'Military Objective and Collateral Damage: Their Relationship and Dynamics' (2004) 7 *Yearbook of International Humanitarian Law* 35.

who would refrain from concluding that a breach of international humanitarian law has occurred and that a war crime has been committed. Under the law of armed conflict, this may be wrong in a whole series of situations. Apart from this example, there are many other issues. For instance, the use of force will be considered unlawful as an intervention in internal affairs, overlooking the fact that the legitimate government has invited the foreign power to become involved (Russia in Syria, 2015). A treaty will be considered violated, but the observer will not ask himself whether it was yet in force (even if ratified), whether there was an applicable reservation, whether the treaty was suspended on some recognised ground. Was there not another norm prevailing in the conflict of norms, eg as *lex posterior*? Was the purported breach not covered by countermeasures? Or perhaps a customary norm of international law is not followed by some States—a manifest breach! But was that norm not simply derogated from by an agreement applicable between those States (*lex specialis*)? True, these and others are complex legal questions, which suppose some knowledge of the dossier. All the more reason to be cautious as to the frequent and easy findings that international law has (again) been 'violated'.

II. Elements Pushing States towards Compliance

There is a series of elements tending to push States (and other subjects) towards spontaneous compliance with the rules of international law. Some examples follow:

1. *Bearer of the interests.* In municipal law, the bearer of many relevant interests is the individual acting in pursuit of his or her personal aims. Therefore, the temptation to flout the law is greater: I have an interest in leaving my car in a prohibited area when I am in a hurry; I have in interest in stealing an object when I want to benefit from it; I have in interest in hiding my income when I do not want to pay more taxes, etc. In international law, the organs executing the law are almost exclusively the staff of a State or an organisation, acting on behalf of that entity and not in the pursuit of their own interests. Thus, these persons have nothing to gain from the non-application or breach of the law. On the contrary, their professional training predisposes them to silently implement the obligations falling on the entity for which they work. This automatism will be interrupted only if there are 'vital' contrary interests and, say, a minister makes a phone call to the civil servant calling on him or her to discontinue the ordinary implementation. But in how many cases will that occur?
2. *Number of norms.* The number of applicable norms is much greater in municipal law than in international law. Moreover, the municipal law norms are often much more detailed. Therefore, the number of actual or potential violations is

also bound to be greater. International law, on the contrary, contains fewer and less detailed norms. Many of its provisions are flexible and context-related. In consequence, the number of violations decreases. In short, sovereign States remain freer in international relations than is the individual in municipal settings. This has a consequence for the number of breaches of the law.

3. *Quest of the powerful for stability*. Power needs stability so as to be able to impose its influence. Rapid political upheavals and endemic instability jeopardise the foreign policies of States, including those of the Great Powers. Even hegemony means peace: *pax romana*, *pax americana* and so on. Therefore, the Powers have only a limited interest in international disorder. The same is true in a much more radical sense as regards small and medium-sized States. Deprived of sheer strength, those States have an eminent interest in a strong and stable legal order to protect them. It is no surprise that a small State like Switzerland has constantly emphasised its interest in the strengthening and proper functioning of the international legal order.[7] For the promotion of its interests, an entity may look to power or law. Those who do not possess the former are bound to seek the latter. The net result is that States will violate the rules only if important interests dictate such a course. The threshold for violation is elevated.
4. *Reciprocity*. Reciprocity is a potent factor pushing towards compliance. If State A violates rule *x*, it knows that State B may suspend the application of rule *x* or *y* in response, and this may matter to that State.[8] This situation elevates the opportunity cost of a violation. There is also the danger of creating a precedent that may inspire other States in other contexts (so-called 'loaded guns'). It remains true, however, that reciprocity does not carry the same weight in the relations between a strong and a weak State as it does between States of roughly equal power.[9] There are also collective sanctions: collective countermeasures, sanctions within an international organisation, etc. In these latter contexts, even relatively stronger States are in danger.
5. *Moral repercussions*. In a small society of less than 200 subjects (States), where honour and respectability count for much, violations of the law are always seen as a matter for concern. Internationally, they expose the State to criticism and keep it in the spotlight of international scrutiny. A certain stigmatisation and expressions of public opinions may follow (eg boycotts). This state of affairs indicates again that the benefit of the violation must outweigh its costs to be rationally affordable. This will be the case only if important interests are at stake—and even then not in all cases.

[7] D Schindler, 'Die Schweiz und das Völkerrecht' in A Riklin, H Haug and R Probst (eds), *Nouveau manuel de la politique extérieure suisse* (Berne/Stuttgart/Vienna, 1992) 101–02.

[8] Thus Hitler renounced the use of chemical weapons during World War II, mainly for fear of retaliation.

[9] But even in such a situation, it would be inexact to claim that reciprocity does not play any role. The weaker States may pool together. Or consider the situation in armed conflict where a powerful State uses chemical weapons. The fact that the other State is weaker does not preclude it from retaliating with chemical weapons, if it possesses them.

6. *Law created voluntarily*. The will of the State has a decisive role in the creation of international law and in the assumption of particular obligations by the State. No legislation is imposed in international law; essentially there are rules that are accepted either by consent (treaties), or by concurrence in a certain practice (custom). In most cases a State is bound because it wishes to be, and is not bound when it does not so wish.[10] This fact accounts for a generally good record of compliance in international law (apart from certain sensitive matters such as human rights). When you are free to assume an obligation, you will normally assume it if you consider yourself as having an interest in doing so; but then you have also an incentive to honour the regime you have freely accepted, all the more so since there remains the Sword of Damocles that is reciprocity. International law is here in a better position than municipal law, where most obligations are imposed on the subjects by authoritative legislation. The temptation to avoid a burden not freely accepted remains comparatively higher. As an example, we may take the legal regime of the ICJ. No State is bound to accept the jurisdiction of the Court for the settlement of a dispute to which it is a party.[11] The jurisdiction of the Court rests on the consent of States. A State will thus in many cases keenly calculate the advantages and risks of a submission to the Court; if it defends the case, it has already envisaged the probability that it might lose, and has signalled that it can live with this result. This explains why the judgments of the Court are almost always implemented, even if occasionally only after some time (at the PCIJ, from 1922 to 1939, all dispositive judgments were implemented).
7. *Rationality of States*. It has been said that the State is a cold monster. Whether that is true in all contexts may be left open. What is clear, however, is that States calculate with the greatest care their interests, the action most conducive to their realisation and the costs likely to be incurred by the several paths they can follow in their external policies. In this overall calculation, the consequences of a breach of the law are closely computed and assessed. In municipal law, on the other hand, there are many breaches of the law that occur simply because the individual is moved by his or her fleeting and thoughtless passions. In most cases, it stands to reason that a violation of some criminal law provision is a bad choice. The individual, with his or her personal weaknesses, risks stumbling into the trap of irrational action. This risk is reduced for the State. It may occur mainly at times of greatest nervous and ideological tension, notably after violent revolutions.
8. *The role of municipal law*. A number of norms of international law are inserted into the municipal legal order. There, they will be executed by the regular State organs. If the provisions of international law are violated, there will in such cases also be a violation of the internal law into which these obligations have been incorporated (automatically in monist systems, by transformation into municipal statutes in dualistic systems).

[10] Only exceptionally are obligations imposed without or against the will of States. See C Tomuschat, 'Obligations Arising for States Without or Against their Will' (1993-IV) 241 *RCADI* 195ff.
[11] Art 36 of the ICJ Statute.

It must be added that there have also been evolutions carrying with them negative consequences for spontaneous compliance with international law. We have already seen that classical international law essentially had an instrumental and subservient function: it was a tool of the foreign policy of States. For this reason, it was more rarely violated (since its demands on States were minimal).[12] With the advent of modern international law and its much tighter corset of rules binding States, the situation changed. There were now more opportunities for a clash of interests, and a greater number of situations where there would be the temptation to breach the rules. In short, it is easier to respect flexible rules on the conclusion and termination of treaties than to respond to obligations such as the non-use of force, non-intervention in internal affairs, respect for human rights, etc.

III. The Comparison of Municipal Law with International Law

In the preceding section, many references were made to international law in comparison to municipal law. The comparison may be pursued somewhat further at this point. For most persons, the basic assumption is that municipal law is well-respected (since breach of it is subject to sanctions), while international law is not (since it is not 'sanctioned').[13] We have already seen many aspects that considerably relativise this strict distinction. A precise analysis shows that there is a difference at the quantitative and the qualitative levels.

At the quantitative level of the frequency of violations, international law fares better than municipal law in most cases. The number of violations of the law in municipal society (ranging from breach of contract to road traffic offences) is so overwhelming that many volumes of hundreds of pages could not contain them all. Only a small fraction of these deeds gives rise to litigation; and only a fraction of litigated cases lead to a sanction. Conversely, international law deals only with (political) questions of a certain importance and concomitant visibility. A breach of a treaty is not the same as the breach of an obscure contract; a political matter is not the same as a small private question. Hence, the violations of international law are reported in the media. By reading a good newspaper, one daily encounters a number of violations of international law; but this means that one also tends to encounter

[12] This is true to the point that there is hardly any discussion of the issue in legal doctrine. It was only at the time of World War I, and of the (in)famous 'scrap of paper' argument (see at <http://www.firstworldwar.com/source/scrapofpaper1.htm>), that the issue came to the fore. See in the contemporary literature the graphic presentation by O Nippold, *Die Gestaltung des Völkerrechts nach dem Weltkriege* (Zurich, 1917) 34ff. By the same token, in the 1930s it was still believed that the conclusion of a treaty was in itself the solution, without any care for its prospects of being implemented. See the critique in E Giraud, *La nullité de la politique internationale des grandes démocraties (1919–1939), L'échec de la S.d.N., la guerre* (Paris, 1948) 17–18.

[13] But there are sanctions, eg unilateral countermeasures and reprisals, as well as sometimes collective sanctions, such as the measures able to be taken by the Security Council of the UN under Art 41 of the Charter.

almost all of them. There is no need for multiple volumes in this context, provided an exception is made for human rights and humanitarian law in non-international armed conflicts, two subject matters intimately bound up with the municipal sphere. This incredible degree of visibility of the violations of international law explains why the unexperienced observer may lose any sense of proportion. The impression is that international law is 'always' being violated. In reality, the observer has witnessed only the small number of existing violations, and has not perceived the overwhelming number of cases in which international law has been applied without giving rise to any controversy. The error in perspective is massive when one considers the perception of municipal law. There, the observer will often witness various enforcement measures (police, the justice system), but the sheer number of violations means that the vast majority remain unseen in the shadows. Thus, for example, there are roughly 100,000 treaties in force in the world. How many of these give rise to significant legal problems? There are hardly more than 1,000 such treaties, and even this figure is somewhat on the high side. This means that about 1.25 per cent of all treaties are problematic, and therefore roughly 98.75 per cent are applied without significant trouble. Who would say that this proportion is not honourable?

The situation is different when considered from a qualitative perspective. In the domain of the vital interests of States, there are important and serious breaches of the law, and there are few fully satisfactory remedies. Moreover, the domain of States' vital interests unfortunately correlates largely with that of international law's vital interests. It is therefore in the most important part of the international legal order that we witness the most recurrent evidence of ineffectiveness, or even collapse. The first and principal domain of such shared vital interests is the maintenance of peace, ie the non-use of force.[14] A legal order that is weak when its highest stakes are in jeopardy cannot be called fully effective. In a certain sense, the old maxim that international law realises 'Ordnung im Kleinen, Unordnung

[14] Without peace, no other social progress is possible; everything collapses. See LM Goodrich and E Hambro, *Charter of the United Nations, Commentary and Documents* (London, 1949) 93. 'Once the frame of order is broken, we can reasonably anticipate increasingly norm-less violence, pitiless blows followed by monstrous retaliation in a descending spiral of hardly imaginable depths. The Israeli experience could well prove a microcosmic anticipation of the global system's future in this scenario.' (T Farer, 'Beyond the Charter Frame: Unilateralism or Condominum?' (2002) 96 *American Journal of International Law* 364) Or 'Nous touchons ici au cœur même du problème international. Devant cette question, tout recule au second plan, parce que, en définitive, tout est conditionné par elle. La guerre n'est pas seulement une monstrueuse aberration. Elle est l'obstacle qui rend impossible toute organisation solide de la communauté internationale. Quand elle éclate, l'armature du droit se déchire; quand elle prend fin, les souvenirs et les appréhensions qu'elle laisse continuent d'empoisonner l'atmosphère. Aucun résultat décisif ne peut être acquis aussi longtemps que le monde reste ployé sous sa menace. Toute l'histoire de l'humanité l'atteste: guerres privées, guerres civiles, guerres internationales, peu importe; le refoulement de la guerre est la condition *sine qua non* du progrès social.' (M Bourquin, *Vers une nouvelle Société des Nations* (Neuchâtel, 1945) 85). Or even 'Die Rechtsordnung ist Friedensordnung. Das zeigen uns vor allem ihre Anfänge. Der Friede und das Recht kommen gemeinsam; das Recht bringt den Frieden, und Herstellung des Friedens ist Voraussetzung für die Entfaltung des Rechts. Überall, wo Recht sich entwickelt, löst es den gewaltsamen Kampf ab und setzt eine friedliche Lösung an seine Stelle. Rechtsverfahren tritt an die Stelle von Selbsthilfe. In diesem Sinn kann man sagen, dass das Verbot der Eigenmacht der Beginn und die dauernde Grundlage der Rechtsordnung ist.' (H Coing, *Grundzüge der Rechtsphilosophie*, 4th edn (Berlin/New York, 1985) 142) We may leave these passages untranslated.

im Grossen'[15] ('order in the small matters, disorder in the big matters') cannot be completely refuted. To some extent, there is here an analogy with municipal law. There too the legal order is weak when the highest stakes are in play, notably when powerful groups take liberties with the constitution or the laws, or when revolutionary events upset the constitutional order. The difference remains, however, one of magnitude and of frequency: in the municipal law of some well-ordered States, the phenomenon described remains quantitatively marginal and its gravest forms are only transient; in other States, instability attends public life much more closely. International law has never managed to come to grips with that problem. And to some extent, considering where sovereignty lies, it cannot hope to find a satisfactory path through the quagmire. The issue is here one of power and not one of law. The more we approach the core spheres of a Power's vital interests, the less the law can act as an effective brake. This is true in international and in municipal law; but the proportions of that phenomenon are particularly significant in the international legal order. *De maximis non curat praetor*? And *de maximis non curat lex*?

IV. In Search of an Inventory

When the question is about judging the effectiveness of international law (and not only about the effectiveness of its sanctions) it may be useful to take into account a series of relevant circumstances, which help to shed some light on the matter.

First, a search for the single and simple effectiveness of the international legal order must be abandoned in favour of a more nuanced approach. As already suggested, the latter can consist only in the search for an inventory. International law is composed of a great many subject matters. Each one is the bearer of its own effectiveness. There are areas that manifest legal weakness, for example the laws applying to armed conflict (in the extreme situations of fighting), but even there, there is a significant difference between the law of international armed conflicts (where generally professional armies are engaged in battle) and the law of non-international armed conflicts (civil wars, where there is insufficient incentive to respect the law, especially since the rebels do not enjoy any combatant privilege). Conversely, there are areas further removed from highly politicised matters, the effectiveness of which is entirely different: the Universal Postal Union Treaty and the distribution of postal mail are hugely effective. There remains the fact that in the case for and against international law, most often only the heavily controlled branches are mentioned, not those that function well. If an overall inventory were to be attempted, the aggregate effectiveness of international law would fare astonishingly well. For a more balanced judgement, it is essential to weigh up all the elements of the picture.

[15] See A Hold-Ferneck, *Lehrbuch des Völkerrechts*, vol I (Vienna, 1930) 88.

Secondly, the record of international law has to be moderated by time. Like any living thing, international law has its good phases and also periods of disease, rejection and defeat. How many times during World War I was the death of international law proclaimed?[16] But did it die? The same occurred in World War II.[17] But again, did it die? Has there not been a rebirth every time, in a stronger version than before? The last 20 years have again witnessed a time of crisis: the crisis of unilateralism, that is, of unilateral actions by great Powers, the tendency to go it alone.[18] The results of such crisis are many and varied: wars in violation of international law; Guantanamo; Crimea; nuclear proliferation; terrorist proliferation; the multiplicity of internal struggles and violent civil wars, etc. After the current destabilising events, will there again be a stronger rebirth? When unilateral action has brought to fruition the seeds of disorder, there is in most cases once more the search for a new blueprint of a better order. Thus, the celebrated monograph of Grotius on *The Law of War and Peace* (1625), considered by some as the founding story of classical international law, saw the light of day because of the horrors of the Thirty Years War. The Covenant of the League of Nations of 1919 was the response to World War I. The Charter of the UN was founded on the lessons learned in World War II.[19] No final answer has ever been reached, but every defeat has been followed by renewal. This will remain so: international law is necessary to international relations. It will thus constantly reshape itself from its own ashes.

Thirdly, it must be noted that the time factor has an important role in the implementation of international law. It is an interesting matter of fact that great spaces dilate time, whereas small spaces contract it, just as low altitudes compress the air and high altitudes dilute it. The life of the universe is measured in billions of years; the life of a State in hundreds of years; the life of a man in tens of years; the life of an animal in a few years; the life of an insect in a few days, etc. International law is the law of great spaces; it covers the whole world and it is the law of long timespans. Being deprived of the influence securing immediate successes, it is aimed at marathon-like achievements. If it cannot always compel immediate compliance, it can at least obstinately stand firm against the illegal fact and thereby increase the opportunity cost for the wrongdoer. An international sanction is therefore often a long-term prospect. It is composed of a series of small but insistent pressures, of direct and indirect action, of the constant but invisible wearing away of resistance. The law-breaker shall not be left in peace to enjoy his spoils. The effectiveness of

[16] See the discussion in O Nippold, *Die Gestaltung des Völkerrechts nach dem Weltkriege* (Zurich, 1917) 1ff. As has been said in another context, 'In every crisis there were plenty of voices to say: either you settle this one quickly or the Organization [of the UN] is dead. It is still alive and still in the midst of crisis.' (L Fuller, *United Nations and World Community* (Boston, Mass, 1952) 3)

[17] See the references in HA Smith, *The Crisis in the Law of Nations* (London, 1947); see also D Schindler, 'Gedanken zum Wiederaufbau des Völkerrechts' in D Schindler, *Recht—Staat—Völkergemeinschaft* (Zurich, 1948) 233ff.

[18] See, eg, C Tomuschat, 'International Law: Ensuring the Survival of Mankind on the Eve of a New Century' (1999) 281 *RCADI* 51–53; S Sur, *Le Conseil de sécurité dans l'après 11 septembre* (Paris, 2004) 88–89.

[19] See, eg, FA Walters, *A History of the League of Nations* (London/New York/Toronto, 1960) 812; WE Rappard, 'Vues retrospectives sur la Société des Nations' (1947-II) 71 *RCADI* 120ff.

the law must therefore here be measured over the long term. It would be absurd to measure the kilometre per hour performance of a marathon runner as if he were a 100-metre sprinter. Thus, the Baltic States, annexed in 1940, were liberated 50 years later; the aggressors, Japan, Germany and Italy, were finally defeated in World War II; the strategy against apartheid and the quasi-annexation of Namibia succeeded after many years, etc. It is obvious that these results have not been obtained simply because of international law; but the vindication of the law has been one component of the policy in this regard, which has therefore also been a *legal* policy. International law has in most cases no other choice than to opt for these softer means of sanction. Any attempt to react immediately and decisively would ultimately require the marshalling of armed forces to take punitive measures. This might be seen as a necessary interim action to impose a true world order, but most reasonable people would not accept such a drastic remedy. The medicine is here probably worse than the disease. In municipal law, it is often possible to execute the law against a single individual without troubling the social order. In international law, such remedies are ultimately often not available. The benefits and risks of sanctions must thus carefully be weighed in the balance—a particularly delicate exercise, as experience has shown.[20]

Fourthly, there is now a problem with many different people approaching questions of international law and speaking out with apparent authority on this branch of legal science. In the past, international law was the domain of a few eminent but little-known specialists, far removed from the general public. It was also the specialism of some practitioners within States' foreign offices. Today, countless numbers of people have opinions about this legal order: journalists, activists for NGOs, lawyers and non-lawyers of every type, political scientists, philosophers and sociologists, theologians, military personnel, enraged citizens—the list is endless. In a sense, international law has indeed been 'democratised'. Many of these persons are militant and progressive in outlook: international law is basically a tool for the exercise of their ideology (sometimes at the risk of imposing it on others). These are persons engaged in the search for a better world throughout many different subjects, ranging from human rights to the environment. The problem is that they expound international law through their own ideological lens. They do not view it as it is, but as they want it to be, as a function of their needs.[21] There is nothing wrong with the progressive development of the law, or with some merging of *lex ferenda* with *lex lata*: such was the influence of the New Deal on US constitutional law, and this was how the law of non-international armed conflicts

[20] Since the times of the League of Nations sanctions against Italy in 1935. For the historical aspects, see FA Walters, *A History of the League of Nations* (London/New York/Toronto, 1960) 623ff. On the economic aspects, see P Bartholin, *Les conséquences économiques des sanctions* (Paris, 1939). On the legal aspects, A de Geouffre de Lapradelle, *Le conflit italo-éthiopien* (Paris, 1936). Generally, see AE Highley, *The First Sanctions Experiment—A Study of League Procedures* (Geneva, 1938).

[21] S Sur, 'Les phénomènes de mode en droit international' in Société française pour le droit international, *Colloque de Paris* (Paris, 2000) 49ff; S Sur, 'Quelques observations sur les normes juridiques internationales', (1985) 89 *RGDIP* 903ff.

developed. The problem lies in the magnitude and extent of the phenomenon. The observer will be confronted with an unreal exposition of the law that does not correspond to what he or she witnesses in practice. Here the real facts and real law as practised, there the expounded law deprived of effectiveness; here the law in practice obscured behind a veil, and there the law trumpeted in books but at the same time ignored. This duality is not necessarily beneficial. The observer will rather be confronted with a great number of disappointments. He or she will most often see the supposed rules not being observed in practice. This state of affairs discredits international law and prepares the ground for cynicism—after all, a cynic is but a disappointed idealist.[22] But if one remains within the four corners of positive international law as it actual exists and is practised, there are fewer breaches than at first appears. Many apparent breaches are directed against a phantom rule that does not exist in fact. Overall, it is consequently better to remain within the bounds of the law as it stands, and if necessary to proffer trenchant criticism of this state of the law. Instead, many activists prefer to mix together the law as it is and the law as they wish it was, so as to reap the advantage of buttressing their arguments with a supposed international legal background. In short, they prop up their arguments with apparent legal authority. International law here becomes a collateral casualty of this strategy of mass persuasion.

Fifthly, the criticism directed against the effectiveness of international law is in reality more often than not geared towards the weakness of the 'rule of law' in international affairs, that is, the pre-eminence of the law over political considerations and over amendment of the law. The rule exists, but it is prone to be deflected from its standard trajectory by self-judging interpretations and selective application. Thus, the implementation of the law is less impersonal and regular than it usually is in internal law. The rule exists, but rather than apply it in case of dispute, the States concerned may prefer to conclude a new agreement modifying the legal situation. Overall, there are limits to the growth of the rule of law in international affairs, at least as long as the basic rule of the system is State sovereignty. But legal history has shown that the question is one of degree. It is not at all impossible to increase the impact of international control mechanisms for the application of the law.[23]

[22] As has been very aptly written in the context of the law of armed conflicts, 'The second category of manipulators may deserve more sympathy, but is equally dangerous for IHL: those who claim that every one of their humanitarian wishes is already fulfilled by the existing law binding upon States. … [T]hey weaken the rules which are actually accepted by States by giving belligerents the impression that IHL is the agenda of professional do-gooders, which cannot be respected in actual warfare' (M Sassòli, 'The Implementation of International Humanitarian Law: Current and Inherent Challenges' (2007) 10 *Yearbook of International Humanitarian Law* 49–50, at 50). These words are generalisable.

[23] L Condorelli, 'La Charte, source des principes fondamentaux du droit international' in R Chemain and A Pellet (eds), *La Charte des Nations Unies, Constitution mondiale?* (Paris, 2006) 167: 'Chacun sait que c'est bien là que le bât blesse! En effet, c'est sans surprise que l'on retrouve immanquablement ici l'inadéquation flagrante subsistant—dirait-on en permanence—entre les avancées normatives du droit international et les 'instruments de service' qui devraient en permettre la mise en œuvre.' ('Everyone knows that the problem lies there. It is no surprise that one is confronted here with the flagrant hiatus existing—apparently permanently—between the normative advances of international law and the instruments allowing the servicing of its implementation.')

True, even this has some inherent limits.[24] The quest of humanity for a better order will not, however, cease.[25]

Sixthly, even when ultimately ineffective, international law still has a sort of substitutive effectiveness. If the law cannot provide sanctions so as to bring actual behaviour into line with required behaviour, there remains the fact that international law provides a normative guide, devises criteria of legality and offers rules that operate as yardsticks for the evaluation of actual conduct. Without this measuring rod, it would become impossible to criticise particular conduct on the basis of objective legal considerations; it would be impossible to speak of 'illegal' conduct. It must be noted that social condemnation is often triggered in the first place by the unveiling of a norm-deviant attitude.[26] The social utility of international law thus exists as much in the case where it is respected, where breach of it is subject to sanctions and where it is merely breached without a proper response. All the more will it consequently be necessary to maintain the distinction between the existence of the norm and the degree of its effectiveness. The violation of the norm can affect its existence only through legally recognised mechanisms: derogatory agreements, desuetude, subsequent practice, *lex posterior*, etc. For the rest, an ineffective norm is not simply a non-existing norm.

There is a last point to be made. There are two approaches to international law, both of which are prejudicial to its understanding and growth, albeit in a different way and to a different degree. The first consists in the argument that international

[24] 'The rule of law in a community requires ways of making two different kinds of decisions, both of them needed and both complementing each other: the decisions made by applying rules of law; and decisions made by applying reasons of policy. The notion once taught by academic international lawyers, that a court of law can and should deal with any kind of dispute is, in this writer's opinion, fundamentally erroneous. The organs of government must include, alongside courts, other organs for making policy decisions, and in respect of those policy decisions the function of the court of law should be confined to determining whether the political organ is acting *intra vires* its powers as defined by the applicable constitutional and administrative law.' (RY Jennings, 'General Introduction' in A Zimmermann, C Tomuschat, K Oellers-Frahm and C Tams (eds), *The Statute of the International Court of Justice, A Commentary*, 2nd edn (Oxford, 2012) 5.

[25] N Politis, *La neutralité et la paix* (Paris, 1935) 210: 'De toute manière, les peuples tendront sans cesse à l'établissement d'un état des choses où le droit l'emportera sur l'arbitraire, où les intérêts particuliers seront subordonnés à l'intérêt général et où la force cessera de plus en plus d'être à la disposition des Etats pour être mise à celle de la collectivité.' ('In any event, peoples will relentlessly tend towards the realisation of a state of affairs where the law will prevail over the arbitrary, where the particular interest will be subordinated to the common weal and where the use of force will be progressively reduced as an instrument of State policy and become a power of the collectivity.')

[26] See M Bedjaoui, 'L'humanité en quête de paix et de développement—Cours général de droit international public (2004)' (2006) 324 *RCADI* 56: 'Mais nier l'existence du droit international serait en vérité ajouter une autre catastrophe à son inapplication. Car comment concevoir une société sans droit ? … Nous devons d'abord nous convaincre … que le droit international existe et que, s'il venait à ne pas exister, il faudrait l'inventer, car toute vie en commun serait impossible sans un minimum de règles en jeu. … Et même s'il ne joue qu'un rôle de placebo comme cela lui arrive parfois, le genre mineur de performances qu'il accomplirait en tant que "produit" inoffensif aurait son utilité.' Bedjaoui adds, with respect to the non-use of force rule, 'Même insuffisant ou lacunaire [le droit international], méconnu ou violé, partiellement appliqué ou grossièrement transgressé, il a l'avantage d'exister. … Ce droit existe en effet au moins comme corps de principes et de règles servant d'étalon et d'instrument de mesure des comportements étatiques et appelant sans cesse à une plus grande observance de ses prescriptions.' (*ibid*, at 109)

law must perforce correspond to what a State or group of States wants it to be as a function of their interests, and that otherwise it is simply irrelevant. In substance, this is tantamount to saying that the legal norm may be followed if it allows States to do what they want to do; otherwise, the normative injunction will be ignored and tactically qualified as outdated, inadequate, obsolete, impracticable or as reflecting a 'suicide pact'. This type of argument has been used many times by Great Powers in connection with the law relating to the non-use of force, when they have wanted to go it alone. It was used in an emblematic manner by the George Bush Jr administration after the Twin Towers attack in 2001.[27] This argument is the twin of unilateralism: it is built upon exceptionalism, repudiation of the common law and of multilateralism, and on the primacy of domestic over international interests. Legally it corresponds to the claim for an immediate modification of the law under the cover of extreme urgency, a sort of omnipotent *rebus sic stantibus* doctrine. The attack against the common law is direct and frontal. The effort is not to try to reinterpret the law under the mantle and colour of the particular interests at stake, neither is it to uncover doubtful exception clauses within the legal body. On the whole, this type of argument is thus less toxic for the international legal order than it could seem at first sight. The challenge launched allows other States and actors to react; those reactions can lead to the stigmatisation of the violator of the law, but it can also lead to revision of the rules at stake, for instance by the creation of new exceptions. The toxicity of this course of conduct rests in the fact that the Great Power and its allies will openly defy the rule, and thereby create in the public eye the impression of a weak and precisely 'irrelevant' law—a sort of self-fulfilling prophecy. The protests may be impotent and symbolic outcries by some guardians of the temple, deprived of any means of action.

The second course is at once more common and also more pernicious. It consists in a manipulation of the facts, or in the absurd interpretation of the texts, so as to obtain the desired result. Falsity and bad faith are here triumphant. The State does not pose as a solitary hero fighting for the adaptation of an anachronistic and ill-balanced rule. It rather manipulates the rule in order to make it say what it wants it to say. This will almost in all cases be accompanied by a manipulation of the facts and by projections of a subjective nature presented as truth. At first sight, it might seem that this practice is less corrosive for international law than that mentioned above. Virtue must—and sometimes does—pay tribute to hypocrisy:

[27] See the presentation and critique of the arguments by R Falk, 'What Future for the UN Charter System of War Prevention?' (2003) 97 *AJIL* 590. The argument is used with a sharp unilateralist edge in CC Posteraro, 'Intervention in Iraq: Towards a New Doctrine of Anticipatory Counter-Terrorism, Counter-Proliferation Intervention' (2002) 15 *Florida Journal of International Law* 153ff. See also MN Schmitt, 'Preemptive Strategies in International Law' (2003) 24 *Michigan Journal of International Law* 546, '[t]he world has changed and international law must evolve to remain relevant'. The argument is presented in a more tempered form in JE Stromseth, 'Law and Force After Iraq: A Transitional Moment' (2003) 97 *AJIL* 637, '[i]f international rules governing resort to force are to endure, they must be built upon and reflect the realities of power and the security needs that confront States in the real world'. The formula probably best translates the thought of the author if one replaces the word 'States' with 'United States'; and see finally WM Reisman, 'Assessing Claims to Revise the Laws of War' (2003) 97 *AJIL* 82.

when the State ultimately affirms that its behaviour is conforming to the rule, it thereby confirms the rule and also its relevance. The rule can then paradoxically be reinforced rather than weakened, since a positive *opinio juris* has been implicitly expressed in its regard. The ICJ has formulated this position in a slightly different context as follows:

> If a State acts in a way prima facie incompatible with a recognized rule, but defends its conduct by appealing to exceptions or justifications contained within the rule itself, then whether or not the State's conduct is in fact justifiable on that basis, the significance of that attitude is to confirm rather than to weaken the rule.[28]

In short, the exception confirms the rule, even if it is ill-founded on the facts. It must be said, however, that this course of conduct is from another perspective highly damaging to the international legal order, even more than open defiance. If the belief spreads that it is always possible to manipulate and tear apart any rule to obtain the desired result, international law will disappear off the horizon of the law and plunge into the realm of mere instrumental discourse.[29] The essential functions of the legal order are no longer performed: the legal obligation becomes a mere cloak; legal certainty is an ill-founded fiction; the legal norm is a factor sowing discord and unilateralism, rather than a guarantor of social peace. This is the reason why certain authors[30] have held that when its supreme interests so demand, a State will do better to lay open the reasons why it cannot, in the given circumstances, honour the international legal rule, rather than seeking refuge behind a crooked and manipulated legality. Such an honest claim does not change the rule; the latter remains intact. The State recognises the applicability and relevance of the rule but requires a dispensation on a single occasion. It may assume international responsibility for breach of the rule.

A definitive answer as to the pros and cons of falsity and virtue cannot be given when their impact on the international legal order has to be assessed. Much depends on the circumstances. What can safely be said is that a purely rhetorical use of international law should be avoided as much as possible. Open violations of the rule can in most cases be digested by the system better than hidden manipulations. The latter touch at its root the faith that the legal order is bound to inspire if it wants to be effective.

The question of the effectiveness of international law has thus proved to be much more multifaceted than the simple formula of the cynics, 'power bends law'. This complexity and ambivalence is a mirror of the contradictions and fluctuations proper to human affairs. For more than 2,000 years international law has, in whatever form, accompanied humanity. It will continue to do so. But there is one last aspect impacting on its effectiveness: its perception in public opinion.

[28] *Military and Paramilitary Activities in Nicaragua* (Merits) [1986] ICJ Rep 98, §186.

[29] Critical legal studies have indeed explored this dark side of international law, ie its being a mere instrumental discourse. See, eg, M Koskenniemi, *From Apology to Utopia: The Structure of International Legal Argument* (Cambridge, 2005); D Kennedy, *Of Law and War* (Princeton, 2006).

[30] W Friedmann, 'General Course in Public International law' (1969-II) 127 *RCADI* 78ff.

V. The Public Perception of International Law

The image of international law in public opinion has significantly evolved over time. At the beginning of the twentieth century, especially in common law societies, there was an aversion to the idea of sanctions, and an almost blind faith in the strengthening of international law through the natural growth of civilisation[31] and educated public opinion (which had already pushed through the creation of the League of Nations).[32] International law was thought to be the natural ally of peoples rather than of governments. The latter were considered as remaining caught up in the Great Power ideologies of the nineteenth century. Governments could fail to apply the rules; peoples therefore had to throw their weight into the balance so as to obtain redress. Modern international law had to be known to the peoples; and informed public opinion became an important asset to the effectiveness of the international legal order.

The heyday of this 'popular faith' in international law was from 1919 to 1939—at least, paradoxically, amongst the elite.[33] Modern international law was based on a series of community-orientated issues. From there flowed the effort to 'organise' international society institutionally, so as to be able to respond to these common needs.[34] World War I gave considerable impetus to these movements: this was the 'war to end all wars', meant to lead to an era of peace. This belief was accompanied by that in the natural growth of things. International interdependence was constantly increasing; it could not be confined to technical and economic matters but must perforce encompass political issues too. To achieve this, it was not considered necessary to do much at all. The desired state of affairs would rather realise itself automatically through the very fact of smooth social and ideological evolution.

Politically speaking, the centre favoured international law; and the moderate right- and left-wing press reported favourably on international law and on the League of Nations. The conservative press and the extreme left were opposed

[31] On the idea of continuous progress see T Skouteris, *The Notion of Progress in International Law Discourse* (The Hague, 2010). More generally, see Y Burgess, *The Myth of Progress* (Glasgow, 1996); JB Bury, *The Idea of Progress: An Inquiry into its Origins and Growth* (London, 1920).

[32] This idolatry of public opinion later came to be criticised as being excessive. See, eg, C de Visscher, *Théories et réalités en droit international public*, 3rd edn (Paris, 1960) 77; E Giraud, *La nullité de la politique internationale des grandes démocraties (1919–1939), L'échec de la S.d.N., la guerre* (Paris, 1948) 127ff; W Schiffer, *The Legal Community of Mankind* (New York, 1954) 142ff. On public opinion and international law see, eg, M Merle, 'Le droit international et l'opinion publique' (1973-I) *RCADI* 373ff. For an earlier account, see A Cavaglieri, *L'opinione pubblica nelle relazioni internazionali* (Florence, 1907). See also T Toyoda, 'Influence of Public Opinion on International Law in the Nineteenth Century' (2009) 46 *Albany Law Review* 1099ff. From a more general perspective analysing the rise and fall of expectations linked with international law, see M Koskenniemi, *The Gentle Civilizer of Nations, The Rise and Fall of International Law 1870–1960* (Cambridge, 2001).

[33] The environment was thus favourable for international law: see R Redslob, *Das Problem des Völkerrechts* (Leipzig, 1917). As to the internationalism of the elite, see WE Rappard, 'Le nationalisme économique et la Société des Nations' (1937-III) 61 *RCADI* 97ff.

[34] See, eg, C Denfeld, *Hans Wehberg (1885–1962)* (Baden-Baden, 2008) 158, 172ff; P Guggenheim, *L'organisation de la société internationale* (Neuchâtel, 1944).

to international organisation. For the conservatives, anything that transformed received ways of thinking was in itself an evil. Moreover, the empire of international law and organisation appeared to them as a chimera put together by idealists (which is a sort of self-fulfilling prophecy). Finally, international organisation was opposed because it was placed above the State, and was therefore intended to limit its sovereignty. On the other hand, for the extreme left, international law was a bourgeois construction for the oppression of the workers and the weak. The League of Nations could not be supported, since its Covenant authorised the imposition of sanctions (a war of sanctions).[35] For extreme pacifists this was utterly unacceptable: you cannot fight war with war. They considered that the only beneficiaries of such rules would be the weapon-selling industrialists (*les marchands de canons*).

In fact, public opinion was not the ally of international law or of the League of Nations that had been expected. When the crisis arose in the inter-war period, peoples backed their nation State and derided the League. Truth remained nationalised and did not become international. Immediately after World War II, however, the elite had still not abandoned the idea of international law. It is astonishing to see how many projects aiming at federalisation of the world saw the light of day in this short period[36]—and were realised locally in Europe with the then European Economic Community. International law was still seen in these circles as conducive to peace and order ('peace through law'). But in the US many of the the elite turned towards realism, and the teaching of international law was reduced or abandoned. There was an ever-growing perception of crisis in the law of nations.[37] The Cold War and its tensions; the profound ideological rifts; the rise of totalitarian regimes nourished with contempt for international law; the race for international hegemony; the return to partial alliances; diplomacy outside the UN; the pressure on the laws of war (progress of total war, weapons of mass destruction); manipulative discourses and propaganda; the cultural and intellectual crises; the crises of the elite; the concentration camps, deportations and politicised tribunals—all these events, reported by the press, created an environment in which faith in 'peace through law' needed be replaced, at best, by the maxim 'security by power'. There was thus a sharp division of opinion, in favour of or against international law.

Over the next few decades, other factors came to the fore. With the growing number of States, the world became increasingly more complex. The result was a crisis of multilateralism: it was difficult to achieve the urgently needed results in matters of international concern when one had to achieve compromises between more than 190 States. The tendency was then to accuse multilateralism (and international law) of being ineffective, and to shift towards unilateralism (which is hardly conducive to lasting results). Multilateral international policy had become

[35] See Art 16, Covenant of the League of Nations.

[36] See, eg, JG Guerrero, *L'ordre international* (Neuchâtel, 1945) 121ff; W Schiffer, *The Legal Community of Mankind* (New York, 1954).

[37] J Kunz, 'La crise et les transformations du droit des gens' (1955-II) 88 *RCADI* 9ff.

so complex that people could no longer understand it; their impatience replaced informed scrutiny, their ignorance enlightened knowledge.[38] Unscrupulous politicians did little to rectify this state of affairs, feeling all the benefits of having a scapegoat that did not even have a powerful lobby to defend it.[39] Open attacks and defiance of the UN became fashionable, for example with the Ronald Reagan administration (and even though the pressure applied produced some positive results in the reform of the UN).[40]

Even more recently, the problem has been multifaceted. For example, the militant and often leftist approaches to international law, already mentioned above, led to a rejection of international law as espoused by moderate and right-wing circles. Moreover, international law is now often portrayed as an 'undemocratic' law, made by the executives in back rooms with the participation of a number of dirty political regimes scattered all over the world. By comparison, the democratically legitimised internal law is considered to have a much higher value.[41] In the event of conflict between internal and international law, precedence should be given to the former—a complete reversal of the applicable rule under international law, which ensures its binding force. In Switzerland, international law appears to the general public to be relevant only in particular, isolated contexts: human rights (the expulsion of criminal aliens, the prohibition of minarets, etc) and in bilateral agreements with the European Union. And even then it is viewed in a doubtful light: as a law that protects criminals, does not allow local people to fight against Islamism, etc. We are far from achieving 'peace through law'.

Overall, public information about international law has reached a disturbingly low level—and to some extent this cannot be otherwise, since international law is and remains a technical and complex matter. The conceptions held are in many cases grotesque deformations of reality and at best over-simplifications. For many people, however, ignorance is unfortunately no reason to refrain from making quick, vocal and harsh judgements; on the contrary, it is often a cause of and reason for reaching such judgements. Moreover, the mass media fall far below the requirements of their mission in this regard. There are hardly any correct treatments of international legal issues, ranging from the vocabulary used to technical or ideological misinformation. Technical misinformation flows either from excessive simplification, so that the message supposedly can be understood by the man in the street, or from the ignorance of the makers of these statements. Thus, for example, on Swiss State television, the ICJ was confused with the ICC—the

[38] See H Nicolson, *Diplomatie* (Neuchâtel, 1948) 78, 80. See also D Schindler, 'Contribution à l'étude des facteurs sociologiques et psychologiques du droit international' (1933-IV) 46 *RCADI* 73, 75.

[39] On this psychological mechanism, see S Freud, *Malaise dans la civilisation* (Paris, 1971) 68.

[40] See P Gerbet, *Le rêve d'un ordre mondial—De la S.d.N. à l'ONU* (Paris, 1996) 269ff, 323ff, 357ff. On some difficulties flowing from such attacks, see B Boutros-Ghali, *Mes années à la maison de verre* (Paris, 1999) 29ff.

[41] See the virulent attack against international law in the Swiss right-wing newspaper *Die Weltwoche*, no 50, 10 December 2009, 5, 30, international law being presented as the diktat of foreign powers and judges. Electorally speaking, the political party backing this newspaper is at the current time in Switzerland that which enjoys the greatest electoral share (between 25 and 30% of the votes).

misfortune is clearly that both tribunals have their seats in The Hague! By the same token, the ICJ has been treated as an arbitral tribunal,[42] it having been said that States can seek advice from the Court, that the Court demands an advisory opinion (from itself?), that it has universal compulsory jurisdiction, etc.[43] It has also been said that the judgments of the European Court of Human Rights are not (legally) binding but exert only a moral influence.[44] The fundamental error is to believe that anybody can write on these matters without solid technical knowledge. The financial problems of the written press and the requirements for quick results have long led to the disuse of professional correctors. Ideological misinformation, for its part, flows from the intention to dismantle international law. It is then loaded with a number of purported defects and deficiencies so as to make it an easy target for attack. This occurs mainly in the right-wing press; in the left-wing press international law will rather be manipulated towards a greater share of 'generosity'.

The press is not solely responsible for the poor state of public information. Schools and universities must accept a share of the blame. All too often, the learning process is reduced to modules and building blocks, approaches that are wholly unsuited to the subject matter. The sheer number of students also lowers the overall quality of the teaching. Multiple-choice exams complete the picture. In legal matters in particular, such methods are inadequate. Law requires creativity, independence and imagination: *pectus facit jurisconsultum*. In the law faculties a number students (though fortunately not all) are distinctly unenthusiastic about international law: Is it really necessary to study this somewhat odd legal order (is it really law?), which spreads its arms far away in some unknown international circles? Must I really know it when I mean to practise as a solicitor?

In sum, the following pessimistic conclusions can be drawn:

1. The image of international law has deteriorated in many public circles. The most common question tends to be: You are an international lawyer. Do you think that international law really exists? Look at what happens in the world!
2. This negative projection often revolves around an imaginary international law, which does not exist in fact.
3. The tendency is towards a return to politics and a relative decline in the law, be it in the guise of neo-realism, critical studies, national independence or the need for changes to be effected more quickly than the law seems to allow.[45]

[42] This occurs even in non-legal technical literature. See, eg, JP Favennec, *Géopolitique de l'énergie, Besoins, ressources, échanges mondiaux* (Paris, 2009) 83.

[43] See the examples in C Rousseau, 'Un siècle d'évolution du droit international (1873–1973)' in Université de Neuchâtel (ed), *Le droit international demain* (Neuchâtel, 1974) 21.

[44] *Tages-Anzeiger*, 29 August 2012, 6: 'Ein Urteil des Europäischen Gerichtshofes für Menschenrechte hätte nur politische Kraft und wäre juristisch nicht verbindlich.' ('A judgment of the ECtHR would have only political strength and would not be legally binding.') Compare Art 46, §1 of the ECHR of 1950 (amended in 1994), which stipulates the binding force of the judgments of the Court.

[45] E Luard, *International Society* (New York, 1990) 267.

4. Most people view the application of international law norms as being imposed by politicians, rather than as the impersonal implementation of the law.[46] How often are sanctions regarded as the application of international law, and how often are they simply seen as a selective political tool (again, for example, the Crimean sanctions in 2014)? If the Security Council takes action in some matter, how many perceive this as also being conduct relevant under international law and not simply a political device? Most people are utterly incapable of seeing the legal dimensions of political phenomena. Conversely, they are all too ready to spot the political side of legal processes. This leads to an imbalance.
5. Unilateralism has increased in the last decade. Even small States are now encouraged to go it alone and to promote their own interests.[47]
6. Dissatisfaction with international law and international organisation is augmented by similar dissatisfaction with internal public institutions and politics. Institutions are in crisis; the elite are in crisis; civilisation is in crisis. In this context, international law is more a collateral casualty than a prime issue.

The overall conclusion can only be that international law will remain with us as a necessary legal order. The disaffection of the public is transient and not decisive; the essential point is that States themselves are satisfied with the services of the international legal order (even if in democracies public opinion carries greater weight than elsewhere). Conscious of its necessity and superiority, international law can afford to be lenient with its detractors. In the long run, facts and necessities are more important than fleeting images and grudging acceptance. At the same

[46] C de Visscher, *Théories et réalités en droit international public*, 3rd edn (Paris, 1960) 118: 'Que l'on compare à ce sujet l'action de la contrainte dans le milieu international à la coercition au sein de l'Etat. Celle-ci est conçue et acceptée comme l'émanation impersonnelle du droit dans un ordre de subordination. Dans l'ordre de juxtaposition, qui est actuellement celui des rapports internationaux, l'action collective internationale n'est pas réellement dépolitisée; au mieux, elle apparaît encore comme celle d'une majorité contre une minorité, exposée par conséquent à être détournée vers des fins particulières. Il en sera ainsi tant que l'idée d'un bien commun supranational n'aura pas implanté dans les consciences un sens nouveau des solidarités humaines et des disciplines qu'elles imposent.' In English (our translation): 'We may compare in this regard coercion in the international sphere and in the municipal sphere. The latter is conceived and accepted as law's impersonal emanation in an order of subordination. In the coordinative international legal order, collective international action is not truly de-politicised. In the best scenario, it will appear as the action of a majority against a minority, exposed as being skewed towards particular aims. This will not change as long as the idea of a supranational common weal has not created in the conscience of human beings a new sense for international solidarities and for the disciplines they impose.'

[47] *Die Weltwoche*, no 50, 10 December 2009, 5. Switzerland is invited to accept as international law only what it would accept itself in a popular referendum. What is not said is that if all the States of the world were to adopt such criteria, there would be endless international anarchy, to the detriment of all. Compare H Nicolson, *Diplomatie* (Neuchâtel, 1948) 78–79 (our translation): 'This irresponsibility is encouraged by part of the popular press. It does not hesitate to ask for the repudiation of certain engagements and does not remind the people that these engagements have not only been incurred by a government democratically elected, but have also been ratified after a long discussion in the Chambers. The same owner of a newspaper who would be profoundly disgusted if a publicity agency or a producer of paper were able to repudiate his contracts, will not refrain from preaching to the whole nation a repudiation similar in all points.'

time, international law must be careful not to give the impression that it is a tool to be used to create a hegemony of the strong. It must therefore be at pains to ensure some 'democratic' input. The issue is now being hotly discussed in the context of the European Union. We have to confess that the problem is exceedingly complicated and suggestive of squaring the circle. The aim is to combine legitimate local freedom and necessary collective discipline, ie particular and collective interests. There is no easy conclusion to such a quest. It is simply the red thread running through the whole history of international affairs.

7

International Society or International Community?

I. General Aspects

For some years now, it has been fashionable to speak of the 'international community'.[1] International legal instruments increasingly refer to this community: we find it in treaties (eg Article 53 of the Vienna Convention on the Law of Treaties

[1] On this notion, mainly from the legal point of view, see A Verdross, 'Règles générales du droit de la paix' (1929-V) 30 *RCADI* 318; M Giuliano, *La comunità internazionale e il diritto* (Padua, 1950); G Vedovato, *La Comunità internazionale* (Florence, 1950); T Ruyssen, *La société internationale* (Paris, 1950); G Maturi, *Il problema giuridico della Comunità internazionale* (Milan, 1956); A Migliazza, *Il fenomeno dell'organizzazione e la Comunità internazionale* (Milan, 1958); L Legaz y Lacambra, 'Völkerrechtsgemeinschaft: Ideologie, Utopie und Wirklichkeit' in *Essays in Honor of C. Schmitt* (Berlin, 1959) (reprinted 1989) 123ff; A Truyol y Serra, 'Genèse et structure de la société internationale' (1959-I) *RCADI* 553ff; C de Visscher, *Théories et réalités en droit international public*, 4th edn (Paris, 1970) 110ff; H Mosler, 'The International Society as a Legal Community' (1974-IV) 140 *RCADI* 17ff; RJ Dupuy, 'Communauté internationale et disparités de développement, Cours général de droit international public' (1979-IV) 165 *RCADI* 1; H Mosler, 'International Legal Community' (1982) 7 *EPIL* 309ff; A Truyol y Serra, 'Cours général de droit international public' (1981-IV) 173 *RCADI* 53ff; RJ Dupuy, *La Communauté internationale entre le mythe et l'histoire* (Paris, 1986); E Luard, *International Society* (New York, 1990); M Lachs, 'Quelques réflexions sur la Communauté internationale' in *Essays in Honor of M. Virally* (Paris, 1991) 349ff; PM Dupuy, 'Humanité, Communauté et efficacité du droit' in *Essays in Honor of R.J. Dupuy* (Paris, 1991) 133ff; G Abi-Saab, '"Humanité" et "Communauté" dans l'évolution de la doctrine et de la pratique du droit international', *Essays in Honor of R.J. Dupuy* (Paris, 1991) 1ff; G Herczegh, 'The International Community of States' in *Questions of International Law*, vol 5 (Budapest, 1991) 75ff; GC McGhee, *International Community: A Goal for a New World Order* (Lanham, 1992); G Abi-Saab, 'International Law and the International Community: the Long Road to Universality' in *Essays in Honor of W. Tieya* (Dordrecht/Boston, 1994) 31ff; C Tomuschat, 'Die internationale Gemeinschaft' (1995) 33 *Archiv des Völkerrechts* 1ff; G Abi-Saab, 'Wither the International Community?' (1998) 9 *EJIL* 248ff; B Simma and A Paulus, 'The International Community: Facing the Challenge of Globalization' (1998) 9 *EJIL* 266ff; P Moreau Defarges, *La communauté internationale* (Paris, 2000); D Kritsiotis, 'Imagining the International Community' (2001) 13 *EJIL* 961ff; A Paulus, *Die internationale Gemeinschaft im Völkerrecht* (Munich, 2001); PM Dupuy, 'L'unité de l'ordre juridique international—Cours général de droit international public' (2002) 297 *RCADI* 207ff, 245ff; E Jouannet, 'La communauté internationale vue par les juristes' (2005) 6 *Annuaire français des relations internationales* 3ff; C Warbrick and S Tierney (eds), *Towards an International Legal Community?* (London, 2006); PM Dupuy, 'La communauté internationale: une fiction?' in *Essays in Honor of J. Salmon* (Brussels, 2007) 373ff; AL Vaurs-Chaumette, 'The International Community as a Whole' in J Crawford, A Pellet and K Parlett (eds), *The Law of International Responsibility* (Oxford, 2010) 1023ff; M Koskenniemi, 'International Community from Dante to Vattel' in V Chetail (ed), *Vattel's International Law in a XXIst Century Perspective* (Leyde, 2011) 51ff. See also, in a particular domain, S Villalpando, *L'émergence de la communauté internationale dans la responsabilité des Etats* (Paris, 2005).

(VCLT) of 1969;[2] the Preamble to the Statute of the International Criminal Court of 1998);[3] in resolutions of international organs (eg in Resolution 45/100 of the UNGA on Humanitarian Assistance, 1988;[4] in Resolution 1368 of the UN Security Council, 2001);[5] in international judgments (eg ICJ, *Barcelona Traction*, 1970;[6] *Diplomatic and Consular Staff in Tehran*, 1980;[7] *Legality of Nuclear Weapons* Opinion, 1996);[8] and in many other legal documents.[9] Still more frequently we are confronted with this term in the jargon of journalists and politicians. There are here constant references to the need for the mobilisation of the international community, to the culpable passivity of the international community, to the action of the international community and the like—in most cases in the loosest and most shallow use of terminology imaginable. At the same time, use of the neutral and less zealous term 'international society' has declined, leaving an increasingly greater share to the fast-ascending 'international community'.

The differences between the two terms—'international society' and 'international community'—may be expressed as follows:

1. The term 'international society' is neutral because it is fundamentally descriptive. It refers to a series of interactions existing in fact between international subjects. The concept is of a sociological stamp; it implies no precise value, ideology or perspective.[10] All types of relationships transcending national borders fall within the domain of international society, friendly, hostile, neutral or mixed. The national border refers back to the State; without States, there would not be an international society; there would not exist an 'international space'.[11] In its core, the international society is therefore a society of societies, ie a grouping of national societies.[12] International law is produced in the context of this larger society. There are also areas of private trans-boundary relations, giving rise to a private international law writ large.

[2] This provision refers to international *jus cogens*: 'A treaty is void if, at the time of its conclusion, it conflicts with a peremptory norm of general international law. For the purposes of the present Convention, a peremptory norm of general international law is a norm accepted and recognized by the international community of States as a whole as a norm from which no derogation is permitted and which can be modified only by a subsequent norm of general international law having the same character.'

[3] See, eg, §4, 'Affirming that the most serious crimes of concern to the international community as a whole must not go unpunished …'; or §9, 'Determined … to establish an independent permanent International Criminal Court in relationship with the United Nations system, with jurisdiction over the most serious crimes of concern to the international community as a whole'.

[4] Preamble, §6.

[5] At §4.

[6] *Barcelona Traction* [1970] ICJ Rep 32.

[7] *Diplomatic and Consular Staff in Tehran* [1980] ICJ Rep 43.

[8] *Legality of the Threat or Use of Nuclear Weapons* [1996-I] ICJ Rep 254, §67; 255, §73; 258, §82; 263, §96; 264, §100; 265, §103.

[9] See, eg, the Resolution of the Institute of International Law on Humanitarian Assistance (Bruges, 2003), §3 of the Preamble. It can be found on the website of the Institute at <www.idi-iil.org>.

[10] See E Luard, *International Society* (New York, 1990) 1ff.

[11] A Truyol y Serra, 'Genèse et structure de la société internationale' (1959-I) 96 *RCADI* 568.

[12] A Truyol y Serra, 'Cours général de droit international public' (1981-IV) 173 *RCADI* 53ff.

2. The term 'international community' connotes the idea of a certain type of social relations. It is a value-loaded concept, which usually refers not only to trans-boundary relations but also to a superior good, namely, the common weal of all the members of society. These common interests transcend the particular interests of each of them. The State is no longer the ultimate depositary of the highest interests. Above the single unities and their welfare, there is the welfare of the international political body as a whole. This legal-political de-narcissism of the State need not refer to all matters of international concern: it could be limited to certain areas, for example those considered collectively to be the most vital. The common weal or the *utilitas publica* is therefore the core element in the definition of the international community. Through it, the single unit exits its phase of infantile self-absorption; it makes contact with others and becomes aware of its true dimension; and it conceives the interests that it shares with others. In short, the international community refers to a political body superior to the State taken individually and possessing its own dignity. It can refer to the community of States, of humanity or of the biosphere. The so-called 'constitutionalisation' of international law may be seen as one expression of this community-orientated approach.[13]

Ultimately, each 'community' is based on the existence of a higher interest than that of the members of a society taken individually; this higher interest is of a collective nature and gives rise to solidarity; and it is able to some degree to shape action.

II. Short Historical Aspects in the Western World

The concept of the international community is not limited to Western thought. But we may here concentrate on the Western world, since existing public international law historically flowed from European public law. The opposing concepts of society and community appear only late in Western political thought.[14] But the

[13] C Walter, 'International Law in a Process of Constitutionalization' in J Nijman and A Nollkaemper (eds), *New Perspectives on the Divide Between National and International Law* (Oxford, 2007) 191ff; R Chemain and A Pellet (eds), *La Charte des Nations Unies, Constitution mondiale?* (Paris, 2006); S Szurek, 'La Charte des Nations Unies: Constitution mondiale?' in JP Cot, A Pellet and M Forteau (eds), *La Charte des Nations Unies, Commentaire article par article*, vol I, 3rd edn (Paris, 2005) 29ff; TM Franck, 'Is the United Nations Charter a Constitution?' in *Essays in Honor of T. Eitel* (Berlin, 2003) 95ff; PM Dupuy, 'L'unité de l'ordre juridique international' (2002) 297 *RCADI* 215ff; B Fassbender, *UN Security Council Reform and the Right of Veto* (The Hague/London/Boston, 1998) 89ff; B Fassbender, *The United Nations Charter as the Constitution of the International Community* (Leiden/Boston, 2009).

[14] See the classical monograph by F Tönnies, *Gemeinschaft und Gesellschaft* (Leipzig, 1887), where the author sets the atomistic-individualistic society in opposition to the organic community (individualism/corporatism). On the issue, see also P Pasquino, 'Communauté et société' in P Raynaud and S Rials (eds), *Dictionnaire de philosophie politique* (Paris, 1996) 116–19.

conception of both—even if not yet neatly distinguished—has an ancient pedigree. Here we may briefly review some important milestones.

A. Primitive Societies

There was no trace of a global human community in the so-called primitive peoples.[15] Primitive societies were autarkies and were based on a '*morale close*'.[16] That is to say that ethics and law were indissolubly linked to the group or the tribe; they were particular and not universal; the foreigner was outside the law. Law remained associated with rites and religion proper to the group. The law was personal, not territorial. It was coloured by its connection with the group (*lex originis*, or *jura ossibus inhearent*).[17] Later, when the rational elements in the law were developed, an extension to foreigners, or even to the whole world, became imaginable. If aliens were accepted into the group, there were special devices for ensuring their rights, such as the institution of proxeny in Ancient Greece.[18] It stands to reason that no concept of an international community could blossom in such a setting.

B. The Development of a 'Common Humanity'

The idea of common humanity appeared in Hellenistic times. From there, the idea made its way into Christianity.[19] The basis of this doctrine was reason, considered to be inherent in each human being and not limited by group connotations. From this perspective, the law tended to become universal and to take the form of natural law. The individual was a small unity in a rationally ordered cosmos. The concept of universal rationality is well expressed by the phrase '*lex est ratio summa insita natura*'.[20] From there also flowed a new conception of politics: contrary to the teachings of Aristotle,[21] the *polis* (national community) was not considered to be the highest public collectivity. Cosmopolitanism carried with it the idea

[15] See U Wesel, *Frühformen des Rechts in vorstaatlichen Gesellschaften* (Frankfurt, 1985); W Seagle, *Weltgeschichte des Rechts*, 3rd edn (Munich/Berlin, 1967) 13ff, 49ff (original English version: *The Quest for Law* (New York, 1941)).

[16] H Bergson, *Les deux sources de la morale et de la religion*, 9th edn (Paris, 1932) 283ff.

[17] H Mitteis and H Lieberich, *Deutsche Rechtsgeschichte*, 17th edn (Munich, 1985) 86–87. From there also the tendency to distinguish the law according to status, eg trader, churchman, aristocrat, Jew, etc: A Cavanna, *Storia del diritto moderno in Europa—Le fonti e il pensiero giuridico*, vol I (Milan, 1982) 213ff. For the Jews, see the interesting study by V Colorni, *Gli Ebrei nel sistema del diritto comune fino alla prima emancipazione* (Milan, 1956).

[18] On proxeny, see, eg, C Philippson, *The International Law and Custom of Ancient Greece and Rome*, vol I, (London, 1911) 136ff.

[19] A Verdross, *Abendländische Rechtsphilosophie* (Vienna, 1958) 44ff.

[20] Cicero, *De legibus*, I, 6, §18; II, 4, §8.

[21] Aristotle, *Politics*, book I, chs I and II.

of a universal empire, as imagined and partly realised by Alexander the Great. All rational beings were viewed as citizens of one and the same world. The local political body was but a province of the universal political body.

These teachings would plant their early roots in the Roman *jus gentium*.[22] After the Punic Wars (second and third centuries BCE) and up to the *Constitutio Antoniniana* of 212 CE, there were many peoples in the Empire that were not granted Roman citizenship. However, Mediterranean commerce continued to develop steadily. Therefore, the limitation of the civil law to citizens (principle of personality) became untenable. Only adequate legal protection of foreign traders in Rome could attract them to the local markets. The old rule that Roman private law (*ius quiritium*) was applicable only to citizens needed revision. Reform of the law was realised through special magistrates, the *praetores peregrini*. The law developed was intended to be applicable to all persons, whatever their nationality: it was said to be founded on common reason and equity.[23] This universal law laid to rest the old formalism and became centered on the conception of the *fides*, the pledged word, ie good faith.

[22] M Voigt, *Das ius naturale, aequum et bonum und ius gentium der Römer*, 4 vols (Aalen, 1966) (original edition, Leipzig, 1856–75, vols I–IV); P Bonfante, *Histoire du droit romain*, vol I (Paris, 1928) 261ff; G May, *Eléments de droit romain*, 18th edn (Paris, 1935) 39ff; J Bryce, 'The Law of Nature' in J Bryce, *Studies in History and Jurisprudence*, vol II (London, 1910) 586ff; G Grosso, *Lezioni di storia del diritto romano*, 5th edn (Turin, 1965) 272ff, 290ff; S Riccobono, *Lineamenti della storia delle fonti e del diritto romano* (Milan, 1949) 22ff; A Guarino, *Diritto privato romano*, 9th edn (Naples, 1992) 161ff; M Lauria, 'Ius gentium' in *Essays in Honor of P. Koschaker*, vol I (Weimar, 1939) 258ff; P Frezza, 'Ius gentium' (1949) 2 *Revue internationale des droits de l'Antiquité* 259ff; G Lombardi, *Sul concetto di ius gentium* (Milan, 1974); G Lombardi, *Ricerche in tema di ius gentium* (Milan, 1946); M Kaser, *Römische Rechtsgeschichte*, 2nd edn (Göttingen, 1982) 134ff; M Kaser, *Ius gentium* (Cologne/Weimar, 1993). On *jus gentium* in Grotius, see P Haggenmacher, 'Genèse et signification du concept de "ius gentium" chez Grotius' (1981) 2 *Grotiana* 44. This conception has been held outside the Western world too. Thus, Ibn Khaldun, an Arabic author of the 14th century, in his opus *Muqaddimah*, explains the emergence of laws extended to many persons by a process called *asabiyah*, ie social solidarity: F Baali, *Ibn Khaldun's Sociological Thought* (New York, 1988) 43ff. The proximity of *jus gentium* with natural law has remained up to the present day. See, eg, AA Cançado Trindade, 'La *recta ratio* dans les fondements du *Jus Gentium* comme droit international de l'humanité' in AA Cançado Trindade, *Le droit international de la personne humaine* (Paris, 2012) 91ff; AA Cançado Trindade, 'International Law for Humankind: Towards a New Jus Gentium' (2005) 316 *RCADI* 9ff.

[23] Gaius, *Dig.* 1, 1, 9: 'Naturalis ratio inter omnes homines constituit, id apud omnes peraeque custoditur vocaturque ius gentium, quasi quo iure omnes gentes utuntur' (what natural reason has established among all the humans and is equally observed by all or almost all peoples). In a wider version, Ulpian embraced the animal world, where there are also rational institutions, eg the domain of filiation (*Dig.*, I, I, 1): 'Ius naturale est quod natura omnins animalia docuit'. This wider vision has generally been contested, if not ridiculed. See, eg, F Suarez, *De Legibus ac Deo Legislatore* (1612), book II, ch XVII, §2; G Bonjean, *Explication méthodique des Institutes de Justinien*, vol I (Paris, 1878) 13 ('odd idea'); J Ortolan, *Explication historique des Instituts de l'Empereur Justinien*, 12th edn (Paris, 1883) 23–24; G Boehmer, *Grundlagen der bürgerlichen Rechtsordnung, Zweites Buch*, vol I (Tübingen, 1951) 22; but there are also favourable authors: R Marcic, *Geschichte der Rechtsphilosophie* (Freiburg, 1971) 61. On this doctrine of '*natura animalia docuit*', see G Cortius, *De jure quod natura omnia animalia docuit* (Leipzig, 1727); R Weigand, *Die Naturrechtslehre der Legisten und Dekretisten von Irnerius bis Accursius und von Gratian bis Johannes Teutonicus*, part II: *Kanonisches Recht* (Munich, 1967) 121ff; B Tierney, 'Natura Id est Deus: A Case of Juristic Pantheism?' (1963) 24 *Journal of the History of Ideas* 307ff.

C. The Christian Republic in the Middle Ages

The idea of an international community found a local realisation in the European Middle Ages in the context of its religious unity. The Christian Republic was rooted in the West and was one community; the community of the Muslim faith was situated in the East and formed another community. In Europe, the community was identified with the universal powers, the Pope and the Holy Roman Emperor. The two leaders of the Christian community had their own functions in the medieval constitutional order, for example to coordinate the fight against the infidels. Political thought at that time was infused with the search for unity; but conversely, starting in the thirteenth century, local rulers slowly consolidated their own powers at the expense of the universal powers: *rex imperator in regno suo*. This faith in unity was derived from the idea of one God and its corollary, namely, universal fraternity in faith: *reductio ad unum, unitas divina/unitas humana, universitas mortalium*.[24] There were plans for a European federation directed against the danger of a Muslim conquest, or even geared towards the recovery of Christian lands—the most famous being the *De recuperatione terrae sanctae* (1305) of Pierre Dubois.[25] Overall, it can be said that the Middle Ages thus had a vivid conception of an international community. But this community was merely regional. The bond that united it was its common faith. It thus included on the one side, but excluded on the other. Solidarity was rooted amongst persons of the same faith. There was as yet no conception of a universal human community.

D. From the Spanish Scholastics to the Nineteenth Century

In the sixteenth century, the authors of the Salamanca School (de Vitoria, Vasquez, Suarez, Molina) followed in the footsteps of Thomas Aquinas, who had reacted against the voluntarist exegesis of the Bible that preached the primacy of God's inexplicable will over rational reasoning: *voluntas imperat intellectui*. This had led to a literal interpretation of the Holy Scriptures.[26] Aquinas gave primacy to reason: God cannot will things contrary to reason. This way of thinking allowed room for a dynamic, non-literal and teleological reading of the Holy Scriptures.

At the times of the Spanish Scholastics, the New World had been discovered. Could one expand the doctrine of the community of all men to the new peoples,

[24] See, eg, FA von der Heydte, *Die Geburtsstunde des souveränen Staates* (Ravensbrück, 1952) 223, 228–30.

[25] L Lederman, *Les précurseurs de l'organisation internationale* (Neuchâtel, 1945) 32ff. See also EH Meyer, *Die staats- und völkerrechtlichen Ideen von Pierre Dubois* (Marburg, 1909); E Zeck, *Der Publizist Pierre Dubois* (Berlin, 1911); R Charlier, *Pierre Dubois, précurseur du pacifisme et de l'arbitrage international* (Rouen, 1911); A Osiander, 'A Medevial Internationalist?: Pierre Dubois and his Ninteenth and Twentieth Century Interpreters' in EJ Broers, BC Jacobs and JP Coopmans (eds), *Ius brabanticum, ius comune, ius gentium* (Nimègue, 2006) 111ff.

[26] The origin of this conception is in St Paul's *Letters to the Romans*, 3, 23–24 and 28.

even if they were not Christians? Could the local tribes have rights of property over their lands? Could they be subjects of the law? Did international law (natural law) extend to them? The most famous affirmative passage is in Suarez's utterance on the *bonum commune generis humani*.[27] We can still find faint reverberations of this conception in the fictional *civitas maxima* upheld by Wolff.[28] According to these teachings, there was therefore a common good of all States. However, in contradistinction to these generous doctrinal efforts, social forces pulled in the opposite direction. With the consolidation of the sovereign territorial State, the international community of faith or of reason was split into a series of self-contained political unities, each one possessing increasing power. International relations were atomised and individualised. The international community was thus torn asunder; it was a community in name only. Reasons of State, sovereignty, inalienable subjective rights, vital interests, *jus ad bellum*—these and others were the concepts and realities that were gaining momentum. Certain chapters in Machiavelli's writings are emblematic of the new way of thinking.[29] Positivistic empiricism followed this path and continued the dismantlement of the old universalistic edifices.

E. The Concert of Europe in the Nineteenth Century

The nineteenth century was marked by a new conception of the 'international community', far removed from Salamanca. The interdependence at work in an industrialising world created the need for international leadership. The atomistic society of equals projected by Emer de Vattel was no longer practically sufficient. The community conception was thus taken over by a Concert of Great Powers pretending to act in the name and interests of all European countries and peoples.[30] These Powers (England, France, Prussia, Austria-Hungary, Russia and later also

[27] *De legibus ac Deo legislatore*, book II, ch XIX, §9: 'Ratio autem huius partis et jurisest, quia humanum genus quantumvis in varios populos et regna divisum, semper habet aliquam unitatem non solum specificam, sed etiam quasi politicam et morale, quam indicat natural preaceptum mutui amoris et misericordiae, quod ad omnes extenditur, etiam extraneos, et cuiuscumque nationis.' In English: 'The basis of this branch of the law [international law] is the fact that the human family, however much it is split in peoples and empires, retains still a certain unity, not only of a biological nature, but also as a political and moral community. This flows from the natural precept of mutual love and aid, which extends to all aliens from whatever nation they come.' See also F de Vitoria, *De potestate civili*, no 13.

[28] *Ius gentium methodo scientifica pertractatum* (1749), Prolegomena, §21. See WG Grewe, *The Epochs of International Law* (Berlin/New York, 2000) 358–60. Vattel abandoned this conception: see E Jouannet, *Emer de Vattel et l'émergence doctrinale du droit international classique* (Paris, 1998) 96ff; JJ Manz, *Emer de Vattel, Versuch einer Würdigung* (Zurich, 1971) 125ff, 181; F Mancuso, *Diritto, Stato, Sovranità—Il pensiero politico-giuridico di Emer de Vattel tra assolutismo e rivoluzione* (Naples, 2002) 255ff.

[29] *The Prince* (1513), ch XV. See J Burnham, *Les Machiavéliens* (Paris, 1949).

[30] K Wolfke, *Great and Small Powers in International Law from 1814 to 1920* (Wroclaw, 1961); S Hoffmann, *Organisations internationales et pouvoirs politiques des Etats* (Paris, 1954) 23ff; M Schulz, *Normen und Praxis, Das Europäische Konzert der Grossmächte als Sicherheitsrat, 1815–1860* (Munich, 2009); A Truyol y Serra, *Histoire du droit international public* (Paris, 1995) 99ff.

Italy) formed a club arrogating to itself powers of legislation and action. Some of these Congresses of Powers certainly gave rise to important international legal regulations. For example, the Berlin Conference of 1878 on colonial matters.[31] It was possible for a non-European State to be admitted to the 'advantages of European public law' through recognition of that status by the European Powers. Thus Turkey (the Sublime Porte) was admitted to the advantages of European public law by Article 7 of the Treaty of Paris of 1856. Later, Japan (1894), Siam (1895) and Persia (1896) would also be admitted.[32] The international community had been reduced to a club of Powers acting in its name. On the other hand, this was the first time that an international community had escaped the doctrinal limbo and become a real factor of international life. But it was far away from the ideal international community foreshadowed in doctrine.

F. The Twentieth Century and the Return of a Global International Community

The cataclysm of World War I shook consciences[33] and opened the way for new thinking and new action. The anarchy of international relations and the generalised right of States to wage war brokered a reaction. President Wilson was welcomed in Europe as a messiah of peace. International law and organisation had to be strengthened. Something superior to States, able to constrain them, was considered necessary. This was the background to the creation of the League of Nations and the quest for 'peace through law'. True, States managed to blunt the 'superiority' of the League and its power of sanction. They framed it as an organisation based on the equal sovereignty of its members. But the Covenant of 1919 bore all the hallmarks of the new post-war world in some of its key provisions. This was the case in particular in Article 11, proclaiming that international peace was a matter of concern to the League wherever it occurred (ie even when war took place between non-member States) and that the League 'shall take any action … to safeguard the peace'.[34] It is difficult to find a formula more revolutionary for the times. This conception of a universally common bond was the basis for a renewed vision of an international community. It was rooted in an understanding that common concerns and dangers can be handled only multilaterally. Later, other matters of common concern would be added, ranging from human rights

[31] A Anghie, 'Berlin West Africa Conference, 1884–1885' in R Wolfrum (ed), *The Max Planck Encyclopedia of Public International Law*, vol I (Oxford, 2012) 906ff. See also SE Crowe, *The Berlin West African Conference 1884–1885* (London, 1942).

[32] WG Grewe, *The Epochs of International Law* (Berlin/New York, 2000) 497ff.

[33] Serious authors such as Politis could write after the Great War that it 'had shaken the Universe'. See N Politis, *Les nouvelles tendances du droit international* (Paris, 1927) 17.

[34] On this provision, see R Kolb, 'Article 11' in R. Kolb, *Commentaire sur le Pacte de la Société des Nations* (Brussels, 2014) 447ff.

to the protection of the environment.[35] Bilateralism thus gave way to some partial community orientation.[36] An eminent professor of international law could write in 1996, 'the legal order of the international community … has added itself to the traditional dimensions of the international legal order regulating coexistence and cooperation'.[37]

III. Conceptions of the International Community

The term 'international community' may express significantly differing ideas. A careful examination of international literature allows at least three to be distinguished. The first and the second are gradually different; the third is a specification of the second. The three conceptions differ as a function of the criterion constituting the communal link: either a common legal order; or the consciousness of common welfare directing the concrete actions of the subjects; or, lastly, public institutions with the mission to implement the collective interests. The first conception presents the lowest threshold; the second the highest; the third straddles the others.

A. Necessary International Community

According to this view, the mere fact of being linked together by the existence of a common legal order that is equally binding on all members of society, constitutes among these members a minimum form of community. Through the legal order there is more than a mere anarchical juxtaposition. This addition of the law transforms the simple unrelated society into one having a bond of a communal

[35] The depletion of the environment had been sustained by the dominant interpretation of the Holy Scriptures over a long period of time. It is there written that the human being represents the pinnacle of creation (a very self-serving statement) and that nature and animals are dominated by Man. See the fierce critique of such conceptions in C Amery, *Das Ende der Vorsehung—Die gnadenlosen Folgen des Christentums* (Reinbek (Hamburg), 1972); and L White, 'The Historical Roots of Our Ecological Crisis' (1967) 155 *Science* 1203ff. Our 'domination' (if that peculiar notion is to be maintained) can mean no more than a special responsibility for nature: G Altner, *Schöpfung am Abgrund—Die Theologie vor der Umweltfrage* (Neukirchen, 1974); J Moltmann, *Gott in der Schöpfung, Ökologische Schöpfungslehre* (Munich, 1985); G Angelini, 'Il dominio della terra. Genesi 1.28 e la questione ambientale' (1988) 69 *La Rivista del Clero italiano* 407ff; A Autiero, 'Custodire la creazione—Linee di etica ecologica' (1989) 21 *Rivista di teologia morale* 99ff; U Krolzik, '*Dominium terrae*, Storia di Genesi 1.28' (1990) 22 *Rivista di teologia morale* 257ff; R Murray, *The Cosmic Covenant: Biblical Themes of Justice, Peace and the Integrity of the Creation* (Piscataway, 2007); H Bedford-Strohm and C Deane-Drummond (eds), *Religion and Ecology in the Public Sphere* (New York, 2011). See also EM Condradie, *Ecological Theology: A Indexed Bibliography* (Belleville, 2001).

[36] C Tomuschat, 'Die internationale Gemeinschaft' (1995) 33 *Archiv des Völkerrechts* 1ff.

[37] JA Carrillo-Salcedo, 'Droit international et souveraineté des Etats, Cours général de droit international public' (1996) 257 *RCADI* 146, our translation.

nature. Ultimately, the international community is here a simple deduction drawn from the existence of the international legal order. The law creates the community; the community is at the same time the bearer of that legal order. The law is a factor accounting for a degree of order and cohesion; this transforms society into a community.[38] The question remains, however, whether the expectation-driving term 'community' really covers the minimal social bond created by a common legal order. Should that term not be reserved for communities presenting elements of more pronounced solidarity? Is the more demanding vision not the general understanding of 'community'?

B. Specific International Community

For the proponents of this view, the existence of a common law is not sufficient to create a community. There must be an element of real cohesion going beyond the common legal order. For many holding this view, this element must be found in people's political conscience. Thus, the international community depends on the existence of a community spirit, that is, the readiness of the particular collectivities to tailor their actions to the superior good of the universal community.[39] This in itself depends on the existence of factors of material interdependence and on the consciousness of the superior claim of the common welfare which they trigger.

For most authors, international society is still far from being a community.[40] As has been said:[41]

> The State absorbs all fundamental solidarities and in particular the loyalty of its subjects. The situations where vital interests are at stake illustrate this fact: within the State, when supreme interests are in jeopardy, the people stand in full solidarity behind the national State (eg in a situation of war). In the international society, the opposite is true: the greater the danger to its vital interests, as for example the maintenance of peace,

[38] Such a view has been defended, eg, by MK Yasseen, 'Réflexions sur la détermination du *jus cogens*' in SFDI, Colloque de Toulouse, *L'élaboration du droit international public* (Paris, 1975) 216; H Mosler, 'The International Society as a Legal Community' (1974-IV) 140 *RCADI* 33ff; J Verhoeven, 'Considérations sur ce qui est commun—Cours général de droit international public (2002)' (2008) 334 *RCADI* 105.

[39] C de Visscher, *Théories et réalités en droit international public*, 4th edn (Paris, 1970) 111ff. See also E Luard, *International Society* (New York, 1990) 8; Conseil œcuménique des Eglises (ed), *L'Eglise et le désordre international* (Neuchâtel, 1949) 80–81, 98. The international community is then often presented as a building site in need of completion: P Reiwald, *Conquête de la paix* (Genève, 1944) 13–14. One might also refer to the stratified theory of international society of G Schwarzenberger, *Power Politics*, 3rd edn (London, 1964) 198ff: (1) *law of power* in general international society; (2) *law of reciprocity* in the community created within a treaty (conventional community); (3) *community law* within international institutions, for cooperation in the context of questions of common concern (the fight against drug trafficking, the slave trade, etc). The equation society/community depends here on the extension of the group: in the universal system there is antagonism and thus mere society; in particular systems in which some common interests may crystallise, the community model may achieve a firmer hold.

[40] de Visscher, above n 39, 111–16.

[41] *ibid*, 112, our translation.

> the less the international solidarities. The loyalty of peoples, in such cases, reverts back to their national State. Human beings may not contest, in pure reason, the existence of supranational values; in the domain of action, they obey national imperatives.

The situation between Russia and the Ukraine since 2014 has illustrated the point quite clearly. The war in the former Yugoslavia in the 1990s is another telling example. In each case, the peoples concerned backed and continue to back their own nationalistic beginnings; any international criticism regarding the violation of the law was and still is rejected as political manipulation and a monstrous misrepresentation of facts. Thus, to the peoples involved, in international affairs action rarely appears as an impersonal application of the law. It is rather perceived through the lens of power politics, and often considered as an imposition by the powerful on some less powerful States. Some authors reach the same conclusion without voicing any regret. Thus, Weil has written that the fictional international community is just a cloak that masks the true power of States. It carries with it an unrealistic vision and creates non-realisable expectations, whilst promoting the illusion of faint progress.[42]

Other authors affirm the existence of a specific international community. For Tomuschat, for example, States live within an international constitutional order of a moral, political and legal nature. This order is the basis for action through the increasing weight given to collective interests within the net of international relations and law.[43] The community does not flow from the common constitutional order alone; it is rooted in concrete actions that obey, to some extent, community purposes. According to Dupuy, the international community is a founding fiction (ie the law supposes a state of facts, or a situation different from the real one, in order to deduce certain consequences from this assumption). Alternatively, it may be considered under the lens of a Kantian categorical imperative, leading to the corollary that there exists a duty to act as if the community existed. These theoretical underpinnings lead to the assertion that modern international law is orientated towards a series of community purposes.[44]

This community feeling is stronger within regional communities than in the universal one. It must be admitted, though, that more recently this statement may be open to challenge. National independence, euroscepticism, derision regarding the EU's institutions and action, the quest for greater local decision-making and the like, all have become increasingly fashionable mantras. The optimum balance between common regulation and local autonomy is far from having been found.

[42] P Weil, 'Cours général de droit international public: le droit international en quête de son identité' (1992-VI) 237 *RCADI* 306, 311–12. The same rejection can be found in a series of positivist critiques, opposed to the universalistic conception suggested by the notion: see, eg, K Strupp, 'Les règles générales du droit de la paix' (1947-I) 47 *RCADI* 324.

[43] C Tomuschat, 'International Law: Ensuring the Survival of Mankind on the Eve of a New Century, General Course on Public International Law' (1999) 281 *RCADI* 72ff.

[44] PM Dupuy, 'L'unité de l'ordre juridique international—Cours général de droit international public' (2002) 297 *RCADI* 258.

C. Institutional International Community

The essential cohesive factor leading to formation of a community is not the conscience of the people but an institutional fact: the organised community, ie the existing international institutions. The international organisations are the main and concrete support of the international community. These organisations are focal points for the crystallisation of common concerns and for coordinated cooperation among States. Thus, they are the true engine of the international community.[45] Through its universality and the importance of its functions, the UN is in this context presented as the main depositary of the international community.[46] Its Charter is seen as a type of Constitution.[47] This conception of the international community has been upheld by various distinguished authors.[48] We might add that this institutional vision also corresponds to the shallowest journalistic jargon. The international community is here constantly being identified with the UN or—to some extent absurdly in regard of its elitist composition—with the Security Council.

IV. Society or Community?

In the complex structure of today's international relations, it is hardly imaginable that a community could be built on anything other than a combination of social and communal elements. How to balance those elements is the question that needs to be canvassed. An inventory must be made regularly, since the relevant factors

[45] This idea has been defended since the founding of the League of Nations: see P Otlet, *Constitution mondiale de la Société des Nations. Le nouveau droit des gens* (Geneva, 1917).

[46] M Lachs, 'The Development and General Trends of International Law in Our Time' (1980-IV) 169 *RCADI* 248.

[47] K Skubiszewski, 'Remarks on the Interpretation of the United Nations Charter' in *Essays in Honor of H. Mosler* (Berlin/Heidelberg/New York, 1983) 891ff; B Conforti, 'Cours général de droit international public' (1988-V) 212 *RCADI* 129ff; E Suy, 'The Constitutional Character of Constituent Treaties of International Organizations and the Hierarchy of Norms' in *Essays in Honor of R. Bernhardt* (Berlin, 1995) 267ff; B Fassbender, *UN Security Council Reform and the Right of Veto* (The Hague/London/Boston, 1998) 89ff; B Fassbender, 'The United Nations Charter as a Constitution of the International Community' (1998) 36 *Columbia Journal of International Law* 529ff; G Ress, 'The Interpretation of the Charter' in B Simma (ed), *The Charter of the United Nations—A Commentary*, 2nd edn (Oxford, 2002) 15–18; PM Dupuy, 'L'unité de l'ordre juridique international' (2002) 297 *RCADI* 215ff; TM Franck, 'Is the United Nations Charter a Constitution?' in *Essays in Honor of T. Eitel* (Berlin, 2003) 95ff; S Szurek, 'La Charte des Nations Unies, constitution mondiale?' in JP Cot, A Pellet and D Forteau (eds), *La Charte des Nations Unies, Commentaire*, 3rd edn (Paris, 2005) 29ff; R Chemain and A Pellet (eds), *La Charte des Nations Unies, Constitution mondiale?* (Paris, 2006); C Walter, 'International Law in a Process of Constitutionalization' in J Nijman and A Nollkaemper (eds), *New Perspectives on the Divide Between National and International Law* (Oxford, 2007) 191ff; B Fassbender, *The United Nations Charter as the Constitution of the International Community* (Leiden/Boston, 2009).

[48] See, eg, J L'Huillier, *Eléments de droit international public* (Paris, 1950) 180–81.

shift over time. In short, there is always something like society and community, 'me and the group'. But the equilibrium of the relevant factors is constantly changing.

Political scientists have raised certain arguments against the existence of an international community. Thus, Luard[49] emphasises three differences between national societies (true communities) and international society (mere society). We may review them in brief below:

1. *Excessive decentralisation of international society.* We come back to the lack of centralised authorities and of political-legal integration. Haphazard coordination of individual sovereignties is not a community. The centre is weak, the periphery is strong; consequently, centrifugal forces predominate. Military and economic powers are concentrated in the hands of few. This leads to a tendency towards hegemony or oligarchy. Further, there is no monopoly on the legitimate use of force. International relations remain significantly more irregular and haphazard than internal relations. Decentralisation corresponds to society, while centralisation triggers a community.
2. *Lack of a sense of international solidarity.* The sense of connection to a particular group is much stronger, for most peoples, than the sense of connection to humanity as a whole. Allegiances are local and national; universal ones are at best embryonic. In the event of conflict between allegiances, local or national ones will prevail. There is also a lack as regards the legitimacy of international power, institutions and social order. Generally, a political authority is respected because of some ideology, for example acceptance of the democratic rules of the game; education; inertia and habit; reason and reasoning, etc. This sense of a legitimate order, which must be obeyed, is lacking on the international plane. There, the prevailing state of affairs is perceived as the result of ugly power politics or, in the best case, as something obscure and undefinable. There are no international rites and traditions; no universalistic myths and symbols; no international flags and political ceremonies; no citizens of an international collectivity. All these objects, which have the power to capture the collective imagination and direct personal action, are lacking. The role of the UN, of its Secretary General, of the UN flag, of the blue helmets of UN forces, is little known in its true dimensions. In any case, these entities and symbols do not trigger feelings of identification, loyalty and solidarity in the breasts of many human beings.
3. *Excessive division of international society.* International society is replete with very different ideologies and interests. Can there be a community given such a clash of views? In Luard's opinion, 'international society lacks, even more than these [national societies], a common value-system, consensus on the way in which society should be ordered'.[50] Further, 'There is a juxtaposition of

[49] E Luard, *International Society* (New York, 1990) 6–10. In a more moderate form, see also A Truyol y Serra, 'Cours général de droit international public' (1981-IV) 173 *RCADI* 53ff.

[50] Luard, above n 49, 9, our translation.

isolated States, among which there is no moral or spiritual bond.'[51] Still more pointedly:

> Let us detach the labels 'community' and 'universality' which disguise the content. Let us look beyond the legal appearance of unity. One discerns ... an unstable and bloody game between States as opposed as ever in their conception of the law, morals, peace, war, aims and means.[52]

Clearly, there are also profound ideological rifts in internal societies. But the common constitutional order and the national solidarities bridge these gaps better than they can do in international society. True, within international society there are also some seeds of community of varying breadth and strength: they are planted too deep to be brushed away by centrifugal State forces. We have already reviewed the typical common concerns of States and peoples: sanitation and epidemics, the maintenance of peace, the protection of the natural environment, etc.[53]

The deeper reasons for the differences described above lie in people's lack of socialisation and education.[54] Luard[55] mentions some essential aspects:

1. *International socialisation occurs too late*:

> The socialisation that takes place in domestic societies begins at a very early age. From their earliest years children are taught, by parents, teachers and other elders, the kind of behaviour that is expected from them. Since they are still in a very impressionable age, such influences are likely to have a powerful effect in inducing cooperative behaviour. Socialisation within international society, such as it is, comes far later. Only slowly, as he grows up, does the child become aware, from the watching of television, the reading of newspapers and books, and from other sources of information, of the existence of a world society outside the national state.[56]

By the fact of its occurring late, this international socialisation has a lesser impact:

> International socialisation, on the other hand, is superimposed considerably later, over beliefs and loyalties which are already deeply entrenched. This reduces the impact the former can have, especially where any conflict occurs between the two. The sense of international responsibility is nearly always weaker than that of national loyalty.[57]

[51] Conseil œcuménique des Eglises (ed), *L'Eglise et le désordre international* (Neuchâtel, 1949) 80, our translation.

[52] O Delacrétaz, 'Un message trompeur' in Federal Department of Foreign Affairs, *La Suisse et l'ONU* (Lausanne, 1985) 91–92, our translation.

[53] AA Cançado Trindade, 'International Law for Humankind: Towards a New Jus Gentium, General Course on Public International Law' (2005) 316/317 *RCADI* 9, 9–312.

[54] The perception of things by humans may be more important than the things themselves: Epictetus, *Manual*, §5. See also the Preamble, §1, to the Constitution of UNESCO (1945) recalling that wars take shape in the minds of men.

[55] E Luard, *International Society* (New York, 1990) 58–61.

[56] *ibid*, 59.

[57] *ibid*, 59–60.

It must be added that this international socialisation is resisted in certain influential circles, which consider it to be a sort of treason to the nation. Cosmopolitan internationalism is thus seen as being opposed to patriotic duty. The problem of one-sided schoolbooks, presenting national history through the prism of acclamation for oneself and bleak—if not aggressive—disparagement of others, has been known since the times of the League of Nations. Has progress been achieved? Even in Europe, notably in the eastern part, progress in this regard remains at best slow.

2. *The indirect and fragmentary nature of international socialisation.* International socialisation often flows from indirect and fragmentary sources and events, and not from a rational and clearly structured plan for education. Thus, it generally remains superficial. The number of incorrect, or at least partial, representations of what actually happens in international affairs is a consequence of this lack of proper education or experience. On the other hand, we can observe a significant degree of internationalism in those persons who have been exposed early and profoundly to international experiences (eg because a parent was a delegate to the League of Nations;[58] or because the traumas of war have raised the international question as a fact of life;[59] or because of powerful rational thinking, showing the necessity for a better international order).[60] Let us again reflect on the words of Luard:

> [S]ocialisation within the smaller society occurs in the form of direct and clear-cut injunctions which are unmistakable in meaning and immediate in their impact. They are received from parents, teachers and other respected figures, the authority of whom at the time is unquestioned. Even the instruction which is received concerning civic duties and national loyalties ... may be directly instilled, in the home or at the school, in the same personal and persuasive way. Against this, socialisation within the international society occurs, if at all, only in the most indirect manner. Nobody gives an explicit instruction ... The citizen learns slowly, if at all, from reading and discussion, from the view of publicists and politicians, from resolutions of the UN and other sources that certain international actions ... are widely regarded as inadmissible and generally condemned.[61]

The consequences are manifold:

1. *Anarchy of power.* In international affairs, with their weak centre and strong periphery, State sovereignty often leads to self-serving competitiveness.[62] International policy is usually the result of 194 national policies, and of all the difficulties involving in coordinating them. This state of affairs was already well depicted by Immanuel Kant in 1795.[63] There is a state of nature among

[58] Jiri Toman.

[59] Charles de Visscher.

[60] A Verdross, H Kelsen.

[61] Luard, above n 55, 60.

[62] This remains true, whatever the sense attached to sovereignty: D Thürer, 'Staatliche Souveränität und Völkerrechtsordnung' in D Thürer, *Völkerrecht als Fortschritt und Chance* (Zurich/St Gall, 2009) 149ff.

[63] I Kant, *Towards Perpetual Peace* (1795).

States, not a civil State governed by sanctioned law. Thus, international lawyers are but 'sorry comforters' (*leidige Tröster*).[64] The contrast seems to be between international law in an anarchical society, or international federation in an international community. This division is certainly too bold and one-sided, but we constantly return to this basic idea in the context of the distribution of international power.[65]

2. *Associated relative weakness of the law.* International law may function well in most cases, but the fact remains that it easily breaks down when confronted with the most important matters. When there is staunch opposition by a State, especially if powerful, the sanction mechanisms are weak and ineffective. As we have seen, there is no true solution to this problem—at least not if one does not want to wage war every time action needs to be taken. This perennial weakness of international law in the realm of *de maximis* questions has led to dramatic outcomes—such as the suicide of Burckhardt, the eminent Swiss author, who took his own life mainly because he could see no end to international society's inability to find an answer to war.[66]

Ultimately, the existence of the international community depends on the definition of terms. And it also depends on the exact threshold at which one is prepared to speak of a community. There are no final answers to these questions. The relevant conceptions evolve over time; the problem is therefore essentially historical. What remains true is undoubtedly that the international community faces greater obstacles in its path than do national communities. It is easier to develop local solidarities than universal ones. Universal solidarity remains more a postulate of reason than a fact of life. Only certain elites are open to purely rational arguments. Moreover, it is known that local communities integrate in the face of a common external enemy or threat. The universal society has no such external enemy. It therefore lacks a potent centripetal factor. In a sense, the Tower of Babel has primacy over Noah's Ark.[67]

Ideally, the international community remains a philosophical concept, a path to follow, a faith to serve. In this sense, it is independent from all types of inventory. In this form, the concept resembles an act of faith through the unity of humanity and the indivisibility of certain fundamental interests. It calls for action to achieve

[64] *ibid*, Section II, Final Articles, Art 2. On this issue: R Merkel, 'Lauter leidige Tröster? Kants Entwurf zum ewigen Frieden und die Idee eines Völkerstrafgerichtshofes' (1996) 82(2) *Archiv für Rechts- und Staatsphilosophie* 161ff; R Merkel and R Wittmann (eds), *Zum ewigen Frieden—Grundlagen, Aktualität und Aussichten einer Idee von Immanuel Kant* (Frankfurt, 1996); A Simari, *Pace e guerra nel pensiero di Kant* (Milan, 1998).

[65] See, eg, P Reiwald, *Conquête de la paix* (Geneva, 1944) 79, 206.

[66] See the main monograph by this truly eminent author: W Burckhardt, *Die Organisation der Rechtsgemeinschaft* (Basle, 1927) 374ff.

[67] It may be helpful to recall that the plurality of peoples and the division of humanity into different groups (which is also a source of richness and of pluralism) is depicted in The Bible as the result of humanity's insurrection against God's will: *Genesis* 11:19. We might also recall the sharp words of Dante against this 'anarchy': *De Monarchia* (1313), book I, ch XVI.

some greater share of order and justice in the universal community. This action is certainly worthy of being undertaken. It seeks to square discipline and freedom, the two great forces of human life.

It stands to reason that the balance we need has not yet been attained. More needs to be done to realise a better international order, without reducing local independence and autonomy more than strictly necessary. The task is Herculean: it has been the great political goal throughout history, and remains so, in particular, now. In brief, there will always be an international society and an international community along shifting and perfectible lines. But the balance between the two always fluctuates. Which way will the pendulum swing over the next few decades? The fate of humanity may depend on the answer to this.

Part Two

International Law and Politics

8

The Relationship Between International Law and Politics

I. The Influences of Politics and Power on International Law

A. General Aspects

Nowhere other than in international society have the lingering questions about the relations between law and power had such a great impact. At one end of the spectrum, simple power relations were affirmed;[1] while at the other end, pure legal analysis was clinically severed from political elements.[2] Both theories are excessive: law is not completely dissolved in power; and law cannot be realistically analysed in isolation from its social-political surroundings. It is more useful to carefully weigh the stakes and influences of power within the legal body, in the formative, implementing and modifying stages. The particular role power may play in a society deprived of a common superior has to be keenly taken into account. But first of all we need to address the definitional issues: What is power and what are politics? How do they relate to the law?

Power is exercised between human beings, individually or collectively. The power of one person over another is constituted by the sum total of the factors accounting for the ability of the first person to influence or to determine the conduct of the second person. The number of such factors is virtually unlimited. Some are of a moral nature, others are physical, for example prestige, moral influence, wealth, skills, natural authority, knowledge, capacity to manipulate, interests, fear, physical force, capacity to put in motion means of execution or coercion, etc. Power is by no means limited to superior physical force. There are a number of other factors allowing one person to exert an influence over another. David and Goliath's battle is quite instructive in this regard. *Politics* refers to those activities having the aim of organising social life and harmonising many particular interests, with a view

[1] See the discussion in A Truyol y Serra and R Kolb, *Doctrines sur le fondement du droit des gens* (Paris, 2007) 22ff.

[2] Vienna School, see, eg, Hans Kelsen.

to improving the common welfare of society, as it is perceived by the actor.[3] High politics (*haute politique*) concern objects that touch on interests considered to be vital for a certain collectivity at a given time, or questions affecting the distribution of the most intimate aspects of power. Politics naturally seek support in power, ie in the capacity to influence. The latter is a condition of their success.

Power and law entertain a multitude of relationships. In its dimension as an 'ought to be', ie as requiring certain conduct, the law inherently contains an element of power. It lays down an injunction, it utters an imperative, which it intends to see followed; and it might punish deviant attitudes. Law's power is nevertheless only potential. In order to be realised, it must sometimes be backed by the social organs' meting out some concrete sanctions. The power put at the service of the law is therefore a twin of the latter; it is indispensable to the law for fulfilling its proper mission. From this perspective, power and law join forces in a vision of 'sovereignty of the law'. However, power has a larger scope of action. It is not always put at the service of the law; it also creates the law, directs it and limits its reach. Power is essentially a real or factual force; law is a normative phenomenon. There is hence a dialectic relationship between the two:

1. If power wants to last, it must organise and limit itself; it must seek legitimation, which only the law can fully provide (*oboedientia facit imperantem*); law appears here as the measure and limit of power.
2. Power as a fact may seek to liberate itself from the constraints of the law; it may create new facts and try to impose them contrary to the law as it stands; the most extreme example of such a new 'legality' is revolution.

The height of tension or opposition between power and law is attained in totalitarian regimes. Here, the very concept of legality intimidates the rulers. It is replaced by nebulous 'popular wills' or 'popular spirits',[4] by the exigencies of the 'class struggle', by the 'necessities of consolidation of the revolutionary order' and the like.

Independently of these general typologies, it is possible to adopt a sociological perspective and to determine the many reciprocal, gravitational pulls between the two forces. Thus, for example, power is a factor that directs the configuration of a legal order. In feudal, rural, aristocratic, totalitarian, democratic societies and orders, the structure and content of the law will correspond to the described sociological and political basis.[5] Its configuration shifts over time. For example,

[3] The notion of politics as action for the benefit of the public collectivity (or which has a link to the governance of the State) has not found a single meaning over the course of history: see O Höffe, *Politische Gerechtigkeit* (Frankfurt, 1987) 63. The term 'politics' can also be used in a large sense outside the context of action in favour of a public collectivity: see H Henkel, *Rechtsphilosophie*, 2nd edn (Munich, 1977) 125. Politics linked to a particular collectivity gives rise to a political regime, ie a phenomenon of authority based on the distinction between the governing and the governed: see M Duverger, *Institutions politiques*, 9th edn (Paris, 1966) 13. See also the interesting monograph by J Darbellay, *La réflexion des philosophes et des juristes sur le droit et la politique* (Freiburg, 1987).

[4] For Nazi Germany, see B Rüthers, *Die unbegrenzte Auslegung* (Tübingen, 1968); M Stolleis, *Recht und Unrecht. Studien zur Rechtsgeschichte des Nationalsozialismus* (Frankfurt, 1994).

[5] See the still interesting but somewhat too orthodox study by V Tuka, *Die Rechtssysteme* (Berlin/Vienna, 1941).

the mobilisation of land for industrial and commercial ends could not have been undertaken without the modern concept of property. This in turn triggered a shift from feudalism to modern atomistic-constitutional regimes. Thus, the legal and political system changed, passing from feudal law to the modern codifications.

The relations between *law and politics* are as variegated as those between law and power. Primacy of the law theoretically existed in the times of the Enlightenment, through the multiple doctrines of natural law. Politics had the main function of executing the dictates of reason as deduced from natural law. Politics were thus conceived as legal policies—and we therefore understand why a series of authors have insisted on the ideological functions of modern natural law, linked to the liberal State and the rule of law. The primacy of politics was conversely affirmed by doctrines of realism of various shades, inspired to some extent by Machiavelli. Law here reverted to being an instrument for and of political power. Using a more concrete typology, the relations between law and politics can be described as occupying three axes:

1. A certain policy seeks the support of the law to realise its aim, ie to direct social behaviour in the desired sense. From this perspective, politics always seek to some extent a transformation of their content into legal rules.
2. The law for its part needs an underpinning political order and the expression of some fundamental values, normally set out in a Constitution.
3. The law is a limit on political action when the regime is not based on the omnipotence of the government (in the extreme form through the maxim 'government of law and not of men'). In addition, the law provides the political parties with criteria of legitimacy, if and when these parties want to remain faithful to the established constitutional order. This limitation of politics by law supposes a minimum degree of ideological convergence, that is, agreement on a set of constitutional norms and values by an overwhelming majority of the social body, and also a certain accepted autonomy of the law. These conditions are rarely realised in abnormal societies, scarred by deep ideological rifts, deprived of a constitutional-legal organisation of powers or still heavily decentralised. In such contexts, the weight of politics increases in the same proportion as the deficiencies of the legal system.

Law and politics present three essential differences:

1. In politics, the element of flexibility and dynamism predominates; law rather seeks support in stability and certainty. Politics are subjected and must react to constant fluctuations and changes. This fact gives rise to a certain element of opportunism. It is due to the need to react to quickly shifting social and political realities. There is a constant need for new answers to new problems. The major issue with which every society and all politics are confronted is that concerning the (re)distribution of goods, resources and wealth. But there are also various policies that are not dominated by this distributive issue, for example the recognition of some liberties to certain persons not implying cost

or the limitation of other persons' liberty (eg the recognition of non-classical partnerships). Law, on the other hand, seeks consolidation in institutions and regularities, consonant with the normative order. There is clearly also the need for legal adaptation, but there is always some time lag here, and thus a certain conservative tendency in the law.

2. Politics are orientated towards the concrete substance of things, appreciated through the freedom of ideological and other personal convictions. The law, for its part, is inseparable from a certain degree of formalism. There is a gap between spontaneous social activities and ideologies on the one hand, and the formalisation of legal rules seeking to ensure equality, simplification and security on the other.[6] Legal technique is rooted in this formalism. There is some distinction between problem-orientated thought (politics) and category-orientated thought (law).
3. Politics is orientated mainly towards considerations of usefulness and opportunity, while law prefers to view considerations from the double perspective of justice/legal certainty.[7] In politics, the tendency is to consider exactly what is useful or appropriate to the common good as it is perceived (*salus populi suprema lex esto*). In the law, the tendency is to consider, first, what flows from legality and equality (formal and material, *suum cuique*), and then what is generalisable and foreseeable.[8] From these differences emerges a certain tension between the law and politics, between what is useful and what is just and legal: sometimes this tension is fertile; sometimes it results in 'thorns'.

B. International Power and International Law

The role of power in international law has hardly ever been underestimated, so evident is it.[9] In fact, whatever the sometimes aggressive manifestations of political

[6] C de Visscher, *Théories et réalités en droit international public*, 4th edn (Paris, 1970) 165.

[7] See G Radbruch, *Rechtsphilosophie*, 8th edn (Stuttgart, 1973) 164ff, with the three main concepts and paradoxes influencing the law: justice, legal certainty, utility.

[8] These concepts are often discussed in monographs concerning the art of legislation: see, eg, P Noll, *Gesetzgebungslehre* (Reinbek (Hamburg), 1973).

[9] On the relations between international law and politics, see among others: E Giraud, 'De la valeur et des rapports des notions de droit et de politique dans l'ordre international' (1922) 29 *RGDIP* 473ff; C Bilfinger, 'Betrachtungen über politisches Recht' (1929) I (1) *ZaöRV* 57ff; V Bruns, *Völkerrecht und Politik* (Berlin, 1934); Q Wright, 'Law and Politics in the World Community' in *Essays in Honor of H. Kelsen (Law and Politics in the World Community)* (Berkeley/Los Angeles, 1953) 3ff; C de Visscher, 'Quelques réflexions sur la notion du politique en droit international public et privé' in *Essays in Honor of T. Perassi*, vol I (Milan, 1957) 401ff; C Rousseau, 'Principes de droit international public' (1958-I) 93 *RCADI* 381ff; E Giraud, 'Le droit international public et la politique' (1963-III) 110 *RCADI* 419ff; W Friedmann, *The Changing Structure of International Law* (London, 1964) 45ff; K Eustathiadès, 'Evolution des rapports entre le droit international et la politique étrangère' in *Essays in Honor of H. Rolin* (Paris, 1964) 80ff; A Hartung (ed), *Modernes Völkerrecht—Form oder Mittel der Aussenpolitik* (Berlin, 1965); A Tsoutsos, *Politique et droit dans les relations internationales* (Paris, 1967); C de Visscher, *Théories et réalités en droit international public*, 4th edn (Paris, 1970) 19ff, 33ff, 86ff, 130ff; JES Fawcett, *Law and Power in International Relations* (London, 1982); M Virally, 'Panorama du droit international

aims in international relations, the articulation between both aspects of law and politics is no less complex here than it is in municipal societies. There are questions that governments consider to be intimately linked to interests concerning the conservation or development of State power. In such contexts, the influence of political factors increases. This is the case, for example, as regards the use of force, the control of armaments or the transfer of sovereign powers to supranational entities. There are other subject matters, much more technical in nature, where the law plays is a greater role than political considerations, for example postal exchanges or world meteorology. The domain of 'vital interests' is itself shifting (and thus also shifts the weight of politics). Thus, the degree to which a multilateral treaty could be opened to universal ratification was a matter much debated in the 1960s,[10] while today it has retreated to the realm of purely technical questions governed by legal considerations. Conversely, the question of the submerged, 'innocent' passage of military submarines through certain straits now subject to the regime covering territorial waters when the latter were extended to 12 nautical miles, immediately became a highly political matter. It touched upon the second-strike nuclear capability of the USSR and Western States. The point was that the submarine's position had to remain secret if such second-strike capability was not to be jeopardised. The legal rule requiring the submarine to surface and to hoist its flag when effecting innocent passage could not accommodate this need.[11] By the same token, questions relating to intellectual property, which in the past

contemporain' (1983) 183 *RCADI* 29ff; I Brownlie, 'The Relation of Law and Power' in *Essays in Honor of G. Schwarzenberger* (London, 1988) 19ff; M Byers, *The Role of Law in International Politics* (Oxford, 2000); G Niemeyer, *Law without Force: The Function of Politics in International Law* (New Brunswick, 2001); P Bargiacchi, *Contributo allo studio dei fattori giuridici e politici dell'ordine internazionale* (Milan, 2003); Y Onuma, 'International Law in and with International Politics: The Functions of International Law in International Society' (2003) 14 *EJIL* 105ff; A Oyebode, *International Law and Politics: An African Perspective* (Lagos, 2003); SV Scott, *International Law in World Politics* (Boulder, 2004); C Reus-Smith (ed), *The Politics of International Law* (Cambridge, 2004); OA Hathaway and HH Koh, *Foundations of International Law and Politics* (New York, 2005); RH Steinberg and JM Zasloff, 'Power and International Law' (2006) 100 *AJIL* 64ff; M Koskenniemi, *La politique du droit international* (Paris, 2007); E Brimmer, 'International Politics need International Law' in E Jouannet (ed), *Regards d'une génération de juristes sur le droit international* (Paris, 2008) 113ff; C Reus-Smith, 'The Politics of International Law' in C Reus-Smith, *International Law* (London, 2008) 239ff; R Withana, *Power, Politics Law: International Law and State Behaviour during International Crises* (Leiden, 2008); JP Trachtmann, *International Law and Politics* (Aldershot, 2008); M Koskenniemi, *International Law and Politics, Cursos euromediterraneos bancaja de derecho internacional*, vol 8 (Pamplune, 2009); KH Kaikobad and M Bohlander (eds), *International Law and Power, Essays in Honour of C. Warbrick* (Leyde, 2009); S Sur, *International Law, Power, Security and Justice: Essays on International Law and Relations* (Oxford, 2010); A Orakhelashvili, 'International Law, International Politics and Ideology' in A Orakhelashvili (ed), *Research Handbook on the Theory and History of International Law* (Cheltenhem, 2011) 328ff; M Parish, 'International Law and the Great Power Politics' in D Feldman (ed), *Law in Politics, Politics in Law* (Oxford, 2013) 203ff; M Klamberg, *Power and Law in International Society* (London/New York, 2015).

[10] G Czerwinski, *Das Universalitätsprinzip und die Mitgliedschaft in internationalen universalen Verträgen und Organisationen* (Berlin, 1972); TO Elias, *The Modern Law of Treaties* (New York/Leiden, 1974) 15.

[11] RJ Dupuy and D Vignes (eds), *Traité du nouveau droit de la mer* (Paris/Brussels, 1985) 768–70, 784ff (contribution by T Treves). See also LW Kaye, 'The Innocent Passage of Warships in Foreign Territorial Seas: A Threatened Freedom' (1978) 15 *San Diego Law Review* 573ff.

were mainly technical matters concerning private interests, now tend to become increasingly political, in the wake of certain commercial practices of emerging far-eastern economies. On the whole, apart from vital interests, a sensible analysis of the relationship between international law and international politics supposes a careful inventory and meticulous scrutiny of various mutual influences.

On the general plane, it remains necessary to emphasise the absence of an international policy in the proper sense of the word. Policy means organising and reconciling particular interests for the common good. But what is commonly called 'international politics' is not a policy from and for the international society or community; it is an ever-changing basket of national legal policies. This is one of the reasons why political factors so often seem to stand in sharp contrast to the exigencies of the law. The policies are not in themselves a device for cohesion or community, as they may be in internal societies, where they are geared to the national interest. Quite on the contrary, internationally they may appear to be a continual cause of divisions. Any law grows and consolidates as a function of the increase in common values and interests. This mechanism is gravely inhibited in international society by the centrifugal configuration of politics. In short, the politics reflect a society other than that towards which they should be geared: they are in the service of national societies instead of international society. This absence of congruence is at the root of many problems:

1. On the international plane there exist common concerns and the resolution to tackle them, but the proper means to do so are lacking, due to the absence of an organised power able to respond.
2. On the municipal plane there is a glaring insufficiency of means to respond to increasingly global problems; but there is an organised and sometimes strong power, which acts in the particular interests of the State.

In short, on the centripetal plane, which establishes order and unity, there is a lack of any significant power; on the centrifugal plane, which is a factor of anarchy and individualism, significant powers exist. The two are caught in a chasm and rarely come together as they should. They more often than not pull in opposite directions. The effects are felt in particular in the field of the international law of cooperation. The essential challenges of the beginning of the twenty-first century are situated here.[12]

Even supposing that a truly international policy could see the light of day (ie a policy meant for the welfare of international society as a whole), for example as the result of the action of certain secretariats of international organisations[13] or through the action of morally influential persons, this policy could really bear

[12] It has been said with much humour and some exaggeration that either there will one day be a world government, or there will no longer be a world: A Maurois, *Ce que je Crois, avec les objections faites par quelques lecteurs et les réponses à ces objections* (Paris, 1952) 67.

[13] They have sometimes played eminent roles. See, eg, E Ranshofen-Wertheimer, *The International Secretariat, A Great Experiment in International Administration* (Washington, DC, 1945); J Siotis, *Essai sur le Secrétariat international* (Geneva, 1963).

fruit only if powerful States lent it their support. Only the States could effect significant changes in the international legal order. This is tantamount to saying that such a policy would immediately be viewed through the prism of each State's interests. Each State will consider its own interests and those of its people, and it will try to mould any common policy to these interests; if the end result is too far removed from the State's expectations, it will simply refuse to ratify the instrument embodying the policy choices finally made, or will fail to implement the common policy in full. The environmental protection conferences at Rio (1992), Kyoto (1997), Durban (2011) and even later graphically demonstrated this process. True international politics are proposed by persons without power, and real international politics are performed by powerful persons concerned mainly with national interests. From there flows the frequently voiced impression of the complexity, paralysis and ineffectiveness of international politics or of multilateralism. This whole state of affairs is inherent in the actual distribution of power, that is, in the word 'sovereignty' or (better in the plural) 'sovereignties'.

C. Theories on the Relations of Power and Law in International Society

Many different theories have placed emphasis on the role of political factors in international relations. Four conceptions may here serve as an illustration. Each one attempts to provide an overall answer regarding the degree of penetration of political factors into and the impact of policy on international law. However, there remain important doubts as to the utility of such totalising theories. The mutual relationships between law and politics are in reality placed on a spectrum of highly multifaceted influences. A simplifying approach obscures more than it illuminates the issue.

1. *International Relations Under the Exclusive Influence of Force*[14]

The law is here perceived as an *ex post facto* instrument of the stronger for imposing his victory on the weaker. This idea has an ancient lineage: we find it in Ancient India (Kautilya), in Ancient Greece (Calicles, Trasymachos, Thucydides) and in many other contexts of Western thought (eg Spinoza).[15] That such doctrines could find a favourable foothold in international relations is not surprising. They were defended by two quite different categories of writers: on the one hand by theorists

[14] For a short summary of these theories, see A Truyol y Serra, 'Cours général de droit international public' (1981-IV) 173 *RCADI* 105ff.

[15] Power and law are here identified. One may also recall Spinoza's classic words, that the first rule of natural law is that the bigger fish eats the smaller one: *Tractatus theologico-politicus* (1677) ch XVI. On the international law conception of Spinoza, see A Menzel, 'Spinoza und das Völkerrecht' (1908) 2 *Zeitschrift für Völkerrecht* 17ff; A Verdross, 'Das Völkerrecht im System von Spinoza' (1928) 7 *Zeitschrift für öffentliches Recht* 100ff; H Lauterpacht, 'Spinoza and International Law' (1927) 8 *BYIL* 89ff. See also in general JB Whitton, 'La règle pacta sunt servanda' (1934-III) 49 *RCADI* 241ff.

fond of *a priori* categorisations of the concept of law; on the other hand by practitioners who adopted a conflictual ideology of international relations. Among the former was Adolf Lasson.[16] His Hegelian faith pushed him to deny any authority or law superior to the State. Consequently only force could resolve disagreements between States. War became the historical vector of the progress and development of civilisation: the stronger overpowering the weaker. The theorists of the Uppsala School belonged to the same group, influenced by a mixture of positivism and realism (Lundstedt, Olivecrona).[17] For them, the absence of centralised sanctioning mechanisms condemned international relations to remain ruled by force. States used force in pursuit of their own interests. Therefore the use of force to the detriment of the law outweighed by far the use of force in the service of the law. This was tantamount to saying that international relations were simply governed by force.

The group of practitioners espousing a conflictual ideology primarily included those involved in drafting the foreign policy of the Great Powers, who were convinced of the absolute primacy of ideology. This was the case as regards the drafters of the Marxist-Leninist doctrines of the 1920s, before it became clear that the Soviet Revolution would not be immediately exported and that some form of coexistence with capitalist States would remain necessary.[18] This was also the case, at the height of the Cold War, as regards US neo-realists such as Hans Morgenthau[19] and George F Kennan.[20] Power is the axis of international relations; international law cannot tame this primary force. Therefore, only diplomacy can create facts and contain enemies. To rely on the force of promises, rules and proclamations is at best to be gravely naive. The 1930s had furnished many examples of the breach of pledges. And the era of the Cold War was scarcely a favourable time for the continuation of the idealistic 'peace through law' doctrine, attached to international institutions of which the League of Nations had been the most prominent representative.

The same line of thought was defended by Raymond Aron, a famous French political scientist, when he wrote that international relations have always been dominated by power, except for some lawyers drunk with concepts.[21] Overall, his

[16] A Lasson, *Princip und Zukunft des Völkerrechts* (Berlin, 1871).

[17] AV Lundstedt, *Le droit des gens, danger de mort pour les peuples* (Paris, 1925); K Olivecrona, *Law as a Fact* (Copenhagen/London, 1939).

[18] There is an interesting analogy between the early days of the Soviet Revolution and original Christianity. Both started with a rejection of the State and the law, and both later had to revise their views. For Christian doctrine, see G Fassò, *La legge della ragione* (Bologna, 1964) 23ff. For Soviet positions, see K Gryzybowski, *Soviet Public International Law* (Leyden/Durham, 1970) 2; and I Lapenna, *Conceptions soviétiques de droit international public* (Paris, 1954).

[19] H Morgenthau, *Politics among Nations*, 5th edn (New York, 1967).

[20] GF Kennan, *American Diplomacy, 1900–1950* (Chicago, 1951). On this school of thought: JL Kunz, 'Der heutige Stand der Wissenschaft und des Unterrichts des Völkerrechts in den Vereinigten Staaten' (1955/1956) 7 *Oesterreichische Zeitschrift für öffentliches Recht* 405ff.

[21] R Aron, *Paix et guerre entre les nations*, 8th edn (Paris, 1984) 691. See also G Schwarzenberger, *Power Politics: A Study of World Society*, 3rd edn (London, 1964); G de Lacharrière, *La politique juridique extérieure* (Paris, 1983).

judgement was nevertheless more nuanced than these oft-quoted words suggest. A more recent version of such negationism can be found in the 'rational choice theory' of Goldsmith and Posner.[22] The starting-point of their enquiry is concerned with the reasons why international law plays such an important role in international rhetoric while its real efficacy is subject to important doubts. Has it at least some moral authority? Reality shows that States act in a way to realise their interests of the moment to the greatest extent possible. They are not primarily concerned with respect for international law. The rules of international law emerge from the pursuit of personal interests, but they are definitely not a check on State interests. Consequently, international law is only one instrument among others utilised in the pursuit of interests. Thus, States will respect a treaty in accordance with *pacta sunt servanda* as long as their interests dictate that they should do so, taking into account the principle of reciprocity. In the end, international law may provide a faithful map of State interests at a given time, but it cannot exert a decisive influence on compliance. Each change of interests is reflected in a change of the law, and the latter cannot contain this change. Therefore, international law amounts to rhetoric, chimera and fantasy: what remains is politics.

All these theories insist on an undeniable truth: that international law does not occupy the role it could and perhaps should have in international relations. That power and force have frequently had the last word is attested to by history. But these theories are in error by over-simplifying the issues. They tend to confuse politics with high politics, interests with vital interests. It is only at the extremes that power generally has its way and law is brushed aside. The spectrum of vital interests, important and visible as it may be, is only a small segment of international reality. Moreover, many smaller States have an interest (perhaps even a vital one) in the strengthening of international law. Respect for the law can in itself be an interest; it is not simply a fetter on State interests.[23]

It should be added that conceptions such as those of Goldsmith and Posner are drawn from the perspective of a Great Power (and in the case of both these authors, after the Twin Towers attack). For all the other States, the pull towards compliance presents itself wholly differently. It might be asked how intellectually honest it is to elaborate a theory on international law by taking as a basis (i) only a small segment of international life (vital interests), and (ii) only the situation of Great Powers (which can substitute power for law)? In the end, the multiple and subtle relations entertained by law and policy are here reduced to one extreme of the spectrum, and this is presented as the whole truth.[24] International practice shows a much more nuanced picture of mutual influences and of bridges between the political facts and the legal norm. Further, international law itself is manifestly

[22] JL Goldsmith and E Posner, *The Limits of International Law* (Oxford, 2005). And see the critique by HJ Cremer, 'Völkerrecht—alles nur Rhetorik?' (2007) 67 *ZaöRV* 267ff.

[23] Thus, Switzerland most often respects treaties even when its interests are against its doing so: see the discussion in R Kolb, *Réflexions sur les politiques juridiques extérieures* (Paris, 2015) 63ff.

[24] It is as if the illness was considered to represent the whole story in health politics.

little understood by some authors, who do not have an intimate knowledge of its content and application. Non-lawyers often have some difficulty understanding the 'ought' properly; this is particularly so for political scientists, used, as they are, to the primacy of facts. They remain blind to the more subtle categories of the law. Lastly, the most profound reason why the human spirit refuses to see in these cynical theories the ultimate seal of truth is that they cannot point to any method for achieving the better organisation of the world. The sinister realisations of power and the accomplished actions of despots are presented as the final word for all time, and the baby is thrown away with the bathwater. Who can be fully satisfied by such a perspective?

2. The Dichotomy Between the Law of Power and the Law of Coordination

According to Georg Schwarzenberger, there are two distinct domains of international relations.[25] They translate into two concurrent legally normative circles, which remain mutually exclusive and irreconcilable. In the first circle (the law of power), power takes precedence over the law; in the second circle (the law of coordination), the law limits power more or less effectively:

1. *First circle—the law of power.* In each society there are various relations founded on power, such as between master and servant, capital and labour, the ruling class and the underdogs, and international relations are largely founded upon such power realities. In these domains, the function of the law is essentially conservative, that is, it helps power 'in maintaining the supremacy of force and the hierarchies established on the basis of power, and to give to this overriding system the respectability and sanctity law confers'.[26] This is the domain of customary international law: it spans the individualistic environment of State relations and presents itself as a form of *jus strictum* not tempered by considerations of good faith, reasonableness or equity.
2. *Second circle—the law of coordination.* The law of coordination is based on conventional relationships between States. By concluding an agreement, States exit the hostile environment of general international law. They deliberately approach others for the achievement of some common goal (which may extend to the creation of an international organisation). Here, considerations of good faith, reasonableness or equity have their place and impact. Conventional international law is the domain of *jus aequum*.

Here is the clear dichotomy: (i) the strict law, represented by customary international law, where States reject interferences bearing the hallmark of law; and (ii) equitable law, represented by conventional law, where States accept much

[25] G Schwarzenberger, *Power Politics*, 3rd edn (London, 1964). The author here still distinguishes three circles, adding a 'law of reciprocity', which need not concern us here.
[26] *ibid*, 199.

deeper penetration of legal ideas in order to achieve common aims.[27] It may be said that this interesting theoretical approach is not borne out by international practice, where this dichotomy is not found.

3. *The Theory of Social Authority*

According to Rolando Quadri, an eminent Italian international lawyer, the phenomenon of authority is the central fact around which all law crystallises.[28] Thus, there is the following chain: (i) *ubi societas, ibi auctoritas*; and (ii) *ubi auctoritas, ibi jus*. Society—authority—law. It is not decisive whether the society is organised vertically (central power) or horizontally (decentralisation), since authority is inherent in any society. It is manifested by the preponderance of certain entities or persons. Thus, law is first of all a fact, ie an effective power of decision (*jus est factum*). The legal rule draws its binding force from the command of the authority inherent in the social body. This authority may be diffuse, or consist in a Directory of Powers. It takes different shapes in different societies. Ultimately, this theory leads in international relations to the Great Powers as a 'de facto international government'. Quadri insists on the fact that the smaller powers may contribute to the shaping of the decision, notably when the Great Powers seek their cooperation. We see the law here as flowing from power, more precisely from a power-orientated fact. This sociological theory is, however, quite reductive of the reality it seeks to depict. The essence of law and its role cannot be reduced to some powerful decision-making. A perusal of all the sources of international obligations demonstrates this quite clearly.

4. *New Haven's Policy-orientated Approaches*

For the New Haven school of thought, dominated in international law by Myres McDougal, law is not simply reduced to power.[29] It has its own reach and dignity. But there remains the fact that law is a tool at the service of an ideology. The political facts and goals are criteria for the shaping and interpretation of the law. The lawyer is thereby transformed into the guardian of the political ideals of a society.

[27] See also G Schwarzenberger, *A Manual of International Law*, 5th edn (London, 1967) 28–29.

[28] R Quadri, *Diritto internazionale pubblico*, 5th edn (Naples, 1968) 27–31; R Quadri, 'Le fondement du caractère obligatoire du droit international public' (1952-I) 80 *RCADI* 622.

[29] M McDougal, 'International Law, Power and Policy: A Contemporary Conception' (1953-I) 82 *RCADI* 180ff. On this school of thought: C Schreuer, 'New Haven Approach und Völkerrecht' in C Schreuer (ed), *Autorität und internationale Ordnung* (Berlin, 1979) 63ff; DC Daniel, *Clarification and Appraisal of the Policy-Oriented Framework for International Legal Analysis* (Washington, DC, 1971); R Falk, 'New Approaches to the Study of International Law' (1967) 61 *AJIL* 489ff; B Rosenthal, *L'étude de l'oeuvre de Myres Smith McDougal en matière de droit international* (Paris, 1970); S Voos, *Die Schule von New Haven, Darstellung und Kritik einer amerikanischen Völkerrechtslehre* (Berlin, 2000). For a critique, see also G Abi-Saab, 'Cours général de droit international public' (1987-VII) 207 *RCADI* 35ff; C Tomuschat, 'International Law: Ensuring the Survival of Mankind on the Eve of a New Century' (1999) 281 *RCADI* 25, 53–55.

His or her role is mainly political. The principal characteristics of this orientation are as follows:

1. Law is not a sum total of rules embodying normative prescriptions; it is rather an authoritative decision-making process[30] and a body of decisions already taken. In short, law represents the sum of choices and decisions taken by the operators clothed with political functions. The lawyer does not look for rules; he or she makes choices leading to decisions.
2. Law is orientated towards goal values. The choices of the lawyer have the aim of maximising scope values or base values, such as power, wealth, enlightenment, skill, well-being, affection, respect, rectitude, etc.[31] The principal political aims of this school of thought are the 'dignity and freedom of the human being' according to a western (or rather US) constitutional tradition. But it has to be added that behind these lofty aims there often lurked the pursuit of US interests during the Cold War.
3. The law is not fixed *a priori*, since it is not a set body of rules; it is rather in constant flux, emerging from a process of claim and counterclaim. The decision-making organs can at any time inspire themselves to a new set of values or combination thereof. Therefore, the law cannot be predicted:

   > From the perspective of realistic description, the international law of the sea is not a mere static body of rules but is rather a whole decision-making process, a public order which includes a structure of authorized decision-makers as well as a body of highly flexible, inherited prescriptions. It is in other words, a process of continuous interaction, of continuous demand and response, in which the decision-makers of particular nation states unilaterally put forward claims of the most diverse and conflicting character … and in which other decision-makers … weigh and appraise these competing claims in terms of the interests of the world community and of the rival claimants, and ultimately accept or reject them. As such a process, it is a living, growing law …[32]

   The main criterion in the process must be the one of 'shared expectations'. From the continuous process of demand and response emerge some standards and patterns of expectation regarding future behaviour. These expectations take the place of the rule. They are normative, and their violation will be qualified by the legal community as a violation of the law.[33]

   As can be seen, this approach is extremely teleological and dynamic. The normativity of the law dissolves under the weight of open-ended

[30] See R Higgins, 'International Law and the Avoidance, Containment and Resolution of Disputes' (1991-V) 230 *RCADI* 35.

[31] M McDougal, 'International Law, Power and Policy: A Contemporary Conception' (1953-I) 82 *RCADI* 168. Other authors speak out for 'common values' processed on the international plane: Higgins, above n 30, 33.

[32] M McDougal, 'The Hydrogen Bomb Tests and the International Law of the Sea' (1955) 49 *AJIL* 356.

[33] MS McDougal and WM Reisman, 'The Prescribing Function in the World Constitutive Process: How International Law is Made' (1980) 6 *Yale Studies in World Public Order* 249ff; WM Reisman, 'International Law-making: A Process of Communication' (1981) 75 *ASIL Proceedings* 101.

decision-making, with the moderating device of expectations. The 'is' and the 'ought' tend to merge into each other. Law thereby becomes fundamentally an instrument of political justification or rhetoric.[34] Normativity, to the extent that it exists, is reduced to a choice based on a multitude of criteria and of their combination. The integrity of the legal order is thereby heavily jeopardised. Almost any *ad hoc* manipulation can be brought within the four corners of the law. Foreseeability and certainty are reduced almost to nothing. Such a conception—interesting as it is—can in the best case suit a Great Power policy. Smaller States cling to a normative order, which ensures some degree of certainty and protection. They do not conclude treaties in order to see them interpreted according to alien values and US foreign policy interests. The policy-orientated school is thus ultimately a school of unilateralism in disguise. This fact is revealed by the shaping of the values: for the school we are discussing, the values used in the process are not crystallised in the UN organs or on the universal plane (our authors even show a certain contempt for the UN, a place for ugly merchandising with dictatorial States). The values are mainly shaped by the US Government's foreign policy goals. There the meaning of 'human dignity' or 'free world society' is rooted and takes form.[35]

5. *Conclusion*

We have discussed four theories on the relations between law and power:

1. the negation of law by the use of force (so-called realism);
2. the limits imposed on the penetration of law outside conventional relationships;
3. the strong influence of the holders of social authority, mainly the Great Powers;
4. international law utilised in the service of the policy goals of a particular national society (vested with 'manifest destiny').

But in order to reach a fuller understanding of the multiple interactions between the ideal factors (law) and the real factors (power), it will be necessary to pierce the veil of such totalising theories and consider in much greater detail the many influences exerted by and affecting these two fertile sources.

D. Inroads of Politics into the Law: Political Tensions

Before looking at the many influential factors surrounding the two notions of policy and law, it may be useful to consider one extreme of the spectrum, namely 'political tension', in order to see how one pole is affected by disorder at the other.

[34] G Abi-Saab, 'Cours général de droit international public' (1987-VII) 207 *RCADI* 39.
[35] On the concept of human dignity, see the analysis by M Rothhaar, *Die Menschenwürde als Prinzip des Rechts* (Tübingen, 2015).

It is an observable fact that the standing of law in society progresses in times of social calm and order. The tranquility of social relations allows norms and practices to consolidate, precedents to be assimilated, agreements to be concluded and spontaneous norms to see the light of day under the influence of a wide array of shared values. On the other hand, the evolution of the law is hampered in troubled times, when doubts, uncertainties and crises predominate, and where unexpected shifts, accelerations and ruptures put the normative order under heavy strain. These times of political tension affect the collective belief in norms and law. The effectiveness of means for the peaceful settlement of disputes, notably adjudication, dwindles. Psychologically, such times create a state of confusion, distrust and anxiety, which can easily lead to a collective psychosis. Belief in the rule of force gains ground, just as confidence in the rule of law retreats. The former seems to promise some compensatory strength, whereas the latter seems to suggest underlying weakness. In short, in the domain of relationships, the extreme spectrum of 'vital interests' or 'high politics' is stretched almost to breaking point, in a sort of uncontrolled proliferation. These relations are imbued with passionate and irrational elements. The law, reduced in scope and weight, must to some extent absorb these political tensions. It thereby shows further signs of alteration: a loss of continuity; laws being enacted in rapid succession; breaches of the principle of non-retroactivity; a tendency to enact individualised pieces of legislation to deal with unexpected situations; emergency laws; the concentration of laws with political objects; the inflation of norms, in particular of a contingent character; the abandonment of the formal guarantees of the rule of law; the weakening of legal foreseeability and certainty; the growth of exceptional legislation and special tribunals, etc. In international relations, force then starts to predominate over law. History furnishes many examples of such phases: the decline of the Roman Empire, or the 1920s and 1930s. Legal life, like all other life, experiences cycles of progress and prosperity, and of decline and crisis. In international society the times of crisis have been particularly frequent and hostile. They have been marked by great wars and violent disorder.

The relationship of such tensions with international law can be described through the following categories:

1. *General international tensions.* This category encompasses general social and political upheavals, affecting a significant number of States. The events of the 1920s and 1930s were a prime example.[36] The factors triggering the tensions were manifold: the split amongst the Allied Powers after World War I; the rise of totalitarian lawlessness, including Communism; the confrontation between totalitarian ideologies (fascism, Nazism, Communism); the birth of States seeking to subvert the existing order; aggressive nationalistic tendencies; colonialism and the clashes it produced; the growth of the collectivity and the concomitant reduction in the spheres of liberty for individuals; the

[36] See, eg, the thoughtful study by EH Carr, *The Twenty Years' Crisis, 1919–1939* (London, 1946).

widespread politicisation of the masses; inadequate economic policies at the time of the Great Depression; the rivalries flowing from the export of capital; the loss of cultural certainties and the increase of various relativisms, etc. Such general tensions would then lead to the wars of 1931 (Far East) and 1939 (Europe). The League of Nations, bedrock of the legal approach to international affairs, was progressively marginalised and even ridiculed.[37] 'Pactomany' (ie the tendency to constantly conclude new agreements, especially non-aggression pacts) was but a symptom of this degeneration. Moreover, the Geneva Protocol of 1924 and the General Act of 1928 remained largely dead letters; the Locarno Agreements of 1925 led to great ambiguities, especially on the eastern European boundaries; the codification conferences of 1930 under the auspices of the League of Nations proved unsuccessful; the Covenant of the League was increasingly violated without adequate consequences; the plans for disarmament under the aegis of the League reached stalemate; the non-aggression agreements were massively violated, etc.

2. *Mixed situations of tension and détente.* There are periods when significant tensions on the one side are counterbalanced by détente on the other. The end of the 1940s and the 1950s are an example in point. At the universal level there were the massive tensions produced by the Cold War. They were symbolised, amongst other things, by the Berlin crises (1948–49). At the European level there was the détente leading to the European Convention on Human Rights (1950) and the Treaty of Rome (1957) establishing the European Economic Community. The dissonance between the Western and Communist blocs led to the stagnation of universal international law on a number of issues, eg human rights, disarmament, laws of war, non-intervention in internal affairs, self-determination of peoples, control of the use of nuclear energy, the functioning of the UN (veto, admission of new members, etc), the development of criminal international law according to the Nuremberg principles, the use of legal means to settle disputes, etc. Compare this state of affairs with the sometimes robust integrationist statements by the contemporary Court of Justice of the European Communities.[38]
3. *Tensions within hegemonic situations.* In some periods, the major international political fact is the hegemony of some Power. Minor disorders tend to be resolved by the intervention of the hegemon, which imposes order and

[37] But see the remarkable forecast of 'its' victory made during the war: 'Nous voici au seuil d'une épreuve qui peut être longue, mais dont l'issue n'est pas douteuse. Quelle qu'en soit la durée, elle ne peut qu'aboutir à la réaffirmation des principes essentiels du Pacte de 1919.' (JM Yepes and P da Silva, *Commentaire théorique et pratique du Pacte de la Société des Nations*, vol III (Paris, 1939), on a special leaflet inserted at the beginning of the book already printed). In English: 'We find ourselves at the threshold of an ordeal which might be long, but its outcome is not in doubt. However long it lasts, the result can be only the reaffirmation of the essential principles of the Covenant of 1919.' This happened with the creation of the UN and the adoption of its Charter.

[38] JP Jacqué, 'Le rôle du droit dans l'intégration européenne' (1991) *Revue de Philosophie politique* 119ff.

polices proper respect. This was the case as regards the Roman Empire, or of the European Concert in the nineteenth century; later of the US and USSR in their zones of influence; and in the 1990s and 2000s, the predominance of the US in world affairs, reaching its peak at the time of the war in Iraq (2003).[39] In such hegemonic phases, on the one hand international law finds a powerful ally for lending force to some of its provisions. But on the other hand it is weakened by this all-too-awkward 'big brother'. The development of the law becomes haphazard and tends to be one-sided. Multilateralism regresses, unilateralism progresses. Small States are increasingly dissatisfied with the unilateralist influences imposed on the law. The definition of 'internal affairs' tends to shift, interventionism increases. Some vertical or supranational elements tend to be imported into the legal body through the back door, disguised under the mantle of hegemony. The pressure towards legal conformity increases. Equal sovereignty tends, at least *de facto*, to be carved out by a significant number of ill-defined inroads. Overall, international law does not necessarily atrophy in these periods, but its content does change. The second half of the nineteenth century and the last decade of the twentieth century were phases of progress of international law, albeit that they were also marked by the presence of hegemonic tendencies. Over the last 20 years we have seen the decisive breakthrough of international criminal law and the creation of the International Criminal Court by the Rome Statute of 1998—against the wishes of the hegemon.[40]

4. *Tensions notwithstanding the existence of general solidarities*. Political tensions inhibiting the development of the law must not perforce be viewed in the context of general tensions. Among some States there may be a degree of cultural and social solidarity stemming from common religious, linguistic or historic ties, and at the same time an absence of common political interests. The Republics of Central America, at the beginning of the twentieth century, provide a good example. Separating from Spain in 1820–21, in 1824 they formed a federation, which lasted for 14 years and was dissolved in 1838. The common executive had been weak and the Senate was impotent. However, notwithstanding continual personal quarrels, revolutionary movements and boundary disputes, these republics sought other ways to reunite. The idea of a unification through law, ie a common court of justice, also blossomed. The Central-American Court of Justice was inaugurated in 1908. It was quickly caught up in the tentacles of political disputes linked to trans-boundary revolutionary movements. Called to judge highly political affairs, it fell into

[39] M Byers and G Nolte (eds), *United States Hegemony and the Foundations of International Law* (Cambridge, 2003); G Lhommeau, *Le droit international à l'épreuve de la puissance américaine* (Paris, 2005); IW Zartman (ed), *Imbalance of Power: US Hegemony and International Order* (Boulder, 2009). See also I Clark, *Hegemony in International Society* (Oxford, 2011).

[40] See, eg, A Cassese, *International Criminal Law* (Oxford, 2003).

disrepute and ceased to exist in 1918.[41] This experience shows that political tensions may lurk behind factors of solidarity.

5. *Tensions surrounding a particular subject matter.* Political tensions may also surround some specific subject matters, where concurrent interests and ideologies diverge too much to permit legal conciliation. This was the case, for example, with regard to the minimum or national standards for the treatment of aliens at the beginning of the twentieth century; diplomatic protection as a means of intervention in internal affairs; membership of the UN during the hottest years of the Cold War; expropriations and nationalisations in the 1960s and 1970s; the opening of multilateral treaties to 'all States' at the time of elaboration of the VCLT of 1969, etc. All these issues were highly political at some time in history, and thus resistant to the penetration of legal discipline. But the evolution of international relations finally depoliticised them. They could therefore once more be receptive to legal technique. By the same token, it is probable that the most passionately debated subject matters of our day—eg terrorism, the criminal responsibility of the head of State while in office, disarmament—will follow the same trajectory and become the province of dispassionate legal treatment.

   It can also happen that technical subject matters suddenly acquire a highly political profile, as did, for example, the deep seabed. Neglected for a long time, it suddenly became a matter for intense rivalry as soon as its richness in natural resources was discovered at the end of the 1960s. There was intense debate over whether to allow national exploitation (freedom of the high seas), or whether the area needed to be internationalised so that its resources would profit all States and not only the technologically most advanced. From there emerged the concept of 'the common heritage of mankind',[42] but this came to be reduced in scope in the 1990s.[43]

The criteria by which a subject matter is rendered highly political are eminently subjective. The objective importance of a certain question is but an indicator of its political power. The decisive test is what governments consider at any given time to be closely linked to the conservation or development of the essential interests of their collectivity. While the question of even quite substantial damages as reparation for a tort may simply be a technical issue, any reference to a State in a document may trigger a reaction wholly disproportionate to the real importance of the act. The political dimension of a certain question cannot be judged by a notional Martian, landing on Earth swathed in a veil of ignorance, but only by an experienced person with knowledge of history, international relations and human affairs.

[41] See N Politis, *La justice internationale* (Paris, 1924) 139ff. A new Central-American Court was established in 1992: (1995) 34 *ILM* 921ff.

[42] See AC Kiss, 'La notion de patrimoine commun de l'humanité' (1982-II) 175 *RCADI* 99ff.

[43] By the Agreement on the Implementation of Part XI of the Montego Bay Convention: (1994) 33.*ILM* 1309ff.

II. Centrifugal and Centripetal Political Factors

International relations are criss-crossed by centrifugal (State-orientated) and centripetal (community-orientated) elements. As regards the former, these are dominated by the influence of the State and its particular interests. Such factors may be legal (eg the autonomies of the State: domestic jurisdiction, non-intervention in internal affairs, immunities, etc), or mixed legal-political (eg sovereignty) or essentially extra-legal (eg nationalism). There are other, diffuse notions through which power penetrates the law, such as 'effectiveness'[44] or 'practice'.[45] The same is true for the exceptions and derogations allowed by legal regimes, such as the old distinction between legal and political disputes,[46] characterised by the exercise of a certain restraint on the part of international law with regard to the latter.

On the other side, there are pressures on the legal body in favour of collective interests. It stands to reason that these community-orientated institutions (such as international crimes or *jus cogens*) can be abused by States, who will find it easy to cloak their real interests in lofty words. But it would also be excessive to reduce the scope of these institutions to the sole dimension of abuse and hypocrisy.

A. Centrifugal Political Factors: Power at the Service of the State

1. *Sovereignty*

One of the great difficulties with sovereignty is the illusion that lawyers are able to reduce it to purely legal terms. True, sovereignty is a key concept of international law. But it cannot be limited to a general jurisdiction granted by the law and legally sanctioned protection against external intervention. Sovereignty was the point around which the power of the State crystallised at the start of the modern era; and it has retained this orientation ever since. The antagonism between the legal and political aspects of sovereignty came to the fore at the beginning of the twentieth century, when international lawyers attempted to tame it so as to render the concept compatible with the existence of a superior international legal order of cooperation.

Before the consolidation of the modern State, the concept embraced relatively independent human groups vested with the autonomous power to legislate for

[44] See F Couveinhes-Matsumoto, *L'effectivité en droit international* (Brussels, 2014); J Touscoz, *Le principe d'effectivité dans l'ordre international* (Paris, 1964); C de Visscher, *Les effectivités du droit international public* (Paris, 1967); H Krieger, *Das Effektivitätsprinzip im Völkerrecht* (Berlin, 2000).

[45] For treaties, see W Karl, *Vertrag und spätere Praxis im Völkerrecht* (Berlin, 1983). And generally Société française pour le droit international, Colloque de Genève, *La pratique et le droit international* (Paris, 2004).

[46] See, eg, TW Balch, *Legal and Political Questions between Nations* (Philadelphia, 1924).

themselves and to execute these laws.[47] Sovereignty here concentrated on its external aspect, namely independence. The modern conception of the notion, as external independence and internal supreme power, emerged slowly in the Middle Ages from the efforts of kings to escape their nominal subjugation to the universal powers wielded by the Pope and Holy Roman Emperor (*rex imperator in regno suo*). Several lawyers participated in its shaping, for example in France Jean de Paris, Jean Dubois and Jean de Blanot, in Sicily Marino da Caramanico; as did glossators and canon lawyers, who could not ignore that in practice there existed independent princes and entities (eg Azo, Baldus de Ubaldis, Ludwig of Bebenburg or Alanus).[48] At a time when there were no territorial States with exclusivity of jurisdiction, sovereignty designated a bundle of powers. It essentially referred to the ability to render a final decision with regard to the exercise of one or more specific powers. Sovereignty was thus divisible: there was not yet one sovereign, but a series of sovereignties. With the territorialisation of the State in the sixteenth century, the main issue brought under the banner of sovereignty was internal: the elimination of all intermediate powers so as to concentrate the ultimate decision-making power in the hands of one sovereign, be it a king or a republic.[49] The words 'absolute power', used by Bodin, did not signify power untrammelled by law; they referred to independence from any other human will.[50] The limitation imposed on sovereignty by international law was still acknowledged for a long time, as can be seen in Grotius.[51] In the times of absolutism, the notion began its ascent towards a '*summa potestas*', that is, an unrestricted supreme will to do whatever was seen fit. Spinoza, Hegel, Austin and Lasson did much to support such an unlimited concept. Sovereignty here allowed a State to do as it wished; it might wage war or intervene. Moreover, international law, for many authors espousing that conception, was not seen as true law; it was destroyed by sovereignty. It was against this notion of sovereignty that international lawyers reacted at the beginning of the twentieth century. Since then, it has been commonplace for international lawyers to insist on the relativity of the notion. In international law, sovereignty presents itself as a power of ultimate decision within the limits

[47] On the notion of sovereignty and its history, see A Truyol y Serra, 'Souveraineté' in *Archives de philosophie du droit*, vol 35 (Paris, 1990) 313ff. For the Middle Ages, see H Quaritsch, *Souveränität* (Berlin, 1986) 13ff; F Calasso, *I glossatori e la teoria della sovranità* (Florence, 1945). This is a famous passage referring to the notion 'Liber autem populus est is, qui nullius alterius populi potestati est subiectus' (*Dig*, 49, 15, 7, 1).

[48] G Durant, *Speculum iudiciale*, lib IV, pars III, de feudis, 2, 'nam rex Franciae princeps est in regno suo, utpote qui in illo in temporalibus superiorem non recognoscat'. In 1202, in the Decretale 'Per venerabilem', Pope Innocent III said, with regard to the French king, 'rex ipse superiorem in temporalibus minime recognoscat'.

[49] J Bodin, *Les six livres de la République* (1576), book I, ch 8.

[50] Bodin admits several legal limitations to sovereignty: see *ibid*, book I, ch 2, 4 and 8; book VI, ch 4.

[51] *De iure belli ac pacis*, lib I, 3, 6, and 7 ('cujus actus nullius humanae voluntatis arbitrio infirmari potest'). See also F de Vitoria, *Relectio de iure belli*, cap 7 (capacity to govern oneself through one's own laws); F Suarez, *De fide, spe et charitate*, tract III, disp 13 (decision of last resort, no remedy to a superior human tribunal or person); A.Gentili, *De iure belli*, lib I, cap 3 (no superior judge).

of the international legal order. It manifests itself in the first place as the full and exclusive power of the State over its territory. But alongside this legal notion of sovereignty, there remain the political doctrines of the latter. Through 'political sovereignty', States claim unchallengeable liberties to do as they see fit in the pursuit of their own interests. The notion thus remains trapped on a battlefield situated between law and politics. The international lawyer cannot simply ignore these realities. Political sovereignty is not a legal concept, it cannot be squared with the law, but it is nonetheless an existing factor of international life.

When the political objectives pursued by a State can be realised through—or at least without opposition from—international law, legal sovereignty will eclipse political sovereignty. The State can here take the desired measures by producing a valid legal title. Political sovereignty becomes proactive when the political aims and actions of a State cannot be squared with international law as it stands. The conflict can be of limited impact, ie focused on a certain subject matter and taking place between only some States, for example nuclear tests of doubtful legality in a certain area of the Pacific or armed actions orchestrated through irregular bands on the territory of one State. The conflict can also be regular and generalised: this is the case when a State is governed by a regime whose interests and values are far removed from what is generally accepted, eg North Korea. For such utterly isolated States political sovereignty represents an instrument of defiance against legal requirements viewed as the *diktat* of an alien majority, contrary to the local values and interests of the regime. This situation may also occur in the context of violently nationalist governments, as occurred in the Balkans during the 1990s; or in the context of theocratic regimes, as in Iran in the 1980s or the Taliban's Afghanistan at the end of the 1990s (especially with regard to human rights questions); or in the context of totalitarian governments, as was the case under the communist regimes; or, lastly, in the context of regimes pushed to defend an isolated position, as in the case of Israel with regard to the occupied territories (only the unfaltering backing of the US allows Israel to go on with its policies). In such cases, an inflated notion of 'internal affairs' is used as a shield against any type of external pressure. It stands to reason that the legal notion of sovereignty is not at stake here; neither is the point concentrated on the legal notion of 'internal affairs'. Neither concept is legally affected by the existence of, say, human rights obligations embodied in a treaty. The notions of sovereignty or internal affairs are here rather used to carve out a non-legal exception or allowance. International law is thereby recused: sovereignty is used as a basis to invoke liberties contrary to the law. This notion reflects the reasons of power, which cannot be squared with the law. The use of legal arguments against these claims will in most cases be of limited value: the problem is not a legal one; it is primarily political. It would manifestly be otiose to ignore these aspects; after all States are bearers of vital interests and of a consciousness of national destiny. Overall, it is perfectly proper for certain actors (eg judges) to reject such illegal arguments. For the observer of international relations, a larger perspective is necessary, one which takes account of the whole picture. The truly searching perspective must constantly employ two lenses, scrutinising both the legal and the political elements. As has been aptly said, 'The fundamental difficulty of subjecting States to the rule of law is that States possess power.'[52]

There are also situations where legal sovereignty later takes its revenge on political sovereignty. The establishment of egoistic practices covered by the flag of equal sovereignty and liberty will in many cases be conducive to conflicts and disputes. These conflicts, situated on the policy level, can quickly become acrimonious. When these situations last for some time, they result in pressure for harmonisation of the practices according to criteria of reasonableness, justice and regulation. Incessant conflicts put in jeopardy the pursuit of State activities and increase their cost. This is the moment for the return of international law: it is prayed in aid to blunt the sharp edges of 'political sovereignty' in view of the incompressible needs due to life in common. Thus, from a diachronic perspective, the claims of political sovereignty often precede the law; and the latter operates to harmonise competences at a later time. The point is that the one leads back to the other; the freedom conquered under the one finally needs to be brought under the control of the empire of the second. Some examples follow.

A good illustration of the conflicts that may flow from unbridled political sovereignties can be found in the *Casablanca Deserters* case of 1909.[53] The origin of the conflict was rooted in an incident occurring at Casablanca between the French military authorities and the German consular authorities. Six deserters from the French Foreign Legion (*Légion étrangère*), among whom were three Germans, had been escorted by a German official to a ship bound for Hamburg. At the port, they were recognised by French soldiers and arrested. When the prisoners attempted to flee, a violent altercation ensued involving the French soldiers and a German consular employee. Germany demanded the liberation of the prisoners and an apology from the French authorities for the impairment of the prestige of its consular authorities. France refused. The incident was objectively of limited proportions and importance, but as soon as the news of its occurrence spread, a grave conflict between the two States erupted. It involved two opposing exercises of sovereignty (military versus consular authorities) in a domain where international law contained no clear rules on the priority of the one over the other. Moreover, the incident took place in Morocco, where the relationships between both States were already heavily strained. As Politis acutely observed, 'In both States the chauvinistic press inflated the debate … Public opinion, ill-informed

[52] JL Brierly, *The Law of Nations*, 6th edn (Oxford, 1963) 48. Political sovereignty may predominate in areas of vital interests, or in questions where the law remains vague and populated only by some broad and discretionary principles. In the latter context, political sovereignty does not necessarily oppose the law; it merely penetrates where there is no precise legal rule and fills the gap. By doing so, it may nevertheless effectively resist the unfolding of the law within a given subject matter.

[53] *Casablanca Deserters*, XI *RIAA* 126ff. On this case, from the perspective interesting us here, see N Politis, *La justice internationale* (Paris, 1924) 117ff.

and prone to exaggeration, was subject to blind rages and allowed free rein to vent its passions'.[54] The conflict between these two sovereignties not being sufficiently regulated by the law (and being thus of political nature) escalated to the verge of war. Finally, the tension was diminished through an arbitral proceeding. Its diplomatic undertones were more important than the strict application of international law—which was in any case of little help in view of its gaps. The arbitrators created new contextual legal rules for the resolution of the dispute. The law thus tempered the excesses of political sovereignty.

Another example of tensions created by the exercise of 'political sovereignty', which were later calmed by the emergence of international law rules to harmonise the conflicting claims, can be found in connection with the Harmon Doctrine.[55] This notorious doctrine was originally supported by the US, and also by India. It held that each riparian State on an international river was entirely free to adopt such measures as were considered necessary on that part of the waterway traversing its territory, even to the extent of diverting the waters of an international waterway so that the flow was disrupted further downstream. The river and its resources were thus a domain of liberty set apart from legal rules. Each State here exercised its 'political sovereignty' and legal freedom. It stands to reason that each State also had to accept the consequences of the exercise of this freedom by other riparian States, notwithstanding the amount of damage caused. The activities of the States involved inevitably produce frictions and tensions. This rendered impossible any rational exploitation of a waterway. Consequently, in the end the doctrine operated to the detriment of all States. There thus came a time for a paradigm change. Rivers were to be considered a common resource, where a certain degree of harmonisation of the concurrent jurisdictions was to be accepted for the benefit of all the riparian States. The liberties of the one were then put into the balance with the liberties of the other, according to criteria of reasonableness and justice. There would follow a regime of mutual balancing and limitation of jurisdictions, the main rules of which were the equality of riparian States, the duty to abstain from causing significant damage to other riparian States, some equitable sharing of resources, obligations such as mutual consultation, negotiation and information, an obligation to preserve the resources and the natural environment of the river, etc. This evolution reached its height with the New York Convention on International Waterways of 1997.[56] Unlimited sovereignty was thus transformed into an ensemble of rationally limited and distributed jurisdictions

[54] Politis, above n 53, 118–19, our translation.

[55] On this doctrine, see, eg, E Jiménez de Aréchaga, 'International Law in the Past Third of a Century' (1978-I) 159 *RCADI* 188ff.

[56] (1997) 36 *ILM* 700ff. For the older law of rivers, see F Berber, *Rivers in International Law* (London, 1959). For the 1997 Convention, see L Caflisch, 'La Convention du 21 mai 1997 sur l'utilisation des cours d'eau internationaux à des fins autres que la navigation' (1997) 43 *AFDI* 751ff; SC McCaffrey and M Sinjela, 'The 1997 United Nations Convention on International Watercourses' (1998) 92 *AJIL* 97ff; SC McCaffrey, *The Law of International Watercourses*, 2nd edn (Oxford, 2007).

governed by international law. In short, political sovereignty had, at least partially, been transformed into legal sovereignty.

2. *Nationalism*

Nationalism is not a legal notion, yet it has an extremely important impact on international law. It has various forms and shades, ranging from steadfast isolationism to aggressive unilateralism. It is rooted in the more or less extreme attribute of preferring the national interests of one State over even the most elementary ones of other nations. Its rallying cry is 'right or wrong, my country'. It can thus be seen that nationalism orientates power towards particularism, to the detriment of elementary requirements of life in common. The effect of nationalism on international relations is nevertheless not uniform; it depends on the social and political contexts. Thus, nationalistic tendencies can present themselves as a factors of order and stability as much as factors of disorder and tension.

The concept of nationalities was a progressive idea of the nineteenth century. It allowed the particularistic division of collectivities to be overcome, and greater political unities to be brought together within the nation State. This was the case, for example, in Italy and Germany. Nationalism here had been an ordering factor: it had a centripetal orientation, aiming towards consolidation and the centralisation of power. In the twentieth century, however, it quickly developed into a factor of regression. Its tendency was now to consider itself as the ultimate answer to the distribution of power, and thus to resist any attempt to reduce the anarchy *between* States as it had done *within* States. It therefore presented itself as one of the main centrifugal factors checking any advance of the international community. Nationalism fragmented political power, notably in its irredentist form, with 360-degree secessionism and micro-nationalism. It also led to a particular conception of power, worshipped for itself. Consequently it ushered in totalitarian regimes, where the collective national cause greatly outweighed the freedom of individuals.

In the following paragraphs, only this aggressive and centrifugal form of nationalism will be the subject of analysis. The natural attachment of a person to his or her State of origin, its culture and its self-determination will not be discussed. Aggressive nationalism, for its part, is based on the conception that one's own nation is an absolute; it is as if it were alone in the world. This myth[57] of the absolute 'I' is based on a one-sided and complaisant interpretation of history, garnished with a certain unilateral 'manifest destiny'. Aggressiveness is its lifeblood and its rule of conduct. It is the fiercest enemy of international organisation and of peace movements. It is also characterised by its contempt for human values. Not only is it discriminatory with regard to nationality and origin, but its maxim tends to be that the nation is all and the individual nothing, or, more precisely, that the individual realises

[57] That there are often mythical components in nationalistic conceptions is a fact noted by many authors. See, eg, D Schindler, 'Contribution à l'étude des facteurs sociologiques et psychologiques du droit international' (1933-IV) 46 *RCADI* 78.

himself only in serving the former. This type of nationalism is therefore mostly bellicose,[58] totalitarian and military, aspiring to isolation and autarky.

What are the consequences of this sort of nationalism on (international) law? The relationship between nationalism and law is already strained. The law is essentially based on rational principles, with equality of treatment at its core;[59] nationalism is essentially irrational and exalts the solipsistic 'I'. From there flows an almost irreducible tension with the law: the radical 'I' of unilateralism is opposed to legal reciprocity, the singularity of each unit to the rule for social interaction. Reason indicates that if a right is claimed for 'me', I must also concede it to others; but nationalistic feeling cannot concede equal rights to its many enemies. It thus contravenes a rule that intellect, but not the heart, considers unimpeachable: equality and reciprocity. Moreover, narcissistic infantilism takes the place of rational reciprocity.[60] Observation of nationalism in practice shows exactly this: nationalistic thinking constantly claims exceptions for its own nation (justified by some special mission, its manifest destiny, the fact of being chosen by God, etc). It stands to reason that such a nation cannot concede to others the right to attack it with the same aggressiveness as it attacks others, to claim territories from it as it claims territories from others, to insult it as it insults others, etc. On the contrary, it will condemn the scandalous attitudes of the other while concealing its own identical conduct. To paraphrase a famous saying, it looks closely into the eye of its brother but fails to look into its own.[61] Thus, it is no surprise that international facts are judged quite differently according to who is involved. Crimes against humanity are denounced or justified, the persons involved in them described as devils or heroes according to which side they support: my own men are heroes, those of the other side are criminals. This was shown in all its full horror in the Yugoslav Wars of the 1990s. Neither Serbs, nor Croats nor Albanians demonstrated any capacity for dispassionate equal treatment, each accusing the others and excusing itself—and this in the domain of crimes against humanity, presented in legal doctrine as being at the core of universal values shared by all! Another, older example, can be found in the Leipzig Trials after World War I, in the context of the *Llandovery Castle* case (1921).[62] German military personnel had been accused and convicted on the evidence of sinking a ship carrying British shipwrecked military personnel, all of whom died. As soon as the accused were convicted, a mass of persons who had

[58] Europe was marked by nationalism from 1900–45. This led to two World Wars. Nationalism also explains the wars in the Balkans during the 1990s.

[59] See G Fassò, *La legge della ragione* (Bologne, 1964) (reprinted at Giuffrè, Milan, 1999).

[60] On the characteristics of the extreme right, see A Chebel d'Appolonia, *L'extrême droite en France, De Maurras à Le Pen* (Paris, 1996) 32ff. They include: hatred of the other, the exaltation of violence and war, contempt for democracy and Parliamentarism, adhesion to military dictatorships and strong leaders, contempt for intellectualism and for abstract reason, racial prejudices, fear of decadence leading to a search for a return to national values, a tendency to verbal excesses, hostility towards moderate religion, a claim to absolute (own) truth, etc.

[61] Luke 6:41–42.

[62] *Llandovery Castle* (1922) 16 *AJIL* 708. On the Leipzig trials, see C Mullins, *The Leipzig Trials: An Account of the War Criminals' Trials and a Study of German Mentality* (London, 1921).

attended the trial rushed to acclaim them as German heroes. The British observers had to be protected against lynching. Propaganda, nationalism and the sufferings of the German people during the war could to some extent explain this attitude, but only to some extent.

Overall, a profound moral schizophrenia follows:[63] there is on the one hand a private morality, valid between ordinary citizens and rooted in the usual solid principles of faithfulness; and on the other hand there is a public morality, prevailing between public collectivities, tainted by inversions and perversions. It is obvious that killing is prohibited in the former case; but it is not so obvious that it should be prohibited in the latter. This is the reason why the Nazis could be caring fathers for their and their fellows' children, and at the same time actively engage in the deportation of other children.

According to a general rule of nature, the aggressiveness of one leads to the increased aggressiveness of the other. Thus, the constant danger is that the tensions between States may lead to armed conflict. At the same time, any type of compromise and conciliation is decried in nationalistic circles as treason and weakness; there are calls to overthrow those governments that engage in such behaviour. Even modest incidents tend to become inflamed. The *Casablanca Deserters* example[64] is typical of this state of affairs. National honour is at stake at every point. The result is an increase in the number of hostile relationships. Innumerable States and persons are constantly suspected or accused of being 'hostile' to the nation; evidence for this is found everywhere. This attitude is wrapped up in a psychosis. The overall result is that international society remains not only in a state of coordination (which is not curable), but also in a poisoned state of anarchy, fuelled by acrimony, aggression and conflict. Particular interests prevail over any general interest. International relations remain under the sway of force. Force and law are to some extent mutually exclusive, in the sense that the predominance of the one signifies the demise of the other.

Moreover, by its absolute nature nationalism leads to the integral politicisation of international relations. All matters become matters of high politics; vital interests of the nation are seen everywhere. Nationalism leads to a doctrine of 'all-politics'. Every interest of the State—even if objectively minor—is linked to its honour and prestige, and therefore becomes a vital interest. Thus, no dispute is truly justiciable. It cannot present that degree of de-politicisation which allows the application of impersonal legal rules. In the modern interdependent world, with it urgent common concerns, nationalism presents clear and significant dangers. It inhibits international confidence and agreements, renders impossible the resolution of common issues and blockades the development of international law.[65]

[63] T Ruyssen, *La société internationale* (Paris, 1950) 163.

[64] Above n 53.

[65] See the strong words of Politis, considering excessive nationalism as an international disease: N Politis, *La morale internationale* (Neuchâtel, 1943) 78–79. See also M Bourquin, *Vers une nouvelle Société des Nations* (Neuchâtel, 1945) 16; E Claparède, *Morale et politique, ou Les vacances de la probité* (Neuchâtel, 1947) 109–10.

As has been aptly said, 'At the present time nationalism is the chief obstacle to international comity and peace. It may be a myth …, but, if so, it is an extraordinarily potent myth …, one which inspires widespread popular action quite at variance with ideals of human cooperation.'[66] The importance of international confidence-building for improving the content of international law cannot be over-emphasised. When a certain confidence reigns, solutions to even complex problems can be found quickly; when there is no confidence, there is no possible progress and no possible solution. There is hardly any doctrine less conducive to international confidence-building than nationalism.

The future and force of the modern international law of cooperation will depend heavily on the fortunes of nationalism. The stronger the latter, the greater the likelihood of violent anarchy throughout the world; the weaker the latter, the greater the prospects for conciliation and progress in the legal order.

3. *Effectiveness*

Each legal order tries to conciliate to varying degrees the established law and the revisionist fact, that is, '*ex injuria jus non oritur*' and '*ex facto oritur jus*'. This tension between law and power, between the ideal and reality, is constant. It is the basis of law's life. There is not always a tension between the two levels: the fact can also concur in consolidating the law.[67] However, the fact may also attempt to establish a new order of things, requiring, more or less brutally, adaptation of the law.[68] Effectiveness and validity are the two fundamental poles inherent in the rule of law. Each is constitutive of its own spectrum and is not simply engaged in a struggle between a legal (validity) and an extra-legal (effectiveness) element. The error of normativistic schools is to consider only the dimension of formal validity; the mistake of realist schools is to take account only of the dimension of effectiveness.

The linking of the law to these two dimensions flows from certain cardinal legal concepts: legal certainty and the integrity of the positive law. The first is sometimes sustained by effectiveness. This concept diminishes the gulf between what irremediably 'is' and what 'ought to be' according to the norm. The second—integrity of the law—inhibits the recognition of the violation of the law as creative of new titles *contra legem*. The dilemma is that the law cannot eternally ignore the fact established against its prescription. If it did so, it would lose its impact on reality and fail to exercise its pacific mission. But the law cannot altogether systematically defer to the established fact. It would here lose its normative integrity and create an incentive to illegality. To the Scylla of an unreal obligation responds the Charybdis of a reality having become an end in itself. The conciliation between both branches must occur through *legal* doctrines allowing the fact to be taken into account, in order to insert it to some extent into the legal order. Facts alone

[66] CJH Hayes, 'Nationalism' (1941) 369 *International Conciliation* 227.

[67] See C de Visscher, *Les effectivités du droit international public* (Paris, 1967) 13ff, 'effectivités menées à terme'.

[68] *ibid*, 'effectivités en action'.

cannot modify the law; they need some translation into legal categories so as to become legal facts. The relevant legal norms transform effectiveness into validity. In international law, these transforming norms are mainly recognition, acquiescence and prescription. There is a series of further norms referring to effectiveness, for example in the context of the effective blockade of coasts,[69] of effective belligerent occupation,[70] of effective and opposable nationality,[71] etc. A discussion of these matters will follow below.

The issue of effectiveness within the international legal order thus involves the quest for a doctrine of *legal* effectiveness. However, not unlike sovereignty, effectiveness also has some aspects that resist smooth integration into the legal order. It also concerns cases where the fact maintains pressure on the law to fit its own requirements. The issue then is amendment of the law to accommodate the facts created on the ground. To legal effectiveness we must therefore join analysis of political effectiveness.

In international law, where the legal injunction is situated in an environment of decentralised power, the traditional stance was to defer to effectiveness. As we have already seen, in international law there are many individualised and context-related rules. Moreover, the weakness of institutional and executory mechanisms tends to augment the role of forces consolidating the accomplished fact. The same can be said as regards the existence of many gaps and uncertainties within the law, which open the gates to factual arguments and inroads; and also of the important role of politics and power. As was explained in the *Grisbadarna* case of 1909, in international law one should refrain from modifying a state of affairs if it has existed for a long time (*quieta non movere*).[72] The claim has therefore been advanced that effectiveness is the great principle of international law.[73] In any event, by the weight it attaches to facts, effectiveness presents itself as an instrument of consolidation of politics into law.

Forces for the consolidation of facts exist in many areas of international law:[74] customary law as an expression of effective practice; desuetude as the expression of non-practice; the so-called objective regimes within the law of treaties; the birth of the State as a question of fact; acquisitive prescription and acquisition of territory though the *corpus* requirement; the occupation of *terrae nullius*; historical rights over spaces; the principle of the stability of effective boundaries; effective control over territory for the duties to exercise a certain jurisdiction and to grant certain rights (belligerent occupation, human rights guarantees); the effective blockade of coasts; effective nationality and flags of ships; the *de facto* organ in the

[69] London Declaration on Naval Warfare (1909), Arts 1ff. See D Schindler and J Toman, *The Laws of Armed Conflict* (Leiden and Boston, 2004) 1111ff.

[70] Art 42 of the Hague Regulations, 1907. See Schindler and Toman, above n 69, 55ff.

[71] *Nottebohm* [1955] ICJ Rep 23.

[72] *Grisbadarna*, XI *RIAA* 161.

[73] E Giraud, 'Le droit international public et la politique' (1963-III) 110 *RCADI* 691.

[74] See the impressive study by F Couveinhes-Matsumoto, *L'effectivité en droit international* (Brussels, 2014).

domain of international responsibility;[75] the *forum prorogatum* as effective subjection to a competence, etc. The militancy of effectiveness is traditionally at its greatest in the domain of the use of force, where there is pressure to recognise illegal conquests—a fact witnessed most recently in the annexation of Crimea (2014). In the era of the UN Charter, reinforcement of the normativity has taken place in this domain through the doctrine of non-recognition of situations created by the illegal use of force or based on a violation of the rights of self-determination.[76] This rule was recalled by the arbitrator in the *Region of Brcko* case (1997): the rule applies 'where an entity seeks, through aggression in violation of international law [*sic*], to acquire territory with the aim of effecting a change in sovereignty over that territory'.[77] Thus, under UN Charter law aggressive acquisitions of territory cannot be cured, at least so long as the States assembled continue to uphold the opposition.

There follow some examples of the influence of facts on the law.

i. Facts Disciplined by Legal Norms: Effective Occupation of Territory

Occupation designates here the act of appropriation by a State of land without a master. A territory is legally without a master when it is not subject to the sovereignty of a State. The issue turns around the now mainly historical phenomenon of the discovery of new lands. For a long time,[78] the acquisition of territorial sovereignty was considered as a legal act more than as a fact. At the end of the Middle Ages the papacy—on the basis of a supposed gift by the Emperor Constantine (ca 285 CE–337 CE)—claimed to possess the right to distribute uninhabited lands, or land inhabited by pagans, to Christian rulers. From there flowed the Papal Bulls *Dum diversas* (Nicolas I, 1452), *Romanus Pontifex* (Nicolas I, 1455), *Inter caetera* (Callixtus III, 1456) and *Inter caetera* (Alexander VI, 1493).

With the schism of the Christian faith brought about by the Reformation, these titles lost their political and legal weight. Discovery was now considered to confer the main title for territorial acquisition. An effective display of sovereignty was not yet required, since the lands involved were too vast and too far away to allow fully-fledged possession. Towards the middle of the eighteenth century, discovery

[75] On this issue see in particular the studies of P Palchetti, *L'organo di fatto dello Stato nell'illecito internazionale* (Milan, 2007); J Griebel, *Die Zurechnungskategorie der de facto-Organe im Recht der Staatenverantwortlichkeit* (Münster, 2004).

[76] T Christakis, 'L'obligation de non-reconnaissance des situations créées par le recours illicite à la force ou d'autres actes enfreignant des règles fondamentales' in C Tomuschat and JM Thouvenin (eds), *The Fundamental Rules of the International Legal Order* (Leiden/Boston, 2006) 127ff; J Crawford, *The Creation of States in International Law*, 2nd edn (Oxford, 2006) 131ff; J Dugard, *Recognition and the United Nations* (Cambridge, 1987) 13ff.

[77] *Region of Brcko* (1997) 36 *ILM* 422, §77.

[78] See WG Grewe, *The Epochs of International Law* (Berlin/New York, 2000) 229ff, 395ff, 543ff. See also J Fisch, *Die europäische Expansion und das Völkerrecht* (Stuttgart, 1984). For an older contribution, see G Jèze, *Etude théorique et pratique sur l'occupation comme mode d'acquérir les territoires en droit international* (Paris, 1896).

ceded its place to effectiveness as a requirement for acquisition. Discovery was downgraded to conferring an inchoate title, which granted the right to occupation (*jus ad occupationem*). The effective display of governmental functions on the spot (eg police, collection of taxes, adjudication of disputes, etc) created the full title. Thus, Australia was discovered by the Dutch but administrated by England; the latter had the territorial title. Effectiveness progressed at a time when the competition for acquisition of colonial territories was more intense, and when the presence of administrative and military personnel on the spot was much stronger. Certain natural law doctrines strengthened this requirement by holding that lands could not be claimed by formal owners who remained completely inactive but must accrue to those persons effectively working that land.[79] Overall, as can be seen, effectiveness here was entirely incorporated into the legal norm. But the norm simply refers to the fact without altering it. In other words, the norm recognises the result of fierce competition for land and accords title to the most diligent and the most powerful. The political fact comes first; but it is at least ratified by the norm. The law-maker provided for this 'law of the jungle'. The impact of the fact on the norm is thus virtually unlimited; but it took place fully within the four corners of the law as it stood at the time.

ii. Facts Leading to an Adjustment of Legal Competences: Acquisitive Prescription

The term 'prescription' will here be understood in the broad sense of designating the consolidation of a title by the continuous, pacific and uncontested exercise of territorial jurisdiction over time, against which the formal owner registers no protest ('*nec clam, nec vi, nec precario*').[80] Every legal order contains some instrument whereby a new title, accompanied by the loss of a previous title, is conferred on a subject who is not able to claim formal title but who has behaved as the owner over a long period of time without disruption.[81] This transfer is based on the prolonged inactivity of the formal owner, who has failed to claim his or her rights. Equity and the stability of legal relations both support the recognition of a new title. Prescription validates a state of affairs even if it is contrary to the law. In contradistinction to occupation, here there exist prior adverse legal titles of the formal but inactive owner; these titles are displaced by the new situation.[82] Subjective good faith is not required in the process; the possessor may well know that he or she does not have perfect title.[83]

[79] See, eg, E de Vattel, *Le droit des gens* (1756), book II, ch XI, § 141.

[80] For further details and literature see R Kolb, 'La prescription acquisitive en droit international public' in Université de Neuchâtel (ed), *Le temps et le droit* (Basle, 2008) 149ff.

[81] *Se ut dominus gerere.*

[82] Exceptionally a prescriptive title can be used by the lawful owner in immemorial possession so as not to have to produce evidence of the formal title, if that is difficult to obtain. Prescription here confirms the title.

[83] See, eg, N Politis, *La morale internationale* (Neuchâtel, 1943) 123.

Certain authors[84] have developed the idea that acquisitive prescription is a process founded exclusively on the effectiveness of possession, regardless of the reaction of the formal title-holder (acquiescence, renunciation, recognition). This has led to fierce debate.[85] In practice, effectiveness does not have the same weight here as it has in matters of occupation (above). In the context of occupation, the fact is not in opposition to a pre-existing legal title. Prescription, on the other hand, leads to the loss of an existing title. It is therefore understandable that prescription as a legal mechanism is founded on a series of conditions, which must be fulfilled before the old title disappears and the new one is established. Far from being subjected to the pressure of subversive facts, the law imposes on these facts its own conditions of validity. The law first takes account of prolonged possession. But this is not taken only as a fact; it is also seen as a situation creating equities, legitimate expectations and legal security. The effectiveness of possession is therefore also taken into account in view of certain paramount legal values. Secondly, the new title cannot be established if the formal title-holder protests (in the event of *erga omnes* spaces, as the high seas, the right to protest is generalised). The new title emerges because the culpable inactivity of the title-holder can in all good faith only mean that he or she renounces sovereignty over these spaces, or at least does not deserve legal protection. There is thus a double sanction, that of a positive fact (prolonged possession) and that of a negative fact (renunciation or inactivity). The law adds to the facts some legal considerations justifying transfer of the title. Overall, prescription concerns a fact tamed and disciplined by the law.[86]

iii. Facts Fully Mastered by the Law: Colonial *Effectivités*

Effectiveness has in this context an auxiliary role devoted to the proper application of the legal norm. The rule on 'colonial *effectivités*' requires account to be taken of the conduct of colonial administrative authorities as evidence of the effective exercise of territorial jurisdiction.[87] When the *uti possidetis* boundary is not clear, these *effectivités* can provide a decisive criterion for fixing the boundary. The *effectivités* are thus a tool for interpreting and filling gaps in the formal title. However, they cannot brush aside a formal title. The law refuses to sanction purely unilateral

[84] J Touscoz, *Le principe d'effectivité dans l'ordre international* (Paris, 1964) 148ff, 231–32; G Dahm, *Völkerrecht*, vol I (Stuttgart, 1958) 588ff; J Charpentier, *La reconnaissance internationale et l'évolution du droit des gens* (Paris, 1956) 157–58. Others have attempted to bring back the notion of prescription to a legal act (but this makes the notion superfluous): W Wengler, *Völkerrecht*, vol II (Berlin, 1964) 981, fn 3.

[85] M Kohen, *Possession contestée et souveraineté territoriale* (Paris, 1997) 17ff, rejecting the whole notion of acquisitive prescription.

[86] Issues of prescription may also arise in the context of delimitation involving some attribution of land. See, eg, *Kasikili/Sedudu Island (Botswana/Namibia)* [1999] ICJ Rep 1101, §90ff. See also *Georgia v South Carolina* (1990) 91 *ILR* 439, 451 (US Supreme Court), concerning the Savannah River.

[87] See M Kohen, *Possession contestée et souveraineté territoriale* (Paris, 1997) 471ff; LI Sanchez Rodriguez, 'L'*uti possidetis* et les effectivités dans les contentieux territoriaux et frontaliers' (1997) 263 *RCADI* 149ff.

conduct when set up in opposition to an existing and clear title. The Chamber of the ICJ in the *Frontier Dispute* between Burkina Faso and Mali (1986) was very clear on this:

> Where the act corresponds exactly to law, where effective administration is additional to the *uti possidetis juris*, the role of *effectivité* is to confirm the existence of the right derived from a legal title. Where the act does not correspond to the law, where the territory which is the subject of the dispute is effectively administered by a State other than the one possessing the legal title, preference should be given to the holder of the title. In the event that the *effectivité* does not co-exist with any legal title, it must invariably be taken into consideration. Finally, there are cases where the legal title is not capable of showing exactly the territorial expanse to which it relates. The *effectivités* can then play an essential role in showing how the title is interpreted in practice.[88]

As can be seen, law and fact are communicating: the smaller the impact of the law (eg because of the non-existence or obscurity of legal title), the greater the role of fact and vice versa. Unlike the situation regarding occupation, the law does not view fact as a blank cheque; and unlike the situation as regards prescription, fact here cannot be set up in opposition to a formal title. The *effectivités* are certainly a factor impacting on the law, but this process is fully encapsulated within the applicable legal rules.

iv. Facts Irreducible to the Law: The Conception of an Absolute Prescription

The conflict between political facts and law is pushed to its extreme in those areas where effectiveness conceives of itself as liberated from the constraints of law. The issue has been addressed in the context of the violent transfer or occupation of territory. If the reaction of third States does not lead to the dislodging of the aggressor or to a war defeating the latter, the territorial situation brought about by force will continue. Such occupations occurred more than once in the twentieth century. But, contrary to what has been claimed by some, in the long run the law was not always defeated. It is true that the return to 'legality' was due to a transformation of the historical or political situation, and also to a shift in power relations, more than to a pure sanction imposed by the law. But the fact remains that the requirements of the law triumphed in a series of cases, even if this did not occur through legal procedures. We might recall several situations involving unlawful uses of force or unlawful occupation: Manchukuo (1932), Leticia (1933); Abyssinia (1935); the annexations of Austria, Czechoslovakia and Albania (1938–39); the annexation of the Baltic States (1940); Israeli occupied territories (1948, 1967, 1973); Katanga (1960); Goa (1961); Southern Rhodesia (1965); Namibia (1966); Biafra (1967); the Turkish Republic of Northern Cyprus (1974); Transkei,

[88] *Frontier Dispute (Burkina Faso/Mali)* [1986] ICJ Rep 586, §63. See also *Territorial, Insular and Maritime Dispute (El Salvador/Honduras)* [1992] ICJ Rep 408, 418–19, 436.

Bophuthatsawana, Venda and Ciskei (1976–81); Kuwait (1990); Bosnia (1992–95); Crimea (2014), etc.[89]

When faced with these forced territorial changes, the law is not powerless. Acquisitive prescription is not able to be relied upon, since the usurpation of territorial rights will be met with fierce and prolonged protest by the aggrieved State. Third States are obliged to refuse to recognise situations created by the unlawful use of force or established against the right of self-determination of peoples.[90] Sanctions can be imposed on the usurper at the collective level (eg Security Council) or at the individual State level (countermeasures). But the efficacy of these will depend on the determination of the community of States to confront the aggressor, and in particular on the conduct of the Great Powers. There will always be voices and arguments in favour of a more conciliatory attitude towards the aggressor, as the Ukraine crisis has shown once more (2014–date). The more time passes, the more the momentum of legality may diminish; other problems will dominate the agenda; *Realpolitik* may take over. The reactions to the unlawful fact, such as non-recognition, will tend to become diluted. Thus, it may happen that a particular situation is finally established without any hope for a return to the legal *status quo ante*. This is a hard case, known by all legal orders. Power seems to enjoy one of its greatest victories. The law, for its part, is summoned to adapt to the new facts so as not to completely divorce itself from the realities that it ought to regulate. If at all, such brutal penetration by effectiveness into the legal order would be recognised only when inevitable; it would then have to be validated by the community of States in some collective act.[91]

It is nevertheless erroneous to think that the law will simply accept defeat and abandon the fight against the diktat of insolent effectiveness. The law seeks allies in the political world in order to maintain the threat of a possible response to effectiveness. It awaits the opportunity to take its revenge. Thus, after 1940, the annexation of the Baltic States might have seemed irreversible, all the more so since it was the deed of a Great Power. Recognitions *de facto* were progressively

[89] On many of these situations, see R Kolb, 'La maxime "nemo ex propria turpitudine commodum capere potest" (Nul ne peut profiter de son propre tort) en droit international public' (2000) 33 *RBDI* 120, with many references.

[90] See Art 41, §2 of the Articles on State Responsibility, UNGA Resolution 56/83, 2001. The doctrine of non-recognition has a normative effect, it is contra-factual: its meaning is not to change the fact but to impede the fact in producing certain legal effects. The argument that the doctrine is 'ineffective', ie does not change the actual state of affairs, is thus ill-conceived (it is made, eg, in J Verhoeven, *La reconnaissance international dans la pratique contemporaine* (Paris, 1975) 285ff, 308ff, 611, 767ff, 841; R Bierzanek, 'La non-reconnaissance et le droit international contemporain' (1962) 8 *AFDI* 135). The position is correctly stated by various authors, eg, L Oppenheim and H Lauterpacht, *International Law*, vol I, 8th edn (London, 1955) 145.

[91] L Oppenheim, *International Law*, vol I, 9th edn (R Jennings and A Watts (eds), London, 1992) 186, on the necessity to give priority to the fact in the long term. On the capacity of the community of States to cure the illegality by a change of general legal opinion, see, eg, H Lauterpacht, *Recognition in International Law* (Cambridge, 1947) 429, 'There remains the possibility of curing the invalidity of the results of the unlawful conduct by recognition on the part of States proceeding, as it were, as organs of the international community'; and H Krieger, *Das Effektivitätsprinzip im Völkerrecht* (Berlin, 2000) 254–55.

turned into recognitions *de jure*. But the defect of illegality and the will to achieve independence persisted. In 1991, the three republics were independent once more. The victory of the law was even pushed as far as proclaiming the fiction—a true kick up the backside of arrogant effectiveness—that the three States had legally never ceased to exist as independent entities.[92] The modern principles of self-determination, nationalist feeling and sovereign independence have made it more difficult for occupiers and aggressors to cure the illegal territorial situation. Brutal effectiveness is thus to some extent rebuffed, while the law silently and slightly progresses.

4. *The Problem of Practice in International Law*

Only in international law is the practice of the subjects so important in its impact on the normative system. Action and inaction as material facts contemplated by legal norms may even sometimes outweigh in importance the formal law-creating agencies. In all its main sources, international law presents a characteristic weakness as regards the formal elements: in customary international law,[93] in general principles of law and even in conventional law. All these sources are to a remarkable extent sustained by the amorphous effectiveness of 'practice'. The practice followed by the parties is essential to the determination of the extent of their rights and obligations. Practice manifests itself in material acts of various types, but also in some legal categories, such as 'subsequent treaty practice', recognition, acquiescence, estoppel, prescription, obsolescence, historical consolidation of titles and so on. All these concepts are entangled in webs of practice or non-practice, ie action and inaction.

Practice also has an important role within institutional international law. The difficulty of formally modifying the constitutive instruments of international organisations (because of the important majorities required and the time-consuming processes) has led to alternative ways of adapting these 'constitutional' instruments to the changing needs of life. Such informal means of adaptation have already functioned to their full extent with regard to the Covenant of the League of Nations.[94] For example: Article 1, §2 of the Covenant was reshaped in practice, in the sense that non-self-governing States and non-democratic States could be admitted to the League (this opened the way for Siam and Abyssinia); Article 16 of the Covenant was weakened by various interpretive resolutions of the Assembly holding, inter alia, that each member State was entitled to qualify for itself the existence or not of a *casus foederis* or *garantiae*. Through practice, the Council constantly gained ground over the Assembly. The right of the League to conclude treaties (*jus*

[92] See the materials in (1990) 94 *RGDIP* 774ff and (1991) 37 *AFDI* 259ff.

[93] We might here also think of the theory of 'spontaneous law' espoused by Ago, which is based on a certain social effectiveness. See R Ago, 'Science juridique et droit international' (1956-II) 90 *RCADI* 946ff. In any event, the concept of customary law largely revolves around the primary concept of practice.

[94] W Schücking, 'Le développement du Pacte de la Société des Nations' (1927-V) 20 *RCADI* 359ff.

tractatus) was permitted in practice, for example in the context of the mandate agreements or the treaty between the League and Switzerland concerning League personnel (1926). Its right to enter into diplomatic relations was also admitted in practice. Consequently, a diplomatic mission was sent by the League to Mossul and the Åland islands. In the UN Charter, one finds the same propensity to effect changes by a subsequent practice informally accepted as law. One might mention the voting procedure in the Security Council (Article 27, §3), where the abstention of a permanent member was not counted as a veto.[95] Similarly, peacekeeping operations, with the specific rules applying to them, were introduced into the Charter in an informal manner.[96] One often speaks tongue in cheek about Chapter VI½ of the Charter, as these operations constituted a sort of hybrid between the peaceful settlement of disputes (Chapter VI) and concrete action taken to maintain and re-establish peace (Chapter VII). Article 42 was also reinterpreted in practice as authorising member States to use force under a sort of 'mandate' of the United Nations.[97] The powers of the General Assembly by virtue of Resolution 377 (V), called 'Uniting for Peace' or 'Dean Acheson', rebalanced the domains of action between the Assembly and the Council.[98] A constitutional practice thus developed, as nowhere in the Charter is the mechanism 'Uniting for Peace' to be found. Article 12, §1 of the Charter, subordinating the General Assembly to the Security Council when the latter organ is seized of a dispute, has also been the object of exceptions and flexible interpretation. The Assembly, indeed, more than once took a position on a crisis, notwithstanding that the Council was still formally seized of the question or even acting upon it.[99] The reach of decolonisation also affected United Nations practice in the 1950s. It modified the Charter in a profound way, notably in Chapter XI relative to non-autonomous territories.[100] A more recent example is a re-evaluation of human rights law, including the 'responsibility to protect' individuals from grave and systematic violations of their physical integrity. Among the aims of the Charter, human rights law has thus clearly gained more weight than it enjoyed at the time of drafting the instrument.[101] Constitutional practice has therefore enriched the Charter in relation to important issues, and not only with respect to specific or subordinate matters.

The need for the adaptation of institutional law according to practice and the needs of time has been acknowledged by the PCIJ and ICJ in a series of

[95] A Zimmermann, 'Article 27' in B Simma et al (eds), *The Charter of the United Nations—A Commentary*, vol I, 3rd edn (Oxford, 2012) 916–17.

[96] M Bothe, 'Peacekeeping', in Simma et al (eds), above n 95, 1171ff.

[97] N Krisch, 'Article 42', in B Simma et al (eds), *The Charter of the United Nations—A Commentary*, vol II, 3rd edn (Oxford, 2012) 1332ff; LA Sicilianos, 'Entre multilatéralisme et unilatéralisme: l'autorisation par le Conseil de sécurité de recourir à la force' (2008) 339 *RCADI* 25ff.

[98] C Tomuschat, 'Uniting for Peace: Ein Rückblick nach 50 Jahren' (2001) 76 *Die Friedens-Warte* 289ff.

[99] Especially since the 1960s: racial policies in South Africa, the situation in Angola, Southern Rhodesia, Tunisia, Cyprus, etc. See E Klein and S Schmahl, 'Article 12' in Simma et al (eds), above n 95, 509ff. There have in most cases been no notable objections to this practice.

[100] See the contributions in Simma et al, above n 95, 1829ff.

[101] E Riedel and JM Arend, 'Article 55(c)', in Simma et al, above n 95, 1568ff.

cases: *Treatment of Polish Citizens at Danzig* (1932; practice of the League Council on questions of national minorities);[102] *International Status of South-West Africa* (resolutions of the Security Council on international mandates);[103] *Reservations to the Genocide Convention* (practice of the League of Nations and UN organs on reservations to multilateral conventions);[104] *Certain Expenses of the United Nations* (practice of the UN on the creation and financing of peacekeeping forces);[105] *Namibia* (effect of abstention from voting in the Security Council of the UN);[106] *Western Sahara* (practice of UN organs with respect to decolonisation),[107] etc. These practices flow from acts and omissions that governments consider necessary in the pursuit of their interests. Consequently, practice is a window through which political considerations find their place at the heart of the formation of international law. The weight of practice in this legal order is a function of the weight of politics therein. To a non-negligible degree, positive international law is but the sum of such contingent attitudes.

Practice has two main types of influence on the law:

1. *Constitutive function*. In the first place, practice creates rights and obligations by the consolidation of regularities transformed into rules. It also fixes the extent of these rights and obligations. This function is particularly visible in the context of the formation of customary international law. The practice can also abrogate certain rules by desuetude, or modify them through subsequent practice. This occurred, for example, when the new category of private acts (*acta jure gestionis*) carved out an exception to the jurisdictional immunity of States, restricted thenceforward to sovereign acts (*acta jure imperii*). These functions of practice are concentrated at the level of the law-creating agencies (sources). For example, the concept of 'innocent passage', as codified in Articles 17 to 26 of the Montego Bay Convention on the Law of the Sea (1982), is the product of a long-standing practice, which finally settled the precise conditions for the exercise of the right.[108] Thus, the passage of foreign ships must be direct, and also continuous (without halt) and expeditious. Submarines must navigate on the surface and hoist their flag. The passage must not impair the peace and security of the coastal State. Practice has progressively determined the categories of activities not compatible with these requirements, eg military exercises or fishing activities. The freedom of passage may

[102] *Treatment of Polish Citizens at Danzig* (1932) PCIJ Series A/B no 44, 39.

[103] *International Status of South-West Africa* [1950] ICJ Rep 134.

[104] *Reservations to the Genocide Convention* [1951] ICJ Rep 25.

[105] *Certain Expenses of the United Nations* [1962] ICJ Rep 173.

[106] *Namibia* [1971] ICJ Rep 22.

[107] *Western Sahara* [1975] ICJ Rep 29.

[108] On innocent passage, see S Slonim, 'The Right of Innocent Passage and the 1958 Geneva Conference on the law of the Sea' (1966) 5 *Columbia Journal of Transnational Law* 96ff; PB Walker, 'What is Innocent Passage?' (1969) 21 *Naval War College Review (Newport)* 53; W Riphagen, 'Le droit de passage inoffensif' in SFDI, *Colloque de Rouen* (Paris, 1984) 190ff; F Ngantcha, *The Right of Innocent Passage and the Evolution of the Law of the Sea* (London, 1990); G Cataldi, *Il passaggio delle navi straniere nel mare territoriale* (Milan, 1990).

be suspended only for reasons of security of the coastal State, on the basis of equality (non-discrimination of flags), temporarily, in specified areas and via notification. Practice has in this area created a balanced regime. The same was not possible as regards the thorny and disputed question of the breadth of the territorial sea. Practice was here utterly divided. At the beginning of the 1960s, 20 States claimed 3 nautical miles, 3 States 4 miles, 14 States 6 miles, 17 States 12 miles and 10 States 200 miles of territorial sea/patrimonial sea.[109] After the adoption of the Montego Bay Convention in 1982, international practice aligned itself to the 12-mile rule. Conversely, as an example of abrogation, we might recall that practice has extinguished a rule in the context of privateering and letters of marque. Privateering had developed since the fifteenth century as an auxiliary means for State enforcement of maritime laws. The frequent abuses by the mandated vessels, engaging in acts of piracy, brought the whole institution into disrepute, especially in the eighteenth and nineteenth centuries.[110] The Declaration of Paris of 1856 thus abolished privateering. Overall, practice has thus played a role in the creation, modification or termination of rules of international law.

2. *Derogative function*. Practice may also play a sort of derogative role. Wherever a legal order is affirmed, it suggests the presence of certain fundamental legal notions indissolubly linked to legal disciplines. Legal consciousness considers these elements as being to some extent of an incompressible nature. No difference of social structure can obliterate the conception of the lawyer holding that the rule of law prevails over the arbitrary, and the legality of the acts at stake prevails over their simple utility. Moreover, the lawyer will cling to the impartiality of the judge (eg the fact that the judge has not been formerly involved in the case), the (mandatory) settlement of disputes, the centralised administration of legal sanctions rather than private justice, the prohibition of gravely anti-social conduct (eg through the doctrine of abuse of rights), the subordination of the use of force to legal proceedings, the loss of a right to vote on a matter where the voter has a personal interest in the outcome, or the nullity of acts tainted with grave unlawfulness.

   Certain difficulties in the realisation of these precepts in international law flow from the horizontal structure of international society. However, many obstacles to the progress of the law in international relations are derived from the political will not to remain subject to these legal requirements. Political facts resist the expansion of the law in order to maintain a greater margin of undisturbed action. The means of resistance is the device of derogative practice. In maintaining many discretionary domains and ill-defined rules, States ensure the permanence of fluctuations and exceptions. Consequently, the

[109] D Bardonnet, 'La largeur de la mer territoriale' (1962) 66 *RGDIP* 34ff.

[110] H Bonfils, *Manuel de droit international public*, 3rd edn (Paris, 1901) 736ff. See also FR Stark, *The Abolition of Privateering and the Declaration of Paris* (New York, 1897); DJ Bederman, 'Privateering' in R Wolfrum, *The Max Planck Encyclopedia of Public International Law*, vol VIII (Oxford, 2012) 475ff.

law cannot fully regulate any matters fraught with such uncertainties. On the shifting and slippery body thus upheld and cherished, the law, with its instruments of objectivity and reciprocity, cannot find an adequate toehold. In these cases, the practice of States is not constitutive of legal obligations. It rather derogates from the most rational state of the law. At the heart of such derogative practices is the wish to keep certain subject matters apart from a series of legal requirements. Those matters are reserved for the domain of political influence. By this action, derogative practice repositions the respective spheres of law and policy: it diminishes the impact of the law and augments the weight of politics; it derogates from the legal idea and is constitutive with regard to political freedom (whereas constitutive practice does exactly the opposite). This derogative practice fuels the 'reserved domains' or exclusive jurisdictions of States. It stands to reason that from a positivistic point of view, the practices described here are not derogative at all: there is no established legal rule from which derogation is possible; derogation occurs only with respect to what the law 'ought to be', which is a problem of natural law. But there remains the fact that the law is intimately linked to a question of consciousness: when we think of a legal order, we tend to include certain things that we expect to be there; these are linked to the very concept of law in our consciousness. These 'ideal' factors of law and justice tend constantly to penetrate into every legal order, be it through interpretation, analogies, general principles, law-making, etc. Derogative practice combats this type of expansion of the law. It opposes the progress of the fundamental legal exigencies.

Examples of such 'derogative' practice abound, especially in areas of high politics (ie vital interests):

a. In the area of State succession, there remain many vague norms, imprecise exceptions, confused practice and simple references to the will of States, creating important legal uncertainties and thus political room for manoeuvring.[111]
b. The recognition of States and governments has not been reduced to legal criteria, as had been proposed,[112] but has remained coloured by a vast array of political considerations[113] (which may be inescapable, since a government might feel the need to decide freely what type of relations it wants to have with another State).
c. Self-judging reservations, for example under Article 36, §2 of the ICJ Statute, reserving to a State the right ultimately to determine whether the exception to the acceptance of the jurisdiction of the Court applies or not in a given situation.[114]

[111] See the Report of G Ress on State Succession in *Annuaire IDI*, 2000/2001, 119ff, 712ff.

[112] H Lauterpacht, *Recognition in International Law* (Cambridge, 1947).

[113] See, eg, P Dailler, M Forteau and A Pellet, *Droit international public*, 8th edn (Paris, 2009) 624–26.

[114] There is a rich literature on the subject: FO Wilcox, 'The United States Accepts Compulsory Jurisdiction' (1946) 40 *AJIL* 699ff; H Waldock, 'The Plea of Domestic Jurisdiction before International Legal Tribunals' (1954) 31 *BYIL* 96, 131–37; G Guerrero, 'La qualification unilatérale de la compétence nationale' in *Essays in Honor of J. Spiropoulos* (Bonn, 1957) 207ff; HW Briggs, 'Reservations to the

d. More generally some types of reservations to treaties, for example those reserving the primacy of municipal law or some internal religious traditions (even if such reservations are legally void).[115]
e. The strict conditions for the exercise of self-defence according to the UN Charter have been enlarged and weakened in the practice of certain States, while other exceptions to the prohibition of the use of force have been added, for example with regard to anticipatory self-defence, armed reprisals, colonialism as permanent aggression, the use of force against non-State actors, humanitarian intervention, etc.[116]
f. The conditions for the exercise of extraterritorial jurisdiction remain in a state of flux (the main legal conceptions turn around 'effects' doctrines and a reasonable link to territory, a thin cloak for discretionary policies).[117]

Acceptance of Compulsory Jurisdiction of the International Court of Justice' (1958-I) 93 *RCADI* 328–63; K Holloway, *Les réserves dans les traités internationaux* (Paris, 1958/0 317ff; RY Jennings, 'Recent Cases on "Automatic" Reservations to the Optional Clause' (1958) 7 *ICLQ* 349ff; WP Rogers, 'The United States "Automatic" Reservation to Optional Clause Jurisdiction of the International Court of Justice' (1958) 7 *ICLQ* 758ff; HW Briggs, 'The United States and the International Court of Justice: A Re-Examination' (1959) 53 *AJIL* 301ff; B Maus, *Les réserves dans les déclarations d'acceptation de la juridiction obligatoire de la Cour internationale de Justice*, PhD (Genève, 1959) 149–63; P Guggenheim, 'Der sogenannte automatische Vorbehalt der inneren Angelegenheiten gegenüber der Anerkennung der obligatorischen Gerichtsbarkeit des Internationalen Gerichtshofes in seiner neuesten Gerichtspraxis' in *Essays in Honor of A. Verdross* (Vienna, 1960) 117ff; LFE Goldie, 'The Connally Reservation: A Shield for an Adversary' (1962) 9 *University of California Los Angeles Law Review* 277ff; C de Visscher, *Problèmes d'interprétation judiciaire en droit international public* (Paris, 1963) 209–13; G Döker, 'Das Connally Amendment und die obligatorische internationale Gerichtsbarkeit' (1963/1964) 11 *AVR* 155ff; M Dubisson, *La Cour internationale de Justice* (Paris, 1964) 180, 185–89; IF Shihata, *The Power of the International Court to Determine its Own Jurisdiction, Compétence de la compétence* (The Hague, 1965) 271, 284–97; K Holloway, *Modern Trends in Treaty Law* (London/New York, 1967) 654ff, 683ff; DW Greig, *International Law* (London, 1970) 501–06 (2nd edn, London, 1976, 651–57); E Zoller, *La bonne foi en droit international public* (Paris, 1977) 131ff; J Crawford, 'The Legal Effect of Automatic Reservations to the Jurisdiction of the International Court' (1979) 50 *BYIL* 63ff; S Rosenne, *The Law and Practice of the International Court*, 2nd edn (Dordrecht/Boston/London, 1985) 395–99; DW Greig, 'Nicaragua and the United States: Confrontation over the Jurisdiction of the International Court' (1991) 62 *BYIL* 182–86, 206–07; R Szafarz, *The Compulsory Jurisdiction of the International Court of Justice* (Dordrecht/Boston/London, 1993) 52–55; SA Alexandrov, *Reservations in Unilateral Declarations Accepting the Compulsory Jurisdiction of the International Court of Justice* (Dordrecht/Boston/London, 1995) 76–91; R Kolb, *The International Court of Justice* (Oxford, 2013) 503ff. See also the Separate Opinion H Lauterpacht, *Norwegian Loans* [1957] ICJ Rep 43ff and Dissenting Opinion H Lauterpacht, *Interhandel* (Preliminary Objections) [1959] ICJ Rep 97ff.

[115] K Zemanek, 'The Legal Foundations of the International System' (1997) 266 *RCADI* 175ff. For human rights treaties, see in particular W Kälin and J Künzli, *The Law of International Human Rights Protection* (Oxford, 2009) 125ff; JA Carrillo-Salcedo, 'Droit international et souveraineté des Etats' (1996) 257 *RCADI* 181ff. Sometimes, especially in regional systems, the reservation, once held to be invalid, might be severed from the rest of the declaration: see, eg, ECtHR, *Belilos* (1988) Series A no 132, § 60 and *Loizidou* (1995) Series A no 310, §95ff.

[116] For a discussion, see, eg, R Kolb, *Ius contra bellum, Le droit international relatif au maintien de la paix*, 2nd edn (Basle/Brussels, 2009) 255ff; C Gray, *International Law and the Use of Force*, 2nd edn (Oxford, 2004) 29ff.

[117] See the Report of F Rigaux in *Annuaire IDI*, 2000/2001, 87ff.

g. The conditions for the registration of ships have remained vague in practice, so as to fit the practice regarding flags of convenience.[118]
h. The law of extradition has been weakened by subjective determinations of notions such as 'political offences'.[119]
i. The sensitive domain of countermeasures has been kept apart from mandatory judicial control so as to remain a political tool too.[120]
j. A significant number of optional declarations under Article 36, §2, of the ICJ Statute, conferring jurisdiction on the Court, contain a clause whereby they can be denounced at any time with immediate effect; if that were to be allowed, the State would have not accepted any mandatory jurisdiction at all.[121]
k. States resist the introduction of judicial control of acts of international organisations (eg decisions by the UN Security Council).[122]
l. States may often vote even when they are directly interested in the outcome, as is the case for decisions under Chapter VII of the UN Charter,[123] etc.

We might also recall some broader structural choices: the settlement of disputes is not mandatory; private justice is not abolished. But these are structural matters linked to the decentralised structure of international law.

5. *The Domain of 'High Politics': The Distinction Between Legal and Political Disputes and Vital Interests*

Interests that States consider to be intimately linked to the conservation or development of their power have a significant impact in international law. This is the case, for example, as regards the distinction between legal and political disputes, with the adaptation of the suitable means for the settlement of the dispute; or in the existence of a law of 'vital interests', where necessities and urgent needs carve out derogations from and exceptions to ordinary legal regimes.

118 N Aloupi, *Le rattachement des engins à l'Etat en droit international (navires, aéronefs, engins spatiaux)*, PhD (Paris II, 117ff).

119 J Puente Egido, 'L'extradition en droit international: problèmes choisis' (1991-VI) 231 *RCADI* 9ff.

120 G Arangio-Ruiz, 'Counter-Measures and Amicable Dispute Settlement, Means in the Implementation of State Responsibility' (1994) 5 *EJIL* 20ff, and the response of C Tomuschat, 'Are Counter-Measures Subject to Prior Recourse to Dispute Settlement Mechanisms?', *ibid*, 77ff.

121 R Kolb, 'La dénonciation avec effet immédiat de déclarations facultatives établissant la compétence de la Cour internationale de Justice' in *Essays in Honor of L. Caflisch* (Leiden, 2006) 875ff.

122 See M Bedjaoui, *Nouvel ordre mondial et contrôle de la légalité des actes du Conseil de sécurité* (Brussels, 1994).

123 See A Zimmermann, 'Article 27' in Simma et al (eds), above n 95, 919ff.

i. Legal and Political Disputes[124]

Legal disputes are defined by international law in the broadest way as disputes on the interpretation or application of law, on divergence of interests with regard to a legal question and possibly even as disputes on the modification of the law when the parties seek adjudication. In the *Mavrommatis Palestine Concessions* case (1924), the PCIJ defined the notion thus:[125] 'A dispute is a disagreement on a point of law or fact, a conflict of legal views or interests between two persons.' Since 1924, this definition has been relied upon in a constant line of case law, notwithstanding some slight variations in the formula used.[126] In the *Interpretation of Peace Treaties*

[124] On this time-honoured distinction, see C Fenwick et al, 'The Distinction between Legal and Political Questions', *Proceedings of the American Society of International Law*, 1924, 44ff, 125ff; TW Balch, *Legal and Political Questions between Nations* (Philadelphia, 1924); JHW Verzijl, 'La classification des différends internationaux' (1925) 86 *RDILC* 732ff; J Hostie, 'Différends justiciables et non justiciables' (1928) 9 *RDILC* 263ff, 568ff; H Lauterpacht, 'La théorie des différends non justiciables en droit international' (1930-IV) 34 *RCADI* 499ff; J Fischer-Williams, 'Justiciable and Other Disputes' (1932) 26 *AJIL* 31ff; V Bruns, 'Völkerrecht als Rechtsordnung II: Politische und Rechtsstreitigkeiten' (1933) 3 *ZaöRV* 445ff; H Lauterpacht, *The Function of Law in the International Community* (Oxford, 1933) 139ff, 351ff; D Schindler, 'Contribution à l'étude des facteurs sociologiques et psychologiques du droit international' (1933-III) 46 *RCADI* 280ff; S Rundstein, 'Le caractère juridique des différends internationaux' (1934) 15 *RDILC* 377ff; M Habicht, 'Le pouvoir du juge international de statuer ex aequo et bono' (1934-III) 49 *RCADI* 314ff; S Verosta, 'Différends juridiques et conflits d'intérêts' in *Jahrbuch der (österreichischen) Konsularakademie*, 1935, 78ff; O Oncken, *Die politischen Streitigkeiten im Völkerrecht* (Berlin, 1936); G Berlia, *Essai sur la portée de la clause de jugement en équité en droit des gens* (Paris, 1937) 95ff; T Gihl, 'The Subjective Test as a Means of Distinguishing between Legal and Political Disputes' (1937) 8 *Acta Scandinavica Juris Gentium* 67ff; D Schindler, *Die Schiedsgerichtsbarkeit seit 1914* (Stuttgart, 1938) 102ff; M Vaucher, *Le problème de la justiciabilité et de la non justiciabilité en droit international des différends dits politiques ou non juridiques* (Paris, 1951); A. Cassese, 'The Concept of Legal Dispute in the Jurisprudence of the International Court' in *Comunicazioni e studi* (*Essays in Honor of G. Morelli*), vol XIX (Milan, 1975) 173ff; A Beirlaen, 'La distinction entre les différends juridiques et les différends politiques dans la pratique des organisations internationales' (1975) 11 *RBDI* 405ff; H Mosler, 'Political and Justiciable Legal Disputes. Revival of an Old Controversy' in *Essays in Honor of G. Schwarzenberger* (London, 1988) 216ff. See also C Rousseau, *Droit international public*, vol V (Paris, 1983) 253–55. On the approach of the ICJ, T Sugihara, 'The Judicial Function of the International Court of Justice with Respect to Disputes Involving Highly Political Issues' in AS Muller et al (eds), *The International Court of Justice* (The Hague/Boston/London, 1997) 117ff.

[125] *Mavrommatis Palestine Concessions* (1925) PCIJ Series A no 2, 11. As was aptly explained by C de Visscher, *Théories et réalités en droit international public*, 3rd edn (Paris, 1960) 458, 'Evitant d'adopter une position trop formelle qui l'eût conduite à des définitions trop complexes, propres à favoriser l'esprit de chicane, la Cour a ramené la notion du différend à ses données les plus simples.'

[126] See, eg, *Serbian Loans* (1929) PCIJ Series A no 20, 16–18; *Interpretation of Peace Treaties* [1950] ICJ Rep 74; *Right of Passage over Indian Territory* (Preliminary Objections) [1957] ICJ Rep 148–49; *Right of Passage over Indian Territory* (Merits) [1960] ICJ Rep 34; *South West Africa* (Preliminary Objections) [1962] ICJ Rep 319; *Northern Cameroons* [1963] ICJ Rep 27; *Aegean Sea Continental Shelf* (Competence) [1978] ICJ Rep 13; *Applicability of the Obligation to Arbitrate under Section 21 of the United Nations Headquarters Agreement of 26 June 1947* [1988] ICJ Rep 27; *East Timor* [1995] ICJ Rep 99; *Application of the Convention on the Prevention and Punishment of the Crime of Genocide* (Preliminary Objections) [1996-II] ICJ Rep 614–15; *Lockerbie* (Preliminary Objections) [1998] ICJ Rep 17, 123; *Land and Maritime Boundary (Cameroon v Nigeria)* (Preliminary Objections) [1998] ICJ Rep 314; *Arrest Warrant of 11 April 2000* [2002] ICJ Rep 13; *Avena* (Provisional Measures) [2003] ICJ Rep 88; *Certain Property (Liechtenstein v Germany)* [2005] ICJ Rep § 24; *Land and Maritime Dispute (Nicaragua v Colombia)* (Preliminary Objections) [2007-II] ICJ Rep 873, §§ 138ff.

opinion (1950)[127] and *South West Africa* cases (Preliminary Objections, 1962),[128] the ICJ stated that the existence of a dispute had to be established objectively and autonomously by the Court itself. The subjective claim of one party that there was a dispute was not decisive:

> A mere assertion is not sufficient to prove the existence of a dispute any more than a mere denial of the existence of the dispute proves its non-existence. Nor is it adequate to show that the interests of the two parties to such a case are in conflict. It must be shown that the claim of one party is positively opposed by the other.[129]

The Court ultimately decides—if necessary *ex officio*—the question of the existence of the dispute[130] (Article 36, § 6 of the ICJ Statute).

Political disputes have their place within legal disputes: after all, international law regulates public matters and thus political questions. There is hardly any international dispute devoid of some political aspects, underpinnings or tensions. International Courts do not refuse to adjudicate cases where there are important political interests at stake. As regards the ICJ, we might recall the *Diplomatic and Consular Staff in Tehran* case (1980),[131] the *Nicaragua* case (1986)[132] or the *Lockerbie* case (1992/1998).[133] If the dispute cannot be reduced to legal terms (considering the claims of the parties), it will not be justiciable. This is so, for example, for moot questions,[134] for the making of new regulations of a technical nature,[135] for the indication of means to put an end to a situation of asylum in an embassy,[136] etc. The dispute is justiciable if it is engrafted upon a legal question; but it is not justiciable when the political aspect is not based on some legal claim.

It is true that, strictly speaking, all disputes are justiciable: the judge can always reject the claim of the claimant as not being well-founded in law; he can hold that what is not prohibited is allowed; or else he can pronounce a *non liquet*. But the dispute will hardly be resolved in such circumstances. However, and this is the crucial point, any political dispute can be turned into a legal one by the parties to the dispute or by the claimant. When the parties place themselves on the terrain of the law and formulate their claims on legal bases, the dispute is a legal one. The criterion is therefore subjective, that is, related to the will of the parties. This was acknowledged in the old Locarno Treaties of 1925, where legal disputes were defined as those where the parties reciprocally contest a right ('litiges au sujet

[127] *Interpretation of Peace Treaties* [1950] ICJ Rep 65.

[128] *South West Africa* (Preliminary Objections) [1962] ICJ Rep 328.

[129] *ibid.* See also *Northern Cameroons* [1963] ICJ Rep 27; *Nuclear Tests* [1974] ICJ Rep 271, 476; *Genocide Case* [1996-II] ICJ Rep 614, § 29.

[130] See, eg, the *Territorial and Maritime Dispute (Nicaragua v Colombia)* [2007-II] ICJ Rep 874, §138.

[131] *Diplomatic and Consular Staff in Tehran* [1980] ICJ Rep 3.

[132] *Nicaragua* [1986] ICJ Rep 14.

[133] *Lockerbie* (Provisional Measures) [1992] ICJ Rep 3ff; (Preliminary Objections) [1998] ICJ Rep 9, 115ff.

[134] *Northern Cameroons* [1963] ICJ Rep 29.

[135] *Free Zones* (1932) PCIJ Series A/B no 46, 162.

[136] *Haya de la Torre* [1951] ICJ Rep 78–79.

desquels les parties se contesteraient réciproquement un droit'). The distinction between legal and political disputes was extracted from the old conception of 'political disputes by nature' and reshuffled as follows: legal disputes were those where the parties placed themselves deliberately on legal territory by formulating their claims on the basis of legal norms; political disputes were those where the parties demanded a modification of the law by basing themselves on political motives, or where they did not formulate their dispute on the basis of legal claims. The first type of dispute was to be heard by arbitral or judicial organs; the second type was to be handled by diplomatic procedures (without binding decisions).[137] The foregoing means that States can at all times keep their disputes apart from the law, ie not settle them according to the law, and thereby bypass the requirements of the rule of law. The same choice is not permitted to subjects in municipal law. The true meaning of the subjective distinction is therefore that States are free to maintain their disputes on a political agenda and to refuse to compromise. The dispute may then remain active for an immeasurable length of time, as the 'eternal' dispute between Israel and Palestine graphically reveals.

There are also disputes which may not seem ripe for adjudication on account of the tense environment they inhabit. Often such disputes are devoid of any specific object; they are rather 'situations'. Their roots lie in historic and long-standing divisions or recriminations between States. Such situations are often passionate, and can hardly be reduced to the technical terms of a legal reasoning. The relationship to a vital interest (see section II.A.5.ii. below) is so intimate that the government concerned is unable to give up its control over the process, lest its internal social peace be endangered. The mere application of the law to such situations will not resolve the dispute; it might even exacerbate and poison it. Technically, the dispute could be decided, but materially it could not be resolved by the law. The tools of the law are here doubly insufficient: first, the object of the dispute is often not rationally defined and not sufficiently circumscribed; secondly, the legal solution, once devised, would leave too many inflammable materials. The serene voice of justice cannot be heard in such a passionate climate. Beyond the will of one or both parties, the whole context may here indicate that the dispute could be better handled in a political arena with full jurisdiction over all its aspects (political, psychological and so on), rather than by a court of justice with jurisdiction limited to some legal aspects, which are hardly the decisive ones. Such situations must not objectively put at stake important interests; sometimes, the interests at stake may seem entirely futile to the external observer, but they have symbolic or political value for the actors concerned. The placing or planting of a flag may trigger armed clashes; the question of the name of a State may create huge tensions

[137] It is true that the General Act of Arbitration of 1928 attempted to impose mandatory conciliation for political disputes, followed by mandatory arbitration in the event of the failure of the former. The arbitrator was instructed to decide such cases *ex aequo et bono* (quasi-arbitration). This attempt was not successful. The same can be said for the Geneva Protocol of 1924, which never entered into force. It had attempted to impose arbitration for all types of disputes. See P Barandon, *Le système juridique de la Société des Nations pour la prévention de la guerre* (Geneva/Paris, 1933) 23ff.

(eg Macedonia); the arrest of certain persons may provoke an armed conflict, etc. Here again, politics may partially do away with the law.

It is perhaps useful to add that the foregoing considerations on the 'situations' cannot be formalised in a doctrine of inadmissibility of claims. Once validly seized, the ICJ does not have the power to refuse to adjudicate on the basis that the dispute is prone to political tensions and has broader ramifications, and that therefore the Court does not seem to be the forum most indicated. We might just recall the above-mentioned *Tehran* and *Nicaragua* cases of 1980 and 1986. Neither did the 'passionate' relations between the US and Iran at the beginning of the 1980s hamper the establishment of the Iran/US Claims Tribunal, which, after some incidents at the beginning of its life,[138] has developed a remarkable jurisprudence and whose judgments have all been honoured by Iran to date. The Eritrea/Ethiopia Arbitral Tribunal, deciding on questions flowing from the armed conflict between the two States (1998–2000) also worked, successfully overall, in a context of outright tension between both States.[139]

The different types of disputes also lead to a distinction as to the juridical means of settlement, namely, between 'diplomatic arbitration' and 'legal arbitration'.[140] In principle, political disputes in the sense discussed above should be processed through political means (negotiations, mediation or conciliation), while legal disputes are best brought before legal forums (arbitration or courts of justice). Sometimes, however, the States concerned wish to conclude a dispute involving political tensions through a binding decision which they are unable to find themselves. In such a case, they can agree to treat the proposals of the conciliation commission as binding. They can also request arbitration. In order to accommodate this particular situation, the tool of arbitration has been refined. Thus, there are two forms: first, classical legal arbitration, which is an instrument of justice and law in which the application of the law as it stands predominates to the verge of exclusiveness, and where the arbitrator gives force to the positive law and applies it to the facts at hand; and, secondly, diplomatic arbitration, which is an instrument of peace and de-escalation, where the aim is to sooth the tensions and to calm down the passions, while seeking a flexible and reasonable solution to the dispute. The diplomatic arbitrator is thus mainly a conciliator. His task is to find a balanced solution capable of ushering in lasting peaceful relations. Consequently, the arbitrator must, most importantly, take keen account of the susceptibilities of the parties and display more diplomatic tact than mere legal skill.

Confusion between the two types of arbitration can have negative outcomes. The *Beagle Canal* case of the 1970s is an example. Argentina and Chile were in dispute over the boundaries in Patagonia. An arbitration took place. The arbitrators applied the law strictly, which failed to resolve the situation—quite to the contrary. However, the Catholic faith of both peoples opened the way for mediation by the

[138] G Aldrich, *The Jurisprudence of the Iran-United States Claims Tribunal* (Oxford, 1996) 9ff.
[139] See its awards in XXVI *RIAA*.
[140] On this distinction, see N Politis, *La justice internationale* (Paris, 1924) 107ff.

Pope, whose moral authority had great weight. He finally resolved the dispute by his flexible mediation on the basis of a mutually viable compromise.[141] The previously cited *Casablanca Deserters* case of 1909 is another example.[142] There, the arbitrators approached the matter under a diplomatic banner, and could balance the concurrent jurisdictions (on which there was no clear applicable rule of international law) in such a way as to produce the desired result. More recently, the *Region of Brcko* arbitration (1997)[143] duplicated the success of the *Casablanca* case. According to Annex II of the Dayton Agreement of 1995, a line of demarcation had to be established in the zones controlled by the parties, Serbia and Bosnia. To say the least, relations between the parties were strained. They did not manage to reach agreement. The issue was thus brought before an arbitral tribunal according to the aforementioned Annex of the Dayton Agreement. The region of Brcko, where the dispute had manifested itself, was considered vital by both sides. The arbitral procedure was punctuated by incidents and ill-will. The two 'national arbitrators' refused to sign the award; it therefore emanated only from the tribunal's President, Sir Robert Owens. The tribunal refused merely to apply the law. It had recourse to equity, which its constitutive instrument allowed it to apply. It therefore took into account a series of circumstantial factors of an extra-legal nature, such as: the tension reigning in the area; the allegiances of the population; economic interests; the psychological value of the region for the parties; the importance of the lines of communication for those parties; and the interests of the international community in a lasting and peaceful settlement. In view of these factors, the tribunal decided that partition of the area, as envisaged in the Dayton Agreement, was still premature. The arbitrator rather opted for a temporary solution, comprising joint administration under international control. He added, 'not being required to proceed solely on the basis of legal rules, the Tribunal is authorized to render an award that, in its view, best reflects and protects the overall interests of the parties and that has the strongest likelihood of promoting a long-term peaceful solution'.[144] The arbitrator's forecast was largely realised on the ground. The award finally contributed towards defusing the tension. The reconstruction of the region of Brcko progressed more quickly than that of other areas in the boundary region. Legally speaking, the award was close to being an *excès de pouvoir* (but without trespassing into it); diplomatically, it showed great wisdom. Conversely, the *North Atlantic Coast Fisheries* case of 1910 is a classic example of a legal arbitration. It concentrated on technical points of interpretation of a treaty between two States with excellent mutual relations (the UK and the US).[145] Another example can be found in the *Greek Claims against Germany* case (1972).[146] The point turned on a previous arbitral decision that had awarded

[141] See *Beagle Canal* XXI *RIAA* 53ff.
[142] *Casablanca Deserters*, XI *RIAA* 126ff.
[143] *Region of Brcko* (1997) 36 *ILM* 428ff.
[144] *ibid*, 431, §97.
[145] *North Atlantic Coast Fisheries*, XI *RIAA* 167ff.
[146] *Greek Claims against Germany*, XIX *RIAA* 27ff.

certain damages to Greece for unlawful acts by Germany during World War I. Because of the financial situation in Germany in the 1920s, these awards had not been honoured. The dispute now concentrated on the extent of the duty to negotiate a lump sum agreement in application of certain mutual arrangements. These were technical questions, taking place between two governments favourably disposed to the resolution of the dispute. The arbitrators could apply the legal rules and thereby bring the whole dispute to a successful conclusion. Overall, it can be said that the differentiation between the tools of arbitration may render useful service. Diplomatic arbitration may yield excellent results where legal arbitration would be of no help. The experience and political skill of the arbitrator, his wisdom and his authority, will in such cases be decisive assets.

ii. Vital Interests

There are legal techniques in international law through which States try to defend their vital interests. In other words, the vital interests extend their foothold into the realm of positive law. The main device in this regard is to create saving clauses, derogations or exceptions to the ordinary legal regimes. While States cannot resist the creation of legal rules regulating vital questions, they will at least engraft onto the legal norms tools for escaping their application in particularly tricky situations. These saving mechanisms allow a State to preserve its vital interests as perceived at a given moment. Each legal order knows of such grey zones (or black holes), where power holds sway over the law, such as governmental acts doctrines, 'political questions', Acts of State, decisions exempted from a legal remedy, laws of urgency or necessity, etc. Thus, for example, the decision to declare war or to participate in an armed conflict is justiciable in no country on earth. The law has to acknowledge in these contexts its inherent limits as regards the capacity to handle matters not rationalised and objective enough to be subjected to legal norms.

In municipal societies, the progress of the rule of law has reduced the extent and scope of such matters (which has, however, also had the effect of 'politicising' justice). This movement is less advanced in international society than it is in internal societies, amongst other things because of the lesser impact of the rule of law. In international law, there are still important pockets of resistance as regards such exceptional rights. They are covered by sovereignty and the collective psychology of peoples. In the past, an example of such a 'derogative legal institution' was the 'fundamental rights of States'.[147] Within these rights, that concerning

[147] For the analogy between rights of individuals and rights of States, see the early Draft for a Declaration on the Law of Nations by Abbé Grégoire of 23 April 1795, Art 3, 'ce qu'un home doit à un autre, un people le doit aux autres'. See L Le Fur and G Chklaver, *Recueil de textes de droit international public*, 2nd edn (Paris, 1934) 69. On these fundamental rights, see, eg, L Duguit, *Traité de droit constitutionnel*, vol I, 3rd edn (Paris, 1927) 715ff; G Gidel, 'Droits et devoirs des nations. Théorie classique des droits fondamentaux des Etats' (1925-V) 10 *RCADI* 537ff; L Le Fur, *Précis de droit international public*, 3rd edn (Paris, 1937) §§638ff. See also A Pillet, *Recherches sur les droits fondamentaux des Etats dans l'ordre des rapports internationaux et sur la solution des conflits qu'ils font naître* (Paris, 1899); A Pillet, 'Recherches sur les droits fondamentaux des Etats' (1898) 5 *RGDIP* 66ff and (1899) 6 *RGDIP* 503ff;

'self-preservation' held pride of place.[148] The State had the right and the duty to preserve itself; this right was superior to other rights and obligations, and prevailed in the event of conflict. The State could thus oppose any regulation that would impair its right of survival—as subjectively appreciated.[149] The right to survive has primacy over any positive law. Political societies must protect future generations of the nation; they cannot endanger them or leave them defenceless.[150] This 'right to life' of the State was recognised also by the Institut de droit international in 1921,[151] as well as by other learned societies, such as the American Institute of International Law (1916).[152] From this general right to self-preservation, a series of other rights were deduced, for example rights of necessity (state of necessity), self-defence, the right to augment one's own power, the right to seek security (through alliances), etc.

These doctrines of fundamental rights were progressively abandoned in the twentieth century,[153] but the heritage of such rights has remained in part, for example through bold arguments as to the scope of self-defence,[154] the purported exceptions to the prohibition on the use of nuclear weapons,[155] certain arguments regarding military necessity within the law of armed conflicts,[156] etc. Other such questions relate to a state of emergency's allowing 'derogation' (*recte*: suspension) from certain human rights guarantees, subject to a series of quite strict legal conditions.[157] The 1970s were marked by an epidemic of such states

P Fauchille, *Traité de droit international public*, vol I, pt I (Paris, 1922) 395ff; WG Phillimore, 'Droits et devoirs fondamentaux des Etats' (1923-I) 1 *RCADI* 29ff; S Séferiadès, 'Principes généraux du droit international de la paix' (1930-IV) 34 *RCADI* 343ff; E Kaufmann, 'Règles générales du droit de la paix' (1935-IV) 54 *RCADI* 574ff. Due to US interventionism, the doctrine of fundamental rights and duties of States maintained itself for a longer time in Latin America: H Rolin, 'Les principes de droit international public' (1950-II) 77 *RCADI* 353–60, 354. For a Latin American conception, see, eg, RJ Alfaro, 'The Rights and Duties of States' (1959-II) 97 *RCADI* 95ff, the word 'fundamental' being dropped.

[148] See, eg, Fauchille, above n 147, 410ff.

[149] E Kaufmann, 'Règles générales du droit de la paix' (1935-IV) 54 *RCADI* 576ff; C Bilfinger, 'Les bases fondamentales de la communauté des Etats' (1938-I) 63 *RCADI* 140ff.

[150] P Pradier-Fodéré, *Traité de droit international public*, vol I (Paris, 1885) 365.

[151] Draft of M de Lapradelle, Declaration on the Rights and Duties of States: see (1921) 28 *Annuaire IDI* 205ff.

[152] *ibid*, 208.

[153] See the sharp criticisms of such rights in some of the modern legal doctrine, eg, S Séferiadès, 'Principes généraux du droit international de la paix' (1930-IV) 34 *RCADI* 353ff.

[154] See Oppenheim, above n 91, 416ff, 421ff; DW Bowett, *Self-Defense in International Law* (Manchester, 1958).

[155] Right of the State to survive: see *Nuclear Weapons* (Opinion) (UNGA) [1996-I] ICJ Rep 263, §§96–97. This opinion has been criticised in legal doctrine, see, eg, Condorelli, 'Le droit international humanitaire, ou de l'exploration par la Cour d'une *terra* à peu près *incognita* pour elle' in L Boisson de Chazournes and P Sands (eds), *International Law, the International Court of Justice and Nuclear Weapons* (Cambridge, 1999) 229ff. There have been some unilateral undertakings not to use nuclear weapons against a non-nuclear State: see the Declarations in the UN Security Council, S/1995/261-5, and see (1997) 43 *AFDI* 229–30. In legal doctrine, see (1967) 52-II *Annuaire IDI* 1ff.

[156] See R Kolb, 'La nécessité militaire dans le droit des conflits armés—Essai de clarification conceptuelle' in *Colloque de Grenoble de la Société française de droit international* (Paris, 2007) 151ff, with many references. See also, for an extremely thorough study, E Henry, *La nécessité militaire en droit international humanitaire*, PhD (University of Neuchâtel, 2015).

[157] See, eg, M Nowak, *UN Covenant on Civil and Political Rights, Commentary*, 2nd edn (Kehl/Strasburg, 2005) 83ff.

of emergency, especially in the dictatorships in Latin America.[158] For its part, the European Court of Human Rights leaves a certain amount of political discretion to States over decisions on suspension.[159] The now defunct European Commission of Human Rights had been sharply divided on the issue whether the conditions for a state of emergency were met in Greece at the time of the dictatorship of the colonels, in 1967.[160] Overall in such areas, the political facts put up fierce resistance to the further penetration of legal disciplines into the political body. Whether this is welcome or not is another question.

B. Centripetal Political Factors: Power at the Service of the International Community

As we have already seen, there is largely an absence of, or at least a weakness in, a true policy in favour of the international community. Political mandates are exercised in the name of States and nations, not in the name of the universal community. Thus, international politics are generally the sum of a great number of national policies. Some NGOs may well be considered as acting in the name and interest of the whole community, but apart from the fact that they have no real legislative or decision-making powers, there remain problems of particular interests, lobby groups and transparency. If there were public organs acting for the welfare of the community as a whole, we would have made some steps towards a global federal system. However, the result of the foregoing is that policies in favour of the international community are based on precarious convergences of interests at a given moment, without institutional continuity and constantly prone to being diverted from their trajectory.[161] But there remains the fact that there are such moments of convergence and that there is a sort of substitute politics in favour of the whole—weak and precarious as it may appear. The policy of the majority then realises, at least collaterally, sometimes also directly, some collective interest; and the minority is pushed towards compliance by pressure to conform.

Just as there is a law of 'vital interests' (see section II.A.5.ii. above), there has also developed a 'law of community concerns'.[162] This community-orientated law

[158] See the interesting report by L Despouy in the UN Sub-Commission against discriminatory measures and for the protection of minorities, *Human Rights and States of Emergency*, E/CN.4/Sub.2/1997/19, Report dated 23 June 1997.

[159] *Aksoy v Turkey* [1996] ECHR 68.

[160] Report of 5 November 1969, *Yearbook of the European Convention on Human Rights*, vol 12, 71ff, §152ff.

[161] As was proclaimed with a certain strength and bitterness by Wordsworth, *The Excursion*, book V, 'Earth is sick and Heaven is weary of hollow words which States and Kingdoms utter when they talk of truth and justice'.

[162] See, eg, G Gaja, 'The Protection of General Interests in the International Community—General Course on Public International Law (2011)' (2012) 364 *RCADI* 9ff; S Peter, *Public Interest and Common Good in International Law* (Basle, 2012). Such community concerns were often expressed in the Constitutions of International Organisations, eg the WHO Constitution adopted in 1946. In the Preamble of the latter it is written, inter alia, that the health of all peoples is a fundamental right of every individual, that health is fundamental to the attainment of international peace, that health is a value to all, that

is composed of various doctrines, such as *jus cogens*, obligations *erga omnes*, international crimes, universal criminal jurisdiction, objective or collective territorial regimes (eg 'common heritage' or 'global commons'), the exercise of powers of the UN Security Council in favour of peace, etc. Here we shall focus first on the different levels of sources; the actions of the Security Council will be discussed in section II.B.3. below. The community-orientated perspective may be found in what is sometimes erroneously called the super sources (eg *jus cogens*), in the ordinary sources (eg customary international law) and in the quasi sources (eg soft law). The super sources are not truly different from the ordinary sources. But we shall maintain the distinction because of its usefulness, even if it is technically inexact. Lastly, it should be noted that action for the community interest does not require a State to act *only* in view of such collective interests. More often than not, it will act in pursuance of some individual interest that also happens to further a collective interest. Coexistence of interests is much more frequent than exclusivity of interests.

1. The Super Sources: Jus Cogens *and* Erga Omnes *Obligations*

The point is not to discuss in detail these instruments of modern international law, as regards which legal doctrine has often gone well beyond what is actually borne out by practice. However, we might note that it has been claimed that this body of norms forms an emergent law of the international community.[163] From there, the question often turns to the concept of a hierarchically superior law, taking precedence over ordinary norms of international law, at least in cases of conflict.[164] Peremptory norms in particular have had an extraordinary career in international law. From modest beginnings as an exceptional reason for the nullity of treaties, the notion of *jus cogens* has radiated outwards into the whole international legal order. In municipal legal orders, the notion has been known since antiquity.[165] Its aim is to protect the normative integrity of a legal regime against derogative contractual regimes between a restricted number of parties under the *lex specialis* principle. The integrity of the general regime is protected for reasons of the collective interest (*utilitas publica*). In short, a peremptory law is one from which the subject cannot escape by contracting out of it. The issue is thus centered on the restriction of private autonomy, for example against the setting of wages below a minimum as defined by public policy considerations.

unequal development and disease is a common danger, etc. See at <http://www.who.int/governance/eb/who_constitution_en.pdf>. This is a remarkably early document expressing community-concern thinking.

[163] JA Carrillo-Salcedo, 'Droit international et souveraineté des Etats' (1996) 257 *RCADI* 146.

[164] A Orakhelashvili, *Peremptory Norms in International Law* (Oxford, 2006) 7ff, 340ff. The Swiss Legal Directory (Ministry of Foreign Affairs) has also affirmed this hierarchical superiority, see Note of 12 February 1997, (1998) 8 *RSDIE* 616: 'Ainsi ces règles du droit des gens [*jus cogens*] se trouvent au sommet de la hiérarchie et l'emportent sur toute autre règle.' Which, by the way, is legally wrong.

[165] For Roman law, see M Kaser, 'Ius publicum und ius privatum' (1986) 103 *Zeitschrift der Savigny-Stiftung für Rechtsgeschichte, Romanistische Abteilung* 1, 75ff.

The essence of peremptory laws resides in public utility and non-derogability, that is, in a substantive reason and in a legal technique. From these underpinnings, three aspects can be gathered:

1. municipal *jus cogens* is not a set of substantive fundamental rules placed at the apex of the legal system; it is rather a legal technique that protects a legal regime against fragmentation in view of a public interest;
2. municipal *jus cogens* does not protect only the fundamental interests of the community, but also any type of public interest, eg the rules on the packaging to be used for certain foodstuffs are often peremptory;
3. municipal *jus cogens* is not a phenomenon of some normative hierarchy, since it can be found at all levels of public law, from the constitution to the tiniest administrative regulation.

Some authors have attempted to construe international *jus cogens* on roughly the same lines, configuring it as a legal technique against fragmentation by according priority to the more special law.[166] But this approach has remained isolated. It does not correspond to the often ideologically inflated, and in any case different, construction of the majority of authors. The starting-point for this apparent specificity of international 'public policy' was already set at the time of the drafting of the VCLT (1969) with its Article 53. The issue was whether a treaty concluded between sovereign States could be considered legally void by reason of its content, eg its gravely illegal or immoral content. Since the uncontested rule was that sovereign States can agree on whatever object they wish, and given there are no regular judges in international society able to sanction the public policy and to protect the *pacta sunt servanda* principle, it was almost naturally understood that international *jus cogens* could relate only to the most fundamental norms of the law. Thus the commonly proposed lists of *jus cogens* norms based on the prohibition of piracy, genocide, slavery, aggression, fundamental human rights (torture, etc) and the like.[167] These would be the norms from which the States could not validly

[166] R Kolb, *Peremptory International Law (Jus Cogens)* (Oxford, 2015); R Kolb, *Théorie du ius cogens international* (Paris, 2001).

[167] See JA Pastor Ridruejo, *La determinación del contenido del ius cogens* (Madrid, 1972); J Sztucki, *Jus cogens and the Vienna Convention on the Law of Treaties—A Critical Appraisal* (Vienna/New York, 1974); S Kadelbach, *Zwingendes Völkerrecht* (Berlin, 1992). This view is often held still today: see, eg, Z Drnas De Clément, 'Las normas imperativas de derecho internacional general (*jus cogens*). Dimension sustancial' in Z Drnas de Clément (ed), *Estudios de derecho internacional en homenja al professor E.J. Rey Caro*, vol I (Cordoba, 2002) 647. For older sources in international law, see, eg, E de Vattel, *Le droit des gens* (1758), book II, ch XII, §161: 'Par la même raison, par défaut de pouvoir, un traité fait pour cause injuste ou déshonnête est absolument nul, personne ne pouvant s'engager à faire des choses contraires à la loi naturelle'; and book II, ch XV, §228 (the oath does not affect the nullity); L Casanova, *Del diritto internazionale*, 2nd edn (Florence, 1870) 99–100; A Verdross, 'Forbidden Treaties in International Law' (1937) 31 *AJIL* 571ff; A Verdross, 'Trattati contra bonos mores' (1937) 29 *Rivista di diritto internazionale* 3ff. There are still references to natural law: see, eg, S Séfériadès, 'Principes généraux du droit international de la paix' (1930-IV) 34 *RCADI* 207. The issue then became entangled into the debate on the validity of the Versailles Treaty of 1919: H Lauterpacht, 'Règles générales du droit de la paix' (1937-IV) 62 *RCADI* 306, 308; A Verdross, 'Heilige und unsittliche Staatsverträge' (1935/1936) 2 *Völkerbund und Völkerrecht* 164; C Schmitt, *Die Wendung zum diskriminierenden Kriegsbegriff* (Munich, 1938) 4, fn 4.

derogate by agreement. If they did, their compact would be legally void; and its enforcement could therefore not be demanded under the law.

The entry of peremptory laws on to the international scene was thus already heavily angled towards exceptionalism. International *jus cogens* is limited to the most fundamental norms. And it is identified with these norms, that is, becomes a substantive notion and not merely a legal technique. It therefore naturally tends towards occupying a superior position in any hierarchy of these norms. Nevertheless, sovereignty imposed a limitation on the notion of *jus cogens*: since States must remain free to agree as they see fit in most cases (analogous to private autonomy), any peremptory law could only be very limited. Paradoxically, peremptory laws may seem to mark a victory against excessive freedom of sovereignty; but at the same time, these laws have since their creation been heavily limited by sovereignty.[168] The story does not end there. The concept of 'fundamental values or norms of the international community' had such an appeal and momentum that it expanded the notion of *jus cogens* to an unprecedented extent. From a narrow reason for the nullity of treaties (and eventually of other legal acts), the peremptory laws moved to form a sort of super-constitutional law of the international community. Thus, since the 1990s, *jus cogens* has expanded like a Big Bang in all directions.[169] Various effects have been attached to this super *jus cogens*, some of them in practice, most of them in the writings of certain authors. For example,[170] the inapplicability of jurisdictional immunities;[171] the assumption of universal jurisdiction (for so-called *jus cogens* crimes);[172] the admissibility of retroactivity;[173] various effects in domestic legal orders[174] (eg voidance of amnesties;[175] or, in Switzerland, according

[168] Thus it could be said that *jus cogens*, however necessary it was in certain cases, was like a Rolls Royce that was cherished and cared for but which hardly ever quit its garage: see, eg, P Weil, 'Le droit international en quête de son identité: Cours general de droit international public' (1992-VI) 237 *RCADI* 274.

[169] See C Focarelli, 'La dynamique du droit international et la fonction du *jus cogens* dans le processus de changement de la règle sur l'immunité juridictionnelle des Etats étrangers' (2008) 112 *RGDIP* 761ff; C Focarelli, *International Law as a Social Construct* (Oxford, 2012) 312ff. On these various aspects of modern peremptory law, see also notably Orakhelashvili, above n 164; and PM Dupuy, 'L'unité de l'ordre juridique international—Cours général de droit international public' (2002) 297 *RCADI* 269ff.

[170] See C Focarelli, 'Promotional *Jus cogens*: A Critical Appraisal of *Jus cogens*' Legal Effects' (2008) 77 *Nordic Journal of International Law* 439ff.

[171] See, eg, the stocktaking of A Bianchi, 'Gazing at the Crystal Ball (Again): State Immunity and *Jus cogens* Beyond Germany v Italy (2013) 4 *Journal of International Dispute Settlement* 457ff; or S Knuchel, 'State Immunity and the Promise of *Jus cogens*' (2011) 9 *Northwestern University Journal of International Human Rights* 149ff; Orakhelashvili, above n 164, 322ff, with further references. See also *In re Pinochet* (HL) (1998/1999) 37 *ILM* 1302 or (1999) 38 *ILM* 581; *Al-Adsani v Kuwait* (CA) (1994) 100 *ILR* 465; *Princz v Germany* (US Court of Appeals (Columbia)) (1994) 103 *ILR* 610 (the violation of a norm of *jus cogens* does not lead automatically to a waiver of immunity); *Smith and Hudson v Libya* (US Court of Appeals) (1997) 100 *ILR* 104. For State immunities, see now *Jurisdictional Immunities of State (Germany v Italy)*, ICJ Judgment of 3 February 2012, §§81ff.

[172] See, eg, C Bassiouni, 'International Crimes: *Jus cogens* and Obligations Erga Omnes' (1996) 59 *Law and Contemporary Problems* 63ff; Orakhelashvili, above n 164, 288ff.

[173] See the reference in Focarelli, above n 170, 441, quoting the *Ferrini* decision (2004) of the Italian Court of Cassation.

[174] Orakhelashvili, above n 164, 539ff; and *Furundzija* (ICTY Trial Chamber) (1998) 121 *ILR* 260–62.

[175] Orakhelashvili, above n 164, 223ff.

to Article 139, §3 of the Constitution, the invalidation of popular initiatives); a duty to exercise diplomatic protection;[176] the creation of a title of jurisdiction;[177] the duty of non-recognition of and non-assistance to a situation contrary to a peremptory norm;[178] invalidation of general or regional customary norms contrary to a *jus cogens* provision;[179] the non-extradition of an individual if this would lead to the breach of a *jus cogens* norm,[180] notably to torture, etc. Most of these effects are obtained by deductive reasoning: they are considered inherent in the very notion of *jus cogens*. It has even been claimed that State practice has less (or no?) weight in matters of *jus cogens*.[181] Note also that the effects of peremptoriness are not confined to 'nullity', that is to a more or less automatic and limited legal effect. Quite the contrary: the new *jus cogens* imposes on States a series of positive duties. Thus, for example, the concept of *jus cogens* crimes triggers with it the duty of States to prosecute the culprits on the basis of universal jurisdiction. An unlimited number of new duties could consequently be created simply by way of deduction from the concept of *jus cogens*. The separate existence of such obligations in the body of the sources of international law is unnecessary. Whatever may be the correct answer to the question of the construction of *jus cogens*,[182] the genie has left

[176] J Verhoeven, 'Sur les "bons" et les "mauvais" emplois du *jus cogens*' (2008) 5 *Anuario Brasileiro de Direito Internacional* 159. The question was considered by the ILC, and also in judicial practice, in *Kaunda* (South Africa, Constitutional Court) (2004) 136 *ILR* 463, 503–04, the judges not agreeing on the issue.

[177] On this issue, Orakhelashvili, above n 164, 489ff.

[178] See, eg, *ibid*, 372ff; J Dugard, *Recognition and the United Nations* (Cambridge, 19870) 123ff; M Dawidowicz, 'The Obligation of Non-Recognition of an Unlawful Situation' in J Crawford, A Pellet and S Olleson (eds), *The Law of State Responsibility* (Oxford, 2010) 677; N Joergensen, 'The Obligation of Non-Assistance to the Responsible State' in J Crawford, A Pellet and S Olleson (eds), *The Law of State Responsibility* (Oxford, 2010) 687.

[179] Orakhelashvili, above n 164, 340–41; Study of the ILC on *Fragmentation of International Law*, Doc A/CN.4/L.682 (2006), §367; see also *Furundzija* (ICTY, Trial Chamber) (1998) 121 *ILR* 261; *Siderman de Blake* (US Court of Appeals) (1992) 103 *ILR* 472; *Bouzari v Iran* (Canada, Ontario Superior Court of Justice) (2002) 124 *ILR* 442; *Ferrini* (Italian Court of Cassation) (2004) 128 *ILR* 668–69; *Prefecture of Voioitia* (Italy, Court of Cassation) (2011) 150 *ILR* 720–21; Separate Opinion E Lauterpacht, *Genocide* (Provisional Measures), [1993] ICJ Rep 440, §100; Joint Dissenting Opinion Rozakis/Caflisch/Wildhaber/Costa/Cabral Barreto/Vajic in *Al-Adsani v Kuwait* (CA) (1994) 100 *ILR* 465, §1. *Contra*: Separate Opinion Dugard, *Armed Activities (DRC v Uganda)* [2006] ICJ Rep 91, §13. And see generally R Kolb, 'Nullité, inapplicabilité ou inexistence d'une norme coutumière contraire au *jus cogens* universel?' (2013) 117 *RGDIP* 281ff.

[180] For Switzerland: Arrêts du Tribunal Fédéral = ATF 108 Ib 412; ATF 109 Ib 72; ATF 112 Ib 222ff; ATF 121 II 298. The invocation of *jus cogens* is strictly speaking superfluous, since it would suffice to find a customary norm prohibiting extradition in such cases.

[181] Orakhelashvili, above n 164, 301–02.

[182] The correct answer has been given by Focarelli in his searching and seminal studies on *jus cogens* cited in nn 169 and 170 above. The answer is articulated as follows: (i) there can be no other deductive approach to the further effects of *jus cogens* than that of the nullity of contrary legal acts; (ii) it is only through examination of State practice and the concomitant legal opinion that it is possible to determine if a particular further effect is accepted or not; all these effects must be tested in practice and do not flow from the notion of peremptoriness itself; (iii) these effects, if adopted in practice, become free-standing norms of customary international law (determining, for example, to what extent there is a right to access to justice for victims of international crimes, if jurisdictional immunities are to be set aside, or if universal jurisdiction applies); (iv) thus, *jus cogens* is in most cases superfluous, since the

the bottle and will not return to it simply because it is claimed that it should. The new *jus cogens* has become a powerful—but also ideological—tool in the hands of a policy in favour of the international community. It pushes the international legal order towards a greater degree of community orientation. The sequence in the history of peremptory international law is thus as follows: servant of natural law—validity of treaties—international super-legality.

The trajectory of *erga omnes* obligations is not identical, but the legal and axiological foundation of the phenomenon is the same. As is well known, the ICJ set out in paragraphs 33–34 of its *Barcelona Traction* Judgment (1970) the famous distinction between obligations having a bilateral or particular reach, and obligations owed to the international community as a whole.[183] From there, legal doctrine has construed a sort of *actio popularis*, that is, a generalised legal standing where the point turns on the vindication of obligations of a community nature.[184] The content of such obligations was construed by analogy with *jus cogens* norms, but with some shading and nuances. Each State could thus present a claim against the State committing the unlawful act. Moreover, the active legitimation of the adoption of countermeasures has been broadened to include third States.[185] In short, *jus cogens* has been construed as a substantive phenomenon involving 'constitutional norms of the international community', and *erga omnes* obligations (or rights) as a procedural consequence enlarging the legal standing to bring claims. The fact remains that few States avail themselves of the entitlement to bring claims beyond the sphere of their own interests.

2. *The Ordinary Sources: Aggressive Customary Law*

Over the last few years a new form of customary law has developed. It tends to give precedence to *opinio juris* over effective practice. Traditional customary law had already been used increasingly in the second part of the twentieth century

effects flow from the customary provision and not from the concept of *jus cogens*. The role of peremptoriness will here most often be promotional, ie used as an argument in favour of the development of new customary effects said to be attached to *jus cogens* requirements.

[183] *Barcelona Traction* [1970] ICJ Rep 32. On such *erga omnes* obligations, see C Annacker, *Die Durchsetzung von Erga Omnes Verpflichtungen vor dem Internationlen Gerichtshof* (Hamburg, 1994); JA Frowein, 'Reactions by Not Directly Affected States to Breaches of Public International Law' (1994) 248 *RCADI* 345ff; M Ragazzi, *The Concept of International Obligations Erga Omnes* (Oxford, 1997); K Zemanek, 'New Trends in the Enforcement of Erga Omnes Obligations' (2000) 4 *Max Planck United Nations Yearbook* 1ff; CJ Tams, *Enforcing Obligations Erga Omnes in International Law* (Cambridge, 2005); P Picone, *Comunità internazionale e obblighi erga omnes* (Naples, 2006). See also G Gaja, 'Obligations and Rights Erga Omnes in International Law' (2005) 71-I *Annuaire IDI* 116ff.

[184] On the issue, see, eg, F Voeffray, *L'actio popularis ou la défense de l'intérêt collectif devant les juridictions internationales* (Paris, 2004) 73ff.

[185] D Alland, 'Countermeasures of General Interest' (2002) 13 *EJIL* 1221ff; LA Sicilianos, 'Countermeasures in Response to Grave Violations of Obligations Owed to the International Community' in Crawford et al, above n 178, 1137ff. And see the critique by P Weil, 'Le droit international en quête de son identité: Cours general de droit international public' (1992-VI) 237 *RCADI* 282ff, fearing a multiplication of conflictual relationships and of unilateral measures taken under the cloak of community interest.

to serve community purposes. Indeed, in this regard there had been a tendency to conclude quite rapidly that a conventional norm with a multilateral character also had a customary complexion. This allowed certain inherent hurdles of the conventional process to be overcome, namely the length of the time required for conclusion, the need for ratification or accession, the possibility of formulating reservations, etc. To some extent, such inherent limitations of the conventional process were thus 'circumvented'. The customary nature of a norm allowed them to be overcome and for the norm to be imposed on all the States of the world. This process was not simply an abuse or an ideological hammering. It also corresponded to urgent needs of an international society evolving at a increasing pace and manifesting a significant hunger for normative guidance.[186]

Many norms of multilateral conventional law have thus become guest workers in international law, living within a convention but also labouring in the realm of customary law. This tendency towards a softer custom (from the perspective of the evidence of its existence, not from that of its effect) has exerted some influence on the relationship between practice and legal opinion, at least in certain areas of international law. The gist of the matter is that greater emphasis has been placed on legal opinion ('take States by what they say') rather than on practice ('take States from what they actually do'). Vice pays tribute to virtue. The weaknesses and contradictions of effective practice are ousted by focusing on legal opinion, ie the fact that States do not claim to be entitled to act as they actually do. This process lends strength to legitimate community concerns. Thus, for example, many States engage in torture. The practice is not entirely satisfactory in this context. But hardly any State has claimed that it is legally entitled to use torture. Thus, the customary norm is maintained and even strengthened. The ICJ had to some extent opened the way for this conception by relying on UN General Assembly resolutions or draft conventions in the establishment of the customary norm, ie to facts coloured more by opinion than by effective practice.[187] The ICTY and the ICTR followed suit, especially in the context of the filling of gaps in the the law of non-international armed conflicts.[188]

The following two examples show the new customary process exerting its influence: first, in favour of the general interest; and, secondly, in favour of largely shared particular interests:

1. *Non-international armed conflicts*. The number and importance of internal armed conflicts after 1960 raised the question of the applicable law. States were little more than lukewarm as regards the development of an international legal regime for such conflicts. They considered that regulation would

[186] Thus, the criticisms by Weil, above n 185, 160ff, cannot be wholly accepted.

[187] See, eg, *Gulf of Maine* [1984] ICJ Rep 299; *Nicaragua* [1986] ICJ Rep 97, 106ff; *Nuclear Weapons* (Opinion) (UNGA) [1996-I] ICJ Rep253; *Gabcikovo-Nagymaros Project* [1997] ICJ Rep 62. By contrast, compare the meticulous examination of State practice in *Jurisdictional Immunities (Germany v Italy)* [2012] ICJ Rep 126ff, §§62ff.

[188] See, eg, *Delalic* (ICTY, Chamber of First Instance) 1998, §459. And see generally *Tadic* (ICTY, Appeals Chamber) 1995, §96ff.

be an unwelcome inroad into their internal affairs in a highly sensitive matter. It would moreover give the rebels, whom they considered to be mere criminals, a certain undesirable international legal status. The frequency of such conflicts, the atrocities to which they gave rise, and pressure by the ICRC and other humanitarian groups nevertheless led to the adoption of a minimum regime of applicable law in Additional Protocol II of 1977 to the Geneva Conventions of 1949. This conventional regime developed the fundamental but thin content of Common Article 3 to the Geneva Conventions.[189] However, there remained important gaps in the protection: Additional Protocol II of 1977 contained only 20 substantive articles governing such armed conflicts; the rules of the Geneva Conventions and Additional Protocol I for international armed conflicts extended to a total of some 600 provisions. The disproportion is manifest, even when taking into account that not all rules applicable to international armed conflicts (IACs) are suitable for non-international armed conflicts (NIACs). The gaps were partially filled by the bold jurisprudence of the ICTY under the umbrella of a robust customary law. In its *Tadic* (Jurisdiction) Judgment of 1995,[190] the ICTY tried to bridge the gulf between the two types of conflict by postulating a series of rules for NIACs that were taken from those applied to IACs on the basis of a proclaimed customary law. The main paradigm is expressed in the famous §119 of the Judgment, where the Appeals Chamber emphasises that what is inhumane in an IAC must also be inhumane in an NIAC.[191] In the light of this statement, many customary rules proclaimed for NIACs seem to be based on opinion more than on any solid analysis of practice (however, we are not suggesting that this was a legal error). Moreover, the Tribunal developed the new notion of 'war crimes' in NIACs on the basis of an opinion-orientated customary law not underpinned by widespread practice.[192] The overall result has been a remarkable extension

[189] For the law of NIACs, see, eg, F Bugnion, *Le CICR et la protection des victimes de la guerre* (Geneva, 1994) 275ff; R Abi-Saab, *Droit humanitaire et conflits internes* (Geneva/Paris, 1986); L Moir, *The Law of Internal Armed Conflict* (Cambridge, 2002).

[190] *Tadic* (Jurisdiction) (Appeals Chamber) 1995, §§96ff. The decision is printed in M Sassòli and A Bouvier, *How Does Law Protect in War?*, vol III, 3rd edn (Geneva, 2011) 1758ff. The Tribunal had to apply definitions of crimes as established in customary international law: see the Report by the Secretary General of the UN, Doc NU, S/25704, §34.

[191] 'What is inhumane, and consequently proscribed, in international wars [*sic*], cannot but be inhumane and inadmissible in civil strife.' (Sassòli and Bouvier, above n 190, 1781) 'International wars' is a legal misnomer, since war exists only between States, ie is by definition international (pleonasm). It must also be cautioned that not all rules applicable in an IAC, reflecting the capacities of States' armies, are reasonable when the party under an obligation comprises rebels sometimes deprived even of a territorial basis. On the issue, see M Sassòli and J Grignon, 'Les limites du droit international pénal et de la justice pénale internationale dans la mise en œuvre du droit international humanitaire' in A Biad and P Tavernier (eds), *Le droit international face aux défis du XXe siècle* (Brussels, 2012) 146–48.

[192] §§128ff. The Tribunal excepted, however, 'grave breaches' of the Geneva Conventions, which apply only to IACs. There have been Judges of the ICTY who were prepared to extend even these crimes to NIACs: Judge Abi-Saab in *Tadic* (1995) and Judge Rodriguez in *Aleksovski* (1999), Dissenting Opinion, §§29ff. On this jurisprudence of the ICTY, see L Moir, *The Law of Internal Armed Conflict* (Cambridge, 2002) 133ff. The new approach of the ICTY was then codified by the Rome Conference in the Statute of the ICC, Art 8.

of the applicable humanitarian law in NIACs. This jurisprudence reflected a sort of need of the then international community. Most observers were deeply shocked by the fact that the protection of human beings and the punishment of perpetrators could largely depend on whether the conflict was legally international or non-international at a given moment at a given place. Moral and community-ridden exigencies pushed towards a more robust coverage of NIACs, through the device of 'aggressive custom'.

2. *Extension of the territorial sea to 12 nautical miles.* For a long time, there had been disagreement between those States in favour of a three-mile extension of the territorial sea and those supporting an extension of more than three miles. In 1960, 20 States were in favour of the three-mile rule, but 44 States claimed a broader territorial sea.[193] The major maritime powers insisted on the three-mile rule (UK, US, Japan). Greater extension of the territorial waters would have limited their prerogatives of free navigation and of fishing for the numerous ships registered under their flag, and would also have impaired some strategic interests (the free and submerged passage of military submarines).[194] However, many coastal States constantly maintained strong claims to extended maritime zones, territorial or economical. The three-mile States finally had to give way. Article 3 of the Montego Bay Convention on the Law of the Sea recognises that the ordinary and maximal extension of the territorial sea is 12 miles. The pressure towards adopting the extended zones was applied through legal-political opinions, followed only later by actual deeds. Customary law was thus coloured by the widespread opinion of the many. This ensured the breakthrough of a community purpose (a greater share of economic and other rights to the benefit of the many) with its self-serving side (the extension of maritime zones under exclusive State jurisdiction). The same type of pressure led, as we have already seen in section I.D., to the deep seabed's being proclaimed a 'common heritage of mankind' and subjected to a community regime, the latter being partly undone by the reform of 1994.[195] In both situations, customary law developments were based on opinion much more than on effective practice—at least in the first phase.

[193] D Bardonnet, 'La largeur de la mer territoriale' (1962) 66 *RGDIP* 34ff.

[194] By extension of the territorial waters to 12 or more miles, some important straits would have lost their status as international waters and come completely under the sovereignty of the coastal State. Passing submarines would then have to exercise innocent (rather than free) passage, which required their surfacing and flying the flag. Such a situation would have affected the unrecognised passage of second-strike nuclear submarines.

[195] See A/Res/48/263 and DH Anderson, 'Resolution and Agreement Relating to the Implementation of Part XI of the UN Convention on the Law of the Sea: A General Assessment' (1995) 55 *ZaöRV* 275ff.

3. The Quasi-Sources: Resolutions by the UN General Assembly

The recommendations of the UN General Assembly are not legally binding, but their political and moral weight has often been emphasised.[196] In certain subject matters, the resolutions of the Assembly set in motion legal-political regimes that ultimately led to the development of customary norms and to the conclusion of multilateral conventions codifying rules of international law. This was the case with Resolution 217 (III), 1948, the Universal Declaration of Human Rights, which preceded the adoption of the two Human Rights Covenants of 1966; Resolution 1962 (XVIII), 1963, concerning activities of States in Outer Space, preceding the Outer Space Treaty of 1967; Resolution 2749 (XXV), 1970, concerning activities in the Deep Seabed, which prepared Part XI of the Montego Bay Convention of 1982; Resolution 3452 (XXX), 1975, on the protection of persons against torture or inhuman or degrading treatment, which paved the way for the Convention Against Torture of 1984. Other resolutions have exerted their influence mainly on customary international law: Resolution 1514 (XV), 1960, concerning principles of decolonisation; Resolution 2625 (XXV), 1970, relative to Friendly Relations between States, providing a sort of authentic interpretation of Article 2 of the UN Charter; or Resolution 3314 (XXIX), 1974, concerning the definition of aggression.[197]

In the first years of the UN, the prevailing Western opinion was that resolutions of the United Nations General Assembly (UNGA), especially normative resolutions, were to be accorded significant weight. Given the fact that the Western States numerically dominated the Assembly, this was not surprising.[198] With decolonisation this changed.[199] The UNGA was now dominated by so-called Third World States. These States were deprived of power in bilateral relations and were often poor in political, military and diplomatic resources. The UNGA, however, provided an excellent forum for the advancement of their interests and claims. They dominated the Assembly by their sheer number. The UNGA was transformed into an instrument of political pressure of the Third World. Through it, those States attempted to alter international relations and law so that they would accord more closely with their perceived interests. The UN allowed these States to obtain a certain weight in international relations, especially during the Cold War, when the Super Powers were seeking to marshal alliances. In most cases, these States pursued their own interests, especially in economic matters. However, in some situations these particular interests coincided with a community interest. Examples of the

[196] See, eg, the Message of the Swiss Federal Council dated 21 December 1981, concerning the accession of Switzerland to the UN: *Feuille Fédérale*, 1982-I, 539.

[197] On aggression, see now also the criminal law developments under the revised ICC Statute: G Della Morte, 'La Conferenza di revisione dello Statuto della Corte penale internazionale ed il crimine di aggressione' (2010) 93 *RDI* 697, 717ff.

[198] E Luard, *A History of the United Nations, The Years of Western Domination, 1945–1955*, vol I (London, 1982).

[199] E Luard, *A History of the United Nations, The Age of Decolonization, 1955–1965*, vol II (London, 1989).

first category, where mainly particular interests were pursued, and where success remained elusive, were highly political matters (the ban on nuclear weapons)[200] or economic matters (the attempt to reformulate the terms of international economy around the poles of development, aid to development and State control).[201] Conversely, Resolution 1514, relating to decolonisation, reflected a political and moral orientation shared by all groups of States, and which the colonial powers could not resist. Thus, the pressure exerted first on the UK and France, later on Portugal up to the 1970s, or on South Africa concerning Namibia up to the 1980s, ultimately could only be successful. But even in the less successful areas, such as the ban on nuclear weapons, the constant pressure of sheer numbers had some collateral legal effects, for example the conclusion of treaties for the denuclearisation of certain areas (Latin America, the Southern Pacific), some unilateral undertakings not to use nuclear weapons against States deprived of such weapons, etc.[202] The success of the pressure for the sharing of deep seabed resources through the concept of the 'common heritage of mankind', advanced at the end of the 1960s by Malta's ambassador Arvid Pardo,[203] was limited. The Third World States had been alarmed by the ambiguous criteria set out in the 1958 Geneva Convention on the Continental Shelf, which seemed to allow the exploitation of deep seabed resources under the freedom of the high seas according to a flexible criterion of 'exploitability' (ie technical capacity to exploit).[204] These States feared that only the developed Western States would profit from that criterion, while they, lacking the necessary technology, stood to be deprived of their share. The approach set out in Part XI of the Montego Bay Convention proved, however, to be too State-centered. As we have already seen, it was reformed under counter-pressure applied by the Western States—the only ones having the technology to exploit these resources—in a more market-orientated sense. However that may be, community-orientated issues were here at stake. True, behind these issues lurked individual interests, but that is not surprising. The point remains that some compromise between the interests of the many and the interests of the few was the great legal-political issue in all these contexts. The success of the pressures exerted was largely a function of the capacity of the Third World States to mobilise around aspirations that went beyond their own categorical interests, ie around a community interest. Conversely, when

[200] Eg Resolution 1653 (XVI), 1961. See the analysis of the ICJ, *Nuclear Weapons* (Opinion) (UNGA) [1996-I] ICJ Rep 253ff.

[201] Resolution 3281 (XXIX), 1974, Charter of Economic Rights and Duties of States, New International Economic Order. For an appraisal many years after the event, see A Mahiou, 'Le droit international ou la dialectique de la rigueur et de la flexibilité, Cours général de droit international public' (2008) 337 *RCADI* 110ff. For a contemporary point of view, see, eg, J Bhagwati (ed), *The New International Economic Order: The North-South Debate* (Cambridge, 1977); M Bedjaoui, *Towards a New International Economic Order* (Paris, 1979); RJ Dupuy (ed), *The New International Economic Order* (The Hague, 1981); and M Flory, *Droit international du développement* (Paris, 1977).

[202] M Bedjaoui, 'L'humanité en quête de paix et de développement' (2006) 324 *RCADI* 304ff.

[203] UN Doc A/C.1/PV 1515 and A/C.1/PV 1516 (1967).

[204] Art 1 of that Convention. See RJ Dupuy and D Vignes (eds), *Traité du nouveau droit de la mer* (Paris/Brussels, 1985) 301ff.

these States attempted to push through their own interests by vote, as in economic matters, the resolutions adopted remained to a large extent dead letters. Decolonisation on the one hand and the new international economic order on the other are illuminating illustrations. In any case, successful resolutions will exert a certain political influence (diplomats not trained in international law often consider them to be expressions of the position of the majority of States which they cannot ignore). They can also have legal influence, in particular with municipal actors and internal judges not specialising in international law. These may be easily persuaded to draw from such texts arguments relevant to their decisions.[205]

C. Mutual Influences Between Law and Politics

Apart from the general influences of law and politics discussed above, there is a series of much more discreet and 'capillary' mutual influences. These are no less interesting. Ten examples will be given below, with some illustrations. Other situations could be envisaged and framed, but the analysis has to remain reasonably concise.

1. Mutual Indifference Between Law and Politics

Such mutual indifference occurs mainly in technical matters, into which the law can easily penetrate while politics remain aloof. Vital interests are rarely at stake in such circumstances. This fact allows the law to be used with even greater ease, far from the limelight of mass media and public scrutiny. Breaches of the law are rare in these areas. No State or actor risks misguiding the peaceful administration of the regime being deployed in the common interest of all. The sense of interdependence and common concern is plain here. We might mention as examples the universal postal services, the International Telegraph Union or the World Meteorological Organisation (WMO). To a large extent it is possible to add the World Health Organisation (WHO) and the other specialised agencies of the UN. The lack of political interference mentioned above often leads to law-making by majority within these international organisations. The text adopted binds all States, although there is usually the possibility to 'opt out', to be exercised within a certain time span.[206] This is rarely used. The technical areas cover a significant

[205] M Mendelson, 'The Formation of Customary International Law' (1998) 272 *RCADI* 388ff.

[206] I Detter, *Law Making by International Organizations* (Stockholm, 1965) 207ff; JE Alvarez, *International Organizations as Law-Makers* (Oxford, 2005) 217ff. See Art 54, §1 of the Chicago Agreement (1944) on Civil Aviation, creating the International Civil Aviation Organisation (ICAO), whose Council is allowed to adopt international standards for the safety of aviation by a two-thirds majority. Under Art 21 of the Constitutive Treaty of the WHO, the Assembly is allowed to adopt rules on the fight against epidemics and rules on the standardisation of diagnostics and medical drugs. According to Art 9 of its Constitutive Treaty, the WMO can adopt in the Congress of its member States rules on the standardisation of meteorological data. Implied opting-out clauses may also exist, eg, in the UN,

field of institutional international action. But they come to public notice much less than the great political issues and organs.

2. *The Ratification by Law of a Political Fact*

In some circumstances the law becomes entwined with a political fact by attaching certain legal consequences to its existence. A typical example lies in the creation of a new State. There has never been any question that the law could entirely govern that primary fact:[207] the birth of a State is not in itself a legal question or process, it is a fact; and this fact is essentially political in nature. However, the law does accompany this process. Positively, it will attach certain automatic consequences to the existence of the State as a fact;[208] it will also open the way to the recognition of the new State. Negatively, it will require existing States not to recognise or to assist the new entity if it has been created through violation of the non-use of force rule or the rule on the self-determination of peoples.[209] Thus, the issue is not governed by a simple fact: legal considerations have an impact and their own weight, for example the legality of the creation of the new entity under certain rules of international law, the category of puppet States, the role of self-determination, the will to be a new independent State (which might be lacking, as in the case of Taiwan), etc.[210]

Political considerations are part and parcel of the legal judgment in such areas. Sometimes, they lurk behind apparently technical assessments. Thus, the Badinter Arbitral Commission (in the context of the then European Community) was able to judge that the Federal Republic of Yugoslavia had disintegrated,[211] and that

where it is accepted that a State could quit the organisation if it disagreed with a revision of the Charter binding upon it under Arts 108 or 109 UN Charter. See G Witschel, 'Article 108' in Simma et al (eds), above n 97, 2216–17.

[207] But there are voices pleading for a large degree of legalisation of this process: MG Kohen, 'Introduction' in MG Kohen (ed), *Secession, International Law Perspectives* (Cambridge, 2006) 1ff. But peoples do not accept that their political destiny should be completely governed by legal rules and that historical transformations should be subjected to legal authorisation. The legal status quo cannot stop the promise of a different political tomorrow. The *Kosovo* Opinion of the ICJ ([2010-II] ICJ Rep 404) and its political background illustrated this point. On this Opinion, see, eg, P Hilpold (ed), *Kosovo and International Law* (Leiden/Boston, 2012); L Gradoni and E Milano (eds), *Il parere della Corte internazionale di giustizia sulla dichiarazione di indipendenza del Kosovo* (Padua, 2011); M Arcari and L Balmond (eds), *Questions de droit international autour de l'avis consultatif de la Cour internationale de Justice sur le Kosovo* (Milan, 2011). This does not imply that international policy should be favourable to secession; a world with 1,000 to 3,000 States would not be manageable.

[208] In particular the obligation to respect the territorial integrity of that State and the obligation not to use force against it. See Resolution 2625, 1970, of the UNGA. This gave rise, eg, to the condemnation of North Korea when it invaded South Korea in 1950: H Kelsen, *The Law of the United Nations* (London, 1951) 927ff; E Luard, *A History of the United Nations, The Years of Western Domination, 1945–1955*, vol I (London, 1982) 229ff.

[209] M Dawidowicz, 'The Obligation of Non-Recognition of an Unlawful Situation' in Crawford et al (eds), above n 178, 677; N Joergensen, 'The Obligation of Non-Assistance to the Responsible State', in Crawford et al, above n 178, 687ff.

[210] J Crawford, *The Creation of States in International Law*, 2nd edn (Oxford, 2006).

[211] Opinions I and VIII (1992) 92 *ILR* 162, 199ff.

therefore the territorial integrity of that State was no longer protected. The violent armed actions of the secessionists could no longer be viewed as unlawful attacks against the territorial integrity of the former State, since that State had ceased to exist. On the other hand, Bosnia was in all points a sort of Yugoslavia in miniature. When the war of secession started, the territorial integrity of that State was upheld. Thus, the violent actions of the Bosnian Serbs were perceived by most Western States as amounting to an illegitimate use of force against the integrity of Bosnia. On other occasions, the political considerations are palpable: the cause of the secessionists from Yugoslavia was espoused, that of the secessionists from Bosnia was not. More generally, it can be said that the political community will largely determine the category to be applied: disintegration, secession, legitimate new State, puppet State, *de facto* entity, etc. The law will then attach consequences to this political categorisation. Different States and organisations can here have different views, expressed through their recognitions or other political-legal acts. There will thus often be a plurality of judgments and a plurality of legal regimes applicable to the bilateral relations of the entities concerned.

3. *Law Deferring to Politics*

The whole area of States' jurisdictional and diplomatic immunities is a domain in which the law is expected to exercise self-restraint. The point is to avoid subjecting the political actions of States to the scrutiny of foreign municipal tribunals. The issue is, moreover, bluntly, one concerning the equality of States. International law also largely excludes the execution of assets and goods of foreign States serving the exercise of public functions. The same can be said of the 'Act of State' doctrine practised by common law States, according to which internal tribunals must refrain from passing judgment on the international lawfulness of public acts of foreign States when done abroad. The rule is part of municipal law and does not exist in international law. It has been frequently applied in the context of the expropriation of property without adequate compensation.[212] Initially, the rule was mainly intended to protect the political autonomy of foreign States, that is it had an outward reach. *Underhill v Hernandez* (1897, US Supreme Court) is a case in point: 'Every sovereign State is bound to respect the independence of every other sovereign State, and the courts of one country will not sit in judgment on the acts of the government of another, done within its territory.'[213] Following a US Senate amendment limiting the reach of the *Sabbatino* jurisprudence of the US Supreme Court,[214] the emphasis was laid on the necessity to protect the

[212] One of the most famous pronouncements is that of the US Supreme Court in *Sabbatino* (1964) 58 *AJIL* 779ff. The doctrine has also been applied by UK courts, eg, in *Buttes Gas v Hammer* (1981) 64 *ILR* 331ff.

[213] Oppenheim, above n 91, 366.

[214] *Banco Nacional de Cuba v Sabbatino*, 376 US 398 (1964).

internal executive from judicial embarrassment with regard to its foreign policy. The rule was now inward looking, and essentially became an issue concerning the separation of powers. The *Williams v Curtis-Wright Corporation* case (1982, US Court of Appeals) displayed this new orientation:

> The act of state doctrine once rested in the inherent nature of sovereign authority and principles of international law. Now, in this country at least, the doctrine's foundation has shifted to the interest in preserving the separation of powers between the branches of government. A court declines to exercise jurisdiction over a case that may hinder or embarrass the executive in the conduct of foreign affairs in deference to the proper distribution of functions between the judicial and the political branches in the area of international relations.[215]

With the strengthening of considerations of international legality, the Act of State doctrine has tended to retreat to some extent. The *Pinochet* case (1998–99) in the UK is an illustration.[216]

4. *Weakening of the Law by Contingent Political Interests*

We have already seen in the context of 'derogative practice' that there are subject matters in which political interests feed a series of fluctuations, selectivities and contingencies incompatible with mature legal discipline. Two examples may be given.

First, there is the construction of self-defence. In the UN Charter, the maintenance of peace is based on a triptych of provisions: Article 2, §4 (non-use of force); Chapter VII (collective security); and Article 51 (self-defence). Chapter VII is at the centre of the the system. It represents the collective responsibility for the maintenance and restoration of peace. The two external limbs concern the rights, obligations and powers of individual States. The two rules are in reciprocal tension, the first representing the general obligation (non-use of force) and the latter an exception to this rule[217] (self-defence). In practice, the ineffectiveness of the collective security scheme during the Cold War triggered the tendency for certain powerful States to take security issues back into their own hands. Technically, this occurred through a series of narrowing interpretations of Article 2, §4 and a series of broadening interpretations of Article 51 of the UN Charter. The rule/exception

[215] *Williams v Curtis-Wright Corporation* (1982) 81 *ILR* 518–19.

[216] See, eg, (1998) 37 *ILM* 1320ff (Lord Lloyd of Berwick, favourable to the application of the doctrine), 1338–39 (Lord Steyn, *contra*).

[217] This has sometimes been contested: S Sur, 'La créativité du droit international, Cours général de droit international public' (2012) 363 *RCADI* 257–59. The argument cannot be defended when the drafting history and the system of the Charter are taken into account. The correct position is expressed by the majority of authors, eg C Dominicé, 'La société internationale à la recherché de son équilibre—Cours général de droit international public' (2013) 370 *RCADI* 289.

relation was thus disturbed. For Article 51, the broadening interpretations were based on different arguments:[218]

1. The regulation in Article 51 is not exhaustive and is not meant to derogate from the older customary law principles under the famous *Caroline* precedent.[219]
2. Article 51 concerns only massive use of force; lesser uses of force are covered merely by self-preservation and the requirement for proportionality.[220]
3. The restricted right to self-defence as enshrined in Article 51 of the Charter was based on the implied condition that the system of collective security would work; since it did not, the States reverted back to their right to self-help.[221]
4. There is the right to strike by a single and apparently disproportionate act of self-defence in response to a series of earlier small incidents taken together (*Nadelstichtheorie*, pinprick assaults).[222]
5. There is a right to pre-emptive, or at least anticipatory, self-defence against imminent threats,[223] etc.

Such interpretations have found favour with States surrounded by hostile powers (Israel) or by Great Powers (US, UK). Small States, like Switzerland, have always favoured the restrictive interpretation of Article 51 and related customary international law (aligned with the text of the provision). Analytically, the arguments in favour of broadening the concept of self-defence are tantamount to reducing the legal hold of the prohibition on using force in favour of individualised and subjective assessments by the States concerned. This largely opens the door to political considerations.

[218] R Kolb, *Ius contra bellum, Le droit international relatif au maintien de la paix*, 2nd edn (Basle/ Brussels, 2009) 261ff; O Corten, *Le droit contre la guerre*, 2nd edn (Paris, 2014) 657ff; TM Franck, *Recourse to Force* (Cambridge, 2002) 45ff; C Alibert, *Du droit de se faire justice dans la société internationale depuis 1945* (Paris, 1983). For the case law of the ICJ, see JA Green, *The International Court of Justice and Self-Defence in International Law* (Oxford/Portland, 2009).

[219] DW Bowett, *Self-Defence in International Law* (Manchester, 1958) 182ff. As to the *Caroline* precedent, see the materials in JB Moore, *Digest of International Law*, vol II (Washington, 1906) 409ff. The *Caroline* formula is 'an instant and overwhelming necessity, leaving no choice of means and no moment for deliberation'. This corresponds to the old law of a time when the use of force was not generally limited by international law. It means that a State need not wait for an 'armed attack' but can take action in the broader sense of self-preservation, as subjectively appraised, but only if the action is urgent. See the incidents *Caroline* (1837), *Copenhagen* (1807), *Virginius* (1873), *US expeditions in Mexico* (1916–19), *German invasion of Belgium* (1914), *French fleet in Oran* (1940), *Cuban quarantine* (1962), *Israeli raids in Egypt* (1956) or in *Lebanon* (since 1982), *US attack in Libya* (1986), etc. See Oppenheim, above n 91, 417ff.

[220] G Schwarzenberger, 'The Fundamental Principles of International Law' (1955-I) 87 *RCADI* 335ff.

[221] *ibid*, 338.

[222] NM Feder, 'Reading the UN Charter Connotatively: Toward a New Definition of Armed Attack' (1986/1987) 19 *New York University Journal of International Law and Policy* 415.

[223] A Sofaer, 'On the Necessity of Pre-Emption' (2003) 14 *EJIL* 214ff; for anticipatory self-defence in case of imminent threats, see, eg, R Higgins, 'General Course of Public International Law: International Law and the Avoidance, Containment and Resolution of Disputes' (1991-V) 230 *RCADI* 310–11.

Secondly, there is the policy regarding abductions on foreign territory. Many States have had recourse to this means of law enforcement at one time or another. But the US condensed the matter into a fully-fledged doctrine starting in the 1980s. The issue came to the fore in the context of combatting drug trafficking from Latin American countries. Criminal law cooperation with Latin American countries often proved to be difficult and slow. Therefore the US sought a more reliable and quicker, ie unilateral, means of action. In a note, the State Department justified the practice of abductions:

> While the law must be given full respect even in matters of self-defense, we must not permit the law to be manipulated to render the free world ineffective in dealing with those who have no regard for law ... Arrests in foreign states without their consent have no legal justification under international law aside from self-defense. But where a criminal organization grows to a point where it can and does perpetrate violent attacks against the United States, it can become a proper object of measures in self-defense.[224]

The capture of General Noriega was an extreme example of this doctrine. US tribunals agreed to exercise jurisdiction over persons abducted, avoiding imposing sanctions for the violation of the territorial sovereignty of the aggrieved States (doctrine of *male captus, bene judicatus*). The claim was even made that such abductions were compatible with bilateral treaties of extradition to which the US was a party, since such treaties did not expressly rule them out.[225] When followed, such doctrines significantly weaken international treaties and cooperation. They instill a strong dose of unilateralism into the subject matter. Again, analytically, this is tantamount to weakening the law in favour of political approaches. This remains true, however much it may be desirable to bring to justice persons accused of having committed grave offences.

5. *Normative Accommodation of Political Needs*

General principles of law offer flexible normative guidance and value-orientated hotspots that can contribute to the functioning of legal regimes. Such principles can work to accommodate political exigencies within the legal system. This is one of the functions of equity. Equity can serve legal purposes when it displays a corrective function;[226] it can also serve political purposes when it exercises an

[224] (1990) 84 *AJIL* 727.

[225] *US v Alvarez-Machain* (1992) 31 *ILR* 900ff, where the extreme nature of the acts of Dr Alvarez-Machain probably had an influence on the outcome (the doctor had kept alive an American anti-drug agent to allow his prolonged torture). For criticism of this jurisprudence, see DJ Bederman, *Classical Canons—Rhetoric, Classicism and Treaty Interpretation* (Aldershot, 2001) 254ff. On this case, see the commentaries of M Glennon (1992) 86 *AJIL* 746ff; M Halberstam (1992) 86 *AJIL* 736ff; B Baker and V Röben (1993) 53 *ZaöRV* 657ff; R Rayfuse (1993) 42 *ICLQ* 882ff; CB Buner in *Europäische Grundrechte-Zeitung*, 1993, 1ff; DC Smith (1995) 6 *EJIL* 1ff. The Court of Appeals in *US v Verdugo Urquidez (No 2)* 90 *ILR* 668ff still considered that the abduction was incompatible with the extradition treaty.

[226] It here corrects a general legal rule which appears as being inequitable in the context of an unforeseen particular case: see Aristotle, *Nicomachian Ethics*, Book V, Chap X. Example: the legislator has produced a norm whereby the car transporting drugs is automatically confiscated. The case

individualising function. The latter function is material in the present context. International law is a legal system containing many lacunae, not one overburdened with strict rules. In this context, equity principally plays the role of an individualising device. It directs the operator to take account of all the 'relevant circumstances' (which in international law are often quite diverse). Here are some examples.

First, it may happen that during negotiations a solution cannot be found. But the parties may not wish to abandon the idea of agreement altogether. An alternative could then be to rely on the bridging force of equity. It may allow the parties to postpone difficult decisions—on which consensus is now lacking—to later times and to specific contexts, in which an accommodation might prove easier to reach. The same role can accrue to other principles, such as the prohibition on the abuse of rights. Thus, Article 300 of the Montego Bay Convention on the Law of the Sea (1982) provides that the parties must fulfil their obligations and exercise their rights under the Convention in a way that does not constitute an abuse of rights. When the Convention was negotiated, it was necessary to achieve a delicate balance between the many discretionary powers of the States in their coastal zones and the interests in free navigation of the great maritime powers. The latter feared that the former could abuse their discretionary powers and excessively limit their rights. The recognition of a justiciable doctrine of abuse of rights appeared to them to be a necessary counterweight to the recognition of those discretionary powers. Conversely, the coastal States feared that the maritime powers could abuse the procedural remedies offered to them so as repeatedly to contest the measures taken by the coastal States in what they considered their sovereignty domain. Compromise on this point was found through Article 294 of the Convention. It confers on the tribunal seized the power to examine on its own behalf or at the demand of one party, in a preliminary and summary ruling, the question of abuse of procedure in the claims advanced.[227] We are thus confronted with two cross-related compromises: the discretionary powers of the coastal States against the limitation of substantive abuse of rights; and a preliminary check by the tribunal

occurs that an old and poor grandmother had lent her car to a nephew without any knowledge as to its intended use; the nephew had then engaged into this traffic. Should the good faith grandmother forfeit her car? Other examples of this type occur in the context of criminal law: the law may state that in certain cases an automatic sentence shall be pronounced, eg at least one year in prison, or expulsion from national territory. It may happen that a person accused of a crime which leads to expulsion has committed the act many years ago, in particular circumstances, and that in the meantime he has become an important and successful public manager with family links in the country at stake—should he be expelled? See the many telling examples in L. Langer, 'Menetekel oder Musterlösung? Das amerikanische Ausländerrecht und die Umsetzung der schweizerischen Ausschaffungsinitiative', *RSDIE*, vol. 21, 2011, p. 195ff. In both cases the law is too schematic and creates problems when concrete circumstances arise. Equity and proportionality could here serve as useful correctors—to the extent this is possible, eg if there is some constitutional review.

[227] G. Jaenicke, 'Dispute Settlement under the Convention on the law of the Sea', *ZaöRV*, vol. 43, 1983, p. 817; Y. Tanaka, *The International Law of the Sea*, 2nd ed., Cambridge, 2015, p. 427. See generally on the system of dispute settlement: A. O. Adede, *The System for Settlement of Disputes under the United Nations Convention on the Law of the Sea*, Dordrecht, 1987; N. Klein, *Dispute Settlement in the UN Convention on the Law of the Sea*, Cambridge, 2005.

on the abuse of procedural rights so as not to excessively impair the discretionary rights claimed. Thus, the double principle of abuse of rights has facilitated agreement on a complex regime in the context of important political divergences of interests. Solutions to conflicts were postponed to future concrete situations, with a power of decision of the tribunal seized. It would be easier to find solutions in concrete cases than to create general rules in the Convention. The general principle has here the role of pacification; it functions as a midwife in the birth of a legal regime.

Secondly, equity can instill into a treaty the necessary flexibilities in the absence of general rules of international law on a subject matter. The law then refers the parties to later supplementary agreements, which opens the way to further political adjustments. We might here recall the many equitable clauses in the Convention on State Succession in Matters of Property, Archives and Debts (1983).[228]

Thirdly, equity can designate a discretionary power to be accorded to a judge. The latter will then be able to facilitate the necessary political accommodations. The *Region of Brcko* arbitration (1997) discussed above is seminal in this regard. The same can be said of the case law relating to the delimitation of continental shelves and exclusive economic zones: for a time, the ICJ pursued a policy of 'just and equitable share', even if it formally rejected this argument in the *North Sea Continental Shelf* cases of 1969.[229] By the search for individualised equitable results according to all the relevant circumstances, the Court for some years hampered the progress of a more thoroughly legal approach to delimitation and offered in its place a wide array of political-legal considerations. In the practice of States, this could only lead to some uncertainty as to the principles and rules applicable in drawing the boundary lines. This is the reason why many States continued to avail themselves of the equidistance principle, with its greater certainty and ease of application. The ICJ finally changed its jurisprudence and came back to a more normative approach at the beginning of the 1990s.[230]

6. *Politics Seeking to Remain Unaffected by Law*

There are situations in which specific political interests try to escape from the generality, foreseeability and reciprocity characterising legal obligations. For example, *ex gratia* payments. By this device, a State can pay indemnities to foreign nationals for damage suffered through political sensitive activities, without admitting to having engaged in internationally unlawful conduct and without creating a binding precedent. The payment is thus extracted from the chain of practices giving rise to customary norms through an express declaration of *opinio non juris*.

[228] See in particular Arts 37, §2, 40, §1 and 41 of the Convention.

[229] *North Sea Continental Shelf* [1969] ICJ Rep 22, §20.

[230] On this case law, see R Kolb, *Case Law on Equitable Maritime Delimitation, Digest and Commentaries/Jurisprudence sur les délimitations maritimes selon l'équité, Répertoire et commentaires*, English/French (The Hague/London/New York, 2003); P Weil, *Perspectives du droit de la délimitation maritime* (Paris, 1988).

Any pressure towards conformity of future conduct is rejected in advance. Here lies the root of the difference between politics and law: liberty, *ad hoc* arrangements and fluctuations in the first; obligation, rules and reciprocity in the latter. The US payments to Japanese fisherman in the Pacific in the 1950s provides a good example. The atmospheric nuclear tests by the US in the Pacific, notably on the Bikini Islands, had produced significant fallout in the surroundings. Areas of the high seas where the Japanese fishermen had fished for generations were spoiled. Japan brought the matter to the attention of the US, which was sensitive to the claims of a newly-gained ally. There was a certain inclination to pay damages on an equitable basis, but at the same time a firm intention to maintain the position that the tests were lawful under international law. The *ex gratia* payment was the best way out of the quagmire. It allowed the US to pay damages without binding itself in the future.[231]

More recently, the US has used the same instrument for the payment of damages to the family members of those aboard a civilian aircraft shot down by US military forces near the Iranian coast.[232] The official position was that the US acted in self-defence, ie lawfully under international law, and the point was not to impair this position by the payment of indemnities, which could have been interpreted as an implicit admission of guilt. Other States have similarly had recourse to such *ex gratia* payments, for example in a Convention between the UK and Mexico for losses sustained by British citizens during revolutionary acts in Mexico.[233]

7. *Law as a General Framework for Political Action*

The law may offer a general framework for the exercise of certain competences. This occurs, for example, when a jurisdiction remains discretionary in order to fit changing political needs. The substantive action remains essentially political, but it is generally organised under legal colours. This situation can arise within an international organisation or in inter-State relations. Here are some examples.

i. Article 19 of the League of Nations Covenant

A highly political jurisdiction, linked to a legal power of recommendation, was attributed to the Assembly of the League of Nations by Article 19 of the League of Nations Covenant. At issue was the concept of 'peaceful change'. The provision was worded as follows:

> The Assembly may from time to time advise the reconsideration by Members of the League of treaties which have become inapplicable and the consideration of international conditions whose continuance might endanger the peace of the world.[234]

[231] See in (1956) 2 *AFDI* 309ff.

[232] The Agreement is printed in (1996) 35 *ILM* 553.

[233] See in (1965) 14 *ICLQ* 1199–1200, 1231–33.

[234] On this provision see W Schücking and H Wehberg, *Die Satzung des Völkerbundes*, 2nd edn (Berlin, 1924) 661ff; O Hoijer, *Le Pacte de la Société des Nations* (Paris, 1926) 333ff; J Ray, *Commentaire du Pacte de la Société des Nations* (Paris, 1930) 559ff; JM Yepes and P da Silva, *Commentaire théorique*

The norm transferred to some extent onto the institutional plane the time-honoured problem of *rebus sic stantibus*.[235] The questions raised were essentially political: How could the legal situation flowing from treaties be adapted to political transformations? How could the rights of the conventional *beati possidentes* be reconciled with the political claims of the *non beati possidentes*? It stands to reason that the revision of treaties is a political function; it consists precisely of changing the law. The law can here only attribute competences and organise procedures. The absence of unequal peace treaties and the relatively broad powers of the UN Security Council (see below) have down-tuned the issue since 1945. However, Article 14 of the UN Charter makes it clear that the problem has not disappeared,[236] even if the focus of that provision is broader than that of the now defunct Article 19 of the Covenant.

ii. Powers of the UN Security Council

The powers of the UN Security Council are largely discretionary.[237] The Council can in particular determine whether there is a situation threatening international peace, a notion at once vague and open-ended, designed to give it a significant margin of appreciation or discretion.[238] Chapter VII of the UN Charter is replete with discretionary powers: the Council can take decisions on binding measures, or continue to recommend courses of action (Article 39); it can decide to adopt initially peaceful binding measures under Article 41, or pass directly to military enforcement measures under Article 42, as modified by subsequent practice (authorisations by the Security Council); it can decide whether to adopt measures other than those referred to in Articles 41 and 42 (eg the creation of a tribunal like the ICTY)[239] ; and it has discretion as to what type of mandate to confer on States under the authorisation scheme,[240] etc. These discretionary powers are so

et pratique du Pacte de la Société des Nations, vol III (Paris, 1939) 32ff; L Crema, 'Article 19' in R Kolb, *Commentaire sur le Pacte de la Société des Nations* (Brussels, 2015) 763ff. See also V Böhmert, *Der Artikel 19 der Völkerbundsatzung*, Kiel, 1934; PB Potter, *Article XIX of the Covenant of the League of Nations* (Geneva, 1941); H Lauterpacht, 'Règles générales du droit de la paix' (1937-IV) 62 *RCADI* 371ff; M Bourquin, 'Stabilité et mouvement dans l'ordre juridique international' (1938-II) 64 *RCADI* 351ff. Further references in WG Grewe, 'Peaceful Change' in HJ Schlochauer (ed), *Wörterbuch des Völkerrechts*, vol II (Berlin, 1961) 752ff.

[235] See C Rabl-Blaser, *Die* clausula rebus sic stantibus *im Völkerrecht* (Zurich/St Gallen) 2012.

[236] M Zöckler and D Riznik, 'Article 14' in Simma et al (eds), above n 95, 318ff; R Maison, 'Article 14' in JP Cot, A Pellet and M Forteau (eds), *La Charte des Nations Unies—Commentaire article par article*, vol I, 3rd edn (Paris, 2005) 745ff; VD Degan, 'Peaceful Change' (1981/1982) 16 *RBDI* 536ff.

[237] This was confirmed by the ICTY's Appeals Chamber in the *Tadic* case (1995), above n 188, §31.

[238] M Zambelli, *La constatation des situations de l'article 39 de la Charte des Nations Unies par le Conseil de sécurité* (Geneva/Basle/Munich, 2002) 81ff. Thus, a threat to the peace was perceived in the non-extradition of some persons (Resolution 748, 1992, Libya); the flow of refugees (Resolution 875, 1993, Haiti); the non-ratification of the chemical weapons ban convention by Iraq, amongst other circumstances (Resolution 687, 1991).

[239] Resolution 827, 1992.

[240] See LA Sicilianos, 'Entre multilatéralisme et unilatéralisme: l'autorisation par le Conseil de sécurité de recourir à la force' (2008) 339 *RCADI* 25ff.

numerous and potentially so broad that a lively discussion of the control of legality by international tribunals was launched in the 1990s.[241] In sum, a series of legal powers of constraint are conferred on an organ in view of the exercise of a political function, namely, the maintenance or restoration of international peace. International law limits itself to providing a framework for this action: it grants competences and could develop further limits to their exercise. In the long run, the legitimacy of action of the Council could benefit from slightly more detailed legal regulation.

iii. Classic Peacekeeping Operations[242]

Peacekeeping operations are not regulated in the UN Charter, since they were not foreseen in 1945. Being executive actions of a non-coercive nature, these operations straddle and hover over Chapters VI and VII of the Charter.[243] Their prima facie legality under Charter law was confirmed by the ICJ in the *Certain Expenses* Opinion of 1962.[244]

Traditional peacekeeping operations are based on certain principles developed in practice: the consent of the receiving State; the absence of military personnel of permanent members of the Security Council; the use of force only in self-defence; etc. In the cases of both peacekeeping and peace enforcement under Chapter VII, the law remains a flexible tool for political action; and it accompanies that political action.

iv. Recognition of States and Governments

There have been attempts to reduce the process of recognition of States and governments to objective criteria governed by the law, with the result that when certain factual conditions were met there would be a legal duty to recognise the new entity.[245] The obligation proposed is rooted in an attempt to provide a better and less anarchical order for international society. Practice has not confirmed this conception. Recognition is not simply the acknowledgement of a fact, namely, the existence of an entity; it is also a subjective and political act, whereby a State chooses to normalise its relations with a new entity or not, according to its interests and to the existence or not of outstanding disputes. Thus, recognition is also used as a political tool.[246] A State may bargain the recognition of another against

[241] See section II.C.10 below.

[242] See, eg, M Bothe, 'Peacekeeping' in Simma et al (eds), above n 95, 1171ff.

[243] We may here recall an anecdote about Sheridan. One day, two Dukes encounter Sheridan and say, 'Hello Sherry, we were asking ourselves whether you are weak or cunning.' Sheridan puts his arms around the two Dukes and responds, 'Between the two, I think.'

[244] *Certain Expenses of the United Nations* [1962] ICJ Rep 168.

[245] See, eg, H Lauterpacht, 'Règles générales du droit de la paix' (1937-IV) 62 *RCADI* 224ff.

[246] M Virally, 'Panorama du droit international contemporain' (1983-V) 183 *RCADI* 53–55; C Tomuschat, 'International Law: Ensuring the Survival of Mankind on the Eve of a New Century' (1999) 281 *RCADI* 115ff; J Verhoeven, *La reconnaissance internationale dans la pratique contemporaine* (Paris, 1975) 576ff.

the payment of debts due to it; or recognition may be made prematurely so as to enhance the effectiveness of a politically welcome entity, etc.

The law provides only a framework for the act of recognition; it also regulates the consequences under international law when recognition is performed. As to the conditions for recognition, the law imposes mainly limitations, such as: the duty to ascertain that the factual conditions for the existence of a State are met (government, population, territory, independence); the duty not to recognise before there is a certain degree of effectiveness of the State (non-intervention in internal affairs); the duty not to recognise entities created by the unlawful use of force or in violation of the right of self-determination of peoples; and possibly also the prohibition on using recognition as a tool that would offend the principle of abuse of rights. Within particular international law, further conditions for recognition can be agreed. Thus, the European Communities (as they then were) agreed to recognise the new States in Eastern Europe and of the former USSR subject to the following conditions: (i) respect for the provisions of the Charter of the UN and the Helsinki Final Act, notably concerning the rule of law, democracy and human rights; (ii) the guarantee of minority rights; (iii) respect for the inviolability of inherited boundaries; (iv) the acceptance of all relevant obligations relating to disarmament and nuclear non-proliferation, as well as to regional stability and security; (v) the promise to settle by agreement, and if necessary by arbitration, all disputes relating to State succession or regional issues.[247] These eminently political conditions resemble to some extent lists of requirements for establishing diplomatic relations.

v. The Law on the Peaceful Settlement of Disputes

The law organises a wide array of means for settling international disputes, without binding States to use them in all cases and without indicating mandatory means having precedence. In municipal law, the mandatory competence of the judge ensures in most cases the priority of application of the law, ie the rule of law. In international law, on the other hand, States are free to elect settlement by law or settlement by diplomacy. International law is thus not primarily at pains to ensure its own promotion; it is rather at pains to ensure the settlement of the dispute. Direct agreements allow the actors to take account of a wider range of circumstances than can the judge, who is kept within the confines of litigation. Moreover, the solution is often more stable when it is agreed and accepted by the parties. Consequently, the PCIJ and the ICJ have repeatedly affirmed that they are but substitutes ('*succédanés*') for the direct and amiable settlement of the dispute between the parties, even when proceedings at the particular Court have already been initiated.[248] The aim of settlement is more important than the means to

[247] See (1992) 96 *RGDIP* 261. For a critique, see J Salmon, 'Reconnaissance d'Etats' (1992) 25 *RBDI* 234.

[248] *Free Zones* Order (1929) PCIJ Series A no 22, 13; *Passage Through the Great Belt*, Order [1991] ICJ Rep 29.

achieve such settlement. The main rule is the 'free choice of means' principle.[249] Overall, once more, the law provides a framework and a toolbox for reaching certain politically desirable results. This is one of the reasons for the relative lack of legal detail in the branch relating to the settlement of disputes, notably when compared with that on sources.

8. *Politics Seeking to Consolidate its Realisations in a Legal Regime*

Politics may seek to transform its realisations into a legal regime capable of providing some legal certainty instead of the fluctuations proper to the political realm. Politics here attempts to clothe its achievements in legal robes. This may be to cover an initially illegal fact, to impose an objective regime,[250] or else to fight against an established fact through the doctrine of non-recognition. The politics that seeks such consolidation can be in the service of individual States, a group of powers or the international community.

i. Legal Regimes to the Benefit of Individual States

The concept of historic titles[251] to territory provides a first example. Sometimes, economic and political interests may push a State to extend its spheres of activity as a sovereign and to claim special rights over some adjacent areas. In a large sense, historic titles are part of the doctrine of acquisitive prescription. However, more often than not, historic titles refer to common areas, and notably to the sea (the sea is *res communis*, or more precisely *res extra commercium*). Since the areas thus claimed are part of the common domain, all other States are entitled to protest against the extension of the sphere of jurisdiction of a single State. The ICJ emphasised this entitlement in the *Norwegian Fisheries* case of 1951, when it mentioned the general tolerance of the international community to the Norwegian baseline system.[252] Historic titles are acquired only if certain conditions are met:

1. the spaces must be situated close to the territory of the claiming State, eg historic waters (adjacency);
2. the claim over the spaces must be made as a sovereign;
3. the public authority of the State must have been exercised in the area for a prolonged period of time and effectively;

[249] See the Manila Declaration on the Peaceful Settlement of Disputes by the UNGA, Resolution 37/10, 15 November 1982. On some problems, see, eg, E Jiménez de Aréchaga, 'International Law in the Past Third of a Century' (1978-I) 159 *RCADI* 147. There are rules providing some guarantees against unfair dealing, notably during negotiations between States: see R Kolb, *La bonne foi en droit international public* (Paris, 2000) 580ff.

[250] See P Dailler, M Forteau and A Pellet, *Droit international public*, 8th edn (Paris, 2009) 271ff.

[251] On historic titles, see YZ Blum, *Historic Titles in International Law* (The Hague, 1965); A Gioia, *Titoli storici e line di base del mare territoriale* (Padua, 1990); MW Clark, *Historic Bays and Waters* (New York, 1994); CR Symmons, *Historic Waters in the Law of the Sea* (Leiden, 2008).

[252] *Norwegian Fisheries* [1951] ICJ Rep 139.

4. the exercise of authority must have been notorious, ie notified or objectively known;
5. third States, notably those that had previously exercised rights in the area, must have accepted the claims, stopped protesting or never protested against these claims (acquiescence).

These criteria were applied by the US Supreme Court in the *US v Alaska* case (1975).[253] Overall, the function of law, in such cases, is to allow the consolidation of an effective state of affairs. The divorce between law and fact is thereby nullified The historical titles are based on the equitable consideration, which is to allow a State having ancient ties with some area to enjoy exclusive rights over it. The law provides a tool to transform political claims into legal entitlements.

Another example relates to the self-determination of peoples.[254] Originally, this concept had only a political reach and no legal status. In this regard it resembled the 'principle of nationalities' of the nineteenth century. The concept of the self-determination of peoples appeared as early as the Draft Declaration on the Law of Nations of Abbé Grégoire, dated 23 April 1795. Article 17 provided that a people can have recourse to war to defend its sovereignty, its liberty or its property.[255] Fresh evolutions followed President Wilson's Fourteen Points and the Soviet Revolution of 1917. In the second part of the twentieth century, the principle was largely linked to decolonisation. It appears in this guise in Resolutions 1514 (XV), 1541 (XV) and 2625 (XXV) of the UN General Assembly.[256] Later, the focus was on the protection of minorities, once the decolonisation phase had passed. The gist of the principle has thus constantly shifted, while maintaining connections with territorial transformations and political struggle: (i) first, a link with the French Revolution and popular sovereignty; (ii) later, a link with the principle of nationalities and national minorities, up to the time of the League of Nations; (iii) later still, a connection to decolonisation; and (iv) finally, a link with all types of minorities (internal self-determination), occupied peoples (eg Palestine) or peoples already constituted as States (sovereign self-determination). The common point is that various political aspirations have found natural prolongation

[253] *US v Alaska* (1975) 14 *ILM* 1017; see also the commentary by A Zimmermann in (1986) 23 *San Diego Law Review* 763ff. The concept of 'historical bays' is but a special case of historical titles (see, eg, JL Bouchez, *The Regime of Bays in International Law* (Leiden, 1963) 199ff): relevant cases here are the claims of Norway over Varangerfjord (1881), of Canada over Hudson Bay (1906), of Russia over Vladivostok Bay (1957), of Libya over the Bay of Syrte (1973) (there has here been a vigorous protest by third States: (1986) 80 *AJIL* 668ff). Sometimes the essentially political argument of 'vital bays' has been advanced: see UN Memorandum on Historical Bays, Doc A/CN4/143 (1962), §§151ff. As to Canada, see D Pharand, *Canada's Arctic Waters in International Law* (Cambridge, 1988).

[254] For a short discussion of this right, see, eg, C Tomuschat, 'International Law: Ensuring the Survival of Mankind on the Eve of a New Century' (1999) 281 *RCADI* 239ff. For a more detailed analysis, see, eg, D Raic, *Statehood and the Law of Self-Determination* (The Hague/London/New York, 2002) 171ff; K Knop, *Diversity and Self-Determination in International Law* (Cambridge, 2002).

[255] L Le Fur and G Chklaver, *Recueil de textes de droit international public*, 2nd edn (Paris, 1934) 69.

[256] On the historical evolution of the principle, see, eg, S Calogeropoulos-Stratis, *Le droit des peuples à disposer d'eux-mêmes* (Brussels, 1973) 15ff.

through a legal doctrine. The latter remains highly coloured by political aspects, with all their fluctuations and changes.

Legal literature has identified the main legal aspects of the principle of self-determination:

1. There are external and internal types of self-determination.
2. Internal self-determination concerns the relations of a people (minority) within a State with that State. It does not give rise to a right of secession but only to the protection of human and minority rights, as well as to a right to good governance. It is further composed of the right to resist foreign intervention, granted to all peoples already constituted as States.
3. External self-determination concerns the ability, given to a people, to resist by force any domination and/or to exercise a right to secession. This limb of self-determination is in tension with the principle of the territorial integrity of States. Thus, it is recognised only in certain well-defined contexts: the fight against colonisation; and oppression by foreign occupiers (eg Palestine) or racist regimes (the previous apartheid regime in South Africa). Some authorities also include the situation in which a minority is systematically excluded from representation in the State institutions and is the object of massive persecution (remedial secession).[257] But this latter doctrine is not yet part and parcel of positive international law.[258] Lastly, there is the right to reunification of divided peoples, such as the two Germanys or the two Koreas. Here stops the objectivisation operated by legal rules.

On the cardinal issue, namely the definition of what is a 'people', the law does not give any clear indications.[259] Politics remains the master of the process. There is no *a priori* definition of peoples. What a people is depends on historical processes and political projections, on self-definition and sometimes stigmatisation by others. Thus, outside the context of peoples already constituted as States, the 'people' vested with rights of self-determination must be recognised by States, regional or universal organisations each and every time. The concept of a people itself remains to a considerable extent political; and political considerations will play a great role in the recognition operated by political organs. Politics clothes a part of the principle in law; and it keeps it subjected to important gaps *intra legem* so as to remain the master of those crucial *ad hoc* judgements necessary to put it into operation. The principle of self-determination is amphibious; it straddles law and politics.

[257] See, eg, *In re Secession of Quebec*, Canada, Supreme Court, Opinion of 20 August 1998, (1998) 37 *ILM* 1373.

[258] See the analysis in R Kolb, 'Autodétermination et 'sécession-remède' en droit international public' in *Essays in Honor of G. Ziccardi-Capaldo* (*Global Community Yearbook*) (New York, 2013) 57ff.

[259] JF Guilhaudis, *Le droit des peuples à disposer d'eux-mêmes* (Grenoble, 1976) 32ff. This is also the reason why some authors claimed that the principle itself was a purely political doctrine and not part of the legal order. See, eg, W Friedmann, 'General Course in Public International Law' (1969-II) 127 *RCADI* 185ff; or the legal philosopher M Villey, *Leçons d'histoire de la philosophie du droit* (Paris, 1962) 162.

ii. Legal Regimes to the Benefit of a Group of Powers

The clearest example here is that of 'objective territorial regimes'.[260] Sometimes Great Powers created through various conventions territorial regimes considered to be valid *erga omnes*. This occurred mainly in the nineteenth century through the Concert of Europe, concerning: neutralisations (eg the neutrality of Switzerland, Vienna Treaty 1815); demilitarisation (eg the Treaty of Paris of 1856); regimes for the freedom of navigation (eg Convention of Constantinople of 1888); or later treaties on denuclearisation (eg Treaty of Rarotonga, 1985, which was, however, not principally sponsored by Great Powers). In this area, some Powers tend to act as a sort of *de facto* international government for the collective interest. In reality, the interests pursued are often both general and particular. The Commission of Lawyers, constituted under the auspices of the League of Nations in the context of the *Aland Islands* case (1920), to a certain extent recognised the legal validity of such regimes: 'Les Puissances ont, en effet, dans de nombreux cas, depuis 1815, et notamment lors de la conclusion de Traités de Paix, cherché à établir un véritable droit objectif, de vrais statuts politiques, dont les effets se font sentir en dehors même du cercle des parties contractantes.'[261] The Antarctic Treaty of 1959[262] is based on the same approach. There is a group of States who are the masters of the regime, with a concomitant expectation that third States will respect this regime, perhaps on the basis that it has matured into customary international law. The question whether these 'objective legal regimes' are a recognised exception to the principle of the *inter partes* effect of treaties, or whether they can rather be said to be based on customary rules, is secondary for our purposes. The main point is that political aspirations to territorial stability seek to clothe themselves with legal rules.

iii. Legal Regimes to the Benefit of the International Community

One example in this category has already been mentioned more than once in the present study: the doctrine of the 'common heritage of mankind'.[263] At the end of

[260] See E Klein, *Statusverträge im Völkerrecht* (Berlin, 1980); SP Subedi, 'The Doctrine of Objective Regimes in International law and the Competence of the UN to Impose Territorial or Peace Settlements on States' (1994) 37 *GYIL* 162ff.

[261] In English: 'The Powers have, indeed, in numerous cases since 1815, and notably through the conclusion of peace treaties, attempted to establish a truly objective law and political statutes, whose effects can be felt beyond the circle of contracting parties.' *Journal officiel de la Société des Nations*, 1920, Supp no 3, 17.

[262] See, eg, A Watts, *International Law and the Antarctic Treaty System* (Cambridge, 1992); F Francioni and T Scovazzi (eds), *International Law for Antarctica*, 2nd edn (The Hague, 1996).

[263] K Baslar, *The Concept of the Common Heritage of Mankind in International Law* (The Hague/Boston/London, 1998); A Blanc Altemir, *Patrimonio Común de la Humanidad* (Barcelona, 1992); A Cassese, *International Law in a Divided World* (Oxford, 1986) 376ff; RJ Dupuy, 'La notion de patrimoine commun de l'humanité appliquée aux fonds marins' in *Essays in Honor of C.A. Colliard* (Paris, 1984) 197ff; R Goy, 'The International Protection of the Cultural and Natural Heritage' (1973) 4 *NYIL* 117ff; C Joyner, 'Legal Implications of the Concept of the Common Heritage of Mankind' (1986) 35 *ICLQ* 190ff; AC Kiss, 'La notion de patrimoine commun de l'humanité' (1982-II) 175 *RCADI* 99ff;

the 1960s, there was a political effort to transform the deep seabed into an international common space to the benefit of all States, and not just for the benefit of the technologically most advanced. The legal-political tool for this was the 'common heritage' principle, which then found its way into the Montego Bay Convention on the Law of the Sea (Part XI of the Convention).[264] The institutional framework for the exploration and exploitation of the deep seabed, and for the redistribution of its revenues, was highly detailed.[265] Its bureaucratic complexity led to marked-orientated reform at the beginning of the 1990s. However, the idea of the redistribution of revenues remained.[266] The concept of common heritage has moreover extended to other spaces: this is the case, for example, in Article 1 of the Treaty on Outer Space of 1967 and later Article 11 of the Treaty on Activities of States on the Moon and other Celestial Bodies of 1979. No institutional arrangements of the kind described above for the deep seabed were made in these latter contexts. Community pressures continue to be exerted for the extension of the domain of global commons. Arguments relating to 'common heritage' have, for example, been advanced in the context of geostationary orbits or Antarctica. There have also been efforts by ecological groups to achieve recognition of 'global ecological commons', such as the atmosphere, the ozone layer, tropical forests, etc.[267] In these cases, the idea of protection replaces that of common exploitation.

The common heritage principle has certain normative aspects:

1. non-appropriation under national sovereignty;
2. the sharing of the resources and revenues, if any, among all peoples and States;
3. exclusively peaceful utilisation of the spaces and the non-stationing of weapons of mass destruction;
4. freedom of scientific research and the duty to make the results accessible to all;
5. duties of prevention of damage to and protection of the environment;

V Postyshev, *The Common Heritage of Mankind: From New Thinking to New Practice* (Moscow, 1990); W Stocker, *Das Prinzip des Common Heritage of Mankind als Ausdruck des Staatengemeinschaftsinteresses im Völkerrecht* (Zurich, 1993); S Sucharitkul, 'Evolution continue d'une notion nouvelle: le patrimoine commun de l'humanité' in *Essays in Honor of S. Rosenne* (Dordrecht/Boston/London, 1989) 887ff; R Wolfrum, *Die Internationalisierung staatsfreier Räume* (Berlin, 1984) 328ff; R Wolfrum, 'The Principle of the Common Heritage of Mankind' (1983) 43 *ZaöRV* 312ff.

264 Montego Bay Convention on the Law of the Sea, Arts 133ff.

265 FH Paolillo, 'The Institutional Arrangements for the International Sea-Bed and Their Impact on the Evolution of International Organizations' (1984-V) 188 *RCADI* 135ff.

266 On the current state of affairs, see, eg, DR Rothwell and T Stephens, *The International Law of the Sea* (Oxford/Portland, 2010) 136ff; Y Tanaka, *The International Law of the Sea*, 2nd edn (Cambridge, 2015) 177ff.

267 See, eg, MS Soroos, 'The Evolution of Global Commons' in *Global Environmental Policies* (2001) 39ff; R Warner, 'Implementing the Rule of Law for nature in the Global Marine Commons: Developing Environmental Assessment Frameworks' in C Voigt (ed), *Rule of Law for Nature: New Dimensions and Ideas in Environmental Law* (Cambridge, 2013) 347ff; M Kotzur, 'Das Völkerrecht von der Menschheit her denken: einige Ueberlegungen zu den global commons' in A Blankenagel and P Häberle (eds), *Den Verfassungsstaat nachdenken* (Berlin, 2014) 43ff.

6. non-discrimination of access and the duty to take due account of the activities of other States in the area.

At the heart of the institution lies the protection of the common space and its sustainable exploitation to the benefit of all. In short, the basic idea seems to be an 'expropriation' of a certain good to the benefit of the international community as a whole. Political will is put at the service of individual interests of the mass of the States, and sometimes of the have-nots; but indissolubly linked to those interests are the interests of the international community.

Another matter already mentioned relates to the duty of non-recognition of territorial situations created through the use of unlawful force or in violation of the principle of self-determination.[268] The principle of legality has here made an important inroad into the principle of effectiveness.[269] The former principle was mentioned for the first time in Article 13 of the Treaty of Union of American States at Santiago of Chile in 1856. It was later generalised in the Manchurian crisis in 1932/1933, with a League of Nations Resolution leading to the Stimson Doctrine.[270] After World War II, it was applied to a great number of unlawful territorial situations, for example the annexation of territories by Israel, Northern Cyprus, the South-African Townships or Kuwait. Thus, a political conception anchored in a collective interest crafted a legal tool. The latter operates on behalf of the collective interest within the legal order.

A last example concerns the avoidance of a gap that would be politically unwelcome. This occurred in the context of the creation of the category 'crimes against humanity' at the end of World War II.[271] This category was inserted into Control Council Law no 10 of the Allied Control Council for Germany (1945)[272] and in the Statute of the International Military Tribunal annexed to the London Agreement on the Criminal Prosecution of War Criminals of European Axis Powers (1945).[273] It allowed criminal prosecutions to be brought for atrocities committed by Germans on Germans (whereas the category 'war crimes' would have covered only persons having an enemy nationality). The issue of how a State treated its

[268] See J Dugard, *Recognition and the United Nations* (Cambridge, 1987) 123ff; M Dawidowicz, 'The Obligation of Non-Recognition of an Unlawful Situation' in Crawford et al (eds), above n 178, 677; N Joergensen, 'The Obligation of Non-Assistance to the Responsible State' in Crawford et al (eds), above n 178, 687ff.

[269] On its historical evolution and practice, see, eg, R Kolb, 'La maxime "nemo ex propria turpitudine commodum capere potest" (nul ne peut profiter de son propre tort) en droit international public' (2000) 33 *RBDI* 84ff; Oppenheim, above n 91, 183ff.

[270] Among the contemporary literature, see mainly AR Tullié, *La Mandchourie et le conflit Sino-Japonais devant la Société des Nations* (Paris, 1935); WW Willoughby, *The Sino-Japanese Controversy and the League of Nations* (Baltimore, 1935).

[271] On crimes against humanity, see, eg, O Triffterer (ed), *Commentary on the Rome Statute of the International Criminal Court*, 2nd edn (Munich/Oxford) 159ff; A Cassese, P Gaeta and JR Jones (eds), *The Rome Statute of the International Criminal Court, A Commentary*, vol I (Oxford, 2002) 353ff.

[272] Art 2, §1.

[273] Art 6, letter c.

own nationals had formerly been a matter for domestic jurisdiction.[274] True, the offences to be punished were criminal according to all the criminal codes in the world, but they had not yet been framed as an international crime. The universal reach of the category 'crimes against humanity', attaching to the fact of being human and not to a nationality, has been emphasised in the case law.[275] A political and moral interest of universal reach has found its way into the law.

9. *Politics and Law on Separate Tracks*

An example of this situation can be found in the parallel activities of the UN Security Council and the ICJ when seized of different aspects of the same dispute. The Council is called on to treat the political aspects of the dispute, the Court the legal aspects as submitted by the parties. The Court has developed in its case law the doctrine according to which the jurisdictions of both organs are separate and each is pursued *pari passu*. There is here an attempt to carve out a sort of 'legal reserved domain', protected against inroads by politics.[276]

The Court has affirmed the autonomy of its own proceedings with respect to those before the Security Council in a remarkably straight line of jurisprudence: *Aegean Sea Continental Shelf* (1978);[277] *Diplomatic and Consular Staff in Tehran* case (1980);[278] *Military and Paramilitary Activities in Nicaragua* (Jurisdiction and Admissibility) (1986).[279] The usual chain of arguments is as follows: The Court's jurisdiction is not hampered by the parallel seizing of the Security Council: the Council deals with the political aspects and the Court with the legal ones.

274 See, eg, the *Bernheim* case, brought before the organs of the League of Nations after enactment of the Nuremberg race laws, which were obliged to decline jurisdiction: (1933) 12 *Revue de droit international (Paris)* 502ff.

275 *Judgment of the International Military Tribunal*, London, 1946, Cmd 6964, 60ff; *Altstötter* Trial (1947), US Military Tribunal, *Law Reports of Trials of War Criminals*, United Nations War Crimes Commission, vol VI (London, 1948) 39–40; *Flick* Trial (1947), US Military Tribunal, *Law Reports of Trials of War Criminals*, United Nations War Crimes Commission, vol IX (London, 1949) 51–52.

276 See, eg, E Klein, 'Paralleles Tätigwerden von Sicherheitsrat und Internationalem Gerichtshof bei friedensbedrohenden Streitigkeiten' in *Essays in Honor of H. Mosler* (Berlin/Heidelberg/New York, 1983) 481ff. There are also cases where the consensual title of jurisdiction of the Court is limited by a clause or a reservation whereby the Court shall be competent only if and when another procedure for the settlement of the dispute has proved unsuccessful. The Court may then defer, as the case may be, to this conventionally stipulated primacy. See *Border and Transborder Armed Actions (Nicaragua v Honduras)* [1988] ICJ Rep 88ff.

277 *Aegean Sea Continental Shelf* [1978] ICJ Rep 12.

278 *Diplomatic and Consular Staff in Tehran* [1980] ICJ Rep 21, §40; and with regard to a Commission created by the Secretary General, *ibid*, 23, §43.

279 *Military and Paramilitary Activities in Nicaragua* (Jurisdiction and Admissibility) [1984] ICJ Rep 435, §98. For a critique, see PM Norton, 'The Nicaragua Case: Political Questions before the ICJ' (1987) 27 *Virginia Journal of International Law* 459ff. *Contra*: A Chayes, 'Nicaragua, the United States, and the World Court' (1985) 85 *Columbia Law Review* 1449ff; PW Kahn, 'From Nuremberg to the Hague: the United States Position in Nicaragua v US and the Development of International Law' (1987) 12 *Yale Journal of International Law* 1ff; J Verhoeven, 'Le Droit, le Juge et la Violence, Les arrêts Nicaragua c. Etats-Unis' (1987) 91 *RGDIP* 1183ff; PM Eisemann, 'L'arrêt de la CIJ du 26 novembre 1984 (Compétence et recevabilité) dans l'affaire des activités militaires et paramilitaires au Nicaragua et contre celui-ci' (1984) 30 *AFDI* 385ff.

The Security Council has only a primary and not exclusive competence on matters concerning the maintenance of the peace (Article 24, §1 of the Charter). Moreover, Article 12, §1 of the Charter does not contain any limitation on parallel activities of the Security Council and ICJ as it does as regards the relationship between the Security Council and General Assembly (argument *a contrario*). In the *Lockerbie* case (1992/1998),[280] the Court considered that the Security Council could not put to an end the dispute before the Court: the existence of the dispute had to be judged solely with regard to the moment of the seizing of the Court; subsequent Security Council resolutions could not extinguish it so as to deprive the Court of jurisdiction; the legal effect of the resolutions had to be considered at the merits stage. At the same time, the Court took pains not to interfere with the exercise of its political powers by the Security Council.[281]

10. Legal Inroads into Politics

In a broad sense, any adoption of conventional provisions and any development of customary norms represents an extension of the legal domain, and therefore the progress of the law within the enveloping body of politics. The aim of international law is to regulate various political relations between States by introducing legal considerations such as objectivity, reciprocity or obligation. In a narrower sense, the law can penetrate into a political body previously resistant to the progress of the rule of law. The law makes an inroad into a sensitive political area and imposes a certain regularity with regard to the aims to be pursued. In the first phase, some general principles of law will flow into a legally virgin space. These principles will give rise to deductive reasoning, analogies and concretisations. The result will be the progressive augmentation of the legal content. This triggers its own requirements of generality, a certain level of abstraction, reciprocity, equality, justice and equity, legal certainty and the like. Three examples of this process can be given here.

i. Judicial Review of Political Acts

In municipal law, judicial review of the legality or constitutionality of political and administrative acts has mainly been the result of the progress of the rule of law during the twentieth century.[282] Formally, judicial review of constitutionality confirms the primacy of the constitution over derived sources. Substantively, the process implies legal control of political choices, which must remain within the four corners of the constitutional order. Not all systems confer such power on the judiciary. There are peoples sensitive to the danger of a 'government of judges';

[280] See particularly [1998] ICJ Rep 23, §37ff.

[281] A due regard that the Council has not always paid to the Court. See M Bedjaoui, *Nouvel ordre mondial et contrôle de la légalité des actes du Conseil de sécurité* (Brussels, 1994) 89.

[282] M Hertig Randall, 'L'internationalisation de la juridiction constitutionnelle: défis et perspectives' (2010) 129 *Revue de droit suisse* 221.

they prefer to leave the question of constitutionality to the political process, for example the popular vote. This is the case in Switzerland. In other systems, either from the outset (US)[283] or following appalling experiences (Germany),[284] a constitutional judge was entrusted with the supreme guardianship of the law. In international society, the general relations of law and power, the absence of a clearly defined constitution, as well as the weakness of the rule of law, have all hampered any comparable function. A Belgian proposal to confer such a power on the ICJ was overwhelmingly defeated at the San Francisco Conference of 1945.[285]

The Court has nevertheless developed in its case law a certain doctrine on judicial review.[286] It concentrates on acts of international institutions; control of the

[283] On constitutional review in the US, see, eg, L Tribe, *American Constitutional Law* (Minnesota, 1988).

[284] On constitutional review in Germany, see, eg, S Korioth and K Schlaich, *Das Bundesverfassungsgericht* (Munich, 2015).

[285] See the discussion in M Bedjaoui, *Nouvel ordre mondial et contrôle de la légalité des actes du Conseil de sécurité* (Brussels, 1994) 20.

[286] See among others H Thierry, 'Les Résolutions des organes internationaux dans la jurisprudence de la Cour internationale de Justice' (1980-II) 167 *RCADI* 393ff; E McWhinney, 'The International Court as Emerging Constitutional Court and the Co-ordinate United Nations Institutions (especially the Security Council): Implications of the Aerial Incident at Lockerbie' (1992) 30 *CYIL* 261ff; GR Watson, 'Constitutionalism, Judicial Review and the World Court' (1993) 34 *Harvard International Law Journal* 1ff; M Bedjaoui, *Nouvel ordre mondial et contrôle de la légalité des actes du Conseil de sécurité* (Brussels, 1994); L Condorelli, 'La Corte internazionale di Giustizia e gli organi politici delle Nazioni Unite' (1994) 77 *RDI* 897ff; V Gowlland-Debbas, 'The Relationship between the International Court of Justice and the Security Council in the Light of the Lockerbie Case' (1994) 88 *AJIL* 643, 663ff; DW Bowett, 'The Impact of Security Council Decisions on Dispute Settlement Procedures' (1994) 5 *EJIL* 89ff; LC Caflisch, 'Is the International Court of Justice Entitled to review Security Council Resolutions accepted under Chapter VII of the United Nations Charter?' in N Al-Nauimi and R Meese (eds), *International Legal Issues Arising under the United Nations Decade of International Law* (The Hague, 1995) 633ff; K Roberts, 'Second-Guessing the Security Council: The ICJ and its Powers of Judicial Review' (1995) 7 *Pace International Law Review* 281ff; JE Alvarez, 'Judging the Security Council' (1996) 90 *AJIL* 1ff; B Martenczuk, *Rechtsbindung und Rechtskontrolle des Weltsicherheitsrats. Die Überprüfung nichtmilitärischer Zwangsmassnahmen durch den Internationalen Gerichtshof* (Berlin, 1996); D Akande, 'The ICJ and the Security Council: Is there Room for Judicial Control of Decisions of the Political Organs of the United Nations?' (1997) 46 *ICLQ* 309ff; A Leporatti, 'Some Aspects of the Relationship between the ICJ and the Security Council in the Light of Recent Cases: In Particular, are there Limitations to the Security Council's Powers?' in K Koufa (ed), *International Justice, Thesaurus Acroasium* (Thessaloniki, 1997) 723ff; MN Shaw, 'The Security Council and the ICJ: Judicial Drift and Judicial Function' in AS Muller et al (eds), *The International Court of Justice, Its Future Role after Fifty Years* (The Hague, 1997) 219ff; F Lenze, 'Une compétence expresse de la Cour en matière de contrôle de légalité des actes des autres organes principaux de l'ONU, notamment du Conseil de sécurité?' in K Koufa (ed), *International Law at the Turn of the Century, Thesaurus Acroasium* (Thessaloniki, 1998) 565ff; M Fraas, *Sicherheitsrat der Vereinten Nationen und Internationaler Gerichtshof* (Frankfurt, 1998); J Herbst, *Rechtskontrolle des UN-Sicherheitsrates* (Frankfurt, 1999); N Meyer-Ohlendorf, *Gerichtliche Kontrolle des Sicherheitsrates der Vereinten Nationen durch den Internationalen Gerichtshof: kann der IGH die Rechtmässigkeit von Zwangsmassnahmen nach Kap. VII UNO-Charta kontrollieren?* (Berlin, 2000); E de Wet, 'Judicial Review of the United Nations Security Council and General Assembly through Advisory Opinions of the ICJ' (2000) 10 *RSDIE* 237ff; D D'Angelo, 'The "Check" on International Peace and Security Maintenance: The ICJ and Judicial Review of Security Council Resolutions' (2000) 23 *Suffolk Transnational Law Review* 561ff; D Schweigman, *The Authority of the Security Council under Chapter VII of the UN Charter: Legal Limits and the Role of the ICJ* (The Hague, 2001); M Zambelli, *La constatation des situations de l'article 39 de la Charte des Nations Unies par le Conseil de sécurité* (Geneva/Basle/Munich, 2002) 336ff; MS Amr, *The Role of the International Court of Justice as the Principal Judicial*

legality of acts of States with regard to international law falls within the ordinary contentious function of the Court. The following aspects are the pole stars of 'constitutional control':

1. There is a presumption of the validity of acts of international organisations.[287] This protects legal certainty and gives a proper margin of political action to international institutions. It further protects the legitimate expectations of States as to the legality of decisions, and protects the acts of such institutions from excessive subversion. A permanent threat of findings of illegality, responsibility and nullity would hamper the action of international institutions. But the presumption of legality can be rebutted. No blank cheque is given to politics.
2. The question of the legality of a legal act of an organ can be posed directly through a request for an advisory opinion.[288]
3. The same question of legality can also arise in the context of so-called incidental control, when the Court is required to pronounce on the legality of a resolution or some other act in order to be able to respond to the legal question asked.[289] This can occur in either an advisory[290] or a contentious proceeding.[291] The Court will not in such cases declare the nullity of the resolution at issue, but only refrain from applying it with effect between the parties in the case at hand (Article 59 of the ICJ Statute). The political effect of the pronouncement by the highest judicial body of the UN will manifestly extend beyond the the parties to the proceedings.

Organ of the United Nations (The Hague/London/New York, 2003) 279ff; E de Wet, *The Chapter VII Powers of the United Nations Security Council* (Oxford/Portland, 2004) 25ff; I Petculescu, 'The Review of the United Nations Security Council Decisions by the ICJ' (2005) 52 *NILR* 167ff; MI Papa, *I rapporti tra la Corte internazionale di Giustizia e il Consiglio di sicurezza* (Padua, 2006) 287ff; R Kolb, *The International Court of Justice* (Oxford, 2013) 879ff. See also E de Wet and A Nollkaemper, 'Review of Security Council Decisions by National Courts' (2002) 45 *GYIL* 166ff. For a control of an international treaty (concerning the EU) by an internal Constitutional Court (German *Bundesverfassungsgericht*) with regard to the compatibility of the transfer of sovereign powers to the EC/EU, see *Brunner and others* (1993) 98 *ILR* 197ff.

287 *Namibia* (Opinion) [1971] ICJ Rep 22; *Certain Expenses of the UN* (Opinion) [1962] ICJ Rep 168.

288 *Constitution of the Maritime Safety Committee of the IMCO* (Opinion) [1960] ICJ Rep 151.

289 For example, there is a dispute between two States on the execution of a commercial treaty: State A claims that State B has breached that treaty by non-performance; State B responds that it could not perform the treaty since it is bound by an embargo decision of the Security Council under Art 41 of the UN Charter; State A responds that the resolution of the Security Council is invalid. If the Court is seized on the issue of the violation or non-performance of the treaty, it may have to decide incidentally (ie as a preliminary point) whether the resolution is valid and applicable.

290 See *Certain Expenses of the UN* (Opinion) [1962] ICJ Rep 168: a certain number of members of the UN contested the legality of a resolution allocating to the UN budget the expenses of peacekeeping operations; *Namibia* (Opinion) [1971] ICJ Rep 22: South Africa had contested the validity of UN resolutions on Namibia and the Court responded.

291 The issue would have been prominent in the *Lockerbie* case, if it had not been discontinued. See [1992] ICJ Rep 15, §§39–40. Chapter VII resolutions of the Security Council were here at stake.

4. Substantively, the review will bear on respect for the constitutive instrument of the organisation, the functions and aims entrusted to the organs and/or the rules on jurisdiction and procedure. The level of control can be high or lower, for example defining those matters in which there will be only minimal control of manifest irregularity, improper motives, abuse of procedure or arbitrariness; defining matters over which more control is required, for example with regard to fundamental rights of persons or fundamental norms, as indicated; by carving out certain matters where non-justiciability prevails and where political discretion is thus granted; by modifying the degree of scrutiny according to the type of procedure, ie direct or incidental control, etc.[292] Overall, the spaces left for political discretion are here coloured and restrained by legal considerations.

ii. Restriction of State Immunities[293]

Immunity does not exempt a subject from a legal obligation but only from a certain procedure for its execution. It is conferred with regard to the public authority manifested in the acts of States and presents itself as a space left to politics by the law. For a long time there have been efforts to limit this exceptional institution of the common law. Thus, jurisdictional immunities of States have been progressively limited since the beginning of the twentieth century to State conduct under public authority, to the exclusion of State conduct as a private person (distinction *acta jure imperii* and *acta jure gestionis*). When the State exercises its public functions, the tribunals of foreign States cannot subject them to their jurisdiction; when the State engages on the markets as a private person would do,[294] the jurisdiction is not impeded. This distinction ensures judicial protection without impinging on the political freedom of States. There are nevertheless also tendencies nowadays to limit immunities in one core area of public action, that is in the context of the violation of fundamental norms of international law through grave crimes. If admitted, such exceptions would have a direct impact on the domain of politics by significantly restricting its reach.

Such restrictive tendencies have enjoyed some success in the context of criminal international law.[295] They have been less successful in the context of States'

[292] See, eg, JE Alvarez, 'Judging the Security Council' (1996) 90 *AJIL* 26–27.

[293] G Hafner et al, *La pratique des Etats concernant les immunités des Etats* (Leiden, 2006); R van Albeek, *The Immunity of States and Their Officials in International Criminal Law and International Human Rights Law* (Oxford, 2008); A Bellal, *Immunités et violations graves des droits humains: vers une evolution structurelle de l'ordre juridique international?* (Brussels, 2011); S El-Sawah, *Les immunités des Etats et des organisations internationales* (Brussels, 2012); H Fox and P Webb, *The Law of State Immunity*, 3rd edn (Oxford, 2013).

[294] Eg labour contracts with subordinate personnel in the service of an embassy; the purchase of commodities; etc.

[295] This has been the case mainly in the context of torture. In *Filartiga v Pena-Irala* (1980) 77 *ILR* 169ff, the son of an opponent was abducted by Mr Pena-Irala and tortured to death. When the torturer came onto the territory of the US, where the father and sister of the deceased had sought refuge, a

jurisdictional immunities.[296] In particular in the context of mass violations during an armed conflict, there can hardly be anything to be gained by opening the gates to uncontrolled litigation all over the world.[297] In such situations, lump sum agreements between governments, or international schemes, such as the UN Compensation Commission for Iraq,[298] are the best ways to deal with the issue. However that may be, the tendencies towards a restriction of immunity are, analytically speaking, inroads made by the law into the sphere of politics.

iii. The Juridification of Political Aspirations: Soft Law Becoming Hard

Sometimes, flexible legal-political general principles form a bridge for the progressive penetration of the law. This may be the case, for example, as regards principles such as 'right to a healthy environment'[299] under the limb of human rights. Initially, there may be nothing more than a program or a political aspiration; it does not have, as such, any tangible legal value, or is at least not justiciable. The same can be said of principles such as the 'right of future generations to a healthy environment' or 'trans-generational equity'.[300] In the traditional approach these are only political slogans not founding any legal claim. But even here the law has sometimes progressed in unexpected directions. The *Oposa Minors* case (1993), decided by the Supreme Court of the Philippines,[301] is an interesting, if not extravagant, precedent—but possibly also a welcome one. The claimants were minors represented by their parents. They demanded that certain licences to exploit wood in virgin forests should not be renewed. As a legal basis for this claim, they cited Article 16, §2 of the Philippines Constitution of 1987, which emphasises that the

claim was brought before US tribunals. The tribunals rejected the immunities of the foreign State with regard to the acts committed. The situation was similar in *Letelier v Chile* (1980) 63 *ILR* 378ff, where a Chilean politician and his secretary were killed by a bomb in the US. The bomb had been planted by agents of the Chilean secret service. Chile's immunity was brushed aside: see S Schmahl, 'Letelier and Moffitt Claim' in R Wolfrum, *The Max Planck Encyclopedia of Public International Law*, vol VI (Oxford, 2012) 819ff. In *Al-Adsani v Kuwait* (1994) 100 ILR 465, the Court of Appeal had this to say (per Evans LJ at 471), 'no State or sovereign immunity should be accorded even under the State Immunity Act in respect of acts which it is alleged are properly to be described as torture in contravention of public international law' (reversed by the High Court and the Court of Appeal: see the Judgments of 15 March 1995 and of 12 March 1996, (1995) 103 *ILR* 420ff and (1996) 107 *ILR* 536 respectively). One might also recall the *Pinochet* proceedings in England: (1998) 37 *ILM* 1302, particularly at1332ff. See also, in a different context (expropriations founded apparently on an anti Semitic motive), *Siderman de Blake v Argentina* (1992) 103 *ILR* 468.

296 *Jurisdictional Immunities of the State* [2012-I] ICJ Rep 105ff.

297 J Bröhmer, *State Immunity and the Violation of Human Rights* (The Hague/Boston/London, 1997) 206: 'War, war crimes and genocide *per definitionem* inflict pain on thousands, sometimes millions of individuals. Municipal courts are just not equipped to deal with the sheer number of cases which could arise from such crimes.'

298 See eg J. A. Crook, 'The UN Compensation Commission: A New Structure to Enforce State Responsibility' (1993) 87 *AJIL* 144ff; RB Lillich (ed), *The United Nations Compensation Commission* (New York, 1995); V Jütte, *Die United Nations Compensation Commission* (Bern/Frankfurt, 1999).

299 Principle I of the Rio Declaration of 1992.

300 Principle II of the Stockholm Declaration of 1972.

301 *Oposa Minors* (1994) 33 *ILM* 173.

State must protect and develop the right of each person to a healthy environment in conformity with international instruments. The claimants also relied on the concept of 'inter-generational responsibility and justice'. The Supreme Court reversed the decision of the district court and allowed the claim. It considered that the claimants had legal standing to act on behalf of future generations under the principle of inter-generational responsibility: '[E]very generation has a responsibility to the next to preserve that rhythm and harmony [of nature] for the full enjoyment of a balanced and healthful ecology.'[302] There was thus a duty to protect the forests. In view of the considerable scope of the licences, the right of the claimants to contest them could not be doubted.[303] The decision was taken unanimously by the 14 signatory judges. The style of argument can seem strange to the traditionally trained Western lawyer. There may be a flavour of legalisation of politics, or of the politicisation of law. But it cannot be denied that the law here extended into the political realm. The decision is also a milestone in the protection of a collective interest of the international community, namely the environment.

III. Conclusion

The relationships between international law and international politics are constantly shifting, mutually reinforcing or opposing one another. There is no simple relationship where the one always predominates over the other. It is true that international law—the political law of nations—is closer to politics than any other legal branch, with the exception of constitutional law. This is true with regard to its object, the diplomatic-political relations among States, and also the mobility of its sources, never petrified into a code. It is equally true with regard to the decentralisation of international society, where the constitutional functions remain largely in the domain of State jurisdiction. Lastly, it is true with regard to the permanence of sovereignty and of national allegiance in the common feeling. All these factors explain the intimate relationships between the two poles in international society.

For sceptics, there can be no true law in an anarchical society. Thus, so-called international law is but a cloak for politics, merely a changeable discourse for the justification of any deed. International society is from this perspective governed only by politics. For legalists, conversely, international society is progressively legalised. Everywhere the law lurks behind the scenes. The States use the tool of law in all their political dealings. In robust versions of this view, politics seems to disappear beneath the weight of legal constraints. The truth lies in between. Even if it is permeable to politics more than any other legal order, international law is a legal order; its particularity simply stems from the type of society it regulates. Profoundly marked by politics (as to some extent also internal law, which is the result

[302] *ibid*, 185.
[303] *ibid*, 188.

of political dealings in parliament) it also influences the latter and imposes its own requirement. In every negotiation, there is a complex web of political and legal aspects that have to be taken into account—if only because the result of the negotiations will often have to be consigned to a legal document. The proper course is thus to avoid the two main pitfalls: on the one hand, to exaggerate the role of law in constructing lofty conceptual orders floating beyond the reach of political influence; on the other hand, to indulge in open cynicism, accompanied by a sense of superiority as one who has understood it all. Modesty and nuance are necessary on both sides, as in all other realms of life.

Part Three

International Law and Certain Fundamental Legal-Political Notions

9

The Relationship of International Law with Certain Cardinal Legal Notions

Eight important legal values will be the object of review in this part of the book:

1. the common good;
2. justice;
3. legal certainty;
4. reciprocity, equality and proportionality;
5. freedom;
6. morals and social morals;
7. will and reason;
8. sanctions.

Initially, the material content of these concepts, as developed through social experience, needs to be delineated. The issue will then turn on how these notions apply in the context of international law, that is, the extent to which there are analogies with the general legal experience, and the extent to which specificities and alterations prevail in international society. The answers given may deepen our understanding of the characteristics of international law and its links to the universal legal phenomena.

I. The Common Good

A. General Legal Experience

The common good (*bonum commune*) has since ancient times rubbed shoulders with political bodies as a notion referring partly to ideals but also to reality. It indicates the means and aims of government. Thus, for Plato and Aristotle, the concept refers to the art of taking care of matters concerning all citizens of the *polis*, ie designating what is beneficial to all. This is linked to the ultimate end of the political body, namely a good life (*eu zoïn*). In the phrase the 'common good', the 'good' is defined as a function of the cardinal virtues: intelligence, courage, measure and justice; the word 'common' refers to the collective space, ie the political collectivity.

The common good is thus a finalistic notion referring to a series of moral, political and legal values. The term '*bonum commune*' seems to have been used first by Albertus Magnus: '*omnis politia est ad commune bonum et nulla ad privatum*'.[1] He refers—rather too simplistically—to the two main *utilitates* found in each society: the good of the whole (*utilitas publica*) and the good of the individual (*utilitas singulorum*).

Thomas Aquinas completes the picture. Given that a human being needs the collectivity for protection and perfection, he must recognise a good that transcends his needs as a single unit. This greater good is a goal towards which one must strive.[2] It refers to good order,[3] peace and justice,[4] proportionality of the charges,[5] respect for the other[6] and the blessings of life.[7] Thomas Aquinas refuses to set the interests of the individual and those of the collectivity in opposition to each other. The individual can only have a good life in a well-ordered collectivity.[8] Conversely, the collectivity cannot prosper if it crushes the individuals comprising it. Harmonisation of the two is required. This is achieved though political action set out in positive legislation. The latter must strive towards the common good.[9] This implies that the appreciation of the common good changes over time and throughout history. Some natural law limits to positive law are nevertheless formulated by Thomas Aquinas. Their transgression renders the law either defective or, in more serious cases, void.[10] The edifice can be summed up thus:

1. There exists a common good of the collectivity, transcending the individual good of its members.
2. This good is an end that can never be completely realised but towards which one must strive.
3. The common good is nourished by a series of social virtues, for example the good life of the whole or the justice of the whole collectivity, etc.
4. Even if the common good can command a certain superiority over the individual good, it cannot altogether demand any type of sacrifice from the component members of society; there are minority and individual rights that must be observed.
5. What comprises the common good has changed throughout history, and it is the task of the legislator to define it in positive laws.
6. The power of the legislator is limited with regard to certain individual and minority rights, and also by natural and divine law.

[1] *Commentaries to the Sentences of Peter Lombard*, book II, ch XLIV, §12.
[2] *Summa Theologica*, I, q 193, a 2.
[3] *ibid*
[4] *ibid*, II, II, q 58, a 2ff.
[5] *ibid*, II, I, q 96, a 4
[6] *ibid*, II, I, q 90, a 2.
[7] *ibid*
[8] *ibid*, II, II, q 58, a 9, 3.
[9] *ibid*, I, q 90, a 4.
[10] *ibid*, II, I, q 96, a 4 and q 95, a 2.

The edifice is remarkable for its clarity, equilibrium, modesty and realism. A new dimension was added to it by the Salamanca School at the time of the great discoveries of the Americas. With Francisco de Vitoria (1499–1556) the concept of the common good of humanity was born (*bonum commune humanitatis*). The analysis by Thomas Aquinas was extended to the relations among States. The States are part of a great human family and pool together in a community having its own common good. This greater common good must prevail over the particular good of one State to the same extent than the good of the political collectivity prevails over that of the single individual.[11]

What is the relationship of the law to the common good? Law is an integral part of the social phenomenon; it regulates certain relations within it. Viewed from this perspective, the law is not an end in itself; it is a means to realise the aim of a good collective life. It follows that the main juridical values, namely justice, legal certainty and reciprocity, remain connected to a superior aim and value. To a certain degree, there follows therefrom a primacy of politics over law: politics has to seek the best way to realise the common good; the law, as a means to achieve that goal, must follow suit. But this reasoning should not be pushed too far. The common good itself demands the fine-tuning of policy to comply with the law (rule of law). Boundless fluctuations and arbitrariness cannot be reconciled with the good of the collectivity. From this perspective, the law is not simply a means to an external end; it is also an end in itself, a condition for realising order and justice. This duality reflects the two main functions of law: on the existential plane it is a means for the realisation of a political program; on the essential plane, it constitutes a society through a set of rules allowing some justice to exist.[12] The concept of the common good is thus marked by many polarities; it must be seen as a notion harmonising various streams, and thus essentially as a complex balancing mechanism.

What sense can be attached to the notion of 'good'? It stands to reason that the content of the term has evolved throughout history and is relative to place and culture. Any final and locked definition of the 'good' would be tantamount to trying to terminate history. In its broad sense, the concept of 'good' refers to anything that, at a given moment and place, is considered to represent a positive and useful tool or value. This covers material and economic goods, but also spiritual, moral and artistic goods. These goods allow individuals to realise themselves, but also to realise the things they desire. The attempts to define the 'good' more precisely have led to markedly different doctrines:

1. For one school of thought, the common good cannot possess any fixed object whatsoever; it varies radically throughout history. The only stable point is

[11] *De potestate civili* (1528), no 13. See A Verdross, 'Der klassische Begriff des bonum commune und seine Entfaltung zum bonum commune humanitatis' (1977) 28 *ÖZöRV* 143ff.

[12] 'Das Recht stellt … einen unmittelbaren Ausdruck des Sozialen selbst dar, das gar nicht ist, ohne dass es (auch) rechtlich geformt wäre, das, wenn es sich verwirklicht, unmittelbar rechtliche Formen entfaltet, weil sie in seinem Wesen notwendig enthalten sind, und weil das Soziale so wenig ohne Recht … entstehen und bestehen kann, wie die Materie ohne molekulare Struktur nicht Materie ist.' (E Fechner, *Rechtsphilosophie*, 2nd edn (Tübingen, 1956) 202)

the formal category of the 'weal' or 'good'; its material content depends only on time and place. Once some content has been added to the formal notion by specific men in a specific place, the good is transformed into a tool of social action.[13] But is there really only relativity? Is there nothing constant in history?

2. According to another view one must distinguish between individualistic and collectivistic societies. In the former, the collective goods are at the service of individuals and of their freedoms; in the latter, the individual goods are put at the service of the collectivity (incidentally, in the pure form this would lead to individualistic anarchy or to collectivistic totalitarianism). Between both basic systems there is but a political choice.[14] The error in this conception lies the extreme opposition of the two terms. The conciliatory and measured flavour of Thomas Aquinas's doctrines were lost in the harsh realities of the twentieth century.
3. According to the utilitarian school, happiness lies at the heart of the common good. As money is the basic unit of comparison for economic goods, happiness is the unit of comparison for all others. The common good is represented by 'the greatest happiness of the greatest number'.[15] The empirical, scientific, liberal and optimistic tone is manifest. The crux of the matter, however, is that happiness cannot be quantified and is not something that means the same for all of us. Moreover, an arithmetic process does not guarantee that in the pursuit of the greatest sum total of happiness, excessive sacrifices will not be demanded from some members of society. Negative utilitarian approaches are perhaps more subtle in this regard, by taking the opposite perspective, that is, the minimisation of unhappiness or misfortune.[16] This approach may cover a significant part of the common good but cannot exhaust its content.
4. Lastly, still other theories emphasise some particular aspects of the common good, renouncing a general approach. Thus, for example, the principle of responsibility has been presented as a cardinal aspect of the common good in the context of environmental depletion.[17] By the same token, human rights are often presented as a key element of a good society.[18]

The foregoing shows that an adequate doctrine of the common good requires the balancing of individual and collective interests. In particular, it would be wrong to identify the common good with the collective interest. Individual interests are part

[13] R Stammler, *Die Lehre vom richtigen Rechte* (Berlin, 1902) 196ff.

[14] G Radbruch, *Rechtsphilosophie*, 8th edn (Stuttgart, 1973) 142ff.

[15] F Hutcheson, *An Inquiry into the Origin of our Ideas of Beauty and Virtue* (1725), book II, ch 3, §8; J Bentham, *An Introduction to the Principles of Morals and Legislation* (1789), ch 1, 7, 13, 17.

[16] EN Kahn, *The Sense of Injustice* (New York, 1949); I Tammelo, *Zur Philosophie der Gerechtigkeit*, Frankfurt, 1982) 127ff; A Kaufmann, *Negativer Utilitarismus: Ein Versuch über das bonum commune* (Munich, 1994); A Kaufmann, 'Die Lehre vom negativen Utilitarismus, Ein Programm' (1994) 80 *Archiv für Rechts- und Sozialphilosophie* 476ff.

[17] H Jonas, *Das Prinzip Verantwortung*, 10th edn (Frankfurt, 1992).

[18] See, eg, the Preamble to the Universal Declaration of Human Rights (Resolution 217, 1948) of the UN General Assembly.

and parcel of the common good, otherwise society could not prosper. Individual and collective interests remain autonomous realities entertaining many interactions; these interactions take place on the field of the common good. From here stems the intimate link between the common good and justice, politics and law. It stands to reason that collective interests possess an inherent superiority over individual ones in the very narrow area in which they are the determining factor for minimum social cohesion; and it also stands to reason that collective interests often have a predominant influence in the processes of balancing constitutional law and adjudication.[19] But it is no more than that; and even in such cases, balances must be sought: for example, the expropriation of property in the public interest must be conceded, but private interests must be given their proper place by the payment of adequate (or full) and prompt compensation.

The overarching notion of the common good is thus ultimately one of a proper middle path, of proportionality and of prudence.[20] Too much accorded to the one leads to a diminution of the common good. The equation is not one of additions, whereby the total result increases, but rather one of a normal distribution, where the peak of the curve lies towards the middle of the picture. But much also depends on the type of society and on the free choices of its members. Thus, communist economic regimes applied to societies as a whole tend to diminish the common good, on the political plane (through dictatorships) and on the economic plane (by impoverishment through lack of private incentive to create wealth). But there are cultural differences as to the degree of collectivisation supported in a society (compare the US with the Scandinavian States). And in small societies based on personal adherence, such as a monastic community, community of goods may yield beneficial results.

We might also note that the common good is at one and same time an ideal and a real notion. It is an ideal in the sense that it indicates an aim and a direction for human efforts, a summit to conquer. In this sense, it provides a measuring rod for the political efforts of legislation. Each good law will contribute to consolidating society; and each ill-conceived instrument will sow the seeds of discord. The notion of the common good is also a subjective ethos by which the individual members of society should be inspired: the consciousness of each individual's responsibility for the health of the society in which we live. In this sense, the common good cannot actively exist if it does not inform the individual members of society, that is, if there is no community spirit manifested through the readiness to make some sacrifice for the good of the collectivity as a whole. This supposes a keen regard for the social bond. At the same time, the common good represents

[19] See, eg, the excellent analysis in JP Müller, *Eléments pour une théorie suisse des droits fondamentaux* (Berne, 1983).

[20] Tax policy illustrates the point. Excessively low taxes put at risk the sustainability of the collectivity, render the proper execution of the collective tasks more difficult and jeopardise social peace in the long run. The richer members of society have nothing to gain from the development of a growing class of poor and revolutionary-minded people. On the other hand, excessive taxation impoverishes the middle classes, atrophies life and inhibits private initiative: the collectivity loses, since overly heavy taxes kill the tax income.

a historical reality, from the efforts made in that regard from the first, more ritualistic peoples to the modern, more reason-based societies.[21] Various factors are decisive in this context: economic structures, culture, intellectual and moral canons, religion, relationships with other collectivities, etc.[22] This concrete common good is fixed in the constitutional order of a society. The good is reflected first in the organisation of the collectivity, eg the separation of powers or the rule of law; then in the prerogatives of the State, eg a liberal and social State; and lastly in the rights and protections granted to the subjects, eg fundamental human rights, minority rights, etc. The great constitutional theories, from Dante to Locke, from Montesquieu to Rousseau, from Burke to Constant or Marx, are fundamentally theories of the common good. And each theory of the common good is thus a political theory.[23]

B. The Common Good in International Society

The main characteristic of international society, namely its decentralisation (or better: 'de-centration'[24]), has been emphasised and discussed on many occasions. This decentralisation is the main hallmark of the weakness of the international common good. The component units (States) have a time-honoured conception of their own perfection, centered upon their 'inalienable' sovereignty. To paraphrase Aristotle, they are like the gods, remaining aloof from the general law of sociability. Concomitantly, there is a grave deficit in the community layer. In short, the periphery is strong and the centre is weak; the solidarities are mainly national

[21] Compare, eg, the Nuer people, dominated by their links with their livestock (names of persons were based on the colour and type of cattle owned, marriage was linked to the possession of cattle, etc), with our modern societies. On the Nuer, see EE Evans-Pritchard, *The Nuer* (Oxford, 1950), eg at 18–19.

[22] B Tuka, *Die Rechtssysteme, Grundriss einer Rechtsphilosophie* (Berlin, 1941) has distinguished social types based on the predominant values, thus presenting different types of good and laws. Thus, there would exist carnine (dominated by birth), domine (dominated by wealth), merzine (dominated by commerce) artines (dominated by art of technique), tumultine (dominated by migration) or vizine (dominated by neighborhood) societies. Let us take the first type (carnine societies) as an example. The gist of the matter is here birth, social extraction or cast. This fact determines the rank, social honours and role of an individual. Honour is a good particularly protected. There are legal consequences, for example the laws on marriage are based on the effort to reflect social segregation and to preserve the purity of the blood; patrimony remains linked to the family or clan, and its circulation is hampered, etc. The common good of the society revolves around birth. In a domine society, on the other hand, marriage would be based on wealth and on the buying of brides; the rights of a subject increases or decreases according to his wealth, etc. These categorisations are interesting, but it is clear that they represent merely ideal types and do not reflect the complexity of real societies. As has been rightly said, the definition of the common good will also indicate the spiritual height of a society: 'Je nach der Stufe der materiell-geistig-sittlichen Entwicklung einer Sozietät und je nach der Reife der Urteilsbildung über das ihr angemessene Gemeinwohl bestimmt sich die Höhenlage des sozialen Ideals' (H Henkel, *Einführung in die Rechtsphilosophie*, 2nd edn (Munich, 1977) 468).

[23] O Höffe, *Politische Gerechtigkeit* (Frankfurt, 1987).

[24] This term might avoid the incorrect conception according to which international society has decentralised power to the periphery; in reality, in modern international society, power was never centralised at all.

and not international; the elected constituencies are responsible to the various peoples and not to an abstract international community; the manifest destiny is national, not universal. However, many problems and concerns are international, without, though, a proper political body to tackle them. From that flows the often-expressed feeling that international problems are not adequately addressed and resolved; that they become protracted and lead to stalemate; that cacophony and anarchy prevail. The more this perception takes root, the less propensity there is in certain circles to make international efforts at improvement. Quite on the contrary, the sense of disappointment, weariness and harassment leads to disengagement and to a return to apparently better-suited national politics. True, this is only one side of the coin, but it would be foolish to brush it aside.

Analytically, it is essentially the aforementioned balance between the two *utilitates* that is missing. The common good is made up of a reasonable balance between the private good and the collective good. In international society the collective good is too weak, while the private good is too strong. There follows a disequilibrium, characterised by a certain tendency towards anarchy. The good of the component units takes precedence in too many cases over the good of the collectivity. The international common good thus leans too far towards one side of its spectrum; there is an inherent lack of balance. The exaltation of sovereignty and nationalism is merely an extreme form of this disequilibrium, which already, in its ordinary complexion, is overly influenced by private or individual interests. The cohesion of national society is ensured by the feeling of pooling together against external threats:[25] this powerful tool of integration operates for internal societies and provides ample space for collective interests; conversely, it is wholly absent from international society, which has no outside enemy receiving the blows (in the words of Sigmund Freud).[26]

The weakness of the common good is reflected and perpetuated in the absence of a proper 'organisation' of international society. No collective organs have been created with real powers of determination of the law and enforcement. And even when international organs do seem to possess significant powers, as does the Security Council of the UN under Chapter VII of the UN Charter, there remains the fact that the Council can take decisions but only the member States have the

[25] See notably C de Visscher, *Théories et réalités en droit international public*, 2nd edn (Paris, 1955) 118–19: 'C'est au contact du dehors que tout groupe social se différencie et prend conscience de lui-même; sa solidarité ne s'affirme intégralement qu'envers l'étranger. L'Etat moderne doit sa cohésion historique et sa forte individualisation aux pressions extérieures, aux sentiments de loyauté à la collectivité nationale qu'elles ont suscités et stimulés. … La communauté internationale ne bénéficie pas de ce facteur décisif de cohésion sociale. Elle ne peut y substituer que l'appel infiniment moins puissant à des sacrifices consentis à un bien commun supranational dont la perception … reste peu accessible à l'immense majorité des hommes'. See also *ibid*, 124: 'Autant les hommes répugnent à voir dans la force brutale la loi unique des rapports sociaux, autant ils sont enclins à transférer leurs aspirations morales au groupe auquel ils appartiennent, à hypostasier le pouvoir qui en est l'émanation, à idéaliser en lui leurs convoitises et leurs revendications. De l'Etat, pouvoir éthique aussi bien qu'instrument de puissance, ils attendent cette combativité vigoureuse qui est capable de leur procurer ce qui reste inaccessible à leur faiblesse individuelle.'

[26] S Freud, *Malaise dans la civilisation* (Paris, 1971) 68.

power to implement them (Article 25 of the Charter). In other words, a decision of the Council is not of a supranational character, it is not directly applicable in the municipal legal orders, it is not self-executing; the State must adopt the necessary legislation to insure implementation. Even here, ultimate control lies with the political organs of the States. If they are willing to breach Article 25 of the Charter, or if they boldly claim that a resolution is not legally binding for excess of authority, they can derail its implementation within their national legal system. The sanctions adopted by the Council can thus be considerably weakened. The saga of the anti-terrorist sanctions over the last few years has shown that the resolutions of the Security Council are not the last word;[27] their implementation has undergone

[27] A Tzanakopoulos, 'Collective Security and Human Rights' in E De Wet and J Widmar (eds), *Hierarchy in International Law* (Oxford, 2012) 42ff; M Milanovic, 'Norm Conflict in International Law: Whither Human Rights?' (2009) 20 *Duke Journal of Comparative and International Law* 69sff; G Thallinger, 'Sense and Sensibility of the Human Rights Obligations of the UN Security Council' (2007) 67 *ZaöRV* 1015ff. See also HP Aust and N Naske, 'Rechtsschutz gegen den UN-Sicherheitsrat durch europäische Gerichte?' (2006) 61 *ZöR*, 587ff; V Bore Eveno, 'Le contrôle juridictionnel des Résolutions du Conseil de sécurité: vers un constitutionnalisme international?' (2006) 110 *RGDIP* 832ff; M Bulterman, 'Fundamental Rights and the United Nations Financial Sanctions Regime: The Kadi and Yusuf Judgments of the Court of First Instance of the European Communities' (2006) 19 *Leiden Journal of International Law* 753ff; E Sciso, 'Fundamental Rights and Article 103 of the UN Charter Before the Court of First Instance of the European Communities' (2006) 15 *ItYbIL* 137ff; C Tomuschat, 'Case Law (Yusuf, Kadi, 2005 Judgments, CFI)' (2006) 43 *Common Market Law Review* 537ff; M Payandeh, 'Rechtskontrolle des UN-Sicherheitsrates durch staatliche und überstaatliche Gerichte' (2006) 66 *ZaöRV* 41ff; E Cannizzaro, 'A Machiavellian Moment? The UN Security Council and the Rule of Law' (2006) 3 *International Organizations Law Review* 189sff; U Haltern, 'Gemeinschaftsgrundrechte und Antiterrormassnahmen der UNO' (2007) 62 *Juristenzeitung* 537ff; J Klabbers, 'Kadi Justice at the Security Council?' (2007) 4 *International Organizations Law Review* 293ff; N Lavranos, 'United Nations Sanctions and Judicial Review' (2007) 76 *Nordic Journal of International Law* 1ff; S Zasova, 'La lutte contre le terrorisme à l'épreuve de la jurisprudence du TPICE' (2008) 19 *Revue trimestrielle des droits de l'homme* 481ff; S Griller, 'International Law, Human Rights and the European Community's Autonomous Legal Order: Notes on the European Court of Justice Decision in Kadi' (2008) 4 *European Constitutional Law Review* 528ff; LM Hinojosa Martinez, 'Bad Law for Good Reasons: The Contradictions of the Kadi Judgment' (2008) 5 *International Organizations Law Review* 339ff; E Cannizzaro 'Sugli effetti delle risoluzioni del Consiglio di sicurezza nell'ordinamento comunitario: la sentenza della Corte di giustizia nel caso Kadi' (2008) 91 *RDI* 1075ff; A Gianelli, 'L' "autonomia" del sistema giuridico comunitario rispetto al diritto delle Nazioni Unite' (2008) 91 *RDI* 1078ff; P Palchetti, 'Può il giudice comunitario sindacare la validità internazionale di una risoluzione del Consiglio di sicurezza?' (2008) 91 *RDI* 1085ff; P De Sena and MC Vitucci, 'The European Courts and the Security Council: Between "Dédoublement Fonctionnel" and Balancing of Values' (2009) 20 *EJIL* 193ff; P Hilpold, 'EU Law and UN Law in Conflict: The Kadi Case'(2009) 13 *Max Planck Yearbook on United Nations Law* 141ff; E Cannizzaro, 'Security Council Resolutions and EC Fundamental Rights: Some Remarks on the ECJ Decision in the Kadi case' (2009) 28 *Yearbook of European Law* 593ff; R Pavoni, 'Freedom to Choose the Legal Means for Implementing UN Security Council Resolutions and the Kadi Judgment: A Misplaced Argument Hindering the Enforcement of International Law' (2009) 28 *Yearbook of European Law* 626ff; M Scheinin, 'Is the ECJ Ruling in Kadi Incompatible with International Law ?' (2009) 28 *Yearbook of European Law* 637ff; C Tomuschat, 'The Kadi case: What Relationship is there between the Universal Legal Order under the Auspices of the UN and the EU Legal Order?' (2009) 28 *Yearbook of European Law* 654ff; P De Sena, 'Sanzioni individuali del Consiglio di sicurezza, Articolo 103 della Carta della Nazioni Unite e rapporti fra sistemi normativi' in F Salerno (ed), *Sanzioni 'individuali' del Consiglio di sicurezza e garanzie processuali fondamentali* (Padua, 2010) 45ff; JF Flauss, 'La primauté de la Charte et la Convention européenne des droits de l'homme' in F Salerno (ed), *Sanzioni 'individuali' del Consiglio di sicurezza e garanzie processuali fondamentali* (Padua, 2010) 71ff; S Marchisio, 'Il primato della Carta e la Comunità europea' in F Salerno (ed), *Sanzioni 'individuali' del*

often several twists and turns before achieving *terra firma*. It stands to reason that the action of the Security Council cannot simply be equated with a collective interest, especially when the Powers there assembled take liberties with the law. But there remains the fact that the collective action of the Council, in the name of the membership (see Article 24 of the UN Charter), is reduced and refracted in a way that does not have any equivalent in national legal systems.

We may leave this subject here. In previous chapters, we have already reviewed the community interests of the twentieth century, and there is little point in repeating ourselves. There remains the fact that some progress in the collective interests limb seems to be urgently required if the world is to be better governed. But that would imply some sacrifices as regards individual freedom and sovereignty. Never more so than now does it seem utopian to imagine that peoples are ready to set foot on this path. We are witnessing more or less aggressive returns to unilateralism, isolationism and sovereignty, which hardly augur well for an optimistic outlook over the next few years. But having said that tides turn. The annoying aspect of the matter is that new ground is likely to be broken only if a major catastrophe befalls humanity.

II. Justice

A. General Legal Experience

The common good is the supreme principle of the social-political realm; justice is the supreme principle of legal regulation. Law is orientated towards justice and justice towards the common good. This is the supreme triptych of the social constitution. Since ancient times, it has been suggested that the law has as one of its main aims the effort to realise justice.[28] As an ideal principle towards which law should strive, justice remains superior to law. The latter takes the form of positive enactments, while the former is in constant movement and requires critical reflection

Consiglio di sicurezza e garanzie processuali fondamentali (Padua, 2010) 87ff; S Cassella, 'Les suites de l'arrêt Kadi de la CJCE: quel équilibre entre protection de la sécurité internationale et respect des droits de l'homme?' (2010) 56 *AFDI* 709ff; F Naert, *International Law Aspects of the EU's Security and Defence Policy* (Oxford/Portland, 2010) 427ff; A Garrido Muñoz, *Garantías judiciales y sanciones antiterroristas del Consejo de seguridad de Naciones Unidas* (Valence, 2013) 335ff. For an overview over legal doctrine on this issue, S Poli and M Tzanou, 'The Kadi Rulings: A Survey of the Literature' (2009) 28 *Yearbook of European Law* 533ff. For the situation in Switzerland, T Gazzini and I Fellrath, 'La procédure de gestion des listes de personnes affectées par les sanctions des Nations Unies devant le Tribunal fédéral' (2009) 65 *Revue de droit administratif et de droit fiscal* 146ff.

[28] In the Accursian gloss to the *Digest* one reads, 'Est autem ius a iustitia, sicut a matre sua, ergo prius fuit iustitia quam ius': glose no 9 *ad Dig*, 1, 1, 1. For the perversion of legal orders, see the classical monograph by F von Hippel, *Die Perversion von Rechtsordnungen* (Tübingen, 1955). Law cannot be based on coercion alone: even the Mafia has an effective normative order, though it hardly seems that this can be called 'law'.

upon what has been realised. But what is justice? Centuries of reflection have not reduced this notion to a certainty. A fully-fledged definition is impossible, since to pin down 'justice' would be to lose its fluid and critical character, leading to its petrification. This would utterly alter its function. The notion thus remains open-ended. However, it can be analysed and given some degree of greater precision.

In the first place, justice indicates a harmonious proportion, ie a conformity or congruence.[29] This principle of proportion is applied to the coordination of equal subjects in a society. Thus, Dante writes that justice is a 'proportion from man to man'.[30] This proportion touches only on the typical or interchangeable nature of these subjects, not on their unique characteristics, which cannot be compared and do not give rise to any proportion. Thus justice is not love, or compassion, or truth. Its geometry is governed by laws, not by feelings. Through its proportionality orientation, justice is essentially a relational notion. Radical individuality is beyond justice and law. In its equity limb, justice nevertheless also has an individualising aspect.

Secondly, there are four elements of justice when considered on a general plane.[31] In the first place, justice is directed to the other, to interpersonal or intersubjective relations; it is based on 'other-directedness'.[32] It provides a measuring rod for these external relations. In the second place, justice allows rights and duties to be derived. Claims based on justice are considered legitimate, duties based on justice are considered to be burdens rightly carried. In the third place, justice is fundamentally linked to equality.[33] Every subject recognised as a person should be treated like every other such subject; this is a fundamental conception of justice. This means that the same treatment must be meted out when two or more persons are in the same situation, and a different treatment is called for when people's situations are different. The treatment must then be different to exactly the same extent as the difference in the situation, no more and no less. The concept of proportionality here again breaks through. The political agenda is in significant part dominated by the effort to ensure such relative equality. In the fourth place, justice is linked to the concept of fairness,[34] which manifests itself in different contexts, for example: fair trial guarantees; the right to be heard (*audiatur et altera pars*); the propensity to give persons a fair chance at self-realisation and development; fair reward for work done, etc. Justice sometimes refers to one of these four aspects and sometimes to another, but all four facets are part of it. In this sense, justice

[29] Thus for Leibniz it is 'congruitas ac proportionalitas quaedam', and Bellarmino adds 'Id enim est iustum, quod rectum et adaequatum et cum sua regula optime congruens'. See G del Vecchio, *La giustizia* (Rome, 1946) 2.

[30] 'Hominis ad hominem proportio'. See *De Monarchia*, II, V, 1. As feeling creatures, this equation should be extended to animals: see Bentham, above n 15, ch VIII, §1.

[31] See W Huber, *Gerechtigkeit und Recht* (Gütersloh, 1996) 149–50.

[32] J Finnis, *Naturel Law and Natural Rights* (Oxford, 1984) 161.

[33] See A Kaufmann, *Rechtsphilosophie*, 2nd edn (Munich, 1997) 151ff. For a complex analysis of justice, see M Walzer, *Spheres of Justice* (New York, 2000); J Rawls, *A Theory of Justice* (Cambridge, Mass, 2005).

[34] JR Lucas, *On Justice* (Oxford, 1980) 1ff, with the opening title 'Unfair'.

is a source of and limit on resolutions to social problems: one the on hand, it is a measuring rod (eg equality and proportion); on the other hand, it acts as a limit against arbitrary, excessive or unjust results (eg disproportionate solutions, violation of fundamental rights, unfairness, etc).

Thirdly, justice is a directive principle whose character remains open-ended. Its directions are not self-standing; they must be influenced by the moral, social, political and legal criteria of a given society at a given moment. Thus the notion of justice cannot itself determine what is 'equal': Only free citizens and not slaves? Only men and not women? Only humans and not animals? By the same token, the maxim '*suum cuique tribuere*' ('give to each what is due to him') cannot in itself indicate what is due (the *suum*). This can be done only in context, and this means by given social ideologies and orders, and also through the lens of subjective ideologies. Justice is therefore based on certain conditions and orders, which it cannot itself create but which it must presuppose. The criticism that the notion is empty is therefore only part of the truth: it is more precise to say that the notion must be given concrete form by additional criteria which it cannot contain within itself, so as to allow history and conceptions to change. The changing criteria, once added to the general concept, give it concrete meaning.

Certain schools of thought have reduced justice to simpler strands. Thus, in some positivistic conceptions, justice is mainly realised in the positive law.[35] But the human spirit has some difficulties with reducing the scope of justice to the historically contingent and imperfect realisations of a legislator. For sociological schools, the criterion of justice is determined only by the dominant opinions in a given society. However, this conception ignores the trans-temporal aspects of justice, which, however non-self-sufficient, are manifested by experience. Is it an accident that justice has long been explained through the use of concepts such as equality or fairness? For neo-idealistic schools of thought, justice is only a form that the dialectics of the spirit will fill with content.[36] Again, it is doubtful that the trans-temporal dimension of justice is devoid of any content. Lastly, for certain natural law schools, justice is manifested in the natural order reflecting the divine order.[37] Such versions of justice are over-optimistic, and also over-dogmatic. Overall, these reductive conceptions are extreme simplifications of a notion comprising openness, polarity and experience.

Fourthly, some difficulties exist regarding the determination of justice; they flow from the open-endedness mentioned above. Three layers of relativity may be mentioned:

1. In the first place, as already noted, there are *inter-temporal problems*. Massacres were considered glorious in ancient Assyrian society and the surrounding

[35] H Kelsen, *Was ist Gerechtigkeit?* (Vienna, 1953). A wider vision would be to include general principles of law and other general legal conceptions.

[36] G Maggiore, *Filosofia del diritto* (Palermo, 1921).

[37] E Brunner, *Gerechtigkeit* (Zurich, 1943); or, with a Catholic complexion, A Sériaux, *Le droit naturel*, 2nd edn (Paris, 1999) 53–54.

regions; they were commanded by divine glory and justice. Fortunately, times have changed. So have conceptions. For example, what is just access to a vote? Does it apply only to men, or only to men owning a certain amount of property? What about women? Prisoners? There is, as we know, a temporal relativity in the conceptions of justice, given that the concretising criteria are not fixed once and for all.

2. In the second place, there are *ideological problems*. There will be differences on questions of taxation, of social assistance, of grants; on criteria such as retribution according to performance or need, of capacity or equality. In all questions relating to redistribution, which are essentially matters of proportion and thus of justice, liberalism (taken in the European sense of the word) and communism will not view matters through the same lens.[38] But this is fundamentally a matter of freedom: if justice demanded absolute criteria in which everyone had to believe, freedom would be heavily curtailed.
3. In the third place, there are *psychological problems*. The conception of justice is also heavily influenced by an individual's personal biography, by education and experiences (eg any violence suffered), by upbringing and family, by socialisation processes, by profession, by culture, by interest (eg wealth or poverty triggering different perspectives and interests)[39]—perhaps also by genes. Thus, justice is subject to an inescapable perspectivism. It is almost miraculous that it can survive as a notion cherished by many persons and remain socially necessary when the range of perspectives on justice is so wide. In a sense, though, this perspectivism is welcome: in human affairs, progress always has a better chance of emerging from competition and confrontation of opinion than through the utopia of 'lock, stock and barrel' tailored truths.[40] The darker side of the matter is a certain tendency towards dogmatism and extreme militancy in the name of the great and lofty value of justice. This quickly leads to self-righteousness, to a self-centred existence, to the claim of rights and dues in all directions (almost an extremist thought process: all is due to me), instead of considering one's own limitations, one's own preferences, one's own concomitant duties, others' reasons, the mote in one's own eye. A keen consciousness of perspectivism can avoid this pitfall.

Fifthly, reflections on justice have allowed three main forms of the concept to be defined. The first is 'divine justice' (*justitia Dei*). Justice is here configured as the commandment of God to which the righteous man submits without questioning.[41] This conception dominated in monotheistic and closed societies, with the Hebrews and later the first Christians, with Augustine and later the Franciscans,[42]

[38] C Perelman, *Justice et raison* (Brussels, 1963).

[39] B Rüthers, *Das Ungerechte an der Gerechtigkeit* (Zurich, 1991) 7ff.

[40] *ibid*, 10.

[41] Ezekiel 18:5.

[42] P Stuhlmacher, *Gerechtigkeit Gottes bei Paulus*, 2nd edn (Göttingen, 1966); E Plutta-Messerschmidt, *Gerechtigkeit Gottes bei Paulus* (Tübingen, 1973); U Wilckens, *Der Brief an die Römer I*, 2nd edn (Zurich/Neukirchen, 1987) 202ff.

and also with Islam. Faith renders justice, and outside faith there is no justice; law and morals are incorporated into religion. Reason is not enough; original sin has blurred Man's capacity to attain the light of justice without God's grace.[43] From there flows an often radical devaluation of human justice in comparison with the light of divine justice.[44] In the words of Augustine, 'Et hoc quod [Deus] vellet, ipsa iustitia est'.[45] It is not necessary to emphasise all the dangers of such a one-sided and dogmatic conception.

The second is 'universal justice' (*justitia universalis*). Justice is here configured as a supreme virtue, ie as a cardinal virtue; it embodies the harmony between all the virtues.[46] As an objective virtue it hinges on perfection, together with beauty, temperance, prudence and good. In the social order, it refers to the execution of duties by each member so that the body as a whole can function properly. The advent of Christianity operated two significant shifts in this doctrine of justice as a virtue: (i) justice became one virtue among others (eg prudence, temperance, courage) and was now subordinated to the theological virtues (faith, hope and charity); and (ii) justice was defined with a more subjective bent, as referring to a righteous will and action. For example, 'constans et perpetua voluntas ius suum cuique tribuens';[47] 'honeste vivere, neminem laedere, suum cuique tribuere'; or the Golden Rule, 'Do to others all that you would have them do to you.'[48] From these general concepts, subjective or objective moral consequences can be drawn.[49] In this light, the following may appear to be unjust: inconsistent attitudes (which we tend to overlook or justify when they are our own, while spotting them constantly in the behaviour of others, possibly ignoring relevant differences of fact);[50] opportunistic action; complaisant identification of our own interests with the collective good or with altruistic interests (so as to avoid unwelcome thoughts about our own standards); constant overestimation of one's own interests and positions, self-righteousness; oppressive or totalitarian beliefs; the utterance of emphatic judgements without a full knowledge of the relevant facts and reasons; excessive weight accorded to one's ability to pass judgement, without taking account of the benefit of checking the facts; over-emphasis on one aspect of a more complex problem; the upholding of a position that may be satisfactory for

43 See the discussion in Thomas Aquinas, *Summa Theologica*, II, I, q 91, a 6.

44 Saint Gregory wrote, 'Humana iustitia divinae iustitiae comparata, iniusta est: quia et lucerna in tenebris fulgere cernitur, sed in solis radio posita tenebratur'. Ballarmin added, 'Tanta est puritas Dei, ut comparatione ejus omnis alia iustitia, iniustitia esse videatur' (*Explication Psalmorum*, cxlii, 2). Godefroy distinguished as follows, 'Justitia Dei est reddere bonum pro malo; Justitia hominis est reddere bonum pro bono, malum pro malo'. See G del Vecchio, *La giustizia* (Rome, 1946) 26, 30.

45 *Sermo*, cxxvi, 3. See Del Vecchio, above n 44, 24, fn 3.

46 O Höffe, *Politische Gerechtigkeit* (Frankfurt, 1987) 222ff; RC Cross and AD Woozley, *Plato's Republic, A Philosophical Commentary* (London, 1964).

47 See *Institutiones*, book I, 1.

48 On this Golden Rule, see A Dihle, *Die Goldene Regel* (Göttingen, 1962); H Reiner, 'Die Goldene Regel und das Naturrecht. Zugleich Antwort auf die Frage: Gibt es ein Naturrecht' (1997) 9 *Studia Leibnitiana* 231ff. See also T Hobbes, *Leviathan* (1651), chs 14 and 26.

49 On morals and justice, R Spaemann, *Moralische Grundbegriffe*, 2nd edn (Munich, 1983).

50 E Claparède, *Morale et politique ou les vacances de la probité* (Neuchâtel, 1947).

what it includes but defective for what is excluded; giving free rein to passions and over-statement;[51] unilateralism in all its forms, not reflecting reciprocities; indulging the propensity to believe that one is (always) right and others (always) wrong, etc. Many of these are issues of subjective righteousness.[52] They are rooted in personal psychology and the attempt at rational control over one's own impulses.

The third form of the concept of justice is particular justice (*justitia particularis*). The notion is here exclusively social, that is, reflecting proportionality between members of a society.[53] At its heart lies inter-subjectivity: justice concerns a relationship with another placed on an equal footing. Hence, this form of justice involves outwards projection, towards the other. It is a measure for the rational integration of mutual subjectivities. Thomas Aquinas defines this very aptly: 'Justitia … ordinet hominem in his quae sunt ad alterum. Aequalitas autem ad alterum est.'[54] And 'Justitia … est communis radix totius ordinis ad alterum.'[55] Equality becomes essential to the functioning of this form of justice. The point is relative equality: treat equally what is equal; and treat unequally what is unequal in the exact same proportion as its inequality. Equality here refers to proportionality,[56] not necessarily to formal identity (eg retribution, an eye for an eye, a tooth for a tooth).[57] This proportionality differs for coordinative relations between subjects placed on an equal footing (commutative justice) and for subjects placed in a relationship of superiority and inferiority (distributive justice). The first is found mainly in private law (eg contracts, responsibility), the second mainly in public law (taxes, social services, etc); the first is based on relations of equality, the second on relations of inequality. Thus, in the first the formal or arithmetic proportion is paramount: there must be objective or subjective equivalence of the acts, goods or assets. In the second, the question turns on the distribution of wealth, positions and charges in a society. This must be done on account of the special qualities of persons, in particular their merit. Proportion is here geometrical: thus, taxes are not arithmetically the same but depend on the amount of income and wealth, and vary with it. The differences in taxation will be justified when they reflect as exactly as possible the differences in income and wealth. Many relationships are both commutative and distributive in different aspects: if a State expropriates an

[51] Classical authors caution that serenity is necessary for a well-balanced judgement: Aristotle, *Nicomachean Ethics*, I, 13; Thomas Aquinas, above n 43, II, I, q 91, a 6 and q 109, a 2.

[52] See, eg, P Briñol, KG DeMarree and RE Petty, 'Processes by which Confidence (vs. Doubt) Influences the Self' in RM Arkin, KC Oleson and PJ Carroll (eds), *Handbook of the Uncertain Self* (New York, 2010) 13ff; P Briñol and RE Petty, 'Self-Validation Processes' in G Haddock and GR Maio (eds), *Contemporary Perspectives on the Psychology of Attitudes* (London, 2004) 205ff.

[53] Sometimes this is also called political justice: O Höffe, 'Justice' in P Raynaud and S Rials (eds), *Dictionnaire de philosophie politique* (Paris, 2003) 366.

[54] Thomas Aquinas, above n 43, II, II, q 57, a 1.

[55] *ibid*, II, II, q 58, a 8, 2. And 'iustitia ordinat hominem in comparatione ad alium' (*ibid*, II, II, q 58, a 5). See also Aristotle, *Nicomachean Ethics*, V, 3, 1129b, 25 and 32; 1130 a 13; V, 4, 1130b, 1; Dante, *De Monarchia*, I, XI, 7.

[56] Aristotle, above n 55, V, 1131a–b, 1132a.

[57] Kant gives pride of place to this rule: I Kant, *Metaphysics of Morals, Doctrine of Law*, pt II, § 49, letter E.

estate, there will be on the one hand a relationship of subordination (the decision to expropriate) and a relationship of coordination (payment of adequate compensation). Other forms of particular justice have been added to the two main forms defined by Aristotle. Thus, 'protective justice' concerns the protection of the subordinated subject with regard to his superior: State/subjects, parents/children, employer/employee, commander/soldier, etc.[58] Protective justice commands the prohibition of arbitrary acts, the grant of protective fundamental rights, judicial control of action, etc. On the other hand, 'legal justice' has to do with the duties of the citizen towards the State, ie of the subordinated subject towards the superior.[59] In a larger sense, protective and legal justice can be encompassed within distributive justice. Equity completes this picture and offers an individualised justice for particular situations where the general rule produces unsatisfactory results.

In the times of the Enlightenment, various great systems of morals and justice were proposed. For example, Thomasius suggested a tripartite system: the *honestum*,[60] concerning good and evil in relation to internal peace (morals); the *decorum*,[61] covering those rules unconcerned with internal or external peace, ie the social rules of *savoir vivre*; and the *justum*,[62] concerning good and evil in relation to external peace. This was the basis of law. The aim was the repression of social action troubling the peace of society. The main rule here was 'neminem laedere'. Since it ensured social peace, the rule of law must be enforceable, unlike moral rules.[63] Leibniz[64] also proposed a tripartite system, where law and morals were less separated: the *jus strictum* was based on the precept *neminem laedere*, and therefore on commutative justice; the *jus aequum* was based on the precept *suum cuique tribuere*, and therefore on distributive justice; the *jus pietatis* was based on the precept *honeste vivere*, and therefore on justice as virtue. Lastly, we might mention the tripartite system of Cardinal Thomas Cajetan:[65] here, legal justice concerned the relation of the individual towards society; distributive justice the relation of society towards the individual; and commutative justice the relations of individuals among themselves. Interesting as they are, these classifications are not exhaustive.

The order of justice is fragmentary. It contains flexible signposts and principles, directives and finalities, and is not a closed and ready-made system for easy application. It would be wrong, however, to say that the doctrine of justice is but an empty edifice. If there are many contingent elements, there are also some permanent markers; and with the addition of choices made at a certain time in a certain

[58] H Coing, *Die obersten Grundsätze des Rechts* (Heidelberg, 1947) 70ff.
[59] Thomas Aquinas, above n 43, II, II, q 58, a 5.
[60] 'Quod vis ut alii sibi faciunt, tu te tibi facies': C Thomasius, *Fundamenta iuris naturae et gentium* (1705), book I, ch VI, §40.
[61] 'Quod vis ut alii tibi faciant, tu ipsis facies': *ibid*, §41.
[62] 'Quod tibi non vis fieri, alteri ne feceris': *ibid*, §42.
[63] *ibid*, book I, ch VI, §43ff.
[64] G Leibniz, *Codex iuris gentium diplomaticus, Dissertatio* I, 11–13.
[65] T Cajetan, *Commentaria in Secundam Secundae divi Thomae de Aquino* (1518), II–II, q 61, a 1.

society, the doctrine gains still further strength. There are at least three constants.[66] *First*, justice contains a negative criterion: it indicates certain attitudes which are incompatible with it. It is easier to say what is unjust than to determine what is just (negative philosophy). This fact allows certain judgments to be made. The murders carried out under the regimes of Hitler or Pol Pot were and remain injustices. *Secondly*, justice requires that differences in practice are always justified by the facts. This excludes the arbitrary, according to the maxim *sic volo sic jubeo* … It is moreover not sufficient to have a single measuring rod if it is not used taking any relevant difference of facts into account. Thus, it would be unjust to calculate taxes not according to wealth but according to race or corporeal weight. On the other hand, if foodstuffs must be rationed, it is compatible with justice to make distinctions according to the special calorific needs, say, of pregnant women or of manual workers, etc—but not with regard to ideology, race, political affiliation and so on. Justice therefore requires a *distinctio rationis cum fundamento in re*. Enquiry into the proper criteria for making a distinction is the day-to-day work of constitutional tribunals. *Thirdly*, justice requires action using a single and uniform measuring rod. This supposes a value judgement as to what is 'equal' or 'similar', and thus to be measured by that rod. The value judgement here at stake is external to the doctrine of justice; and as a value judgement it is made in time and in context. But once the criterion of what is similar has been adopted, the cases will have to be treated in a coherent way according to the same measure. If the measuring rod is changed from one case to the other, while these cases may be similar, an injustice will follow. This injustice may occur in two situations. First, there may be unequal treatment of what are essentially equal things. There are many examples of such injustices: the privileges accorded to some persons due to sympathy or recommendation; the remorseless increments in tax law (ie the higher rate of tax payable due to the adding together of the incomes of married persons rather than their separate taxation), etc. Secondly, there is equal treatment of what is essentially unequal. For example, a prohibition on using the minority language extending to a region where the minority lives; a uniform tax regime applying to any unmarried person, regardless of whether that person has children to support or not, etc. It may also occur that an apparent injustice follows from an inadequate distributive proportion. Thus, a crime involving danger to life and limb may be punished less severely than a theft; or a road traffic offence may be sanctioned more severely than sexual abuse of a child. The legislator may nevertheless want to maintain such a distinction: thus, in a federal system, the differences in taxation from state to state may be welcomed as an element of tax competition, thereby keeping overall taxes lower; or it may be justified to require that at least one non-alcoholic drink be sold at a price lower than the cheapest alcoholic drink (the aim being to avoid drunkenness), but it would be exceeding that aim and thus unjust, to fix the price of all non-alcoholic drinks at three times less than the cheapest alcoholic drink (no necessity and disproportionality).

[66] H Henkel, *Einführung in die Rechtsphilosophie*, 2nd edn (Munich, 1977) 395ff.

As a whole, justice is riddled with many opposites. For example, traditionally the demands of material justice are set up in opposition to those of legal certainty. However, security is also an essential element of justice. If foreseeability of the normative content were to be absent, arbitrariness would raise its head; if there was no steady measuring rod, justice could not be done. Thus, on the one hand, legal security is in tension with the needs of individualising justice (equity); but at the same time, on another hand, both concepts are aligned and allied. Another example of polar opposites within justice may illustrate the point. In certain Swiss cantons there had been a popular vote for deciding whether a special and favourable tax regime should be maintained for rich foreigners not working in Switzerland but having a residence there.[67] On the one hand (on the left) the argument was that these persons should be taxed like anybody else, without any 'privilege'. Here, the accent was placed on justice as equality. This clearly presupposed that the situations of Swiss workers and foreign non-working residents were indeed equal. On the other hand (on the right), the arguments were manifold. First it was argued that the situations were not equal at all. The persons concerned were foreigners; they did not work in Switzerland; if they did, they could not benefit from the special regime. Moreover, given that these persons earned the greatest part of their revenue outside Switzerland, it would be administratively extremely difficult to determine their total income so as to fix the applicable tax rate. The difficulty stemmed from the fact not only that all this revenue and wealth was situated abroad, but also that it was scattered throughout many countries. Therefore, lump sum taxation might seem adequate here. This limb of the argument denied that the situations were equal or similar. There were, on this view, relevant differences, which should lead to another result. The second limb of the argument was that if these persons were taxed like any other, many of them would quit the cantons. There would thus be significant financial losses in those areas. The argument is not just opportunistic, it affects justice: if there is less revenue for the State, there will be cuts in State services; these cuts will in many cases affect the less wealthy who are dependent on those services; and that would be unjust. Whether one follows one or the other line of the reasoning is not relevant here; what counts is simply the structure of the argument. In the second limb of the opponents' argument, there would seem to be a conflict within justice: justice as (strict) equality versus upholding the means for social distributive justice. There is here a tension within the notion of justice. Such situations of internal conflict occur in a non-negligible number of cases. They render the handling of the concept still more complex, but also more fascinating.

A last aspect may be mentioned, although it exceeds the competence of a lawyer. Justice is not only an external measuring rod for ensuring equality; as we have seen, it also embodies a subjective and inner propensity to be just (virtue). The two

[67] Later the issue was made the object of a federal vote, where the same arguments relating to justice were put forward. See, eg, M Amrein, 'Von Prinzipien und Privilegien', *Neue Zürcher Zeitung*, no 229, 3 October 2014, 19.

aspects cannot be entirely separated. But this propensity to be just often increases as a proportion of the justice, serenity and happiness achieved, and decreases as a proportion of the injustice, upheaval and violence suffered. Psychological studies have found as a fact that injustice suffered does not in most cases lead a person to become just, as a sort of compensation, but rather to become unjust, to reproduce the injustice and to retaliate for the wrong suffered.[68] Machiavelli's remark that formerly oppressed people often become the worst oppressors has much psychological truth. Even the thirst to compensate injustice through a particular attachment to justice is also rarely conducive to the desired result. Persons of this type are generally stubborn, self-righteous and unyielding, if not petulant. It seems that the capacity to be just, being a quality requiring balance and equanimity, depends on inner serenity and detachment, as well as empathy. This is much easier to realise when one has received (or considers oneself to have received) justice than when one has been on the receiving end of injustice.

A general theory of justice stops at this point. Throughout history, the specific content of justice has been coloured by the current ideology; and the propensity of the individual to be just depends on his cultural and personal character. In a number of cases, we know what justice requires, but we simply do not want it enough.[69]

B. Justice in International Law

In international society, there is a manifest imbalance between commutative justice and distributive justice. The precepts of commutative justice, regulating the exchange of relations between equals, traditionally carried much greater weight than distributive aspects supposing a hierarchical structure and some redistribution. Equal sovereignty and not collective power—that is the gist of the matter. International law has always been 'private law' in its structure, while being 'public law' in its content. It has evolved around the notions of contract (treaty), property (territory) and responsibility (diplomacy, war). The 'public law' institutions of international law, institutional law, organs controlling States, the maintenance of peace, *jus cogens* and the like, rest upon a layer of private law, in which they cannot truly put down roots. Public justice, in the full sense of the term, can only be based on the improvement of international institutions vested with powers; this supposes some reduction in the spheres of sovereignty. Conversely, private justice is well developed. This is one of the reasons why so many municipal private law analogies were suggested for transposition into the body of international law.[70]

[68] See, eg, I Boszormenyi-Nagy and RB Krasner, *Between Give and Take* (New York, 1986).

[69] Euripides, in *Hippolyte*, puts the following remark into the mouth of Phaedrus, 'we understand what is just and convenient, but we let it not enter into our actions'.

[70] H Lauterpacht, *Private Law Analogies in International Law* (London, 1927).

1. *International Commutative Justice*

Modern international commutative justice is organised around three axes: (i) contracts (treaties) based on the principles of equivalence and reciprocity; (ii) *neminem laedere*, ie the protection of the 'private' sphere recognised to each State; (iii) procedure, with equality of arms and due process. It is hardly necessary to insist on the importance of treaties in a society dominated by 'equal States'. The law of treaties seeks to realise equivalence between the contracting parties through reciprocity of obligations and rights, and reciprocity in the application of reservations and the like. The aim of the conventional bond is to maintain the equilibria stipulated (or to adapt them by agreement) in full reciprocity.

The '*neminem laedere*' limb is found in the protection of the sovereign sphere of every State, including the integrity of its territory, domestic jurisdiction, non-intervention in internal affairs, the immunities of States, the duty to ensure that the territory is not used to violate the rights of other States, etc. The same principle informs the whole law of international responsibility, and in particular the duty to make reparation. The main principle governing the amount of reparation is equivalence. As the PCIJ emphasised in a famous passage, it must 'as far as possible, wipe out all the consequences of the illegal act and re-establish the situation which would, in all probability, have existed if that [unlawful] act had not been committed'.[71] Many other principles delimit the respective spheres of action of States and ensure that one cannot legally injure another: good faith and the protection of legitimate expectations; exceptions of *inadimplendi contractus*, proportionality, etc.

Lastly, there are procedural rights. They are based on equality of arms. The oral and written procedures are based on strict equality as to the time allotted and the items permitted.[72] Moreover, the ICJ has refused to hear the arguments of an international organisation orally when that would have created a glaring inequality with regard to a staff member complaining of the decision of an international administrative tribunal, a staff member who could not be heard for lack of legal standing of the individual in ICJ procedures.[73] We might also recall the extension of the benefit of reservations contained in optional declarations of the opposing party by way of reciprocity.[74]

2. *International Distributive Justice*

International distributive justice is cast in an open-ended and moving net. Some illustrations of the five main forms of distributive justice in international law are given below.

[71] *Chorzow Factory* (1928) PCIJ Series A no 17, 47. Compare the slightly differently worded Art 35 of the State Responsibility Articles (2001), where reference is made to 'the situation which existed before the wrongful act' without referring to its probability (which is of easier application). On the whole issue, see J Crawford, *State Responsibility* (Cambridge, 2013) 506ff.

[72] See, eg, Arts 45, §2 and 57 of the Rules of ICJ, 1978.

[73] *Judgment no 2867 of the Administrative Tribunal of the ILO upon Complaint filed against the International Fund for Agricultural Development* (Opinion) [2012-I] ICJ Rep 29, §§44–45.

[74] See, eg, *Norwegian Loans* [1957] ICJ Rep 23–24; and *Interhandel* [1959] ICJ Rep 23.

i. Constitutional Justice

In certain subject matters, community interests have given rise to a public law-type organisation. This is the case mainly in the context of the maintenance of international peace. Public order rules governing the non-use of force, and international institutions vested with powers of decision, have developed here, starting with the League of Nations and then the UN. Overall, the tendency has been to expropriate the individual sovereign right to wage war or use force, and to concentrate the power of legitimate violence in a centralised organ representing the community.[75] Equality, peace and justice were all to be promoted by this paradigmatic shift: international society should try to make the same leap undertaken by State society some centuries earlier.

Justice is here distributive: powers are unevenly distributed according to the needs of the community. Issues of protective justice also appear: States have to be protected against possible abuse by an excessively powerful Security Council (hence the issue of judicial review). In the 1990s, the system of collective security gained some momentum—and it has not lost it since.[76] A similar approach exists in the context of freezing international boundaries against unilateral action. The matter is sensitive from the perspective of the maintenance of peace. Thus, the principle of stability of international boundaries has been stressed more than once by the ICJ, for example in the *Preah Vihear* case (1962).[77] It has been applied in the context of the heritage of colonial boundaries (*uti possidetis*),[78] in the context of the law of State succession to treaties[79] and in the context of the law of treaties in general.[80] The general interest has here created some public law norms—but in this case there is no particular institutional scheme to guard them. The overall aim remains to safeguard peace as the first condition for justice. Such norms contain duties owed by States to the collectivity in view of its own needs; the issue is thus one of constitutional distributive justice.

[75] A system of collective security. See, eg, A Orakhelashvili, *Collective Security* (Oxford, 2011).

[76] See M Zambelli, *La constatation des situations de l'article 39 de la Charte des Nations Unies par le Conseil de sécurité* (Geneva/Basle/Munich, 2002); C Denis, *Le pouvoir normatif du Conseil de sécurité des Nations Unies: portée et limites* (Brussels, 2004); R Cadin, *I presupposti dell'azione del Consiglio di sicurezza nell'articolo 39 della Carta delle Nazioni Unite* (Milan, 2008).

[77] *Preah Vihear* [1962] ICJ Rep 34. See also the *Dubai/Sharjah* arbitration, (1981) 91 *ILR* 578. On the stability of boundaries, see, eg, G Abi-Saab, 'La pérennité des frontiers en droit international' (1990) 64 *Relations internationales* 341ff.

[78] *Frontier Dispute (Burkina Faso v Mali)* [1986] ICJ Rep 567, §§24–25. The arbitral Commission on Yugoslavia (EC) considered in its Opinion II that the principle of *uti possidetis* had precedence even over the principle of self-determination of peoples, ie the right of self-determination must be exercised within the given limits of the inherited boundaries. See (1992) 92 *ILR* 170–72. On *uti possidetis*, G Nesi, 'Uti Possidetis Doctrine' in R Wolfrum (ed), *The Max Planck Encyclopedia of Public International Law*, vol X (Oxford, 2012) 626ff and the literature indicated therein.

[79] See Arts 11 and 12 of the Vienna Convention on State Succession in Treaties, 1978.

[80] See Art 62, §2, letter a of the VCLT of 1969, concerning the non-availability of the argument of fundamental change of circumstances to reject a boundary treaty.

ii. Protective Justice

In situations where there are superiors and persons subjected to their power, the question arises as to the protection of those subjects against the arbitrary acts of their superiors. In municipal law, the response has been to develop the rule of law, fundamental rights and freedoms, judicial control and limiting doctrines, such as the prohibition on abuse of rights. The tools cannot be wholly different in the international legal order. But the fact remains that international law is insufficiently developed in this respect. Its horizontal structure (relations between equals) has long kept it aloof from the sorts of problems that arise in vertical relationships involving subordination. Nevertheless some distinctive mechanisms of protective justice have developed since 1945, notably in international human rights law. The protection of the individual against the abuses of a superior power is, however, not limited to the core human rights set against the pre-eminent power of States. It also exists in other, properly international areas, for example in the protection of the personnel of an international organisation through the grant of administrative law remedies allowing the seizing of an international administrative tribunal. When the ICJ was called to advise on the legality of the creation of such a tribunal by the UN General Assembly, it considered that an implied power must exist to that effect in view of the compelling need for proper protection of the staff:

> It would, in the opinion of the Court, hardly be consistent with the expressed aim of the Charter to promote freedom and justice for individuals and with the constant preoccupation of the United Nations Organization to promote this aim that it should afford no judicial or arbitral remedy to its own staff for the settlement of any disputes which may arise between it and them.[81]

But the classic human rights protection was and remains that used to counter abuses by States.[82] Initially, this branch of the law developed as a response to the massive oppression exercised by the Axis Powers in the totalitarian years of the twentieth century. The Universal Declaration of Human Rights of 1948 led the way, followed by the two Covenants of 1966. The regional systems have created tribunals that have the power to issue binding judgments on matters of human rights violations. Among the protective rights recognised to individuals, we might

[81] *Effect of Awards of Compensation made by the United Nations Administrative Tribunal* (Opinion) [1954] ICJ Rep 57.

[82] The literature in this area is extensive. See, eg, A Mandelstam, 'La protection internationale des droits de l'homme' (1931-IV) 38 *RCADI* 129ff; H Lauterpacht, 'The International Protection of Human Rights' (1947-I) 70 *RCADI* 1ff; R Brunet, *La garantie internationale des droits de l'homme* (Geneva, 1947); CE Rittgerband, *Universeller Menschenrechtsschutz und völkerrechtliches Interventionsverbot* (Berne/Stuttgart, 1982); P Alston (ed), *The United Nations and Human Rights* (Oxford, 1992); C Tomuschat, *Human Rights: Between Realism and Idealism* (Oxford, 2003); U Villani, *La protezione internazionale dei diritti umani* (Rome, 2005); E Decaux (ed), *Les Nations Unies et les droits de l'homme* (Paris, 2006); W Kälin and J Künzli, *The Law of International Human Rights Protection* (Oxford, 2009).

mention the right of *habeas corpus*:[83] thus, a deprivation of freedom must be grounded on a sufficient legal basis and respect for procedural guarantees, and must have a proper motive (eg to impede flight or to serve a criminal sentence). The UN Human Rights Committee under the ICCPR Covenant of 1966 consequently has had occasion to lend precision to the term 'arbitrary arrest';[84] and the Inter-American Court applies these *habeas corpus*-related aspects to enforced disappearances.[85]

More recently, the issue of individual protection has expanded to affect decisions of the UN Security Council under Chapter VII of the Charter. The desire to grant the UN Security Council strong powers, that is to give it teeth unlike the toothless Council of the League of Nations, led the drafters of the Charter to give it almost free rein once the political requirement for a majority, according to Article 27, §3 of the Charter, has been fulfilled. If the Powers within the Council agree, and the smaller States at least in part vote for the resolution, the Council has its way. Legally, there is hardly any limit to its powers. Those under Chapter VII are almost completely discretionary: Whether to recommend, or to issue a decision? To take any measure, or none at all? Which measure should be taken? Peaceful coercive measures, or forcible measures? Should authorisation be given to member States? Should blanket authorisation be granted, or do further details need to be drafted? Whether to impose time limits or not. All these issues may be freely decided by the Council.

For a long time, the Security Council was impeded in its acts. The dissension caused by the Cold War rendered enforcement action impossible. Since the 1990s, the situation has changed. The Council has taken many and powerful measures, sometimes imposing sanctions, sometimes issuing authorisations to use force. Western States, principally the US, discovered that the Council could be a valuable asset to their foreign policy. But are there any checks or balances?[86] In the 2000s, the issue attained significance in the context of the listing and de-listing procedures in the war against terror. The Council took action against persons suspected of supporting terrorist acts, in particular by freezing the assets of a number of named persons.[87] However, it did not allow protective justice mechanisms to come sufficiently into play. In particular, the sanctioned persons had no judicial remedy to establish the legality of the measures taken against them. Some States, including Switzerland, fought for the better compatibility of the sanctions regime

[83] L Doswald-Beck and R Kolb, *Judicial Process and Human Rights—United Nations, European, American and African Systems, Texts and Summaries of international Case-law* (Kehl/Strasbourg/Arlington, 2004).

[84] See, eg, *Mukong v Cameroon* (1994) Communication no 458/1991, A/49/40. On the case law, M Nowak, *UN Covenant on Civil and Political Rights, Commentary*, 2nd edn (Kehl/Strasburg/Arlington, 2005) 210ff.

[85] See the famous case *Velasquez Rodriguez v Honduras* (1988) 95 *ILR* 292.

[86] Since any man confronted with the absence of limits tends to abuse his powers: Montesquieu, *De l'esprit des lois*, book XI, ch 4.

[87] Res 1373, 1377 (2002); Res 1438, 1440, 1450 (2003); Res 1455, 1456 (2005); Res 1611, 1617 (2006); Res 1735 (2007), etc.

with human rights guarantees, ie the right to a remedy.[88] This right is all the more important when one knows that some individuals were added to the list by mistake, due to false accusations or the confusion of similar names in the Arabic language. In the meantime, a series of municipal tribunals or regional international tribunals have affirmed their jurisdiction to establish whether the measures taken in implementation of the Security Council Resolution have been compatible with applicable human rights guarantees, and more often than not have refused to validate the implementing measures for incompatibility with the constitutional standard of observance of core human rights.[89] Important standards of protective justice have developed here. The extent to which such control can and must be balanced with the efficacy of collective security action against terrorism is the great question of the day. The jurisprudential adventures in this regard are not at an end.

iii. Just Distribution of Rights in Situations of Inequality

Can or must one accord more rights to a subject exercising greater responsibilities in a particular area? Is the same true when that subject financially contributes more than another to a certain action? Can or must one distinguish the rights according to material factors, such as wealth? Such questions are always delicate, since they reveal a tension with the great principle of formal equality. The issue is further complicated in international law by the attachment of States to their formal equality, and their utter suspicion of any measure that might cast a shadow on this fundamental axiom. Thus, for a long time, the right of veto of each State participating in a conference made the adoption of multilateral conventions very difficult. The same was true as regards the creation of organs with restricted membership, like the Prize Court in 1907–09. It stumbled on the fact that no State would accept a call to renounce its own seat.[90] In modern international law, there are two main examples of 'unequal justice': in the composition of organs; and in weighted voting systems.

Many organs now have a restricted membership, reflecting special responsibilities, greater financial shares and so on. Thus the UN Security Council is composed mainly (permanent members) of the victorious Powers of World War II. The device of the League of Nations had been 'peace through law', the maxim of

[88] JF Paroz, 'Les droits et les devoirs d'un Etat membre: l'expérience et les initiatives de la Suisse depuis son adhésion aux Nations Unies' in R Kolb, *Introduction au droit des Nations Unies* (Basle/Brussels, 2008) 270ff. See, eg, the de-listing procedure created by Res 1730 (2006) of the Security Council.

[89] See, eg, Tribunal of First Instance of the EC, *Yusuf* (2005), §277ff (the Security Council cannot depart from *jus cogens* human rights); *Kadi* (2005), *ibid*; *Ayadi* (2006), *ibid*; *Hassan* (2006), *ibid*; *Al-Aqsa* (2007), *ibid*; Court of Justice of the European Communities, *Kadi* (2008), *ibid* (primacy of the whole European public order human rights guarantees over implementing measures for Security Council decisions); *Sayadi* case (UN Human Rights Committee, 2008), Communication no 1472/2006, CCPR/C/94/D/1472/2006 (again full standard of control under the ICCPR). See also national jurisprudence, eg in Switzerland: *Nada* (2007), Federal Tribunal (ATF 133 II, p 450ff) (on the lines of the *Yusuf* case quoted above), etc.

[90] See N Politis, *La justice internationale* (Paris, 1924) 13ff, 198ff.

the UN is 'peace through power'. The organ entrusted with the maintenance of peace[91] must reflect this fundamental policy choice, hence the restriction of its composition to the Great Powers of the day. Weighted voting systems exist mainly within international financial institutions, eg the International Monetary Fund (IMF). It also occurs that weighted voting is a consequence of the composition of an organ, as the Deep Seabed Authority shows. In the IMF,[92] the dominant principle is that each member State possesses a voting power proportional to the capital subscribed. In practice, this ensures that the lion's share of power goes to the US. There are, however, palliative mechanisms: there is a minimum voting strength for small subscribers; the necessity to obtain the assent of certain categories of States for certain decisions; the requirement for qualified majorities in certain subject matters, etc. In international commodities organisations (coffee, cocoa, etc) there is a weighted voting system within each group of States, ie exporters and importers. In the then EC a weighted voting system was installed with the following weights, calculated according to the population of the individual State: Germany, France, Italy and the UK, 10 votes; Spain, 8 votes; Belgium, Greece, The Netherlands and Portugal, 5 votes; Austria and Sweden, 4 votes; Denmark, Finland and Ireland, 3 votes; Luxemburg, 2 votes. Article 161, §1, letters a)–d), of the Montego Bay Convention on the Law of the Sea (1982) creates a complex weighted voting system within the Seabed Authority. It takes account of the importance of States as producers, consumers or investors with regard to the basic commodities to be exploited in the Area. There are here efforts towards the realisation of distributive justice.

iv. Just Distribution of Charges in Situations of Inequality

The dominant idea in this context is that of 'compensating' inequality or of affirmative action. Justice requires what is different to be treated differently, in proportion to its relevant difference. The weaker shall obtain certain privileges reflecting their weakness and contributing to their advancement. Legitimate as it may be, this approach must be considered carefully. First, one must take care not to use inappropriate criteria to measure the relevant inequality and/or the degree or proportion of that inequality. Secondly, one must avoid creating rigid systems of permanent compensation, which will contribute towards cementing existing inequalities and create in the weaker a mentality of permanent assistance, of passivity and of living off the back of others. Thirdly, one must be careful when assessing the beneficiaries. When one group is privileged because it employs loud political lobbyists, while another does not, this may lead to skewed perceptions. These will later fall to be corrected by other regimes dealing with compensatory

[91] Art 24 of the UN Charter.

[92] On the IMF, see L van Houtven, *Governance of the IMF: Decision making, Institutional Oversight, Transparency and Accountability* (Washington, DC, 2002); S Schlemmer-Schulte, 'International Monetary Fund (IMF)' in R Wolfrum (ed), *The Max Planck Encyclopedia of Public International Law*, vol V (Oxford, 2012) 1037ff.

inequality. In international law, the compensation here at stake has founded certain special branches of the law entirely dominated by this conception (the law of development). It has also partially influenced other legal regimes, such as that of State succession.

In the first situation, action on compensatory inequality is generally organised. The law of economic development in favour of Third World States warrants special attention.[93] It is composed of several layers: the new international economic order and the issue of redistribution; preferential treatment; aid to development; transfer of technology and know-how; technical assistance; governance of debts, etc. In its Resolution 3201 (1974) on the new international economic order, the UN General Assembly insisted on the link between the right to economic development and compensatory justice.[94] The development of fair trade and compensatory mechanisms has dominated UNCTAD since 1961. Within the developing States, certain categories were progressively singled out: (i) the least advanced countries; (ii) insular and land-locked States; (iii) those States most affected by economic crisis. Special compensatory mechanisms were projected for these States. Such distinctions have also found their way into hard international law, for example the Montego Bay Convention on the Law of the Sea (1982). It was negotiated in the 1970s, the heyday of the new international economic order. The Convention tries to balance a great number of interests by creating special statuses. Thus, it distinguishes between developed and developing States,[95] and also geographically disadvantaged States[96] or land-locked States,[97] producers and consumers of certain commodities,[98] etc. Special rights are attributed to archipelagic States,[99] which are more often than not developing States.

Another characteristic example is the system of preferential rights under the GATT system of 1994 (later the WTO). The norms on commerce were not the same as regards North–North relations and North–South relations. The inequality of development was reflected in a normative distinction unilaterally favouring the developing States. First, the principle of reciprocity was not applied to developing States. Thus, Article 35, §8 of the GATT stipulated that developed States could not

[93] SFDI, *Pays en voie de développement et transformation du droit international, Colloque d'Aix* (Paris, 1974); M Flory, *Droit international du développement* (Paris, 1977); BO de Rivero, *New Economic Order and International Law* (Oxford, 1980); M Bennouna, *Droit international du développement* (Paris, 1983); F Snyder and P Slinn (eds), *International Law of Development* (Abingdon, 1987); A Pellet, *Droit international du développement*, 2nd edn (Paris, 1987); G Feuer and H Cassan, *Droit international du développement*, 2nd edn (Paris, 1991); J Bouveresse, *Droit et politique du développement et de la coopération* (Paris, 1990); FV Garcia-Amador, *The Emerging International Law of Development* (New York, 1990); M Bulajic, *Principles of International Development Law* (Dordrecht, 1993); A Mahiou, 'Droit international et développement' (1999) III *Cours euro-méditérannéen Bancaja de droit international* 7ff.

[94] See the Preamble to the Resolution.

[95] See, eg, Arts 140, §1, 143, §3, letter b, 144, 148, 150, 152, letter d, 155, §1, letter f, 155, §2, 160–61, 164, 173, §2, letter c, 202–03, 207, §4, 244, §2, 271–74, 276, §1.

[96] See Arts 69–70, 160–61, 254, 266, 269, 272.

[97] See Arts 69–70, 140–41, 148, 152, §2, 160, §2, letter k, 266, §2, 269, letter a, 272, 274, letter a.

[98] See Art 161.

[99] See Arts 46–54.

invoke the lack of reciprocity to avoid reducing or eliminating custom restrictions on developing States. A similar system dominated the Lomé Agreements (1975–95) between the then EC and African States. Secondly, the 'most favoured nation treatment' was replaced by preferential treatment of the developing States. Thus, concessions could be accorded to developing States without concomitant duties to extend them to all other States. This meant that tariff preferences could be granted to one group of States. The main pillars of international commercial law, namely reciprocity and most favoured treatment, were here abandoned in favour of a compensatory justice scheme.

Still another example can be found in the domain of the transfer of technology. It covers the transfer of technical instruments, techniques, services and know-how. The need for such a transfer had already been emphasised in the Declaration relative to a New International Economic Order of 1974.[100] On the basis of this Declaration, a Code was prepared and adopted by UNCTAD in 1978.[101] The Montego Bay Convention on the Law of the Sea (1982) was the first hard-law instrument to largely translate these aspirations into positive law. Part XIV is generally devoted to this topic; there is also a special regime for the deep seabed. Part XIV of the Convention is based on obligations of cooperation culminating in *pacta de contrahendo*.[102] Developed and developing States cooperate with a view to 'promot[ing] actively the development and the transfer of maritime science and marine technology on fair and reasonable terms and conditions'.[103] The various bilateral and multilateral frameworks in which this cooperation has to take place are spelled out in Articles 270–274 of the Convention. The transfer of technology in the context of the deep seabed regime is organised mainly in Article 5 of Annex III to the Convention. The aim of the provision is to ensure that the Enterprise, representing humanity, can operate in the exploitation of the Area on the basis of conditions that are not too unequal with respect to the technologically advanced and licensed actors. For this reason, the licensed private actors must put at the disposal of the Authority, on fair and reasonable terms and conditions, the relevant technologies. Similar rights exist for the developing States, to the extent that they wish to engage in deep seabed mining.[104] In addition, Articles 144 and 274 oblige the Authority to promote the transfer of technology in various ways: by the training of the personnel of the Enterprise or of developing States;[105] by engaging interns within this personnel;[106] by placing technical documentation at the disposal of developing States;[107] by favouring the acquisition of know-how and

[100] Res 3201 (1974), UNGA, §4.

[101] UNCTAD Code on Transfer of Technology (1980) 19. *ILM* 773ff. See D Thompson, 'The UNCTAD Code on Transfer of Technology' (1982) 16 *Journal of World Trade Law* 311ff.

[102] See Y Tanaka, *The International Law of the Sea*, 2nd edn (Cambridge, 2015) 371ff; T Treves, 'Le transfert de technologie et la Conférence sur le droit de la mer' (1977) 104 *JDI* 43ff.

[103] Art 266, §1.

[104] Art 5, §3, Annex III.

[105] Art 144, §2, letter b.

[106] Art 274, letter a.

[107] Art 274, letter b.

technical assistance for developing States,[108] etc. This very bureaucratic regime was corrected by the reform of 1994. The developed States feared provoking market distortions by the transfer of technology; they also emphasised the danger of discouraging investment; and, lastly, they highlighted intellectual property right problems. The Enterprise and developing States have been referred to the free market and joint-venture agreements to be concluded among them. The Deep Seabed Authority may here help to obtain the necessary contracts by organising consultations.[109] The initial distributive justice approach has thus been curtailed. To this day, significant schemes for technology transfer have not been drafted (as, incidentally, is also the case as regards the exploitation of deep seabed resources).

Inequality can also occur in an *ad hoc* manner. This happened, for example, in the domain of State succession. In both the Vienna Conventions of 1978 and 1983 (on treaties and on State property, archives and debts) a distinction is made between ordinary cases of succession and those cases involving the 'newly independent States' (ie the former colonies). Compensatory advantages are granted to the latter, such as the clean-slate rule (under which there is no obligation to continue the treaties of the colonising State)[110] or the much greater rights of those States to participate in a share of the goods of the predecessor State.[111] In principle, no debt should pass from the colonising predecessor to the newly independent State, unless a strictly conceived derogative agreement is concluded.[112] Notwithstanding the fact that decolonisation is now complete, it should be noted that some States emerging from the collapse of the USSR claimed to be 'newly independent States' in the sense of the Conventions on State succession.

Overall, the conception of redistribution and compensatory advantage is only partly realised in international society. Through the marked-orientated tendencies of the last few years, redistributive approaches have further lost their attractiveness. But it would be wrong to ignore the existing mechanisms.

v. Equity

It is superfluous to come back to equity in international law. We may simply refer to the discussion in section II.B.i. above.

C. Conclusion

Each legal order presents itself as a constant effort to reconcile the demands of justice and other needs. The precise combination of the factors of justice realised and the degree of their realisation allows us to grasp the political spectrum of a society.

108 Art 274, letters c and d.
109 1994 Agreement (Resolution 48/263 UNGA), A/48/950, Part V, Arts 1 and 2.
110 Arts 16 and 30 of the 1978 Convention on Succession in Treaties.
111 Art 15 of the 1983 Convention on State Property Archives and Debts.
112 *ibid*, Art 38.

These elements are variable in time and place; they differ from legal order to legal order; and they differ according to the branches of the law involved. In international law, the most characteristic feature is the predominance of individualism, and to some extent even of 'private justice'. The spectrum of international justice is more largely horizontal and commutative than it is vertical and distributive. From this perspective, international law is more markedly private law than public law. However, any overly weighty predominance of one type of justice over the other is the hallmark of social disequilibrium. The strength of the commutative aspect can be seen in the powerfulness of reciprocity, in the relativity of legal situations, in the number of duties to abstain (*neminem laedere*) and so on. The concomitant weakness of the distributive aspect is rooted in the absence of a supranational power. We always come back to this fundamental fact: commutative justice and law can blossom in the top soil of the normative dimension; distributive justice and law need an organic layer replete with powers. Progress in distributive justice is thus linked with the 'organisation of the international society', ie its progressive institutionalisation. For the time being, great leaps forward cannot be expected.

III. Legal Certainty

A. General Legal Experience

Security, ie certainty and foreseeability, is a fundamental need of individuals and social groups. The action an individual plans and finally undertakes is based on the expectation of normal conduct by other subjects, or conduct that can be required in a certain context. The orientation of human behaviour is significantly driven by the internalisation of external signs. An understanding of their meaning allows individuals to undertake and to participate with efficacy in social interaction. Society in itself is but a network of regularities resulting in a certain order. Life in common is possible only through the acceptance of such regularities. Just as the universe could not exist if it were not governed by certain physical laws, so society would descend into chaos if there were no regularities fed by expectations.

Justice and security are both 'other orientated', ie projections out towards the external world. Through the characteristics described, security is hugely relevant for the law. It takes the form of 'legal certainty'. However, security plays a role in many different areas too—anthropological, economic, sociological and animal:

1. Legal *sociology* defines norms as generalised expectations of conduct accompanied by sanctions. Thus, the expectation (which is mid-way between a pure fact and a pure 'ought') becomes the central pivot for the definition of norms. It concerns a real psychological fact in the mind of individuals; but it differs from the mere effectiveness of real situations in that it contains a normative element. The generalisation of social expectations allows the stabilisation of

society. Regularity condenses itself into rules. Moreover, expectations reduce the domain of complexity: they allow a subject to avoid envisaging each time all the possible avenues of conduct and result, and to concentrate on the expectable and legitimate behaviour in regard to the social role of other persons. The sociological definition of norms is thus engrafted upon the idea of the security of inter-individual interaction.[113] The same could be said of economic interaction, which is a special aspect of social interaction. Apart from devices geared at retaining a certain flexibility in case of unforeseen developments (eg safeguard clauses), economic interaction is fundamentally based on the foreseeability of exchanges and transactions. Without such foreseeability, the exchange of goods is hampered, as instances of important monetary or other types of crisis show.

2. Security also plays an eminent role in *anthropology and psychology*. The foreseeability of conduct and the ability to harmonise one's own acts and aspirations with the external world are important factors of psychological stability. Security reduces anguish and the pressure of having to take often complex decisions. The burden of having to constantly weigh up all the many alternatives is considerably reduced.[114] This need for stability is more pronounced in human beings than in (other) animals. The latter are more importantly driven by instinct. Human beings, less prone to instinctive conduct, suffer from a lack of inner security. The cultural institutions (including the law) must compensate for the deficits left by nature.[115] Brutal social upheavals provide evidence for this: the growing insecurity ushers in disorder and tension; all exchanges suffer, from black markets to hyper-inflation; the individual shows signs of trauma, anxiety and fear, often leading to aggression and hate. Periods of rejection of received certainties are also periods of violence. This is true to a large extent in the animal world too.[116] Studies of animals living in groups have shown that they often follow a rigid social order, based on hierarchy and the prohibition of inappropriate conduct. Security and the credibility of the signs displayed are central to the ability of the group to survive many external threats. In such cases it is essential to be able to rely on the conduct of the other members of society. Security, moreover, allows the efficacy of social life to be improved by the division of tasks. This sharing of tasks supposes that legitimate confidence in the proper execution of these roles is honoured in most cases.

[113] *Encyclopedia of Social Sciences*, vol 11 (New York, 1968) 204ff, 208ff; N Luhmann, *Rechtssoziologie*, vol I (Reinbeck, 1973) 53ff.

[114] U Beer, *Optimisten leben länger* (Geneva, 1985); M Koller, *Sozialpsychologie des Vertrauens* (Bielefeld, 1990); K Salmelaaro and J Nurmi, 'Uncertainty and Confidence in Interpersonal Projects' (1996) 13 *Journal of Social and Personal Relationships* 109ff.

[115] A Gehlen, *Moral und Hypermoral* (Frankfurt/Bonn, 1969) 95ff.

[116] K Lorenz, *Über tierisches und menschliches Verhalten* (Munich, 1974); K Lorenz, *Vergleichende Verhaltensforschung* (Vienna/New York, 1978); GE Pugh, *The Biological Origin of Human Values* (London, 1977); GS Stent (ed), *Morality as Biological Phenomenon* (Berlin, 1978); EO Wilson, *Sociobiology* (Cambridge, 1982).

3. Lastly, security is also a cardinal notion of *moral* life. Legitimate expectations create confidence and faith; they should not be deceitful or deluded. *Fides est credulitas*, as Isidor of Sevilla rightly observed.[117] The duty to honour the confidence created is at the root of the contractual bond (*pacta sunt servanda*, good faith).[118] It stands to reason that such a duty is intimately linked with justice and correctness. These are at bottom moral values.

Within the law, the notion of security takes on the complexion of 'legal security' or 'legal certainty'.[119] This is composed of many different aspects. The need for security is first of all realised through the existence of a legal order. Its primary function is to effect an ordering of society through normative regularities and guidance. This is security *through* law. But there is also security *within* the law. The latter manifests itself in two domains: (i) objective or *erga omnes* legal certainty, concerning the legal order in general; and (ii) subjective or *inter partes* legal certainty, concerning the legal relations of some specific subjects. The first type of certainty touches on the functioning of the legal order in its entirety, for example through the requirements for accessibility of the law, clarity and precision of the norms, etc. The second type of security concerns interpersonal relationships. It demands that a subject honour the confidence and expectations it has created through its conduct, when another subject is legitimately entitled to rely on them. Security here requires a certain coherence or continuity of conduct when it affects third parties. This type of certainty is mainly rooted in the principle of good faith with its many sub-aspects, such as estoppel, acquiescence, prescription by inaction, responsibility for representations (*Anscheinshaftung*), etc. This concerns the subjective legal certainty between the parties to some transaction or exchange (*fides*).

Objective legal certainty has two main categories: (i) certainty with regard to legal norms; and (ii) security with regard to the execution of the law. The concrete legal certainty felt by a subject, or of benefit to a legal operator, is the sum of both *certitudo* and *securitas*, that is, it lies in the quality of the norms posed *and* in their concrete realisation.

The first limb concerns *normative certainty* (*certitudo*). It can be limited to a given existing positive legal order, or touch on the changing of legal norms within that legal order. *First*, with regard to the existing law, certainty means mainly the need for clarity, simplicity and the systematic ordering of the legal material. The legal operator (and ideally also the citizen) should be able to orientate himself within the legal norms without getting lost in a mass of vague, disordered or labyrinthine regulation. This type of certainty is jeopardised by an excessive number of vague norms or lengthy formulas. The same is true if too many rules grant a discretionary power to the operator, either concerning the elements of the norm (too many generic terms, such as 'reasonable') or concerning the application of the norm (discretion as to whether to take action or not). The same also occurs

[117] Isidor of Sevilla, *De Differentiis*, I, 486.
[118] Cicero, *De officiis*, lib I, cap VII.
[119] On legal certainty, see, eg, T Piazzon, *La sécurité juridique* (Paris, 2009).

when the norms are riddled with too many saving clauses, exceptions, suspension or equity clauses, in particular when these allow unilateral qualifications. A pronounced tendency to individualise the normative content has the same effect. There are other factors influencing this type of certainty: inadequate, complicated, ill-styled, contrived or overblown wording; insufficient systematisation of the norms, which thus remain scattered and haphazard; the lack of proper coordination of the various sources of a legal order; and the inflation of norms, devaluing their sense and favouring lack of respect for and ignorance of the law (*plurimae leges, pessima civitas*).

Secondly, with regard to the changing of norms, certainty mainly refers to stability and continuity of the law and the legal rights acquired. Law must be allowed to project some certainty into the future. If it did not, the realisation of projects and the investment of resources would become difficult or otiose. There can be no certainty if everything can be put legally at risk at any time, if everything can be reopened on a whim. On the legislative plane, this implies avoiding overly frequent and unexpected amendments of the law. A comprehensive and well-planned one-off reform of a branch of the law will be better than a number of small and poorly coordinated modifications.[120] Transitory legislative measures may be necessary to accompany the changes. Moreover, this type of certainty calls for the avoidance of retroactive laws, which the subject could not have expected at the moment he or she acted (but more favourable new laws may sometimes be retroactively applied, as with the *lex mitior* in criminal law).

Lastly, normative certainty calls for the continuity of acquired legal positions, such as acquired rights. To the fullest measure possible (and subject to compatibility with public policy), such situations should not be disturbed, even if certain of their aspects may have to be harmonised *pro futuro* with the new regulation. That the law has to be modified so as to respond to new needs and realities is beyond doubt. But it has to be appreciated that this change conflicts with the concurrent need for legal stability, and prompts a series of inter-temporal law problems. A careful balancing of the stakes has to take place here.

The second limb concerns *executive security* (*securitas*). In the first place, this type of security demands that judgments rendered on the basis of legal norms be reasonably foreseeable, so that the risk of process can be adequately assessed. There are other aspects regarding judgments that fall into this category, for example: the principle of *res judicata*, terminating the dispute and creating security; the strict conditions for revision of a judgment rendered; and the assumption of coherence and continuity of jurisprudence, potentially even including the announcement of a prospective overruling (future probable change in the case law).[121] The most

[120] P Noll, *Gesetzgebungslehre* (Reinbek (Hamburg), 1973) 214ff.

[121] On this last point, see B Weber-Dürler, *Vertrauensschutz im öffentlichen Recht* (Basle/Frankfurt, 1993) 234ff. The Swiss Federal Tribunal has held that a change of jurisprudence, which would result in the loss of certain remedies, must be announced in advance: ATF 106 Ia, p 92; ATF 109 II, p 176; ATF 116 II, p 496; ATF 120 Ia, p 26.

essential aspect of this type of security lies in the execution of the law in general, that is, in its real efficacy and in the ability to ensure its realisation through some remedy, if necessary by coercion (*Realisierungssicherheit*).[122] Executive security depends mainly on the chance to see the legal provision realised, or alternatively on the possibility to have it realised by procedural devices. The legal regulations creating organs for the enforcement of the law and giving the necessary powers to these organs are part and parcel of this type of security. The same can be said of the abilities given to persons to denounce violations of the law, to formulate claims and to set in motion executive measures. It is true that legal certainty, and more fundamentally the concept of law, suffers when the subjects cannot rely on the realisation of the norms the system has set out. However, in this regard, it should be recalled that the factors encouraging respect for the law amount to more than the simple fear of a sanction or coercion in case of lack of respect. A legal order that could count only on the hammer of a sanction after the fact would paradoxically be appallingly ineffective: its norms would be constantly violated; and some redress after the fact would have to be sought, where possible. How could such an order provide security? The main aspect of effectiveness is and remains spontaneous compliance: *oboedientia facit imperantem*. International law does not fare too badly in this regard, since its norms are seldom imposed on the subjects but rather flow from consent.

The third and last limb concerns *security between the parties* (*fides*). Modern legal orders create rights and duties flowing from social interaction, in which one subject conducts himself in such as way as to arouse legitimate expectations in some other subject. Confidence in a certain regularity of legally relevant conduct is protected by the principle of good faith. The law does not allow the first subject to plead his true but concealed intention to displace the socially legitimate expectation created by his effective conduct. He is bound by the manifestation, representation or appearance deliberately or objectively created. This protection of legitimate expectations has different manifestations in the legal orders. For example: (i) a prohibition, in certain cases, on contradicting previous deeds (estoppel, *venire contra factum proprium*, *doctrina de los actos proprios*)—eg if a debtor induces the creditor not to apply a time-bar, the former cannot after the fact plead prescription in order not to pay the debt; (ii) prolonged inactivity may result in the loss of rights, ie the transformation of the legal situation (acquiescence, *qui tacet consentire videtur si loqui potuisset ac debuisset*)—eg a married partner draws no consequences from adulterous conduct but later tries to derive rights from it; (iii) the acquisition of rights in the case of prolonged and uncontested possession (acquisitive prescription); (iv) responsibility for representation, for example, in German law, the fact of having held oneself out as being the representative of a business leads to subjection to the stricter regime of responsibility applicable to such persons; (v) in the conclusion of contracts, the true intention of a party cannot be pleaded against the fair and reasonable meaning of words

[122] T Geiger, *Vorstudien zu einer Soziologie des Rechts* (Aarhus, 1947) 64.

which the other party could and should have understood; (vi) in public law, there is protection of the public faith (*öffentlicher Glaube*), ie the individual is protected as to the confidence he or she places in the truth of certain public registers or in certain information officially conveyed.[123]

B. Legal Certainty in International Law

The most characteristic feature of international law for our present purposes is the predominance of subjective security over objective security, that is, of the *inter partes* limb over the *erga omnes* limb. This once again reflects the intimate structure of international society, where private law or horizontal elements predominate over public law or vertical elements. In such an environment, relativity and bilateralism of legal situations generally prevail. The ensuing fragmentation is easier to fit into a system of 'localised' legal certainty, and conversely more difficult to square with a uniform notion of certainty detached from the bilateral or particular situations. Simply put, objective legal security is based on the integrated governance of public affairs, with a hierarchy of organs and sources. International law is not constructed along these lines. It must be added that international law mainly regulates political relations between States. In such surroundings, legal certainty tends to weaken, leaving the lion's share to considerations of utility or equity, linked to particular situations. This is the case in municipal law too: constitutional law, which is the political branch of the legal order, tends to be the least permeated by considerations of legal certainty, unlike largely non-political branches of the law such as private law.

1. Objective Legal Certainty

The weaknesses of objective legal certainty can be felt at three levels: normative, structural and organic. First, there is a great deal of normative insecurity. It concerns the organisation, formulation and precision of the norms. There are many aspects of legal insecurity here. *First*, the international legal order is weakly systematised. The law is largely unwritten; it grows spontaneously; its articulation is defective, non-linear and sometimes circuitous. Thus, customary international law is based on a sum of more or less convergent practices. This existential process, whereby haphazard acts and omissions lead to a certain regularity which in turn evolves into a rule, cannot result in a well-ordered and well-thought-out edifice. Moreover, many international rights and obligations exist only between certain parties. The share of particular law is particularly important in the international legal order when compared to that of the common law. This fact contributes to the

[123] For example, if an erroneous time limit for exercising a remedy is indicated in an official letter by an apparently competent State organ, and if there is no negligence on the side of the addressee, he or she may benefit from it, if necessary through an extension: Swiss Federal Tribunal, ATF 115 Ia, p 12ff; ATF 117 Ia, p 421ff.

fragmentation of the law, and thus to legal uncertainty. The relations between the various sources themselves become uncertain. The 1986 *Nicaragua* case before the ICJ revealed such uncertainty in the—still simple—situation of the relationship of the UN Charter with customary international law.[124] Overall, the abovementioned uncertainties lead to absence of clarity and foreseeability. This fact also impacts on the propensity of States to bring disputes to the fore.

Secondly, international law is not based on a hierarchy of its sources. In municipal law, the hierarchy of the legal sources is an expression of the hierarchy of the organs adopting them. In international law, the legislator is always the States, with no hierarchical distinction. The absence of hierarchy leads to the fact the normative conflicts can be resolved only by *ad hoc* interpretations based on flexible maxims, such as *lex posterior* or *lex specialis*. These maxims are applicable only with regard to the same group of parties and have no effect for third States. The lack of hierarchy as to the sources and acts leads to fragmentation and uncertainty where a subject matter is regulated by many different legal instruments, as occurred, for example, in the legal regime governing the River Danube through the two main conventions of 1856 and 1948, which were not accepted by the same States—a solution could ultimately be found on some aspects only through the Sofia Convention of 1994.[125]

Thirdly, there is a lack of precision in many international norms. It stands to reason that it is more difficult to find consensus among 194 States than among a smaller number of subjects. Thus, the text expressing such consents is often watered down to reflect the lowest common denominator. Such texts are open to vague formulas, which increase legal uncertainty. Moreover, as we have already seen, international law deals with political matters; it thus often has recourse to techniques bestowing flexibility, such as equity clauses, standard or other saving clauses, with a view to allowing adaptations to accommodate fluctuating social and political conditions. The impact on legal certainty of such vague notions is even greater in respect of the same clauses in municipal law: in the case of the latter, though, there is normally a judge to review then and apply to them some degree of objective interpretation; in international law, there is no such regular judge. This means that the clauses at stake will normally lead to unilateral action. In general, the presence of self-interpretation and the significant weight of soft law increase the impact of legal uncertainty. The latter will in particular tend to dilute the boundary between hard and soft law. The result is a certain lack of clarity as to what is legally due and what is merely politically opportune. Even in subject matters dominated traditionally by strict standards with regard to clarity, namely criminal law, international law is much less demanding than sensitive internal systems, like that in Germany after the Nazi regime. The formulation of some

[124] *Military and Paramilitary Activities in and Against Nicaragua* [1986] ICJ Rep 92ff.

[125] See AF Zeilinger, 'Danube River' in R Wolfrum (ed), *The Max Planck Encyclopedia of Public International Law*, vol II (Oxford, 2012) 1012ff.

offences under the heading 'crimes against humanity' ('intentionally causing great suffering') are emblematic in this regard. One might also recall, in the domain of State responsibility, the defunct Article 19 of the ILC Draft on International Responsibility of States from the 1970s (on international crimes of States).[126] The same can be said for many norms of the law on State succession; we have already discussed this issue in section II.A. above. Moreover, the effect of a series of rules of international law is ill-defined, for example the rules on maritime delimitation based for a certain time on 'equitable results', the effects of *jus cogens* or *erga omnes* norms, etc. Thus, for example, does *jus cogens* lead to a hierarchy of norms exhibiting priority over, or even sometimes leading to the nullity of (all), inferior norms? Is there a hierarchy within the hierarchy of *jus cogens* norms? What exactly are the rights of third States and entities in the context of *erga omnes* positions: an enlarged *jus standi*, or also new substantive rights in the context of countermeasures? And so on.

Fourthly, international normativity is fragmented. The system is polynormative and multi-polar. The absence of a sole legislator leaves the whole edifice of norms resting on shaky foundations. There is often a plurality of norms on the same subject-matter. There may be superposition of old and new provisions, of legal and soft-law norms, and so on. General international law can on most points be derogated from by particular legal regimes, conventional or other (prescriptive situations, estoppels, acquiescence, recognitions, other normative unilateral acts, etc). This leads to a kaleidoscopic legal order; and this in turn diminishes legal certainty. There are also gaps in the legal order, that is, areas which remain under the domination of uncoordinated political action. Giraud has written, in words which are perhaps overly critical, 'Gaps are comparable to breaks easy to fill—but international law resembles sometimes more an unfinished palace, where some fundamental parts for a proper functioning are missing, eg a part of the roof or the staircase.'[127]

Fifthly, international normativity is traversed by unilateralism. A series of norms within this legal order allow States unilaterally to determine the content of the obligations assumed.[128] The bywords of this legal order are in any case self-interpretation and self-qualification, in the absence of a regular judge to carry out checks and controls. Thus, to the fragmentation of the norms is added the fragmentation of qualifications under these norms. The constraints of reciprocity and interest in the application of the agreed regimes somewhat temper the subjective and centrifugal force, but they do not do away with it altogether. Unilateral,

[126] ILC Draft on International Responsibility [1996-II.2] *ILC Yearbook* 60.

[127] E Giraud, 'Le droit international public et la politique' (1963-III) 110 *RCADI* 584.

[128] See the hardly complimentary study by G de Lacharrière, *La politique juridique extérieure* (Paris, 1983) 105ff. See, eg, *Hartford Fire Insurance Co v California* (1993) 100 *ILR* 566ff (US Supreme Court), where the Court adopts a stand with regard to extraterritorial jurisdiction which unilaterally suits US interests: the real links to the US were tenuous; they were much stronger with regard to the UK (this was recognised by the minority, see, eg, Judge Scalia, *ibid*, 600). See also the massive US interference with the Swiss legal order in the *Marc Rich* affair (1984) 40 *ASDI* 160ff.

tainted and self-interested interpretations limit the certainty of the international legal order. States quite commonly insist on their positions. In such cases, disputes can rumble on, be it over The Falklands/Malvinas, Palestine or elsewhere.

Sixthly, international normativity is often controversial. These controversies are not limited to subordinated or marginal questions but are strongest in the most vital areas of the law, such as that relating to the use of force. The construction of customary international law or of general principles of law has remained uncertain. There are many different theories concerning the most important law-creating agencies of international law. It is hardly surprising that a legal order based on such foundations cannot offer a sufficient level of objective legal certainty.

The absence of superior organs guaranteeing the application of the rule of law creates significant room for political action, for power-related outcomes, for the reign of effectivities (*quieta non movere*)—that is for legal insecurity. The calm and flat surface of the waters is undermined by rocks, sandbanks and reefs. The application of the law remains asymmetrical and depends on a network of external factors, most of them being of a political nature. The absence of superior organs entrusted to enforce the law leads to the relative weakness of the law's sanction—and thus to a weakness of the *securitas* aspect discussed in section III.A. above.

All these factors contribute to an inadequate level of objective legal certainty. It has been said that in international law, legal certainty remains a 'chimera'.[129] This description goes too far, in particular considering its generality and boldness; but it would be foolish to deny part of its truth.

2. *Subjective Legal Certainty*

Conversely, as has been said, subjective legal certainty is quite strongly developed in international law. Considerations of good faith and legitimate expectations, viewed from the horizontal perspective of interacting subjects, have led to a series of legal concretisations.[130] The principles of *pacta sunt servanda* and good faith lie at the root of respect for treaties.[131] In the *Port of Portendick* case (1843), the French authorities had informed the UK authorities that a port would be kept open. Later, the port was closed without proper notice. The UK Government complained about this lack of information, which led to economic losses for some ships of its nationality. The French Government was ordered by the arbitrators to pay an indemnity in view of the legitimate expectations first created and later breached.[132] In the *Schufeldt* case (1930),[133] the arbitrator rejected a plea for

[129] K Zemanek, 'The Legal Foundations of the International System' (1997) 266 *RCADI* 288.

[130] See R Kolb, *La bonne foi en droit international public* (Paris, 2000).

[131] Art 26 VCLT. See J Salmon, 'Article 26' in O Corten and P Klein (eds), *The Vienna Convention on the Law of Treaties, A Commentary*, vol I (Oxford, 2011) 659ff; K Schmalenbach, 'Article 26' in O Dörr and K Schmalenbach (eds), *Vienna Convention on the Law of Treaties, A Commentary* (Heidelberg, 2012) 427ff.

[132] A de la Pradelle and N Politis, *Recueil des arbitrages internationaux*, vol I: *1798–1855* (Paris, 1905) 526.

[133] *Schufeldt* (1930) II *RIAA* 1094.

nullification of a concession when the investor, in the belief of its validity, had gone on to invest considerable sums of money, and when the government for many years had not claimed any default in the concession. The same has been said regarding legislation that had not been applied for a long time, so as to create a legitimate expectation as to its lapse.[134] By the same token, treaties or contracts can exceptionally be ratified through conduct (regular application).[135] A treaty can also be modified by subsequent practice, creating legitimate expectations as to its permanence.[136] The binding force of unilateral promises is grounded on good faith and legitimate expectations.[137] Acquiescence has been applied to maritime or territorial disputes,[138] among others. And so on.

Overall, it can be said that in international law, legal certainty concentrates on bilateral or special relationships, ie that it is more strongly *ratione personae* than *ratione materiae*.

IV. Reciprocity and Proportionality

A. General Legal Experience

The root of reciprocity lies in the relations of one subject with another. This 'other-relatedness' accounts for its relevance to the legal phenomenon. It has been contended that reciprocity is the elementary feature of any law.[139] In its various shades—equality, reversibility, equilibrium, proportionality, the Golden Rule—it certainly profoundly influences the legal order. In primitive societies,[140] reciprocity creates a simple framework of spontaneous order: I bind myself to the extent that you bind yourself; I base my obligations on yours; I respect the agreement to the extent that you respect it, etc. This inter-subjective equilibrium is at once an ideal principle of equality *and* a powerful factor ensuring compliance. It stands to reason that it plays an increased role in societies deprived of a superior power enforcing the law. In such cases, reciprocity, with all its imperfections, replaces the missing regulatory mechanism, ie the organic structure. It is an *Ersatz*.

[134] *DJ Adams* (1921), *Annual Digest of Public International Law Cases*, vol 1: *1919–1922*, 237–38, *obiter*.

[135] *Textron* case (1981) 6 *Iran / US Claims Tribunal Reports* 345–46; or *Union of India c Sukumar Sengupta* case (1990) 92 *ILR* 570 (Supreme Court, India). See also *Kamiar* (1968) 44 *ILR* 262–63 (Israel Supreme Court).

[136] *US/French Air Services Agreement (1963)* (1965) 69 *RGDIP* 249–50.

[137] *Nuclear Tests* [1974] ICJ 268 and 473.

[138] See, eg, *Norwegian Fisheries* [1951] ICJ Rep 138–39; *Temple of Préah Vihéar* [1962] ICJ Rep 23, 27–28.

[139] E Fechner, *Rechtsphilosophie*, 2nd edn (Tübingen, 1956) 101.

[140] See, eg, for the Trobiand society in Papua-New Guinea B Malinowski, *Crime and Custom in Savage Society*, 9th edn (London, 1970).

Reciprocity is first of all a principle of justice, notably of commutative justice. It permeates the field of exchanges and of compensation for damage inflicted. This 'justice reciprocity' manifests itself in the idea of equilibrium, mainly of equals (eye for eye, tooth for tooth) or of the one by its equivalent (*do ut des* in proportionality). The latter opens the way to a richer and more modulated equality through 'equivalence', for example a certain degree of reaction as a function of the gravity of the triggering illegal act. Proportionality here becomes paramount. This form of 'justice reciprocity' is linked to morals. The link is particularly strong with the Golden Rule, especially in its negative form: 'Do not do to others what you do not want to be done to yourself.'[141] It is understandable that this form of reciprocity found some way into the law. In the time of the Enlightenment, the whole legal order was perceived by some authors as representing a proportional and reciprocal cession of parts of liberty.[142] Thomasius had claimed that the main maxim of politics was the positive Golden Rule (*quod vis ut alii tibi faciant, tu et ipsis facias*) and the main maxim for law the negative Golden Rule (*quod tibi non vis fieri, alteri ne feceris*).[143] In modern legal orders, reciprocity profoundly impacts on areas where subjects placed on a footing of equality confront each other, ie in the domains of private law. In this context, the public law principle of the duties according to the law is to a large extent substituted by the private law principle of *do ut des*. But the enforcement of these private duties is not left mainly to reciprocity. It is a question of public law, through the organs entrusted with the enforcement of the law. Conditional obligations (on the basis of reciprocity) of pre-State legal orders finally usher in unconditional obligations guaranteed by the State organic machinery.

The content of reciprocity can be viewed through four different lenses placed in order of increasing strength: (i) 'relation reciprocity', relating to the equality of the subjects involved and thus to the measure of equivalence; (ii) 'correlative reciprocity', which concerns the mutual dependence of rights and obligations in a legal relationship; (iii) 'equilibrium reciprocity', which concerns the force of the measures permitted to be taken to re-establish the situation in case of breach of the law (proportionality); and (iv) 'moral reciprocity', which gives the measure of correct conduct towards the other once he is recognised as an equal. The last culminates in the Kantian categorical imperative, 'So act as to treat humanity, whether in your own person or in another, always as an end, and never as only a means.'

1. *Relation Reciprocity*

Being a relational notion, reciprocity supposes a definition of 'equivalent' relations within which the notion will be called to apply. This question essentially turns

[141] This is universal rule of morality: *Mahabharata*, XIII, 5571; Confucius in *Lun Ju*, XV, 23; Talmud (see in A Dilche, *Die Goldene Regel* (Göttingen, 1962) 8); or the Holy Bible, Matthew, 7:12; and for the Old Testament, see Tobias 4:15 (see H Reiner, 'Die Goldene Regel' (1948) 3 *Zeitschrift für philosophische Forschung* 74ff).

[142] See I Kant, *Metaphysics of Morals*, 'Doctrine of Law', letter c: the liberty of the one must coexist with the liberty of the other according to a universal law of coexistence.

[143] C Thomasius, *Fundamenta iuris naturae et gentium* (1705), lib I, cap VI, §§40–42.

around the notion of equality: reciprocity will apply to the full extent in relations between equal subjects, and less or not at all in relations between unequal subjects. Thus, in Roman law there was inequality between the *paterfamilias* and the other non-emancipated members of family, or between the free individual and slaves. The network of equality and reciprocity was thereby restricted to certain relations and could not be applied to others. In the Middle Ages, there was a distinction according to status: nobleman, merchant, clergyman, Catholic, Jew, etc. Reciprocity was here restricted and fragmented into a plurality of different circles. The more the empire of the equality of men increases, the firmer the hold of reciprocity; and vice versa. This is a first function of the legal order: to define the spheres of equality.

2. *Correlative Reciprocity*

This type of reciprocity interlinks the two poles—the right and the obligation—within a legal relationship. It renders the one dependent on the fulfilment of the other. Reciprocity in this sense first of all limits the rights: I cannot demand performance if I have not rendered performance. It limits also the obligations: I do not have to perform if the other party has not performed. The role of reciprocity is to bring these two unilateral attitudes together into one single relationship. This unity is based on conditionality or correlativity: (i) first with regard to the 'if': I bind myself if you bind yourself; I perform if you perform; I refuse to give if you do not give, etc; (ii) secondly with regard to the measure: I engage myself in the same proportion to which you engage; I perform in proportion to your execution; I give in proportion to what you gave, etc. The overall aim is to reach a relative equivalence between parties. In a positive sense, reciprocity serves to modulate among themselves rights and obligations. This is the case, for example, in the context of optional declarations under Article 36, §2 of the ICJ Statute, when each party to a proceeding can invoke by way of reciprocity reservations contained in the declaration of the other party.[144] The modulation can also occur with regard to an external criterion, say in the context of 'most favoured nation clauses'. A specific substantive customs regime may, for example, be transferred to the benefit of other parties. In a negative sense, reciprocity goes beyond the modulation of rights and duties. It affects here the permanence of a legal relationship as a whole, notably when it allows non-performance and even termination on account of breach (*inadimplendi non est adimplendum*; *fidem frangenti non est fides servanda*).[145] Reciprocity also leads to the creation of substitutive legal positions, notably the ability to take countermeasures.

[144] See, eg, *Norwegian Loans* [1957] ICJ Rep 27.

[145] On the origin of the rule, see F Merzbacher, 'Die Regel fidem frangenti fides frangitur und ihre Anwendung' (1983) 99 *Zeitschrift der Savigny-Stiftung für Rechtsgeschichte, Kanonistische Abteilung* 339ff.

3. *Equilibrium Reciprocity*

Reciprocity does not stop at the interlinking of rights and obligations. It also requires a certain measure of response so that one party's reaction in cases of breach will lead to a new balance and not to further and aggravated imbalance. Reciprocity is therefore not only a relation but also a proportion; not only reversibility but also substantive equality; in short, it also refers to proportionality. Thus, for example, countermeasures must be proportionate to the gravity and scope of the unlawful act. If they go beyond this, the aggrieved State will be taking advantage of the situation to create—on the occasion of the wrongful act—a new disequilibrium in its own favour. This is a sort of punishment. But this is not what the institution of countermeasures is meant to achieve.

Proportionality has three main facets. They were developed in constitutional and administrative law.[146] *First*, proportionality means adequacy: the means used must be capable of realising the aim pursued. This is a question of ability to produce the required result. If there is no adequacy, the act at stake cannot produce the purported effect and it is therefore without foundation in the law. It is arbitrary, in the sense of being manifestly unjustified with regard to the facts. For example, the aim to avoid alcoholic excess cannot be pursued if only one alcoholic beverage is prohibited while others can be sold without restriction. *Secondly*, proportionality means necessity: the adequate means chosen must also be the least intrusive leading to the aim pursued; in other words, there must be no other measure, less invasive of the interests and/or rights of third parties, that would lead to the same result. Others must not be affected more than is necessary to achieve the aim pursued. For example, a prohibition on a suspect's travelling abroad might be disproportionate in the sense indicated when the aim pursued by the restriction can also be realised by the deposit of a bail bond. *Thirdly*, proportionality in the strict sense means that there must be a reasonable relation between the means employed and the aim pursued, or between the generating act and the reaction thereto. There are here two categories: one between the action and the aim; and the other between the gravity of the violation of the law and the gravity of the response thereto. The law can either impose sanctions on manifest disproportion, or require proportionate responses in a much stricter way, eg by adjusting the indemnities of each party in exact proportion to their fault. The main problem with this type of proportionality is the variety of possible criteria for establishing the correct measure. For example, in the case of a breach of the law and the adoption of countermeasures, will it be the gravity of the generating act in the abstract sense, or rather the gravity of concrete but perhaps unexpected results? Will one also need to take account of the practical effects of the countermeasure on the wrongdoing

[146] See, eg, JP Müller, *Eléments pour une théorie suisse des droits fondamentaux* (Bern, 1983) 138.

State? Does the existence of a subjective fault modify the equation, allowing graver countermeasures? Can the aim of the countermeasures enter into the calculation of its permissible intensity? These are potentially complex questions.[147]

4. *Moral Reciprocity*

In this last category, reciprocity elevates itself to the sphere of morals. It attempts to find a measure for conduct that can be universalised. The other is thought of as being myself. This is at the root of the categorical imperative and of the Golden Rule. When the other is considered as a morally equal subject, the just conduct must depend on its capacity to be generalised and thus to be acceptable to the other. From there stems the double rule: (i) think of your conduct under the guise of its generalisation; (ii) do not inflict on others what you do not want to be inflicted upon you. The measure of this judgement is not purely empirical but normative (reasonableness). In other words, the test is not what an individual, with all his or her idiosyncrasies, may consider good, but what can reasonably be considered good by the vast majority of humans. The sadomasochist likes to beat and to be beaten; he or she cannot reasonably claim that others will too.

It can be noted that this moral reciprocity turns towards the other. Its projection is fundamentally external. Correlative reciprocity (section IV.A.2. above), on the other hand, is turned towards the inner workings of legal relations, and towards subjects each considering his or her own legal position. Moral reciprocity tends to erase the 'I' in favour of a universal rule of good action. Relation reciprocity (section IV.A.1. above) and correlative reciprocity, on the contrary, concern concrete relationships the equilibrium of which must be maintained in the light of the rule *neminem laedere*: the 'I' here remains pivotal; his or her rights are protected. Within the law, moral reciprocity has both a structural and an operational role. On the structural level, the point is that the law realises to some degree the injunctions of this type of reciprocity. It does so by limiting equally the rights of the subjects in view of the preservation of the equal liberty of all; and the law prefers impersonal and abstract rules so that the peculiarities and idiosyncrasies of each individual remain marginal; and so on. On the operational level, moral reciprocity can be used in the interpretation and application of the law. An attitude that is shown to be unreasonable, capricious, unbalanced or excessively onerous for others will tend not to receive legal protection. The legal operator may find that such a non-commendable attitude, which ought not to be generalised, either does not fall within the limits of the applicable norm, or contravenes an applicable principle of law (such as abuse of rights, abuse of procedure, arbitrary acts, trespass, etc).

[147] For international law countermeasures, see the reflections in R Kolb, 'La proportionnalité dans le cadre des contre-mesures et des sanctions—Essai de clarification conceptuelle' in Académie de droit international de La Haye, LA Sicilianos and L Forlati-Picchio (eds), *Les sanctions économiques en droit international/Economic Sanctions in International Law* (Leiden/Boston, 2004) 379ff.

Moral reciprocity tends here to be realised within the positive law through the work of various legal operators.

B. Reciprocity in International Law

Reciprocity plays a particularly important role in international law. This is due to its decentralised and horizontal structure, giving rise to many bilateral or potentially bilateral legal relationships.[148] In a society marked by the absence of a centralised superior power, reciprocity attempts to tame anarchical sovereignty by mutually conditioning performance and introducing thereby some element of order. But this order is and remains precarious: it is an order comprising multiple Swords of Damocles hanging over the heads of States, recalling that the other will react to your own deeds or breaches. But it is also an order of escalating countermeasures, to the point where the whole legal order might collapse (as occurred in World War I with the law of maritime warfare).[149] Societies based on the equality of subjects without superior power display strong elements of commutative justice. This fact translates itself into the equilibrium of obligations. Reciprocity is the primary sanction of this substitutive equilibrium. This reciprocity is mainly expressed in self-help: as you do, so shall I. There are important branches of international law where the rights and obligations of States mirror each other and where, for this reason, reciprocity is one of the main factors leading to compliance. This is the case, for example, in the context of diplomatic law, or arms reduction and control law. There is a reciprocal interest in compliance; and there is an interest in avoiding the countermeasures of the other party in the event of of breach. Conversely, in subject matters where so-called 'absolute obligations' are paramount, and where reciprocity therefore plays a smaller role, the problem of compliance is significantly greater. This is the case, for example, in human rights law. In the latter context, only institutionalised control and certain sanction mechanisms can make up for the relative lack of spontaneous compliance. Other factors also increase or diminish the strength of reciprocity, such as the power or lack of power of a State to effectively take the reciprocal measures.

We may now return to the four previously mentioned categories of reciprocity and look at their functioning in international law.

[148] On reciprocity in international law, see, eg, M Virally, 'Le principe de réciprocité dans le droit international contemporain' (1967-III) 122 *RCADI* 1ff; E Decaux, *La réciprocité en droit international* (Paris, 1980); F Parisi and N Ghei, 'The Role of Reciprocity in International Law' (2003) 36 *Cornell International Law Journal* 93ff. For treaties: C Campiglio, *Il principio di reciprocità nel diritto dei trattati* (Padua, 1995); B Simma, *Das Reziprozitätselement im Zustandekommen völkerrechtlicher Verträge* (Berlin, 1972). For customary international law: B Simma, *Das Reziprozitätselement in der Entstehung des Völkergewohnheitsrechts* (Munich/Salzburg, 1970). From an historical perspective, see J Lambert, *La vengeance privée et les fondements du droit international public* (Paris, 1936).

[149] See, eg, JA Hall, *The Law of Naval Warfare*, 2nd edn (London, 1921); AP Higgins, 'Submarine Warfare' (1920/1921) 1 *BYIL* 149ff; A Laurens, *Le blocus et la guerre sous-marine (1914–1918)* (Paris, 1924).

1. Relation Reciprocity in International Law

International law offers an ideal playing field for reciprocity. The decentralisation of power, but also the great homogeneity of the subjects of the law (some 194 or so States), sharpens its edges and smoothes its operation.[150] Most of the other subjects of international law have also remained linked with the State: international organisations (associations of States and platforms for cooperation between States) or collectivities having the aim to become States (*de facto* regimes, insurgents, movements of national liberation, etc). As long as international law remains centered on the sovereign State, reciprocity will find an ample field of application.

2. Correlative Reciprocity in International Law

This type of reciprocity plays a significant role in the context of the creation of rights and obligations. Thus a treaty balances the respective rights and duties by conditioning one with regard to the other. To this global reciprocity, inherent in the structure of agreements, one must add a voluntary reciprocity left to the consent of the parties. Thus parties to a treaty may or may not insert reservations, which will in turn be applicable reciprocally. Reciprocity extends the equilibrium between the parties to this micro-regime, as it has been freely chosen by the parties or by one party. Conversely, reciprocity was tamed, if not ousted, by the old unequal treaties, which were to the benefit of one party and to the detriment of the other.[151]

From the perspective of rights and obligations, reciprocity ensures their correlation and creates new rights, for example the right to raise a reservation, contained in the optional declaration of compulsory ICJ jurisdiction of the other party.[152] Moreover, this type of reciprocity plays a role in the execution of obligations. It determines their exact reach by modulating the respective dues as a function of effective compliance: I perform in the same measure as you have performed. On the level of decentralised 'sanctions', reciprocity manifests itself in countermeasures and material breach of treaties (Article 60 VCLT), with a view to re-establishing, provisionally or finally, a unilaterally disturbed equilibrium. This type of reciprocity can also play a role in the interpretation of norms. Under the principle of good faith or estoppel, there are some situations where a State must agree to be bound by an interpretation which it has itself proposed in analogous circumstances.[153]

[150] That the homogeneity of a society has repercussions on the law has been noted for a long time. See, eg, C Schmitt, 'La question clé de la Société des Nations' in R Kolb (ed), *Deux textes de Carl Schmitt* (Paris, 2009) 61ff.

[151] L Caflisch, 'Unequal Treaties' (1992) 35 *GYIL* 52ff.

[152] *Norwegian Loans* [1957] ICJ Rep 27.

[153] The argument had been made (but was in this case rejected by the Court) that Mexico should not be allowed to propose an interpretation of consular duties which it did not honour in its own practice: *Avena* [2004-I] ICJ Rep 38, §45.

3. Equilibrium Reciprocity in International Law

As we have seen (section IV.A.3. above), this principle mainly concentrates on the issue of proportionality when unilateral measures affect the legally protected sphere of other subjects (*neminem laedere*).[154] The measuring rod for proportionality has two functions: either it concentrates on a correspondence between the means used and the aim pursued, or it seeks a correspondence between the gravity of the triggering act and the response thereto. These are 'aim proportionality' and 'reactive proportionality' respectively.

Aim proportionality applies to a variety of subject matters. The laws on self-defence or necessity are heavily influenced by the notion. The lawfulness of the measures taken must be decided in view of the aim to repel the attack or to safeguard an essential interest of the State against a grave and imminent peril. Thus, since the time of the League of Nations, emphasis has been laid on the fact that self-defence supposes proportionate means justified by the persistance of the danger.[155] The ICJ has insisted on many occasions on this type control with regard to the aim, eg in the famous *Nicaragua* case of 1986.[156] As regards necessity, one may recall the *Torrey Canyon* incident in 1967.[157] The wreck of a ship, SS *Torrey Canyon*, leaking oil after an accident, was bombed from the air so that it would catch fire and burn off the oil. This means had been chosen after all the other options had been carefully weighed up, it being concluded that such bombardment was the only effective means to achieve the aim. The action was taken as *ultima ratio*. The same 'aim proportionality' control is effectuated by human rights monitoring bodies. The measures taken against individuals are here scrutinised with regard to the aim pursued and the lesser or less onerous means available.

International humanitarian law is also profoundly influenced by issues of 'aim proportionality'. It requires that some reasonable relation (or absence of excess) must exist between the military advantage expected to be realised (aim) and the collateral damage likely to be inflicted upon protected persons, notably civilians. Articles 51, §5, letter b, 57, §2, letter a, and 57, §3 of Additional Protocol (AP) I of 1977 to the Geneva Conventions of 1949 are expressive of this effort. The cardinal principle of military necessity itself, in its restrictive version, calls for such a limitation, since '"Imperative necessity" means that there is no equally effective lawful military means, involving less damage or suffering, which is sufficient to

[154] On the principle of proportionality, see mainly D Bardonnet, 'Quelques observations sur le principe de proportionnalité en droit international', *Essays in Honor of E. Jiménez de Aréchaga* (Montevideo, 1994) 995ff; E Cannizzaro, *Il principio della proporzionalità nell'ordinamento internazionale* (Milan, 2000). On a particular topic, see J Gardam, *Necessity, Proportionality and the Use of Force by States* (Cambridge, 2004).

[155] Report of M Brouckère, 1926, Doc Société des Nations, A.14, 1927, V, p 60.

[156] *Military and Paramilitary Activities in and against Nicaragua* [1986] ICJ Rep 94, 103.

[157] See E Brown, 'The Lessons from the Torrey Canyon: International law Aspects' (1968) 21 *Current Legal Problems* 113ff.

the legitimate end'.[158] We might take the example of Article 57, §3 of AP I.[159] The texts is as follows:

> When a choice is possible between several military objectives for obtaining a similar military advantage, the objective to be selected shall be that the attack on which may be expected to cause the least danger to civilian lives and to civilian objects.

The rule can be applied only in a particular set of circumstances. There must be a precise military aim to be pursued and a plurality of military objectives, each one allowing the full realisation of that aim. For example,[160] a line of supply is to be cut off. We are in a mountain region. There are three bridges over large precipices. Bridge A is situated in a village; bridge B is used for military and civilian purposes, such as transporting medical supplies; bridge C is situated in an uninhabited region. The choice here should be to attack bridge C. However, it may appear that an attack on two or all three of the bridges would ensure a more lasting disruption of the enemy's military supply line. It is not prohibited in such a case to attack all three bridges, if that is necessary to obtain the purported military advantage. Conversely, if the cutting off of the line of supply is militarily relevant only for a short time, say during the conduct of a particular military operation in the region, only an attack on bridge C would be warranted under the provision here at stake.

With regard to collateral damage in general and its avoidance, Article 57 of AP I received significant application during the NATO operation 'Unified Protector' in Libya (2011). Different precautionary measures were taken under Article 57 of AP I:[161] care in the choice of weapons (laser- or GPS-guided); renunciation of the use of weapons of dubious legality, such as cluster bombs; use of light weapons in order to contain or limit the range of the blast and fragments spilling out; use of ammunition programmed to explode after impact, so as to avoid damage to persons or objects external to the target, etc. Moreover, some operations were suspended or cancelled with the aim of gathering better information or of sparing civilians.

Reactive proportionality is paramount in the law on countermeasures.[162] The point is here to balance the gravity of the generating acts and the measure of the response. The old *Naulilaa* case (1928) is still good law on this point.[163]

[158] WV O'Brien, 'The Meaning of Military Necessity in International Law' (1957) 1 *World Polity* 141.

[159] An analogous rule can be found in Art 6 of Protocol II (1999) to the Hague Convention on Cultural Property in Time of War (1954): see V Mainetti, 'De nouvelles perspectives pour la protection des biens culturels en cas de conflit armé: l'entrée en vigueur du Deuxième Protocole relatif à la Convention de La Haye de 1954', *Revue internationale de la Croix-Rouge* vol 86, no 854, 353.

[160] The Commentary on the Protocol gives as an example an attack on a railway line, either in the railway station or in the countryside, expecting that the latter choice should prevail: Y Sandoz, C Swinarski and B Zimmermann (eds), *Commentary of the Additional Protocols of 8 June 1977 to the Geneva Conventions of 12 August 1949* (Geneva, 1987) 687.

[161] See G Bartolini, 'L'operazione "Unified Protector" e la condotta delle ostilità in Libia' (2012) 95 *Rivista di diritto internazionale* 1050–53.

[162] See R. O'Keefe, 'Proportionality', in: J. Crawford / A. Pellet / K. Parlett (eds), *The Law of International Responsibility*, Oxford, 2010, p. 1157ff.

[163] *Naulilaa* (1928), II *RIAA* 1028.

Disproportionate armed reprisals during an armed conflict can amount to a war crime.[164] In the context of non-armed countermeasures in peacetime, the *Air Services (US/France)* case (1978) contains important developments on the issue of reactive proportionality.[165]

International law also knows the categories of adequacy, necessity and proportionality in the strict sense, as developed in municipal administrative law:

1. *Adequacy*. For example, in the *French Owners of the Mont Cenis* (1938), the French authorities contested the urgent reasons advanced by the Italian Government to expropriate property belonging to certain French citizens. They claimed that the whole exercise was a ruse, the aim of which was to chase the French owners from the area in issue.[166] This claim was tantamount to saying that the expropriation served no recognised public purpose. It thus could not be adequate given the aim pursued. Another example is that of the destruction of objects, committed by a retreating army in wartime in order to halt the progress of the enemy. Such destruction would not be lawful if it could not contribute to this aim.[167]
2. *Necessity*. The previously mentioned examples of the *Torrey Canyon* and Article 57, §3 of of AP I (1977) illustrate this category. It is particularly frequently applied by human rights bodies. Paragraphs 2 of Articles 8 to 11 of the ECHR (1950) require that any limitation of the human rights there enshrined must be 'necessary in a democratic society'. Article 15 of the ECHR allows for so-called derogations (ie suspension of rights) 'to the extent strictly required by the exigencies of the situation'. The Court has interpreted these formulas as referring to a double standard of necessity: the necessity to have recourse to such measures in the first place, and also the absence of less onerous measures to reach the same result. Thus, in the *Lawless* case (1961),[168] it was claimed that the Government could have taken less onerous measures than detention of certain persons without immediate judicial control under emergency legislation. For example, it had been said that travelling restrictions could have been used instead. The Court scrutinised but rejected this argument in the circumstances. It held that ordinary legislation would not have sufficed and an interruption of international traffic would have been disproportionate due to its effect on the whole population. Conversely, in *Hentrich v France*

[164] *Mackensen and Maelzer* (1945), United Nations War Crimes Commission, *Law Reports of Trials of War Criminals*, vol VIII (London, 1949) 7.

[165] *Air Services (US/France)* (1978), XVIII *RIAA* 417ff.

[166] AC Kiss, *Répertoire français du droit international public*, vol II (Paris, 1966) no 204, p 114ff.

[167] *Von List (Hostages Trial)*, US Military Tribunal at Nuremberg (1948) 15 *ILR* 647–49.

[168] *Lawless* ECtHR (1961) Series A no 2, 57–58. In *McBride v UK* (1993) Series A no 258-B, 52, §54, the Court rejected the argument that a provisional derogation under Art 15 was unlawful since it was not foreseen in the text of the provision; it argued that if a State can suspend without limitation in time, it can also suspend for a certain time, which is less intrusive. See also *Handyside v UK* (1976) Series A no 24, 23, where the issue was whether a schoolbook on sex education had to be prohibited or could simply have some passages expurgated (less onerous measure).

(1994),[169] the Court affirmed that a general right of pre-emption granted to the State in certain circumstances was disproportionate (in the sense of not necessary), since there were less intrusive means to safeguard the fiscal interests of the State. In the domain of State responsibility, a claim for reparation of damage may be excessive when the damage could have been easily avoided by the injured State (duty of mitigation). In such a case, the amount of damages allotted can be equitably reduced by deducting the quantum of losses that could have been avoided by the exercise of proper diligence.[170]

3. *Proportionality in the strict sense.* The issue is here a balancing of contrary interests and legal positions. Control of this type of proportionality can be stricter or looser, according to the subject matter. When there is a regular judge and the issues concern protective justice, the test tends to be strict. This is the case, for example, in the context of international administrative tribunals. In direct inter-State intercourse, where the unilateral and subjective allegations of each subject predominate, the test is generally limited to ruling out manifest disproportion or abuses. But even here the judge sometimes attempts to apply stricter criteria. Many examples of a strict application of proportionality can be found in international administrative law. Here the judge regularly rules on whether a sanction imposed on a civil servant presents a reasonably proportionate link to the faults committed.[171] Thus, in the *Ferecchia* case (1973), the ILOAT (ILO Administrative Tribunal) held that the sacking of a staff member could not be considered proportionate in view of his demonstrable abilities and the services rendered by him over a time-span of six years.[172] Conversely, in the domain of countermeasures and outside the judicial context, the test more often focuses on the avoidance of disproportion and abuse.[173] But even here counter-tendencies exist, for example in

[169] *Hentrich v France* (1994) Series A no 296-A, 21. See also *Tinnelly and Sons Ltd v UK* (1998), *Reports*, 1998-IV, p 1663, §78.

[170] 'International law recognizes … an obligation on the part of an injured party to mitigate his or her losses. In this respect an injured party may not recover damages for a loss which he or she ought to or could have avoided by reasonable efforts. In addition he or she must take into account any "benefit" that may have resulted.' *Category 'C' Claims (First Instalment)* (1994) 109 *ILR* 383; see also *ibid*, 388–89.

[171] But even here, it exceptionally occurs that the judge refers only to 'significant disproportion'. See, eg, the *Gregorio* case (1983), *World Bank Administrative Tribunal Reports*, 1983-II, decision no 14, p 20.

[172] ILOAT, Judgment no 203. A similar situation is exposed in the *Planthara* case (1995), *WBAT Reports*, 1995, decision no 143, 14–15. A contrary example can be found in Case 13/69 *Van Eick v Commission* [1970] ECR 3.

[173] See, eg, *Air Services (US/France)* (1978) XVIII *RIAA* 465–66, 483. See also the US sanctions in the context of the Tehran Hostages crisis of 1979: O Schachter, 'International Law in Theory and Practice' (1982-V) 178 *RCADI* 179. See also the shooting down of the Korean Airliner by Soviet military aircraft in 1983: (1983) 29 *AFDI* 749ff. The same criterion can be found in the domain of environmental damage created in the territory of one State on the territory of another (significance of the damage): see the old case case *Donauversenkung* (1927/1928) 4 *Annual Digest of Public International Law Cases* 131 (and H Lauterpacht, *The Function of Law in the International Community* (Oxford, 1933) 286ff). Still, the criterion is applied in anti-trust law: W Meng, *Extraterritoriale Jurisdiktion im öffentlichen Wirtschaftsrecht* (Berlin, 1994) 416. Another example—straight baselines in the law of the sea must follow the 'general direction' of the coastline; the issue is manifestly only one of disproportion, the criterion being too vague for positive or strict proportionality: *Norwegian Fisheries* [1951] ICJ Rep 142, where the Court refers to the absence of manifest abuse.

Article 51 of the Articles on State Responsibility (2001)[174] and in the specific area of the law on self-defence according to the newer jurisprudence of the ICJ.[175]

4. *Moral Reciprocity in International Law*

There are here no relevant differences from municipal law. Moral reciprocity is first of all realised by the existence of the legal order and its norms. However, the profound influences of political factors in the shaping and implementation of international law to some extent overshadow the reign of this type of reciprocity.

5. *Limits to Reciprocity in International Law*

Lastly, some limits to the principle of reciprocity in international law have to be mentioned. There are, first, some logical limits: for example, there can be no direct reciprocity between a coastal State and a land-locked State with regard to certain issues a maritime nature. Secondly, there are axiological limits: reciprocity is limited or inapplicable in the context of systems of distributive justice, of affirmative action, of compensatory inequality, etc. Thirdly, reciprocity is limited with regard to absolute obligations and international public order.[176] In particular, public order limits the domain of reciprocity. Public order obligations are due unconditionally; their performance does not depend on the attitude or acts of the other party; the *tu quoque* argument is not admissible. Thus, if State A mistreats certain prisoners of war from State B, State B cannot argue that it is therefore permissible for it to mistreat prisoners of war from State A. Such absolute obligations exist mainly in the area of the maintenance of international peace, environmental law, human rights law and international humanitarian law.[177] Fourthly and lastly, within international organisations and other institutional mechanisms, and even more strongly in supranational organisations, reciprocity is largely replaced by the guarantee of legality. The multiple layers of spontaneous and unilaterally driven equilibria of reciprocity are here replaced by an objective legal regime under the control of the organisation. The situation approximates that prevailing within the public law of a State.

[174] See J Crawford, *The International Law Commission's Articles on State Responsibility* (Cambridge, 2002) 296.

[175] See *Oil Platforms* [2003] ICJ Rep 196ff, §73ff.

[176] B Simma, 'From Bilateralism to Community Interest in International Law' (1994-VI) 250 *RCADI* 229ff.

[177] For example, through the ruling out of reprisals against protected persons. See Arts 46, 47, 13, §3 and 33, §3 of Geneva Conventions I–IV, 1949, and Art 51, §6 of AP I of 1977. On reprisals in international humanitarian law, see J Hebenstreit, *Repressalien im humanitären Völkerrecht* (Baden-Baden, 2004), with many references.

V. Liberty

A. General Legal Experience

It has been claimed that liberty must seek the support of the law if it wants to last. But there is another aspect, at least as essential: liberty is a constitutive value of the law; law, mainly in its modern conception,[178] exists only because there is this basic fact called liberty. There seems to be a reciprocal and existential relationship: no law without liberty; but also no liberty without law. That the law supposes liberty lies in its normative character formulating an obligation; it is not a fact of nature rooted in necessity. Having its roots in the prescriptive domain (the 'ought') and not in the descriptive domain (the 'is'), law cannot exist but through a liberty of action. The movements between inanimate bodies are determined by physical laws; they need no legal law, if that inappropriate expression may be ventured. Their movement is necessary and self-sufficient; a normative injunction is superfluous and nonsensical. Conversely, human action is not yet determined action. It is directed by numerous options between which the will chooses. An external principle is here demanded to direct the wills towards the socially desirable or compatible attitudes. If there is no possible transgression, there are no legal norms; but there is the possibility for transgression where there is a choice of action; and a choice of action is a liberty. Thus, the law may order the driver not to pass when the traffic signal shows red; but it cannot instruct that same person not to digest the food he has swallowed.

The effect of the law on liberty is two-fold: (i) first, the law frames liberty so that the liberty of the one becomes compatible with the liberties of the other subjects within a society (the law is here a limit on liberty); (ii) secondly, the law organises liberty so as to guarantee and preserve it (the law as a guarantee of liberty). In both cases, we are dealing with legal liberty. This is unlike liberty pure and simple, notably the total absence of any constraint, that is arbitrary liberty. The latter is not a legal notion, since it suggests anarchy and chaos.

The basic idea of the Enlightenment, that law is a system of mutual limitation of liberty with regard to life in common,[179] is to a large extent true for all legal orders at all times. It represents a sort of formal concept of the law. Each legal system is an attempt to find the golden point of equilibrium between rights, obligations and competencies of a plurality of subjects, to coordinate life in plurality. This formal

[178] The modern conception of the law is anthropocentric; it is based on the subjective rights of Man. See Thomas Hobbes, *Leviathan* (1651), ch XIV, where he meaningfully claims that law consists in the liberty to do something or to abstain from doing something. The link between liberty and law is often emphasised in modern literature: see, eg, W Huber, *Gerechtigkeit und Recht* (Gütersloh, 1996) 222.

[179] JJ Rousseau, *Du contrat social* (1762), book I, 8, 9; C de Montesquieu, *De l'esprit des lois* (1748), book XI, 3; I Kant, *Über den Gemeinspruch* (1793), ch 2; JG Fichte, *Grundlage des Naturrechts* (1796), ch 8; *Déclaration française des droits de l'homme et du citoyen* (1789), art 4.

mechanism is necessary in any society, inasmuch as it is necessarily composed by more than one individual. The concrete manner in which to effect it is left to historical choices, in particular to the predominating doctrines of the common good and justice, as well as to the dominant interests and persons within the social order. For the individualistic thinkers of the Enlightenment, the point was to find the maximum liberty of each individual still compatible with ordered life in society. For the socialist authors of the twentieth century, individual liberties were secondary to collective exigencies. Formal liberty is here attacked as a facade, while effective liberty through State-sponsored equality is demanded. The liberty from (or against) the State is to a great extent transformed into a liberty with the State.

But what is liberty? Assuredly, such concepts are not easy to define. At its core, liberty concerns the ability of a subject to act according to his autonomous determination. The individual subject is considered to be the creator of his proper destiny by following his own path according to his personal knowledge and will. From this perspective, liberty consists in being set free or absolved from pre-established authority in favour of one's own subjective conscience. Thus, such a liberty can evolve only in those times when the conception of absolute truth or a dominant religious order has been abandoned. Liberty has a relativistic and will-orientated root; it is also based on democratic thought. If it is postulated that absent an absolute truth the individual has moral autonomy, this liberty is naturally extended towards a democratic regime by the very fact that the choice of every subject counts the same, ie has the same weight.

The autonomy discussed here has three facets: empirical, deontological and transcendental. *First*, from the empirical point of view, liberty presents itself as a fact: a real possibility of unlimited, or only partly limited, choice; of decision and execution of the decision. This is the liberty of the free arbiter: '*quicumque enim est liberi arbitrii, facit quod vult*' or '*liberum arbitrium nihil aliud est quam voluntas*'.[180] This form of radical liberty does not directly interest the law. Applied to social life, it would lead to anarchy and chaos, to the absolute will of each subject. *Secondly*, from the deontological perspective, liberty calls for an ethical complement, which can be found in the categorical imperative (see section IV.A. above). This liberty is not dissociable from reason. Thus, in exercising my liberty, I have to take account of the liberty of others if I want others to take account of mine. Liberty is no longer an unlimited or rarely limited subjective projection but an ability to obey oneself as a rational being. The deontological aspect means that a subject can autonomously determine not only its freedom but also its duties.[181] It is obvious that this notion directly affects the law. *Thirdly*, liberty tends to decline when Kantian reason is replaced by Hegelian transcendental reason, which determines the actions

[180] Damascenes, *De Fide Orthodoxa*, ch 14.

[181] A Kaufmann, *Rechtsphilosophie*, 2nd edn (Munich, 1997) 24–42: 'Wichtig ist, dass Kant Freiheit nicht indeterministisch und also rein negativ als ursachloses Wollen, als Willkür, liberum arbitrium, versteht, sondern positiv auf die praktische Vernunft gründet, nämlich als eine Bedingung von Sittlichkeit in praktischer Absicht … [E]rst am Gebot entsteht die Freiheit des Handelns' (italics omitted).

of the individual. Here, individual liberty retreats; it is replaced by the objective spirit and its incarnation, the State, whose dialectic actions determine history. The subjective limb is identified with the objective one; liberty cannot be dissociated from deterministic laws. Consequently, Kant's subjective idealism has found its way, in the latest epigones, with Hegel and Marx, into doctrines ultimately negating individualistic freedom. While Hegelianism profoundly influenced Italian and German legal thinking at the end of the nineteenth century,[182] its notion of liberty, presented here, had no (and even less a lasting) impact on the law. It was too philosophical to be of tangible legal use. Summing up, these doctrines of freedom accented different aspects: in the first case, liberty as correspondence to subjective will; in the second, as correspondence to subjective reason; in the third, as correspondence to objective laws. A legal doctrine of liberty can flourish only in the middle ground. As was said in ancient times, '*Libertas est naturalis facultas eius quod cuique facere libet, nisi si quid vi aut iure prohibetur.*'[183]

The concept of liberty has its positive and negative sides,[184] both entertaining complex relationships. Negative liberty is central in liberalistic conceptions of society. It grants the subjects spheres of liberty against the intervention of the State. This liberty has no precise content; it is a form concentrated on autonomy, independence, negation of interference. Locke, Mill and others have discussed the underpinnings of this liberty. Positive liberty is based on the conception that in order to develop an effectively meaningful set of freedoms, a series of material conditions must first be created and thereafter maintained. This is the role of the State. Proudhon or Marx developed this. The interplay between the two freedoms is exemplified by modern human rights law: there is on the one hand protection against State interventionism (civil rights), and on the other the grant of rights for obtaining State action (social rights). It stands to reason that neither of these branches of liberty can exist alone; and also that one must not trump the other. The point will always be to balance one and the other in an open-ended political and historical process, where the scales will swing at times towards the individual and at other times more towards the State. When the balance leans too much towards negative liberty, society will become riddled with inequalities and might become unstable (sowing seeds of violence and revolution of the have-nots); moreover, the law of the jungle will come to the fore and there will be a risk of totalitarian deviance.[185] On the other hand, when the balance leans too much towards positive liberty, the political body will stifle individual initiative and sacrifice individual autonomy; totalitarian State control will grow and permeate society. The whole history of legislation and competing conceptions of justice can be written as a history of the tensions between negative and positive liberty. It

[182] Through authors such as Binder, Schönfeld, Larenz, Spaventa, Gentile, Maggiore, Csarini-Sforza, etc. On this influence, see, eg, G Fassò, *Storia della filosofia del diritto*, vol III: *Ottocento e Novecento* (Bari, 2001) 79ff, and the bibliography at 471–74.

[183] Florentinus, *Dig*, 1, 5, 4, *de statu hominum*.

[184] I Berlin, 'Two Concepts of Liberty' in I Berlin, *Four Essays on Liberty* (London, 1969) 118ff.

[185] W Huber, *Gerechtigkeit und Recht* (Gütersloh, 1996) 222–23.

also stands to be noted that in international society, 'negative liberty' still largely prevails over 'positive liberty'. It is anchored in the concept of sovereignty, which gives rise to such notions as non-intervention in internal affairs, the immunities of States, the presumption of validity of State legal acts, etc. There was a certain progression of the concept of positive liberty in the twentieth century, for example in the domain of human rights (social and economic), but also in general international law (such as in the area of development aid). The fact remains, however that the negative conception reflects the basic structure of international society.

The dominant conceptions of liberty have evolved throughout history. In antiquity and during the Middle Ages, the conception of person-centered subjectivism culminating in moral autonomy was largely absent. Man remained confined in a cosmos governed by the Greek Logos or by Christianity. He remained a small cog in an overwhelming heteronomous order, under the weight of which his moral self-determination disappeared. With the anthropocentric revolution of modern times, the Protestant Reformation and the development of empirical sciences, Man progressively placed himself at the centre of the cosmos. He occupied the epicentre of that subjective reason to which all expressions of reality were now subjected (this is the root of the so-called idealism). Man was therefore now the supreme legislator; he legislated with a liberty that progressively increased; natural law constraints were abandoned, while positivism approached its heyday. Objectivistic heteronomy was thus replaced with subjectivist autonomy.[186]

This notion of freedom then found its way into modern constitutionalism. There were two main aspects here: the construct of the social contract; and the fundamental rights and freedoms. The legal order of the State was explained by the model of the 'social contract'.[187] This contract reconciled primary liberty and secondary obligation. The basis of the law was the natural subjective right to liberty. Thus, the social contract was concluded by the free choice of the people. It introduced a measure of rational limitation of liberty, ie mutual obligations. The precise consequences of this social contract were construed differently by different authors. For some, the social contract was a tool of subjection to power (Hobbes).[188] Liberty was exercised to constitute a civil society and to leave behind the state of nature. Thereby, the individual renounced his liberty and subjected himself to an absolute monarch, vested with full powers enabling him to keep the social peace by the sword. For others, the social contract could be accompanied by a contract of subjection (Pufendorf). The people elected the power to which they subjected themselves. But the people remained the ultimate unit of self-determination, whence a dualism arose between the people and the monarch—a split sovereignty. For still others, the social contract was a contract of subjection,

[186] E Opocher, *Lezioni di filosofia del diritto* (Padua, 1983) 135ff.

[187] On the social contract, see, eg, JW Gough, *The Social Contract, A Critical Study of its Development* (Oxford, 1957); P Riley, *Will and Political Legitimacy: A Critical Exposition of Social Contract Theory in Hobbes, Locke, Rousseau, Kant and Hegel* (Harvard, 1982); SC Kolm, *Le contrat social libéral* (Paris, 1985).

[188] On this contract of subjection, see J Voigt (ed), *Der Herrschaftsvertrag* (Neuwied/Berlin, 1971).

but individuals kept for themselves certain inalienable rights (Locke). If these spheres of intangible liberty were violated by the government, the people were vested with a right to resist. Lastly, for still others, the social contract was a contract of subjection, but the identity of the subjects exercising power and bound by the contract meant that each subject remained as free after the conclusion of the contract as he was before (Rousseau).[189] It is thus around the notion of liberty that the three main forms of government cluster: absolutism (today, totalitarian regimes); liberalism (today, the rule of law and fundamental freedoms); and democracy (today linked with liberalism): Hobbes—Locke—Rousseau.

The fundamental and inalienable freedoms and human rights are based on the same conception of liberty.[190] The gist of the matter was to reserve to individuals certain spheres of life in which the State would not, or not arbitrarily, interfere. There was here protection of minorities and of the individual against decisions taken by the majority. These rights are a necessary complement to the democratic principle. We might recall the English Petition of Rights (1628), the Habeas Corpus Act (1679), the Bill of Rights (1689), later the Bill of Rights of Virginia (1776) and the French *Déclaration des droits de l'homme et du citoyen* (1789). Supreme and often justiciable subjective rights were thus granted to individuals. In international law, for a long time there has been the already mentioned doctrine of the 'fundamental rights of States', which attempted to draw some analogies from the municipal constitutional developments mentioned above. But in international society, there was no superior power against which these rights could be turned. In effect, they rather meant that States could subjectively and unilaterally repudiate international legal obligations when their fundamental rights (eg of survival) were at stake. These rights were abandoned in the twentieth century. There remained only certain doctrines, like the state of necessity or *rebus sic stantibus*, to take their place. The issue of these fundamental rights has already been discussed above; but we may briefly return to them below, from the present perspective.

B. Liberty of States in International Law

The 'state of nature' model for a time influenced international relations, characterised as they are by the juxtaposition of sovereign States. At the times of Grotius, the law was considered to limit liberty on two planes: through heteronomous natural law constraints; and through autonomous positive law constraints, based on conventional and thus voluntary bonds. Progressively, the heteronomous limb

[189] JJ Rousseau, *Contrat social*, ch I, 6; ch II, 1, 3, 4.

[190] On the Bills of Rights: W Hubatsch, *Die englischen Freiheitsrechte* (Hannover, 1962); RA Rutland, *The Birth of the Bill of Rights, 1776–1791* (Chapel Hill, 1955); G Ostrander, *The Rights of Man in America, 1606–1861* (Columbia, 1960); G del Vecchio, *La déclaration des droits de l'homme et du citoyen dans la révolution française* (Paris, 1968); SJ Samwer, *Die französische Erklärung der Menschen- und Bürgerrechte von 1789/1791* (Hamburg, 1970); S Rials, *La déclaration des droits de l'homme et du citoyen* (Paris, 1988); J Morange, *La déclaration des droits de l'homme et du citoyen* (Paris, 1988); CA Colliard (ed), *La Déclaration des droits de l'homme et du citoyen de 1789* (Paris, 1990).

diminished in scope and the autonomous limb increased its influence. International society thereby transformed from a necessary to a voluntary society. This fact manifested itself clearly in the nineteenth century, where States were admitted to the advantages of the public law of Europe by an act of recognition which allowed them to enter the 'club'.[191] As a whole, the domain of liberty of the constituted States thereby increased: the scope of imposed obligation retreated in favour of chosen obligations. Moreover, the identification of the monarch with the State led to a personification of the latter. This trend was pursued within republican regimes, when the nation-State became the supreme expression of an historically unique people. For neo-idealistic authors such as Hegel, Fichte or von Stein, the State was the supreme reality of collective life. This led them to reject the idea that States could be bound by superior laws, including truly binding international law. The domain of liberty reached its peak and crossed the line into anarchy and potential chaos.

Further, the anthropomorphic conception of the State, moulded on its people, led to the formulation of a series of fundamental rights of States,[192] considered to be inalienable, positions which even international law could not restrict or cast aside. Political claims were thereby legalised through the mantle of supreme subjective State rights. States enjoyed a 'right to liberty', a 'right to life' or to 'existence', a right of 'self-preservation', a right 'to honour', a right to 'free commerce and communication'. In short, such rights assumed the function of a series of rights of necessity or of a law of vital interests.[193] They allowed States to bracket out the application of the ordinary laws by a unilateral claim that the conditions for the application of these vaguely shaped fundamental rights were fulfilled. This frankly excessive conception of State liberty—which goes to the detriment of the 'other'—was subject to harsh criticism at the beginning of the twentieth century. The personification of the State, its inalienable supreme rights, were attacked as incompatible with the existence and rule of an international legal order. Contrary to internal law, where such supreme individual rights remained situated within the four corners of the legal order and the jurisdiction of tribunals, in international law they were rather used as legal black holes creating a permanent threat of 'exceptions'. Legal doctrine now developed the concept of the relativity (versus absoluteness) of rights.[194] The rights of the one had to be reconciled with those of

[191] WG Grewe, *The Epochs of International Law* (Berlin/New York, 2000) 497ff.

[192] On this issue, see above p 323.

[193] See, eg, E Kaufmann, *Das Wesen des Völkerrechts und die Clausula Rebus Sic Stantibus* (Tübingen, 1911) 193ff.

[194] Thus, it was claimed that an absolute or unlimited right is an anarchical and non-legal concept. See, eg, G Scelle, 'Règles générales du droit de la paix' (1933-IV) 46 *RCADI* 408. See also N Politis, *Les nouvelles tendances du droit international* (Paris, 1927) 41: 'Jadis absolus [les droits des Etats], ne rencontrant que les limites imposées par des accords volontaires, ils sont maintenant relatifs, n'ayant que la portée indispensable pour répondre au but social qui les a créés; en d'autres termes, tandis qu'autrefois on les fondait sur l'individualisme, on les base désormais sur la solidarité.' We may again leave this sentence untranslated. This doctrine of relativity of rights also gave way to the development of the doctrine of prohibition of abuse of rights in international law. See, eg, N Politis, 'Le problème

the other; the law could not allow subjective projections to remain unlimited and produce conflicts which the legal order had no rule to absorb. Thus, the concept of absolute sovereignty (the State unbound by any superior legal rule) was criticised and abandoned in favour of the concept of relative sovereignty (the State as not subject to any superior decisional power but subject to the international legal order). Relativity of rights predominantly meant that these rights could not be considered in isolation, as unlimited entitlements of a single subject, but that they were cast in social life and thus limited by the equal rights of others. This common space was necessarily adjusted by international legal rules, which could not be subverted by unilateral claims to exceptions. The perspective changed: the point was no longer to concede equal rights to unilateral exceptionalism (which anyway could be exercised only by the powerful) but to construe an international law equally binding on all. This construction took the leap from 'arbitrary' liberty to 'deontological' liberty. However, in the 'anarchical' international society, empirical or arbitrary liberty is constantly engaged in a struggle with deontological or legal liberty. The tendency to claim unlimited and unfettered rights remains; the law's fight against such legal black holes has not ended, as events such as detention at Guantanamo Bay have shown in a specific subject area.[195]

However that may be, evolution towards a tamed liberty can be seen in many domains. Thus, the conception of 'domestic jurisdiction' evolved from its ancient complexion, whereby certain subject matters were by their nature non-international (and thus internationally black holes), to the modern conception, according to which a subject matter comes under domestic jurisdiction as long as it is not regulated by international law. And a subject matter is regulated by international law, through the adoption of norms, when it becomes a matter of international concern. This concept of the reserved domain was sanctioned by the PCIJ in the famous *Nationality Decrees* opinion of 1923.[196] Liberty is thus coordinated in a space of coexistence and does not simply refer to a subjective unconditional

des limitations de la souveraineté et la théorie de l'abus des droits dans les rapports internationaux' (1925) 6 *RCADI* 1ff; EC Stowell, *International Law* (New York, 1931) 122: 'The exercise of every right is subject to the proviso that it be not abusive so as to interfere unduly with the exercise of the rights of others or cause them undue inconvenience or injury. This rule against the abusive use of rights lies at the foundation of every system of law. It may be called the rule of the relativity of rights.' The PCIJ itself recognised the applicability of the doctrine of abuse of rights in two cases: *Certain German Interests in Upper-Silesia* (1926) PCIJ Series A no 7, 30, 37–38; *Free Zones* (1930) PCIJ Series A no 24, 12 and (1932) PCIJ Series A/B, no 46, 167. The abuse of rights doctrine was a legal tool against the tradition of 'absolute' rights. With the progress of the relative rights conception, the doctrine of abuse of rights featured less prominently in international law.

[195] D Thürer, 'Guantanamo: Ein Legal Black Hole oder ein System sich überschneidender und überlagernder Rechtskreise?' (2004) 14 *RSDIE* 1ff.

[196] *Nationality Decrees Issued in Tunis and Morocco* (1923) PCIJ Series B no 4, 23, 24: 'The question whether a certain subject matter is or is not solely within the jurisdiction of a State is an essentially relative question; it depends upon the development of international relations.' See also the alternative legal construction of G Arangio-Ruiz, 'Le domaine réservé—L'organisation internationale et le rapport entre droit international et droit interne' (1990-VI) 225 *RCADI* 9ff, not based on a *ratione materiae* approach.

faculty. This novel approach also opened the way for the protection of human rights,[197] a matter that historically was exclusively a domestic affair. We might also recall the evolution of the residual rule of liberty (all that is not prohibited is permitted), discussed above.

All these evolutions had to do with the taming of liberty within the horizontal sphere: the liberty of the one must be reconciled with the liberty of the other. In the twentieth century, an additional layer of limitation of liberty came into play, this time in a vertical setting: the pressure of 'international community'-related norms or of international public order. Thus, the very concept of *jus cogens* is rooted in the restriction of 'liberté de traiter', that is, in the nullity of agreements when their content is contrary to certain public policy prescriptions of international law. These aspects have already been discussed and need not be visited again here.

Overall, it can be said that the vast amounts of State liberty accumulated in the nineteenth century through the demise of natural law constraints were progressively reined in in the twentieth century, on the one hand by the horizontal device of relativity of rights (or primacy of international law) and on the other hand by the vertical device of public order. The transition of State liberty from arbitrary to deontological is far from over. Anarchy continues to lurk everywhere, in fact, and sometimes also in law.

VI. Morals and Social Morals

A. General Legal Experience

Morals can be defined as a concept the aim of which is to serve the idea of the good.[198] As much as the common good or justice, morals are principally a driving idea, a value indicating a goal at which to strive. In this context, morals have the function of disciplining human will so as to direct it towards satisfying the needs

[197] E de Vattel, *Le droit des gens*, book II, ch VI, para 71 and ch XVIII, para 347, examined diplomatic protection in the case of wrongs committed against aliens. The later human rights movement would drop the requirement of foreign nationality for having international standing to demand a certain standard of treatment.

[198] On morals, see, eg, the following publications covering a large range of approaches: PS Atiyah, *Promises, Morals and Laws* (Oxford, 1981); H Hart, *Law, Liberty and Morality* (London, 1981); D Gauthier, *Morals by Agreement* (Oxford, 1986); S Lee, *Law and Morals* (Oxford, 1986); S Theron, *Morals as Founded on Natural Law* (Frankfurt, 1987); JQ Wilson, *The Moral Sense* (New York, 1997); M Baumann (ed), *Norms and Values* (Baden-Baden, 2010). As to the structure of moral language, RM Hare, *The Language of Morals* (Oxford, 1978). See also R Dreier, *Recht, Moral, Ideologie* (Frankfurt, 1981); W Enderlein, *Abwägung in Recht und Moral* (Freiburg/Munich, 1991); H Geddert, *Recht und Moral* (Berlin, 1984); E Winter, *Ethik und Rechtswissenschaft* (Berlin, 1980); S Vöneky, *Recht, Moral und Ethik* (Tübingen, 2010); B Beck (ed), *Moral und Recht* (Passau, 2011); H Kress, *Ethik der Rechtsordnung* (Stuttgart, 2012); S Vöneky (ed), *Ethik und Recht* (Heidelberg, 2013).

of the good. They attempt to impose a certain attitude on the will, and can thus be considered as giving rise to duties. Morals essentially direct and educate the will.[199] But at the same time, morals are a fact. They are configured differently in the various historical societies in which they have taken shape, and in the various human beings whose actions they command. Some moral concepts are eternal but of a very general nature, for example the honouring of promises made, or respect for the other. At the same time, morals contain more than one aspect interacting with the law. Here, two categories of morals first need to be distinguished: (i) individual morals, either of a subjective (morals of conscience) or of an objective (religious morals) complexion; and (ii) social morals, which are attached to the existence of an individual within society and to his or her inter-subjective relations. The latter can concern certain constant human necessities as well as the contingent moral requirements of a given historical society.

Individual morality takes different forms. *First*, it can consist of a very personal appeal to the individual conscience. This type of morality is autonomous and subjective; it is not deduced from a heteronomous set of norms. It flows directly from a personal sense of duty rooted in accepted values. Its content and functioning largely depend on the internalisation of social values, but are also marked by unique traits of personality. This type of morality will rarely be shared in all its points among different people, except within small circles of the like-minded. In any case, it does not entertain close ties to the law. It is too subjective and insufficiently inter-subjective to have legal significance. But there are certain aspects through which this 'conscience morality' becomes relevant to the law. This is the case, for example, when the law protects the liberty of the individual to act as his conscience dictates, through the grant of human rights and fundamental freedoms. Also, in criminal law, motives rooted in such conscience may lead to mitigation of the sentence, for example when death is caused to save a person from further grave suffering. It must be added that legal rules are followed in most cases not because the individual envisions and fears punishment, but because he or she is convinced of the (moral) justification for the rule. The criminal code is not primarily respected by most persons most of the time because they do not want to go to prison; it is respected because they do not consider it right to kill or to steal. However, the law can come into a sharp conflict with this type of morality in the situation of individuals breaching legal prescriptions out of moral conviction. The law will normally be vindicated in these cases through the imposition of a sanction. This confronts the individual concerned with a personal dilemma.

Secondly, individual morality can present itself in the shape of an articulated ethical system, as found in religious doctrines or in secular beliefs (such as, say,

[199] In the apt words of an Italian legal philosopher, '[l]a legge morale riguarda l'intimità stessa del volere, impera sulla determinazione e decisione del subietto morale, esigendo motivi incondizionati, la volizione del bene per l'incondizionato motivo del bene': F Filomusi-Guelfi, *Lezioni e saggi di filosofia del diritto* (Milan, 1949) 53. In English, 'moral law concerns the innermost will, and governs the determination and decision-making of the moral subject. It calls for unconditional motives, the wish for good simply because it is good'.

Stoicism). These systems are based on personal convictions. They remain far removed from the practical precepts of the law, which do not seek to realise perfection or illumination. As much as subjective 'conscience morality', the present type remains to a large extent alien to the law. But throughout history, and still today in Islamic theocratic regimes, the law has been used as a tool to impose such religious systems and to punish deviance by legal processes. While this use of the law is technically possible, both systems, the religious and the legal, are tainted by such a forced union. The use of legal tools to impose religious prescriptions leads to totalitarian abuse and terror of expressing an opinion. It negates freedom of conscience. Moreover, religious morals can never be truly sanctioned through the law, since they cannot be realised by external sanction; ethics can only exist through subjective and internal adhesion. The law should not be used as a tool or a weapon to impose morals; this must be left to the subjective conscience. The law rather addresses the average human being in demanding actions and omissions necessary for life in society. If more is demanded from it, the law is alienated from its true function and ultimately infected. In a liberal society, the tensions between religious morals and the law can be manifold: divorce, polygamy, euthanasia, abortion, the treatment of sacrificial animals, etc. When public order prescriptions are at stake, the law should take priority and be enforced. If this is not the case, the cohesion of society is shaken. But where enforcement takes place, significant conflicts with minority groups may ensue.

Social morality is constituted by norms of conduct generally recognised in society in regard to the good and proper common life. The links between this form of morality and the law are manifold. Like the law, this form of morality touches on the relations of one subject with another. The point is no longer 'What do I owe to my conscience, or what to I owe to God?'; it is rather 'What do I owe to the other?' Some of these norms of social morality have been transformed into legal norms. This is the case, for example, as regards the basic loyalty in inter-subjective transactions: *pacta sunt servanda* and good faith are embodiments of moral precepts. Another moral idea received within the law is the concept of due diligence, or conversely the one of fault, that is, defects in application, attention, custody and so on. The moral idea of assistance has led to the duty to assist a person in danger. Conversely, other moral norms have not led to clear legal *alter egos*. But they can still influence the formative process of the law, for example compassion, which opens the way to euthanasia. A significant number of moral ideas thus have a certain connection with the law, and some have legal prolongations. There are also moral norms that do not pretend any legal status. This is the case mainly with lower morals, notably the simple usages, and with higher morals, notably love.

As with other important concepts, social morality has contingent and absolute spheres. In the narrow sense, social morality is empirical and thus fully contingent. It consists of the ethical conceptions dominant at a certain time in a certain society, concerning the duties triggered by life in common. The morals of seventeenth-century Puritan society and those of the pluralistic post-modern Western societies of the twenty-first century can hardly be said to coincide.

Contingent social morality is based on the average morals of the majority of members of society (*quod plerumque fit*). These conceptions of what is demanded by life in society have a profound influence upon the law, in its formative stage and in its interpretation. Only this link allows the law to remain rooted in society and to avoid a conceptional gulf that would prejudice the efficacy of its application. Such morals also allow the legal operator to choose a measure that is not simply a subjective whim: rather, it is based on the dominant conception in the given society, which ensures acceptability by the majority of its members. In this way, standards such as 'reasonableness', 'due diligence', 'legitimate expectations' (or '*bonos mores*') will be filled with concrete legal sense by referring back to dominant legal-moral conceptions on what ought to be done. The law does not here seek moral truth; it merely seeks to anchor its functioning in the feelings and actions of social participants. Such contingent morals can possess an elevated spirit or a lower nobility (as is shown by the oppressive local usages described by Flaubert in *Madame Bovary*).

At its lower end, such contingent morality touches on the world of simple social usages without true moral connotations (ie not touching on the concept of the good), and at its higher end it involves absolute human morals. Usage is a norm of behaviour whose sanction lies in social disapproval of contrary conduct. It is situated in a sphere of indifference with regard to the idea of good. This is the case as regards educational standards, or the rules of *savoir vivre*, lack of respect for which will lead at most to ostracisation of the boorish individual. There are also many professional usages, for example applying to vineyard farmers. The expectation of conduct is clearly condensed into a plurality of norms. But these norms are neither legal (obligations, legal sanctions) nor moral (idea of the good); they are simply social and linked to the idea of utility. Towards its higher end, contingent morality elevates itself to configure that small group of values that are so intimately linked with elementary human existence on earth that they transcend time and space. These general criteria of the good are like the general principles of the legal realm; most of them are linked with the law in some more or less important way. Such moral precepts are notably linked to the law when they concern the common good, that is, respect for the law (which is principally a moral idea), the fundamental individual freedoms, the fight against arbitrary action, etc. Other precepts are expressive of virtues, such as moderation, loyalty, charity, mutual respect, justice, courage, etc. Again, there are here intense interactions with the law. And as we have already seen, a small number of these higher morals stand aloof from the law, as is the case with love or heroism.

The relationship between the law and the good has been the object of complicated and profound commentaries. It is useful to distinguish the higher part of the legal order, with its main principles, from the lower part, where the innumerable detailed positive rules have their seat. The spheres of the law and those of the good progressively converge as one ascends to the highest levels of the legal order, its principles and theoretical foundations; and they diverge just as progressively when one descends to the lower regions of the many positive and contingent norms. At the upper end, it must be said that the very existence of law and the configuration of the legal obligation can ultimately be justified only with regard to the idea of the good. Without any link to morals, an obligation remains a constraint; it hardly becomes an 'ought' in the full sense of this word. The ultimate foundation of the duty to obey legal rules can rest only in the pursuit of the common good and in the idea of justice though legal provisions. It is true that partly unjust law must be obeyed out of consideration for the paramount importance of social peace, legal security and subjectivity of judgment. But a law making no effort towards justice can compel only by the sword. This may occur for a certain time, but the situation remains precarious and superficial, and it risks being overthrown. As de Visscher has written most lucidly:

> The problem of obligation ... is a moral problem. The distinction between legal and ethical categories ... cannot be pushed to the point of divorcing the law of the primary notions of morality from where all normative disciplines flow. ... The law is part of morality to the extent that the idea of justice, which forms its specific content, is inseparable from the idea of good, which is a moral idea.[200]

There is, however, another side of the coin. As we have seen, the law cannot be based on a maximum morality; it cannot force adherence to the good. A legal order purporting to realise morality loses itself in the sands of oppression; it annihilates liberty, which is one of its great lifelines. Human liberty—itself a moral idea—requires the limitation of the impact of morals on the law.[201] This is the reason why, as it becomes more concrete through its many positive norms, the legal order emancipates itself and puts some distance between itself and morals. From there comes the conception of law as the 'minimum of morality' or the 'ethical minimum'.[202] Through this legal self-restriction, the moral act remains largely based on the only possible ground on which it can flourish, namely free will to realise the good. There remains, however, the fact that certain legal orders or branches of the law are more connected to morals than others. Thus canon law and those provisions of the criminal code reflecting some of the Ten Commandants are closer to morals than most of the more or less dull provisions of administrative law.

There is a series of factors distinguishing law from morals. The distinction is merely phenomenological—and complex—since the ultimate bases of the two normative phenomena remain closely linked. Different criteria of distinction have been proposed. The first, and most important, is that morality is an internal phenomenon, while law has an external reach.[203] In other words, morals concern the

200 C de Visscher, *Théories et réalités en droit international public*, 4th edn (Paris, 1970) 122.

201 See S Pufendorf, *De officio hominis et civis* (1673), *Prefatio*; C Thomasius, *Fundamenta iuris naturae et gentium* (1705), lib I, cap V.

202 G Jellinek, *Die sozialethische Bedeutung von Recht, Unrecht und Strafe*, 2nd edn (Berlin, 1908) 45.

203 C Thomasius, *Fundamenta iuris naturae et gentium* (1705), book I, ch VI, §35. The external reach of law had already been stressed in the Middle Ages: Thomas Aquinas, above n 43, II, II, q 58, a 2, ad quartum, '[A]ctiones quae sunt hominis ad seipsum sufficienter rectificantur rectificatis passionibus per alias virtutes morales. Sed actiones quae sunt ad alterum indigent speciali rectificatione, non solum per comparationem ad agentem, sed etiam per comparationem ad eum ad quem sunt. Et ideo circa eas est specialis virtus, quae est iustitia.'

inner life of individuals, their volition and their search for the good; law concerns the external life of individuals, in the domain of what is due to others. The same idea was developed by Kant, but with a slight shift of accent. For Kant, legality is distinguished from morality from the point of view of the reason for respecting the norms: in the legal realm, what counts is only the conformity of the action with the legal requirement, whatever the motives for this action; in the moral realm, the motive for the action is paramount, since it must itself be based on the search for the good.[204] There are many variants of this exterior/interior criterion:

1. with regard to the object of the rules: *ad alterum* for the law, *ad forum internum* for morals (Thomasius);
2. as we have seen, with regard to the motive of respect for the norms: indifferent for the law, essential for morals (Kant); and also
3. with regard to the foundation of the norms: heteronomous will for the law, autonomous will for morals;
4. with regard to the aim of the norms, geared towards the good of the action as such or towards the good of the action in view of relations with others.[205]

Thus, del Vecchio insists on the subjectivity of morals (the judgement being made in relation to the subject itself) and the trans-subjectivity of the law (the judgement being made in relation to actions of others).[206] The criterion can also be found in those constructions that insist on the bilateralism and interrelatedness of rights and obligations in the law, and on the predominance of obligations in the domain of morals;[207] or in the pluralistic character of the law (regulating society) and the monistic approach of morals (regulating the individual himself).[208]

All these conceptions are certainly useful, but they should not be pushed too far. It is only for the most part that the law is turned outwards and morals inwards. Morals can also affect social action: this is the case, as we have seen, with social morals. Conversely, the law sometimes takes into account the motives for action, for example in criminal law (mitigating or increasing a sentence) or in the context of the doctrine of abuse of rights, when directed at ruling out the subjective intention of harming another. It also does so when certain standards apply, such as that of 'good morals' (*bonos mores*). The inner and the outer are too closely connected to be completely separated; will and action are consequentially linked; Confucius rightly said, 'pay attention to your thoughts, they are the beginning of your actions'. By the same token, as the Golden Rule shows, it is impossible to neatly separate those actions due to oneself and those actions due to the others. In a certain measure, we owe something to another because we owe it to ourselves, and vice versa. This is the ultimate root of legal rules such as estoppel. Moreover, the law can technically formulate duties towards oneself. For a time, at the urging of

[204] I Kant, *Introduction to the Metaphysics of Morals* (1797), ch III.
[205] G del Vecchio, *Lezioni di filosofia del diritto*, 3rd edn (Rome, 1936) 199ff.
[206] *ibid.*
[207] I Vanni, *Lezioni di filosofia del diritto* (Bologna, 1920) 99.
[208] M Virally, *La pensée juridique* (Paris, 1960) 76.

the Church, criminal codes contained norms prohibiting suicide. The attempted suicide could then be criminally prosecuted. Lastly, we might note again that most people follow the law not simply because of the fear of punishment, but because they are convinced that it is right to do so, ie because of a moral impulse.

Other differences relate, for example, to the different scope of both phenomena, the law being confined to representing an 'ethical minimum'.[209] The law can and should remain below any requirement for perfection. Only those duties indispensable to social life should be imposed by legal constraint and sanction. Moral choices, on the other hand, should be left to individuals as far as possible, all the more so in a pluralistic and secular society (*in dubiis libertas*). In a sense, law represents neither minimum nor maximum ethics; it embodies average ethics, those that can and must be demanded of the average person living in society.[210] Law can therefore seize only those domains where it can demand something in some measure of many or all members of society.

It has also been emphasised that morals lack the external sanction mechanisms with which the law is provided. But once more, the distinction is only relative. Violation of norms of social morality can lead to meaningful social sanctions, such as boycott and ostracism. And international law does not in any case possess the institutional sanctioning mechanisms known to municipal law. The reactions to violations of its norms are partly legal (countermeasures), but also to a great extent simple social reactions (disapproval, hostile foreign policy towards the State breaching the law, reactions of public opinion, etc). Both are in a larger sense legal 'sanctions', in that they react to the breach of a legal norm and seek to remedy it.

The position sometimes held that moral norms are vague and legal norms precise is too generic to be true. There are precise moral norms (eg honour the promise you made) and vague legal norms (eg legal standards).

Overall, there are many and intense exchanges between the law and morals. The two notions were originally twinned, even if each later took its own path in life.

B. International Morals

International morals[211] are social morals. Individual morality does not apply to the State, since the latter is not a living being gifted with conscience. But again

[209] G Jellinek, *Die sozialethische Bedeutung von Recht, Unrecht und Strafe*, 2nd edn (Berlin, 1908) 45. Others have considered from another perspective that the law represents an 'ethical maximum', in the sense of rules provided with sanctions: G Schmoller, *Grundriss der allgemeinen Volkswirtschaftslehre*, pt I (Munich, 1918) 57.

[210] A Kaufmann, *Rechtsphilosophie*, 2nd edn (Munich, 1997) 217, 'Das Recht, das seine Forderungen an alle richten muss, auch an diejenigen, die zu anspruchsvollen moralischen Leistungen nicht imstande sind, kann immer nur Durchschnittsanforderungen gegenüber Durchschnittsmenschen aufstellen'.

[211] On the morals of international law, compare, eg, the two following publications: N Politis, *La morale internationale* (Neuchâtel, 1943); SR Ratner, *The Thin Justice of International Law—A Moral Reckoning of the Law of Nations* (Oxford, 2015).

this distinction should not be overstressed. There are many great moral rules, found in individual or religious systems, that also concern life in society (eg in the Decalogue). The first question to be asked is, however, to what extent can international morality exist at all? Among States as political and sovereign entities, is there any place for moral rules? If the answer is affirmative, to what extent do these rules differ from those applicable to human individuals? The answers given to these questions have varied significantly. For some, international society and international law are subject to moral rules more than any other society or law, since the power that States possess is that most fundamental to the destiny and survival of humanity as a whole. Thus, this international space must all the more be governed by moral rules.[212] A variant of this argument holds that since international law is more precarious and more prone to gaps than any other legal order, considerations of justice and ethics are essential to nourish its skinny frame. In particular the absence of a superior power makes it necessary to rely on the palliative of ethics.[213] For others, arguing on the same lines, the norms of international morality correspond to those of individual social action. The great moral rules are thus universal. They apply to whatever subjects, to the extent that these subjects are vested with autonomy of action. At the end of the day, these universal rules flow from precepts such as *honeste vivere*, *neminem laedere* and the like, which cannot be different for individuals and for groups of individuals (States).[214]

On the other hand, there are authors rejecting the idea of applying moral rules to States. The reasons given are many: that international law has no need of a moral foundation, since it is not based on subordination but on coordination, and thus respects the autonomy of its subjects (only in relationships involving subordination are moral rules for the protection of the weaker necessary);[215] or that the universalisation of international law has been pushed so far that the links with concrete moral rules rooted in particular cultures have been severed;[216] or that the State is an expression of evil and thus cannot be the holder of moral positions (Nietzsche, Tolstoy); or that the State is the supreme reality on earth and thus establishes its own morality, not being subjected to any other.[217]

Lastly, there are certain authors who accept the existence of moral rules between States. Nevertheless, they modify the complexion of these rules in comparison with ordinary morals as applicable between human individuals. Thus, it has been said that international morality is nation-orientated and particularistic.[218] Further, it has been emphasised that the State can breach an international obligation when a vital national interest is at stake—an option the individual is not granted in the municipal realm.[219]

[212] R Coste, *Morale internationale—L'humanité à la recherche de son âme* (Tournai, 1964) 555ff.
[213] M Huber, *Grundlagen nationaler Erneuerung* (Zurich, 1934) 56.
[214] Politis, above n 211.
[215] A Raestad, *La philosophie du droit international public* (Oslo, 1949) 63.
[216] A Papaux and E Wyler, *L'éthique du droit international* (Paris, 1997).
[217] GWF Hegel, *Grundlinien der Philosophie des Rechts* (Berlin, 1821).
[218] A Trendelenburg, *Naturrecht auf dem Grunde der Ethik* (Leipzig, 1860).
[219] M Rümelin, *Rechtsgefühl und Rechtsbewusstsein* (Tübingen, 1925).

None of the objections to the existence of an international morality is convincing. Morality is certainly not limited to protective justice. For example, as a deontological norm limiting the reach of liberty so as to take account of the equal liberty of the other, or else as a requirement to honour promises, morality has a distinctive role to play in relations involving coordination. Morality is also not limited to universal norms. Social and other types of morality exist wherever there is human action. Further, speculation as to whether the State represents good or evil is of metaphysical nature. In reality, the State is the main form of collective political organisation. It seems doubtful that it could be considered only as an evil. But even assuming it were, morals would have the role of pushing it towards the 'lesser evil'. The negation of a law placed between and above States is a dogmatic excess producing appalling practical results. For all these reasons, we must reject the idea that there is no morality in international relations. There are standards of social morality (and also of higher morality) in the society of States—as they also exist in any other society. But what is the precise content of this international morality? Is there one morality for States and a different one for individuals? Are there some common precepts for both, and some differing rules for each? Before answering these questions, we must first look at the types of morality that exist in the context of political bodies.

There are three main forms of political morals: universal, international and national. National morals have as a point of reference the good of the national collectivity or State. The spectrum of this morality ranges from aggressive nationalism to international cooperation on the basis of perceived self-interest. There is also international morality, which concerns the good of the international community of States. It attempts, for example, to impose peaceful relations and to avoid war. Lastly, there is universal morality, which concerns the good of all human beings on earth. Human rights precepts are based on it. The differences between general moral theories and morals for State relations can be analysed according to the following two aspects:

1. *Apology of egoism*. For the individual, in the wake of the civilising missions of the major religions and secular philosophies, the concept of morality has been progressively centred on the idea of the universal good. Its maxims are mainly altruistic: 'What I owe myself I also owe the other.' The Sermon on the Mount is emblematic of this approach. The evolution of the moral notion in international affairs is still far from this.[220] There is no universal religion able to influence and tame international society in the sense of furnishing a moral network of precepts. The great monotheistic religions either historically ignored the State and the international community (Christianity), or developed frankly bellicose doctrines (Islam). The State remains a supreme entity and is hardly subjected to moral values. The interests of the State continue to

[220] However, Wolff and Vattel have claimed that the moral rule requires a people to love another people as it loves itself. See H Kraus, 'La morale internationale' (1927-I) 16 *RCADI* 497–98.

be elevated to supreme heights, whereas in municipal society similar attitudes displayed by individuals would provoke the greatest disapproval. Thus when statesman declare that their State and people are a 'great nation', or even the 'greatest among the nations', the masses applaud cheerfully. But what of an individual who boasts 'I am great', 'I am the greatest'? The best that can be said is that such utterances would cause some embarrassment to those who heard them. This simple example shows the distance between the normally altruistic moral tone of municipal societies and the mostly egoistical tone of State morality.[221] This difference manifests itself in a series of consequences, mainly the plea that the State be allowed to act in a way that would be considered immoral if an individual acted in the same way. This moral dualism allows the masses to passionately represent as necessary, useful and moral actions that common moral sense condemns (eg annexation). This strange state of affairs flows from the national loyalty of the individual: 'my country, right or wrong' or, more precisely, 'my country, always right'. Overall, international society is still characterised by the predominance of national or egoistic morality. However, the progress accomplished by international morality is considerable. The three forms mentioned above—national, international and universal—constantly interact.

2. *Utilitarianism?* International morals (taken here as encompassing all the three forms previously mentioned) have often been linked to utilitarian considerations,[222] unlike the higher moral precepts applicable to individuals, which are said to be valid unconditionally. The moralisation of international relations has long sought support in rational arguments seeking to persuade the decision-makers that their true interest lay in adopting a stance compatible with this or that moral rule. Morality alone was considered insufficient to that end; it had to be buttressed by interest. Hence, international morality became a function of utility; and consequently it became largely a matter of circumstance and less a matter of principle. It is inspired by reciprocities, mutual expectations and variable calculations. Since rational man knows that not all subjects will realise their true interest, which is to follow moral rules, he will introduce political considerations into the moral equation. This is also the profound sense of Machiavelli's opus: he affirms morality, but he tries

[221] The 'reason of State' has led to similar analysis: CJ Friedrich, *Constitutional Reason of State* (Providence, 1957); F Meinecke, *L'idée de la raison d'Etat dans l'histoire des temps modernes* (Geneva, 1973); S Hoffmann, *Une morale pour les monstres froids: pour une éthique des relations internationales* (Paris, 1982); LC McDonald, 'Three Forms of Political Ethics' (1978) 31 *The Western Political Quarterly* 7ff; SS Monoson and M Loriaux, 'The Illusion of Power and the Disruption of Moral Norms: Thucydides' Critique of Periclean Policy' (1998) 92 *The American Political Science Review* 285ff. For international lawyers on this subject, see, eg, H Lauterpacht, *Collected Papers*, vol II (Cambridge, 1975) 336ff; R Phillimore, *Commentaries upon International Law*, vol III (London, 1885) 879; FW Jerusalem, *Kriegsrecht und Kodifikation* (Breslau, 1918) 52.

[222] Especially in the English school of thought, inspired by Bentham, Austin, Sidwick, Paley and others, particularly in international law by teachers such as E Creasy, *First Platform of International Law* (London, 1876).

to make it compatible with life in a dishonest society. The danger of such an approach is clear: cause and effect are linked; each liberty taken will lead to another one; guns will be loaded on both sides; calculating will take the place of rules. The many calculations will inevitably spiral down.[223] It might have seemed useful (and even moral) for some to use force in Kosovo and later in Iraq without the proper backing of international law; but the annexation of the Crimea[224] is the latest poisonous fruit of such doctrines of lawlessness.

Social morals influence international law in two main ways: (i) they exert pressure on the formation of the law; and (ii) they exert pressure on the application of legal norms. The illustrations given in the next paragraphs concern the influence of international or universal morals on international law, since the influence of national morals (and nationalism) has already been mentioned in several other contexts.

1. *Formation of the Law*

The creation of legal rules influenced by moral considerations is perhaps more frequent in international society than it is in municipal law. The reason is the state of fluidity of international law, which is a law in a constant state of formation and transformation. Given its normative gaps and uncertainties, moral (as also political) considerations can permeate more easily than in a solid body of codified law; sandstone allows water to penetrate more deeply than does granite. The absence of a regular legislator makes amendment of the law slower and more burdensome. Moral arguments will then sometimes be mustered to take liberties with legal rules felt to be anachronistic and inequitable. In order to exert their influence, morals will have to seek an alliance with international politics, and to some extent with public opinion.

From an historical perspective, moral considerations had a great impact at the formative stage of modern international law, notably at the time of Grotius. International law was progressively composed of pieces of Roman law, *jus gentium*, natural law and moral considerations. The diplomatic documents of the seventeenth century were replete with political, justice-related and equitable arguments.[225] Later, certain protagonists in the French Revolution sought to moralise—at least on paper—international relations. The *Project on the Law of Nations*, written by

[223] On these dilemmas, see O Höffe, *Politische Gerechtigkeit* (Frankfurt, 1987) 412ff.

[224] On this annexation, see amongst others L Wildhaber, 'Ostukraine und Völkerrecht' (2015) 25 *RSDIE* 159ff; P Hilpold, 'Die Ukraine-Krise aus völkerrechtlicher Sicht: ein Streitfall zwischen Rechts, Geschichte und Politik' (2015) 25 *RSDIE* 171ff; O Luchterhandt, 'Der Anschluss der Krim an Russland aud völkerrdchtlicher Sicht' (2014) 52 *AVR* 137ff; M Geistlinger, 'Der Beitritt der Republik Krim zur Russischen Föderation aus der Warte des Selbstbestimmungsrecht der Völker'(2014) 52 *AVR* 175ff; C Santulli, 'La crise ukrainienne: position du problème' (2014) 118 *RGDIP* 799ff; TD Grant, 'The Annexation of Crimea' (2015) 109 *AJIL* 68ff; O Merezhko, 'Crimea's Annexation by Russia—Contradictions in the New Russian Doctrine of International Law' (2015) 75 *ZaöRV* 167ff; T Christakis, 'Self-Determination, Territorial Integrity and Fait Accompli in the Case of Crimea' (2015) 75 *ZaöRV* 75ff.

[225] H Wheaton, *Histoire des progrès du droit des gens*, vol I, 4th edn (Leipzig, 1865) 109–10.

Abbé Grégoire in 1795, holds in Article 1 that nations are in a state of nature and linked among themselves by a universal morality; in Article 3 that a nation should behave with regard to another as it would like to be treated itself, and that what a man owes to a man a nation owes to another; in Article 4 that nations should, in peacetime, do each other the greatest possible good, and in wartime, the least possible evil; in Article 5 that the particular interest of a nation is subordinated to the common interest of the human family; in Article 15 that attempts against the liberty of one nation are an attack on all nations; and lastly, in Article 21, that treaties are inviolable and sacred.[226] This project had little influence on the French Government. Emer de Vattel—a much more influential author—wrote that each nation shall contribute as much as possible to the happiness and perfection of other peoples.[227] In legal doctrine, many passages, or even whole chapters, were devoted to the moral rule in international law.[228] Moreover, the nineteenth century flew the flag of progress and civilisation[229] (even if largely limited to white men): the idea of humanity—eg through the Red Cross movement[230]—took wing; there was a movement to abolish slavery[231] and to justify (selective) humanitarian interventions.[232]

The twentieth century was also full of moral elements influencing legal positions. For example: the construction of the modern *jus contra bellum* and the maintenance of international peace; the significant development of *jus in bello* and the protection of civilians in warfare; the Fourteen Points of President Wilson, including the ban on secret treaties, and the establishment of the League of Nations for the maintenance of international peace;[233] the organisation of international cooperation in many matters; the advent of human rights protection, including in the Carter Doctrine in the US;[234] the prosecution of the great war criminals and later of international law criminals; the decolonisation movement (the moral dimension can be seen in personalities such as Gandhi or Senghor); discussions around the notion of humanitarian intervention, including now the responsibility to protect;[235] the development of an international public order; pressure in

[226] L Le Fur and G Chklaver, *Recueil de textes de droit international public*, 2nd edn (Paris, 1934) 68–69.

[227] E de Vattel, *Le droit des gens* (1758), Préliminaires, §13.

[228] See, eg, GF de Martens, *Précis du droit des gens* (1788), Introduction, §1; E Creasy, *First Platform of International Law* (London, 1876) chs I and II, 1–48.

[229] See still Art 38, §1, letter c of the ICJ Statute.

[230] See, eg, F Bugnion, *Le CICR et les victimes de la guerre* (Geneva, 1994); or P Boissier, *History of the International Committee of the Red Cross: From Solferino to Tshushima* (Geneva, 1985).

[231] D Weissbrodt, 'Slavery' in R Wolfrum (ed), *The Max Planck Encyclopedia of Public International Law*, vol IX (Oxford, 2012) 216ff.

[232] WG Grewe, *The Epochs of International Law* (Berlin/New York, 2000) 445ff (in general), 487ff (humanitarian intervention).

[233] J Schwietzke, 'Fourteen Points of Wilson (1918)' in R Wolfrum (ed), *The Max Planck Encyclopedia of Public International Law*, vol IV (Oxford, 2012) 203ff, with further references.

[234] On the latter, see O Schachter, 'Les aspects juridiques de la politique américaine en matière des droits de l'homme' (1977) 23 *AFDI* 53ff.

[235] See O Corten, *Le droit contre la guerre, L'interdiction du recours à la force en droit international contemporain*, 2nd edn (Paris, 2014) 801ff; C Antonopoulos, *The Unilateral Use of Force by States in*

favour of the better protection of the natural environment, including animals; pressure for the moralisation of the international economy, etc. It stands to reason that these moral pressures were accompanied by political agendas and tools; but it would be wrong to completely ignore the moral flavour of some of the positions, which had and has a manifest influence on international normativity.

Some examples show that the law and moral arguments can conflict, even if it often pertains to the application of the legal rule rather than to its formation. Thus under international law no exception has evolved allowing the use of force for humanitarian reasons, if only because the great majority of Third World States are resolutely against this notion.[236] In the Kosovo crisis (1999), this led to many arguments of the type 'unlawful but legitimate', ie moral but against the letter of the law. Why, it was asked in certain circles, should the authorisation of the Security Council always be considered necessary, when one knows the mainly political composition and agenda of this organ? Why should this always be better than unilateral action by States in cases of humanitarian urgency, for example in the case of massacres? It should be added that there have also been tensions between moral perspectives. The predominant Western view on humanitarian intervention may perhaps have been 'morally justified' in some instances, but many other States cast doubt on the perspective adopted: is intervention really only humanitarian, or is there not always some other agenda? Is intervention really in the name of the international community, or are self-serving interests concealed beneath the surface? Is intervention not selective on account of such interests? Who has ever intervened to halt massacres committed by an ally or a friend? Is intervention not based simply on taking sides in a civil war? Are abuses not unavoidable, as the intervention in Libya showed? Authorised to protect civilians, it was used as a tool

International Law (Athens, 1997) 452ff; BP Lepard, *Rethinking Humanitarian Intervention* (Pennsylvania, 2002); D Liakopoulos, *L'ingerenza umanitaria nel diritto internazionale e comunitario* (Padua, 2007). For a more developed bibliography, see V Lowe and A Tzanakopoulos, 'Humanitarian Intervention' in R Wolfrum (ed), *The Max Planck Encyclopedia of Public International Law*, vol V (Oxford, 2012) 47ff. See also R Kolb, 'Note on Humanitarian Intervention' (2003) 85 *Revue internationale de la Croix-Rouge* 119ff. On the notion of responsibility to protect, see, eg, JM Genser and I Cotler (eds), *The Responsibility to Protect: The Promise of Stopping Mass Atrocities in Our Time* (New York/Oxford, 2012); J Hoffmann and A. Nollkaemper (eds), *Responsibility to Protect: From Principle to Practice* (Amsterdam, 2012); A Hehir, *Responsibility to Protect: Rhetoric, Reality and the Future of Humanitarian Intervention* (Basingstoke, 2012); A Rausch, *Responsibility to Protect: Eine juristische Betrachtung* (Frankfurt, 2011); AJ Bellamy, SE Davies and L Glanville (eds), *The Responsibility to Protect and International Law* (Leiden, 2011); A Orford, *International Authority and the Responsibility to Protect* (Cambridge, 2011); P Cunliffe (ed), *Critical Perspectives on the Responsibility to Protect: Interrogating Policy and Practice* (London, 2011); RC Thakur, *The Responsibility to Protect: Norms, Laws and the Use of Force in International Politics* (London, 2011); CG Badescu, *Humanitarian Intervention and the Responsibility to Protect: Security and Human Rights* (London, 2011); J Pattison, *Humanitarian Intervention and the Responsibility to Protect: Who Should Intervene ?* (Oxford, 2010); C Verlage, *Responsibility to Protect: Ein neuer Ansatz im Völkerrecht zur Verhinderung von Völkermord, Kriegsverbrechen und Verbrechen gegen die Menschlichkeit* (Tübingen, 2009). See also N Michel, 'La responsabilité de protéger: Une vue d'ensemble assortie d'une perspective suisse' (2012) 131 *Revue de droit suisse* 5ff.

[236] See mainly the very clear analysis in O Corten, *Le droit contre la guerre, L'interdiction du recours à la force en droit international contemporain* 2nd edn (Paris, 2014) 801ff.

for regime change.[237] And is a door opened to unilateral uses of force not inviting a slew of precedents, potentially leading to greater international disorder and uses of force in the future? If that is taken as a starting-point, the moral issue is blurred. The lines shift, matters appear to be less clear-cut. The result is this: there is also morality in the application of the law, not only in the apparently moral reasons to act *contra legem*.

2. *Application of the Law*

In the implementation of international law, national morality predominates over international morality when States are implementing the law, and international morality tends to play a much greater role when implementation is carried out by international organs. The general principles of law constitute a significant vector for the penetration of moral considerations into the legal body at the stage of its application. The link between many of these principles and moral considerations has rightly been noted: '[general principles of law] are the paths which civilised mankind has learned in its long experience in the municipal sphere to be those leading to justice'.[238] The connection is particularly visible in principles such as good faith, estoppel, proportionality, reciprocity, undue enrichment,[239] the principle that reparation is due for damage caused, the right to be heard, the need for clarity in the law,[240] etc. Through their application, such principles allow moral considerations to exert some influence.

There are, further, political principles with some moral colour. This was the case as regards the many UN General Assembly resolutions formulating principles in the context of decolonisation (which were later to become legal principles),[241] including resolutions on permanent sovereignty over natural resources[242] or on the status of combatants in wars of national liberation.[243] Such political principles are often founded on moral arguments, for example, in the context of

[237] M Payandeh, 'The United Nations, Military Intervention, and Régime Change in Libya' (2012) 52 *Virginia Journal of International Law* 355ff; D Tladi, 'Security Council, the Use of Force and Regime Change: Libya and Côte d'Ivoire' (2012) 37 *South African Yearbook of International Law* 22ff; G Wilson, 'The United Nations Security Council, Libya and Resolution 1973: Protection of Civilians or Tool for Regime Change?' in C Panara and G Wilson (eds), *The Arab Spring: New Patterns for Democracy and International Law* (Leiden, 2013) 101ff.

[238] B Cheng, *General Principles of Law—As Applied by International Courts and Tribunals* (London, 1953) 386.

[239] See Pomponius, 'Iure naturae aequum est neminem cum alterius detrimento et iniuria fieri locupletiorem': *Dig*, 50, 17, 206; and *Dig*, 12, 6, 14. See also *Liber Sextus, Corpus iuris canonici, de regulis iuris, regula* 48.

[240] See Case 169/80, *Société Gondrand* [1981] ECR 1931; see also <http://eur-lex.europa.eu/legal-content/EN/TXT/HTML/?uri=CELEX:61980CJ0169&from=EN>.

[241] See M Virally, 'Le rôle des principes dans le développement du droit international' in M Virally, *Le droit international en devenir* (Paris, 1990) 195ff. For the development of environmental protection in the Rio Conference of 1992, see SP Johnson, *The Earth Summit: The UN Conference on Environment and Development* (London/Dordrecht, 1993).

[242] UNGA Resolution 1803 (1962).

[243] UNGA Resolution 3103 (1973).

decolonisation, on the immoral nature of colonial domination. Such principles are intended to influence the application of the law. Lastly, many international awards or judgments contain references to moral considerations influencing the law. The 'elementary considerations of humanity' in the *Corfu Channel* Judgment of the ICJ (Merits, 1949) are particularly well known;[244] the Aboriginal right to land recognised by municipal courts in Australia is a less well-known example.[245] In political relations, moral considerations also play a certain ill-defined role, for example in the refusal to conclude commercial governmental contracts with oppressive governments.

3. *Conclusion*

International morality is cast in a state of profound tension between universal morality and national morality, the good of the wider community and the good of national communities. The rivalry between the two branches is vivid: convergence is difficult and the pressures of international morality are increasing.

International morality has three roles to play. First, at the level of the ultimate foundation of legal obligation, moral considerations are inescapable. Secondly, on the plane of the creation of the law, morality sometimes leads to the creation of new norms (eg human rights) and the amendment of old norms (eg colonialism). Thirdly, at the level of implementation of the law, international morality faces the greatest difficulty in making an adequate place for itself. Most often, it can at best aspire to exerting partial, temporary and precarious influence. State power organised around the notion of national morality opposes any challenge to its growth.

VII. Will and Reason

A. General Legal Experience

Each legal order lives in a state of fertile tension between two of its main elements, namely, reason and the will. Legal phenomena are nourished by the multiple convergences and divergences between intellectualism and voluntarism, heteronomy and autonomy, objectivism and subjectivism, transcendence and immanence. Through reason, the 'natural' element within the law is emphasised, ie its association with the realm of values; whereas through the will, the 'positive' element of the law is affirmed, ie its association with reality, and also its dependence on power. The mutual place accorded to the ideal and to real factors within the law, the relations between natural and positive law, form the underlying theme of the legal

[244] *Corfu Channel* (Merits) [1949] ICJ Rep 22. But see also the *South-West Africa* (Second Phase) [1966] ICJ Rep 287.

[245] *Mabo v Queensland* (1992) 112 *ILR* 412, 457ff.

'fugue' that has been played since time immemorial. The overlapping of the two elements is so close that it is impossible to treat reason without the will, or the will without reason; the one calls for the other and exists only in the light of the other. This overlap and the constant shifts between these elements can be grasped only from an historical perspective. Here they will be assessed only relatively briefly.[246]

The gist of the matter is that whenever reason is riding high, optimistic natural law conceptions seeking to realise justice take precedence. Conversely, when the will is at its peak, pessimistic positive law conceptions, where power makes law, tend to predominate. Reason seeks justice, the will calls for power. For reasons of space, the following historical outline will mainly consider European thinking. Given the essentially European elaboration of legal science, this limitation may not appear too arbitrary.

1. Antiquity

Greek thought was orientated towards objective laws governing the universe (*Logos*) more than towards the expression of subjective divine or human wills. The Logos and the cosmos led to natural law conceptions. Sophistic approaches, with their subjectivism, moral positivism and relativism, were an exception to the rule. For the Sophists, reason could not know the objectively good; thus, there remained only the will. Therefore, there was no natural law but only positive law imposed by power and interest. These theories were rejected in the intellectualist response of Plato and Aristotle. These intellectualist conceptions were then adopted by Rome. Through the Stoics natural law thinking entered Roman *mores*. However, the Romans had a more genuinely legal approach to the matter. They thus developed the idea of rights and duties, notably the concept that the law must delimit the spheres of action and of liberty of each individual.[247] Hence the criticism levelled at the so-called 'liberal touch' of Roman law by the totalitarian regimes of the 1930s. The autonomy of the will in legal transactions was recognised, eg in contracts and testamentary documents. It was a source of private rights and entitlements ('subjective legal positions'). In the private law sphere, there was discussion and rational coordination. In public law, as time passed and the Emperor consolidated his power, the will expanded and reason retreated. The domain of reason was thus private law, the domain of the will public law. This public

[246] For a more detailed account, see H Welzel, *Naturrecht und materiale Gerechtigkeit*, 4th edn (Göttingen, 1990); G Fassò, *La legge della ragione* (Bologna, 1964) (reprint in Milan, 1999); E Benz, *Marius Viktorinus und die Entwicklung der abendländischen Willensmetaphysik* (Stuttgart, 1932).

[247] The concept of subjective rights may not yet be highly developed, but rights and duties (realisable through claims, *actiones*) are the core of the legal system. See the probably overly restrictive view of M Villey, 'L'idée du droit subjectif et les systèmes juridiques romains' [1946–1947] *Nouvelle revue historique de droit français et étranger* 201ff; M Villey, *Leçons d'histoire de la philosophie du droit* (Paris, 1962) 167ff; A Sériaux, *Le droit naturel*, 2nd edn (Paris, 1999) 66ff. See also G Pugliese, *Actio e diritto subiettivo* (Milan, 1939); C Gioffredi, 'Osservazioni sul problema del diritto soggettivo nel diritto romano' (1967) *Bollettino dell'Istituto di diritto romano* 227ff; G Pugliese, *Istituzioni di diritto romano* (Padua, 1986) 38–39.

tendency towards the '*imperatoria majestas*'[248] and the concomitant '*quod principi placuit legis habet vigorem*',[249] '*princeps legibus solutus*'[250] or '*princeps lex animata in terris*'[251] constantly increased throughout the third and fourth centuries, and later in the Byzantine Empire. In these times of crisis, private law declined and hypertrophic public law developed.[252] The will expanded its empire and reason took flight.

2. Christianity

Original Christianity was based—through its links to Judaism—on voluntaristic metaphysics, clearly expressed in the Old Testament. God is the creator of the world and its moral legislator. God is almighty; thus, his liberty is absolute and no reasonable limits constrain it. God cannot be judged by Man and Man's reason.[253] Man cannot attain truth by his own efforts. Original sin has clouded his senses; he can attain illumination only through God's grace, and possibly through faith. Reason is suspect; it can be used to subvert the word of God, to cast doubt upon it. And is not reason common to non-believers and believers? Lack of faith cannot liberate Man. Man cannot emancipate himself from God and pretend to become self-sufficient in the light of his own reason. At the same time, the early Christians were suspicious of the State and its laws: this was the domain of worldliness, of power, lust and decadence.

As is well known, Saint Augustine would built his doctrine on the bedrock of these original conceptions:[254] the supreme principle of action is the will (*voluntas imperat intellectui*); it alone can be morally judged as good or evil. Thus, there is only the arbitrary will of God, who can, if He wishes, condemn the just and save the unjust, predestining some to be saved and others to be lost. This doctrine was then taken over by the nominalists around Duns Scot and William Occam,[255] but also by Saint Anselm,[256] Hugh St Victor[257] and others,[258] including, later, the

248 *Dominus terrarum: Dig.*, 14, 2, 9.

249 *Dig*, 1, 4, 1, Ulpian.

250 *Dig*, 1, 3, 31, Ulpian. There were certain passages to the contrary in the *Digest*, but they had no influence on practice: Codex, 1, 14, 4, 'Digna vox est maiestate regnantis, legibus alligatum se Principem profiteri: adeo de auctoritate iuris nostra pendet auctoritas. Et re vera maius Impero est, submittere legibus principatum.'

251 *Novellae*, 105, 4.

252 D Liebs, *Römisches Recht*, 2nd edn (Göttingen, 1982) 82ff.

253 Paul, Rom 9, 11–20.

254 He thereby reacts to certain early tendencies within the Church to come back to Greek intellectualism: Filon, *De vita Mosis*, II, 14; Atenagoras, *De resurrectione mortuorum*, 24; Clement of Alexandria, *Stromata*, I, 29; Origenes, *Contra Celsum*, V, 37 and *In numeros homilia*, X, 3; Tertullien, *Adversus Judaeos*, II, 3ff and *De corona*, V, 4, VI, 1; Lactantius, *Divinae Institutiones*, VIII, etc. See G Fassò, *La legge della ragione* (Bologna, 1964) 32ff. See Augustine, *Contra Faustum*, XXII, 27; *Contra Duas Epistolas Pelagianorum*, III, 7, 20.

255 William Occam, *Opus Oxoniense*, II, d. 3, q. 5-6, n. 15. And *ibid*, I, d 8, q 5, a 3, n 24, 'quare voluntas voluit hoc, nulla est causa, nisi quia voluntas est voluntas'. See also *ibid*, d. 17, q 1–3, a 3, n 5.

256 Saint Anselm, *Proslogion*, XI.

257 H St Victor, *De sacramentis christianae fidei*, I, IV, 1.

258 See, eg, in the late Middle Ages, P D'Ailly, *Commentaire aux sentences*, I, q 9, S ('divina voluntas nullam habet rationem, propter quam determinetur ut velut'); J Gerson, *De consolatione theologiae*, II,

Protestant tradition of Luther or Calvin. Politically, such doctrines would pave the way for Hobbes and absolutism: if reason is dead, only the will of the powerful remains; the ruler will impose his unquestioned will; and the ruler, for most of these authors, is a monarch, reflecting the image of the one God. Such a political construction leads not only to absolutism, but also later to totalitarian regimes.

Thomas Aquinas reacted against this construct; he tried to return to a more balanced conception, drawing on Greek intellectualism and relaxing the considerable tension between reason and the will. He was particularly vexed by utterances to the effect that God's will could have any object whatsoever, even the damnation of the just. That seemed to be blasphemous to him, suggesting, as it did, that God could will evil.[259] But in order to say that something is evil at all, we need the light of reason. God created an ordered cosmos; and Man can take part in that order through the light of reason. The law is more reason than will, that is, the participation of Man in the divine order.[260] The will is subordinated to reason[261]—one must will what is good and just, that is conform to the order of God—and not the other way round. Reason must thus indicate the path to be followed by the will (*lex indicans*). Through such an approach, a huge measure of harmonisation between the will and reason, terrestrial and celestial life is achieved. Natural law takes its place once more, and positive law must remain compatible with it.[262] Thomas Aquinas's theories would influence Gregory of Rimini, the Spanish Scholastics (de Vitoria, Molina, Suarez, Vasquez), a moderate branch of Protestantism (Melanton, Hemming, Winkler) and authors such as John Locke. Politically, this doctrine led to modern constitutionalism, that is, to power limited by law and by the rule of law (or: the will limited by reason).

3. *The Enlightenment and Modern Times*

There were contrasting currents in this period. On the one hand, there was the constitutional tradition seeking to impose, at the highest level of power and law, the rule of law (Locke, Montesquieu, Rousseau). The main aim was to limit the arbitrary expression of power and to guarantee liberty. On the other hand, the anthropocentric revolution, leading to German idealism, put the human being and its autonomy at the centre of the world.[263] And in practice, the modern legislator

1, 147, A and *De vita spiritualis animae*, III, 13, C, 'nihil est malum nisi quia prohibitum'; G Biel, *Collectorium sententiarium*, I, d 43, q 1, 'voluntas divina est prima regula omnis justitiae et rectitudine'; F Vasquez, *Controversiae illustres*, I, 27, 6ff. On these passages, see H Welzel, *Naturrecht und materiale Gerechtigkeit*, 4th edn (Göttingen, 1990) 89ff.

259 Thoman Aquinas, above n 43, II, I, q 90, 1 and q 100, a 8; Thomas Aquinas, *De Veritate*, q 23, a-6, 'Dicere autem quod ex simplici voluntate dependeat iustitia est dicere quod divina voluntas non procedeat secundum ordinem sapientiae, quod est blasphemum.'

260 Thomas Aquinas, above n 43, II, I, q 91, a 2.

261 *ibid*, I, q 82, a 3 and 4, 'Si ergo intellectus et voluntas considerentur secundum se, sic intellectus eminentior invenitur … intellectus sit altior et nobilior voluntate' (3); 'intellectus movet voluntatem … movet ipsam ut finis' (a 4).

262 *ibid*, II, I, q 95, 2 and 96, 3.

263 Kant would write that there was nothing in the world that could be held to be good without restriction other than a good will: I Kant, *Metaphysics of Morals*, Foundation, I.

took firm hold and legislated according to the opinion and will of the majority. Modern constitutionalism was thus a construct requiring a delicate balance between human freedom and heteronomous constraint. From the eighteenth century onward, the positive pole orientated towards the will would constantly trump the the limiting pole orientated towards reason. There were manifold reasons for these developments: centralisation of the State and power; the build-up of nation-States conscious of their own interests and missions; the progress of the natural sciences and the positive method ('*verum ipsum factum*'), and thus the progress of positivism;[264] the codification of natural law systems in the modern codes; the success of historicism and particularism; the advent of analytical jurisprudence; the excessively deductive rationalistic schemes providing a negative image of reason (eg Wolff); the exaltation of the State and its power (Hegelianism),[265] etc. The will appeared to be a principle for practical action through which Man could determine his own destiny.

4. *Other Cultures*

Islam is based on the command of God, which the believer must obey. Islam signifies submission to the will of God. Voluntarism therefore lies at is heart, in a way similar to Saint Augustine's doctrine. Politically, power is not separated from religion; political power is an expression of God's will on earth. It is interesting to note that here too there were attempts at intellectual reform, even if they did not ultimately succeed. Thus, the Mutazilite sect (founded by Wacil Ibn'ata in the eighth century) affirmed the primacy of reason (*aql*) over will.[266] In this philosophy there exists a good and an evil in themselves, which can be known through the light of reason. God is limited by the order he created and his will is but an instrument of a justice that precedes it. We might note with interest the parallelism of these efforts with those of Origen and Thomas Aquinas in the Christian world—efforts which constituted in themselves a tribute paid to reason.

The same tension between reason and will existed in the Far East. Thus, for Buddha the wheel of power turned as a function of the wheel of justice. Moral reason (*dhamma*) was supreme.[267] But there were also schools contesting these views and centered on the will (eg Makkhali Gosala).[268]

[264] Positivism had a more limited impact in the English common law system, where reason continued to play a greater role. See, eg, CH McIlwain, *The High Court of Parliament and its Supremacy* (Hamden, Conn, 1962) 105ff.

[265] A lawyer belonging to this school of thought could still write after World War II that the constitutive principle of the law is the will: W Cesarini Sforza, *Rechtsphilosophie* (Munich, 1966) 15ff.

[266] On this sect, see at <www.britannica.com/topic/Mutazilah>.

[267] KN Jayatilleke, 'The Principles of International Law in Buddhist Doctrine' (1967-I) 120 *RCADI* 441ff.

[268] *ibid*, 466.

5. The Relations Between Reason and the Will in Law

What exactly are the relations between reason and the will in the context of the law? It seems obvious that both notions are necessary in human affairs, and that the only question is that of their proper articulation. Within the law, a merely rational legal order without the complement of the will suffers from grave defects as regards positivity and adaptation to changing societies and needs. Conversely, a merely positive legal order without the complement of reason suffers from a lack of justification and of moderation. Only a synthesis of both elements can lead to a satisfactory position: the will ensures the effectiveness of the law and reason its justice. This synthesis between the real and ideal elements does not require a meeting in the middle. The balance to be found will differ from branch to branch and also on the vertical plane (reason predominating in the higher spheres of the law, the will in the lower ones). This means that the synthesis between the two elements is in constant flux.

On the one hand, there is a predominance of reason over the will. In particular, it may be noted that the great constitutional principles are based on reason more than on will. They were developed at the time of the Enlightenment as flowing from natural law, and remarkably are still paramount in our constitutional law today: the rule of law, the separation of powers, equality before the law (and 'equality of arms' in judicial process), the subordination of the judge to the legislator, the independence and impartiality of the judge, publicity of laws, the impersonality of the law, fair trial principles, etc. Such a system, centered on the rule of law, requires a rational conception of society. The same can be said of the general principles of law. For example, each society, especially when it develops, is confronted with the protection of legitimate expectations or the curbing of abuses of rights; or else with the regularisation of situations having prevailed since time immemorial. Such principles of justice are close to natural law conceptions and thus to reason.[269] There is here a rational and non-voluntary layer of the law; principles are not created by intelligent will but are to some extent inherent in the spontaneous order of life.

On the other hand, the will predominates over reason. This is the case as regards the minutiae of positive law rules, which are made to fit changing interests and day-to-day needs. This is also the case in public law, through ordinary legislation and rules adopted by the executive; and in the domain of private law, through the creation of subjective legal acts, eg contractual engagements. In the former domain, there may be limits of constitutional law to respect, and in the latter there is public order to be respected (*jus publicum privatorum pactis mutari non potest*).[270]

[269] See, eg, P Melanchthon, *Loci communes rerum theologicarum, de lege*, vol II, pt I (Gütersloh, 1952) 41–42: 'Ut sunt in disciplinis theoricis …, quaedam communia principia … regulae omnium humanarum functionum. Has recte vocaveris leges naturae.'

[270] See *Dig*, 2, 14, 38, Papinian.

B. Reason and Will in International Law

In the history of international law, there have been considerable oscillations between reason and the will. We may here shortly discuss two extremes: the rational *jus gentium* rooted in ancient times; and the will-orientated positivistic order of the nineteenth century. In between there is the Grotian system in search of a balance between both elements.

1. *International Law as Reason:* Jus Gentium[271]

Jus gentium started out as a branch of Roman law. It was geared towards the relations of Roman citizens with foreigners and formed the transnational part of the Roman legal order. With the consolidation of the Empire, Rome came into close contact with many other peoples. Moreover, following the Punic Wars (264 BCE to 146 BCE), Mediterranean commerce started to develop. However, Roman civil law, like all ancient laws, was limited in its application to Roman citizens (the personality principle; it was not until 212 CE that all subjects of the Roman Empire would become citizens). It nevertheless proved impossible to leave others outside the reach and protection of the law. How could international commerce take place if no legally sanctioned contracts could be concluded between a Roman and a foreign citizen? Thus, Roman magistrates (*preator peregrinus*) developed a common law for all. It was—at least in spirit—founded on the common reason (*ratio naturalis*)[272] applicable to all people, since it could not pretend to be binding on foreigners if it were founded on the will of the Roman legislator alone. Thus, according to the famous Roman jurist Gaius, 'naturalis ratio inter omnes homines constituit, id apud omnes pereaque custoditur vocaturque ius gentium, quasi quo iure omnes gentes utuntur'.[273]

The formalism of Roman civil law was thus abandoned in favour of a law based on reason. Within *jus gentium*, recourse to justice, equity, teleological considerations, analogies and general principles was frequent. All these instruments are typically rational tools of the law. For example, the validity of contract was not based on the correct recitation of the ritual formulas (which were not accessible to non-Romans) but on faith in the promise deliberately given, ie on good faith. Through the *jus gentium* reform, Roman law could progressively elevate itself to the *ratio scripta* it was later perceived to be.

[271] M Kaser, *Ius gentium* (Cologne/Weimar, 1993). The proximity of *jus gentium* with natural law has remained to this day. See, eg, AA Cançado Trindade, 'La *recta ratio* dans les fondements du *Jus Gentium* comme droit international de l'humanité' in AA Cançado Trindade, *Le droit international de la personne humaine* (Paris, 2012) 91ff; AA Cançado Trindade, 'International Law for Humankind: Towards a New Jus Gentium' (2005) 316 *RCADI* 9ff.

[272] Cicero, *De legibus*, 2, 5, 13.

[273] *Dig*, 1, 1, 9 and *Institutiones*, 1, 1.

2. *International Law as Reason and Will: The Grotian System*

A cardinal aspect of the doctrine of Hugo Grotius is the articulated effort to find some equilibrium between reason and will within the edifice of classical international law. When the new continents were discovered and the unity of faith was broken through the Protestant Reformation, a common law could be based only on common reason. This is why Grotius, after a will-orientated phase in his younger days, placed the 'right reason' at the core of his *De jure belli ac pacis* (1625). From there flows natural law, that is, what right reason shows to conform to human nature. Grotius then pushed intellectualism to the point where he affirmed that God himself could not alter these precepts. However, he was also sensitive to empirical facts and effective practice. This is the domain of positive law. To an *a priori* knowledge of natural law through reason is added an *a posteriori* knowledge of positive norms through the common opinion of peoples manifested through their consent and practice. Natural law contains the fundamental precepts of social life; the voluntary law of nations spells out and fixes their content. The voluntary law of nations draws its binding force from the will of all peoples, or at least many of them.

As can be seen, Grotius created the basis for a synthetic doctrine of the law of nations, mid-way between speculation and empiricism, reason and will, idealism and reality.[274] This famous Dutch jurist influenced a whole school of thought following the path thus opened, notably Rachel, Wolff, de Vattel and de Martens.[275] This synthetic doctrine predominated over the Pufendorf school of thought, which reduced all international law to natural law.[276] The binding force of international law was founded by Pufendorf on the conscience of the ruler; and a positive international law was denied in the absence of a regular and centralised sanction.

3. *International Law as Will: Nineteenth-century Positivism*

Towards the end of the nineteenth century, positivism had entirely replaced natural law thinking. The latter remained present in the moral philosophy of law, ie outside legal science, but public international law was now construed as positive law of a distinct type. Municipal legal positivism had insisted upon the centralised sanction as the necessary hallmark of all law, but international law could not be based on such a centralised notion. Was it thus to be expelled from the realm of legal phenomena? Or was it simply a non-positive law? Is the latter not a contradiction in terms? The answer was to lay emphasis on the sources rather than on the sanction, ie on legal opinion rather than on institutions. International law could not be heteronomous: it could not be created by a centralised legislator and imposed on society. But it could be autonomous: it could be created by agreement

[274] See, eg, A Truyol y Serra, *Histoire du droit international public* (Paris, 1995) 58ff.
[275] *ibid*, 87ff.
[276] *ibid*, 86–87.

between equally sovereign entities. Objective international law thus flows from subjective legal acts and not subjective entitlements from objective law, as is the case in municipal law. The root of international law is subjective: the exercise of a will, which gives rise to consent, and thus to a binding rule between equals. International law represents the convergence of individual wills (self-limitation), or combined wills (consent, *Vereinbarung*) or superposed wills (the doctrine of common consent).[277] In sum, international law is a receptacle of agreements, based on a significant initial pact, that is, the agreement on the binding force of agreements: *pacta sunt servanda*. Agreements are the sole basis of international law, from its top (basis of obligation) to its bottom (sources of particular law). The coherence of the system is perfect. The most rigid positivists do not hesitate to draw drastic consequences from their premises: since a State does not exist before its recognition by other States (recognition being a manifestation of will), before such recognition it is lawful to invade its territory, annex it and massacre its population. This may be scorned politically, but it is legally unimpeachable.[278] Other consequences are often drawn too: a residual rule of freedom (the *Lotus* rule); a hostility to general principles of law (too reason-related); a hostility to analogies (extending the obligation beyond clear-cut consent); a hostility to objective or teleological interpretation and a preference for subjective and historical constructions; the reduction of customary international law to a tacit pact; the favour shown to the unanimity rule in decision-taking (respectful of equal autonomy); the preference for separatism between legal orders rather than monism; the reduction of many legal questions to questions of fact (was there intention or not?); the claim that international law is cast in an 'individualistic' environment so as to combat the extension of legal obligation;[279] the refusal of subjects of the law other than States, etc. Positivistic

[277] See A Truyol y Serra and R Kolb *Doctrines sur le fondement du droit des gens* (Paris, 2007) 59ff. For authors following such a doctrine most coherently in the 20th century, see, eg, D Anzilotti, *Droit international* (Paris, 1929); A Cavaglieri, *Lezioni di diritto internazionale* (Naples, 1925) 34ff; K Strupp, 'Les règles générales du droit de la paix' (1934-I) 47 *RCADI* 301. See also H Triepel, *Völkerrecht und Landesrecht* (Leipzig, 1899) 83–84. And see the famous decision in *SS Lotus* (1927) PCIJ Series A no 9, 18.

[278] A Cavaglieri, 'Règles générales du droit de la paix' (1929-I) 26 *RCADI* 348.

[279] Thus, it has been said that restrictions on the sovereignty of a State should be interpreted restrictively, or that the doctrine of abuse of rights cannot be countenanced in international law since it is an individualistic legal order. But what is not said is that if restrictions on the sovereignty of one State are interpreted restrictively, this is tantamount to encroaching upon the equal sovereignty of the other State. A legal relationship is bilateral: if I give more to the one, I take away from the other. Why should this be compatible with equal sovereignty? The same discussion has been conducted as regards the doctrine of abuse of rights. M Scerni, *L'abuso dei diritti nei rapporti internazionali* (Rome, 1930) sets out the basic argument (at 80): '[La regola che proibisce l'abuso dei diritti] ['The prohibition on the abuse of rights'] è certamente inaccettabile per l'organizzazione giuridica della vita internazionale tuttora informata al principio individualistico di libertà e di indipendenza' (Summarised in English: the unacceptability of the principle in a social environment based on individualism). The answer is proffered by G Salvioli, 'Les règles générales de la paix' (1933-IV) 46 *RCADI* 69: 'On parle de caractère individualiste, mais le rapport international est un rapport entre deux sujets. Auquel de ces deux sujets faut-il alors assigner la prépondérance quant à ce caractère individualiste? Pourquoi devrait-on affirmer le principe individualiste seulement en faveur d'une de ces Parties, le titulaire du droit?' (Summarised in English: Why should individualism apply only to the benefit of the holder of a right and not to the holder of the concomitant obligation?)

voluntarism is centered on the unchallengeable and supreme power of the sovereign. As has been aptly remarked, '[t]he essence of positive law is power'.[280]

We have already seen how, at the beginning of the twentieth century, there was a reaction against this reductionism of positivistic approaches (see the chapter on the 'Constitutionalisation of international Law'). International law was not to remain a purely instrumental law placed at the disposal of States for the formulation of their foreign policies. It was also to become a common law for common concerns; it was called on to develop a limb of general international law and not to remain a purely specific law, based on expressions of consent by changing numbers of States; it was finally to become a *Rechtsordnung* (legal order) and not to remain solely a *Rechtsgeschäftsordnung* (legal acts order). There is no point in returning to all these issues here.

4. *The Tempering of Will in Modern International Law*

It may be noted that modern international law has tempered the reach of its will-orientated limb. Here are some examples:

1. The paramount role of the principle of good faith is to limit the reach of the will and to instil some proper balance with regard to reason. Good faith is the 'anti-voluntarist' principle par excellence. It requires account to be taken not only of the true or possibly hidden intention of a subject, but also of how the other subjects parties to the legal interaction could and should have understood the relevant conduct. Their legitimate expectation is in certain cases legally protected. Thus, legal effects are attached to socially relevant conduct, even without the existence of a relevant or real intention. Good faith may, for example, apply to the conclusion of agreements, in the context of estoppel or elsewhere.[281]
2. The growth of international public order (namely *jus cogens*) has directly curbed the reach of the will. A legal expression of will can no longer have any object whatsoever. If the object of the agreement contravenes peremptory legal positions, it will be void. Thus, *jus cogens* limits the legal capacity to create voluntary norms of international law.
3. Lastly, it should be noted that tremendous progress has been made in the domain of the density of international law. In particular the growth of the 'international law of cooperation' has created a whole limb of the law informed more by social necessities than by arbitrary will.

The foregoing does not mean—by far—that the will disappears as a fundamental tool for shaping international law and adapting it to the changing concerns of States. The point is rather that the international law of the twentieth and twenty-first centuries has struggled to find a renewed and adapted balance between the two basic forces of the law discussed here. The journey is never over; it continues in perpetuity.

[280] Ortolan, quoted by E Creasy, *First Platform of International Law* (London, 1876) 14.

[281] See the many examples in R Kolb, *La bonne foi en droit international public* (Paris, 2000).

VIII. Sanctions

A. General Legal Experience[282]

Is the attachment of sanctions to legal rules a matter concerning the existence of the law (a normative question), or is it a matter concerned with the efficacy of the law (a factual question relating to its implementation and enforcement)? It would seem that sanctions are a matter relating to the realisation of the law. From this perspective, they seem to be external to the notion of law but linked to its practice. Historical evolution has over many centuries kicked against this duality. The existence of sanctions became the hallmark of the law itself for certain doctrines. The primary function of the modern State was to consolidate an order formerly troubled by endemic private (private justice) and public (religious) warfare. If law was to maintain order and to constrain social actors, it had perforce to become a vector of real power and effective authority. Thus, the law was progressively identified with the command of the sovereign enforced by the sword. The whole body of the law became positive and subject to sanctions for breach; a non-positive or non-sanctioned law was no longer considered to be law. The peaceful order so longed for depended on this primary fact: the effective capacity of the State to impose the rules, if necessary through sanctions.

This 'guarantee' function of modern law has made the sanction a non-dissociable element of the notion of law. A legal order or a norm regularly breached by the social actors without a sanctioned consequence is expelled from the realm of the law. But there remain many questions. What exactly is a 'legal sanction'? Does it refer only to centralised sanctions meted out through an organised procedure? And is it the effectiveness of the sanction or the possibility of a sanction that is the deciding factor? A brief historical overview of the question of sanctions may be helpful. The following aspects are shown by a study of European history:

1. Until relatively recent times (the sixteenth to eighteenth centuries), sanctions were not part of the concept of law. Law was defined through its sources and its finality (justice) rather than through its efficacy or its sanctions. This way of thinking flowed from the time-honoured predominance of finalistic over causal thinking. The whole realisation of the law was for many centuries perceived as a meta-juridical fact. A profound change occurred only in the sixteenth century with the emergence of the modern State and thinkers such as Spinoza, Hobbes, Pufendorf, Thomasius, Kant and Fichte.

[282] See, eg, R Zippelius, *Rechtsphilosophie* (Munich, 1982) 34ff; H Henkel, *Einführung in die Rechtsphilosophie*, 2nd edn (Munich, 1977) 117ff; HLA Hart, *The Concept of Law* (Oxford, 1961) 188ff; CA Morand, 'La sanction' (1990) 35 *Archives de philosophie du droit* 293ff; Faculté de droit et des sciences sociales de Poitiers (ed), *La sanction du droit* (Paris, 2001).

2. As a meta-legal phenomenon, the realisation of the law was largely left, in the Middle Ages, to the subjects of the law, ie in the domain of private justice. This state of affairs often led to private wars. In a broad sense, private wars and reprisals were methods of legal sanction. Notwithstanding all their imperfections and abuses, they served to enforce the law. Private war was progressively subjected to rules. However, it was never considered a fully-fledged legal means. It largely remained a violent fact, which the legal order tolerated at best.
3. The rise of the importance of sanctions was a direct function of the strengthening of State structures, that is, of the vertical element of the law. When superior organs entrusted with legal authority were created, the concept of the sanction tended to become legalised. This was also the case in ancient Rome. Conversely, in a horizontal society deprived of superior organs, the concept of the sanction remained underdeveloped. This can be seen from the life of the Germanic clans in the early Middle Ages. In analytical terms, it can be said that in a centralised society the sanction is a legal phenomenon, whereas in a decentralised society it tends to remain an extra-legal element leading, however, to some efficacy of the law. The first type of legal order tends to focus on efficacy of the norms, the latter remains concentrated on the creation of norms. For the first, sanctions are a necessary complement, for the second they tend to be an excessively ambitious tool. From there flows the extraordinary ambiguity of the concept of sanctions in coordinative legal orders: on the one hand, they are an essential element for some minimum degree of realisation of the law; but on the other hand, their exercise increases the anarchy within the legal order and attacks social peace.

In the course of historical evolution, the following steps and epochs can be recalled:

1. In primitive societies, the law was not clearly distinguished from other social norms.[283] A series of legal historians have maintained that sanctions were essential even in such primitive legal settings. They accepted, however, the enlargement of the notion of sanctions to cover decentralised responses, such as reprisals and countermeasures.[284] For others, a sanction was, even in those times, only an external element strengthening the legal rule, together with other factors such as the consciousness of being legally bound.[285] Other authors laid stress on the existence of primitive institutions for guaranteeing the imposition of sanctions, such as tribunals, councils of elders, and so on.[286] In all these conceptions, sanctions were and remain fundamental to the concept of law. However, they can be defined in a broader way than is usual within

[283] And yet it was law. On the issue, see AR Radcliffe-Brown, 'Primitive Law' in AR Radcliffe-Brown, *Structure and Function in Primitive Society* (London, 1952) 212. See also U Wesel, *Frühformen des Rechts in vorstaatlichen Gesellschaften* (Frankfurt, 1985).

[284] EA Hoebel, *The Law of Primitive Man* (Cambridge, Mass, 1954) 26.

[285] L Pospisil, *Anthropology of Law—A Comparative Theory* (New York, 1971), Chapter 3.

[286] B Cardozo, *The Growth of the Law* (New Haven/London/Oxford 1924) 31ff, emphasising the role of the general body of doctrine and tradition coalescing in judgments of tribunals.

a modern State, not as comprising a procedurally organised mechanism but as empowering a reaction in case of breach of the law. In a sense, this view of sanctions refers back to the binding nature of the norm. The binding nature of the rule suggests some consequences; it implies that the aggrieved party will react in some way. Overall, it may be said that consciousness of the obligatory character of the law still seems more important at this stage in history than the organisation of special procedures for sanctioning.

2. Roman law presents an example of a legal order in which the concept of sanctions grew in parallel to the consolidation of State power. In primitive Rome, the private element predominated over the public one. Family and clans were at the core of social power. Legal sanctions thus rested on private justice. However, from the times of the Twelve Tables (in the fifth century BCE), parties to a dispute could agree to arbitration. Progressively, this arbitral function was exercised by special magistrates coming from the sacral-religious orders. They developed legal actions (*legis actiones*) to which the citizens could subject themselves by *litis contestatio*. The procedure led to a judgment. The execution of the judgment remained, however, a private matter: for example, through the *manus iniectio*, a creditor would seize hold of the debtor and take him to his (the creditor's) home; if the judgment was not implemented within 60 days, the captive could be killed or sold as a slave; alternatively, the debtor might work to pay off his debt. If objects were the subject of litigation, the magistrate might allow the creditor to seize them. The recourse to judges became mandatory in the course of the third century BCE, at a time when the power of the State consolidated. A new judicial procedure developed. The execution of the judgment mainly focused on seizing objects belonging to the debtor and selling them in order to liquidate the debt when its repayment was not made within a given period (*venditio bonorum*). With the advent of the Empire, the State increasingly imposed a procedure to be followed at imperial tribunals (*cognition extra ordinem*). By the time of Diocletian and Constantine (third to fourth centuries CE), this procedure was firmly established. The execution of judgments was carried out by imperial staff (*exsecutores*) acting on behalf of the State. The whole process now involved public law.[287]

3. In the Middle Ages, power was split up into innumerable jurisdictions. Thus, the question of sanctions tended to return to the private sphere. But the strong propensity of the Germanic peoples to think in terms of law[288] led to the application of rules for limiting the deleterious effects of private wars (*faida*, *inimicitia*). An unlawful act created a duty of vengeance, imposed on the whole clan of the injured subject. Arbitral procedures were known, and

[287] On this evolution of Roman law, see M Kaser, *Römische Rechtsgeschichte*, 2nd edn (Göttingen, 1982); G Dulckeit, F Schwarz and W Waldstein, *Römische Rechtsgeschichte*, 8th edn (Munich, 1989).

[288] F Kern, *Recht und Verfassung im Mittelalter* (Basle, 1953). See also H Mitteis and H Lieberich, *Deutsche Rechtsgeschichte*, 17th edn (Munich, 1985).

the award could be executed through private justice. The party not honouring his obligations would be expelled from his clan and could be killed by anyone; his goods and objects could be seized by the injured party. This system was brushed aside by the consolidating Frankish Empire. A public procedure took its place. The judge had the power to impose his jurisdiction through the threat of sanctions (*bannitio*). The judgment handed down was liable to be executed through State organs. Any measure taken under the flag of private justice had to be authorised by the judge. The seizing of property was effected by a State official (*grafio*). With the weakening of the Empire, the domain of anarchic private justice came to the fore once again. Reprisals became a means to execute the law, as well as a means to fulfil criminal enterprises (there were those who provoked incidents on purpose, so as to be allowed to proceed to private justice through their private armies, with the aim of enrichment). There were attempts to limit the violence provoked by these reprisals and wars, but they were not very effective.[289]

4. The modern State placed the concept of sanctions at its core. The endemic legal uncertainty and violence of the Middle Ages resulted in a significant shift towards certain and efficacious law. Spinoza,[290] Hobbes[291] and later Pufendorf[292] insisted on there being an element of sanction. This position was also taken by many subsequent authors: Thomasius,[293] Kant,[294] Fichte,[295] Rousseau[296] and others.[297] The law now tended to be defined by and through the presence of sanctions: no law without sanction. The decentralised reprisals had created so much confusion that they were no longer considered a legal tool to ensure respect for the rule but rather as an excuse for private violence.
5. In the twentieth century, the question of sanctions gave rise to different ways of thinking: for some, they remained an element essential to the existence of law (eg del Vecchio); for others, the consciousness of being legally obligated was sufficient for the existence of a legal rule (eg Bierling); for yet others, the concept of the sanction was enlarged to cover all sort of reactions to unlawful acts, including reprisals and war (eg Kelsen); for still others, the sanction was

[289] See an example in A Erler, E Kaufmann and D Werkmüller (eds), *Handwörterbuch zur deutschen Rechtsgeschichte*, vol 5 (Berlin, 1998) 1029. On reprisals, see the main treatise of that time: Bartolus, *On Reprisals* in *Consilia, Quaestiones et Tractatus* (Lyon, 1547).

[290] B Spinoza, *Tractatus theologico-politicus* (1670), XVI.

[291] T Hobbes, *De cive* (1642), *Leviathan* (1651), Prefaces. See also M Luther, *Von weltlicher Obrigkeit* (1523).

[292] S Pufendorf, *De iure naturae et gentium* (1672), lib I, cap II, 6; lib II, cap VI.

[293] C Thomasius, *Fundamenta iuris naturae et gentium* (1705), lib I, cap V, para XXI, 'At vero obligatio iuri correspondens semper externa est, metuens coactionem aliorum hominum.'

[294] I Kant, *Metaphysics of Morals* (1797), 'Introduction to the Doctrine of Law', letter D.

[295] JG Fichte *Fondement du droit naturel* (1796), sect III, ch II, §13ff.

[296] JJ Rousseau *Contrat social* (1762), I, 7.

[297] Eg J Austin, *Lectures on Jurisprudence or the Philosophy of Positive Law*, vol I, 5th edn (London, 1885) 79ff.

a pure element of fact external to the legal order (eg Marcic); and lastly, some considered that the sanction was not constitutive of the law but, if completely absent, would deprive a rule of its positivity (eg Henkel).[298]

So what is a legal sanction? Different terms are used: sanction (connoting the means of realisation of the law in general, or an institutional mechanism created to react to violations of the law); coercion (connoting the physical or moral force exerted on the violator of the norm so that he will repair his wrongdoing and abstain from violating the law again); execution (connoting either the real chance to see the realisation of a norm in social conduct or the means conducive to that); or even coercibility (concerning the possibility to exercise constraint). There is thus a constant fluctuation between the normative and the factual element, between the realisation of the law and the threat of its realisation. There also remains a doubt as to the means to be adopted in applying sanctions. Only centralised devices? Spontaneous social reactions? Reprisals? We may here briefly consider certain issues:

1. *Sanction as a norm or as a fact?* For normative legal theories, the law is based on the unconditional will to impose itself, ie on the obligatory character of the norm. The sanction remains an external adjunct to this end. If the sanction were the distinctive element of the law, each norm providing for a sanction would in its turn have to be protected by a further norm providing for a sanction, and so on *ad infinitum*. It is added that those theories placing the sanction at the core of the legal phenomenon are prone to become power theories. The essential element of the law is then perceived in the hammer to be swung in case of breach rather than in the norm directing human affairs in the first place. From this perspective, norms are themselves part of the sanction: for example, the rules on the international responsibility of States, the duty to make reparation, etc. For other theories, the sanction must be looked at under the guise of effectiveness, ie as a fact. This position is expressed in an emblematic way by the Uppsala School of law. An intermediate position has also been developed: it refers to the coercibility of the law. The sanction lies mid-way between the norm and the fact: it is a normative fact, ie conduct that is foreseeable. A legal norm supposes the possibility to use constraint. But it does not suppose that the constraint will really be exercised. The ability to exercise constraint varies according to the branch of the law, the type of obligation, etc. In a slightly different formulation, the law is characterised by a tendency to have recourse to constraint. The sanction should remain the *ultima ratio*; other means to induce respect have to be tried first.
2. *Sanction solely as a legal fact, or also as a social fact?* Are legal sanctions only those organised and channelled through legal procedures? Or can other social pressure in favour of implementation be added? The State-centred authors

[298] On the whole question, see H Henkel, *Einführung in die Rechtsphilosophie*, 2nd edn (Munich, 1977) 117ff.

admit only the former option; but other authors take the broader view, to the extent that it allows effective realisation of the norm at stake.[299] In particular, reprisals are added to the panoply of the sanctioning mechanisms.[300] In this latter view, sanctions are not the monopoly of the State. It is essentially in the realm of international law that this broader view is of paramount importance. It allows to international law to be presented as 'sanctioned law', however imperfect the process may be.

3. *Sanction attached to any single norm or to the legal system as a whole?* For some authors, a legal norm to which no sanction is attached is denied legal status.[301] Such a norm would automatically become a solely moral one. It imposes an obligation only through conscience. Such a view is excessively narrow. It stands to reason that there are certain norms—the inclusion of which in the legal system cannot seriously be contested—for breach of which no specific sanction is levied, or indeed can be levied. This is the case, for example, as regards a series of constitutional law norms, situated at the apex of the system. Their breach could be sanctioned only by a revolution or by civil disobedience. And even *leges imperfectae* are not necessarily non-legal: for example, so-called 'natural obligations' are essentially moral obligations, but the legal order recommends them. They are thus not legally irrelevant. The better view is to consider that sanctions must attach to the legal order as a whole, that is, to a significant number of its norms. If too many norms are breached too many times with too few legal consequences, the legal order will suffer from a low degree of effectiveness, and in extreme cases may lose its positivity.[302] The exact threshold of required effectiveness varies from subject matter to subject matter, and from legal order to legal order.

B. The Sanction in International Law[303]

The weakness of sanctions in international law is regularly put forward as a topic for debate. The issue of sanctions has principally been used in judging the law's existence; or as a promise for its evolution; and lastly as an expression of its structure. Thus, there are three schools of thought: (i) the absence of proper sanctions

[299] See, eg, G Jellinek, *Allgemeine Staatslehre*, 3rd edn (Berlin, 1914) 337.

[300] See notably H Kelsen, 'Unrecht und Unrechtsfolge im Völkerrecht' (1932) 12 *Zeitschrift für öffentliches Recht* 481ff.

[301] See, eg, W Burckhardt, *Einführung in die Rechtswissenschaft* (Zurich, 1939) 163ff.

[302] H Henkel, *Einführung in die Rechtsphilosophie*, 2nd edn (Munich, 1977) 121.

[303] For some earlier literature, see, eg, MS Kebedgy, *Contribution à l'étude de la sanction du droit international* (Brussels, 1897); J Cabral, *The Sanction of International Law* (The Hague, 1916); O Brück, *Les sanctions en droit international public* (Paris, 1933); J Lambert, *La vengeance privée et les fondements du droit international public* (Paris, 1936). For more recent literature, see the overview in A Pellet and A Miron, 'Sanctions' in R Wolfrum (ed), *The Max Planck Encyclopedia of Public International Law*, vol IX (Oxford, 2012) 1ff, with an extensive bibliography.

as a reason for the non-existence of international law as law; (ii) the weakness of its sanctions as a reason to see in international law only a law *in fieri*; and (iii) the organisation of sanctions in international law as a reason to qualify international law as being different. Each of these is examined in further detail below:

1. *Existential argument: absence of sanction as non-existence.* This argument is well-known and often canvassed; we may thus be brief. For a series of authors, there is no law without a regular legislator, judge and enforcer. Thus, the law exists only within the State. International law is a misnomer. It has no organised sanctioning mechanism at its disposal. Consequently, it is either a positive morality or a sort of rational (natural) law, but not a positive law. Ultimately, it is no law at all. This conception was espoused by Spinoza and Hobbes. States live in a state of nature, not in a civil society with its legal rules. The so-called rules of international law obligate rulers only through their conscience. This position was later developed within the science of international law by Pufendorf, who refers to Hobbes.[304] The lack of sanctions lies at the heart of his system.[305] Relating to external conduct, international law is, however, not a simple morality. It is a system of natural law, not of positive law.[306] This conception has since been defended by many authors, such as Austin,[307] Burckhardt[308] and Somló.[309] The problem with all these constructions is that they are based on logical *a priori* considerations. The main criticism brought against these wonderfully coherent doctrines is therefore that they neglect experience. The State legal order may perhaps be considered the most perfect legal achievement, but law has never been the monopoly of the State. Legal phenomena existed before the State and continue to exist outside the State. The 'sanction' is organised differently according to social context. To use this difference in order to deny the legal character of international law is nothing more than a dogmatic *petitio principii*.[310]

[304] S Pufendorf, *De iure naturae et gentium* (1672), lib II, cap III, 23: 'Nec praetera aliud ius gentium voluntarium seu positivum arbitramur, quod quidem legis propriae dictae vim habeat, quae gentes tamquam a superiore profecta stingat.'

[305] *ibid*, lib I, cap II, 6; lib II, cap VI.

[306] *ibid*, lib II, cap III, 23.

[307] J Austin, *Lectures on Jurisprudence or the Philosophy of Positive Law*, vol I, 5th edn (London, 1885) 79ff.

[308] W Burckhardt, *Die Organisation der Rechtsgemeinschaft* (Basle, 1927) 374ff.

[309] F Somló, *Juristische Grundlehre*, 2nd edn (Leipzig, 1927) 153ff, 167ff.

[310] See also the remark by E Giraud, 'De la valeur et des rapports des notions—De droit et de politique dans l'ordre international' (1922) 29 *RGDIP* 513, 'le droit est une croyance. Ce qui fait sa force, comme celle de toutes les croyances, c'est le nombre et la valeur des adhésions qu'il recueille. La contrainte qui sanctionne le droit n'est pas la cause première de son autorité; cette cause, c'est la croyance en la justice et l'utilité de la règle de droit chez la plupart de ceux qu'elle régit. Le développement du droit international, comme celui du droit interne, est une œuvre de propagande.' ('Law is a belief. What gives it force, as with all beliefs, is the number and quality of its adherents. The sanction of the law is not the first cause of its authority. This cause lies in the belief in justice and utility of the rule for most of the persons subjected to it. The development of international law, like that of municipal law, is an exercise in seeking to convince.')

2. *Evolutionary argument: weakness of sanctions accounting for an international law in making.* A legal order well provided with sanctions, such as municipal law is meant to be, remains for a series of authors the ideal to be attained. But the fact that international law does not reach such standards does not mean that it is not law. It shows, however, that international law is still evolving, remaining to some extent in its infancy. In a sense, international law must be perceived as being in transit from an imperfect legal system to a progressively more perfect one. This occurs through the development of sanctioning mechanisms. That may take time, as it took time in municipal societies. This evolutionary view has been presented by many legal philosophers,[311] but also by some eminent international lawyers.[312] The response to this theory has been given in the chapter on the so-called primitive character of international law. The different organisation of international law sanctions is not so much an expression of any deficiency as an expression of the difference of the societies being regulated. In a decentralised society, sanctions may progress within some institutional settings, but they can never become like sanctions within a State—unless we live in a world State.
3. *Structural argument: the organisation of sanctions as a reason to perceive international law as a different law.* According to this view, international law and municipal law regulate different societies. The different organisation of their sanctioning mechanisms is but a reflection of this state of affairs.[313] This modest and realistic argument is difficult to rebut.

In conclusion, a series of factors influencing the realisation of international law and its sanctions may be mentioned:

1. International law concentrates more on its sources than on its sanctions.[314] The latter are left to State organs or to political procedures.
2. International law utilises indistinct and pluralistic sanctions, ranging from UN Security Council decisions to countermeasures, from legal procedures to economic, social, cultural or political pressures, or to the pressure of public opinion. It sometimes includes normative opinions, such as the duty to make reparation, non-recognition, deprivation of membership advantages, systems of control, etc.[315]

[311] See, eg, I Vanni, *Filosofia del diritto* (Bologna, 1920) 81; G del Vecchio, *Lezioni di filosofia del diritto*, 3rd edn (Rome, 1936) 230ff; W Schönfeld, *Die logische Struktur der Rechtsordnung* (Leipzig, 1927) 56; H Ryffel, *Rechts- und Staatsphilosophie* (Neuwied/Berlin, 1969) 188. See also the private international lawyer E Zitelmann, *Die Unvollkommenheit des Völkerrechts* (Munich/Leipzig, 1919).

[312] See mainly H Lauterpacht, 'Règles générales du droit de la paix' (1937-IV) 62 *RCADI* 118–21.

[313] See, eg, A Truyol y Serra, 'Théorie du droit international' (1981-IV) 173 *RCADI* 118.

[314] For a long time, ie up to the First World War, the issue of sanctions was hardly perceived as deserving of special treatment in international law. The basic presumption was that a sovereign State would 'obviously' honour its obligations. It was only at the time of the 'scrap of paper' doctrine (see Ch 6, n 12) that a change in legal consciousness occurred. See, eg, O Nippold, *Die Gestaltung des Völkerrechts nach dem Weltkriege* (Zurich, 1917) 34ff. But there were still authors who maintained the old view of the marginal position of sanctions in international law: JW Garner, 'le développement et les tendances récentes du droit international' (1931-I) 35 *RCADI* 711.

[315] See L Forlati Picchio, *La sanzione nel diritto internazionale* (Padua, 1974) 20ff.

3. The implementation of many rules of international law is achieved through State organs. In most cases, this occurs without any difficulty. The risk lies, however, in a *détournement de but*, the pursuit of national interests under the guise of implementation of international law. If both notions are compatible, the alliance is perfect; if the former differs from the latter, there is sometimes the risk of abuse.
4. International law sanctions are not based on objective qualification by a tribunal or some other international organ. In most cases, they remain based on the self-judging attitudes of States. The risk here is that the sanctioning mechanisms may dissolve into larger political action. The concomitant tendency towards selectivity undermines the effort to achieve impersonal application of the law.
5. As in every decentralised society, the sanctions remain embedded in a political process and in a series of discretionary powers granted by the law. These instruments may be used by an aggrieved State, but they can also be forgone or neglected. Consequently, sanctions often remain simply an option for the aggrieved party. The situation is different when an organ of an international institution is obliged to take some measures under its Statute in the event of the breach of some rule. In such a decentralised environment, the sanctioning function cannot be entirely legalised. More than in a centralised, rule of law-orientated society, the question remains one of (legal) policy. The sanction is hardly founded on the law, but it can at least be possibly limited through law.
6. Since international law cannot rule out decentralised countermeasures, the attempt must be to impose legal limits. This has been done with the rules of the International Law Commission on State Responsibility (2001), in Articles 49ff.[316]
7. Sanctions under international law are often long-term enterprises. Their effectiveness must be measured in the medium or long run (a dimension not on the radar of the daily press). It may take years or decades to undo apartheid or unlawful annexations (eg the Baltic States).
8. A great problem in this context is linked to the inroad made by international politics into the realm of sanctions, and to the absence of a 'veil of ignorance' regarding the situations at stake. If an academic exercise is carried out in which no concrete States are named but only State A and State B are referred to, almost all legal analysts will agree that State A is responsible for breach of the laws of war and of the prohibition on aggression when some sort of annexation is abstractly described and a type of unregulated warfare is posited. Probably the only condition is that the facts as described do not too closely mirror some real situation in the world, or do not re-enact that real-life situation too obviously. However, if we replace the abstract labels 'State A'

[316] For discussion, see, eg, J Crawford, *State Responsibility* (Cambridge, 2014) 684ff.

and 'State B' with the names of actual States, and the events described with hard facts of international life, prejudice, interests, allegiances, political considerations and the like can affect the analysts' reasoning to such a point that the law is often marginalised. Thus, if State A is Russia, China, Israel or the US, we may immediately witness a mind-shift, even of readers of the present text. A series of considerations alien to the 'pure application of legal norms' then enters into play. Thus, for example, the ICJ may have given a proper representation of international law in the *Wall* Opinion of 2004,[317] and most Israelis would have utterly agreed with that Opinion if the Occupying Power had been their enemy; but they cannot bring themselves to so agree when their State is subject to international scrutiny and criticism. This state of affairs diminishes the capacity of the international law on sanctions to gain firmer ground in international society.

9. Lastly, we might mention in passing that the extraordinary doctrinal multiplicity in questions of international law, ie the existence of many contrasting and opposing constructions of the relevant legal duties, even in core areas of international law like that on the use of force and self-defence,[318] may excite the scientific spirit but at the same time weaken the force of the international legal order, its effectiveness and the capacity of its proper sanctioning. If the impression is that most constructions are possible, and are indeed defended by eminent lawyers, this fact gives wrongdoers an easy way to try to justify their actions, and at the same time a greater scope for confidently asserting, if those actions are ultimately made subject to sanctions, that the meting out of the sanctions was not made under legal considerations but merely followed a political logic. Neither path really leads to a strengthening of international law. However, and obviously, there is no easy way out of that quagmire. The contrasting positions under the law reflect deeply entrenched convictions and interests of different States or persons, and they cannot simply be crushed under the hammer of some dictatorial mainstream.

Overall, we may note the considerable extension of the domain of sanctions and control mechanisms in international law over the last 50 years. Most important treaties today contain implementation and control mechanisms, for example the human rights treaties or the Convention on the Ban of Chemical Weapons of 1993, or the Paris Convention on Climate Change (2015). The Security Council

[317] *Legal Consequences of the Construction of a Wall in the Occupied Palestinian Territory* [2004-I] ICJ Rep 136ff.

[318] Compare, eg, the legal positions of DW Bowett, *Self-Defense in International Law* (Manchester, 1958) and I Brownlie, *International Law and the Use of Force by States* (Oxford, 1963); or, more recently, the positions of S Sur, 'La créativité du droit international, Cours général de droit international public' (2012) 363 *RCADI* 257ff and O Corten, *Le droit contre la guerre*, 2nd edn (Paris, 2014). On many subtle questions with regard to self-defence, see T Ruys, *'Armed Attack' and Article 51 of the UN Charter* (Cambridge, 2010).

of the UN has adopted innumerable measures under Chapter VII of its Charter. Schemes for responsibility, such as the UN Compensation Commission for Iraq,[319] have been adopted. The international criminal courts have opened the way for an international criminal sanctions regime. Far removed from the lofty theoretical debates, these realities impose themselves on the critical observer. They may in themselves be imperfect, but they cannot be called wholly ineffective.

[319] On the UNCC, see, eg, JA Crook, 'The UN Compensation Commission: A New Structure to Enforce State Responsibility' (1993) 87 *AJIL* 144ff; RB Lillich (ed), *The United Nations Compensation Commission* (New York, 1995); V Jütte, *Die United Nations Compensation Commission* (Bern/Frankfurt, 1999).

General Conclusion

There is no point in trying to sum up the long journey undertaken in this monograph. Two contrasting reflections can be proffered as a farewell.

First, if one takes account of all the specificities and the hostile environment engendered by the sovereignty of States for a fully-fledged legal order, international law is an astonishing realisation of the human spirit and forms an amazing bedrock of undeletable reality. Its system is so well-tailored to the environment in which it has to perform, its doctrine of sources, responsibility, relations with internal legal orders and the settlement of disputes so perfectly articulated with its real possibilities, that a close look at the matter should elicit not the usual derision shown by the man in the street but admiration. For millennia, some form of international law has been with us; it has grown and suffered defeat, but it has persisted and will remain. The power of States may dislike it in certain circumstances, but it also needs its legal fabric. And so international law is a fact, as an instrument for use, but also as a norm for compliance.

Secondly, the greatest problem of international law remains the lack of balance between the private law layer and the public law layer, ie between the individual element of coexistence and the community element of common action over common concerns. The former remains overdeveloped. This reflects the structure of international society, based on sovereign States considered as almost self-sufficient political bodies. Conversely, the latter remains underdeveloped, sometimes to a dramatic degree: it has to fight uphill to try to create international rules of common concern through the burdensome process of consent, and then to realise international institutions to control and guarantee common cause-orientated implementation. True, the goal cannot be to deprive peoples of their independence and of the greater efficacy of local rule. However, if humanity wants to avoid obsolescence it must find some way or other to increase the 'common good' limb of international law, that is, to give greater normative density to it and to ensure its proper implementation through adequate international organs. The domains of necessity and freedom constantly need to be adjusted, as it were: *in necessariis unitas, in dubiis libertas* … In view of the ever more urgent common concerns regarding the survival of Man on this blue planet, the time has come for a new attempt at a better delimitation of the respective spheres of action, the 'me' and the 'we'. International justice, cooperation, common interest and other notions are not simply hollow terms;[1] they are now increasingly lit by the flames of urgency and necessity. In view of humanity's inability, from the dawn of civilisation, to respond in any adequate way to these basic precepts, its destiny has been to endure the eternal torment of conflict, disorder and fear.

[1] As was said by Jacques Maritain at the General Conference of UNESCO in 1947: '[Il est nécessaire] que les esprits arrivent à se persuader profondément de principes tels que les suivants: qu'une bonne politique est d'abord et avant tout une politique juste; que chaque peuple doit s'appliquer à comprendre la psychologie, le développement et les traditions, les besoins matériels et moraux, la dignité propre et la vocation historique des autres peuples, parce que chaque peuple doit avoir en vue non seulement son propre avantage, mais aussi le bien commun de la famille des nations; que cet éveil de la compréhension mutuelle et du sens de la communauté civilisée, s'il suppose, étant donné, hélas, les habitudes séculaires de l'histoire humaine, une sorte de révolution spirituelle, répond à une nécessité de salut public dans un monde qui désormais est un pour la vie ou pour la mort tout en restant désastreusement divisé quant aux intérêts et passions politiques; que placer l'intérêt national au-dessus de tout est le moyen le plus sûr pour tout perdre; qu'une communauté d'hommes libres n'est pas concevable s'il n'y est pas reconnu que la vérité est l'expression de ce qui est, le droit, de ce qui est juste—et non pas de ce qui sert le mieux à un moment donné l'intérêt …' See UNESCO (ed), *Paix sur la terre, Anthologie de paix* (Paris, 1980) 204.

SELECTED READING

The present selected reading list does not include all the many monographs and articles quoted in the footnotes. Neither does it include the many manuals and digests of international law. Rather, it provides the reader with some guidance as to interesting works reflecting on the state of international law in general at a given time or from an historical perspective. It is far from being complete; it is based on a personal choice. Only monographs, and not articles, are listed. Some newer or important monographs on international relations have been included, but the list remains centered on international law studies.

Ago R, *Caratteri generali e origine storiche della Comunità internazionale e del suo diritto*, Naples, 2002.

——, *Scienza giuridica e diritto internazionale*, Milan, 1950.

Allot P, *Eunomia: New Order for a New World*, Oxford, 2001.

Alting von Geusau FAM, *Neither Justice nor Order: Reflections on the State of the Law of Nations*, Nijmegen, 2014.

Alvarez A, *Le droit international nouveau—son acceptation, son étude*, Paris, 1960.

——, *Le droit international nouveau dans ses rapports avec la vie actuelle des peuples*, Paris, 1959.

——, *Exposé des motifs et déclaration des grands principes du droit international moderne*, Paris, 1936.

Americano J, *The New Foundation of International Law*, New York, 1947.

Anand RP (ed), *Asian States and the Development of Universal International Law*, Delhi, 1972.

Anghie A, *Imperialism, Sovereignty and the Making of International Law*, Cambridge, 2005.

——, Chimni BS, Mickelson K and Okafor O, *The Third World and International Legal Order: Law. Politics and Globalization*, Leiden, 2003.

Apostolidis C, *Doctrines juridiques et droit international*, Paris, 1991.

Asser Institute (ed), *International Law and the Grotian Heritage*, The Hague, 1985.

Bargiacchi P, *Contributo all studio die fattori giuridici e politici dell'ordine internazionale*, Milan, 2003.

Beck RJ, Arend AC and Van der Lugt RD (eds), *International Rules: Approaches from International Law and International Relations*, New York/Oxford, 1996.

Baty T, *International Law in Twilight*, Tokyo, 1954.

Bederman DJ, *Globalization and International Law*, New York, 2008.

——, *The Spirit of International Law*, Athens, 2002.

——, *International Law in Antiquity*, Cambridge, 2001.

Ben Achour Y, *Le rôle des civilisations dans le système international, Droit et relations internationales*, Brussels, 2003.

Berman PS (ed), *The Globalization of International Law*, Aldershot, 2005.
Besson S and Tasioulas J (eds), *The Philosophy of International Law*, Oxford, 2010.
Betti E, *Problematica del diritto internazionale*, Milan, 1956.
Bleckmann A, *Allgemeine Staats- und Völkerrechtslehre: Vom Kompetenz- zum Kooperationsvölkerrecht*, Cologne, 1995.
——, *Grundprobleme und Methoden des Völkerrechts*, Freiburg/Munich, 1982.
——, *Die Funktionen der Lehre im Völkerrecht, Materialien zu einer allgemeinen Methoden- und Völkerrechtslehre*, Cologne, 1980.
Bobbio N, *The Age of Rights*, Cambridge, 2001.
Boisson de Chazournes L (ed), *International Law and the Quest for its Implementation*, Leiden, 2010.
Bos M, *A Methodology of International Law*, Amsterdam, 1984.
Bourquin M, *L'Etat souverain et l'organisation internationale*, New York, 1959.
Boyle A and Chinkin C, *The Making of International Law*, Oxford, 2007.
Boyle FA, *Destroying World Order*, Atlanta, 2004.
——, *The Future of International Law and American Foreign Policy*, Dobbs Ferry (New York), 1989.
Bozeman AB, *The Future of International Law in a Multicultural World*, Princeton, 1971.
Brierly JL, *The Basis of Obligation in International Law and Other Papers*, Oxford, 1958.
——, *The Outlook for International Law*, Oxford, 1944.
Brown SJ, *The Spanish Origin of International Law: Francisco de Vitoria and his Law of Nations*, London, 1934.
Brownlie I, *The Rule of Law in International Affairs*, The Hague, 1998.
Bull H, *The Anarchical Society: A Study of Order in World Politics*, 3rd edn, New York, 2002.
Brunée J and Toope SJ, *Legitimacy and Legality in International Law*, Cambridge, 2010.
Buzan B and Little R, *International Systems in World History*, Oxford, 2000.
Byers M (ed), *The Role of International Law in International Politics*, Oxford, 2000.
Byers M and Nolte G, *United States Hegemony and the Foundations of International Law*, Cambridge, 2003.
Cançado Trindade AA, *International Law for Humankind: Towards a New Jus Gentium*, Leiden/Boston, 2010.
——, *Evolution du droit international au droit des gens*, Paris, 2008.
——, *A Humanizaçao do direito internacional*, Belo Horizonte, 2006.
Carty A, *Philosophy of International Law*, Edinburgh, 2007.
——, *The Decay of International Law? A Reappraisal of the Limits of Legal Imagination in International Affairs*, Manchester, 1986.
Cassese A (ed), *Realizing Utopia: The Future of International Law*, Oxford, 2012.
——, *International Law in a Divided World*, Oxford, 1986.
—— and Gaeta P, *Le sfide attuali del diritto internazionale*, Bologna, 2008.
Cheng B, *International Law: Teaching and Practice*, London, 1982.
Cheng TH, *When International Law Works*, Oxford, 2012.
Cimbali G, *Dall'anarchia internazionale alla dichiarazione dei diritti die popoli*, Florence, 1920.
Clark G and Sohn LB, *World Peace Through World Law*, 3rd edn, Cambridge, Mass, 1966.
Clark I, *International Legitimacy and World Society*, Oxford, 2007.
Claude IL, *Swords into Plowshares*, 4th edn, New York, 1971.
Collins R, *The Institutional Problem in Modern International Law*, Oxford, 2015.
Conforti B, *International Law and the Role of Domestic Legal Systems*, Dordrecht, 1993.

Coplin WD, *The Functions of International Law*, Chicago, 1966.
Corbett PE, *The Growth of World Law*, Princeton, 1971.
——, *Law in Diplomacy*, Princeton, 1959.
Corten O, *Méthodologie du droit international public*, Brussels, 2009.
Craven M, Fitzmaurice M and Vogiatzi M (eds), *Time, History and International Law*, Leiden, 2007.
Crawford J and Koskenniemi M (eds), *The Cambridge Companion to International Law*, Cambridge, 2012.
Creveld M van, *The Rise and Decline of the State*, Cambridge, 1999.
Danilenko GM, *Law-Making in the International Community*, Dordrecht, 1993.
D'Aspremont J, *Epistemic Forces in International Law—Fundamental Doctrines and Techniques of International Legal Argumentation*, Cheltenham, 2015.
—— (ed), *Participants in the International Legal System: Multiple Perspectives on Non-State Actors in International Law*, London, 2011.
——, *Formalism and the Sources of International Law*, Oxford, 2001.
De La Pradelle A, *Maîtres et doctrines du droit des gens*, Paris, 1950.
De Lacharrière G, *La politique juridique extérieure*, Paris, 1983.
De Luca P, *La sovranità degli Stati nella comunità dei popoli*, Milan, 1956.
Detter De Lupis I, *The Concept of International Law*, Stockholm, 1987.
De Visscher C, *Théories et réalités en droit international public*, 4th edn, Paris, 1970 (English edn: *Theory and Reality in International Law*, Princeton, 1968).
Delos JT, *La société internationale et les principes du droit public*, Paris, 1929.
Domingo R, *The New Global Law*, Cambridge, 2010.
Dominicé C, *L'ordre juridique international entre tradition et innovation*, Paris, 1997.
Dupuis C, *Le droit des gens et les rapports des Grandes Puissances avec les autres Etats avant le Pacte de la Société des Nations*, Paris, 1921.
Dupuy P and Chetail V (eds), *Les fondements du droit international*, Leiden/Boston, 2014.
Dupuy RJ, *La clôture du système international*, Paris, 1989.
——, *La Communauté internationale entre le mythe et l'histoire*, Paris, 1986.
——, *Le droit international*, 7th edn, Paris, 1986.
Eagleton C, *International Government*, New York, 1948.
Edmunds SE, *The Lawless Law of Nations*, Washington, DC, 1925.
Elias TO, *New Horizons in International Law*, Alphen aan den Rijn/New York, 1979.
Emmerich-Fritsche A, *Vom Völkerrecht zum Weltrecht*, Berlin, 2007.
Eriksen CC and Emberland M, *The New International Law: An Anthology*, Leiden, 2010.
Etzioni A, *From Empire to Community: A New Approach to International Relations*, New York, 2004.
Falk RA, *Law, Morality and War in the Contemporary World*, London, 1963.
Falk RA, *Law in an Emerging Global Village: A Post-Westphalian Perspective*, Ardsley, NY, 1998.
Falk RA, *The Status of Law in the International Society*, Princeton, 1970.
Fassbender B, *The United Nations Charter and the Constitution of the International Community*, Leiden/Boston, 2009.
Fastenrath U, Geiger R, Khan DE, Paulus A, von Schorlemer S and Vedder C (eds), *From Bilateralism to Community Interest*, Oxford, 2011.
Feller AH, *United Nations and World Community*, Boston, 1952.
Fenwick CG, *Foreign Policy and International Law*, New York, 1968.

Finch GA (Carnegie Foundation), *The International Law of the Future*, Washington, DC, 1944.
Finnemore M, *National Interests in International Society*, New York, 1996.
Fisch J, *Die europäische Expansion und das Völkerrecht*, Stuttgart, 1984.
Focarelli C, *International Law as a Social Construct, The Struggle for Social Justice*, Oxford, 2012.
——, *Lezioni di storia del diritto internazionale*, 2nd edn, Perugia, 2002.
Franck TM, *Fairness in International Law and Institutions*, Oxford, 1998.
——, *The Power of Legitimacy among Nations*, Oxford, 1990.
Frei M, *Von einem liberalen zu einem konstruktivistischen Völkerrechtsverständnis*, Zurich/St Gallen, 2007.
Friedmann W, *De l'efficacité des institutions internationales*, Paris, 1970.
——, *The Changing Structure of International Law*, London, 1964.
Garner JW, *Recent Developments in International Law*, Calcutta, 1925.
——, *International Law and the World War*, London, 1920.
Gaurier D, *Histoire du droit international: auteurs, doctrines et développement de l'Antiquité à l'aube de la période contemporaine*, Rennes, 2005.
Giuliano M, *La comunità internazionale e il diritto*, Padua, 1950.
Goldsmith J and Posner EA, *The Limits of International Law*, Oxford, 2005.
Green LC and Dickason OP, *The Law of Nations and the New World*, Edmonton, 1989.
Grewe WG, *The Epochs of International Law*, Berlin/New York, 2000.
Guerrero JG, *L'ordre international, Hier—aujourd'hui—demain*, Neuchâtel/Paris, 1945.
Guillaume G, *Les grandes crises internationales et le droit*, Paris, 1994.
Guzman AT, *How International Law Works: A Rational Choice Theory*, Oxford/New York, 2008.
Heilborn P, *Grundbegriffe des Völkerrechts*, Stuttgart, 1912.
Heinrich-Böll Stiftung (ed), *Die Zukunft des Völkerrechts in einer globalisierten Welt*, Baden-Baden, 2006.
Henkin L, *How Nations Behave: Law and Foreign Policy*, 2nd edn, New York, 1979.
Higgins AP, *The Binding Force of International Law*, Cambridge, 1910.
Hill DJ, *L'Etat moderne et l'organisation internationale*, Paris, 1912.
Holland TE, *Studies in International Law*, Oxford, 1898.
Hoof GJH, van, *Rethinking the Sources of International Law*, Deventer, 1983.
Hosack J, *On the Rise and Growth of the Law of Nations*, London, 1882.
Huber M, *Die soziologischen Grundlagen des Völkerrechts*, Berlin, 1928.
Hudson MO, *Contemporary Developments of International Law*, Washington, DC, 1925.
Jellinek G, *Die rechtliche Natur der Staatsverträge—Ein Beitrag zur juristischen Construktion des Völkerrechts*, Vienna, 1880.
Jenks CW, *The Common Law of Mankind*, London, 1958.
Jessup PC, *Transnational Law*, New Haven, 1956.
Jitta J, *La rénovation du droit international sur la base d'une communauté juridique du genre humain*, The Hague, 1919 (English edn: *The Renovation of International Law on the Basis of a Juridical Community of Mankind*, The Hague, 1919).
Johnston DM, *The Historical Foundations of World Order: The Tower and the Arena*, Leiden/Boston, 2008.
Jouannet E, *Le droit international libéral-providence—Une histoire du droit international*, Brussels, 2011 (English edn: E Toume-Jouannet, *The Liberal-Welfarist Law of Nations: A History of International Law*, Cambridge, 2012).

——, *Qu'est-ce qu'une société internationale juste? Le droit international entre développement et reconnaissance*, Paris, 2011.
Kampto M, *Droit international de la gouvernance*, Paris, 2013.
Kaplan M and Katzenbach NB, *The Political Foundations of International Law*, New York, 1961.
Kaufmann E, *Das Wesen des Völkerrechts und die Clausula Rebus Sic Stantibus*, Tübingen, 1911.
Keeton GW and Schwarzenberger G, *Making International Law Work*, 2nd edn, London, 1946.
Keller H and Thurnherr D, *Taking International Law Seriously*, Bern/New York/Athens, 2005.
Kelsen H, *Peace Through Law*, Chapel Hill, 1944.
——, *Das Problem der Souveränität und die Theorie des Völkerrechts*, 2nd edn, Tübingen, 1928.
Kennedy D, *Nouvelles approches sur le droit international*, Paris, 2009.
——, *International Legal Structures*, Baden-Baden, 1987.
Kingsbury B and Straumann B, *The Roman Foundation of the Law of Nations: Alberico Gentili and the Justice of Empire*, Oxford, 2010.
Kolb R, *Réflexions sur les politiques juridiques extérieures*, Paris, 2015.
——, *Esquisse d'un droit international public des anciennes cultures extra-européennes*, Paris, 2010.
——, *Réflexions de philosophie du droit international*, Brussels 2003; new and augmented edn as *Théorie du droit international*, Brussels, 2013.
——, *Les cours généraux de droit international de l'Académie de droit international de La Haye*, Brussels, 2003.
Korowicz MS, *La souveraineté des Etats et l'avenir du droit international*, Paris, 1945.
Koskenniemi M, *La politique du droit international*, Paris, 2007.
——, *From Apology to Utopia: The Structure of International Legal Argument*, Helsinki, 1989 and Cambridge, 2005.
——, *The Gentle Civilizer of Nations, The Rise and Fall of International Law, 1870–1960*, Cambridge, 2001.
Kosters J, *Les fondements du droit des gens*, Leiden, 1925.
Krasner SD, *Sovereignty: Organized Hypocrisy*, Princeton, 1999.
Krisch N, *Beyond Constitutionalism: The Pluralist Structure of Postnational Law*, Oxford/New York, 2010.
Kunz J, *The Changing Law of Nations*, London, 1968.
Lachs M, *The Teacher in International Law: Teachings and Teaching*, 2nd edn, The Hague, 1987.
Laghmani S, *Histoire du droit des gens, Du jus gentium impérial au jus publicum europaeum*, Paris, 2003.
Lambert J, *La vengeance privée et les fondements du droit international public*, Paris, 1936.
Lauterpacht H, *The Function of Law in the International Community*, Oxford, 1933.
——, *Private Law Sources and Analogies of International Law*, London, 1927.
Leben C (ed), *The Advancement of International Law*, Oxford, 2011.
Lissiztyn OJ, *International Law Today and Tomorrow*, New York, 1965.
MacDonald RSJ and Johnston DM (eds), *The Structure and Process of International Law, Essays in Legal Philosophy, Doctrine and Theory*, The Hague, 1983.

—— and —— (eds), *Towards World Constitutionalism: Issues in the Legal Ordering of the World Community*, Leiden, 2005.
Manning CAW, *The Nature of International Society*, London, 1962.
Mapel DR and Nardin T (eds), *International Society: Diverse Ethical Perspectives*, Princeton, 1999.
Marks S (ed), *International Law on the Left: Re-Examining Marxist Legacies*, Cambridge, 2008.
Martin PM, *Les échecs du droit international*, Paris, 1996.
Maturi G, *Il problema giuridico della comunità internazionale*, Milan, 1956.
McDougal MS, *Studies in World Public Order*, New Haven, 1960.
—— and Reisman M, *International Law in Contemporary Perspective, The Public Order of the World Community*, New York, 1981.
Midgley EBF, *The Natural Law Tradition and the Theory of International Relations*, New York, 1975.
Miele M, *La comunità internazionale*, Turin, 1997.
Morgenthau H, *Politics among Nations: The Struggle for Power and Peace*, 5th edn, New York, 1973.
——, *La réalité des normes: En particulier des normes du droit international*, Paris, 1934.
Mosler H, *The International Society as a Legal Community*, Alphen aan den Rijn/Germantown, 1980.
Moynihan DP, *On the Law of Nations*, Cambridge, Mass/London, 1990.
Mukherjee SK, *A New Outlook for International Law*, Calcutta, 1964.
Müllerson R, *Ordering Anarchy, International Law in International Society*, The Hague/Boston/London, 2000.
Nardin T, *Law, Morality and the Relations of States*, Princeton, 1983.
Nathan M, *The Renascence of International Law*, London, 1925.
Nawaz MK, *The Changing Law of Nations: An Indian Focus*, Calcutta, 2000.
Neff SC, *War and the Law of Nations: A General History*, Cambridge, 2008.
Neuchâtel University, Law Faculty (ed), *International Law Tomorrow*, Neuchâtel, 1974.
Nijman JE, *The Concept of International Legal Personality*, The Hague, 2004.
Nippold O, *Die Gestaltung des Völkerrechts nach dem Weltkriege*, Zurich, 1917 (English edn: *The Development of International Law after the World War*, Oxford, 1923).
Nolte G, *Le droit international face au défi américain*, Paris, 2005.
Nussbaum A, *A Concise History of the Law of Nations*, New York, 1954.
Nys E, *Etudes de droit international et de droit politique*, Brussels/Paris, 1896.
Nys E, *Les origines du droit international*, Brussels/Paris, 1894.
O'Connell ME, *The Power and Purpose of International Law: Insights from the Theory and Practice of Enforcement*, Oxford, 2008.
Okeke CN, *Controversial Subjects of Contemporary International Law*, Rotterdam, 1974.
Onuma Y, *A Transcivilizational Perspective on International Law*, Leiden, 2010.
Oppenheim L, *The Future of International Law*, Oxford/Washington, DC, 1921.
Orakhelashvili A (ed), *Research Handbook on the Theory and History of International Law*, Cheltenham, 2011.
Orford A (ed), *International Law and its Others*, Cambridge, 2006.
Osiander A (ed), *The States System of Europe, 1640–1990*, Oxford, 1994.
Paech N and Stuby G, *Völkerrecht und Machtpolitik in den internationalen Beziehungen*, Hamburg, 2001.

Pahuja S, *Decolonizing International Law: Development, Economic Growth and the Politics of Universality*, Cambridge, 2011.
Papaligouras P, *Théorie de la société internationale*, Zurich, 1941.
Papaux A and Wyler E, *L'éthique du droit international*, Paris, 1997.
Paradisi B, *Storia del diritto internazionale nel Medio Evo*, vol I, Milan, 1941.
Parlett K, *The Individual in the International Legal System: Continuity and Change in International Law*, Cambridge, 2011.
Parry C, *The Sources and Evidences of International Law*, Manchester, 1965.
Paulus A, *Die Internationale Gemeinschaft im Völkerrecht: Eine Untersuchung zur Entwicklung des Völkerrechts im Zeitalter der Globalisierung*, Munich, 2001.
Picone P, *Comunità internazionale e obblighi* erga omnes: *Studi critici di diritto internazionale*, Naples, 2006.
Pillet A, *Les fondateurs du droit international*, Paris, 1904.
Poggi G, *The Development of the Modern State: A Sociological Introduction*, London, 1978.
Politis N, *La morale internationale*, Neuchâtel, 1943.
——, *Les nouvelles tendances du droit international*, Paris, 1927 (English edn: *The New Aspects of International Law*, Washington DC, 1928).
Portmann R, *Legal Personality in International Law*, Cambridge, 2010.
Posner EA, *The Perils of Global Legalism*, Chicago/London, 2009.
Prost M, *The Concept of Unity in Public International Law*, Oxford/Portland, 2012.
Rabkin JA, *Law without Nations? Why Constitutional Government Requires Sovereign States*, Princeton, 2005.
Rajagopal B, *International Law from Below: Development, Social Movements and Third World Resistance*, Cambridge, 2003.
Ralston JH, *Democracy's International Law*, Washington, 1922.
Ramel F, *Philosophie des relations internationales*, Paris, 2002.
Ratner S, *The Thin Justice of International Law, A Moral Reckoning of the Law of Nations*, Oxford, 2015.
Redslob R, *Das Problem des Völkerrechts*, Leipzig, 1917.
Redslob R, *Histoire des grands principes du droit des gens*, Paris, 1923.
Reibstein E, *Die Anfänge des neueren Natur- und Völkerrechts*, Bern, 1949.
Reibstein E, *Völkerrecht—Eine Geschichte seiner Ideen in Lehre und Praxis*, 2 vols, Freiburg/Munich, 1957.
Reisman WM, *International Law in Contemporary Perspective*, 2nd edn, New York, 2004.
—— and Willard AR (eds), *The Law that Counts in World Politics*, Princeton, 1988.
Rodriguez Iglesias GC, *Memoria sobre concepto, método, fuentes y programa de derecho internacional publico*, Madrid, 1982.
Röling BVA, *International Law in an Expanded World*, Amsterdam, 1960.
Romano S, *L'ordinamento giuridico*, 2nd edn, Florence, 1962.
Rosenne S, *Practice and Methods of International Law*, London, 1984.
Rubin AP, *Ethics and Authority in International Law*, Cambridge, 1997.
Salmon J (ed), *Dictionnaire de droit international public*, Brussels, 2001.
Salvioli G, *Studi sui caratteri dell'ordinamento giuridico internazionale*, Spoleto, 1922.
——, *Alcuni concetti generali del diritto internazionale*, Camerino, 1919.
Sandoz Y (ed), *Quel droit international pour le 21e siècle?*, Brussels, 2007.
Sarat A, Douglas L and Umphrey MM, *Law Without Nations*, Stanford, 2011.
Scelle G, *Théorie du gouvernement international*, Paris, 1934.
Schiffer W, *The Legal Community of Mankind*, New York, 1954.

Schindler D, *Recht, Staat, Völkergemeinschaft*, Zurich, 1948.
Schmitt C, *Der Nomos der Erde im Jus Publicum Europaeum*, Cologne, 1950.
Schücking W, *Die völkerrechtliche Lehre des Weltkrieges*, Leipzig, 1918.
——, *Die Organisation der Welt*, Leipzig, 1909.
Schwarzenberger G, *The Inductive Approach to International Law*, London/New York, 1965.
——, *Power Politics, A Study of World Society*, 3rd edn, London, 1964.
——, *The Frontiers of International Law*, London, 1962.
Sereni AP, *The Italian Conceptions of International Law*, New York, 1943.
Shelton D (ed), *International Law and Domestic Legal Systems: Incorporation, Transformation and Persuasion*, Oxford/New York, 2011.
——, *Commitment and Compliance: The Role of Non-Binding Norms in the International Legal System*, Oxford, 2000.
Skouteris T, *The Notion of Progress in International Law Discourse*, The Hague, 2010.
Slaughter AM, *A New World Order*, Princeton/Oxford, 2004.
Smith HA, *The Crisis in the Law of Nations*, London, 1947.
Sperduti G, *La fonte suprema dell'ordinamento internazionale*, Milan, 1946.
Spiropoulos J, *Théorie générale du droit international*, Paris, 1930.
Spruyt H, *The Sovereign State and its Competitors*, Princeton, 1994.
Stadtmüller G, *Geschichte des Völkerrechts*, Hannover, 1951.
Stone J, *Legal Controls of International Conflict*, London, 1954.
Strayer JR, *On the Medieval Origins of the Modern State*, Princeton/Oxford, 1970.
Strupp K, *Eléments du droit international public universel, européen et américain*, vols I–III, Paris, 1930.
Sturzo L, *The International Community and the Right of War*, London, 1929.
Tan KC, *Justice without Borders: Cosmopolitanism, Nationalism and Patriotism*, Cambridge, 2004.
Ter Meulen J, *Der Gedanke der Internationalen Organisation in seiner Entwicklung, 1300–1800*, The Hague, 1917; and *1789–1889*, The Hague, 1929 and 1940.
Téson F, *A Philosophy of International Law*, Boulder, 1998.
Teubner G (ed), *Global Law without a State*, Aldershot, 1997.
Tilly C (ed), *The Formation of the National States in Western Europe*, Princeton, 1975.
Tomberg V, *Grundlagen des Völkerrechts als Menschheitsrecht*, Bonn, 1947.
Trachtman JP, *The Future of International Law*, Cambridge, 2013.
Triepel H, *Völkerrecht und Landesrecht*, Leipzig, 1899.
Truyol y Serra A, *Die Entstehung der Weltsaatengesellschaft unserer Zeit*, Munich, 1963.
——, *Fundamentos de derecho internacional publico*, Barcelona, 1955.
—— and Kolb R, *Doctrines sur le fondement du droit des gens*, Paris, 2007.
Twining W, *Globalization and Legal Theory*, London/Edinburgh/Dublin, 2000.
Vandenbosch A, *Toward World Order*, New York, 1963.
Vedovato, G, *La comunità internazionale*, Florence, 1950.
Verdross A, *Die Verfassung der Völkerrechtsgemeinschaft*, Vienna/Berlin, 1926.
——, *Die Einheit des rechtlichen Weltbildes*, Tübingen, 1923.
Verzijl JW, *International Law in Historical Perspective*, vols 1–10, Leiden, 1968–79.
Vinogradoff P, *Historical Types of International Law*, Leiden, 1923.
Virally M, *Le droit international en devenir*, Paris, 1990.
——, *L'Organisation mondiale*, Paris, 1972.
Vollenhoven C, van, *Du droit de la paix, De iure pacis*, The Hague, 1932.
——, *Les trois phases du droit des gens*, The Hague, 1919.

Walker TA, *A History of the Law of Nations, From the Earliest Times to the Peace of Westphalia*, Cambridge, 1899.
Walker TA, *The Science of International Law*, London, 1893.
Walz GA, *Wesen des Völkerrechts und Kritik der Völkerrechtsleugner*, Stuttgart, 1930.
Watson A, *The Evolution of International Society*, London/New York, 1992.
Weeramantry CG, *Universalizing International Law*, Leiden/Boston, 2004.
Weiss L, *The Myth of the Powerless State*, Ithaca, NY, 1998.
Wheaton H, *Histoire des progrès du droit des gens en Europe depuis la paix de Westphalie jusqu'à nos jours*, 2 vols, 3rd edn, Leipzig, 1853.
Wight M, *Systems of States*, Leicester, 1977.
Winfield PH, *The Foundations and the Future of International Law*, Cambridge, 1942.
Wolfrum R (ed), *The Max Planck Encyclopedia of Public International Law*, vols I–X, Oxford, 2012.
Wolzendorff K, *Die Lüge des Völkerrechts*, Leipzig, 1919.
Wright Q, *The Role of International Law in the Elimination of War*, Manchester, 1961.
Wyler E and Papaux A, *L'extranéité ou le dépassement de l'ordre juridique étatique*, Paris, 1999.
Xue H, *Chinese Contemporary Perspectives on International Law*, The Hague, 2012.
Ziccardi P, *La costituzione dell'ordinamento internazionale*, Milan, 1943.
Ziegler KH, *Völkerrechtsgeschichte*, 2nd edn, Munich, 2007.
Zimmern A, *The League of Nations and the Rule of Law, 1918–1935*, London, 1935.
Zitelmann E, *Die Unvollkommenheit des Völkerrechts*, Munich/Leipzig, 1919.

INDEX

www.ingramcontent.com/pod-product-compliance
Ingram Content Group UK Ltd.
Pitfield, Milton Keynes, MK11 3LW, UK
UKHW020130290926
15471UKWH00003B/393

9 781509 927500